Engineering Design and Graphics with SolidWorks® 2011

James D. Bethune
Boston University

Prentice Hall

Boston   Columbus   Indianapolis   New York   San Francisco   Upper Saddle River
Amsterdam   Cape Town   Dubai   London   Madrid   Milan   Munich   Paris   Montreal   Toronto   Delhi
Mexico City   São Paulo   Sydney   Hong Kong   Seoul   Singapore   Taipei   Tokyo

Editorial Director: Vernon R. Anthony
Acquisitions Editor: Sara Eilert
Editorial Assistant: Doug Greive
Director of Marketing: David Gesell
Senior Marketing Manager: Harper Coles
Senior Marketing Coordinator: Alicia Wozniak
Marketing Assistant: Crystal Gonzalez
Project Manager: Maren L. Miller
Senior Managing Editor: JoEllen Gohr
Associate Managing Editor: Alexandrina
 Benedicto Wolf
Senior Operations Supervisor: Pat Tonneman

Operations Specialist: Deidra Skahill
Art Director: Jayne Conte
Cover Designer: Suzanne Behnke
Cover Image: Fotolia © Gary
AV Project Manager: Janet Portisch
Full-Service Project Management:
 Sudip Sinha/Aptara®, Inc.
Composition: Aptara
Printer/Binder: Edwards Brothers Malloy
Cover Printer: Edwards Brothers Malloy
Text Font: Bookman

Credits and acknowledgments borrowed from other sources and reproduced, with permission, in this textbook appear on the appropriate page within the text. Unless otherwise stated, all artwork has been provided by the author.

SolidWorks® is a registered trademark of DE SolidWorks Corp. Copyright 1997-2008 Dassault Systèmes SolidWorks Corp. All rights reserved.

Disclaimer:

The publication is designed to provide tutorial information about AutoCAD® and/or other Autodesk computer programs. Every effort has been made to make this publication complete and as accurate as possible. The reader is expressly cautioned to use any and all precautions necessary, and to take appropriate steps to avoid hazards, when engaging in the activities described herein.

Neither the author nor the publisher makes any representations or warranties of any kind, with respect to the materials set forth in this publication, express or implied, including without limitation any warranties of fitness for a particular purpose or merchantability. Nor shall the author or the publisher be liable for any special, consequential, or exemplary damages resulting, in whole or in part, directly or indirectly, from the reader's use of, or reliance upon, this material or subsequent revisions of this material.

Many of the designations by manufacturers and seller to distinguish their products are claimed as trademarks. Where those designations appear in this book, and the publisher was aware of a trademark claim, the designations have been printed in initial caps or all caps.

Library of Congress Cataloging-in-Publication Data

Bethune, James D.
 Engineering design and graphics with SolidWorks 2011/James Bethune.
  p. cm.
 Includes index.
 ISBN-13: 978-0-13-274050-0
 ISBN-10: 0-13-274050-8
 1. SolidWorks. 2. Computer graphics. 3. Computer-aided design. 4. Engineering design. I. Title.
 T385.B4833 2012
 620'.0042028553—dc22

                                    2011011139

10 9 8 7 6 5 4 3 2
Prentice Hall
is an imprint of

www.pearsonhighered.com

ISBN 10:   0-13-274050-8
ISBN 13: 978-0-13-274050-0

Preface

This book shows and explains how to use SolidWorks® 2011 to create engineering drawings and designs. Emphasis is placed on creating engineering drawings including dimensions and tolerances and using standard parts and tools. Each chapter contains step-by-step sample problems that show how to apply the concepts presented in the chapter.

The book contains hundreds of projects of various degrees of difficulty specifically designed to reinforce the chapter's content. The idea is that students learn best by doing. In response to reviewers' requests, some more difficult projects have been included.

Chapter 1 and 2 show how to set up a part document and how to use the SolidWorks **Sketch** tools. **Sketch** tools are used to create 2D part documents that can then be extruded into 3D solid models. The two chapters include 42 projects using both inches and millimeters for students to use for practice in applying the various **Sketch** tools.

Chapter 3 shows how to use the **Features** tools. **Features** tools are used to create and modify 3D solid models. In addition, reference planes are covered, and examples of how to edit existing models are given.

Chapter 4 explains how to create and interpret orthographic views. Views are created using third-angle projection in compliance with ANSI standards and conventions. Also included are section views, auxiliary views, and broken views. Several of the projects require that a 3D solid model be drawn from a given set of orthographic views to help students develop visualization skills.

Chapter 5 explains how to create assembly drawings using the **Assembly** tools (**Mate**, exploded **View**) and how to document assemblies using the **Drawing Documents** tools. Topics include assembled 3D solid models, exploded isometric drawings, and bills of materials (BOMs). Assembly numbers and part numbers are discussed. Both the **Animate Collapse/Explode** and **Motion Study** tools are demonstrated. In addition, the title, release, and revision blocks are discussed.

Chapter 6 shows how to create and design with threads and fasteners. Both ANSI inch and ANSI metric threads are covered. The **Design Library** is presented, and examples are used to show how to select and size screws and other fasteners for assembled parts.

Chapter 7 covers dimensioning and is in compliance with ANSI standards and conventions. There are extensive visual examples of dimensioned shapes and features that serve as references for various dimensioning applications.

Chapter 8 covers tolerances. Both linear and geometric tolerances are included. This is often a difficult area to understand, so there are many examples of how to apply and how to interpret the various types of tolerances. Standard tolerances as presented in the title block and demonstrated.

Chapter 9 explains bearings and fit tolerances. The **Design Library** is used to create bearing drawings, and examples show how to select the correct interference tolerance between bearings and housing, and clearance tolerances between bearings and shafts.

Chapter 10 presents gears. Gear terminology, gear formulas, gear ratios, and gear creation using the SolidWorks **Toolbox** are covered. The chapter relies heavily on the **Design Library**. Keys, keyways, and set screws are discussed. Both English and metric units are covered. There is an extensive sample problem that shows how to draw a support plate for mating gears and how to create an assembly drawing for gear trains. The exercise problems at the end of the chapter are supplemented with two large gear assembly exercises.

Chapter 11 covers belts and pulleys. Belts, pulleys, sprockets, and chains are drawn. All examples are based on information from the **Design Library**. There are several sample problems.

Chapter 12 covers cams. Displacement drawings are defined. The chapter shows how to add hubs and keyways to cams and then insert the cams into assembly drawings.

The **Appendix** includes fit tables for use with projects in the text. Clearance, locational, and interference fits are included for both inch and millimeter values.

A complete **Introduction** for new users can be found on the web at http://www.pearsonhighered.com/educator.

SolidWorks® Learning License

Students may get trial access to the SolidWorks® software student version. Instructors should ask their Pearson sales rep and bookstore to package this book with ISBN-10: 0-13-275865-2 at no additional cost. To contact your Pearson rep, please visit www.pearsonhighered.com/educator.

Download Instructor Resources from the Instructor Resource Center

To access supplementary materials online, instructors need to request an instructor access code. Go to www.pearsonhighered.com/irc to register for an instructor access code. Within 48 hours of registering, you will receive a confirming e-mail including an instructor access code. Once you have received your code, locate your text in the online catalog and click on the Instructor Resources button on the left side of the catalog product page. Select a supplement, and a login page will appear. Once you have logged in, you can access instructor material for all Prentice Hall textbooks. If you have any difficulties accessing the site or downloading a supplement, please contact Customer Service at http://247pearsoned.custhelp.com/.

Acknowledgments

I would like to acknowledge the reviewers of this text: Peggy Condon-Vance, Penn State Berks; Lisa Richter, Macomb Community College; Julie Korfhage, Clackamas Community College; Max P. Gassman, Iowa State University; Paul E. Lienard, Northeastern University; and Hossein Hemati, Mira Costa College.

Thanks to editor Sara Eilert. Thanks to my family—David, Maria, Randy, Lisa, Hannah, Will, Madison, Jack, Luke, Sam, and Ben.

A special thanks to Cheryl.

James D. Bethune
Boston University

Contents

Getting Started

CHAPTER OBJECTIVES

- Learn how to create a sketch
- Learn how to create a file/part
- Learn how to create a solid model
- Learn how to edit and modify a sketch

- Learn how to draw angular and circular shapes
- Learn how to draw holes
- Learn how to use the **Sketch** tools
- Change the units of a part

1-1 Introduction

This chapter presents a step-by-step introduction to SolidWorks 2011. The objective is to have first-time users access SolidWorks and be able to start drawing shapes within a few minutes. The use of the tools initially presented in Chapter 1 will be expanded in Chapters 2 and 3.

1-2 Sketching a Line

Figure 1-1 shows the opening SolidWorks screen. This screen should appear when you first access the SolidWorks program. Move the cursor to the icon in the upper left corner of the screen and click the arrowhead to access the **New** tool. The **New** tool is used to create a new drawing.

1 Click the **New** tool.

The **New SolidWorks Document** dialog box will appear. See Figure 1-2.

2 Click the **Advanced** box located in the lower left corner of the box.

Figure 1-1

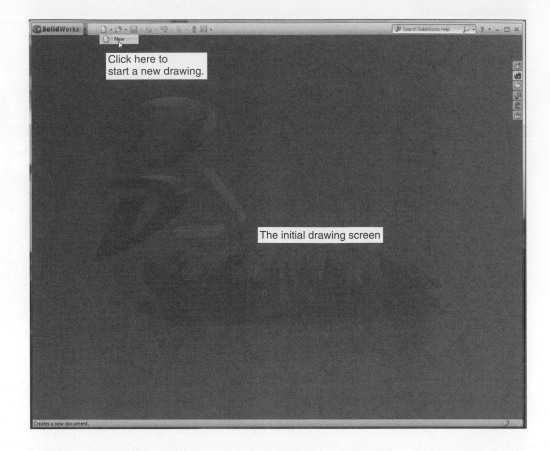

SolidWorks
New
Search SolidWorks Help
Click here to
start a new drawing.
The initial drawing screen
Creates a new document.

> **TIP**
>
> The **Advanced** tool access box may not appear after your first use. Instead, SolidWorks will go directly to the **New SolidWorks Document** box. The **Novice** box can be used to return to the **New SolidWorks Document** box if needed.

Figure 1-2

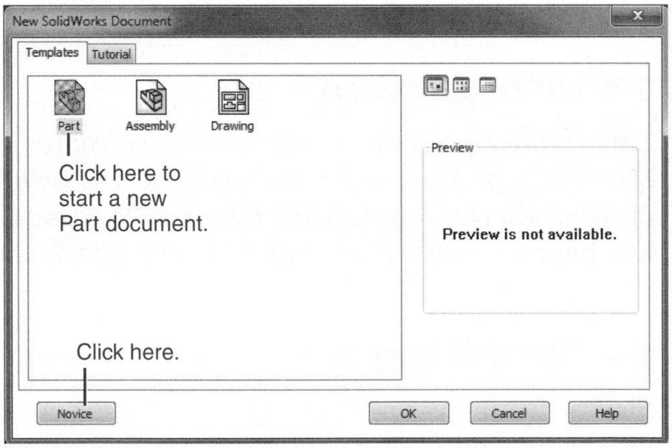

New SolidWorks Document
Templates
Tutorial
Part
Assembly
Drawing
Click here to
start a new
Part document.
Preview
Preview is not available.
Click here.
Novice
OK
Cancel
Help

The next **New SolidWorks Document** dialog box will appear. See Figure 1-3. SolidWorks can generate three different types of drawings: **Part**, **Assembly**, and **Drawing** documents. Individual parts are drawn using the **Part** document. This section will use **Part** documents. **Assembly** and **Drawing** documents will be covered in later chapters.

3 Click the **Part** tool, then click **OK**.

Figure 1-3

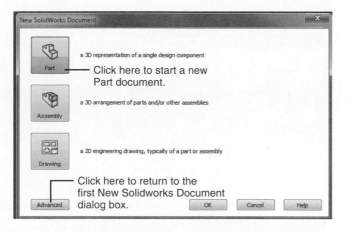

The initial screen display will appear. See Figure 1-4. This screen shows the components of a new **Part** document, which includes toolbars, the **CommandManager,** main menu headings, the **FeatureManager**, and the axis orientation icon.

Figure 1-4

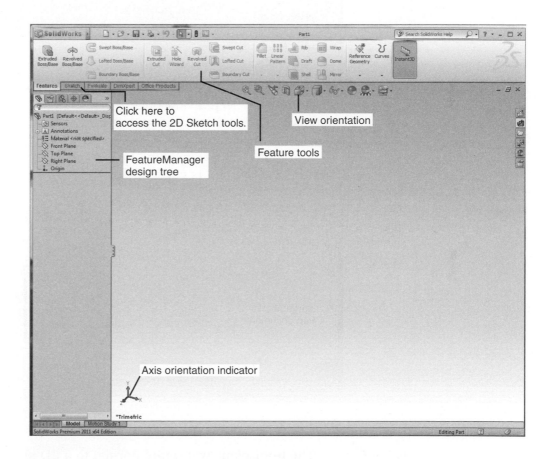

4 Click the **Sketch** tool located on the **CommandManager**.

5 Click **Front Plane** on the **FeaturesManager**.

A reference plane will appear. See Figure 1-5. The plane appears in a trimetric orientation but will automatically be oriented normal (at right

Figure 1-5

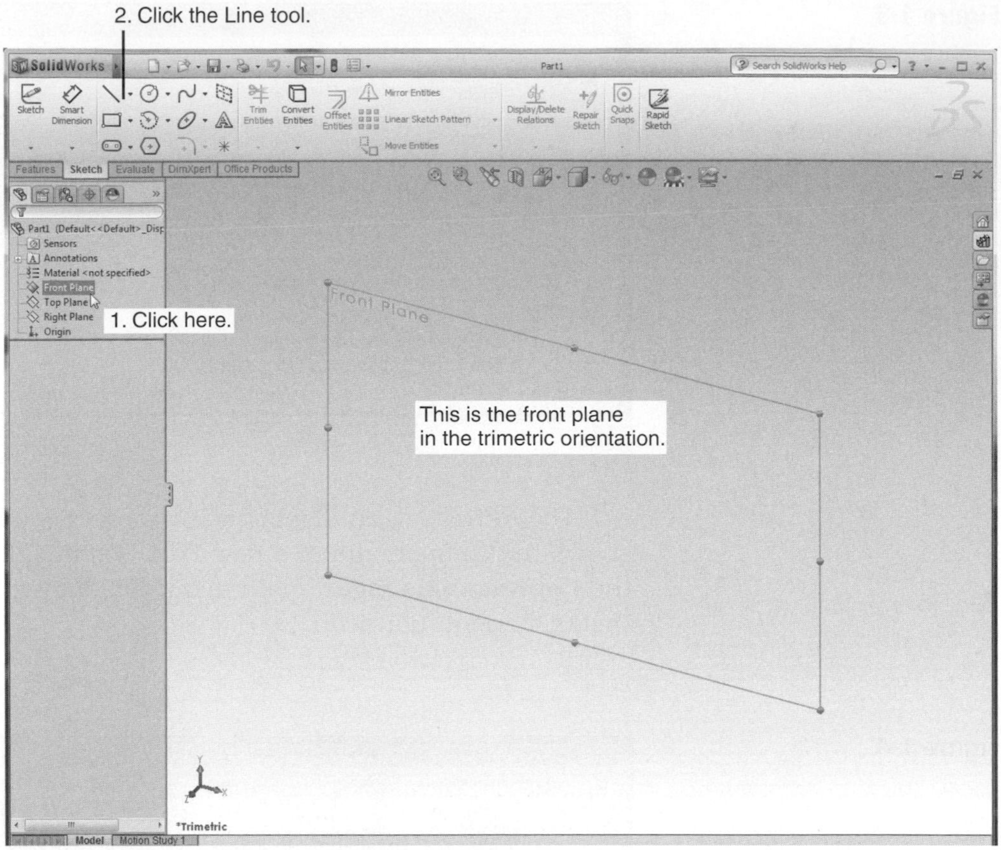

2. Click the Line tool.

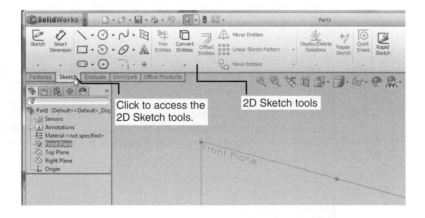

1. Click here.

This is the front plane in the trimetric orientation.

angles to) the selected view once sketching begins. There are three basic sketching planes: front, top, and right side. These views correspond to the three basic orthographic views that will be covered in Chapter 4.

A grouping of 2D sketching tools will appear on the **CommandManager** after the **Sketch** tool is clicked. See Figure 1-6.

Figure 1-6

Click to access the 2D Sketch tools.

2D Sketch tools

6 Click the **Line** tool.

The front plane will rotate normal to a 2D sketching mode. Figure 1-7 shows the default screen display in the sketching environment.

NOTE

The icon with a pencil and arrow located in the upper right corner of the drawing screen indicates that the document is in sketch mode.

Figure 1-7

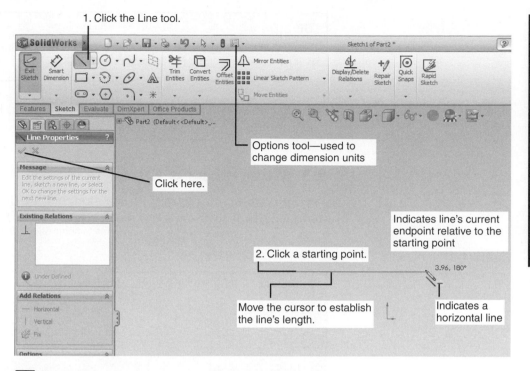

1. Click the Line tool.

Options tool—used to change dimension units

Click here.

Indicates line's current endpoint relative to the starting point

2. Click a starting point.

3.96, 180°

Move the cursor to establish the line's length.

Indicates a horizontal line

7 Locate the cursor in the drawing area, and select a starting point for the line.

8 Click the left mouse button to start the line, and move the cursor horizontally across the screen. Determine an endpoint for the line and again click the mouse button. Click the green check mark on the **PropertyManager**, press the **<Esc>** key, or right-click the mouse and click the **Select** option to end the **Line** tool.

TIP

A line can also be drawn by selecting a starting point and holding the left mouse button down while moving the cursor. The end of the line is defined by releasing the mouse button.

NOTE

As you sketch, the line will change color. The color helps determine the status of the line. When you initially sketch the line it will be light blue, meaning it is not finished; that is, the final length and angle have not been determined. You can complete the line sketch by first clicking a selected endpoint and then either right-clicking the mouse and clicking the **Select** option or by pressing the **<Esc>** key. The line will change to a dark blue color. If you pass the cursor over an existing line, the line will turn red, indicating that the line is active and may be edited. If you click the **Smart Dimension** tool and move the cursor to the line, the line will turn red, meaning it has been identified and is ready for editing. When you click the line, it will turn light blue, and a dialog box will appear. Once the final length of the line has been established, the line will turn dark blue.

NOTE

The examples given in this chapter are dimensioned in inches. To change units,

1. Click the **Options** tool at the top of the screen.

2. Click the **Document Properties** tab, then **Units**, and select the desired **Unit system** radio button.

3. Click **OK**.

See Section 1-9 for a more detailed explanation.

The small shaded square with the horizontal bar across it indicates that the line is a horizontal line.

1-3 Modifying a Line

The line created in Figure 1-8 is a sketched line; that is, it has an approximate length. We will now define an exact length for the line.

Figure 1-8

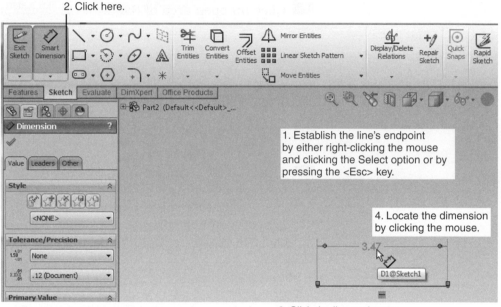

2. Click here.

1. Establish the line's endpoint by either right-clicking the mouse and clicking the Select option or by pressing the <Esc> key.

4. Locate the dimension by clicking the mouse.

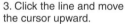

D1@Sketch1

3. Click the line and move the cursor upward.

1 Click the **Smart Dimension** tool in the **Sketch** group on the **CommandManager**.

See Figure 1-8.

2 Click on the line and move the cursor upward away from the line.

3 Determine a location for the line's dimension and click the mouse.

The **Modify** dialog box will appear. See Figure 1-9.

4 Enter a dimension value of **4.00** and click the check mark in the lower left of the **Modify** dialog box.

The line's length will be defined as 4.00 in. The line's length will be modified to this length. See Figure 1-10.

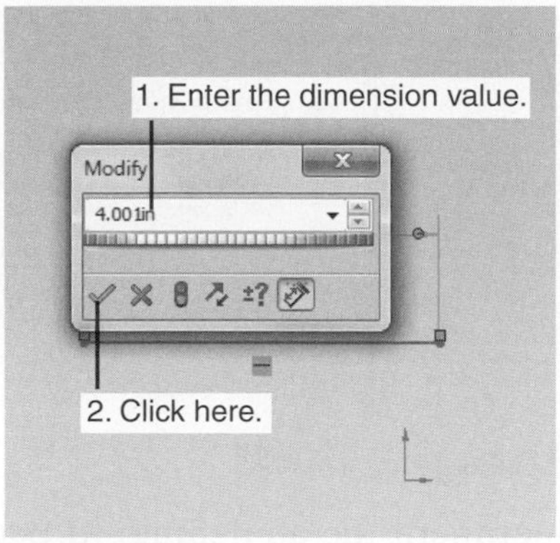

1. Enter the dimension value.

Modify

4.001in

2. Click here.

Figure 1-9

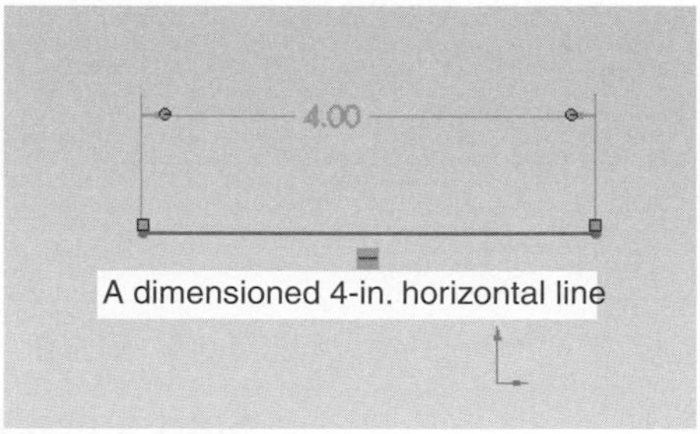

4.00

A dimensioned 4-in. horizontal line

Figure 1-10

5 Click an open area of the drawing screen or press the **<Esc>** key.

> **NOTE**
> A dimension may be changed by double-clicking its numerical value and entering a new value.

The line is now drawn and sized (dimensioned). We will now close the drawing and create another drawing.

6 Select the **File** heading on the main menu. The **File** tool is a flyout from the arrowhead located to the right of the SolidWorks heading at the top left of the screen.

A series of commands will cascade down. See Figure 1-11.

Figure 1-11

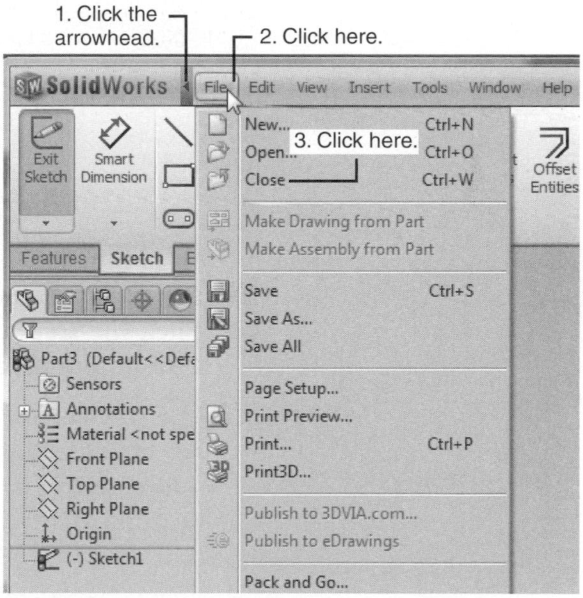

1. Click the arrowhead.

2. Click here.

3. Click here.

7 Select **Close**.

A dialog box will appear on the screen. See Figure 1-12.

8 Select the **Don't Save** option unless you want to save the line.

Figure 1-12

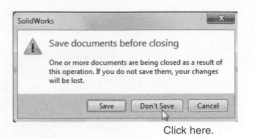

Click here.

1-4 The Rectangle Tool

Start a new **Part** document file as defined in Section 1-2. Click the **Sketch** tab on the **CommandManager** to display the **Sketch** tools. Select **Front Plane** from the **FeatureManager**. See Figure 1-13.

Figure 1-13

Click here.

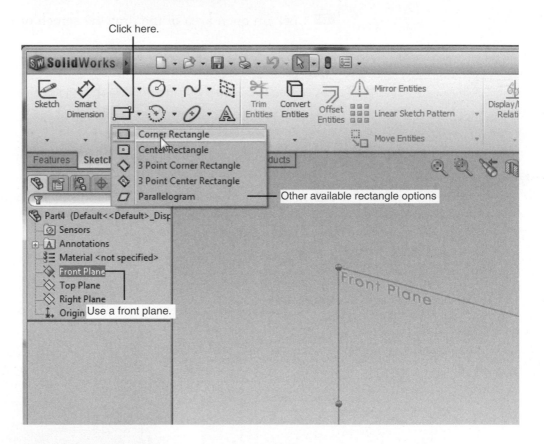

Other available rectangle options

Use a front plane.

1 Click the **Rectangle** tool in the **Sketch** group on the **CommandManager**.

2 Use the **Corner Rectangle** tool to sketch a rectangle by clicking a selected starting point, dragging the cursor down and across the screen, and selecting an endpoint for the rectangle by releasing the mouse button. Right-click the mouse and click the **Select** option.

> **NOTE**
> There are several different way to draw a rectangle. Any tool with an arrowhead next to it means there are other options available.

See Figure 1-14.

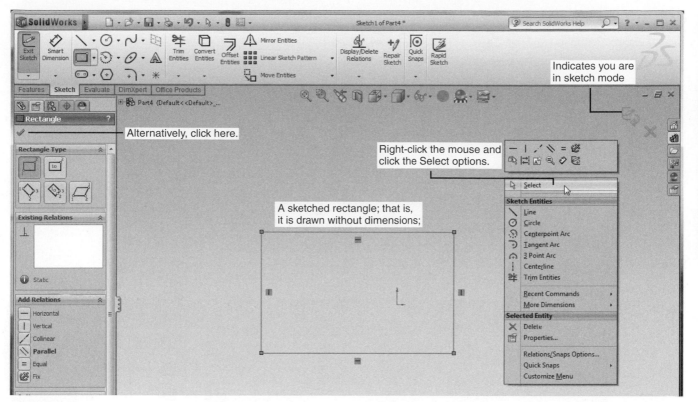

Figure 1-14

3 Click the **Smart Dimension** tool and create a **3.00 × 5.00-in.** rectangle. See Figures 1-15, 1-16, and 1-17.

Select the Smart Dimension tool, click the horizontal line, move the cursor away from the line, and click a location for the dimension.

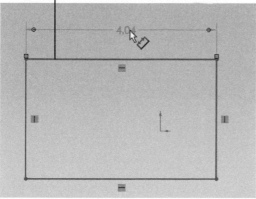

Figure 1-15

Figure 1-16

4 Click the green check mark on the **FeatureManager**, or right-click the mouse and click the **Select** option.

5 Click the **View Orientation** tool located at the top of the drawing screen. See Figure 1-18.

The **Standard Views** toolbar defines 10 different orientations that can be applied to the screen.

Figure 1-17

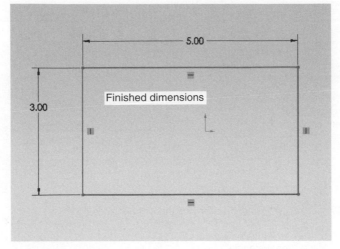

Figure 1-18

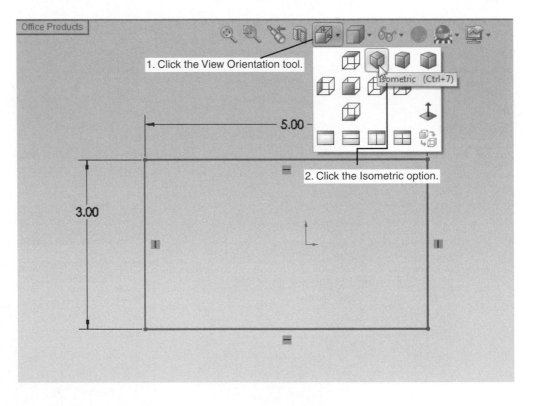

6 Select **Isometric**.

The rectangle will change to an isometric orientation. See Figure 1-19. Now, we will extend the first shape to create a solid feature.

Creating a Solid

1 Click the **Features** tab on the **CommandManager**.

The tools on the **CommandManager** will change from **Sketch** tools to **Features** tools. See Figure 1-20. The **Features** tools are used to convert sketches into solid models. The **Features** tools will be covered in detail in Chapter 3.

Figure 1-19

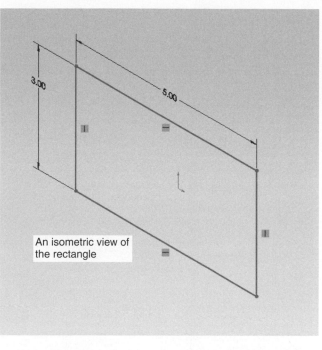

An isometric view of the rectangle

Figure 1-20

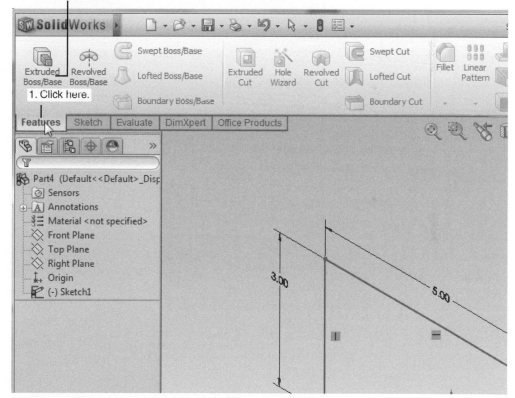

2. Click here.

1. Click here.

2 Click the **Extruded Boss/Base** tool.

The **FeatureManager** will change to display the **Boss-Extrude PropertyManager**. See Figure 1-21. The **Extrude** tool will automatically select the rectangle, as there is only one sketch on the screen.

3 Define the rectangle's thickness as **0.50in**.

Figure 1-21

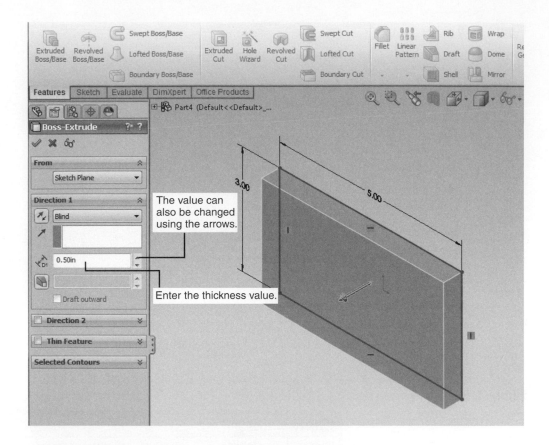

The value can also be changed using the arrows.

Enter the thickness value.

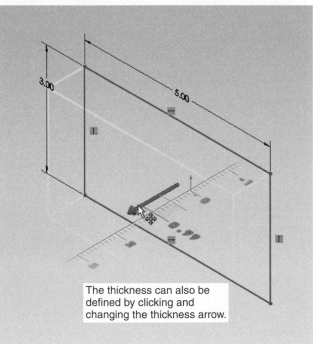

The thickness can also be defined by clicking and changing the thickness arrow.

NOTE

The rectangle can also be transitioned to a solid model by right-clicking the mouse. A list of options will appear. Click the **OK** check mark. See Figure 1-22.

4 Click the OK check mark.

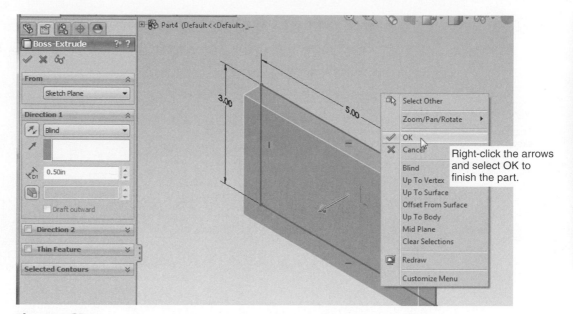

Figure 1-22

TIP

As you click the arrows to the right of the thickness value, the thickness value changes, and the thickness of the rectangle also changes in real time. You may also click and drag the arrow shown in the rectangle to change the thickness.

Figure 1-23 shows the finished rectangle. The rectangle has been used to create a 3D solid model. The shape is now a rectangular prism.

1-5 Drawing a Shape with 90° Angles

Figure 1-24 shows an object that includes only right (90°) angles.

1 Start a new **Part** document as explained in Section 1–2.

2 Select **Front Plane** from the **FeatureManager**.

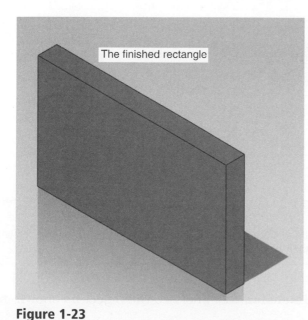

Figure 1-23

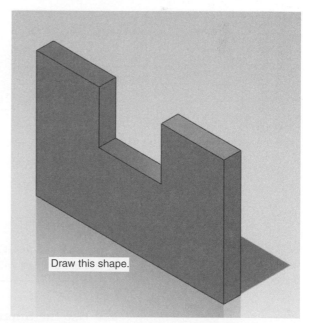

Figure 1-24

3 Select the **Sketch** group and click the **Line** tool.

4 Sketch the shape with horizontal and vertical lines. Approximate the dimensions.

See Figure 1-25.

This broken lines indicates that the endpoint being sketched is aligned with the first horizontal line sketched.

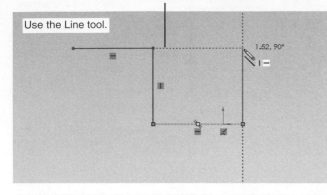

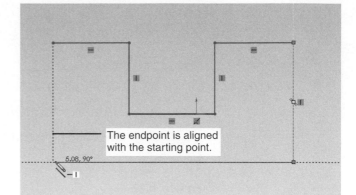

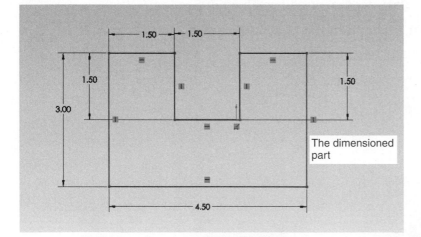

Figure 1-25

TIP

Note that as you sketch lines, other lines and icons appear on the screen to tell you if you are aligned with a point or parallel or perpendicular to other lines.

---

5 Use the **Smart Dimension** tool and size the object as shown in Figure 1-25.

6 Click the check mark in the **Line PropertyManager** and select the **Isometric** option from the selection flyout adjacent to the axis orientation icon. See Figure 1-18.

7 Right-click the mouse and click the **Select** option.

8 Click the **Features** tab, then the **Extruded Boss/Base** tool.

The screen orientation will automatically change to a three-dimensional orientation.

9 Set the object's thickness for **0.60in**. Move the cursor into the drawing area and right-click the mouse.

See Figure 1-26.

10 Click the **OK** option in the menu that appears.

The object should look like the one shown in Figure 1-24.

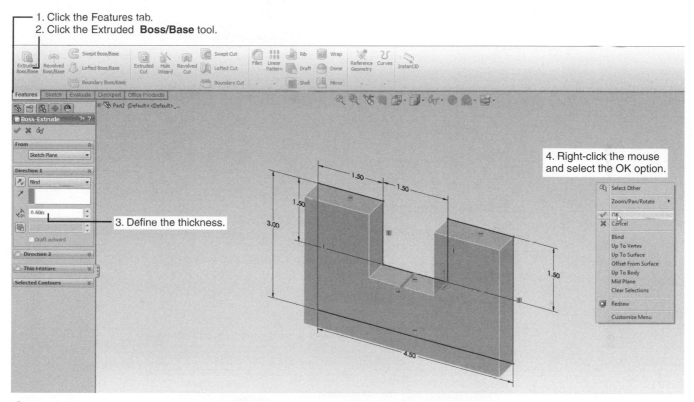

Figure 1-26

1-6 Editing a Sketch

It is possible to edit an existing shape using SolidWorks without resketching the object. For example, the shape created in the last section can be edited to change both the dimensions and the thickness. We will first change the depth of the cutout from 1.50 to 1.25 in. This procedure is called *editing a sketch*. In the next section we will change the thickness of the object from 0.60 to 0.40 in. This is called *editing a feature*. In general, changes to shapes created using the tools included in the **Sketch** group will be called *editing a sketch*, and shapes made using the tools included in the **Features** group will be called *editing a feature*. The **FeatureManager** records all the operations used to define the object. Click on the plus sign next to a feature to see the operations associated with that feature.

To Change the Dimensions

1 Right-click the mouse on the point located on the drawing screen. A listing of tools will appear.

See Figure 1-27.

Figure 1-27

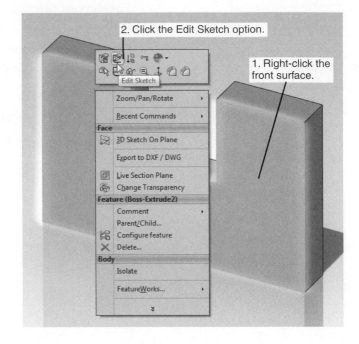

2 Select the **Edit Sketch** tool.

3 Double-click the **1.50** vertical dimension on the cutout.

See Figure 1-28. The **Modify** dialog box will appear.

Figure 1-28

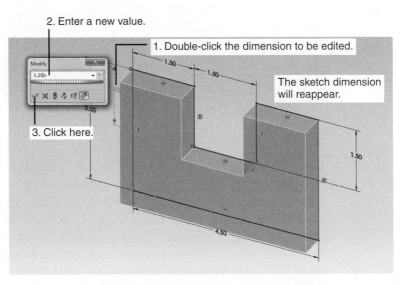

4 Dimension the vertical distance again using a value of **1.25** (the distance was 1.50).

5 Click the **OK** check mark.

See Figure 1-29.

Figure 1-29

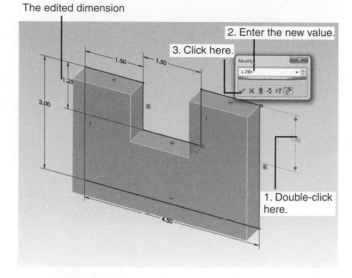

The edited dimension

2. Enter the new value.

3. Click here.

1. Double-click here.

6 Double-click the second 1.50 dimension and change it to **1.25** so that the top surfaces align.

7 Click the **OK** check mark in the **Modify** dialog box to upgrade the dimension.

See Figures 1-30 and 1-31. These figures show the modified sketches. Click the **Exit Sketch** tool or the **Exit Sketch** icon in the triangular-shaped area in the upper right corner of the drawing screen to save the changes and upgrade the 3D feature. Figure 1-32 shows the edited part.

Figure 1-30

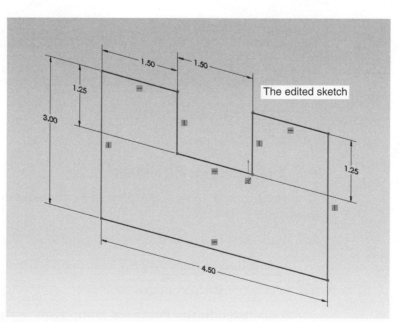

The edited sketch

Figure 1-31

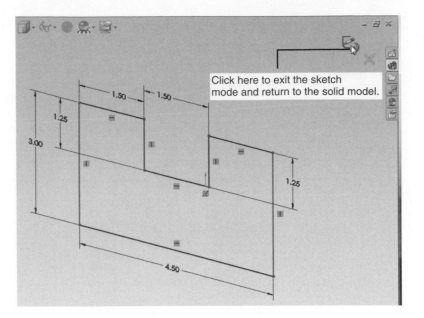

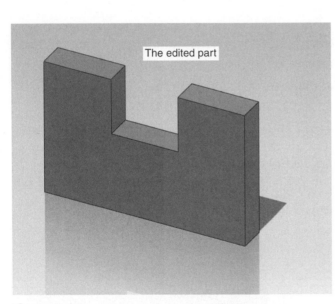

The edited part

Figure 1-32

Figure 1-33

1-7 Editing a Feature

This section will show how to change the extruded thickness of the feature from 0.60 to 0.40 in.

1 With the object on the screen, right-click the mouse button.

A selection of tools will appear. See Figure 1-33.

2 Select the **Edit Feature** tool.

Tools listed in the **Features** group require the **Edit Feature** tool to edit.

3 The **Boss-Extrude2 PropertyManager** will appear on the left side of the screen.

See Figure 1-34.

Figure 1-34

Click here to return to the solid model.

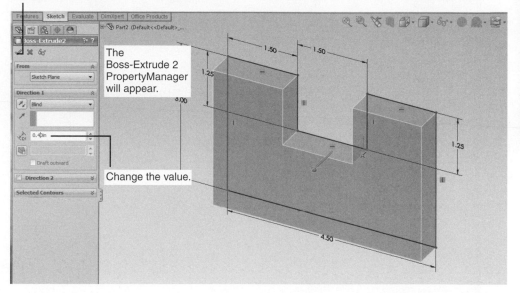

The Boss-Extrude 2 PropertyManager will appear.

Change the value.

4 Change the thickness value from 0.60 in. to **0.40in**, then click the green check mark to save and update the object.

Figure 1-35 shows the edited object.

Figure 1-35

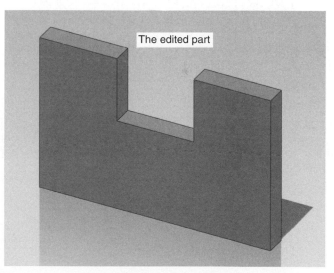

The edited part

1-8 The Circle and Smart Dimension Tools

In this section we will create an object that includes angular corners and holes. It will be drawn in the top plane.

1 Start a new drawing using the procedures presented in Section 1-2.

2 Select the **Top Plane** orientation from the **FeatureManager**.

3 Select the **Sketch** tab on the **CommandManager**.

See Figure 1-36.

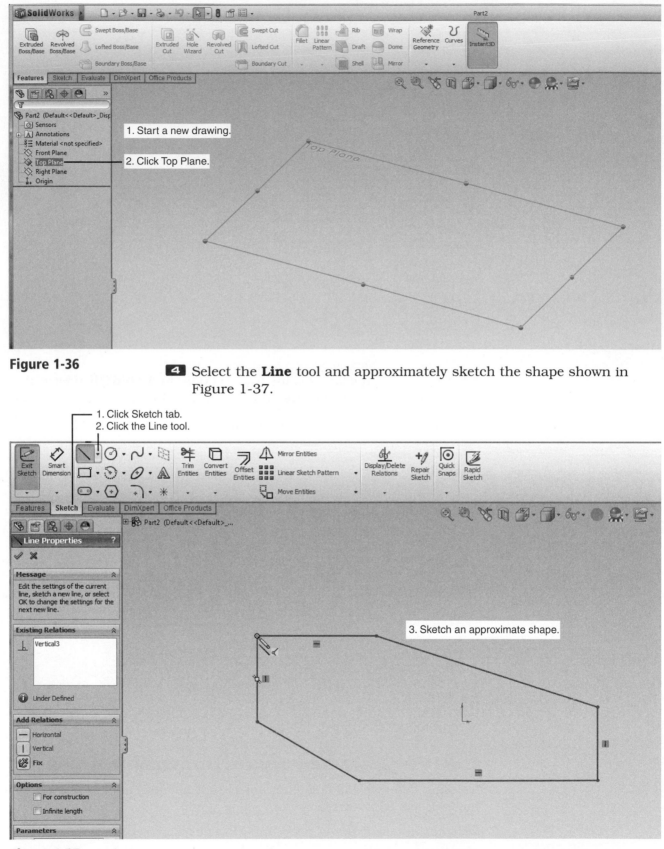

Figure 1-36

4 Select the **Line** tool and approximately sketch the shape shown in Figure 1-37.

Figure 1-37

5 Right-click the mouse and click the **Select** tool or click the green check mark in the **Line PropertyManager**.

See Figure 1-38.

6 Select the **Smart Dimension** tool and dimension the overall width of the part to be **5.00 in**. and the top horizontal line to be **2.25 in**.

See Figure 1-39.

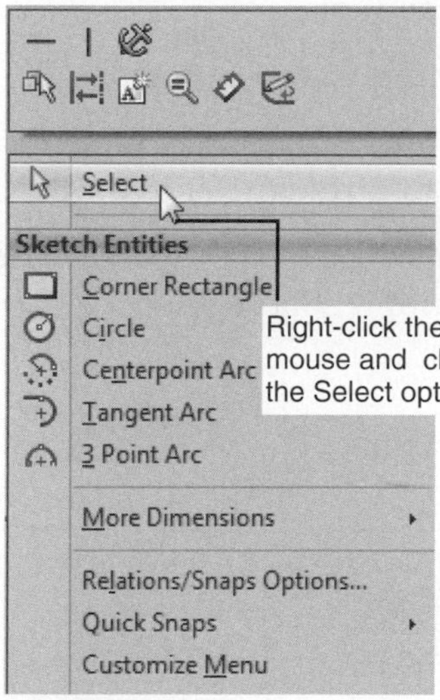

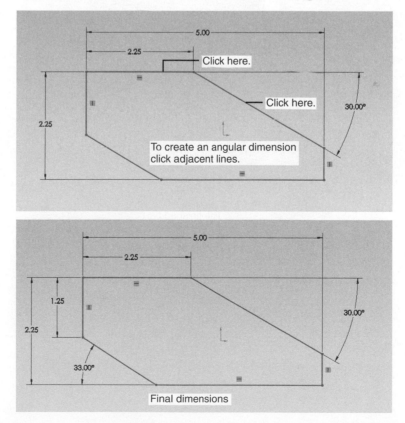

Use the Smart Dimension tool and add dimensions to the part.

Right-click the mouse and click the Select option.

Figure 1-38 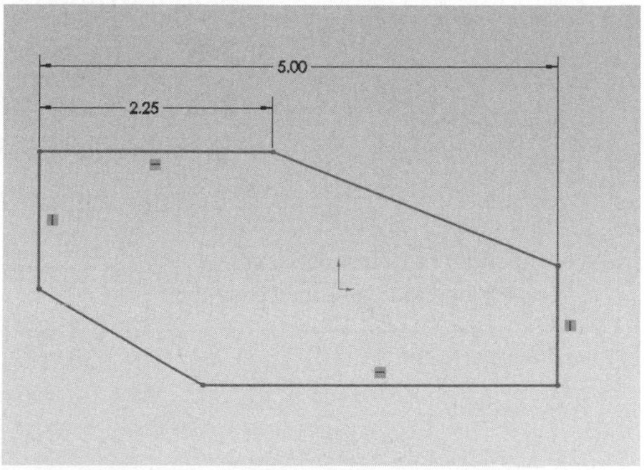   **Figure 1-39**

7 Continue dimensioning the other lines and angles as shown.

To create an angular dimension, click an angular line and then click an adjacent line. Move the cursor away from the lines. The dimension will appear. Insert the dimension as shown in Figure 1-40.

Figure 1-40

Click here.

Click here.

30.00°

To create an angular dimension click adjacent lines.

33.00°

30.00°

Final dimensions

> **TIP**
> Move the cursor around the screen and note how different angular values appear.

Creating the Solid

1 Select the **Features** tab on the **CommandManager** and then the **Extruded Boss/Base** tool.

The drawing's orientation will automatically change to three dimensional (trimetric).

2 Extrude the object to a thickness of **0.50in**.

3 Click the **OK** check mark in the **Boss-Extrude PropertyManager** to change the figure into a solid object.

See Figure 1-41.

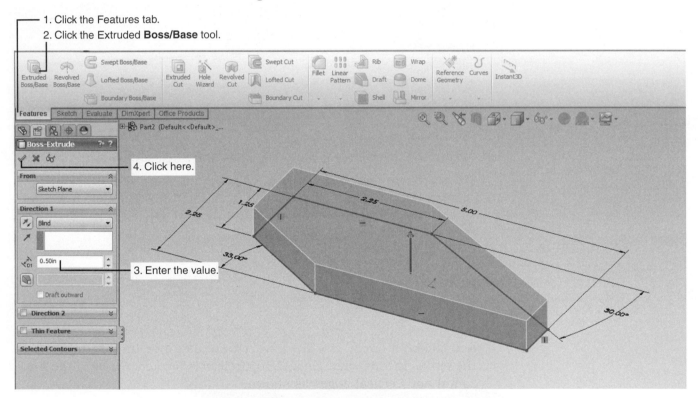

1. Click the Features tab.
2. Click the Extruded **Boss/Base** tool.

4. Click here.

3. Enter the value.

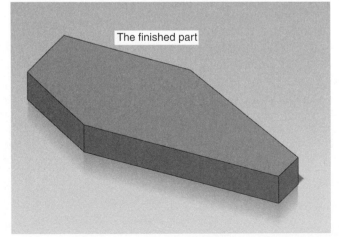

The finished part

Figure 1-41

To Add a Hole

A hole is created in an object by first sketching a circle on a new sketch plane. The circle is then cut out of the object using the **Extruded Cut** tool, creating a hole.

> **NOTE**
>
> Remember that a circle is a two-dimensional shape, and a hole is a three-dimensional shape.

1 Click the top surface of the object.

The surface will change colors, indicating that it has been selected.

2 Right-click the mouse and select the **Sketch** tool.

See Figure 1-42.

Figure 1-42

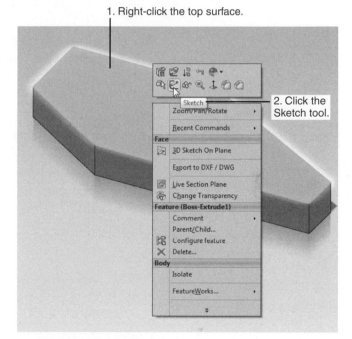

1. Right-click the top surface.

2. Click the Sketch tool.

3 Use the **Circle** tool of the **Sketch** group on the **CommandManager** and sketch a circle. Use the **Smart Dimension** tool to locate and size the circle. In this example a Ø.50 circle was located .75 from the horizontal and vertical edges as shown.

See Figures 1-43 and 1-44.

Figure 1-43

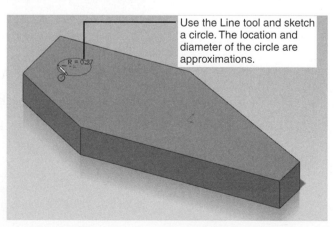

Use the Line tool and sketch a circle. The location and diameter of the circle are approximations.

Figure 1-44

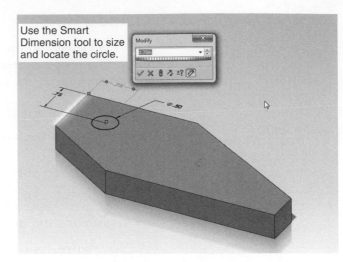

Use the Smart Dimension tool to size and locate the circle.

---

4 Click the **Features** tab on the **CommandManager** and then select the **Extruded Cut** tool.

See Figure 1-45.

Figure 1-45

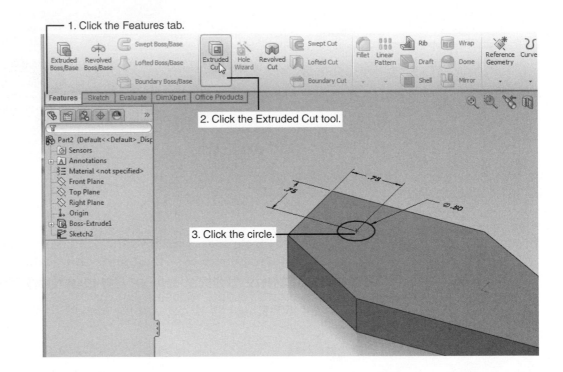

1. Click the Features tab.

2. Click the Extruded Cut tool.

3. Click the circle.

---

5 Click the circle. A preview of the extruded cut will show on the object.

6 Click the green check mark in the **Cut-Extrude PropertyManager**.

See Figure 1-46. Figure 1-47 shows the resulting hole in the object.

NOTE

The cut distance values must be equal to or greater than the thickness of the part.

Figure 1-46

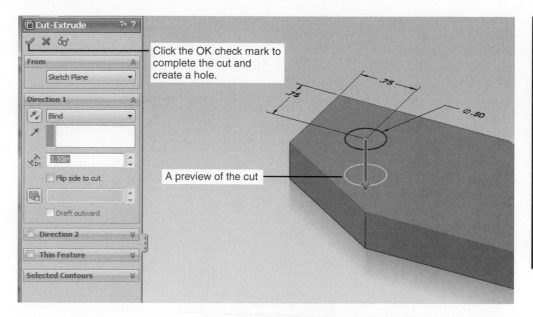

Click the OK check mark to complete the cut and create a hole.

A preview of the cut

Figure 1-47

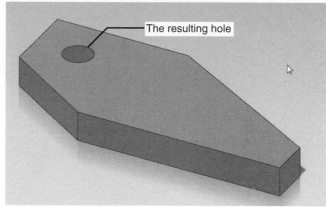

The resulting hole

7 Click the **File** heading at the top left of the screen.

A series of tools will cascade down.

8 Click the **Save As** tool.

9 Define the drawing's file name and click **Save**.

1-9 Setting Units on a Document Properties

The default settings for drawing units may be modified using the **Document Properties** dialog box. In this section we will define the drawing units as millimeters.

1 Start a new **Part** document.

2 Click the **Options** tool located at the top of the screen.

A series of tools will cascade down. See Figure 1-48.

Figure 1-48

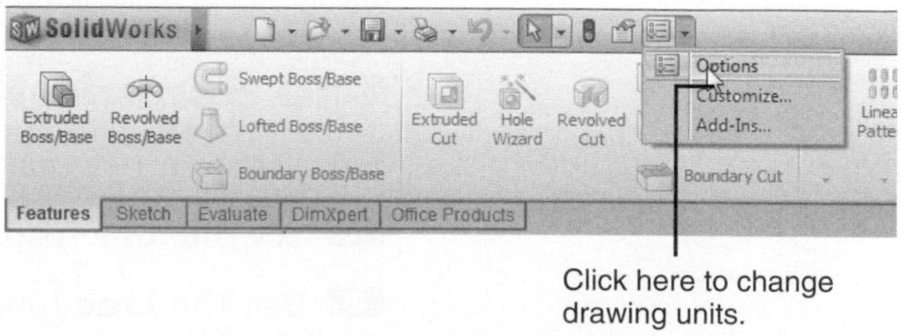

Click here to change drawing units.

3 Click **Options**.

The **Document Properties - Units** dialog box will appear. See Figure 1-49.

Figure 1-49

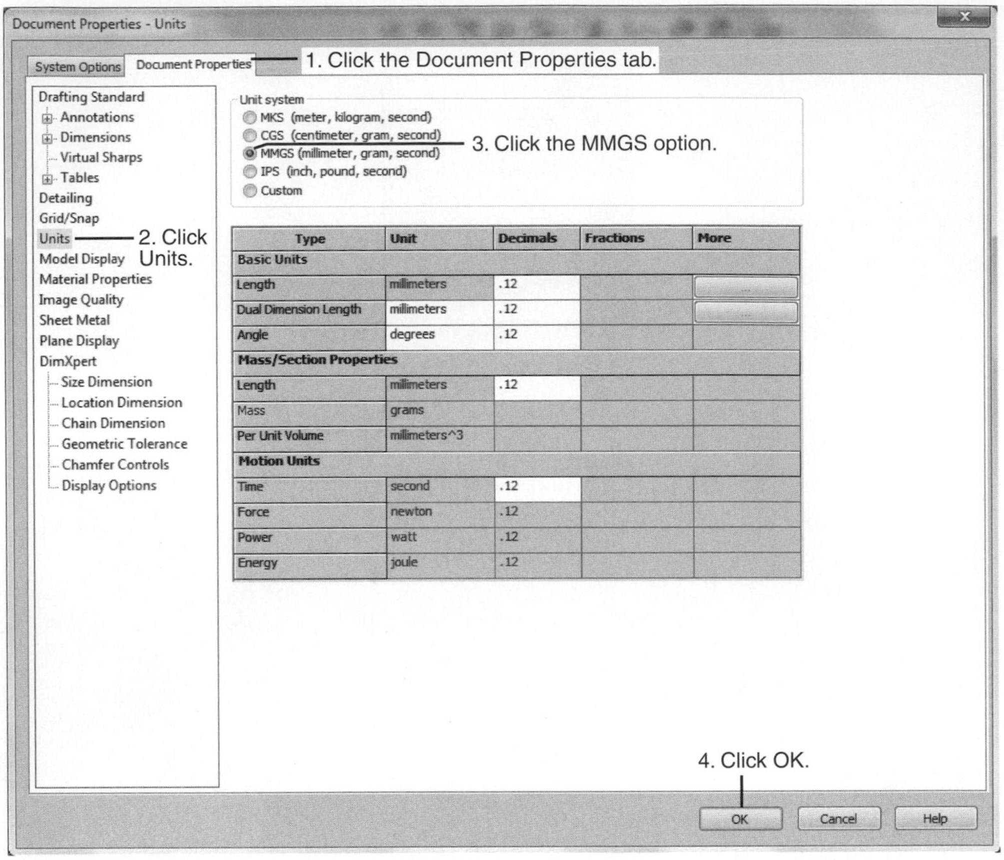

4 Click the **Document Properties** tab.

5 Click **Units** in the left column.

The **Unit system** dialog box will appear.

6 Click the **MMGS (millimeter, gram, second)** tool listed in the **Unit system** box.

7 Click **OK**.

The drawing units are now calibrated to millimeters.

8 Return to the drawing screen and proceed with the following section.

> **TIP**
> In SolidWorks the positive direction is the counterclockwise direction.

1-10 Sample Problem SP1-1

1 Create a new part.

2 Set the dimension units for millimeters.

3 Use the **Line** tool and sketch the profile shown in Figure 1-50.

Figure 1-50

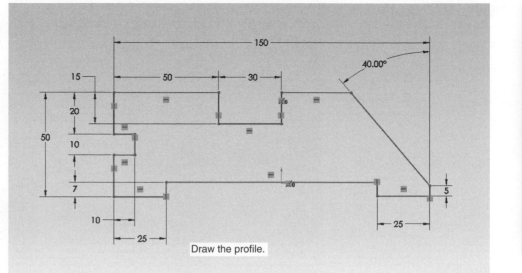

Draw the profile.

All dimensions are in millimeters.

4 Use the **Smart Dimension** tool and add dimensions to the part.

5 Click the **Features** tab and the **Extruded Boss/Base** tool.

6 Set the part thickness to **10.00mm.**

See Figure 1-51.

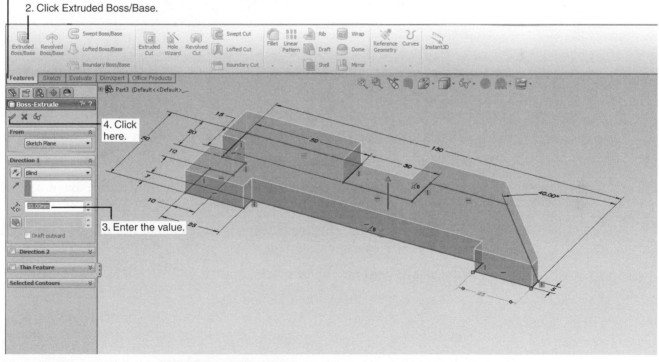

Figure 1-51

7 Click the OK **check mark.**

8 Right-click the top surface of the part and select the **Sketch** option.

See Figure 1-52.

9 Use the **Circle** tool to sketch two circles on the top surface.

10 Use the **Smart Dimension** tool to size and locate the holes.

See Figure 1-53.

Figure 1-52

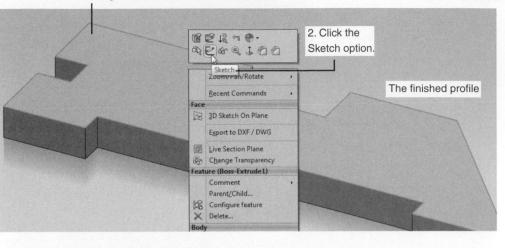

1. Right-click the top surface of the part.

2. Click the Sketch option.

The finished profile

Figure 1-53

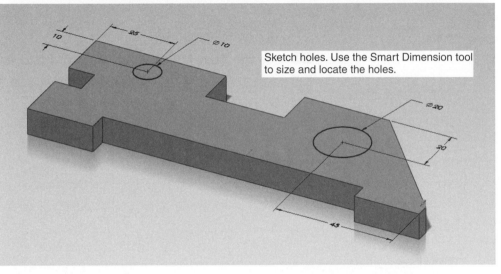

Sketch holes. Use the Smart Dimension tool to size and locate the holes.

11 Click the **Features** tab and select the **Extruded Cut** tool.

12 Select the two holes.

The holes should be selected automatically, but if they are not, click both holes. A preview of the holes will appear.

13 Assure that the thickness value is at least **10,** the thickness of the part, or greater.

14 Click the **green check mark.**

Figure 1-54 shows the finished part.

Figure 1-54

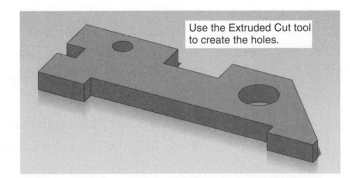

Use the Extruded Cut tool to create the holes.

Chapter Project

Project 1-1:

Sketch the shapes shown in Figures P1-1 through P1-18. Create 3D models using the specified thickness values.

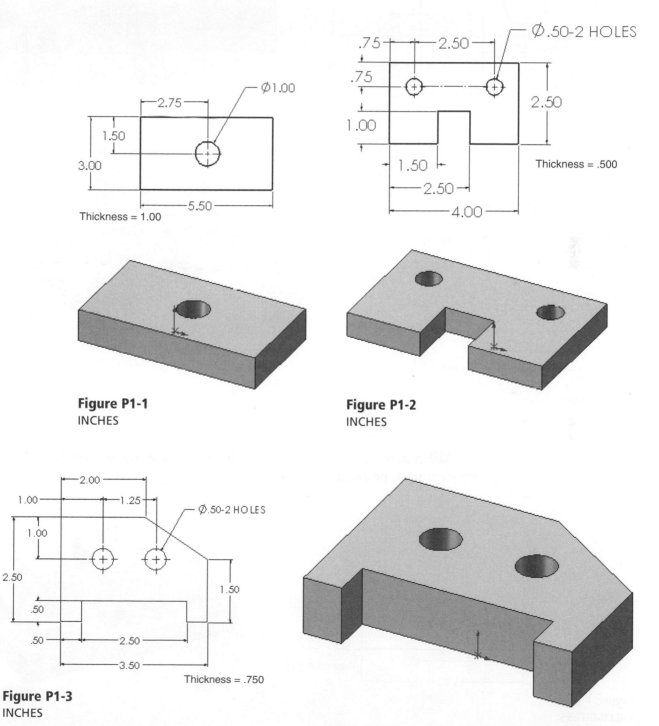

Figure P1-1
INCHES

Figure P1-2
INCHES

Figure P1-3
INCHES

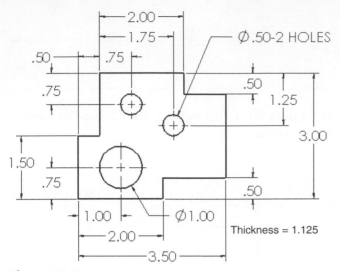
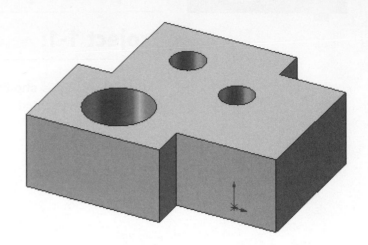

Figure P1-4
INCHES

Thickness = 1.125

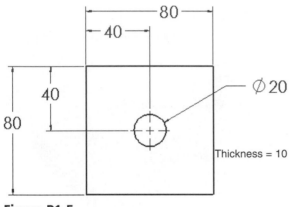
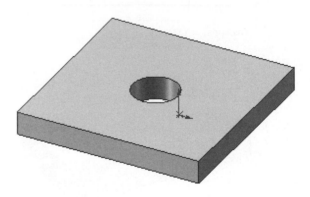

Figure P1-5
MILLIMETERS

Thickness = 10

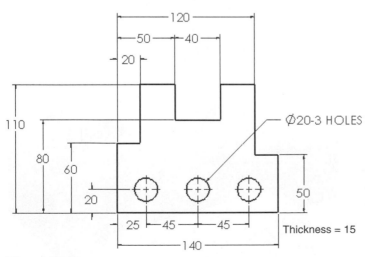

Figure P1-6
MILLIMETERS

Ø20-3 HOLES

Thickness = 15

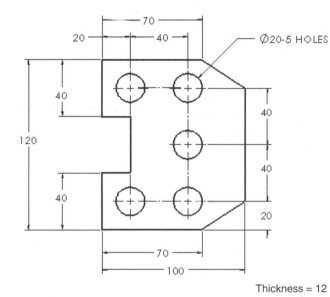

Figure P1-7
MILLIMETERS

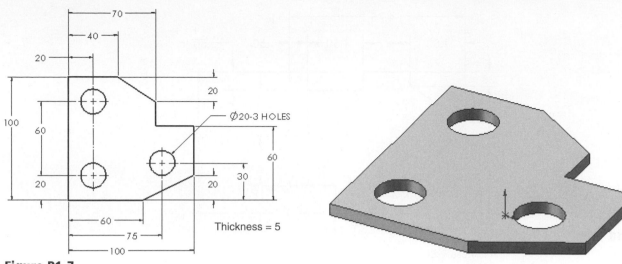

Ø20-3 HOLES

Thickness = 5

Ø20-5 HOLES

Thickness = 12

Figure P1-8
MILLIMETERS

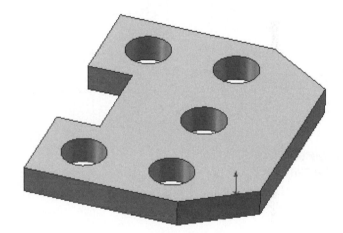

Ø20-2 HOLES

R58.31

Thickness = 20

Figure P1-9
MILLIMETERS

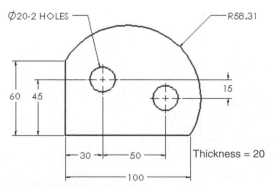

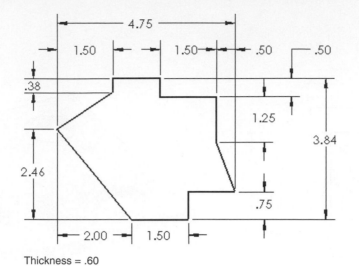

Figure P1-10
INCHES

Thickness = .60

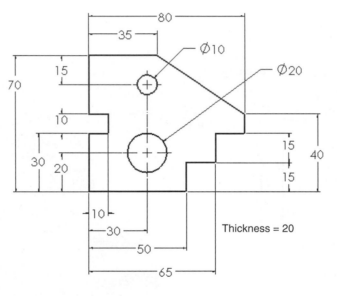

Figure P1-11
MILLIMETERS

Thickness = 20

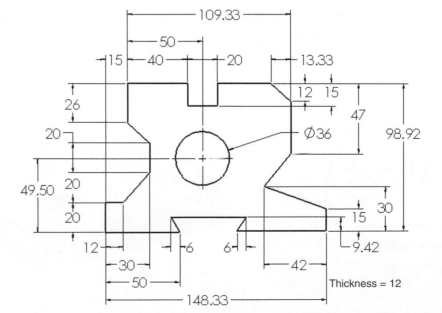

Figure P1-12
MILLIMETERS

Thickness = 12

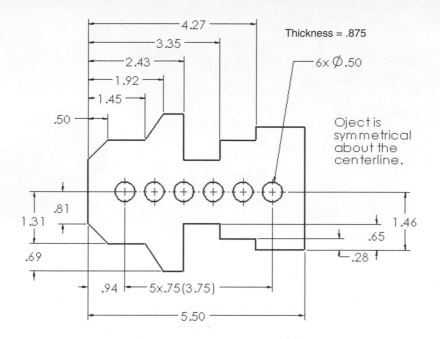

Figure P1-13
INCHES

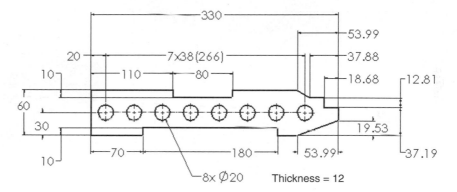

Figure P1-14
MILLIMETERS

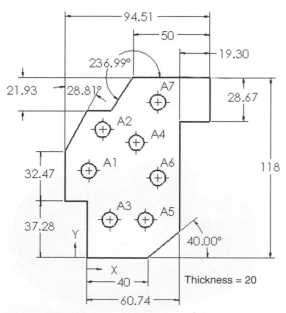

Figure P1-15
MILLIMETERS

TAG	X LOC	Y LOC	SIZE
A1	1.22	57.14	Ø10
A2	10.27	84.04	Ø10
A3	15	25	Ø10
A4	32.38	75.51	Ø10
A5	38.51	25	Ø10
A6	46.50	52.61	Ø10
A7	46.50	101.88	Ø10

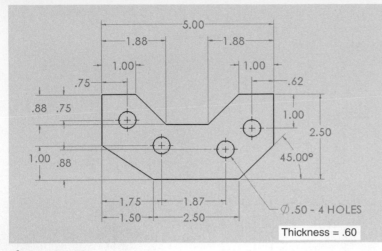
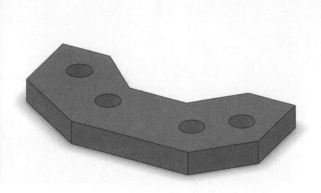

Figure P1-16
INCHES

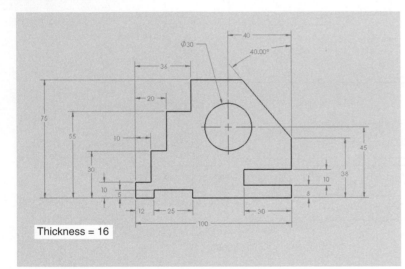
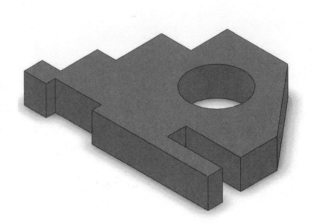

Figure P1-17
MILLIMETERS

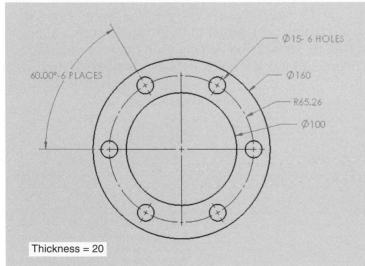
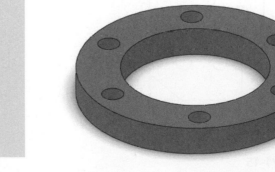

Figure P1-18
MILLIMETERS

2 chaptertwo

Sketch Entities and Tools

CHAPTER OBJECTIVES

- Learn how to create 2D sketches
- Learn how to use most of the sketch tools

- Learn how to create more complex shapes by combining individual sketch tools

2-1 Introduction

Figure 2-1 shows the **Sketch** panel. Most of the tools of the panel will be explained and demonstrated. The **Line** tool was explained in Chapter 1. This chapter starts with the **Circle** tool and explains most of the other 2D sketch tools. The tools will then be combined to form more complex shapes.

Each section is written to explain and demonstrate the particular tool and can be used as a reference later if a quick refresher is needed. However, it is recommended that you work through the entire chapter so you can better understand how to use and combine the different tools available.

Figure 2-1

The Smart Dimension tool, used to add dimensions to a sketch

The 2D Sketch panel

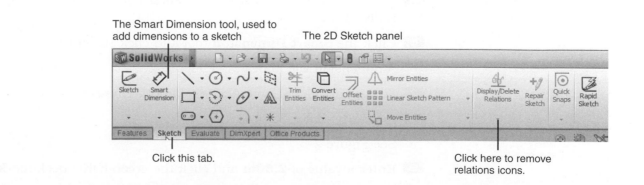

Click this tab.

Click here to remove relations icons.

2-2 Circle

A circle is sketched using the **Circle** tool and then sized, that is, given a diameter value, using the **Smart Dimension** tool. There are two circle tools: **Circle** and **Perimeter Circle**.

To Sketch a Circle

1 Start a new SolidWorks document or **Part** drawing by clicking the **New** tool.

See Figure 2-2. The dimensions for this example are in inches.

2 Click the **Top Plane** option.

3 Click the **Circle** tool.

See Figure 2-3.

4 Click a point on the screen to establish the center point of the circle.

5 Move the cursor away from the center point and click an approximate radius value.

6 Click the **Smart Dimension** tool and click the circle.

A dimension will appear. See Figure 2-4.

7 Locate the dimension by left-clicking the mouse.

8 A **Modify** dialog box will appear.

See Figure 2-5.

9 Enter a value of **2.50in** and click the green (OK) check mark.

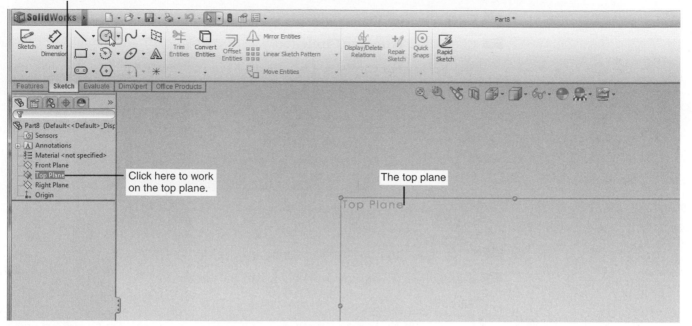

Figure 2-3

Figure 2-4

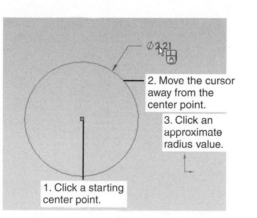

Figure 2-5

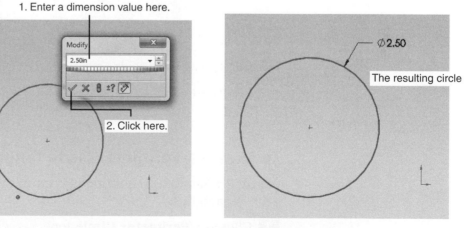

To Sketch a Perimeter Circle Using Three Points

A perimeter circle is a circle drawn using three points. These points may be three individual points or points tangent to an existing object.

1 Start a new SolidWorks document or part drawing by clicking the **New** tool.

The dimensions for this example are in inches.

2 Click the **Top Plane** option.

3 Click the **Perimeter Circle** tool.

The **Perimeter Circle** tool is a flyout from the **Circle** tool. See Figure 2-6.

Figure 2-6

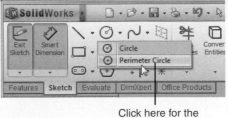

Click here for the
Perimeter Circle tool.

4 Click three points on the screen.

5 Right-click the mouse and click the **Select** option.

See Figure 2-7

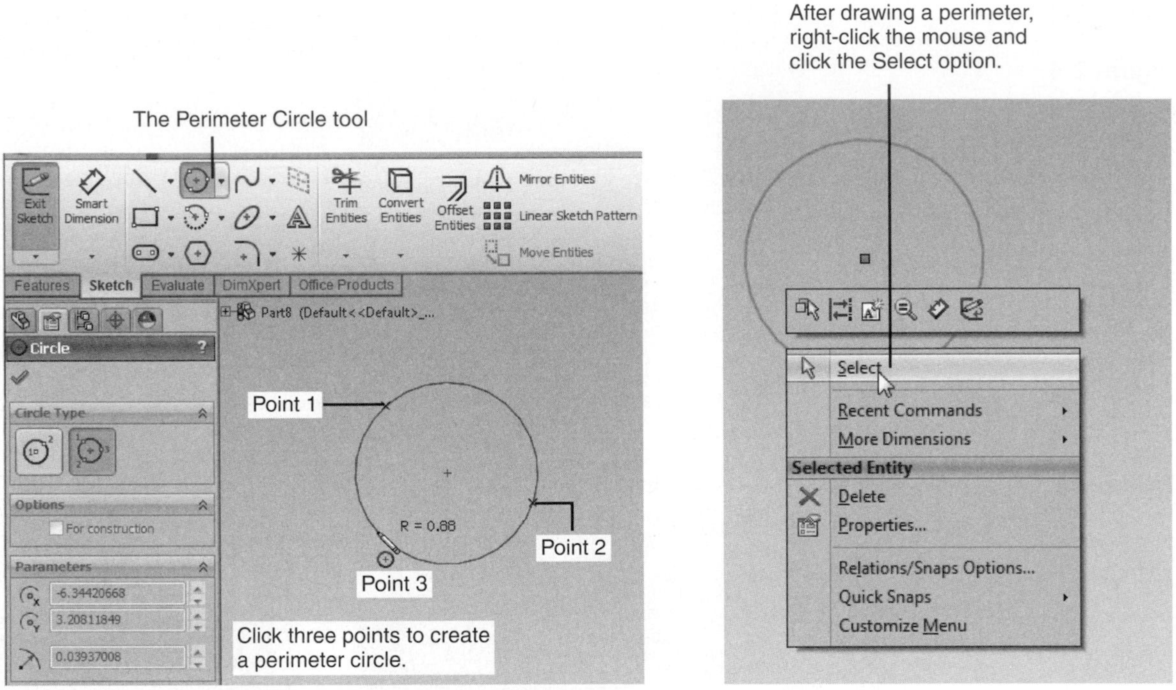

After drawing a perimeter,
right-click the mouse and
click the Select option.

The Perimeter Circle tool

Point 1

Point 2

R = 0.88

Point 3

Click three points to create
a perimeter circle.

Select

Figure 2-7

To Sketch a Perimeter Circle Tangent to Three Lines

Figure 2-8 shows three randomly drawn straight lines. Draw a circle tangent to each line.

1 Click the **Perimeter Circle** tool.

2 Click the approximate center point of each of the three lines.

A circle will appear tangent to all three lines.

3 Right-click the mouse and click the **Select** option.

See Figure 2-9.

Figure 2-8

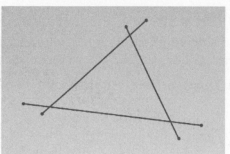

Figure 2-9

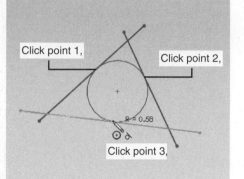
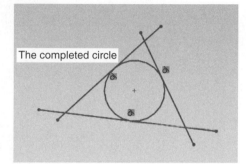

2-3 Rectangle

To Sketch a Rectangle

1 Start a new SolidWorks document or part drawing by clicking the **New** tool.

See Figure 2-10. The dimensions for this example are in inches.

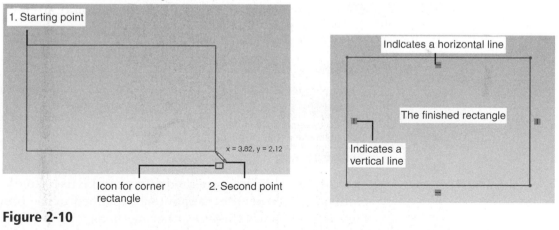

Figure 2-10

2 Click the **Top Plane** option.

3 Click the **Corner Rectangle** tool.

4 Click a start point for the rectangle, then move the cursor away from the point.

5 Select a second corner point and click the mouse.

6 Right-click the mouse and click the **Select** option.

To Delete Relations

The rectangle shown in Figure 2-10 includes small icons that indicate the lines are horizontal or vertical. These icons can be removed as follows.

1 Click the **Display/Delete Relations** tool on the **Sketch** panel. See Figure 2-11.

Figure 2-11

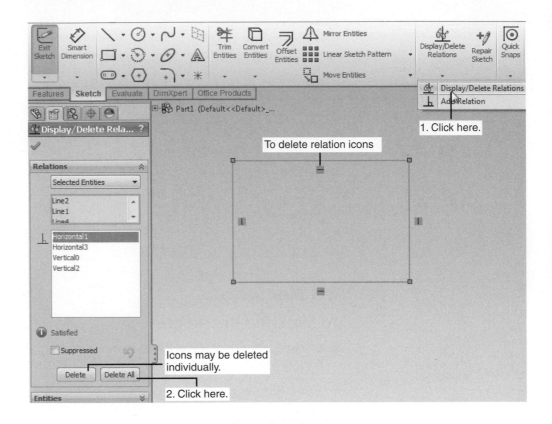

2 Click the **Delete All** option on the **Display/Delete Relations PropertyManager.**

NOTE

The relations icons will disappear when the sketch is converted to a solid model. They are helpful during the sketch phase of the drawing process.

2-4 Other Rectangle Tools

There are five different methods that can be used to create a rectangle, including the **Corner Rectangle** tool explained in the previous section. Figure 2-12 shows the four other methods.

Center Rectangle

1 Click a starting center point.

2 Click a second point that will become the center point of one of the edge lines.

3 Click a third point that will define one of the corner points.

4 Right-click the mouse and click the **Select** option.

Figure 2-12

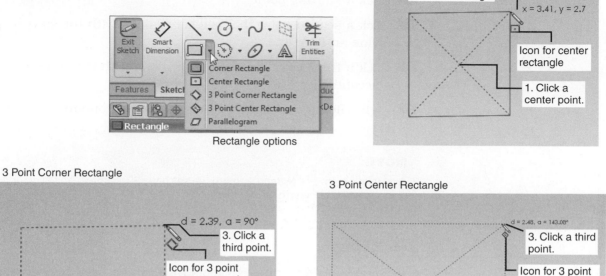

Rectangle options

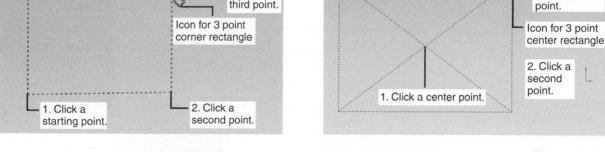

Parallelogram

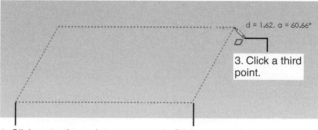

1. Click a starting point.   2. Click a second point.

3 Point Corner Rectangle

1 Click a starting point.

2 Click a second point that will serve along with the starting point to define an edge line.

3 Click a third point that will serve along with the second point to define a second edge line.

4 Right-click the mouse and click the **Select** option.

3 Point Center Rectangle

1 Click a starting center point.

2 Click a second point that will become the center point of one of the edges.

3 Click a third point to define a corner point.

4 Right-click the mouse and click the **Select** option.

Parallelogram

1 Click a starting point.

2 Click a second point that will serve along with the starting point to define an edge line.

3 Click a third point that will serve along with the second point to define a second edge line.

4 Right-click the mouse and click the **Select** option.

> **NOTE**
>
> A parallelogram is a rectangle that does not have 90° corners; however, opposite edges must be of equal length and parallel.

2-5 Slots

SolidWorks has four different tools that can be used to draw slots. The **Slot** tool can be used to create both internal and external slot shapes. Figure 2-13 shows examples of both internal and external slot shapes.

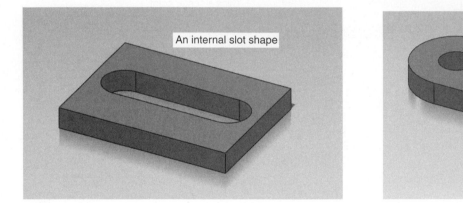

An internal slot shape

An external slot shape

Figure 2-13

See Figure 2-14.

Straight Slot

1 Click the **Slot** tool.

2 Click a starting point.

3 Click a second point that along with the starting point will define the slot's centerline.

4 Click a third point to define the radius of the slot's rounded ends.

5 Right-click the mouse and click the **Select** option.

Centerpoint Straight Slot

1 Click a starting point.

2 Click a second point.

The distance between the starting point and the second point will define half the length to the slot's center point. This tool allows you to center the slot.

Figure 2-14

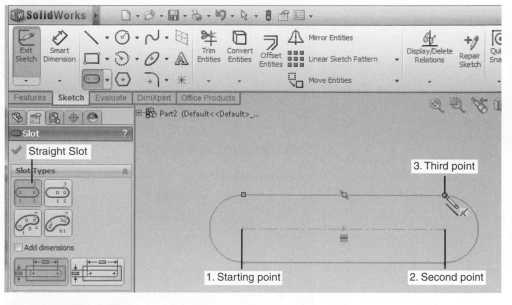

Centerpoint Straight Slot

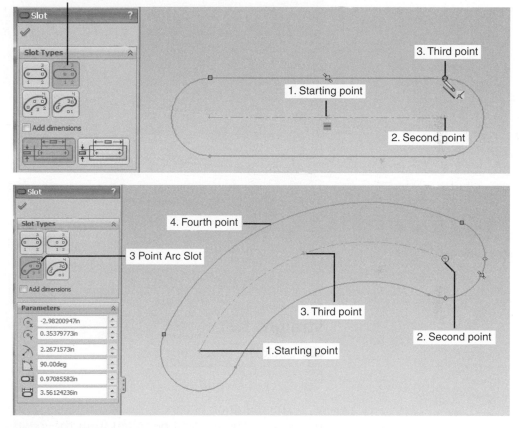

3 Click a third point.

The distance between the second and third points will define the radius of the slot's rounded corners.

4 Right-click the mouse and click the **Select** option.

3 Point Arc Slot

1 Click a starting point.

2 Click a second point.

The distance between the starting point and second point will define the slot's centerline.

3 Click a third point.

The third point defines the radius of the arc used to create the slot relative to the starting and second points.

4 Right-click the mouse and click the **Select** option.

Centerpoint Arc Slot

See Figure 2-15.

Figure 2-15

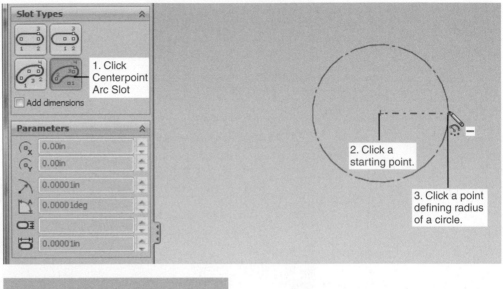

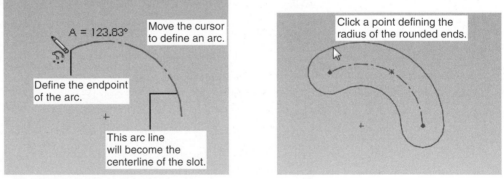

1 Click a starting point.

2 Click a second point.

The distance between the first and second points will define the radius of a circle. The arc will be taken from the existing circle; therefore, the radius of the circle and the radius of the arc will be equal.

3 Move the cursor in a counterclockwise direction and select a third point.

The distance between the second and third points will define the length of the arc's centerline.

4 Move the cursor away from the third point and select a fourth point.

The distance between the third and fourth points will define the radius of the slot's rounded ends.

5 Right-click the mouse and click the **Select** option.

2-6 Polygon

A *polygon* is an enclosed figure containing three or more sides. A hexagon is commonly used in technical drawing to define bolt and nut head shapes.

The **Polygon** tool creates only equilateral polygons, that is, polygons with all sides of equal length. Irregular polygons—those with sides of unequal length—must be created using the **Line** tool.

To Draw a Hexagon

See Figure 2-16.

Figure 2-16

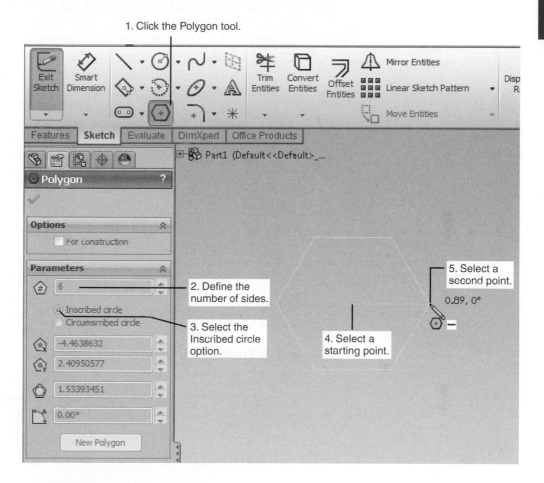

1. Click the Polygon tool.

2. Define the number of sides.

3. Select the Inscribed circle option.

4. Select a starting point.

5. Select a second point.

Right-click the mouse and click the Select option.

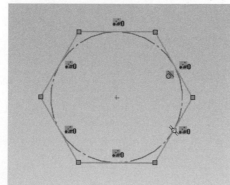

1 Start a new drawing, click the **Sketch** tab, and select the **Top Plane** option.

2 Click the **Polygon** tool located on the **Sketch** panel.

3 Define the number of sides.

In this example six sides were selected, creating a hexagon.

4 Select the **Inscribed circle** option.

5 Click a starting point.

6 Move the cursor away from the center point and click a second point.

The distance between the center point and the second point will define half the distance across the corners of the hexagon.

Figure 2-17 shows an inscribed and a circumscribed hexagon. In general, circumscribed hexagons are more common in technical drawing, as the distance across the flats matches the diameter of the circumscribed circle and the size specifications for hex head screws, bolts, and nuts. The distance is also used to define wrench sizes.

Figure 2-17

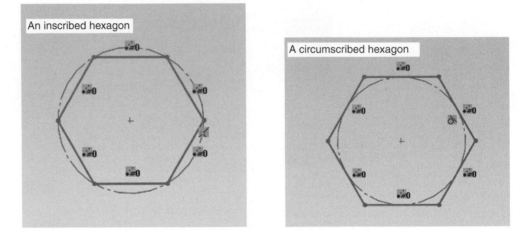

Hexagon Definitions

The size of a regular hexagon (all sides of equal length) may be defined in one of the following ways: distance across the flats, distance across the corners, and edge distance. See Figure 2-18.

Figure 2-18

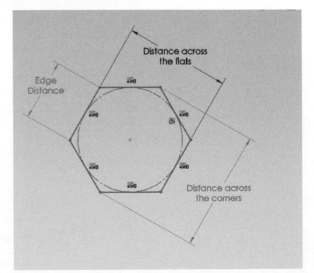

2-7 Arcs

SolidWorks offers three different ways to draw arcs: using a centerpoint, tangent, or three points.

Centerpoint Arc

See Figure 2-19.

Figure 2-19

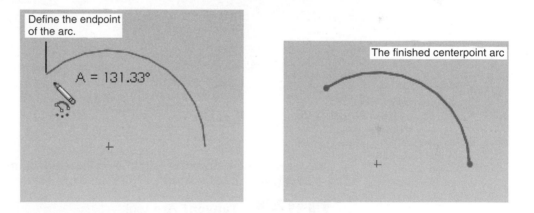

1. Click the Centerpoint Arc tool.

3. Click a second point as the starting point for the arc.

R = 0.69

2. Click a starting point

Define the endpoint of the arc.

A = 131.33°

The finished centerpoint arc

1 Start a new drawing, click the **Sketch** tab, and select the **Top Plane** option.

2 Click the **Centerpoint Arc** tool.

3 Click a starting point.

4 Move the cursor away from the starting point and select a second point.

This point will become the starting point for the arc. The distance between the starting point and the second point will define the radius of the arc.

5 Move the cursor away from the second point and define a third point to define the endpoint of the arc.

6 Right-click the mouse and click the **Select** option.

Tangent Arc

Figure 2-20 shows two randomly drawn intersecting straight lines. Draw an arc tangent to the lines.

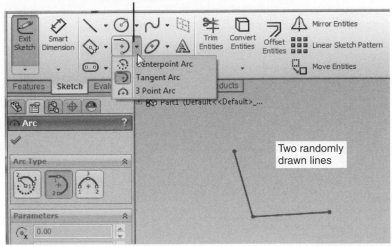

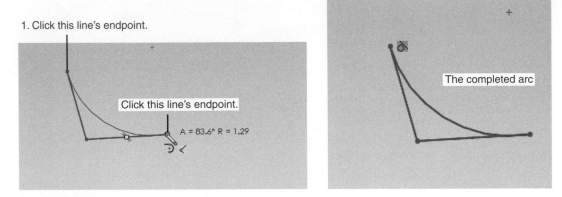

Figure 2-20

1 Start a new drawing, click the **Sketch** tab, and select the **Top Plane** option.

2 Click the **Tangent Arc** tool.

3 Click the endpoint of one of the lines.

4 Click the endpoint of the other line.

5 Right-click the mouse and click the **Select** option.

3 Point Arc

See Figure 2-21.

1 Start a new drawing, click the **Sketch** tab, and select the **Top Plane** option.

2 Click the **3 Point Arc** tool.

3 Click a starting point for the arc.

Figure 2-21

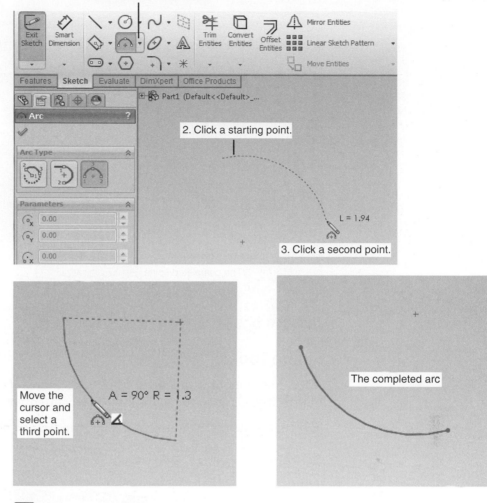

1. Click the 3 Point Arc tool.

2. Click a starting point.

3. Click a second point.

L = 1.94

Move the cursor and select a third point.

A = 90° R = 1.3

The completed arc

4 Select a second point.

5 Move the cursor away from the second point and select a third point.

6 Right-click the mouse and click the **Select** option.

2-8 Spline

See Figure 2-22.

1 Start a new **Part** document, click the **Sketch** tool, and click the **Top Plane** option.

2 Click the **Spline** tool.

3 Select a starting point for the spline and click the point.

4 Select other points and extend the spline.

5 When the spline is complete, right-click the mouse and click the **Select** option or select the check mark in the **Spline PropertyManager.**

A spline may be edited by moving any one of its defining points.

To Edit a Spline

1 Click and hold one of the defining points, drag the point to a new location, and release the mouse button.

Figure 2-22

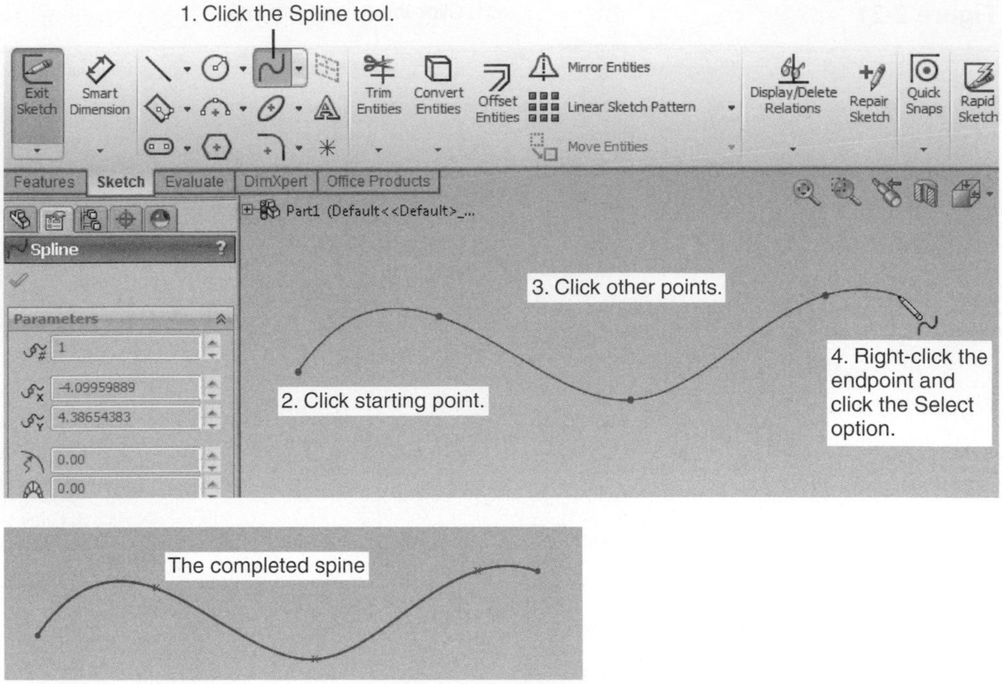

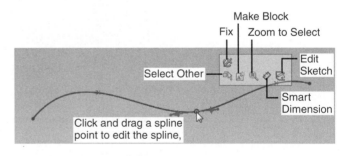

1. Click the Spline tool.

3. Click other points.

4. Right-click the endpoint and click the Select option.

2. Click starting point.

The completed spine

Spline Tools

After a spline point has been relocated, a box of options will appear. See Figure 2-23. These tools are often associated with splines.

1 Right-click the mouse and click the **Select** option.

Figure 2-23

Make Block

Fix   Zoom to Select

Edit Sketch

Select Other

Smart Dimension

Click and drag a spline point to edit the spline,

2-9 Ellipse

Ellipses are defined by their major and minor axes. See Figure 2-24.

Figure 2-24

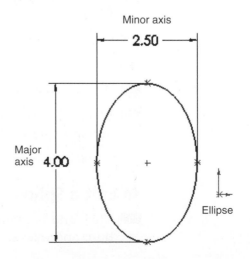

Minor axis

2.50

Major axis 4.00

Ellipse

1 Start a new **Part** document, click the **Sketch** tool, and click the **Top Plane** option.

2 Click the **Ellipse** tool on the **Sketch** toolbar.

3 Locate a center point for the ellipse and drag the cursor away from the center point.

Values for the major and minor axes will appear as the cursor is moved. The initial values will be equal, as the first part of the ellipse construction is a circle. See Figure 2-25. The initial axis can be either the major or minor axis depending on the value of the second axis.

Figure 2-25

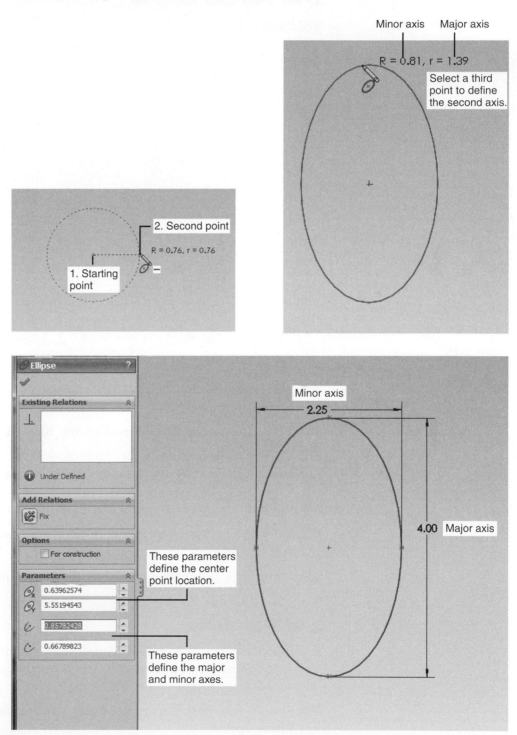

4 Locate the first point for the ellipse; click the mouse.

5 Locate the second point along the second axis; click the mouse.

The finished size of the ellipse may be defined using either the parameter values in the **Ellipse PropertyManager** or the **Smart Dimension** tool.

6 Define the major and minor axes for the ellipse.

7 Click the OK check mark.

2-10 Partial Ellipse

See Figure 2-26.

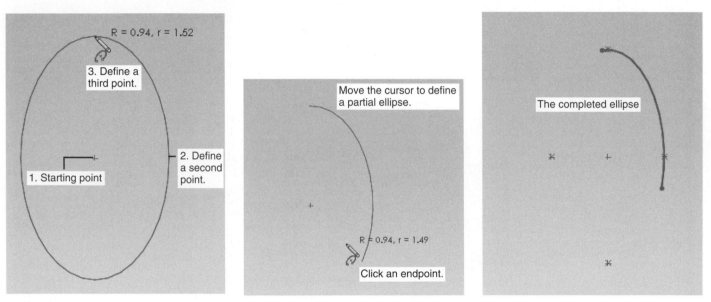

Figure 2-26

1 Start a new drawing, click the **Sketch** tab, and select the **Top Plane** option.

2 Click the **Partial Ellipse** tool on the **Sketch** panel.

3 Click a starting point.

4 Click a second point.

5 Click a third point defining the major and minor axes.

6 Move the cursor to create a partial ellipse based on the original major and minor axes.

7 Right-click the mouse and click the **Select** option.

2-11 Parabola

A **parabola** is the loci of points such that the distance between a fixed point, the **focus,** and a fixed line, the **directrix**, is always equal. See Figure 2-27.

1 Start a new **Part** document, click the **Sketch** tool, and select the **Top Plane** option.

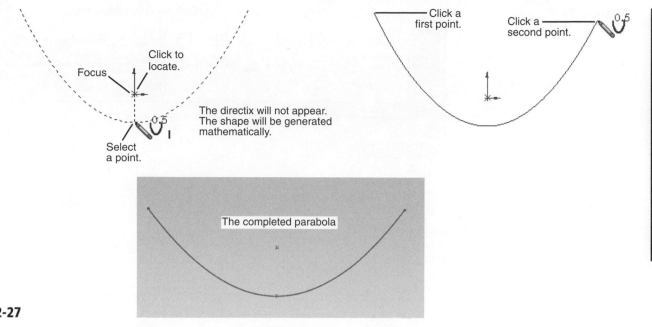

Figure 2-27

2 Click the **Parabola** tool on the **Sketch** toolbar.

3 Select a location for the focus point.

In this example the 0,0,0 coordinate point, or origin, was selected as the focus point. See Figure 2-27. The directrix was added to the illustration to help you understand how the parabolic shape is generated. The directrix will not appear during the SolidWorks construction.

4 Select a point away from the locus; click the mouse.

5 Select the left endpoint for the parabola.

6 Select the other endpoint for the parabola.

The **Parameters** section of the **Parabola PropertyManager** can be used to change the location of the focus point and the orientation of the parabola. The parabola may also be sized using the **Smart Dimension** tool.

7 Click the **OK** check mark.

2-12 Offset

The **Offset** tool is used to draw entities parallel to existing entities. Figure 2-28 shows an existing line. The **Offset** tool is used to draw a line parallel to the exisiting line and of equal length.

1 Start a new **Part** document, click the **Sketch** tab on the **CommandManager,** and click the **Top Plane** option.

2 Draw a random line on the screen using the **Line** tool.

3 Click the **Offset Entities** tool on the **Sketch** panel.

4 Define the distance between the existing line and the offset line by entering the distance into the **Offset Entities PropertyManager.**

NOTE

As the arrows to the right of the box defining the offset value are clicked, the offset line will move in real time to reflect the increase or decrease in the offset distance.

Figure 2-28

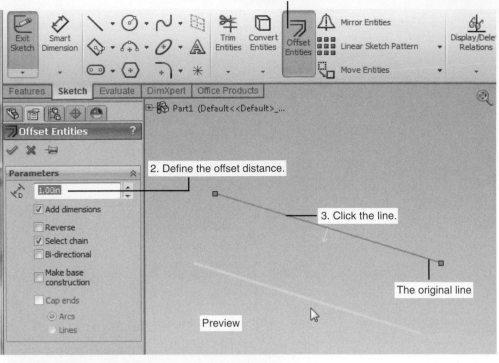

1. Click the Offset Entities tool.

2. Define the offset distance.

3. Click the line.

The original line

Preview

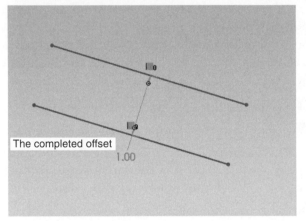

The completed offset

1.00

An arrow will appear on the existing line indicating the default direction of the offset. You can change the direction of the offset by moving the mouse to either side of the line or by checking the **Reverse** box under **Parameters** in the **Offset Entities PropertyManager.**

5 Click the side of the line where the offset line is to be located.

6 Click the OK check mark.

Entities other than lines may be offset. Figure 2-29 shows an offset rectangle and an offset circle.

Figure 2-29

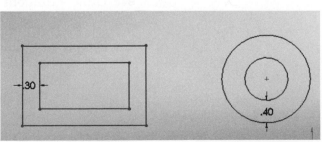

An offset rectangle   An offset circle

2-13 Trim Entities

The **Trim Entities** tool is used to remove unwanted entities from existing sketches.

Figure 2-30 shows an existing configuration consisting of a circle, a rectangle, and a line. The **Trim Entities** tool will be used to remove a segment of the line from within the circle and the rectangle.

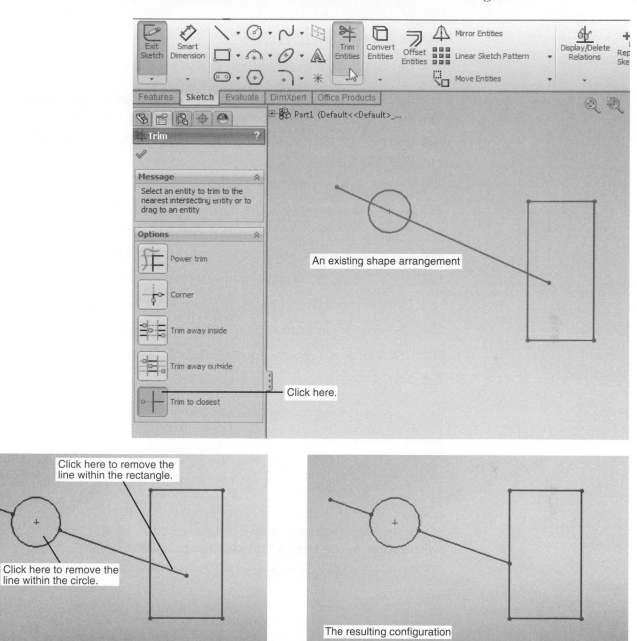

Figure 2-30

1 Start a new **Part** document, click the **Sketch** tab, and select the **Top Plane** option.

2 Draw a line, a circle, and a rectangle approximately as shown. Exact sizes are not required.

3 Access the **Trim Entities** tool on the **Sketch** panel.

In this example, the **Trim to closest** option will be used.

4 Move the cursor to the line segment within the circle; click the line.

The segment will change color when selected. The line segment will be removed when clicked.

5 Select the line segment within the rectangle; click the segment.

6 Click the OK check mark.

2-14 Extend Entities

The **Extend Entities** tool is used to extend existing lines and entities to new lengths or to other sketch entities.

Figure 2-31 shows a 1.50 × 4.00-in. rectangle. This example shows how to extend the rectangle so that it measures 1.5 × 5.5 in.

1 Start a new **Part** document, click the **Sketch** tab, and select the **Top Plane** option.

2 Draw a **1.5 × 4.00-in.** rectangle.

3 Draw a line parallel to the right vertical line of the rectangle. Locate the line **5.5 in.** from the left vertical line of the rectangle.

4 Click the **Extend Entities** tool on the **Sketch** panel.

5 Click the top horizontal line in the rectangle.

The extended line will appear automatically.

6 Click the lower horizontal line in the rectangle.

7 Right-click the mouse and click the **Select** option.

8 Right-click the vertical line located 5.50 in. from the left vertical line.

Figure 2-31

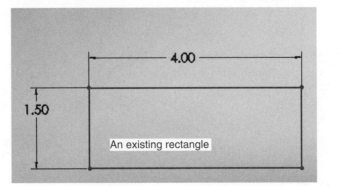

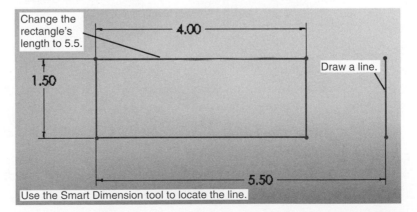

Figure 2-31
(*Continued*)

Chapter 2

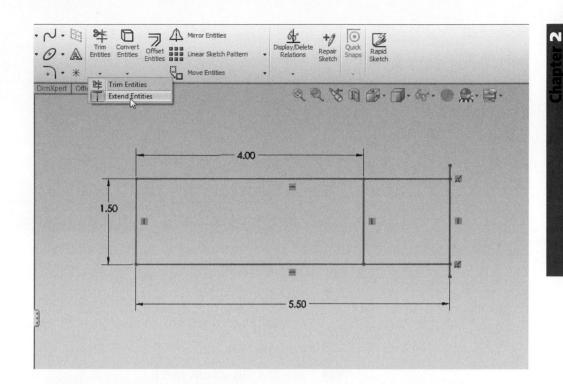

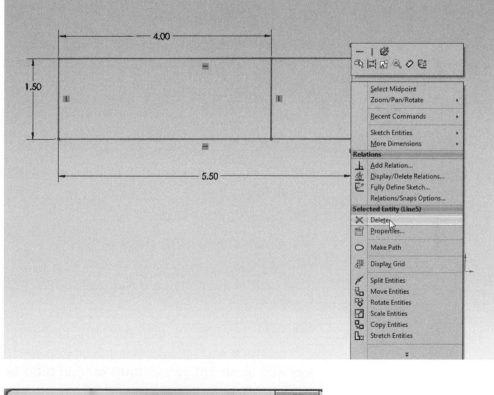

Figure 2-31
(*Continued*)

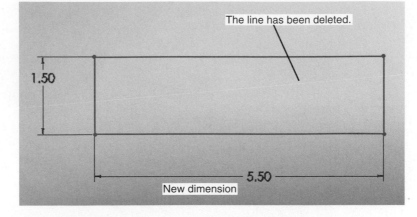

A list of options will appear.

9 Click the **Delete** option.

The **Sketcher Confirm Delete** box will appear.

10 Select the **Yes** button.

11 Click the OK check mark.

2-15 Split Entities

The **Split Entities** tool is used to trim away internal segments of an existing entity or to split an entity into two or more new entities by specifying split points.

Figure 2-32 shows the rectangle created in the last section. Remove a 1.00-in. segment from the top horizontal line so that the left end of the segment is 2.00 in. from the left side of the rectangle. If you have already created a 1.50 × 5.50-in. rectangle, proceed to step 3.

1 Start a new **Part** document, click the **Sketch** tab, and select the **Top Plane** option.

2 Draw a **1.50 × 4.00** rectangle.

3 Access the **Split Entities** tool.

The **Split Entities** tool is accessed by clicking **Tools** on the Standard toolbar, clicking **Sketch Tools,** then selecting the **Split Entities** tool.

4 Click two random points on the top horizontal line.

As the line is clicked, points will appear. Use the **Smart Dimension** tool and locate the points **2.00 in.** and **3.00 in.** from the left vertical line of the rectangle.

5 Right-click the segment between these two points and select the **Delete** option.

The line segment will disappear.

6 Use the **Smart Dimension** tool to size and locate the opening in the line.

7 Click the **OK** check mark.

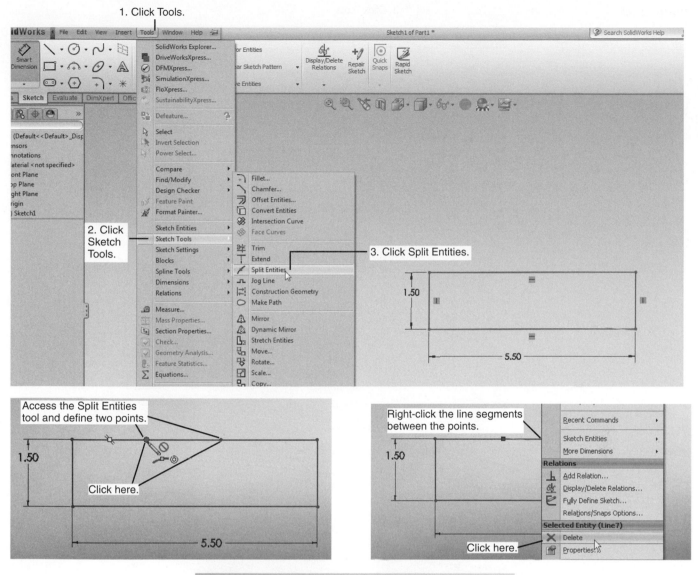

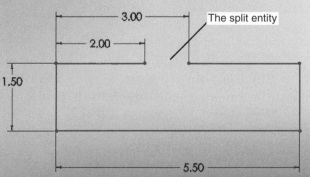

Figure 2-32

2-16 Jog Line

The **Jog Line** tool is used to create a rectangular shape (jog) in a line.

Figure 2-33 shows an existing line. This section will show how to add jogs to the line.

1 Start a new **Part** document, click the **Sketch** tab, and select the **Top Plane** option.

2 Draw a random horizontal line on the screen.

Figure 2-33

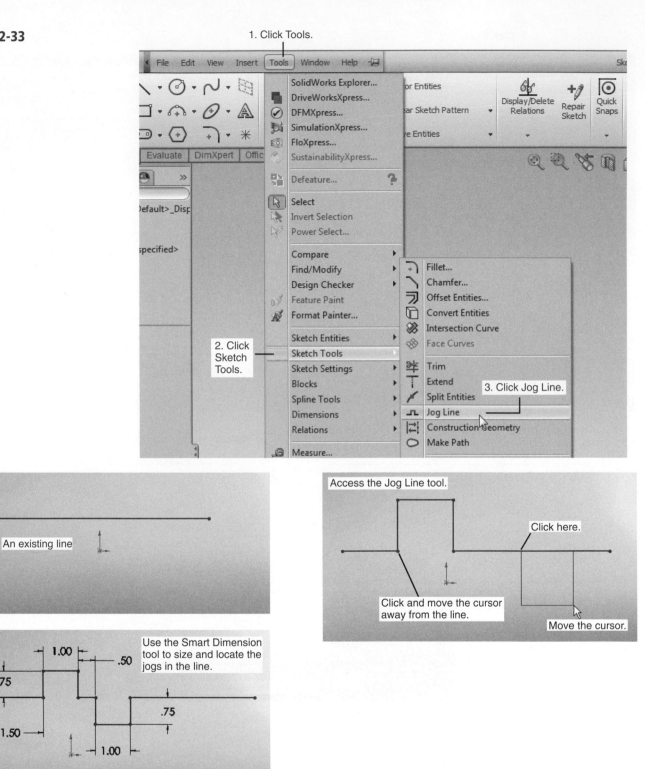

1. Click Tools.

2. Click Sketch Tools.

3. Click Jog Line.

An existing line

Access the Jog Line tool.

Click here.

Click and move the cursor away from the line.

Move the cursor.

Use the Smart Dimension tool to size and locate the jogs in the line.

3 Access the **Jog Line** tool.

The **Jog Line** tool is accessed by clicking **Tools** on the Standard tool-bar, clicking the **Sketch Tools** option, and selecting the **Jog Line** tool.

4 Click a point on the line and move the cursor away from the point as shown.

This will create a rectangular shape in the direction of the cursor movement.

5 Click and move the cursor to create a second jog as shown.

6 Use the **Smart Dimension** tool to size and locate the jogs.

7 Click the **OK** check mark.

2-17 Sample Problem SP2-1

Figure 2-34 shows how the **Jog Line** tool can be used to help shape entities. Two cutouts are added to a 2.00 × 4.00-in. rectangle using the **Jog Line** tool.

1 Draw a **2.00 × 4.00-in.** rectangle in the top plane.

2 Use the **Jog Line** tool to create slots at each end of the object.

3 Use the **Smart Dimension** tool to size and locate the slots.

See Section 1-4.

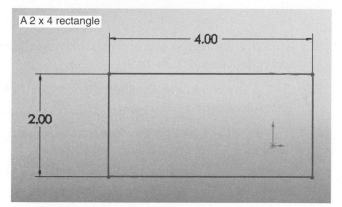

A 2 x 4 rectangle

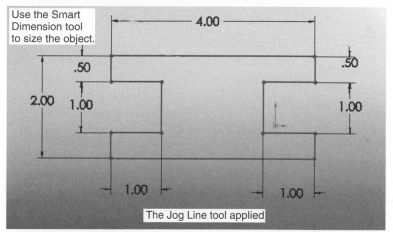

Use the Smart Dimension tool to size the object.

The Jog Line tool applied

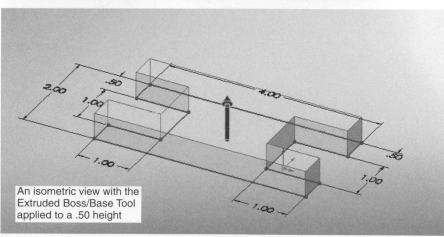

An isometric view with the Extruded Boss/Base Tool applied to a .50 height

Figure 2-34

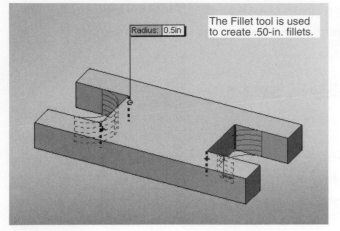

The Fillet tool is used to create .50-in. fillets.

Radius: 0.5in

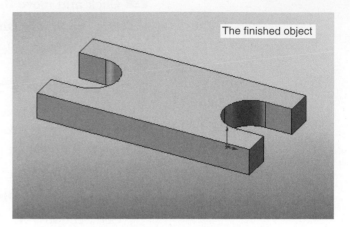

The finished object

Figure 2-34
(*Continued*)

4 Click the **Features** tab on the **CommandManager** and select the **Extruded Boss/Base** tool.

5 Define the thickness by entering a value of **0.50 in.** in the **Boss-Extrude PropertyManager.**

6 Use the **Fillet** tool on the **Features** tab and add **0.50-in.**-radii fillets by clicking the vertical lines as shown.

7 Click the OK check mark to complete the object.

2-18 Mirror Entities

The **Mirror Entities** tool is used to create a mirror image of an entity. A mirror image is different from a copy of an image. Figure 2-35 shows both a mirror image and a copy of the same entity. Note the differences.

Figure 2-35

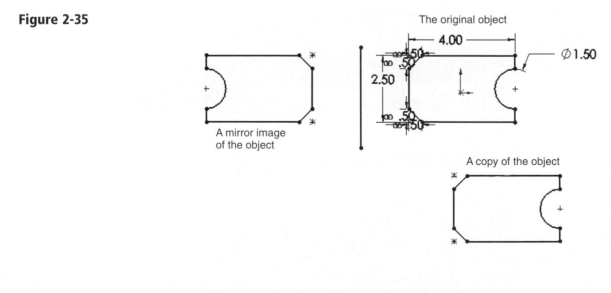

A mirror image of the object

The original object

4.00

2.50

Ø 1.50

A copy of the object

1 Start a new **Part** document, click the **Sketch** tab, and select the **Top Plane** option.

2 Draw the shape and vertical line shown in Figure 2-36.

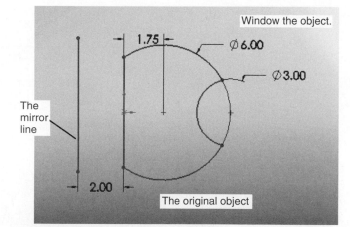

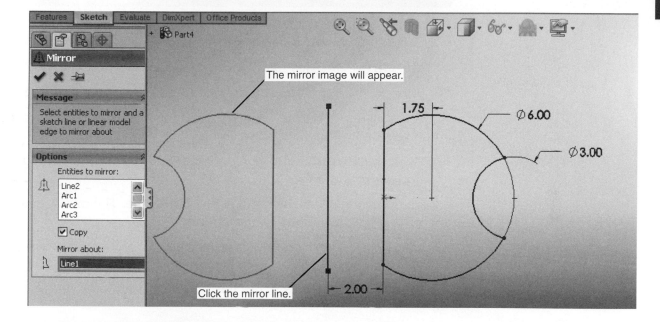

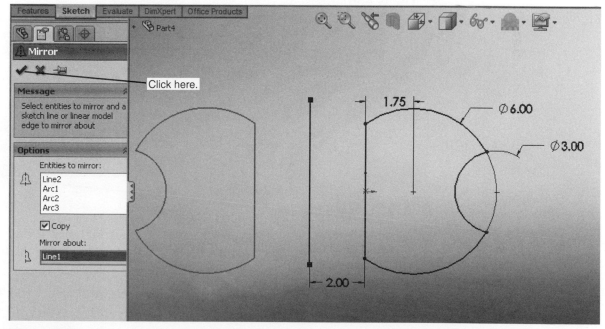

Figure 2-36

Figure 2-36
(*Continued*)

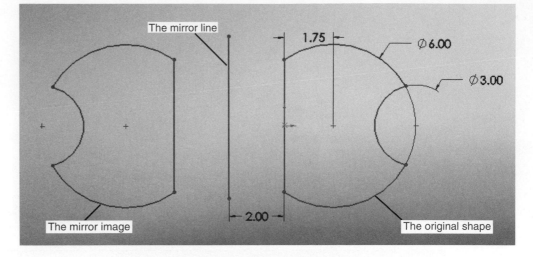

3 Access the **Mirror Entities** tool.

The **Mirror Entities** tool is located on the **Sketch** toolbar.

4 Window the object, but do not include the vertical line in the window.

A listing of the selected entities will appear in the **Options** rollout box of the **Mirror PropertyManager.**

5 Click the **Mirror about:** box to highlight the selection of the mirror line and select the vertical line.

The vertical line will be used as the mirror line. The mirror image will appear as a preview in yellow. See Figure 2-36.

6 Click the OK check mark, or right-click the mouse and click **OK.**

Lines within an object can be used as mirror lines. Figure 2-37 shows the object in the previous figure mirrored about its own edge line.

Figure 2-37

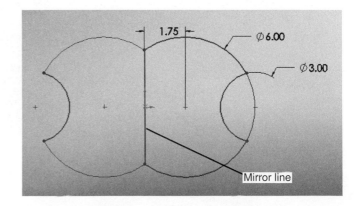

2-19 Fillet

A *fillet* is a rounded corner. Fillets can be internal or external.
Figure 2-38 shows a 2.00 x 4.00 rectangle. Add **R.50** fillets to the top two corners.

1 Start a new drawing, click the **Sketch** tab, and select the **Top Plane** option.

2 Draw a **2.00 × 4.00** rectangle.

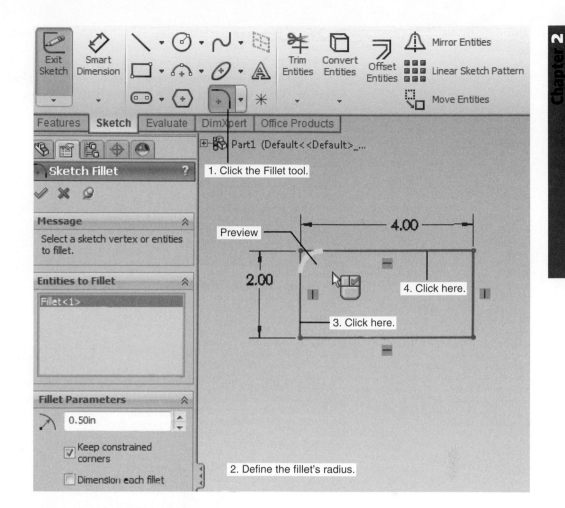

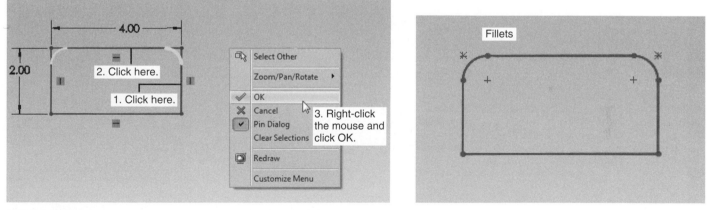

Figure 2-38

3 Click the **Fillet** tool on the **Sketch** panel.

4 Define the fillet's radius as **.50in.**

5 Click the left vertical line and the top horizontal line.

A preview of the fillet will appear.

6 Click the right vertical line and the top horizontal line.

7 Right-click the mouse and click **OK**.

2-20 Chamfer

A *chamfer* is a straight-line corner trim.

Figure 2-39 shows the rectangle used to create fillets in the previous section. Add chamfers to the bottom two corners.

Figure 2-39

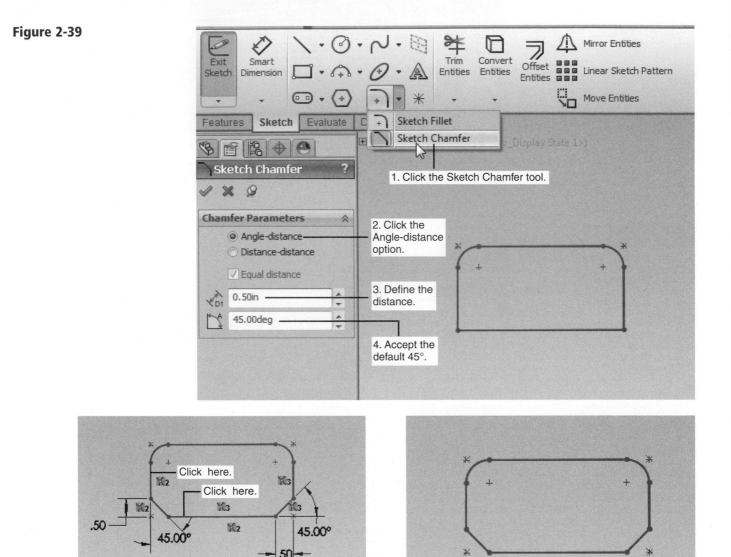

1 Click the **Sketch Chamfer** tool.

2 Click the **Angle-distance** option.

3 Set the distance for **.50in** and the angle for **45.00°**.

4 Click the left vertical line and the bottom horizontal line.

5 Click the right vertical line and the bottom horizontal line.

6 Right-click the mouse and click the **Select** option.

Chamfers may also be drawn by defining equal and unequal distances. Chamfers may also be defined with angles other than 45°. See Figure 2-40.

Figure 2-40

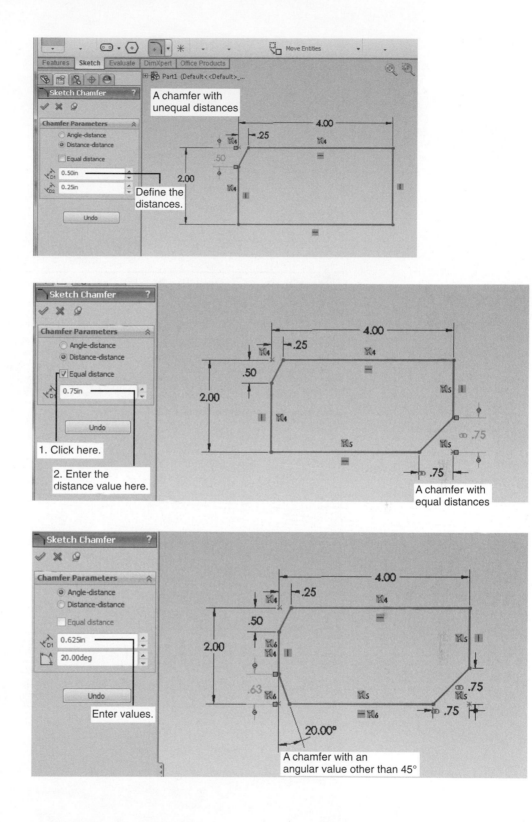

2-21 Move Entities

The **Move Entities** tool is used to relocate entities. See Figure 2-41.

1 Start a new **Part** document, click the **Sketch** tab, and select the **Top Plane** option.

2 Draw the shape shown.

Figure 2-41

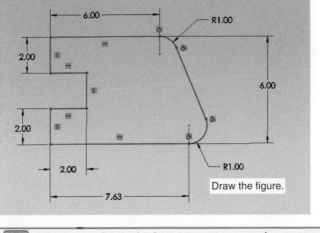

Draw the figure.

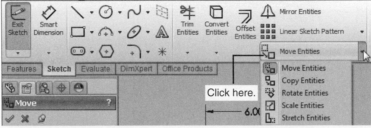

Click here.

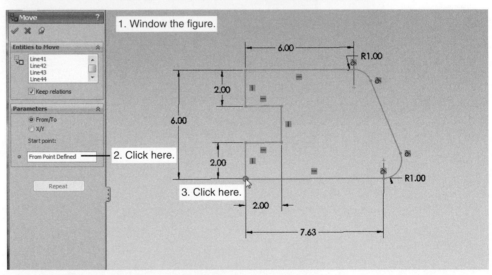

1. Window the figure.

2. Click here.

3. Click here.

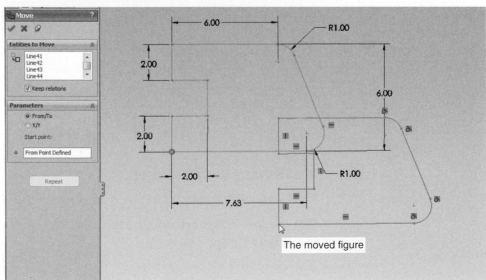

The moved figure

3 Click the **Move Entities** tool located on the **Sketch** panel.

4 Window the object to be moved.

5 Click the **Start point:** selection area in the **Parameters** box of the **Move PropertyManager.**

All the sketch entities will be displayed in the **Entities to Move** box.

6 Select a start point by clicking a point. This point will become the base point.

Any point on the screen can be used as a base point. In this example the lower left corner of the object was selected.

NOTE

The start point does not have to be on the object. Any point on the drawing screen can be used.

NOTE

A move can also be defined using X,Y coordinate values.

---

7 Move the base point to a new location and click the mouse.

Notice that the blue outline of the object in its original position will remain, and the moved object will appear in green.

8 Once the object is in the new location, right-click the mouse and select **OK.**

2-22 Rotate Entities

The **Rotate Entities** tool is used to change the orientation of a sketched entity. See Figure 2-42, which shows the same object used in the previous section on the **Mirror Entities** tool.

Figure 2-42

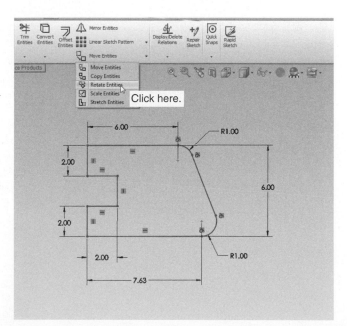

Figure 2-42
(*Continued*)

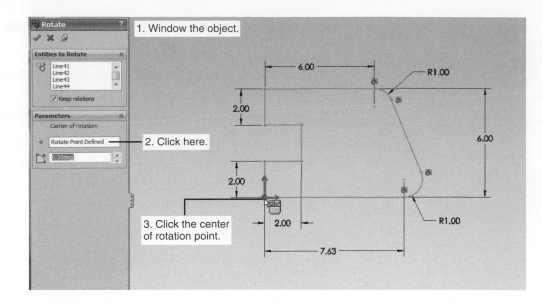

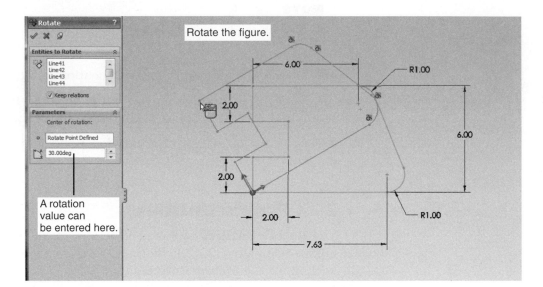

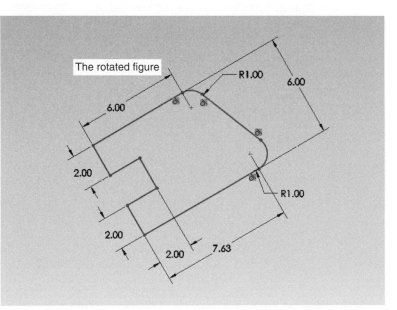

1 Access the **Rotate Entities** tool.

The **Rotate Entities** tool is a flyout from the **Move Entities** tool on the **Sketch** panel.

2 Window the object.

A listing of all the sketch entities windowed will appear in the **Entities to Rotate** box in the **Rotate PropertyManager.**

3 Click the **Center of rotation:** box in the **Rotate PropertyManager.**

4 Select a point of rotation or base point about which the sketch will rotate.

In this example the lower left corner of the object was selected.

5 Drag (click and hold down the left mouse button) the cursor away from the object to rotate the object.

The object will rotate as the cursor is moved. The angle of rotation will appear in the **angle selection** box in the **Rotate PropertyManager.**

6 Click the OK check mark.

> **NOTE**
> The angle of rotation may also be defined by entering angular values in the **Parameters** box in the **Rotate PropertyManager** and clicking the OK check mark at the top of the **Rotate PropertyManager** box.

2-23 Copy Entities

The **Copy Entities** tool is used to create a duplicate of an entity. See Figure 2-43. The difference between the **Move Entities** tool and the **Copy Entities** tool is that the **Copy Entities** tool retains the original object in its original location and adds a new drawing of the object. The **Move Entities** tool relocates the original object.

1 Access the **Copy Entities** tool.

The **Copy Entities** tool is located on the **Sketch** toolbar.

2 Window the object.

3 Click the **Start point:** box in the **Parameters** box to define the base point.

4 Select the base point by clicking on a point.

In this example the lower left corner of the objected was selected as the base point.

5 Move the cursor away from the object.

The preview of the object will be shown in yellow, and the original object will appear in green.

6 Determine the new location for the copy and click the mouse.

7 Click the OK check mark.

Figure 2-43

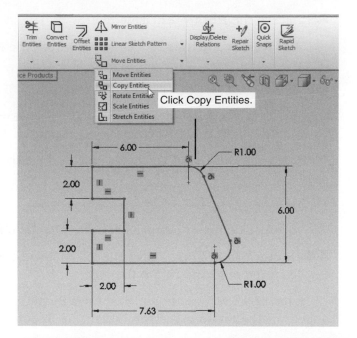

Click Copy Entities.

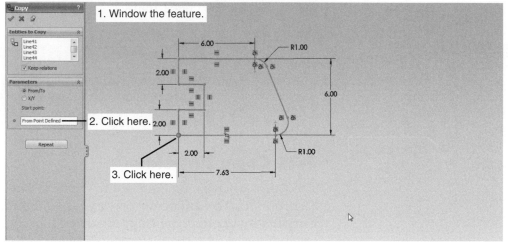

1. Window the feature.

2. Click here.

3. Click here.

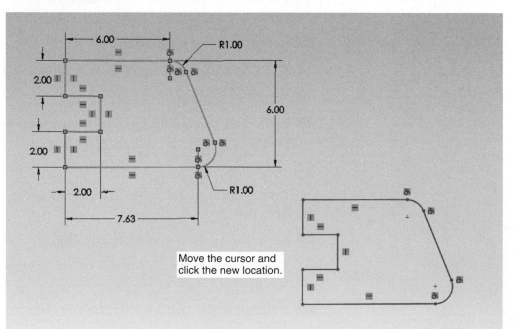

Move the cursor and click the new location.

2-24 Scale Entities

The **Scale Entities** tool is used to change the overall size of an entity while maintaining the proportions of the original object. The **Scale Entities** tool includes a **Copy** option. If the **Copy** option is selected when a scaled drawing is made, the original object will be retained. If the **Copy** option is off (no check mark) when a scaled drawing is made, the original object will be deleted.

Using Scale Entities with Copy On

See Figure 2-44.

1 Access the **Scale Entities** tool on the **Sketch** panel.

2 Window the object.

3 Define the scale factor and the number of copies to be made in the appropriate boxes in the **Scale PropertyManager.**

4 Assure that the **Copy** option is on (there is a check mark in the **Copy** box).

5 Click on **Scale about:** in the **Parameters** box.

6 Select a reference point.

In this example the lower left corner of the object was selected.

7 Right-click the mouse.

The scaled object will appear.

Figure 2-44

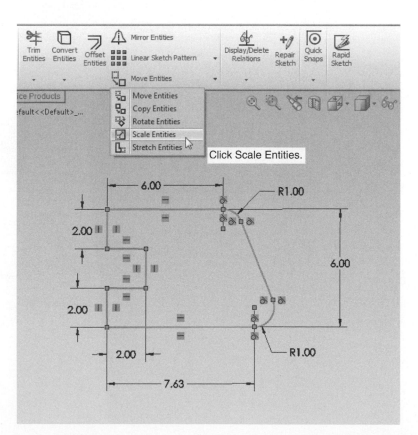

Figure 2-44
(*Continued*)

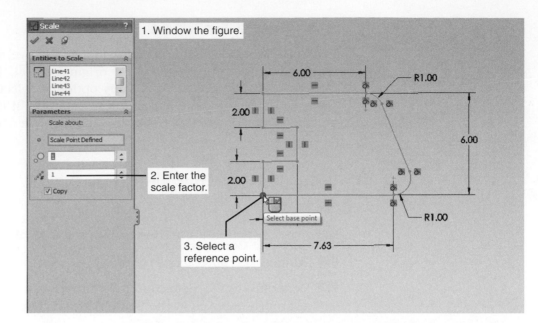

1. Window the figure.

2. Enter the scale factor.

3. Select a reference point.

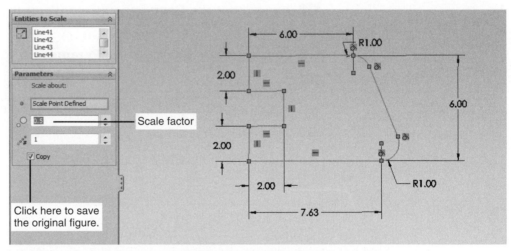

Scale factor

Click here to save the original figure.

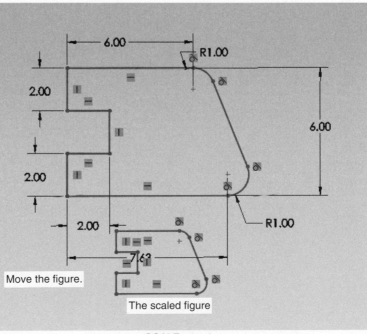

Move the figure.

The scaled figure

SCALE : 1 = 2

8 Separate the original object and the scaled object.

9 Click the OK check mark.

2-25 Centerline

Centerlines are used to help define and locate the center of entities.

The **Centerline** tool is a flyout from the **Line** tool on the **Sketch** panel. See Figure 2-45.

1 Create a new **Part** document, select the **Top Plane** option and draw a **2.00 × 4.00** rectangle.

Draw the rectangle offset from the origin as shown.

2 Click the **Centerline** tool located under the **Line** tool on the **Sketch** panel. Draw a centerline diagonally across the rectangle.

3 Click the origin.

4 Hold down the **<Ctrl>** key, click the centerline, and release the **<Ctrl>** key.

The **Selected Entities** dialog box will appear.

Figure 2-45

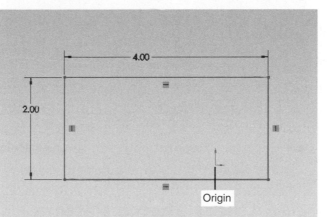

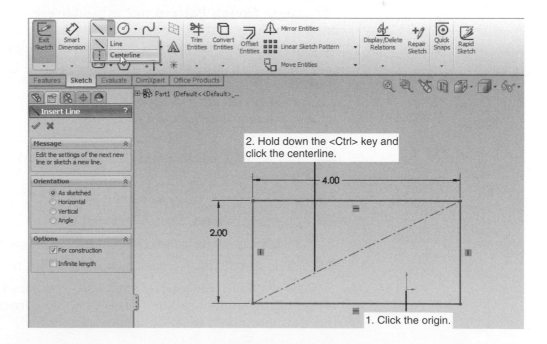

Figure 2-45
(*Continued*)

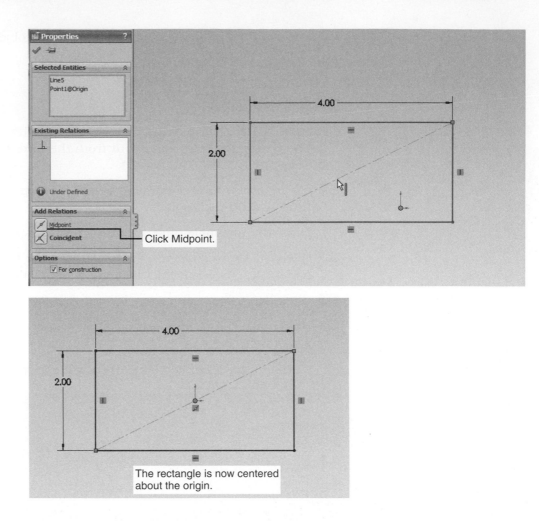

Click Midpoint.

The rectangle is now centered about the origin.

5 Click the **Midpoint** option in the **Add Relations** box.

The figure will be centered on the origin.

2-26 Linear Sketch Pattern

The **Linear Sketch Pattern** tool is used to create patterns of sketched entites in the X and Y directions. Figure 2-46 shows a square. In this section a 3 × 3 linear pattern will be created from the square.

> **NOTE**
>
> A row is defined as a pattern in the horizontal direction, and a column is a pattern in the vertical direction.

1 Start a new **Part** document, click the **Sketch** tab, and select the **Top Plane** option.

2 Draw a **1.00 × 1.00-in.** square as shown.

3 Access the **Linear Sketch Pattern** tool.

The **Linear Sketch Pattern** tool is located on the **Sketch** toolbar.

4 Define the distance between the squares in the pattern.

The distance between the squares is measured from the lower left corner of the original square to the lower left corner of the next square. In this example a distance of 2.00 in. was specified.

Figure 2-46

Chapter 2

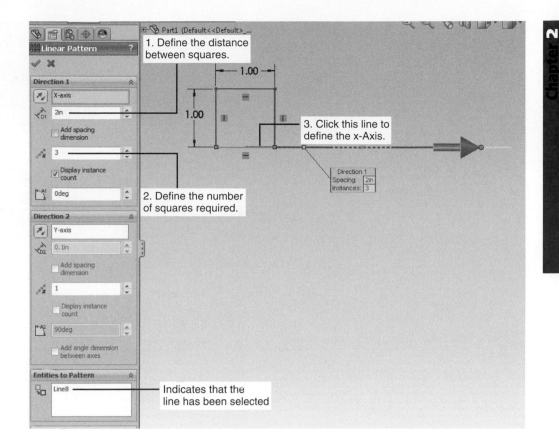

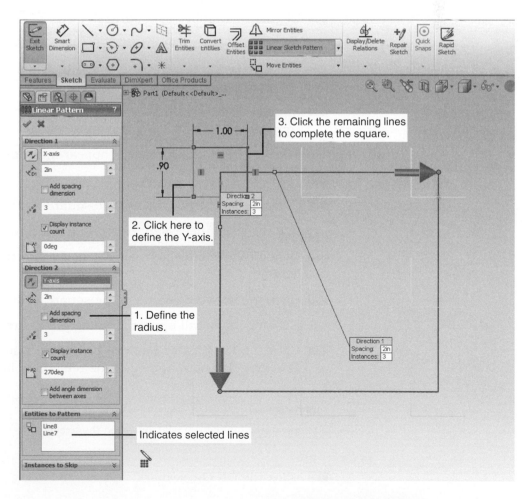

Figure 2-46
(*Continued*)

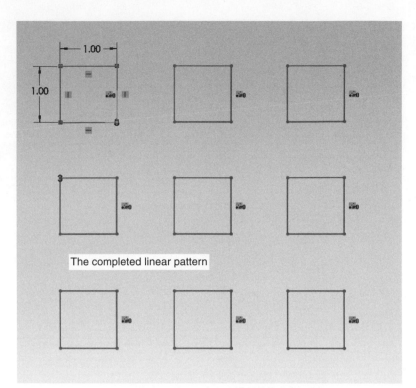

The completed linear pattern

5 Define the number of squares in a row of the pattern.

This example requires three squares in a row of the pattern (X-direction).

The **Linear Sketch Pattern** tool will automatically ask for the definition of the X-axis direction.

6 Initially define the X-axis by clicking the lower horizontal line of the square.

A large directional arrow will appear indicating the X-direction.

7 Click the **Y-axis** box

8 Click the left vertical line of the square.

Use the tool if necessary to create a downward Y-direction.

9 Define the distance between the boxes and the number of boxes in the column.

10 Click the left vertical line of the square to define the Y-direction.

A larger arrow will appear defining the Y-direction.

11 Click the **Entities to Pattern** box in the **Linear Sketch Pattern PropertyManager,** and click the remaining lines of the square.

NOTE
A preview of the pattern will appear on the screen.

12 Click the OK check mark.

TIP

If you edit the dimensions of a pattern formed using the **Linear Sketch Pattern** tool, SolidWorks will readjust the size of the sketch entity and pattern entities.

2-27 Circular Sketch Pattern

The **Circular Sketch Pattern** tool is used to create patterns about a center point such as a bolt circle. See Figure 2-47. In this example a Ø0.75-in. circle will be patterned about a center point located 3.75 in. from the center point of the circle.

Figure 2-47

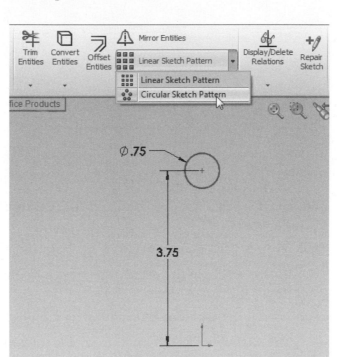

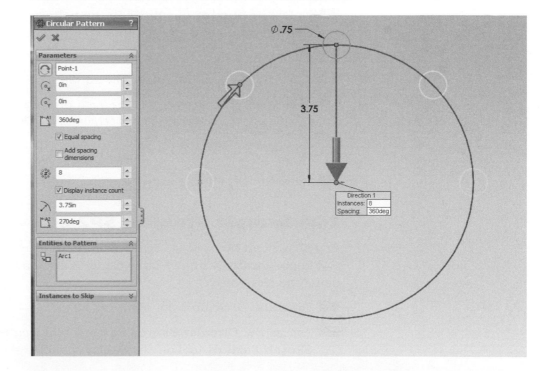

Figure 2-47
(*Continued*)

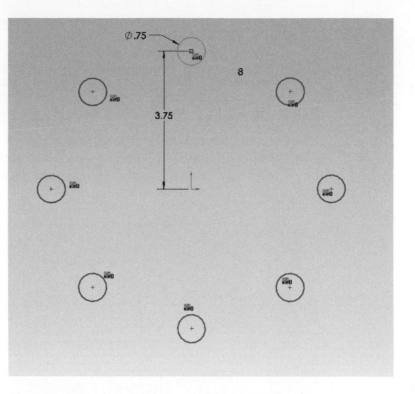

1 Start a new **Part** document, click the **Sketch** tab, and select the **Top Plane** option.

2 Draw a **Ø0.75-in.** circle **3.75 in.** from the screen's origin.

In this example the origin was used for convenience; any starting point can be used.

3 Access the **Circular Sketch Pattern** tool.

The **Circular Sketch Pattern** tool is a flyout from the **Linear Sketch Pattern** tool located on the **Sketch** toolbar.

4 Enter the number of entities in the pattern in the **Circular Pattern PropertyManager.**

5 Click the circle.

NOTE

The circle used in this example contains only one entity. More complex sketches would require all lines in the entity to be identified.

6 Click the OK check mark.

2-28 Sample Problem SP2-2

Any shape can be used to create a circular pattern. Figure 2-48 shows a slot shape located within a large circle. A circular pattern can be created using the slot shape.

1 Draw the circle and slot shown.

2 Access the **Circular Sketch Pattern** tool located under the **Linear Sketch Pattern** tool on the **Sketch** panel.

3 Click the **Entities to Pattern** box and enter all the entities that define the slot.

4 Define the number of entities in the pattern as **12.**

5 Click a point on the drawing screen to create a yellow preview of the pattern.

6 Click the OK check mark.

Figure 2-48

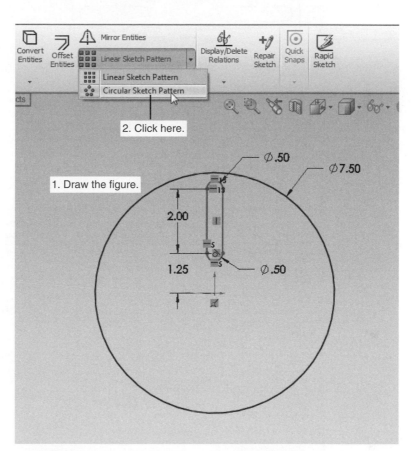

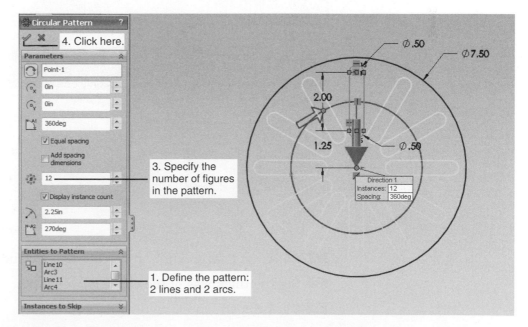

Figure 2-48
(*Continued*)

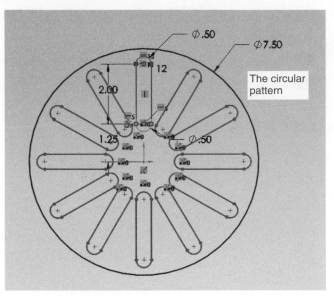

1. Click the Features tab.

2. Click the Extruded Boss/Base tool.

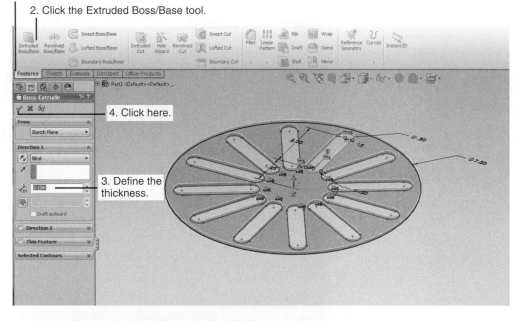

4. Click here.

3. Define the thickness.

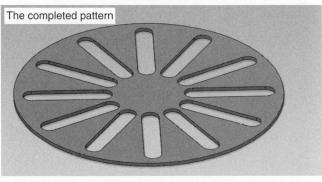

The completed pattern

7 Click the **Features** tab, then click the **Extruded Boss/Base** tool.

8 Set the thickness of the extrusion for **0.30.**

9 Click the OK check mark.

2-29 Sample Problem SP2-3

Figure 2-49 shows a shape that includes fillets. The shape is initially drawn square, that is, with 90° corners, then the fillets are added. See Figure 2-50

Figure 2-49

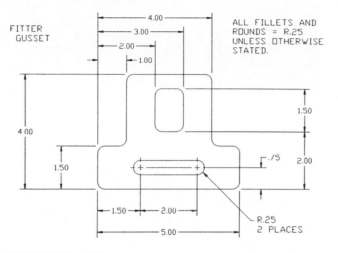

THICKNESS = .375

1 Start a new **Part** document and sketch the T-shape.

2 Use the **Smart Dimension** tool and size the part.

3 Click the **Fillet** tool, set the **Fillet Parameters** for **0.25in,** and add the external fillets.

4 Sketch, locate, and size the **1.00 × 1.50** rectangle as shown.

5 Use the **Fillet** tool and add **0.25** fillets to the rectangle.

6 Use the **Circle** tool and draw two **Ø0.50** circles **2.00** apart, **1.50** from the left edge as shown.

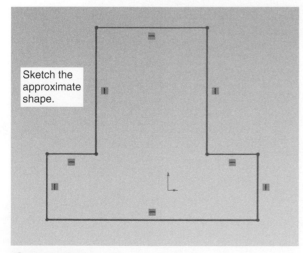

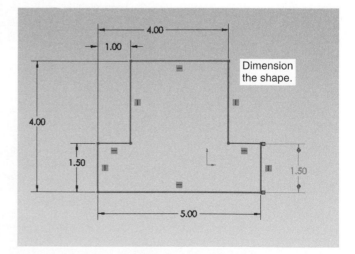

Figure 2-50

Figure 2-50
(*Continued*)

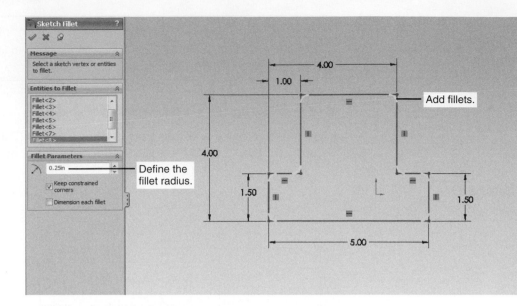

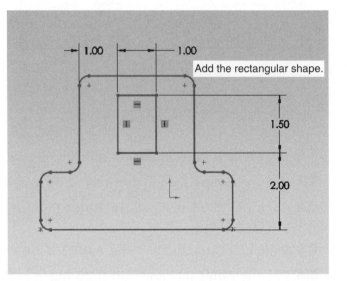

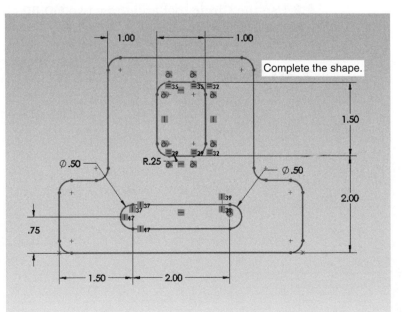

Figure 2-50
(*Continued*)

4. Click here.

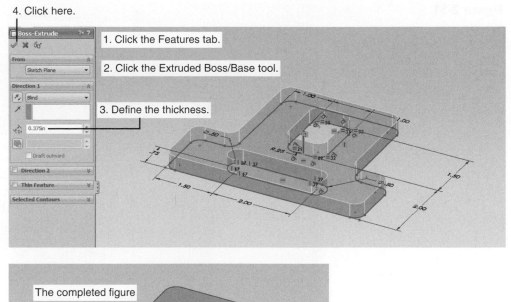

1. Click the Features tab.

2. Click the Extruded Boss/Base tool.

3. Define the thickness.

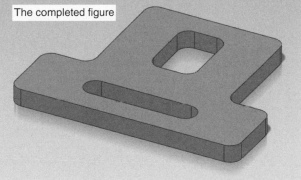

The completed figure

7 Use the **Line** tool and draw two horizontal lines tangent to the two circles.

8 Use the **Trim** tool and delete the internal portions of the circles, creating a slot as shown.

9 Click the **Features** tab and click the **Extruded Boss/Base** tool.

10 Extrude the T-shape to a thickness of **0.375in.**

11 Click the OK check mark.

2-30 Text

The **Text** tool is used to add text to a **Part** document. See Figure 2-51.

1 Create a new **Part** document and select the **Top Plane** option.

2 Click the **Tools** heading, click **Sketch Entities,** and click the **Text** tool.

3 Click the **Text** box in the Sketch **Text PropertyManager** and type the text required.

The text will appear on the screen.

To Change the Font and Size of Text

1 Make sure that the **Use document font** box in the Sketch **Text PropertyManager** is off; that is, there is no check mark in the box.

Figure 2-51

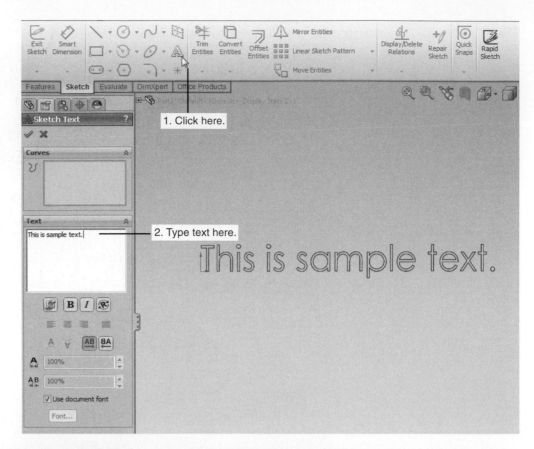

1. Click here.

2. Type text here.

This is sample text.

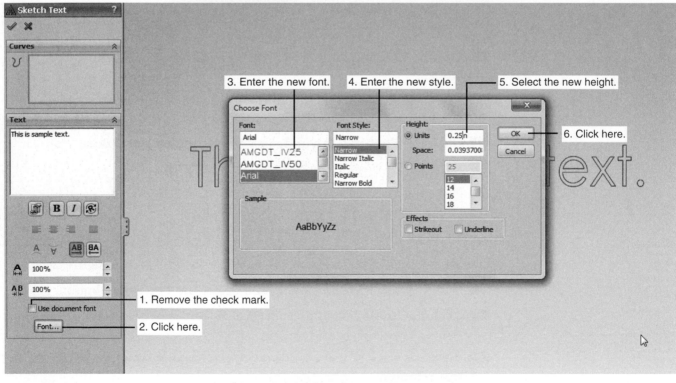

3. Enter the new font.

4. Enter the new style.

5. Select the new height.

6. Click here.

1. Remove the check mark.

2. Click here.

New text font

This is sample text.

Note the difference

2 Click the **Font** box.

The **Choose Font** dialog box will appear.

3 Select the desired font and height.

In this example the **Narrow Arial** font at a height of **.250in.** was selected. Notice the differences in the a between the two fonts.

NOTE

It is best to avoid fonts that are too stylistic. Simple block-type letters are best for engineering drawings.

NOTE

The default font for SolidWorks is Century Gothic.

2-31 Sample Problem SP2-4

Retaining Ring

A retaining ring is used to help prevent longitudinal motion in shafts. Grooves are cut into the shaft and the retaining rings are inserted. There are both internal and external retaining rings. This example will create an external retaining ring.

Figure 2-52 shows a drawing of a retaining ring that uses general dimensions. For this example use the dimensions specified for Part No. BU125. See Figure P2-25. All dimensions are in inches.

Figure 2-52

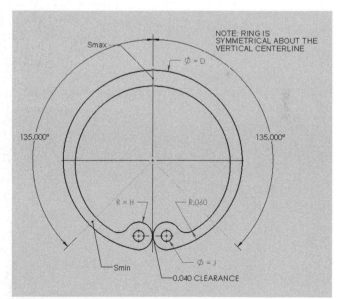

To Draw the Retaining Ring

See Figure 2-53.

1 Start a new **Part** document, select the **Top Plane,** and click the **Sketch** tab.

2 Draw a Ø**1.00** circle.

In this example the center of the circle was located on the origin. Zoom the drawing as necessary.

3 Draw three ray lines from the center of the circle. One line is a vertical line, and the other two are located 135° from the vertical line.

4 Use the **Point** tool and create three points located as shown.

The dimensions for the points came from those given for Figure 2-52.

5 Use the **3 Point Arc** tool and create an arc between the points.

This arc is not concentric about the origin center point.

6 Use the **Centerpoint Arc** tool and create a second arc between the endpoints of the first arc.

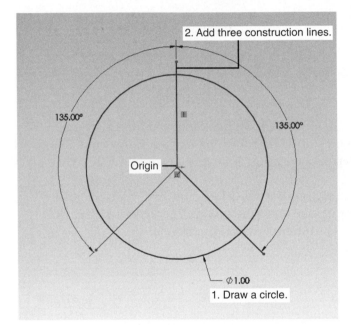

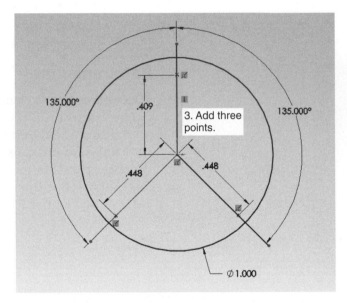

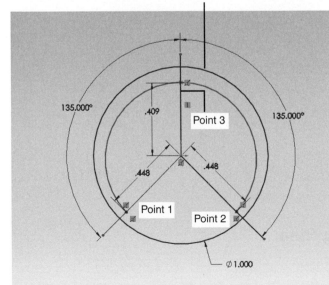

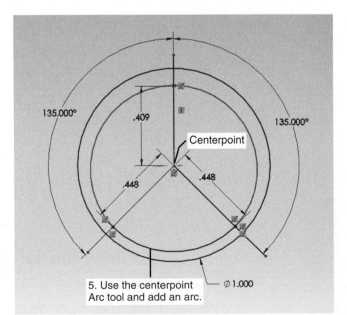

Figure 2-53

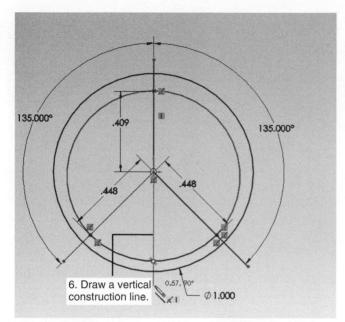

135.000°   135.000°

.409

.448   .448

6. Draw a vertical construction line.   0.57, 90°   Ø1.000

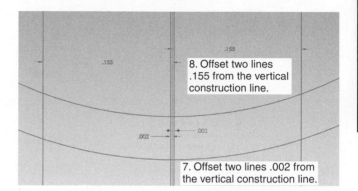

.155   .155

8. Offset two lines .155 from the vertical construction line.

.002   .002

7. Offset two lines .002 from the vertical construction line.

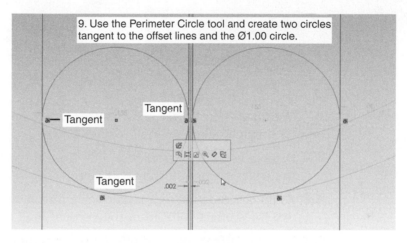

9. Use the Perimeter Circle tool and create two circles tangent to the offset lines and the Ø1.00 circle.

Tangent

Tangent

Tangent

.002   .002

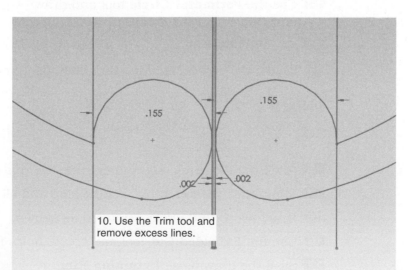

.155   .155

.002   .002

10. Use the Trim tool and remove excess lines.

Figure 2-53
(*Continued*)

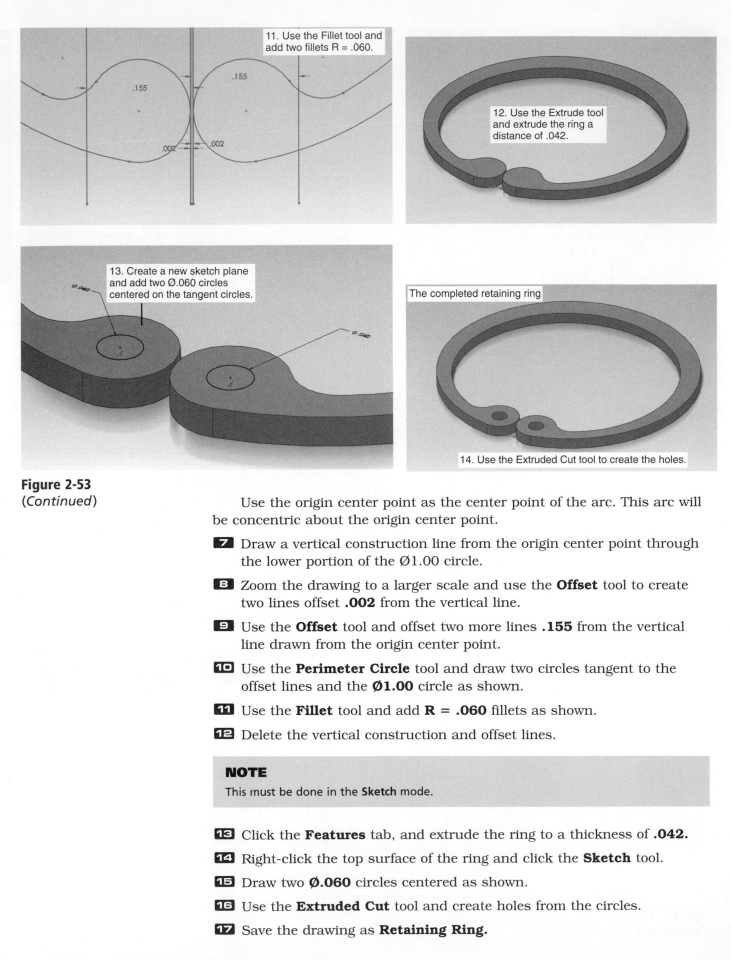

11. Use the Fillet tool and add two fillets R = .060.

.155

.155

.002 .002

12. Use the Extrude tool and extrude the ring a distance of .042.

13. Create a new sketch plane and add two Ø.060 circles centered on the tangent circles.

Ø.060

Ø.060

The completed retaining ring

14. Use the Extruded Cut tool to create the holes.

Figure 2-53
(Continued)

Use the origin center point as the center point of the arc. This arc will be concentric about the origin center point.

7 Draw a vertical construction line from the origin center point through the lower portion of the Ø1.00 circle.

8 Zoom the drawing to a larger scale and use the **Offset** tool to create two lines offset **.002** from the vertical line.

9 Use the **Offset** tool and offset two more lines **.155** from the vertical line drawn from the origin center point.

10 Use the **Perimeter Circle** tool and draw two circles tangent to the offset lines and the **Ø1.00** circle as shown.

11 Use the **Fillet** tool and add **R = .060** fillets as shown.

12 Delete the vertical construction and offset lines.

> **NOTE**
>
> This must be done in the **Sketch** mode.

13 Click the **Features** tab, and extrude the ring to a thickness of **.042.**

14 Right-click the top surface of the ring and click the **Sketch** tool.

15 Draw two **Ø.060** circles centered as shown.

16 Use the **Extruded Cut** tool and create holes from the circles.

17 Save the drawing as **Retaining Ring.**

Chapter Project

Project 2-1:

Redraw the objects in Figures P2-1 through P2-24 using the given dimensions. Create solid models of the objects using the specified thicknesses.

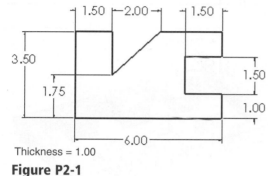

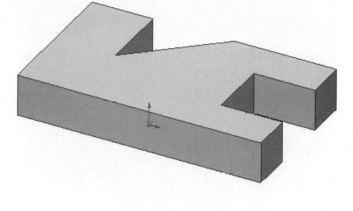

Thickness = 1.00

Figure P2-1
INCHES

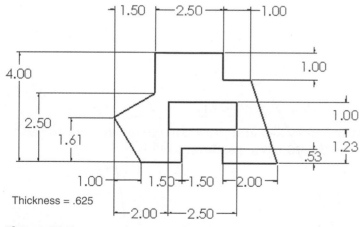

Thickness = .625

Figure P2-2
INCHES

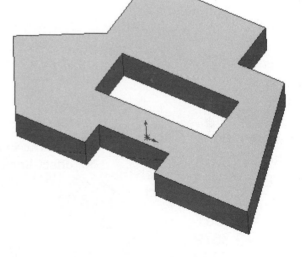

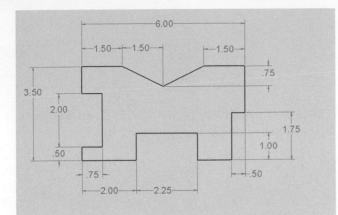

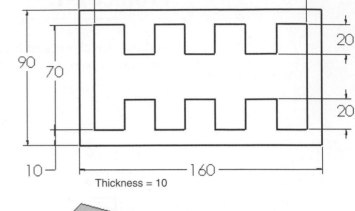

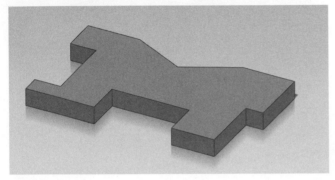

Figure P2-3
MILLIMETERS

Thickness = 10

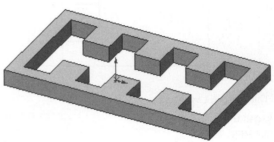

Figure P2-4
MILLIMETERS

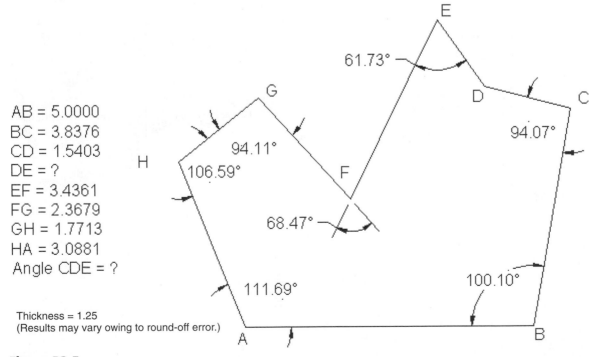

AB = 5.0000
BC = 3.8376
CD = 1.5403
DE = ?
EF = 3.4361
FG = 2.3679
GH = 1.7713
HA = 3.0881
Angle CDE = ?

Thickness = 1.25
(Results may vary owing to round-off error.)

Figure P2-5
INCHES

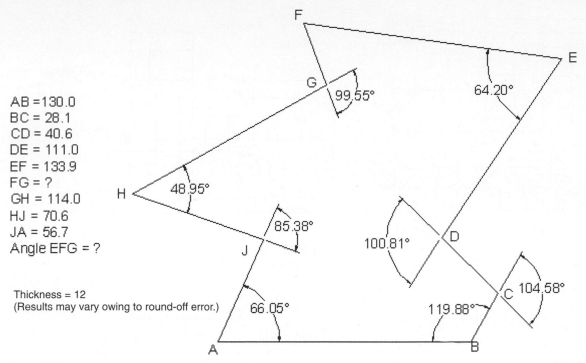

AB =130.0
BC = 28.1
CD = 40.6
DE = 111.0
EF = 133.9
FG = ?
GH = 114.0
HJ = 70.6
JA = 56.7
Angle EFG = ?

Thickness = 12
(Results may vary owing to round-off error.)

Figure P2-6
MILLIMETERS

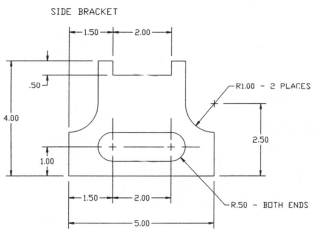

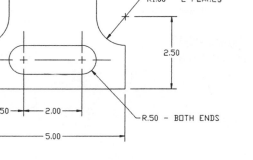

Thickness = 1.25

Figure P2-7
INCHES

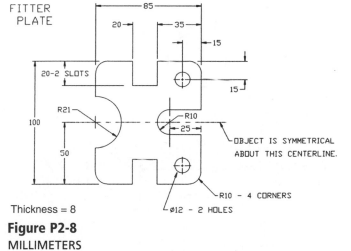

Thickness = 8

Figure P2-8
MILLIMETERS

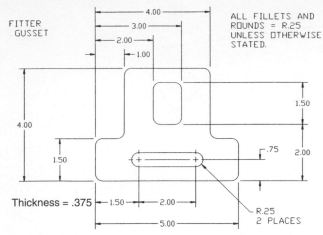

FITTER
GUSSET

ALL FILLETS AND
ROUNDS = R.25
UNLESS OTHERWISE
STATED.

Figure P2-9
INCHES

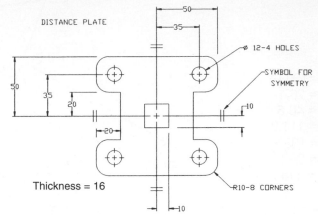

DISTANCE PLATE

Figure P2-10
MILLIMETERS

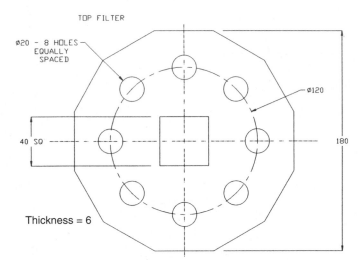

TOP FILTER

Figure P2-11
MILLIMETERS

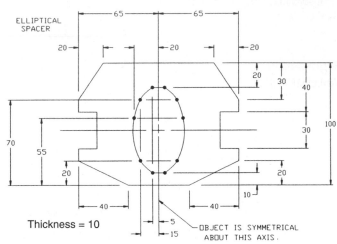

ELLIPTICAL
SPACER

Figure P2-12
MILLIMETERS

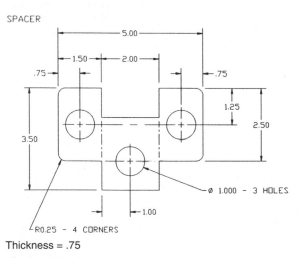

SPACER

Thickness = .75

Figure P2-13
INCHES

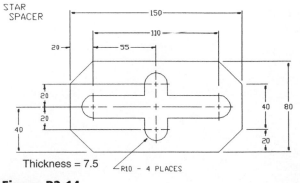

STAR
SPACER

Thickness = 7.5

Figure P2-14
MILLIMETERS

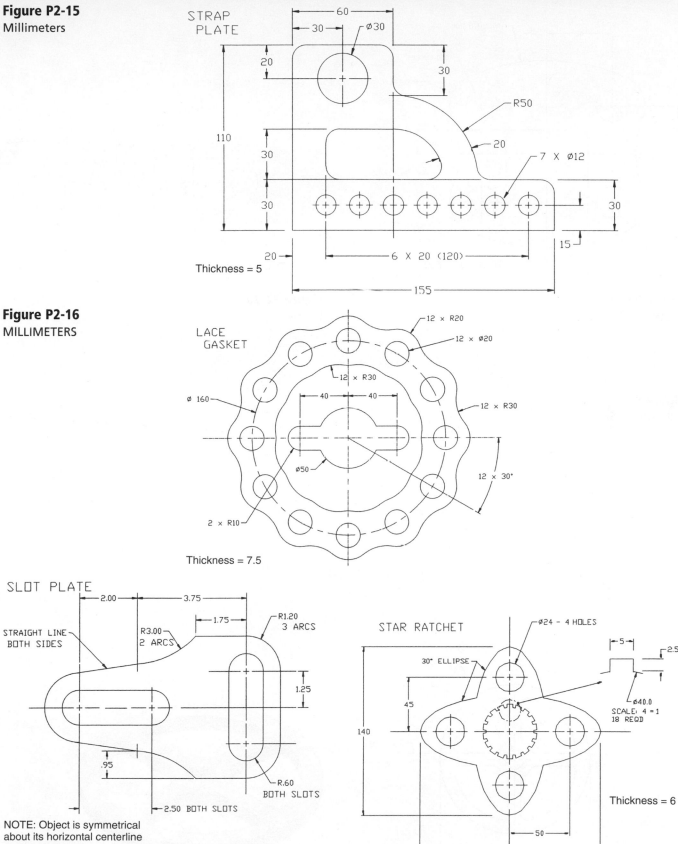

Figure P2-15
Millimeters

STRAP PLATE

Thickness = 5

Figure P2-16
MILLIMETERS

LACE GASKET

Thickness = 7.5

SLOT PLATE

STRAIGHT LINE BOTH SIDES

R3.00 2 ARCS

R1.20 3 ARCS

R.60 BOTH SLOTS

2.50 BOTH SLOTS

NOTE: Object is symmetrical about its horizontal centerline

Thickness = .875

Figure P2-17
INCHES

STAR RATCHET

30° ELLIPSE

Ø24 – 4 HOLES

Ø40.0
SCALE: 4 = 1
18 REQD

Thickness = 6

Figure P2-18
MILLIMETERS

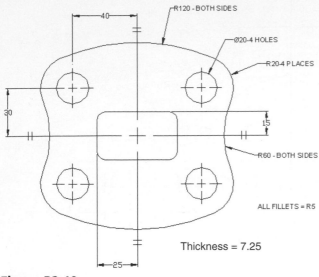

R120 - BOTH SIDES

40

Ø20-4 HOLES

R20-4 PLACES

30

15

R60 - BOTH SIDES

ALL FILLETS = R5

25

Thickness = 7.25

Figure P2-19
MILLIMETERS

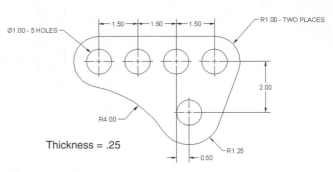

Ø1.00 - 5 HOLES

1.50   1.50   1.50

R1.00 - TWO PLACES

2.00

R4.00

R1.25

0.50

Thickness = .25

Figure P2-20
Inches

Figure P2-21
MILLIMETERS

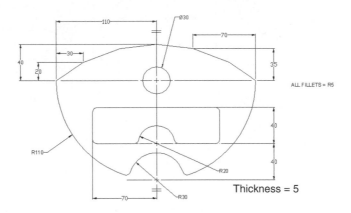

110

Ø30

30

70

40

20

35

ALL FILLETS = R5

R110

40

40

R20

70

R30

Thickness = 5

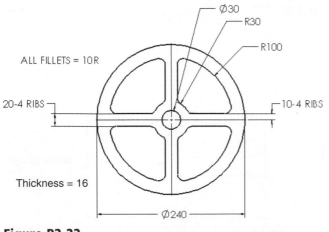

ALL FILLETS = 10R

Ø30

R30

R100

20-4 RIBS

10-4 RIBS

Thickness = 16

Ø240

Figure P2-22
MILLIMETERS

Figure P2-23
Inches

All FILLETS AND ROUNDS = R.25

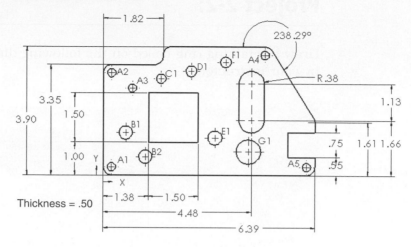

TAG	X LOC	Y LOC	SIZE
A1	.25	.25	Ø.25
A2	.25	3.10	Ø.25
A3	.88	2.64	Ø.25
A4	4.88	3.65	Ø.25
A5	6.14	.25	Ø.25
B1	.68	1.29	Ø.40
B2	1.28	.56	Ø.40
C1	1.76	2.92	Ø.29
D1	2.66	3.16	Ø.33
E1	3.38	1.13	Ø.42
F1	3.71	3.43	Ø.32
G1	4.39	.71	Ø.73

ALL FILLETS AND ROUNDS = 5
UNLESS OTHERWISE STATED

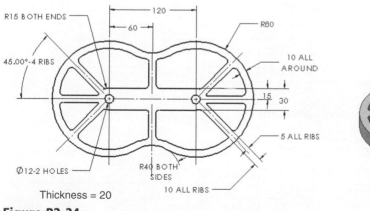

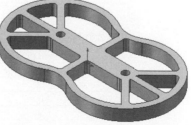

Figure P2-24
MILLIMETERS

Project 2-2:

Draw a retaining ring based on the following dimensions and as assigned by your instructor.

Figure P2-25

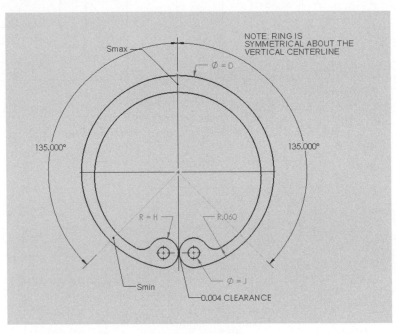

Retaing Ring - Internal - Inches

PART NO	ØD	Smax	Smin	H	A	ØJ	Thk
BU-25	.25	.025	.015	.065	.030	.031	.020
BU-50	.50	.053	.035	.114	.042	.047	.035
BU-75	.75	.070	.040	.142	.055	.060	.040
BU100	1.00	.091	.052	.155	.060	.060	.042
BU125	1.25	.120	.062	.180	.070	.075	.050
BU150	1.50	.127	.066	.180	.070	.075	.050

Retaining Ring - Internal - Millimeters

PART NO	ØD	Smax	Smin	H	A	ØJ	Thk
MBU-20	20	2.3	1.9	4.1	2.0	2.0	1.0
MBU-30	30	3.0	2.3	4.8	2.0	2.0	1.2
MBU-40	40	3.9	3.0	5.8	2.5	2.5	1.7
MBU-50	50	4.6	3.8	6.5	2.5	2.5	2.0
MBU-60	60	5.4	4.3	7.3	2.5	2.5	2.0
MBU-70	70	6.2	5.2	7.8	3.0	3.0	2.5

chapterthree
Features

CHAPTER OBJECTIVES

- Learn about the **Features** tools
- Learn how to draw 3D objects

- Learn how to use **Features** tools to create objects

3-1 Introduction

This chapter introduces the **Features** tools. Several examples are included that show how to apply the tools to create objects.

3-2 Extruded Boss/Base

The **Extruded Boss/Base** tool is used to add thickness or height to an existing 2D sketch. The examples presented use metric dimensions.

To Work with Dimensions in Millimeters

1 Click the **New** tool and start a new **Part** document.

2 Click the **Options** tool at the top of the drawing screen.

See Figure 3-1.

The **Document Properties** box will appear.

3 Click the **Document Properties** tab.

4 Click **Units.**

Figure 3-1

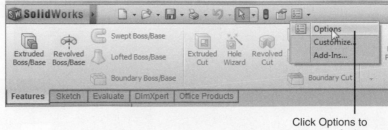

Click Options to access unit changes.

1. Click this tab.

Document Properties - Units

System Options | **Document Properties**

Drafting Standard
  ⊞ Annotations
  ⊞ Dimensions
    Virtual Sharps
  ⊞ Tables
Detailing
Grid/Snap
Units ———— 2. Click
Model Display   Units.
Material Properties
Image Quality
Sheet Metal
Plane Display
DimXpert
  Size Dimension
  Location Dimension
  Chain Dimension
  Geometric Tolerance
  Chamfer Controls
  Display Options

Unit system
- ○ MKS (meter, kilogram, second)
- ○ CGS (centimeter, gram, second)
- ● MMGS (millimeter, gram, second) — 3. Click MMGS.
- ○ IPS (inch, pound, second)
- ○ Custom

Type	Unit	Decimals	Fractions	More
Basic Units				
Length	millimeters	.12		
Dual Dimension Length	millimeters	.12		
Angle	degrees	.12		
Mass/Section Properties				
Length	millimeters	.12		
Mass	grams			
Per Unit Volume	millimeters^3			
Motion Units				
Time	second	.12		
Force	newton	.12		
Power	watt	.12		
Energy	joule	.12		

4. Click OK

OK   Cancel   Help

5 Click the **MMGS (millimeter, gram, second)** button.

6 Click **OK.**

The system is now calibrated for millimeters.

To Use the Extruded Boss/Base Tool

1 Click the **New** tool and create a new **Part** document, click the **Top Plane** option, and click the **Sketch** tab.

2 Use the **Corner Rectangle** tool draw a **60 × 100** rectangle in the top plane. Use the **Smart Dimension** tool to size the rectangle.

See Figure 3-2.

3 Click the **Features** tab.

Figure 3-2

2. Click the Features tab.
3. Click the Extruded Boss/Base tool.

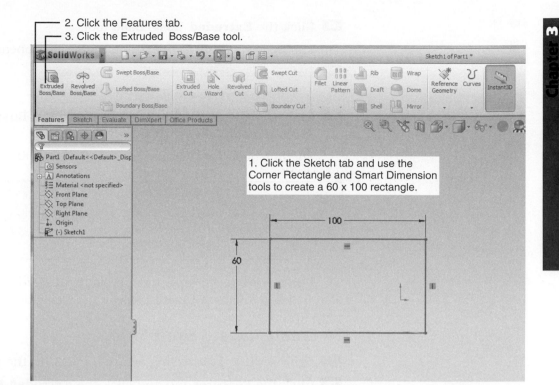

1. Click the Sketch tab and use the Corner Rectangle and Smart Dimension tools to create a 60 x 100 rectangle.

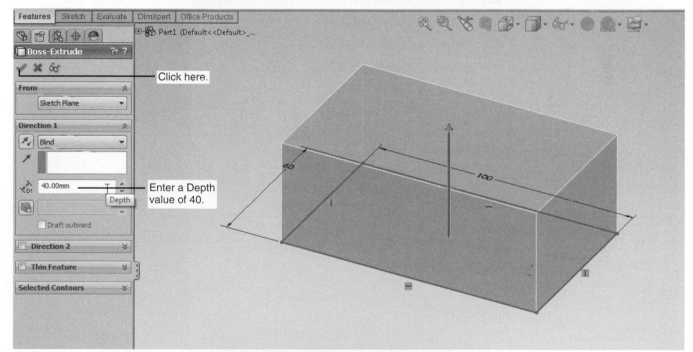

Click here.

Enter a Depth value of 40.

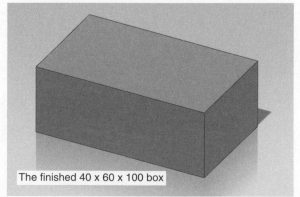

The finished 40 x 60 x 100 box

4 Click the **Extruded Boss/Base** tool.

The **Boss-Extrude PropertyManager** will appear.

5 Define the extrusion height as **40.00mm.**

A real-time preview will appear.

6 Click the OK check mark at the top of the **Boss-Extrude PropertyManager.**

The finished drawing shows a 40 × 60 × 100 box.

> **TIP**
>
> The extrusion depth may be defined by entering a value or by using the arrows at the right of the **Depth** box. The extrusion depth may also be changed by clicking and dragging the large arrow in the center of the box.

The preceding example has perpendicular sides. The **Extrude** tool may also be used to create tapered sides. Tapered sides are called ***draft sides.***

To Create Inward Draft Sides

1 Draw a **60 × 100** rectangle as described in the previous section.

2 Click the **Features** tab and click the **Extruded Boss/Base** tool.

3 Click the **Draft On/Off.**

4 Enter the draft angle value.

In this example a **15°** value was entered. See Figure 3-3.

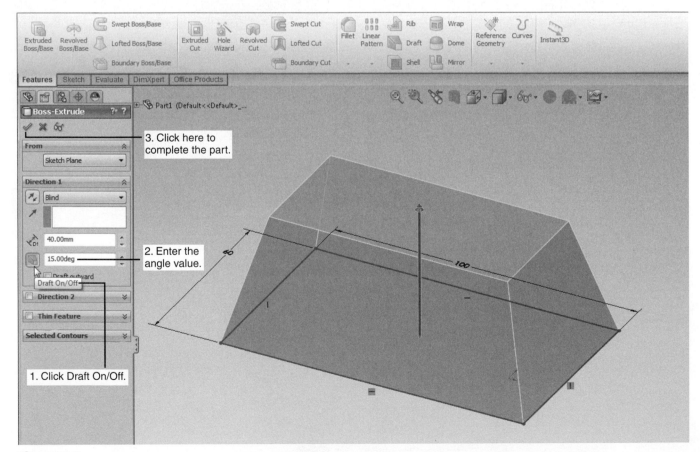

Figure 3-3

5 Click the OK check mark at the top of the **Boss-Extrude PropertyManager** to complete the object.

The draft shown in Figure 3-3 is an inward draft.

To Create an Outward Draft

1 Repeat the same procedure, but this time check the **Draft outward** box.

See Figure 3-4.

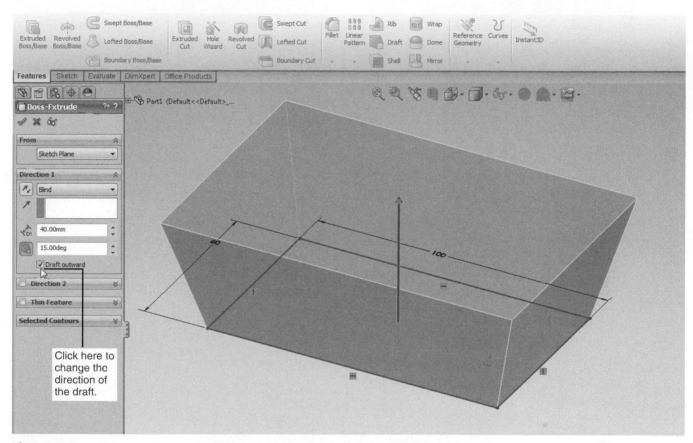

Figure 3-4

3-3 Sample Problem SP3-1

This section shows how to draw a solid 3D model of an L-bracket using the **Extruded Boss/Base** tool.

1 Draw a **60 × 100** rectangle and extrude it to a depth of **20mm** as explained in Section 3.2.

See Figure 3-5.

2 Locate the cursor on the top surface of the box and right-click the mouse. Select the **Sketch** tool.

The 2D sketch tools will be displayed across the top of the screen.

3 Use the **Corner Rectangle** tool to draw a rectangle on the top surface of the box. Use the upper left corner of the box as one corner of the rectangle.

> **NOTE**
>
> The corner points and edge lines will change color when they are activated.

4 Select the **Smart Dimension** tool and dimension the width of the rectangle as **20.0**.

5 Click the **Features** tool, then select the **Extruded Boss/Base** tool.

6 Select the **20 × 100** rectangle to extrude to a depth of **40.00mm**.

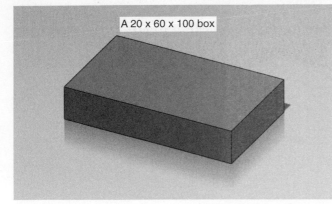

A 20 x 60 x 100 box

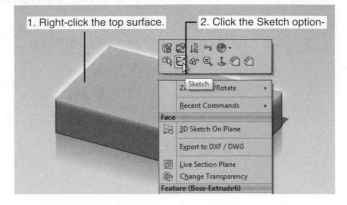

1. Right-click the top surface.

2. Click the Sketch option-

Starting point

3. Use the Corner Rectangle tool and sketch a rectangle.

Second point

The edge line will change color, indicating it has been selected.

4. Click the Features tab.

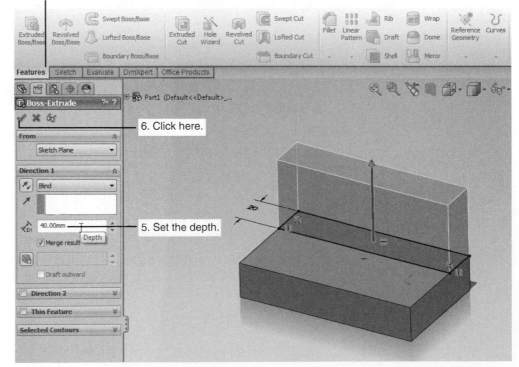

6. Click here.

5. Set the depth.

Figure 3-5

Figure 3-5
(*Continued*)

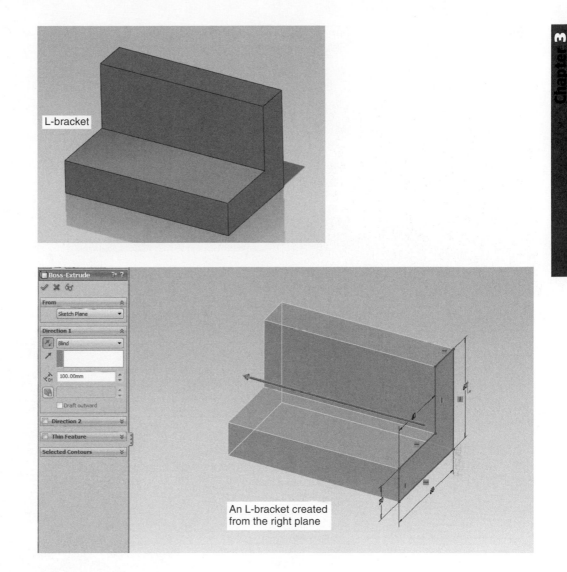

L-bracket

An L-bracket created
from the right plane

7 Click the OK check mark in the **Boss-Extrude PropertyManager.**

SolidWorks offers many different ways to create the same shape. Figure 3-5 shows the same shape created using an L-shape shown on the right plane and extruded.

3-4 Extruded Cut

This section will add a cutout to the L-bracket drawn in Section 3-3 using the **Extruded Cut** tool. See Figure 3-6.

1 Locate the cursor on the lower front horizontal surface and right-click the mouse.

2 Click the **Sketch** option.

3 Use the **Corner Rectangle** and **Smart Dimension** tools to draw and size a rectangle as shown.

4 Click the **Features** tool, then click the **Extruded Cut** tool.

5 Click the OK check mark in the **Cut-Extrude PropertyManager.**

Figure 3-6

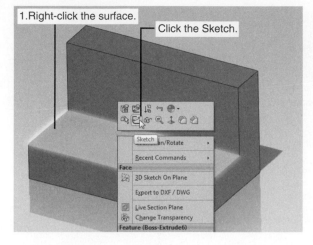

1. Right-click the surface.

Click the Sketch.

6. Click here.

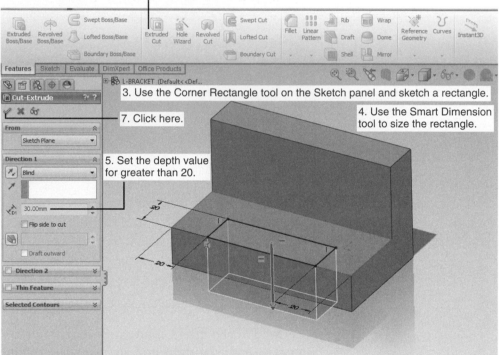

3. Use the Corner Rectangle tool on the Sketch panel and sketch a rectangle.

4. Use the Smart Dimension tool to size the rectangle.

7. Click here.

5. Set the depth value for greater than 20.

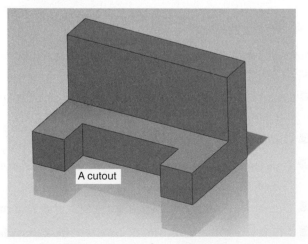

A cutout

3-5 Hole Wizard

This section will add a hole to the L-bracket using the **Hole Wizard.** See Figure 3-7.

1 Click the **Features** tab, then click the **Hole Wizard** tool.

2 Select the type of hole, for example, clear, counterbore, or threaded.

Figure 3-7

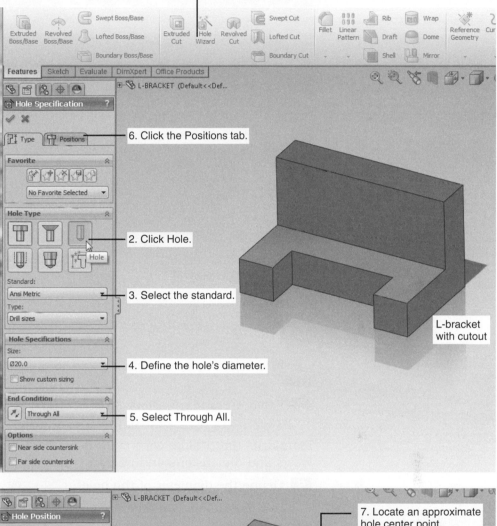

1. Click the Hole Wizard.

6. Click the Positions tab.

2. Click Hole.

3. Select the standard.

4. Define the hole's diameter.

5. Select Through All.

L-bracket with cutout

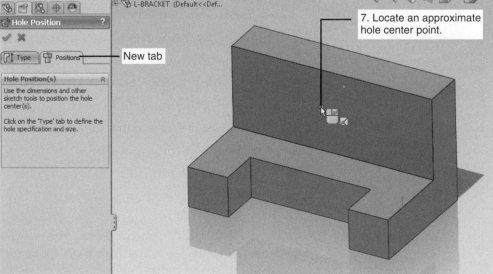

New tab

7. Locate an approximate hole center point.

Figure 3-7
(*Continued*)

8. Use the Smart Dimension tool and locate the hole's center point.

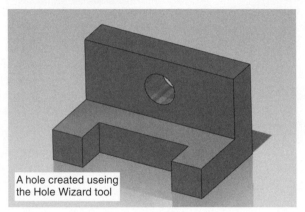

A hole created useing the Hole Wizard tool

In this example a clear hole was selected. SolidWorks calls this option **Hole.**

3 For the **Standard** select **ANSI Metrics.**

ANSI is the American National Standards Institute, which publishes standards that will be covered in detail in the chapter on orthographic views and dimensions and tolerances.

4 Define the diameter of the hole.

In this example a diameter of **20.0mm** was selected.

5 Define the **End Condition** as **Through All.**

6 Click the **Positions** tab on the **Hole Wizard PropertyManager.**

7 Click an approximate location for the hole's center point.

A preview of the hole will appear.

8 Use the **Smart Dimension** tool to locate the hole's center point.

9 Click the OK check mark.

The hole will be added to the L-bracket.

10 Save the L-bracket, as it will be used in later sections.

The hole created in Figure 3-7 is a ***through hole,*** that is, it goes completely through the object. Holes that do not go completely though are called ***blind holes.*** Note that the **Hole Wizard PropertyManager** shows a conical point at the bottom of the hole. Holes created using an extruded cut circle will not have this conical endpoint. Blind holes created using a drill should include the conical point. For this reason, blind holes should, with a few exceptions, be created using the **Hole Wizard** tool.

3-6 A Second Method of Creating a Hole

Holes may also be created using the **Circle** tool and then applying the **Extruded Cut** tool. Figure 3-8 shows a 40 × 160 × 10 object. Add four Ø20 holes.

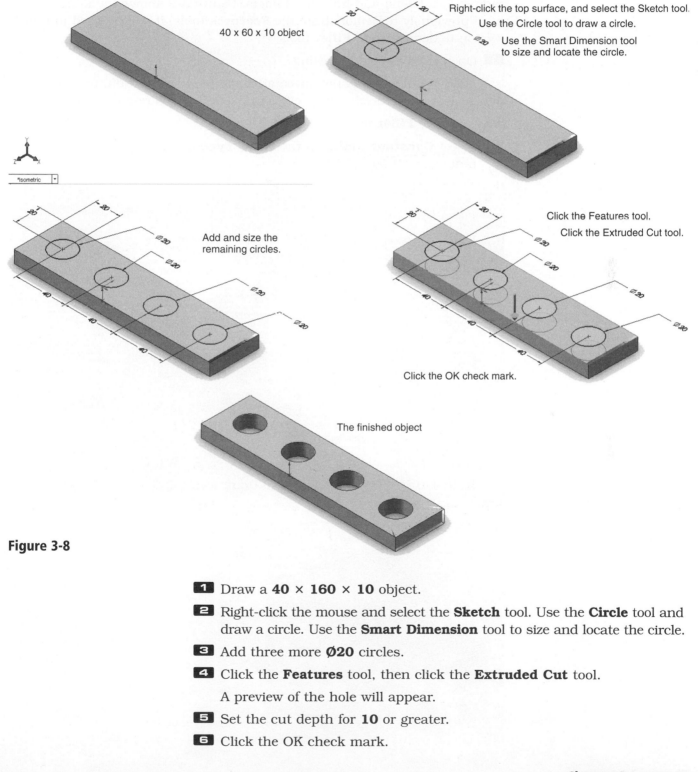

40 x 60 x 10 object

Right-click the top surface, and select the Sketch tool.

Use the Circle tool to draw a circle.

Use the Smart Dimension tool to size and locate the circle.

*Isometric

Add and size the remaining circles.

Click the Features tool.

Click the Extruded Cut tool.

Click the OK check mark.

The finished object

Figure 3-8

1 Draw a **40 × 160 × 10** object.

2 Right-click the mouse and select the **Sketch** tool. Use the **Circle** tool and draw a circle. Use the **Smart Dimension** tool to size and locate the circle.

3 Add three more **Ø20** circles.

4 Click the **Features** tool, then click the **Extruded Cut** tool.

A preview of the hole will appear.

5 Set the cut depth for **10** or greater.

6 Click the **OK** check mark.

3-7 Fillet

A *fillet* is a rounded corner. Specifically, convex corners are called *rounds,* and concave corners are called *fillets*, but in general, all rounded corners are called *fillets*.

SolidWorks can draw four types of fillets: constant radius, variable radius, face fillets, and full round fillets. Figure 3-9 shows the L-bracket used previously to demonstrate the **Features** tools. It will be used in this section to demonstrate **Fillet** tools.

1 Open the L-bracket drawing.

If the L-bracket was not saved after the previous section, use the dimensions and procedures specified in Section 3-3 to re-create the bracket.

2 Click the **Fillet** tool.

3 Select **Constant radius** in the **Fillet Type** box and define the fillet's radius as **10.00mm**.

Figure 3-9

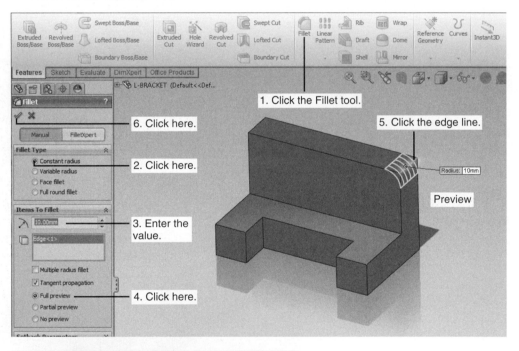

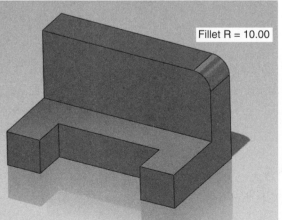

Click the **Full preview** button.

4 Click the upper right edge line of the object,

A preview of the fillet will appear.

5 Click the OK check mark.

To Create a Fillet with a Variable Radius

See Figure 3-10.

Figure 3-10

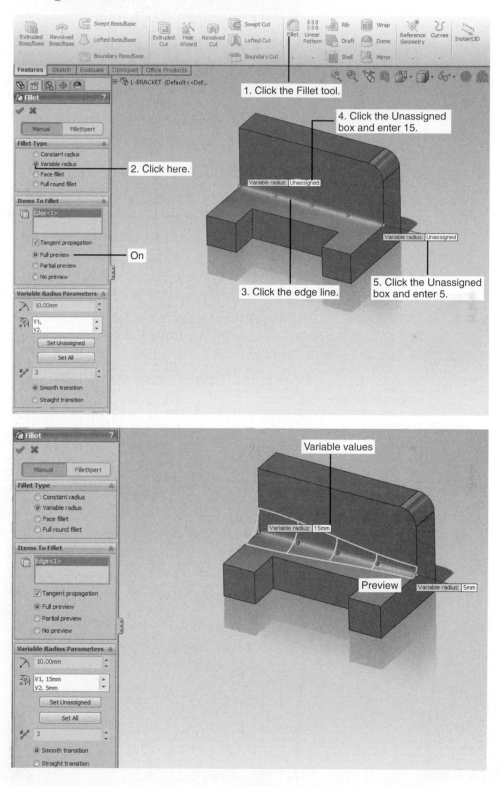

Figure 3-10
(*Continued*)

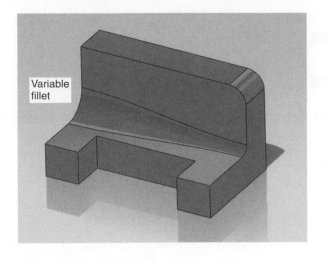

1 Click the **Fillet** tool.

2 Click the **Variable radius** button.

3 Click the edge line shown in Figure 3-10.

Two boxes will appear on the screen, one at each end of the edge line.

4 Click the word **Unassigned** in the left box and enter a value of **15.**

5 Click the word **Unassigned** in the right box and enter a value of **5.**

6 Click the OK check mark.

To Create a Fillet Using the Face Fillet Option

The **Face fillet** option draws a fillet between two faces (surfaces), whereas **Fillet** uses an edge between two surfaces to draw a fillet.

See Figure 3-11.

1 Click the **Fillet** tool.

Figure 3-11

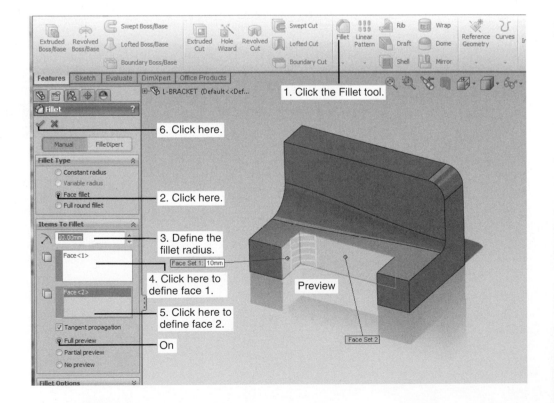

Figure 3-11
(*Continued*)

Chapter 3

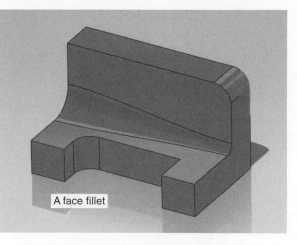

A face fillet

2 Click the **Face fillet** option.

Two boxes will appear in the **Items To Fillet** box. They will be used to define the two faces of the fillet.

3 Define the fillet radius as **10.00mm.**

4 Define **Face 1** as shown.

5 Click the lower box in the **Items To Fillet** box (it will change color) and define **Face 2** by clicking the surface as shown.

6 Click the OK check mark.

NOTE

The top box in the **Items to Fillet** box will be shaded, indicating that it is ready for an input.

To Create a Fillet Using the Full Round Fillet Option

See Figure 3-12.

1 Use the **Undo** tool and remove the fillets created previously.

This will return the original L-bracket shape.

2 Click the **Fillet** tool and click the **Full round fillet** button.

Three boxes will appear. These boxes will be used to define Side Face 1, the Center Face, and Side Face 2.

In this example, the default fillet radius value of **10** will be used.

TIP

Objects can be rotated by holding down the mouse wheel and moving the cursor.

3 Use the **Rotate** tool and orient the object so that the back surface can be selected.

4 Click the back surface.

The back surface is defined as **Side Face 1.**

5 Reorient the object to an isometric view.

6 Click the middle box in the **Items To Fillet** box and click the top surface of the object.

The top surface is defined as the **Center Face.**

7 Click the lower of the three boxes in the **Items To Fillet** box and click the front surface of the object as shown.

Figure 3-12

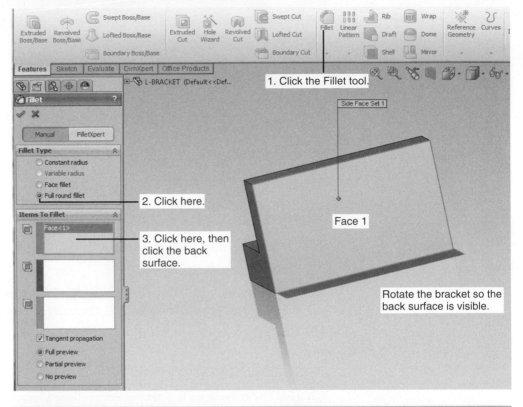

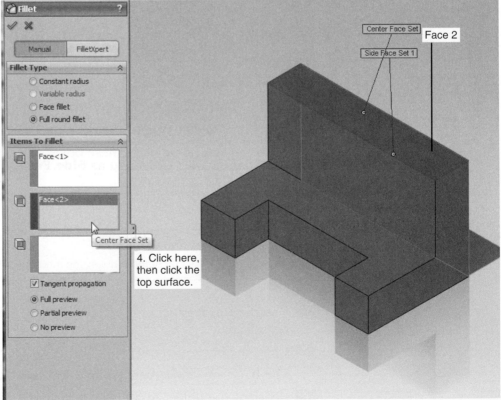

Figure 3-12
(*Continued*)

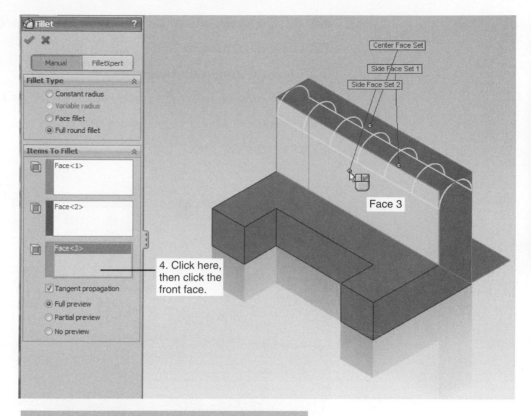

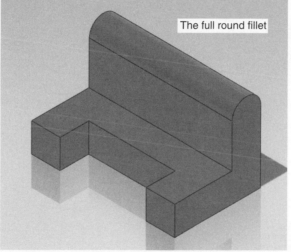

The front surface is defined as **Side Face 2.** A preview of the fillet will appear.

8 Click the OK check mark.

3-8 Chamfer

A *chamfer* is a slanted surface added to a corner of an object. Chamfers are usually manufactured at 45° but may be made at any angle. Chamfers are defined using either an angle and a distance (5 × 45°) or by two distances (5 × 5). A vertex chamfer may also be defined.

To Define a Chamfer Using an Angle and a Distance

See Figure 3-13. This section uses the L-bracket created in Section 3-3 and used in the previous section.

1 Use the **Undo** tool and remove the fillet created in the previous section.

2 Click the **Chamfer** tool.

3 Click the **Angle distance** button.

4 Define the chamfer distance as **5** and accept the **45°** default value.

5 Click the top side edge line as shown.

6 Click the OK check mark.

Figure 3-13

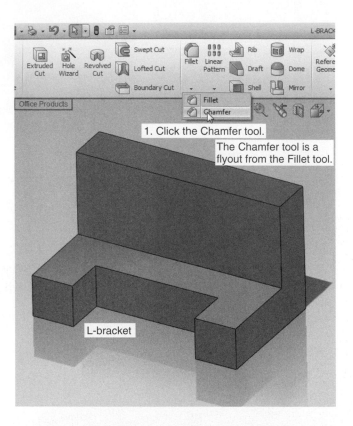

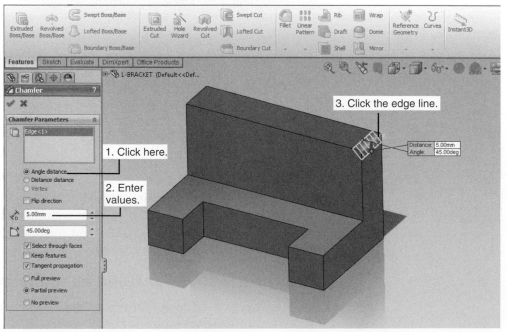

Figure 3-13
(*Continued*)

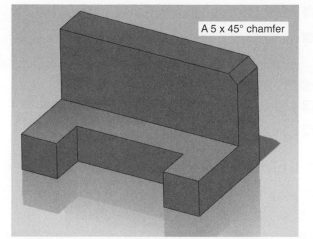

A 5 x 45° chamfer

To Define a Chamfer Using Two Distances

See Figure 3-14.

1 Click the **Chamfer** tool.

Figure 3-14

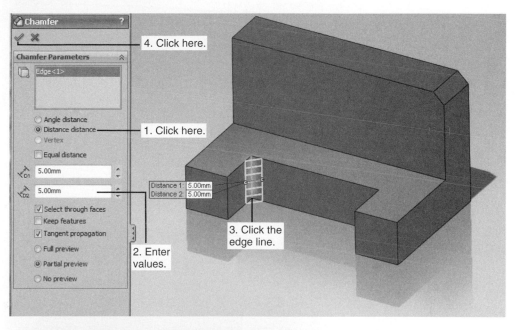

4. Click here.

1. Click here.

Distance 1: 5.00mm
Distance 2: 5.00mm

3. Click the edge line.

2. Enter values.

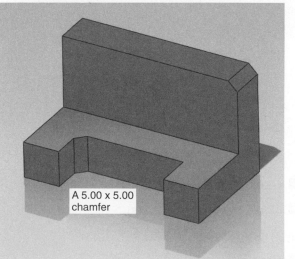

A 5.00 x 5.00 chamfer

2 Click the **Distance distance** button.

3 Define the two distances as **5.00mm** each.

In this example the two distances are equal. Distances of different lengths may be used.

4 Click the inside vertical line as shown.

5 Click the OK check mark.

To Define a Vertex Chamfer

See Figure 3-15.

Figure 3-15

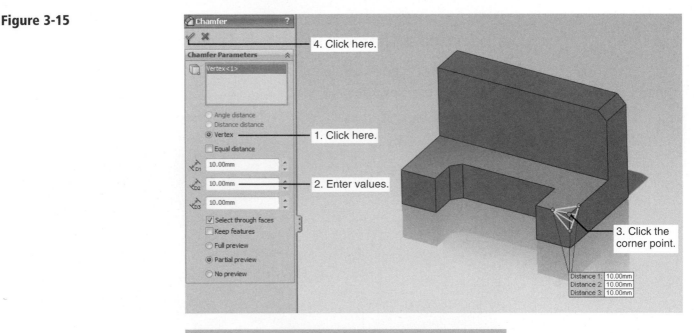

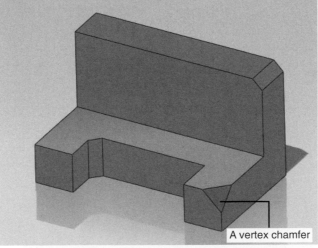

1 Click the **Chamfer** tool.

2 Click the **Vertex** button.

Three distance boxes will appear.

3 Define the three distances.

In this example three equal distances of **10.00mm** were used. The three distances need not be equal.

4 Click the lower top corner point as shown.

5 Click the OK check mark.

3-9 Revolved Boss/Base

The **Revolved Boss/Base** tool rotates a contour about an axis line. See Figure 3-16.

1 Start a new drawing, click the **Sketch** tool, and click the **Top Plane** option.

2 Use the **Sketch** tools to draw a line on the screen and then draw a 2D shape next to the line. All dimensions are in inches.

Draw the shape shown using the given dimensions.

Figure 3-16

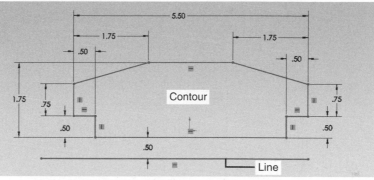

Draw the contour and the line.

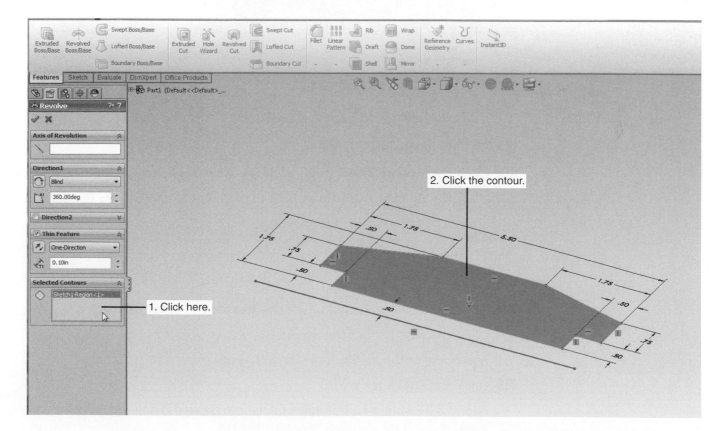

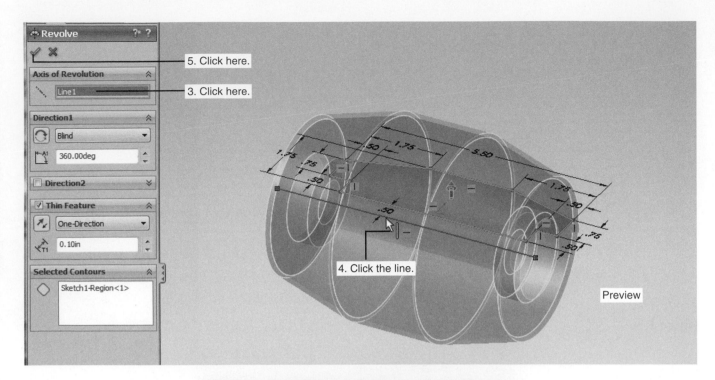

5. Click here.

3. Click here.

4. Click the line.

Preview

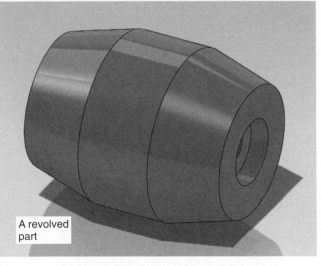

Figure 3-16
(*Continued*)

A revolved part

3 All dimensions are in inches.

4 Click the **Features** tool, then click the **Revolved Boss/Base** tool.

5 Click the **Selected Contours** box, then click the contour on the screen.

> **NOTE**
> If the **Selected Contours** box is already shaded, it means that it has been activated automatically. Click the contour directly.

6 Click the axis box at the top of the **Revolve PropertyManager.**

7 Click the axis line on the screen

A preview of the revolved object will appear.

8 Click the OK check mark.

Figure 3-17 shows an example of a sphere created using the **Revolve** tool.

Figure 3-17

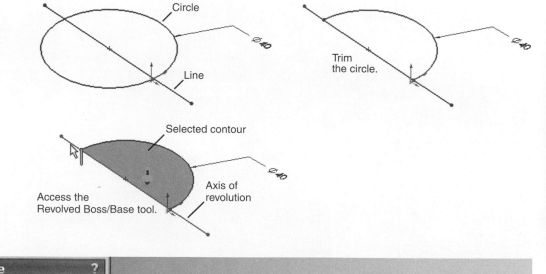

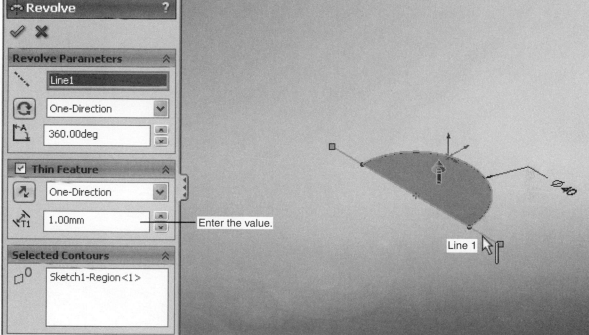

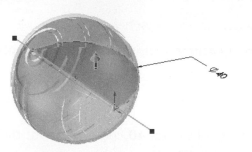

If necessary, click the Reverse Direction box in the Thin Feature box.

Click the OK check mark.

3-10 Revolved Cut

The **Revolved Cut** tool is used to cut revolved sections out of objects. Figure 3-18 shows a 40 × 60 × 100 box.

1 All dimensions are in millimeters. Create a new sketch plane (**Sketch**) on the top surface of the box and use the **Centerpoint Arc** tool to

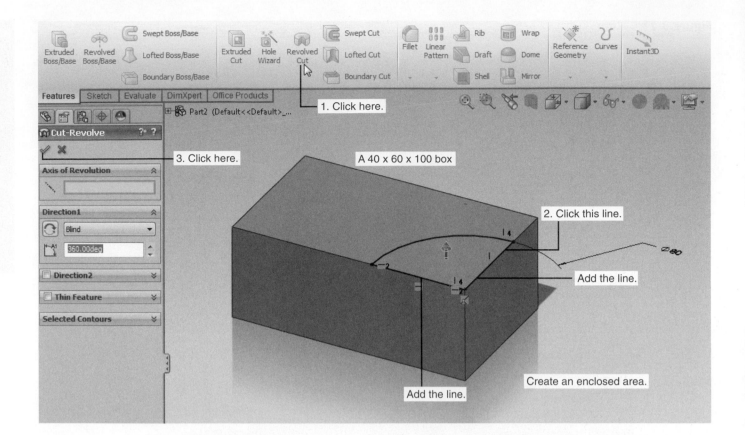

1. Click here.

3. Click here.

A 40 x 60 x 100 box

2. Click this line.

Add the line.

Add the line.

Create an enclosed area.

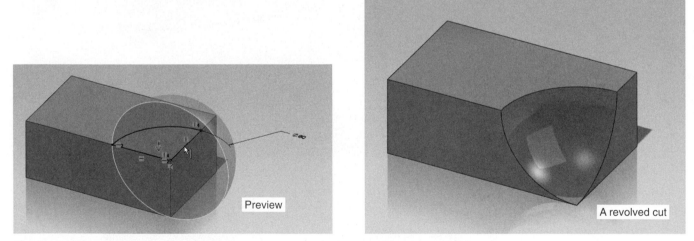

Preview

A revolved cut

Figure 3-18

draw an arc of radius **40** centered about the lower corner of the top surface as shown.

2 Draw two lines from this arc's endpoints to the corner point of the box, creating an enclosed area.

3 Click the **Revolved Cut** tool.

4 Click the **Axis of Revolution** box.

5 Click the top line as shown to identify the axis of revolution.

6 Click the OK check mark.

3-11 Reference Planes

Reference planes are planes that are not part of an existing object. Until now if we needed a new sketch plane, we selected an existing surface on the object. Consider the Ø3.0 × 3.50 cylinder shown in Figure 3-19. The

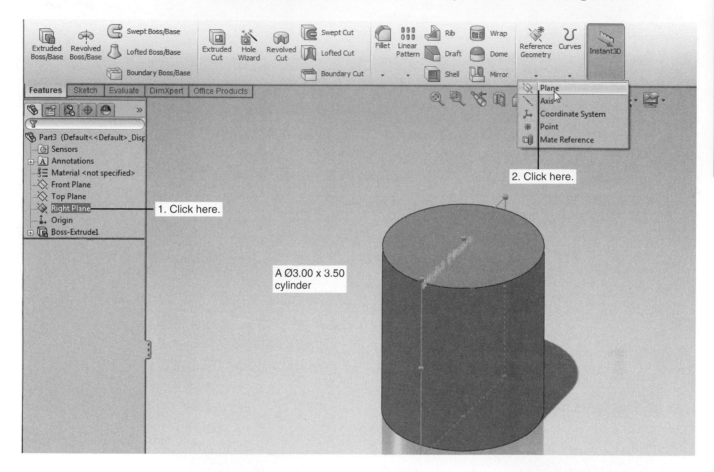

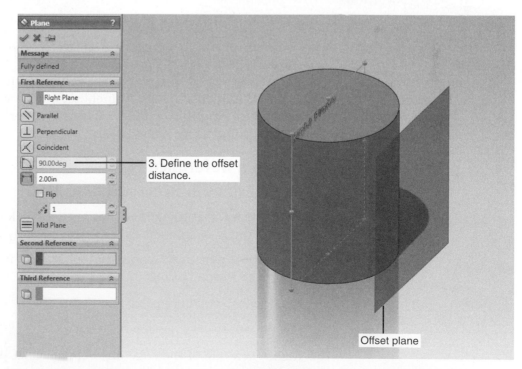

Figure 3-19

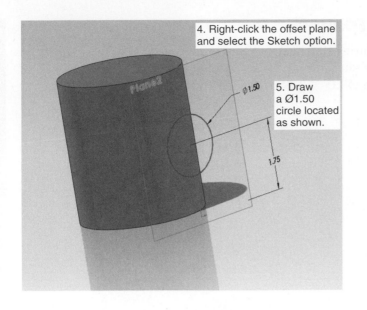

4. Right-click the offset plane and select the Sketch option.

⌀1.50

5. Draw a ⌀1.50 circle located as shown.

1.75

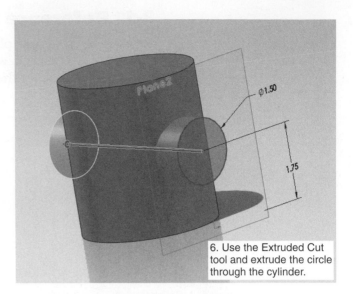

⌀1.50

1.75

6. Use the Extruded Cut tool and extrude the circle through the cylinder.

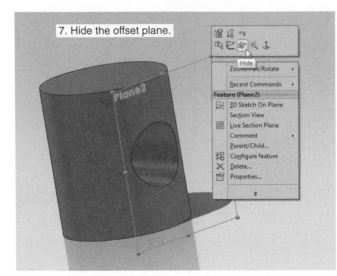

7. Hide the offset plane.

Hide
Zoom/Pan/Rotate
Recent Commands
Feature (Plane2)
3D Sketch On Plane
Section View
Live Section Plane
Comment
Parent/Child...
Configure feature
Delete...
Properties...

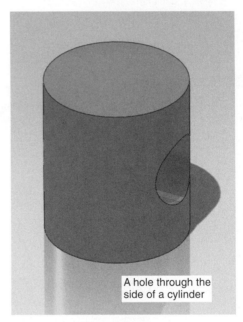

A hole through the side of a cylinder

Figure 3-19
(*Continued*)

cylinder was drawn with its base on the top plane and its centerpoint at the origin. All dimensions are in inches. How do we create a hole through the rounded sides of the cylinder? If we right-click the rounded surface, no **Sketch** tool will appear.

To Create a Reference Plane

1 Click **Right Plane** in the **FeatureManager.**

2 Right-click the **Right Plane** feature and click **Show** to ensure that the right plane is visible. (It will probably already be on.)

3 Click the **Reference Geometry** tool located in the **Features** panel and select the **Plane** option.

The **Plane** box will appear. See Figure 3-19.

4 Set the offset distance for **2.00.**

5 Right-click one of the edge lines of the offset plane.

6 Click the OK check mark.

The new reference plane is defined as **Plane2.**

7 Right-click **Plane2** and click the **Sketch** tool.

8 Use the **Circle** tool and locate a circle with its center point at **X = 0.00, Y = 1.75** on **Plane2.**

Use the origin as a reference to established the X-value. Reference the bottom surface of the cylinder to dimension the hole's center point in the Y-direction.

9 Click the **Circle** tool and draw a Ø**1.50** circle on **Plane2** using the defined point.

10 Click the **Features** tab and click the **Extruded Cut** tool.

11 Define the length of the cutting cylinder as **4.00** to assure that it will pass completely through the Ø3.00 cylinder.

12 Click the OK check mark.

13 Hide **Plane2** and the right plane by right-clicking on the planes and selecting the **Hide** option.

3-12 Lofted Boss/Base

The **Lofted Boss/Base** tool is used to create a shape between two planes, each of which contains a defined shape. Before drawing a lofted shape we must first draw two shapes on two different planes. In this example a square is lofted to a circle.

See Figure 3-20.

Figure 3-20

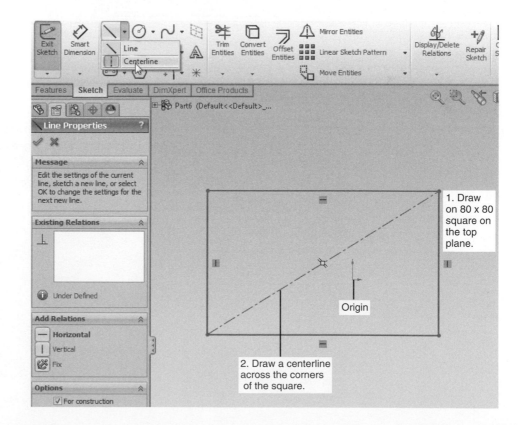

Figure 3-20
(*Continued*)

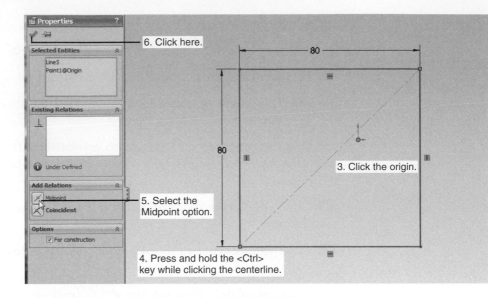

6. Click here.

80

80

3. Click the origin.

5. Select the Midpoint option.

4. Press and hold the <Ctrl> key while clicking the centerline.

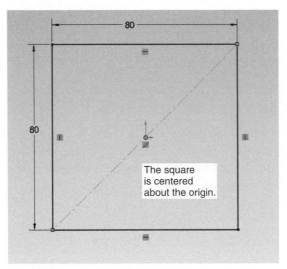

80

80

The square is centered about the origin.

8. Click the Features tab.

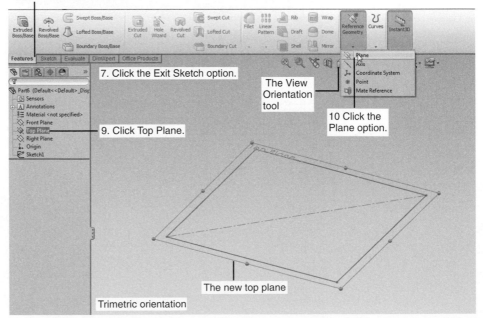

7. Click the Exit Sketch option.

The View Orientation tool

9. Click Top Plane.

10 Click the Plane option.

The new top plane

Trimetric orientation

Figure 3-20
(*Continued*)

Chapter 3

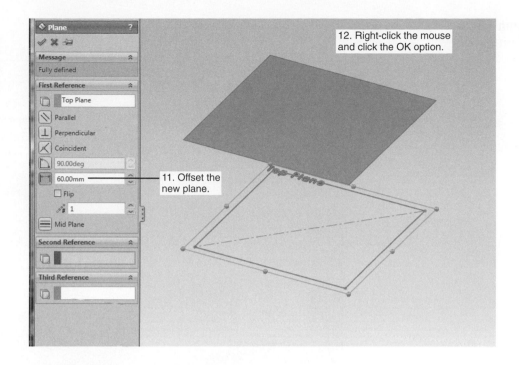

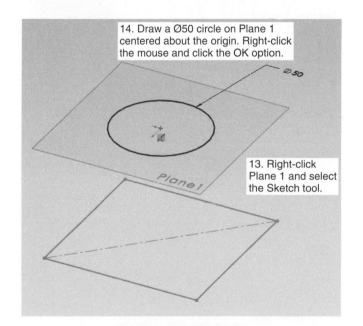

1 Create a new drawing, select the **Top Plane** option, and set the units for millimeters **(MMGS).**

2 Right-click the plane and click the **Sketch** option.

3 Sketch a rectangle about the origin.

4 Use the **Smart Dimension** tool and create an **80 × 80** square.

5 Use the **Centerline** tool and draw a centerline across the corners of the square.

Figure 3-20
(*Continued*)

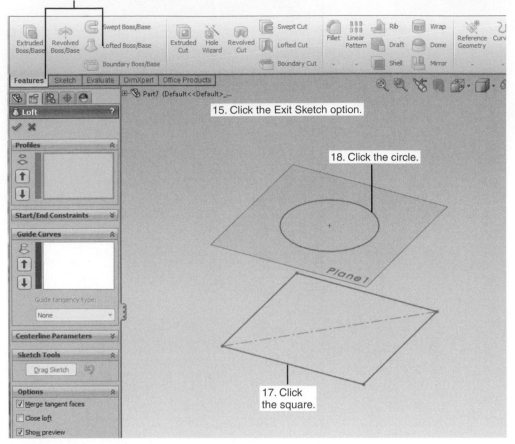

16. Click the Features tab, then click the Lofted Boss/Base tool.

15. Click the Exit Sketch option.

18. Click the circle.

Plane 1

17. Click the square.

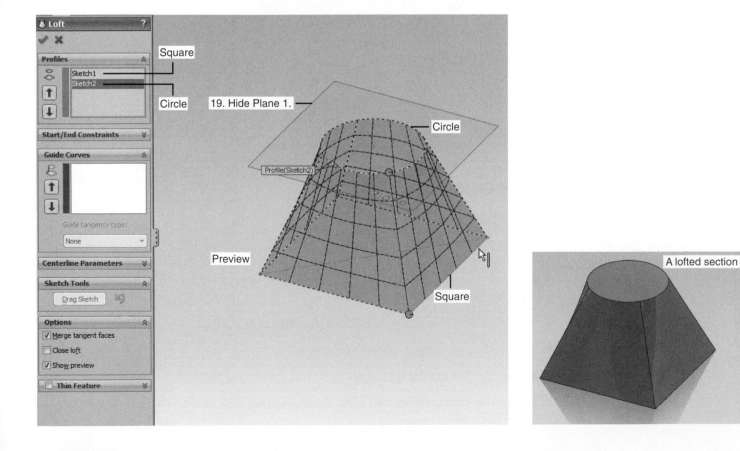

Square

Circle

19. Hide Plane 1.

Circle

Profile(Sketch2)

Preview

Square

A lofted section

6 Click the origin, press and hold the **<Ctrl>** key, and click the centerline.

The **PropertyManager** will appear.

7 Click the **Midpoint** option under the **Add Relations** option.

The square is now centered about the origin.

8 Click the check mark in the **PropertyManager** box.

9 Click the **Exit Sketch** option.

10 Click the **View Orientation** tool and select a **Trimetric** orientation.

11 Click the **Features** tab.

12 Click the **Top Plane** option, click the **Reference Geometry** tool, and select the **Plane** option.

A new plane, called **Plane 1,** will appear.

13 Offset Plane 1 **60** from the top plane that contains the rectangle.

14 Right-click the mouse and click **OK** .

15 Right-click Plane 1 and click the **Sketch** option.

16 Use the **Circle** tool and sketch a circle centered about the origin in Plane 1.

17 Use the **Smart Dimension** tool and dimension the diameter of the circle to **50.0.**

18 Click the **Exit Sketch** option and click the **Lofted Boss/Base** tool.

The **Profiles** box should turn on automatically; that is, it should be blue in color.

19 Click the rectangle.

20 Click the circle.

A preview of the lofted segment should appear.

21 Click the check mark in the **Loft PropertyManager** box.

22 Right-click **Plane 1** and select the **Hide** option.

23 Save the part as **LOFT.**

The LOFT part will be used in the chapter on assemblies.

3-13 Shell

The **Shell** tool is used to hollow out existing solid parts. Figure 3-21 shows a 35 × 40 × 60 box.

The **Shell** tool will be applied to the box.

1 Click the **Features** tab and click the **Shell** tool.

2 Define the shell thickness.

In this example, a thickness of **2.00** was selected.

3 Click the two faces of the box as indicated.

4 Click the **OK** check mark.

Figure 3-22 shows two more examples of how the **Shell** tool can be applied to parts.

Figure 3-21

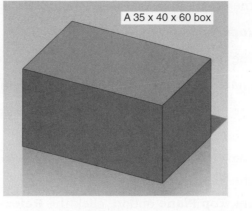

A 35 x 40 x 60 box

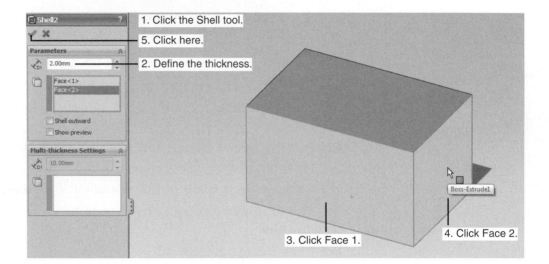

1. Click the Shell tool.
5. Click here.
2. Define the thickness.
3. Click Face 1.
4. Click Face 2.

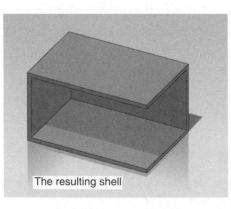

The resulting shell

Figure 3-22

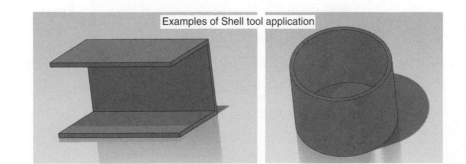

Examples of Shell tool application

3-14 Swept Boss/Base

The **Swept Boss/Base** tool is used to sweep a profile along a path line. As with the **Lofted Boss/Base** tool, existing shapes must be present before the **Swept Boss/Base** tool can be applied. In this example, a Ø.50-inch circle will be swept along an arc with a 2.50-inch radius for 120°. See Figure 3-23.

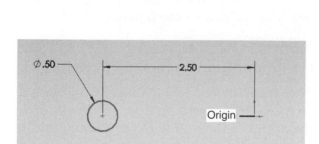
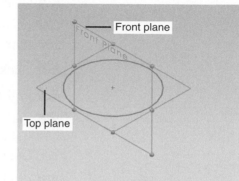

Draw a Ø.50 circle on the top plane as shown.

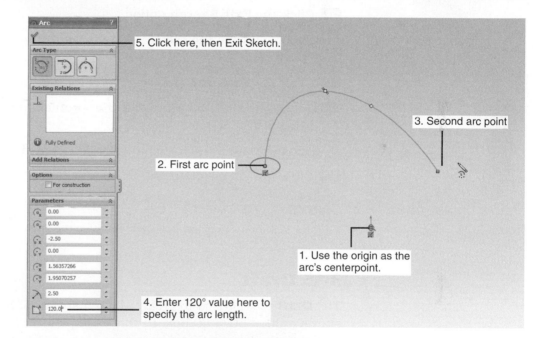

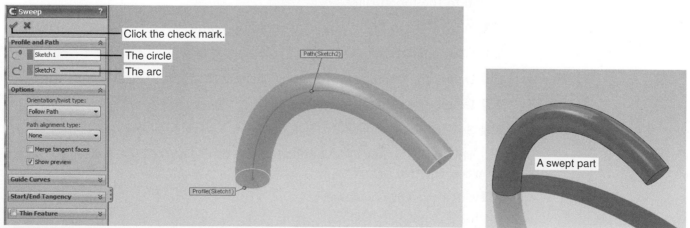

Figure 3-23

1 Start a New drawing and click the **Top Plane** tool. Use the **Circle** and **Smart Dimension** tools to draw a Ø.50-inch circle **2.50** inches from the origin.

2 Use the **View Orientation** tool and change the drawing screen to an isometric orientation.

3 Right-click the mouse and click the **Select** option.

4 Click **Exit Sketch**.

We are now going to create a new sketch on a different sketch plane, so we must exit the top plane sketch plane.

5 Click the **Edit Sketch** tool.

6 Right-click **Front Plane** and click the **Sketch** option.

7 Use the **Centerpoint Arc** tool to draw an arc with a **2.50** radius with the origin as its center point and an arc length of approximately 120°. Define the arc's length as **120°** in the **Parameters** box.

8 Click the OK check mark.

9 Click the **Exit Sketch** option.

This completes the second sketch. The **Swept Boss/Base** tool can now be applied.

10 Click the **Features** tool, then click the **Swept Boss/Base** tool.

11 Select the circle as **Sketch 1** (the profile) and the arc as **Sketch 2** (the path).

The path are a will automatically be selected.

12 Click the OK check mark.

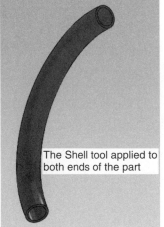

The Shell tool applied to both ends of the part

Figure 3-24

> **NOTE**
> Figure 3-24 shows an object hollowed out using the **Shell** tool.

3-15 Draft

The **Draft** tool is used to create slanted surfaces. See Figure 3-25, which shows a 30 × 50 × 60 box. In this example a 15° slanted surface will be added to the top surface.

1 Draw a **30 × 50 × 60** box on the top plane.

2 Click the **Draft** tool.

3 Define the **Direction of Pull** by clicking the right vertical face of the box.

4 Define the **draft angle** as **15°.**

5 Select the draft face by clicking the top surface of the box.

The draft angle will be applied to the draft face relative to the 90° angle between the two faces.

6 Click the OK check mark.

Figure 3-26 shows a slanted surface created by making the top surface the direction of pull and the front surface the draft face.

A 30 x 50 x 60 box

Figure 3-25

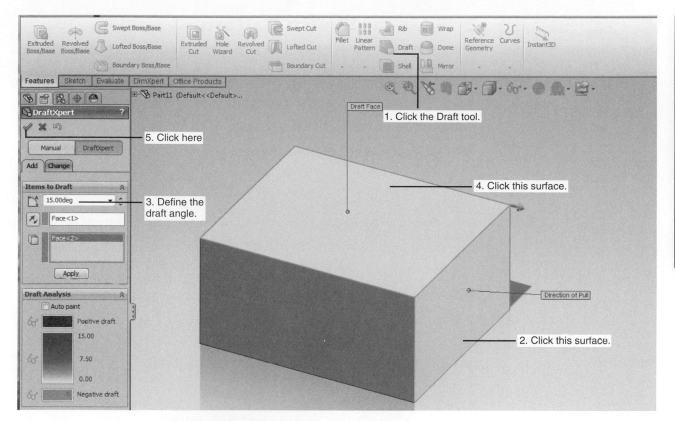

Figure 3-25
(*Continued*)

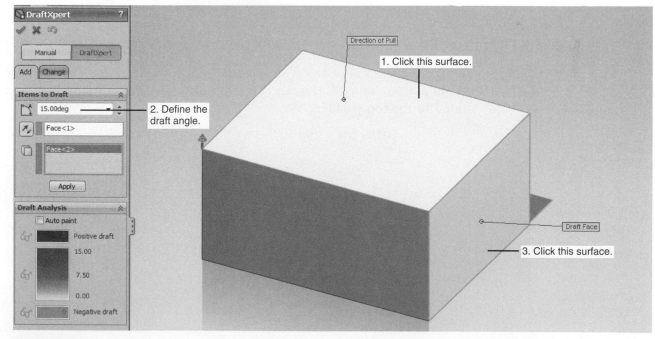

Figure 3-26

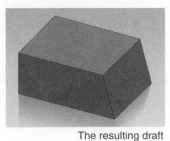

The resulting draft

Figure 3-26
(*Continued*)

3-16 Linear Sketch Pattern

The **Linear Sketch Pattern** tool is used to create rectangular patterns based on a given object.

Figure 3-27 shows a 10 × 15 × 20 box located on a 5 × 80 × 170 base. The box is located 10 from each edge of the base as shown.

1 Draw the base and box as shown.

2 Click the **Linear Sketch Pattern** tool.

NOTE

The box should be selected automatically, but if is not, use the **Features to Pattern** tool to select the box.

---

3 Define **Direction 1** by clicking the back top line as shown.

4 Define the spacing as **30.00mm.**

Figure 3-27

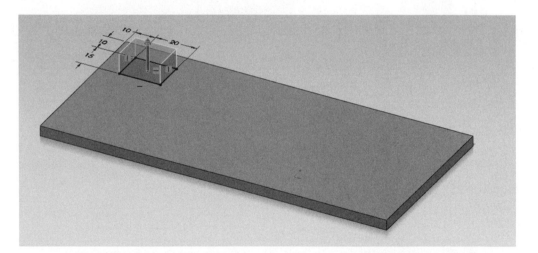

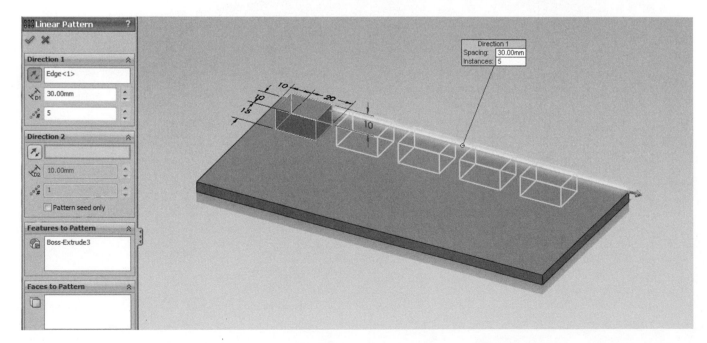

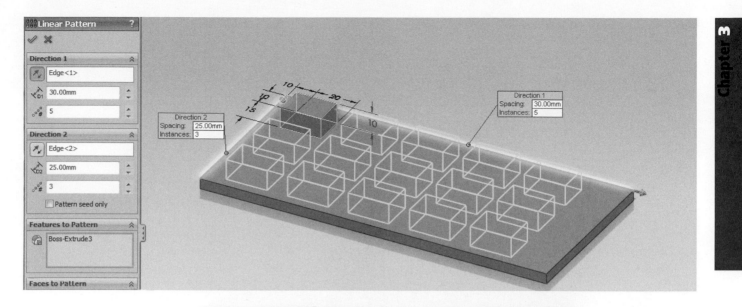

Figure 3-27
(*Continued*)

Spacing is the distance between two of the objects in the pattern as measured from the same point on each object, for example, the distance from the lower front corner on one object to the lower front corner of the next object.

5 Define the number of columns in the pattern **(Instances)** as **5.**

6 Define **Direction 2** by clicking the left edge of the base.

7 Define the spacing for **Direction 2** as **25** and the number of rows in the pattern **(Instances)** as **3.**

A preview of the pattern will appear.

8 Click the OK check mark.

3-17 Circular Sketch Pattern

The **Circular Sketch Pattern** tool is used to create circular patterns about an origin. See Figure 3-28.

1 Draw a **Ø160 × 10** cylinder.

2 Draw a **Ø30** hole centered about the Ø160 cylinder's origin.

3 Define an axis for the Ø30 hole by accessing the **Reference Geometry** tool in the **Features** tools and then clicking the **Axis** option.

Figure 3-28

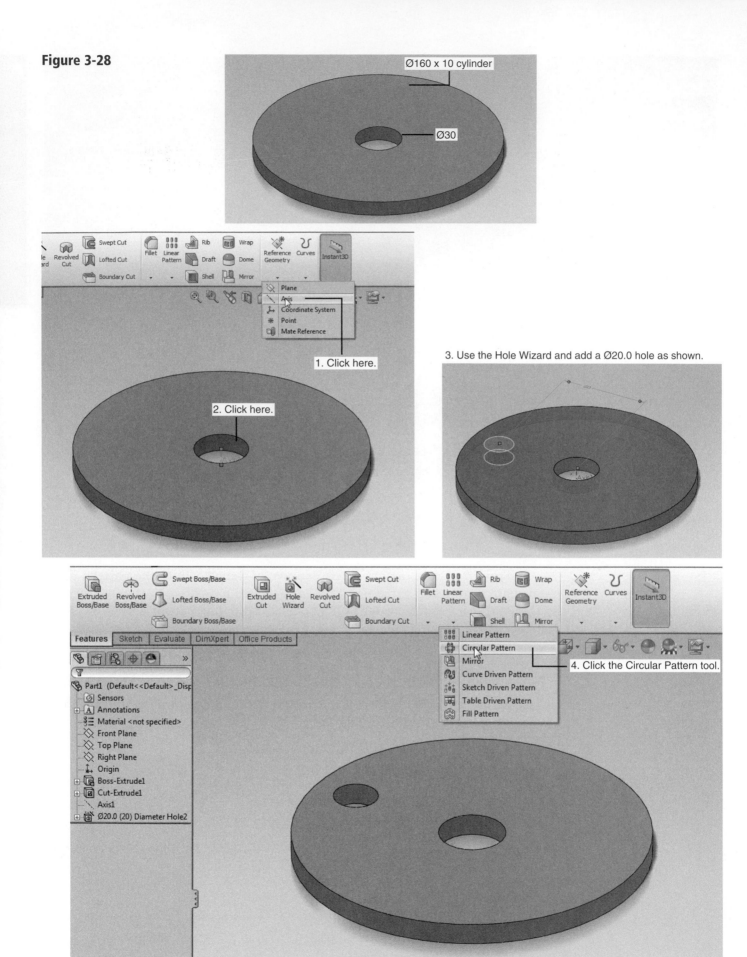

Ø160 x 10 cylinder

Ø30

1. Click here.

2. Click here.

3. Use the Hole Wizard and add a Ø20.0 hole as shown.

4. Click the Circular Pattern tool.

Figure 3-28
(*Continued*)

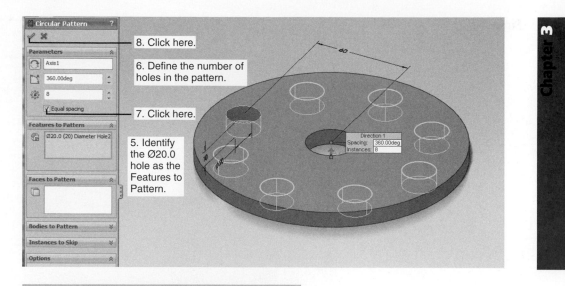

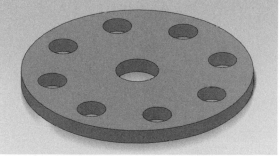

■4 Click the **Cylindrical/Conical Face** option in the **Axis PropertyManager** and click the inside surface of the Ø30 hole.

An axis should appear in the center of the hole.

■5 Use the **Hole Wizard** tool and create a **Ø20.0** through hole **60** from the cylinder's center point.

■6 Click the **Circular Pattern** tool.

■7 Access the **Features** tools and select the **Circular Pattern** tool.

■8 Define the number of features **(Instances)** in the pattern for **8**, click the **Equal spacing** option, select the axis of the Ø30 hole as the axis and the Ø20 hole as the **Features to Pattern.**

A preview will appear.

■9 Click the OK check mark.

■10 Note the axis.

3-18 Mirror

The **Mirror** tool is used to create mirror images of features. A mirror image is not the same as a copy. In this section we will mirror the object shown in Figure 3-29.

■1 Draw the object shown in Figure 3-29. Extrude the object to a thickness of **0.50**.

■2 Access the **Features** tools, and click the **Mirror** tool.

Figure 3-29

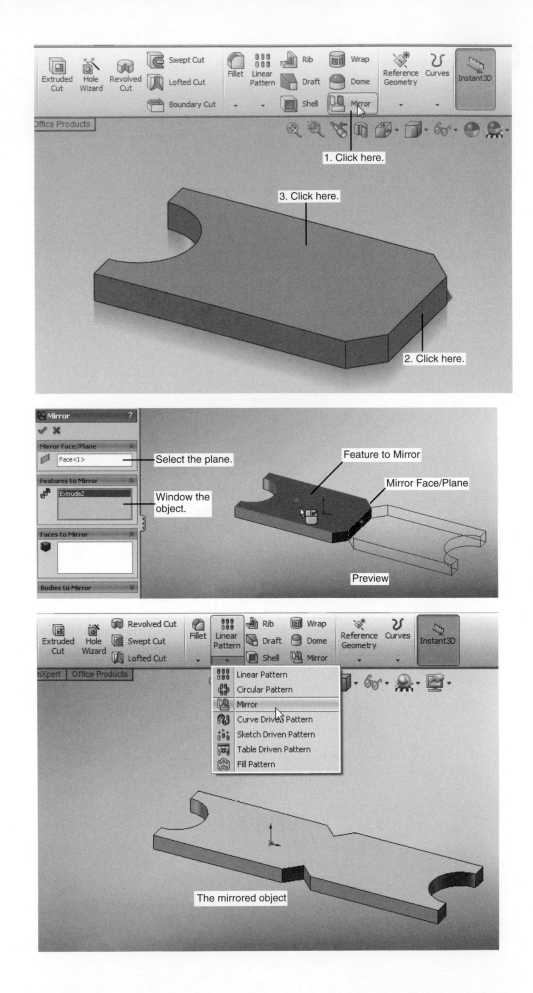

3 Click the **Mirror Face/Plane** box, then click the right surface plane as shown.

4 Click the **Features to Mirror** box, then click the object.

A preview will appear.

5 Click the OK check mark.

3-19 Helix Curves and Springs

SolidWorks allows you to draw springs by drawing a helix and then sweep a circle along the helical path.

To Draw a Helix

See Figure 3-30. All dimensions are in inches.

1 Start a new drawing, select the **Top Plane,** and click the **Sketch** tab.

2 Draw a **Ø1.50** circle.

In this example the circle was centered about the origin. The diameter of this circle will determine the diameter of the helix.

3 Click the **View Orientation** tool and select the **Trimetric** view orientation.

4 Click the **Features** tab, and click the **Helix** tool.

The **Helix/Spiral PropertyManager** box will appear along with a preview of the default helix.

5 Enter a **Height** value of **2.00,** a **Pitch** of **.375,** and **Start angle** of **0.00°.**

Note how the Ø1.50 diameter sizes the helix.

6 Click the OK check mark.

Figure 3-30

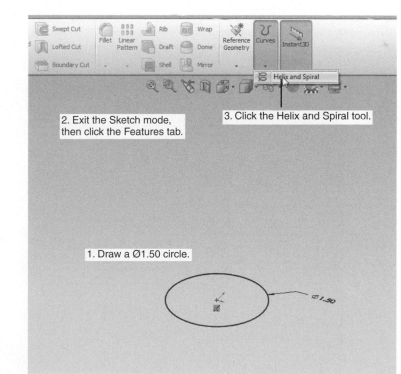

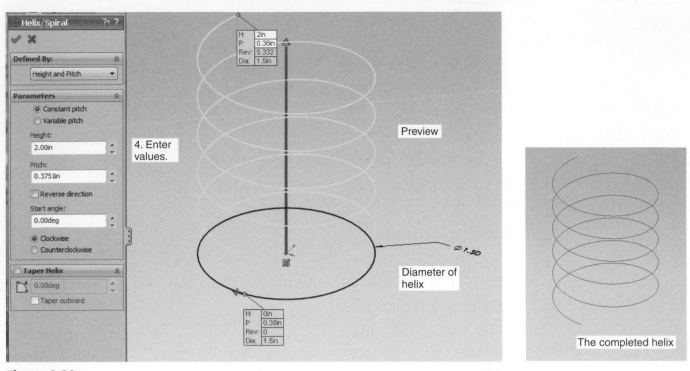

Figure 3-30
(*Continued*)

To Draw a Spring from the Given Helix

See Figure 3-31.

1 Click the endpoint of the helix and click the **Right Plane** option in the **FeatureManager.**

2 Right-click the plane and select the **Sketch** option.

Figure 3-31

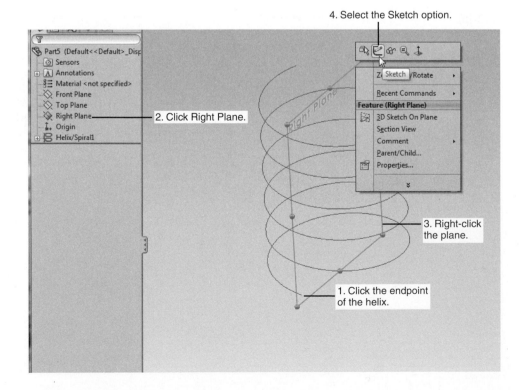

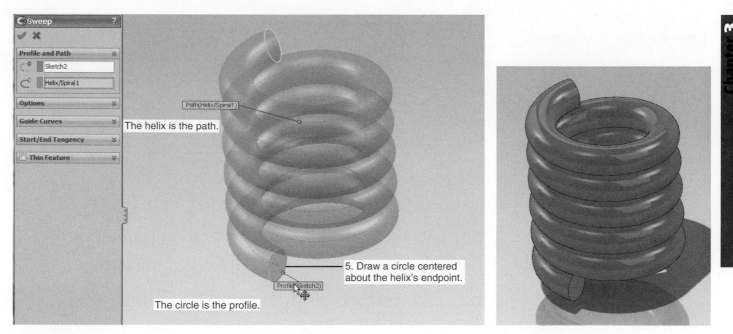

Figure 3-31
(*Continued*)

3 Draw a **Ø.375** circle on the front plane.

The diameter of the circle defines the wire diameter for the spring.

4 Exit the **Sketch** mode, click the **Features** tab, and click the **Swept Boss/Base** tool.

5 Click the circle as the profile and the helix as the path.

A preview will appear.

6 Click the OK check mark.

7 Save the spring.

3-20 Compression Springs

The spring shown in Figure 3-21 is a compression spring. Compression springs are designed to accept forces that squeeze them together. They often include ground ends that help them accept the loads while maintaining their position; that is, they don't pop out when the load is applied.

Figure 3-32 shows a compression spring. It has the following parameters. Dimensions are in inches.

Diameter = 1.00

Pitch = .25

Number of coils = 10

Start angle = 0.00

Wire diameter = .125

To Create Ground Ends

See Figure 3-33.

1 Orient the spring in the **Trimetric** orientation.

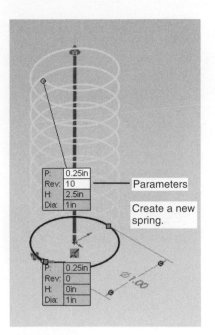

P:	0.25in
Rev:	10
H:	2.5in
Dia:	1in

Parameters

Create a new spring.

P:	0.25in
Rev:	0
H:	0in
Dia:	1in

Ø1.00

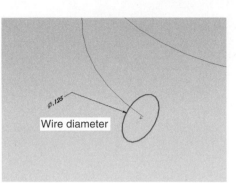

Ø.125

Wire diameter

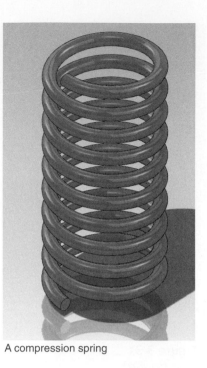

A compression spring

Figure 3-32

2 Click the **Top Plane** option and click the **Plane** option in the **Reference Geometry** tool on the **Features** tab.

3 Create an offset plane **.50** from the top plane.
This is Plane 1.

Figure 3-33

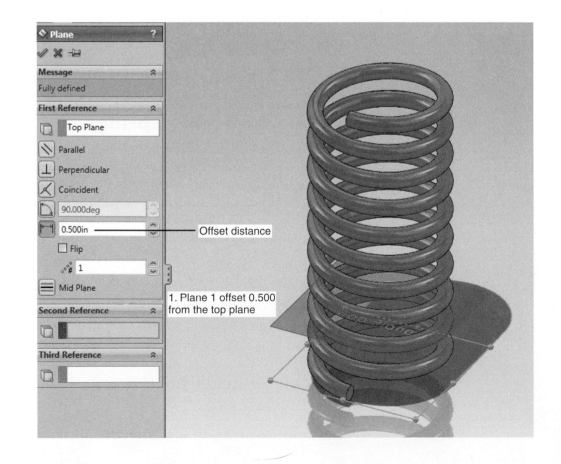

Plane

Message

Fully defined

First Reference

Top Plane

Parallel

Perpendicular

Coincident

90.000deg

0.500in —— Offset distance

☐ Flip

1

Mid Plane

Second Reference

Third Reference

1. Plane 1 offset 0.500 from the top plane

Figure 3-33
(*Continued*)

Chapter 3

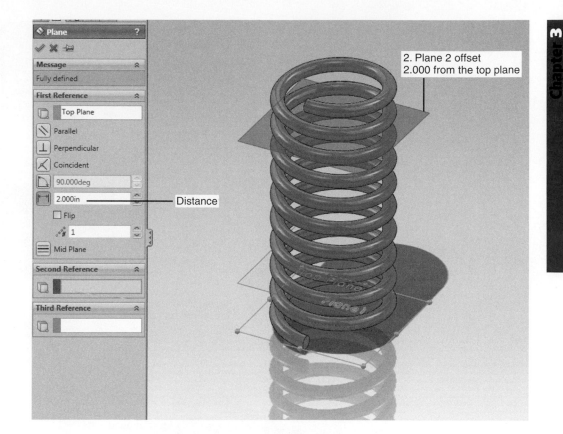

2. Plane 2 offset
2.000 from the top plane

Distance

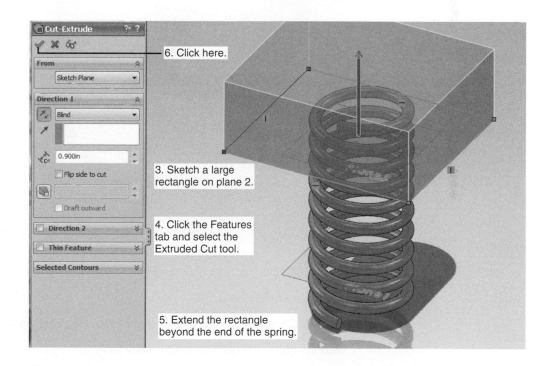

6. Click here.

3. Sketch a large
rectangle on plane 2.

4. Click the Features
tab and select the
Extruded Cut tool.

5. Extend the rectangle
beyond the end of the spring.

Figure 3-33
(*Continued*)

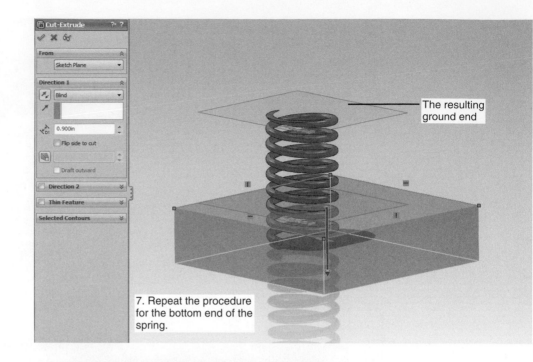

The resulting ground end

7. Repeat the procedure for the bottom end of the spring.

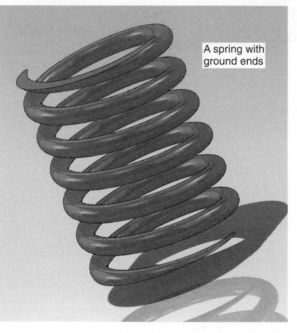

A spring with ground ends

4 Create a second offset plane **2.00** from the top plane.

This is Plane 2.

5 Right-click **Plane 2** and select the **Sketch** option.

6 Sketch a large rectangle on Plane 2.

Any size larger than the spring is acceptable.

7 Click the **Features** tab and select the **Extruded Cut** tool.

8 Create a distance that exceeds the end of the spring.

9 Click the OK check mark.

The top portion of the spring will be cut off, simulating a ground end.

10 Repeat the procedure for the bottom end of the spring.

11 Hide Planes 1 and 2.

The distance between Planes 1 and 2 will be the final height of the spring before compression.

3-21 Torsional Springs

Torsional springs are design to accept a twisting load. They usually include extensions. See Figure 3-34.

To Draw a Torsional Spring

1 Draw a spring as defined in Figure 3-32.

2 Zoom the bottom endpoint of the spring, right-click the end surface, and select the **Sketch** tool.

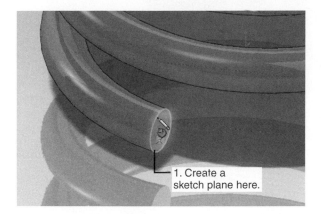

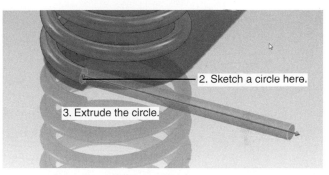

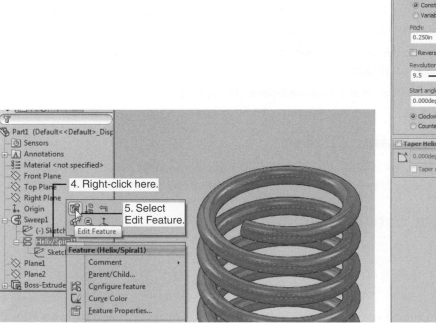

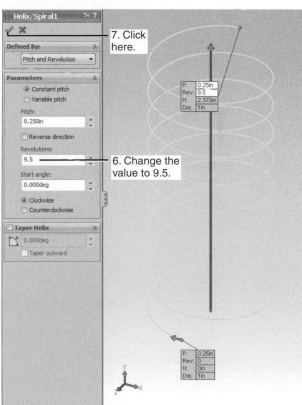

Figure 3-34

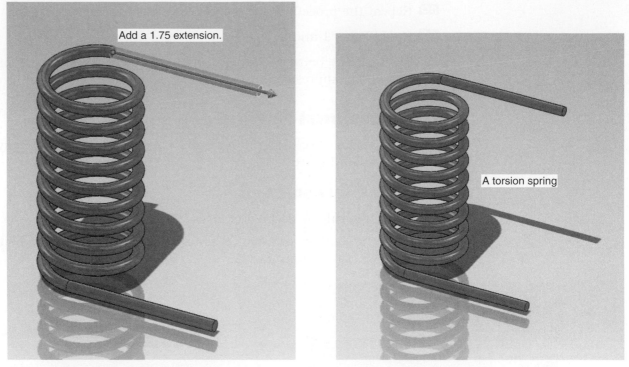

Figure 3-34
(Continued)

3 Click the **Sketch** tab and sketch a circle that exactly matches the existing end diameter.

In this example the **Ø.125** was used.

4 Click the **Features** tab and select the **Extruded Boss/Base** tool.

5 Extrude the circle a distance of **1.75.**

6 Right-click the **Helix/Spiral** heading in the **Manager** box and select the **Edit Feature** option.

7 Change the **Revolutions** value to **9.5** and click the OK check mark.

The **Revolutions** value can be used to create extensions at any angle.

8 Right-click the new top end surface of the spring and draw a **1.75** extension as shown.

9 Click the OK check mark and save the spring.

3-22 Extension Springs

Extension springs are designed for loads that pull them apart, that is, tension loads. Extension springs usually have hooklike ends.

To Draw an Extension Spring

See Figure 3-35.

1 Draw a spring as defined in Figure 2-32.

2 Sketch a circle on the end surface of the spring as shown.

3 Use the **Plane** option under the **Reference Geometry** tool and create an offset front plane through the center point of the circle created in Step 1.

4 Use the **Centerpoint Arc** tool and sketch an arc from the center of the sketch circle a distance of **90°**.

The **Smart Dimension** tool can be used to size the arc.

5 Use the **Swept Boss/Base** tool and sweep the circle along the arc path.

6 Click the OK check mark.

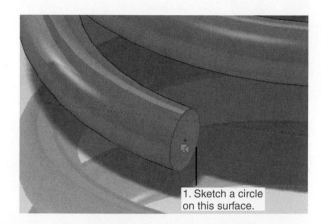

1. Sketch a circle on this surface.

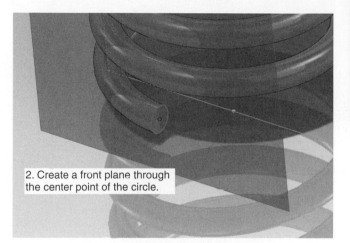

2. Create a front plane through the center point of the circle.

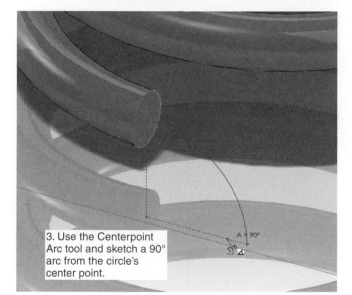

3. Use the Centerpoint Arc tool and sketch a 90° arc from the circle's center point.

A = 90°

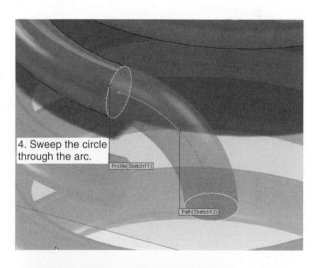

4. Sweep the circle through the arc.

Profile(Sketch11)

Path(Sketch12)

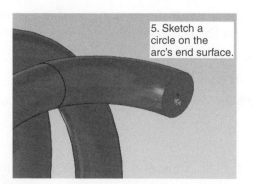

5. Sketch a circle on the arc's end surface.

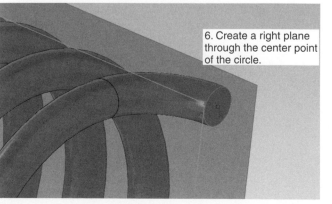

6. Create a right plane through the center point of the circle.

Figure 3-35

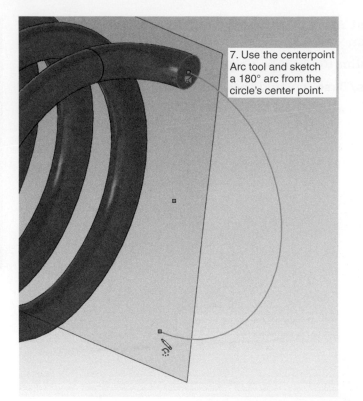

7. Use the centerpoint Arc tool and sketch a 180° arc from the circle's center point.

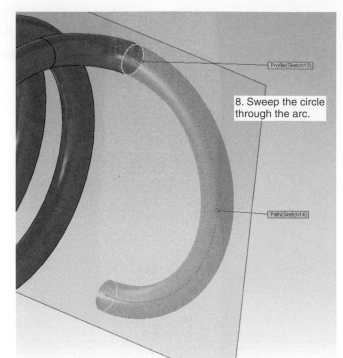

Profile(Sketch13)

8. Sweep the circle through the arc.

Path(Sketch14)

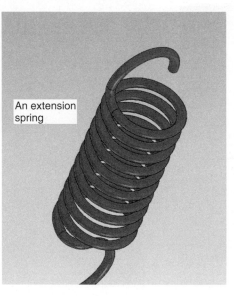

An extension spring

Figure 3-35
(*Continued*)

7 Sketch a circle on the arc's end surface.

8 Use the **Plane** option under the **Reference Geometry** tool and create an offset right plane through the center point of the circle created in Step 5.

9 Create a sketch plane on Plane 2.

10 Use the **Centerpoint Arc** tool and sketch a **180°** arc.

11 Use the **Swept Boss/Base** tool and sweep the circle through the arc.

12 Click the check mark.

13 Hide the planes.

14 Repeat the procedure for the other end surface of the spring.

The spring shown represents one possible type of extension spring.

3-23 Wrap

The **Wrap** tool is used to wrap text or other shapes around a surface. There are three options: emboss, text that stands out from a face; debossed, text that is embedded on a face; and scribe, text that is written directly on the face.

To Create Debossed Text

See Figure 3-36.

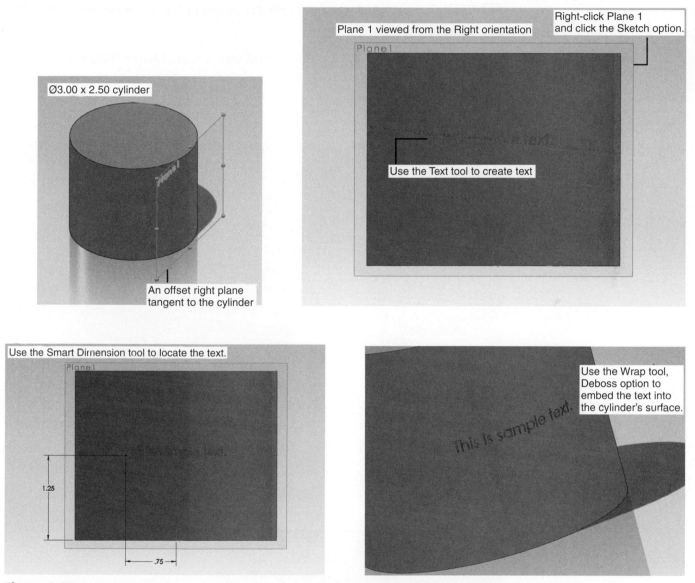

Ø3.00 x 2.50 cylinder

An offset right plane tangent to the cylinder

Plane 1 viewed from the Right orientation

Right-click Plane 1 and click the Sketch option.

Plane1

Use the Text tool to create text

Use the Smart Dimension tool to locate the text.

Plane1

1.25

.75

Use the Wrap tool, Deboss option to embed the text into the cylinder's surface.

This is sample text.

Figure 3-36

1 Draw a **Ø3.00 × 2.50** cylinder based on the top plane.

2 Use the **Plane** option of the **Reference Geometry** tool and create an offset right plane tangent to the outside edge of the cylinder.

This is Plane 1.

3 Change the orientation of the cylinder to the right plane.

4 Right-click **Plane 1** and click the **Sketch** option.

5 Click the **Text** tool and add text to the plane.

6 Use the cursor or the **Smart Dimension** tool to locate the text.

7 Change the drawing orientation to **Trimetric.**

8 Exit the **Sketch** mode.

9 Click the **Wrap** tool.

10 Click the **Deboss** option.

11 Click the edge surface of the cylinder to define the **Face for Wrap Sketch.**

12 Hide Plane 1.

Figure 3-37 shows a sample of embossed text. Figure 3-38 shows a sample of scribed text.

Figure 3-37

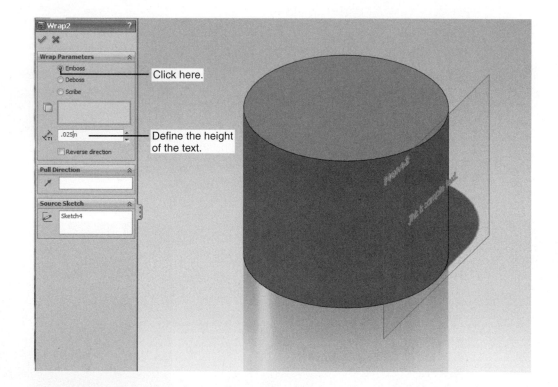

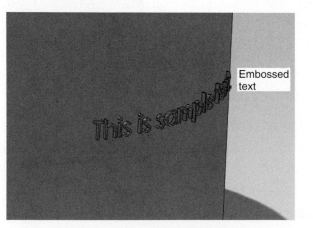

Figure 3-38

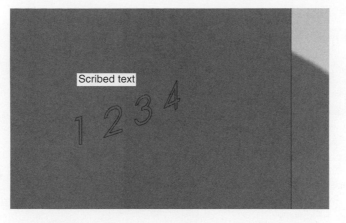

Scribed text

3-24 Editing Features

SolidWorks allows you to edit existing models. This is a very powerful feature in that you can easily make changes to a completed model without having to redraw the entire model.

TIP

The **Edit Sketch** tool is used to edit shapes created using the **Sketch** tools such as holes. The **Edit Features** tool is used to edit shapes created using the **Features** tools such as a cut or extrusion.

Figure 3-39 shows the L-bracket originally created in Sections 3-4 through 3-7. The finished object may be edited. In this example, the hole's diameter and the size of the cutout will be changed.

Figure 3-39

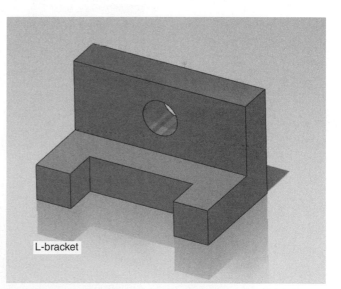

L-bracket

To Edit the Hole

See Figure 3-40.

1 Right-click the **Ø20.0** hole callout in the **FeatureManager** on the left side of the drawing screen and select the **Edit Feature** option.

2. Click the Edit Feature option.

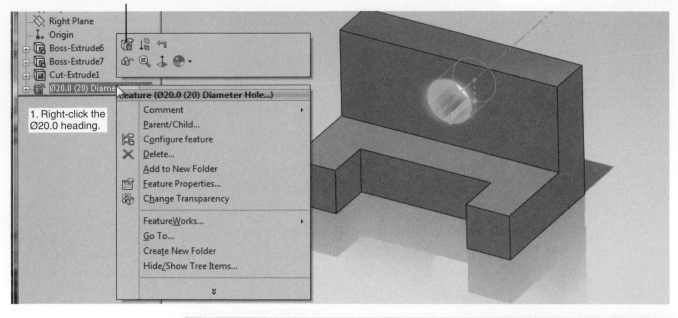

1. Right-click the Ø20.0 heading.

- Right Plane
- Origin
- Boss-Extrude6
- Boss-Extrude7
- Cut-Extrude1
- Ø20.0 (20) Diame...

Feature (Ø20.0 (20) Diameter Hole...)

Comment
Parent/Child...
Configure feature
Delete...
Add to New Folder
Feature Properties...
Change Transparency

FeatureWorks...
Go To...
Create New Folder
Hide/Show Tree Items...

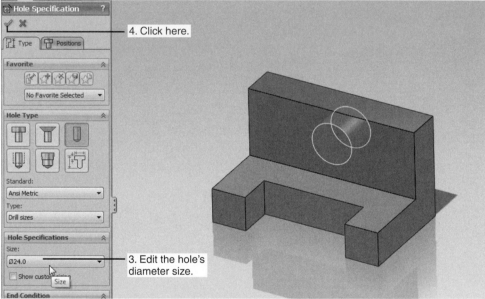

4. Click here.

Hole Specification

Type | Positions

Favorite
No Favorite Selected

Hole Type

Standard:
Ansi Metric
Type:
Drill sizes

Hole Specifications
Size:
Ø24.0
Show custom...
Size

3. Edit the hole's diameter size.

End Condition

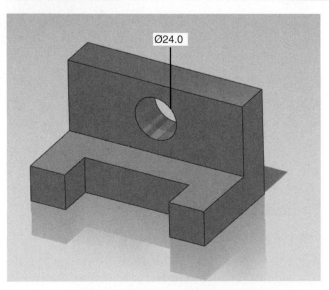

Ø24.0

Figure 3-40

TIP

The hole will be highlighted when selected.

The **Hole Specification PropertyManager** will appear.

2 Select a new hole diameter.

In this example **Ø24** was selected.

3 Click the OK check mark.

To Edit the Cutout

See Figure 3-41.

1 Right-click the **Cut-Extrude1** callout in the **FeatureManager** on the left side of the drawing screen, and select the **Edit Sketch** option.

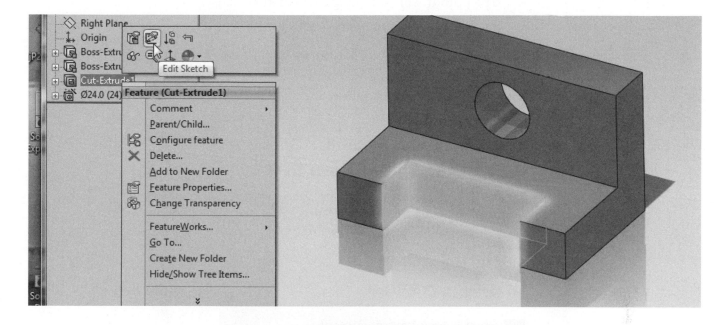

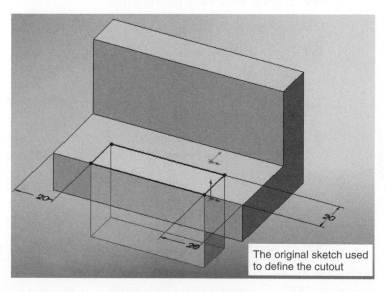

The original sketch used to define the cutout

Figure 3-41

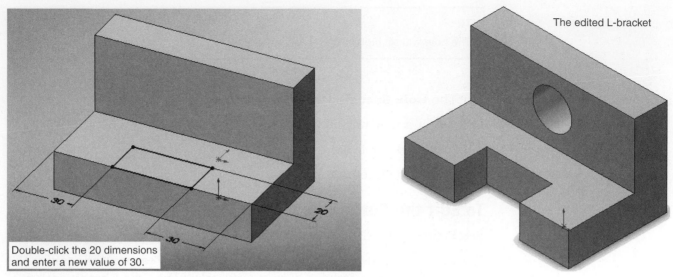

The edited L-bracket

Figure 3-41
(Continued)

Double-click the 20 dimensions and enter a new value of 30.

The cutout will be highlighted when selected.

The sketch used to define the cutout will appear.

2 Double-click the two **20** dimensions that define the length of the cutout and change their value to **30.**

3 Click the OK check mark.

4 Click the **Exit Sketch** option.

3-25 Sample Problem SP3-2

Figure 3-42 shows a cylindrical object with a slanted surface, a cutout, and a blind hole. Figure 3-43 shows how to draw the object. The procedures presented in Figure 3-43 represent one of several possible ways to create the object.

To Draw a Cylinder

1 Start a new **Part** document.

2 Define the units as millimeters **(MMGS)** and access the top plane.

3 Draw a **Ø58** circle and extrude it to **60.**

To Create a Slanted Surface on the Cylinder

1 Click the **Right Plane** option, click the **Reference Geometry** tool under the **Features** tab, and click the **Plane** option.

2 Define the offset plane distance in the **Plane PropertyManager** as **30,** and click the check mark.

3 Right-click the offset plane and select the **Sketch** option.

4 Change the drawing orientation to the **right plane.**

5 Use the **Line** tool and draw an enclosed triangular shape.

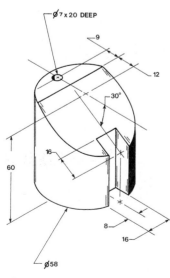

Figure 3-42

Figure 3-43

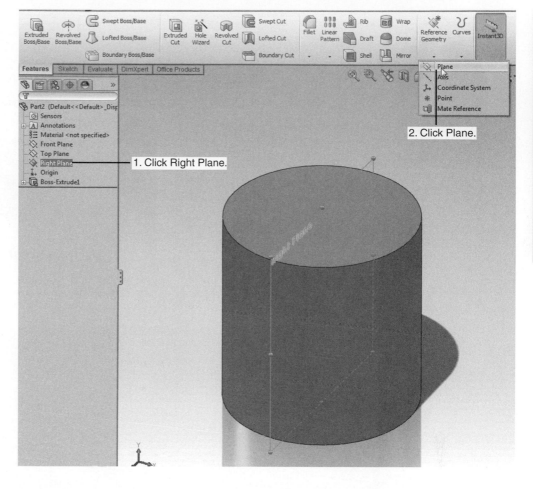

1. Click Right Plane.

2. Click Plane.

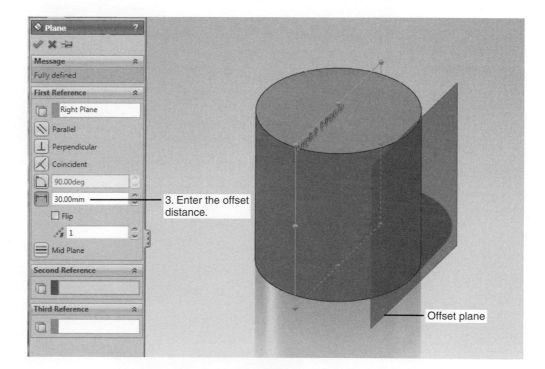

3. Enter the offset distance.

Offset plane

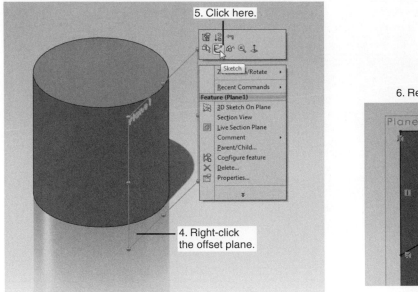

5. Click here.

Sketch
Z _ /Rotate
Recent Commands
Feature (Plane1)
3D Sketch On Plane
Section View
Live Section Plane
Comment
Parent/Child...
Configure feature
Delete...
Properties...

4. Right-click
the offset plane.

6. Reorient the drawing to the right plane.

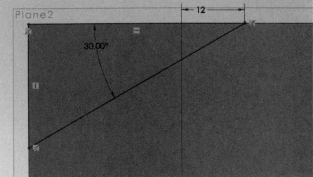

Plane2

12

30.00°

7. Draw an enclosed triangle.

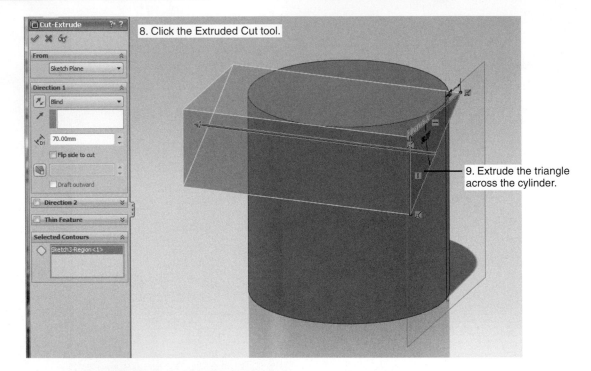

Cut-Extrude

From
Sketch Plane

Direction 1
Blind

70.00mm
Flip side to cut

Draft outward

Direction 2

Thin Feature

Selected Contours
Sketch3-Region<1>

8. Click the Extruded Cut tool.

9. Extrude the triangle
across the cylinder.

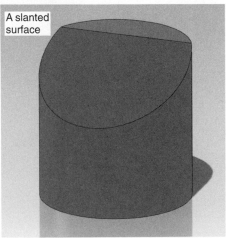

A slanted
surface

Figure 3-43
(*Continued*)

NOTE

The dimensions for the triangle came from Figure 3-42. The triangle must be an enclosed area. No gaps are permitted.

6 Use the **Smart Dimension** tool to define the size and location of the triangle.

7 Change the drawing orientation to **Dimetric** and click the **Extruded Cut** tool in the **Features** tools.

8 Set the length of the cut to **60.00mm** and click the check mark.

9 Right-click the offset plane and click the **Hide** option.

To Add the Vertical Slot

See Figure 3-44.

1 Right-click the slanted surface and click the **Sketch** tool.

2 Click the **View Orientation** tool and click the **Normal to View** tool, or click **<Ctrl-8>.**

3 Draw a vertical construction line through the origin. Start the line on the edge of the slanted surface.

4 Use the **Rectangle** tool on the **Sketch** toolbar and draw an **8 × 16** rectangle as shown. Use the **Smart Dimension** tool to size the rectangle.

5 Draw a second **8 × 16** rectangle as shown.

6 Change the drawing orientation to a dimetric view.

7 Exit the **sketch.**

8 Click the **Top Plane** option, then use the **Reference Geometry** tool on the **Features** toolbar and create an offset top plane **60** from the base of the cylinder.

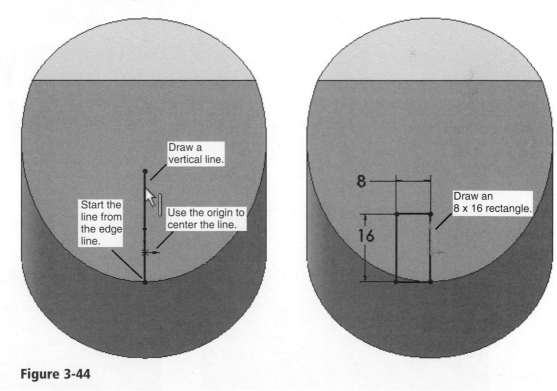

Figure 3-44

Figure 3-44
(*Continued*)

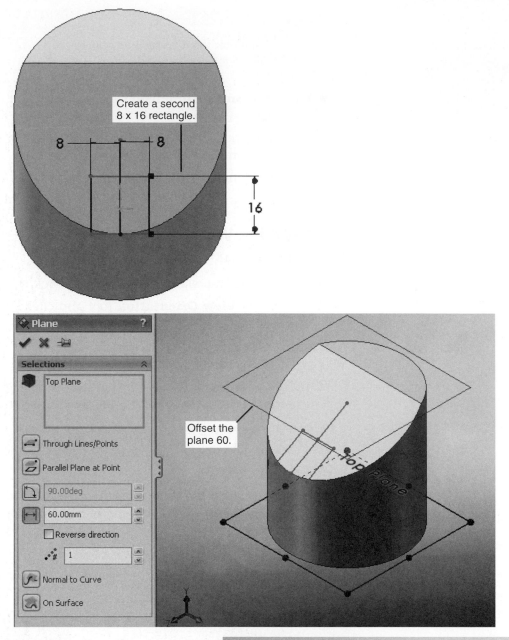

Create a second
8 x 16 rectangle.

Offset the
plane 60.

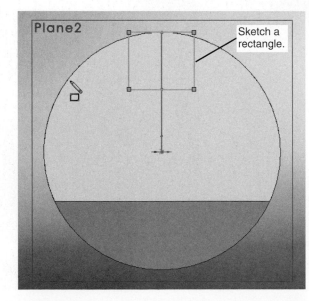

Sketch a
rectangle.

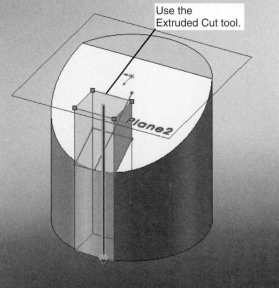

Use the
Extruded Cut tool.

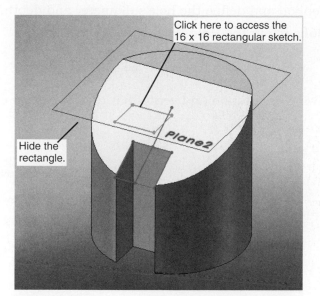

Click here to access the
16 x 16 rectangular sketch.

Hide the
rectangle.

Plane2

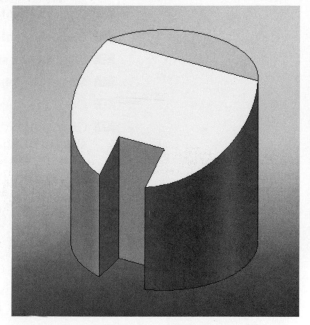

Figure 3-44
(*Continued*)

> **NOTE**
>
> The **Extruded Cut** tool will extrude a shape perpendicular to the plane of the shape. In this example the plane is slanted, so the extrusion would not be vertical, as required. The rectangle is projected into the top offset plane and the extrusion tool applied there.

9 Right-click the 60 offset plane, select the **Sketch** option, and change the drawing orientation to the top view.

10 Sketch a rectangle on the offset plane over the projected view of the 16 × 16 rectangle on the slanted plane, right-click the mouse, and click the **Select** option.

11 Change the drawing orientation to a dimetric view.

12 Use the **Extruded Cut** tool on the **Features** toolbar to cut out the slot.

13 Hide the 60 offset plane and hide the 16 × 16 rectangle on the slanted surface.

14 Click the check mark.

To Add the Ø8 Hole

See Figure 3-45.

1 Use the **Point** tool and sketch a point on the flat portion of the top surface. Use the origin to center the point.

2 Use the **Smart Dimension** tool and locate the point according to the given dimensions.

3 Exit the sketch.

> **NOTE**
>
> There are two ways to draw blind holes (holes that do not go all the way through): draw a circle and use the **Extruded Cut** tool to remove material, or use the **Hole Wizard**. In this example the **Hole Wizard** tool is used because it will generate a conical-shaped bottom to the hole. Conical-shaped hole bottoms result from using a twist drill, which has a conical-shaped cutting end.

4 Click the **Hole Wizard** tool on the **Features** toolbar.

5 Click the **Hole** option and define the hole's diameter and depth.

6 Click the **Positions** tab in the **Hole Wizard PropertyManager**.

7 Click the point.

8 Click the check mark.

9 Change the drawing orientation and verify that the hole has a conical-shaped bottom.

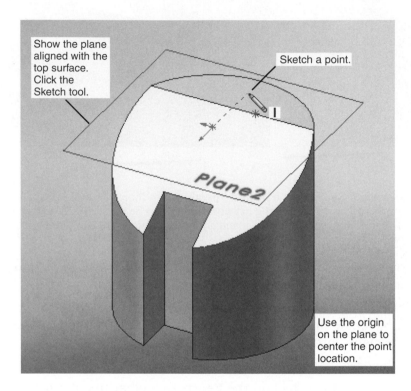

Show the plane aligned with the top surface. Click the Sketch tool.

Sketch a point.

Plane2

Use the origin on the plane to center the point location.

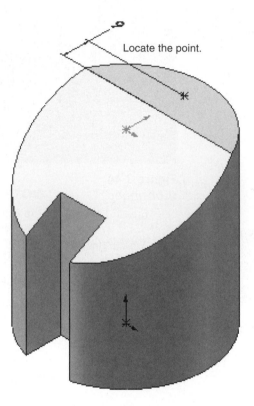

Locate the point.

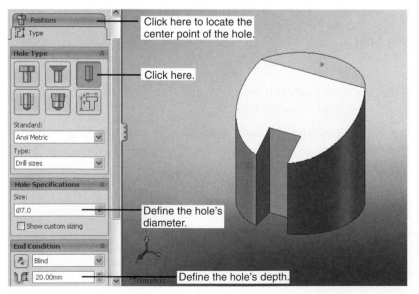

Click here to locate the center point of the hole.

Click here.

Hole Type

Standard:
Ansi Metric

Type:
Drill sizes

Hole Specifications

Size:
Ø7.0

☐ Show custom sizing

Define the hole's diameter.

End Condition

Blind

20.00mm

Define the hole's depth.

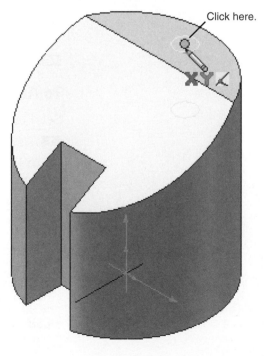

Click here.

Figure 3-45

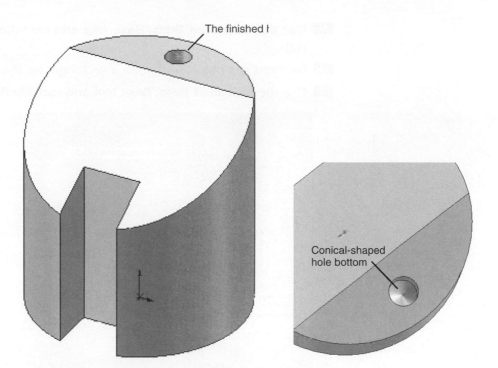

The finished h

Conical-shaped
hole bottom

Figure 3-45
(*Continued*)

3-25 Sample Problem SP3-3

Figure 3-46 shows a dimensioned object. In this example we will start with the middle section of the object. See Figure 3-47.

1 Sketch a profile using the right plane based on the given dimensions.

2 Use the **Extruded Boss/Base** tool to add a thickness of **40** to the profile.

3 Right-click the right surface of the object and select the **Sketch** option.

4 Use the **Rectangle** tool and draw a rectangle based on the given dimensions. Align the corners of the rectangle with the corners of the object.

Figure 3-46

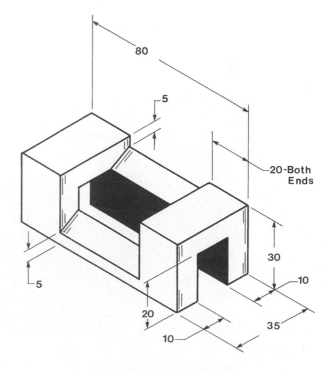

5 Use the **Extruded Boss/Base** tool and extrude the rectangle **20** to the right.

6 Reorient the object and draw a rectangle on the left surface of the object.

7 Use the **Extruded Boss/Base** tool and extrude the rectangle **20** to the left.

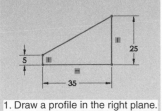

1. Draw a profile in the right plane.

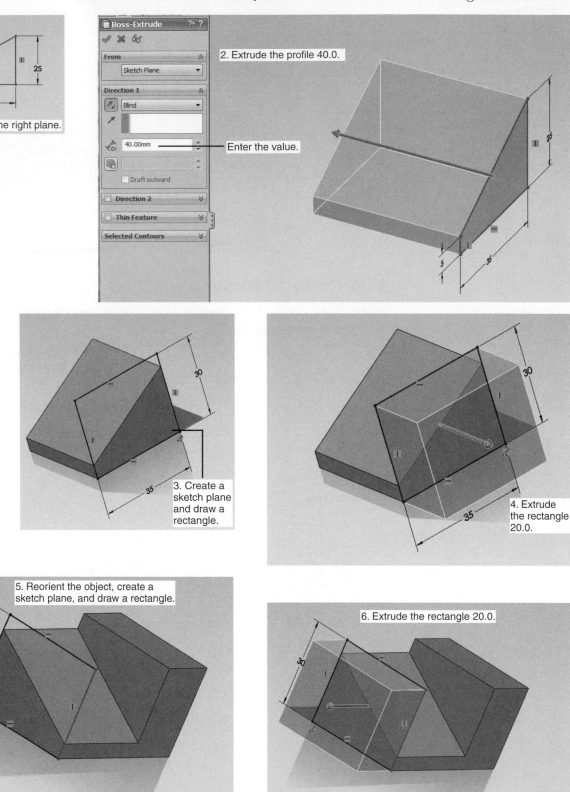

2. Extrude the profile 40.0.

Enter the value.

3. Create a sketch plane and draw a rectangle.

4. Extrude the rectangle 20.0.

5. Reorient the object, create a sketch plane, and draw a rectangle.

6. Extrude the rectangle 20.0.

Figure 3-47

Figure 3-47
(*Continued*)

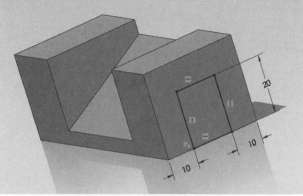

7. Create a sketch plane and draw a rectangle.

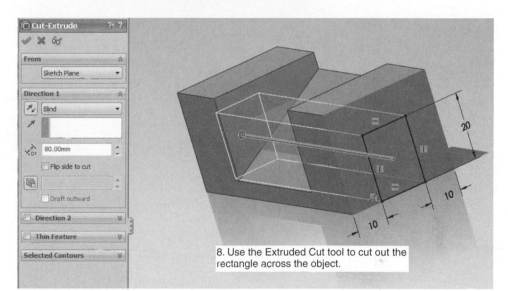

8. Use the Extruded Cut tool to cut out the rectangle across the object.

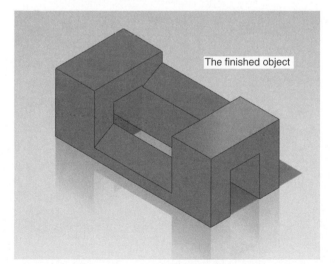

The finished object

8 Re-orientate the object and create a sketch plane on the right side of the object. Draw a rectangle based on the given dimensions.

9 Use the **Extruded Cut** tool on the **Features** toolbar and cut out the rectangle over the length of the object.

Chapter Projects

Project 3-1:

Redraw the following objects as solid models based on the given dimensions. Make all models from mild steel.

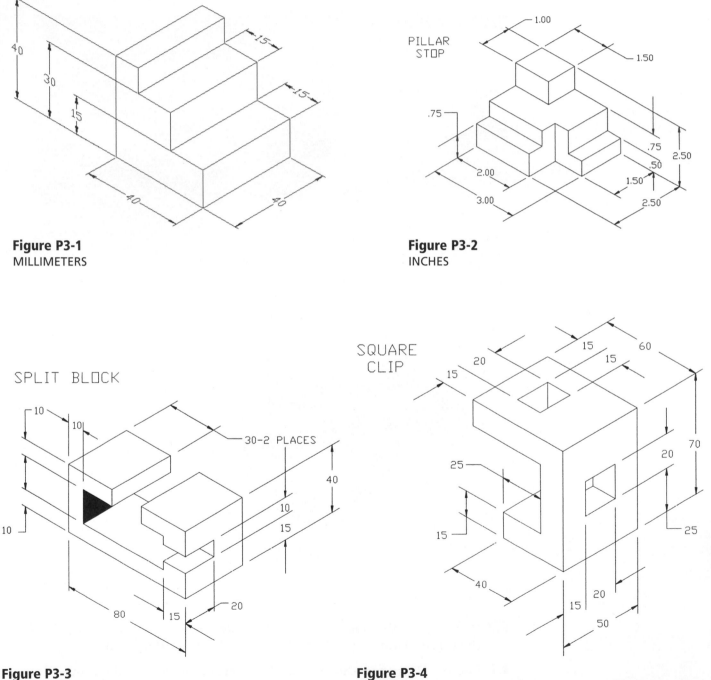

Figure P3-1
MILLIMETERS

Figure P3-2
INCHES

PILLAR STOP

SPLIT BLOCK

SQUARE CLIP

Figure P3-3
MILLIMETERS

Figure P3-4
MILLIMETERS

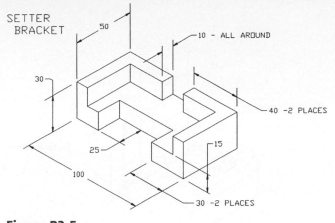

SETTER
BRACKET

50

10 - ALL AROUND

30

40 -2 PLACES

25

15

100

30 -2 PLACES

Figure P3-5
MILLIMETERS

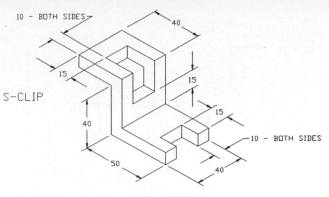

10 - BOTH SIDES

40

15

S-CLIP

15

40

15

15

50

10 - BOTH SIDES

40

MATL = 10mm SAE 1020 STEEL

Figure P3-6
MILLIMETERS

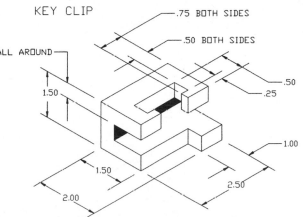

KEY CLIP

.75 BOTH SIDES

.50 BOTH SIDES

.50 ALL AROUND

.50

.25

1.50

1.00

1.50

2.00

2.50

Figure P3-7
INCHES

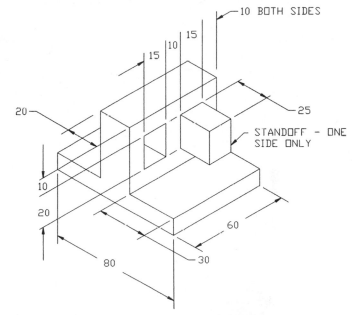

10 BOTH SIDES

15

15

10

20

25

STANDOFF - ONE
SIDE ONLY

10

20

60

80

30

Figure P3-8
MILLIMETERS

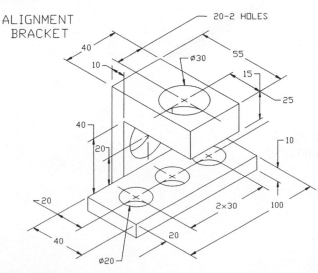

ALIGNMENT
BRACKET

20-2 HOLES

40

10

55

Ø30

15

25

40

20

10

20

2×30

100

40

20

Ø20

Figure P3-9
MILLIMETERS

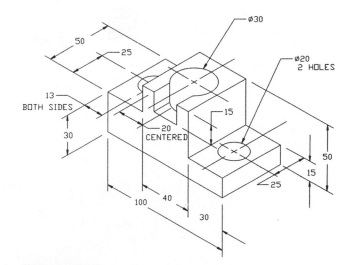

Ø30

50

25

Ø20
2 HOLES

13
BOTH SIDES

15

30

20
CENTERED

50

15

100

40

25

30

Figure P3-10
MILLIMETERS

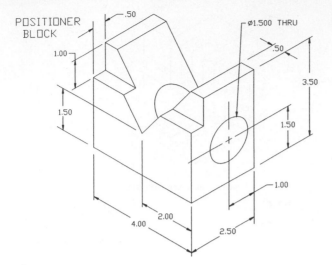

Figure P3-11
INCHES

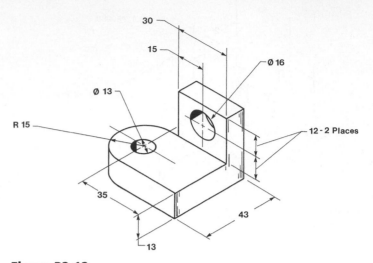

Figure P3-12
MILLIMETERS

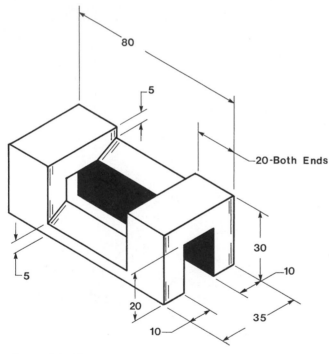

Figure P3-13
MILLIMETERS

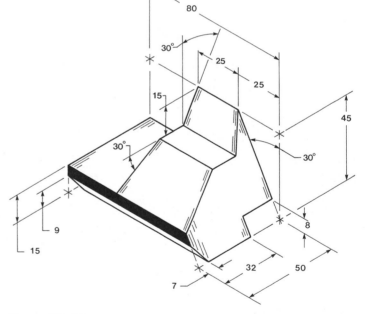

Figure P3-14
MILLIMETERS

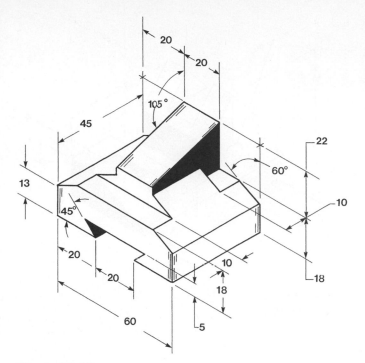

Figure P3-15
MILLIMETERS

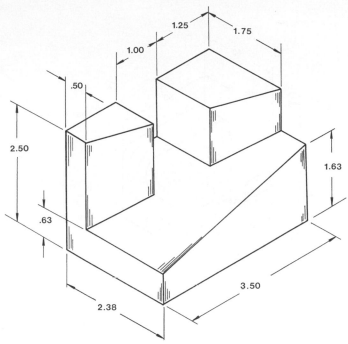

Figure P3-16
INCHES

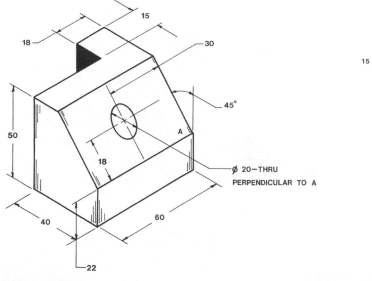

Figure P3-17
MILLIMETERS

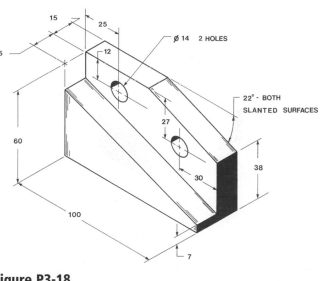

Figure P3-18
MILLIMETERS

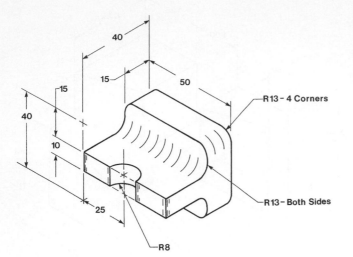

Figure P3-19
MILLIMETERS

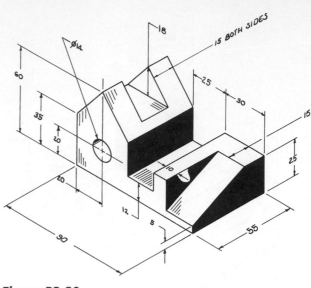

Figure P3-20
MILLIMETERS

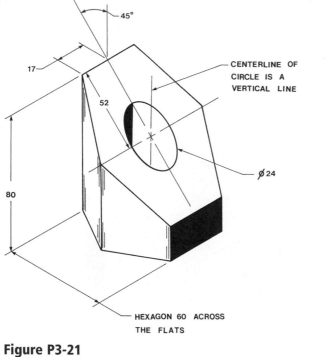

Figure P3-21
MILLIMETERS

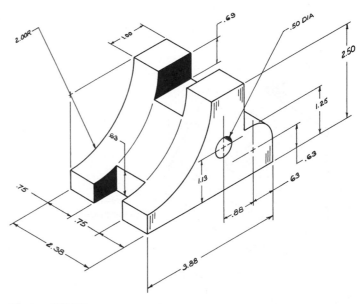

Figure P3-22
INCHES

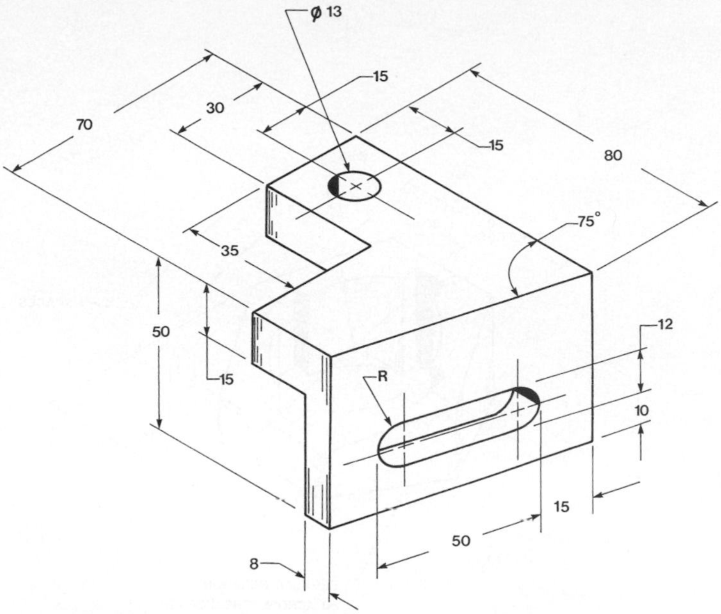

Figure P3-23
MILLIMETERS

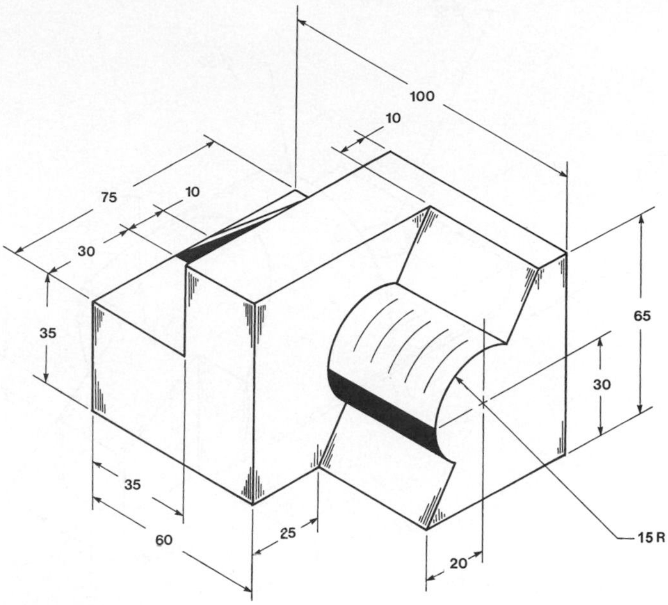

Figure P3-24
MILLIMETERS

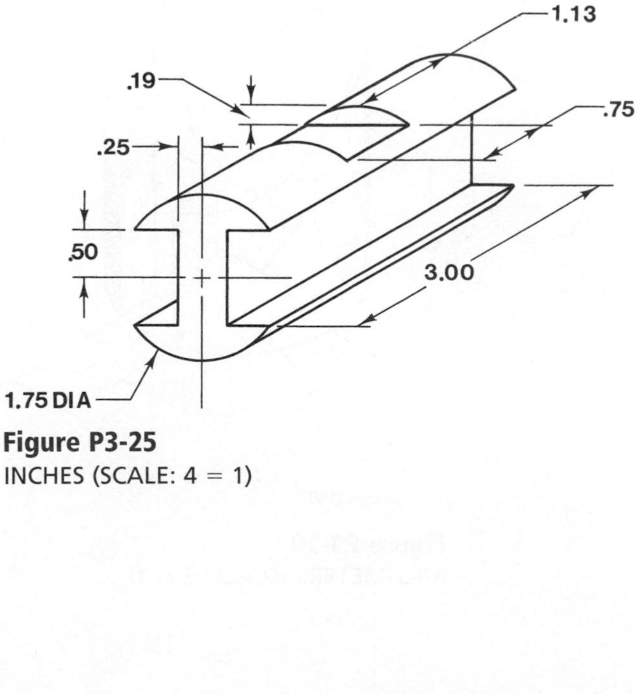

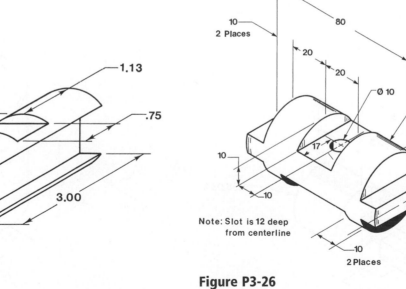

Figure P3-25
INCHES (SCALE: 4 = 1)

Note: Slot is **12** deep
from centerline

Figure P3-26
MILLIMETERS

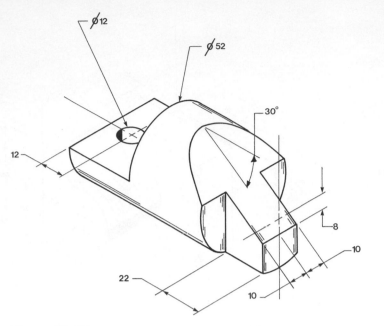

Figure P3-27
MILLIMETERS

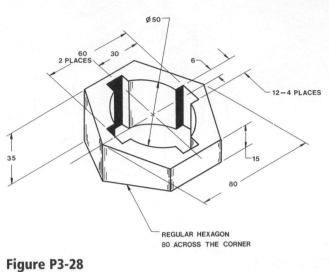

Figure P3-28
MILLIMETERS

Figure P3-29
INCHES (SCALE: 4 = 1)

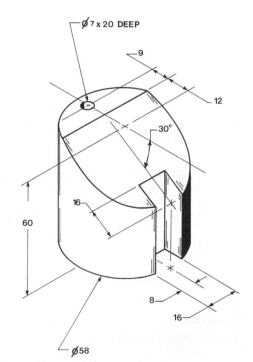

Figure P3-30
MILLIMETERS (SCALE: 2 = 1)

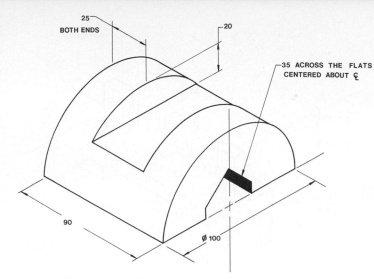

Figure P3-31
MILLIMETERS

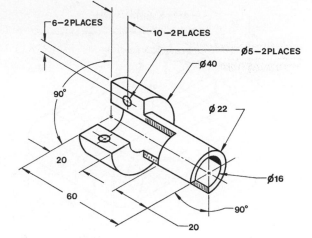

Figure P3-32
MILLIMETERS

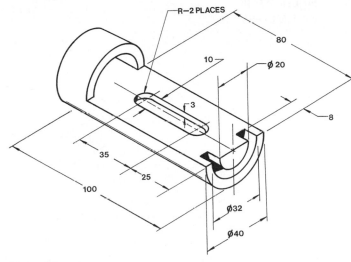

Figure P3-33
MILLIMETERS

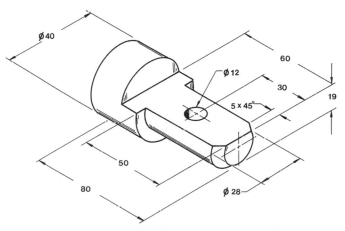

Figure P3-34
MILLIMETERS

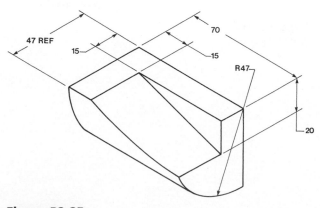

Figure P3-35
MILLIMETERS

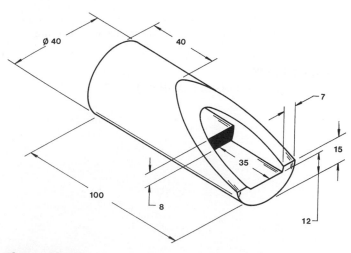

Figure P3-36
MILLIMETERS

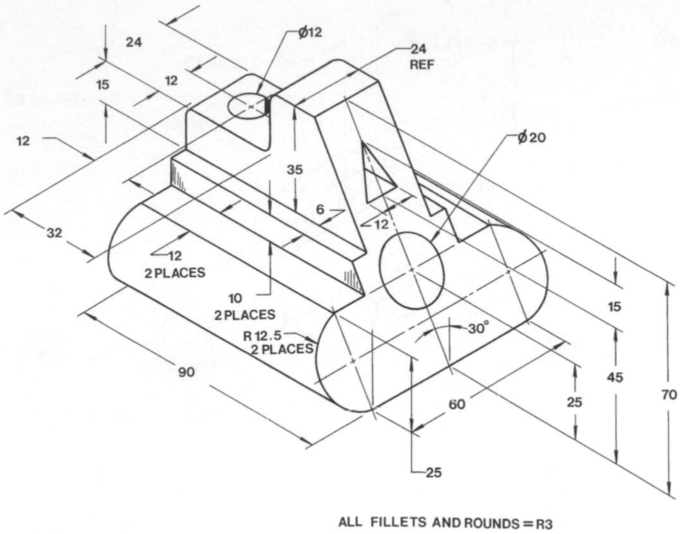

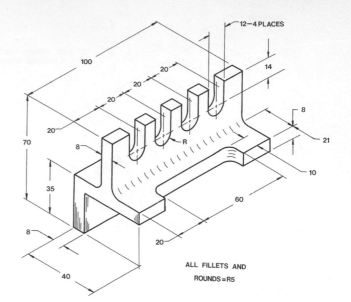

Figure P3-37
MILLIMETERS

ALL FILLETS AND ROUNDS = R3

Figure P3-38
MILLIMETERS

ALL FILLETS AND
ROUNDS = R5

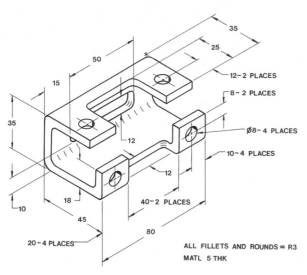

Figure P3-39
MILLIMETERS (CONSIDER A SHELL)

ALL FILLETS AND ROUNDS = R3
MATL 5 THK

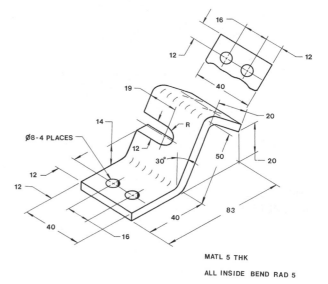

Figure P3-40
MILLIMETERS

MATL 5 THK

ALL INSIDE BEND RAD 5

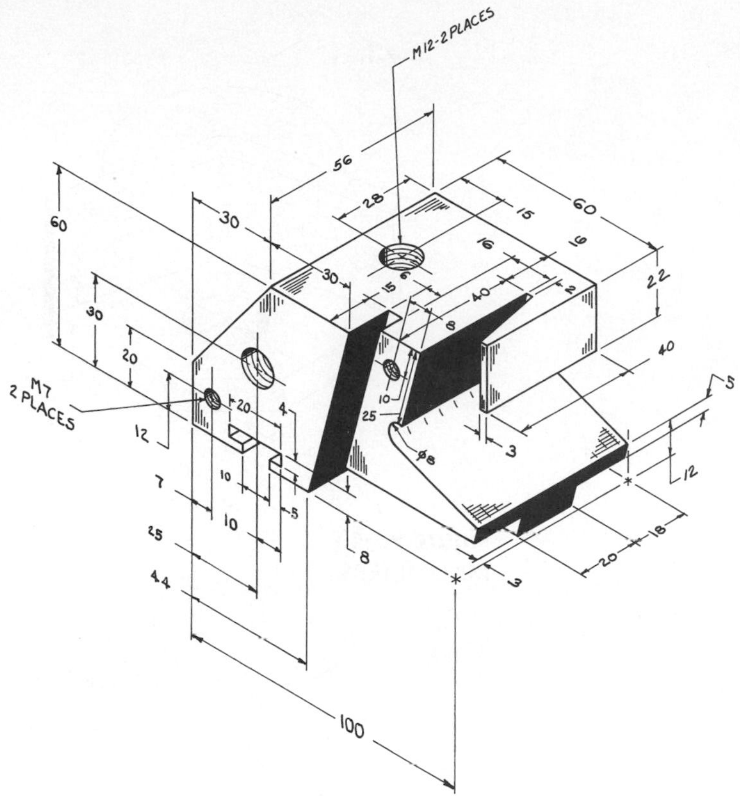

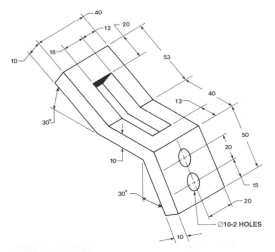

Figure P3-41
MILLIMETERS

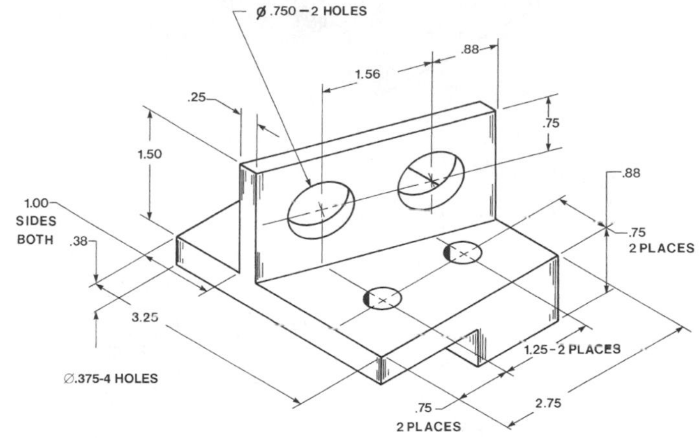

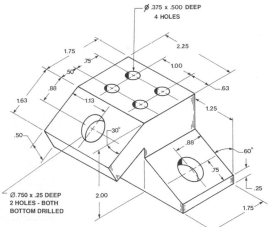

Figure P3-42
INCHES

Figure P3-43
MILLIMETERS

Figure P3-44
INCHES

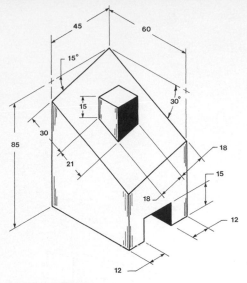

Figure P3-45
MILLIMETERS

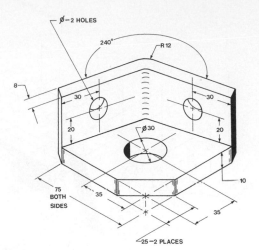

Figure P3-46
MILLIMETERS

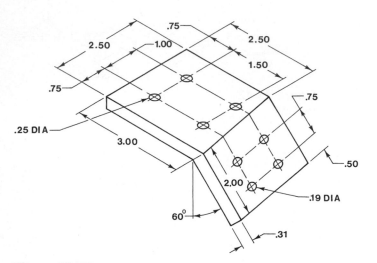

Figure P3-47
INCHES

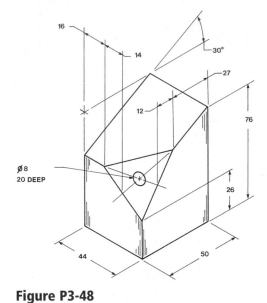

Figure P3-48
MILLIMETERS

Project 3-2:

A. Draw the following spring.
Diameter = 2.00
Wire diameter = .125
Pitch = .375
Revolutions = 16

B. Grind both ends to create a spring 2.00 long in its unloaded position.

Project 3-3:

A. Draw the following spring.
Diameter = 25
Wire diameter = 5 × 5 Square
Pitch = 6
Revolutions = 8

Figure P3-49
INCHES

Figure P3-50
MILLIMETERS

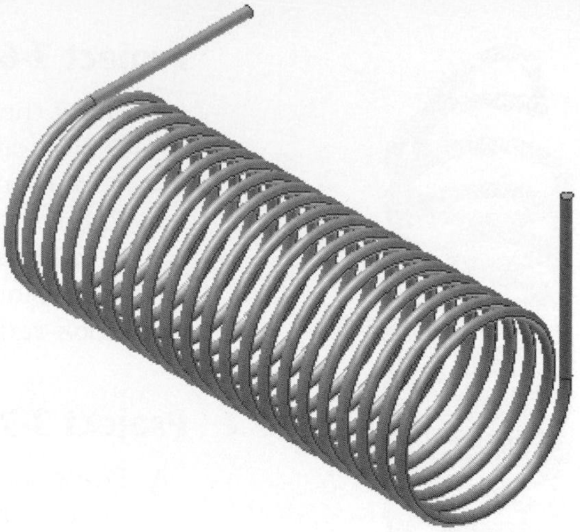

Figure P3-51
INCHES

Project 3-4:

A. Draw the following torsional spring.
   Diameter = .500
   Wire diameter = .06
   Pitch = .125
   Revolutions = 20
   Extension lengths = 1.00, 90° apart

Project 3-5:

A. Draw the following torsional spring.
   Diameter = 12.00
   Wire diameter = 4.0
   Pitch = 6.0
   Revolutions = 18
   Extension lengths = 15, 180° apart

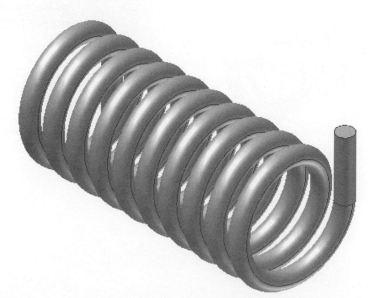

Figure P3-52
MILLIMETERS

Project 3-6:

A. Draw the following extension spring.
   Diameter = 1.00
   Wire diameter = .0938
   Pitch = .180
   Revolutions = 12
   Extension radius = .125
   Hook radius = .50

Project 3-7:

A. Draw the following extension spring.
   Diameter = 30
   Wire diameter = 6
   Pitch = 30
   Revolutions = 10
   Extension radius = 6
   Hook radius = 12

Project 3-8:

Draw a Ø4.00 × 3.00 cylinder and deboss on one of the following. Use a font style and size of your choice, or as assigned by your instructor.
   A. Your name and address
   B. Your school's name and address

Figure P3-53
INCHES

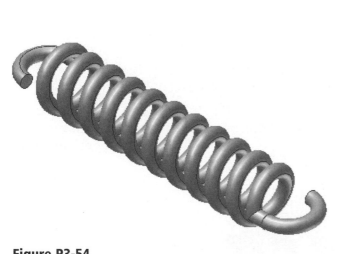

Figure P3-54
MILLIMETERS

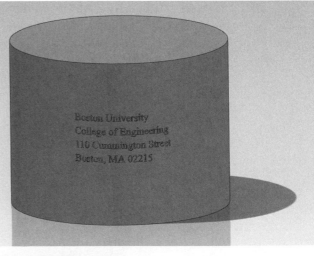

Figure P3-55
INCHES

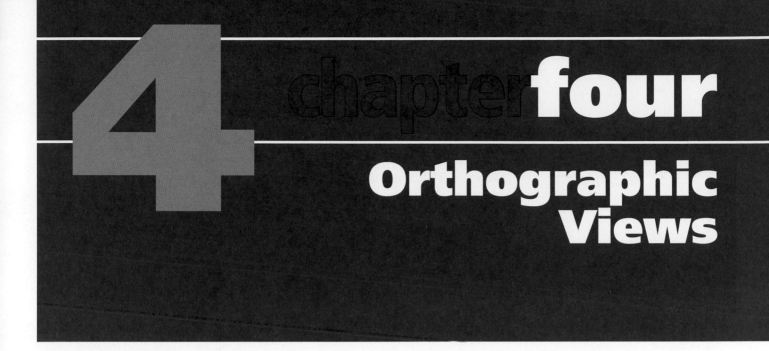

CHAPTER OBJECTIVES

- Learn about orthographic views
- Learn ANSI standards and conventions
- Learn how to draw section and auxiliary views

4-1 Introduction

Orthographic views may be created directly from 3D SolidWorks models. *Orthographic views* are two-dimensional views used to define a three-dimensional model. Unless the model is of uniform thickness, more than one orthographic view is necessary to define the model's shape. Standard practice calls for three orthographic views: a front, top, and right-side view, although more or fewer views may be used as needed.

Modern machines can work directly from the information generated when a solid 3D model is created, so the need for orthographic views—blueprints—is not as critical as it once was; however, there are still many drawings in existence that are used for production and reference. The ability to create and read orthographic views remains an important engineering skill.

This chapter presents orthographic views using third-angle projection in accordance with ANSI standards. ISO first-angle projections are also presented.

4-2 Fundamentals of Orthographic Views

Figure 4-1 shows an object with its front, top, and right-side orthographic views projected from the object. The views are two-dimensional, so they show no depth. Note that in the projected right plane there are three rectangles. There is no way to determine which of the three is closest and which is farthest away if only the right-side view is considered. All views must be studied to analyze the shape of the object.

Figure 4-2 shows three orthographic views of a book. After the views are projected they are positioned as shown. The positioning of views relative to one another is critical. The views must be aligned and positioned as shown.

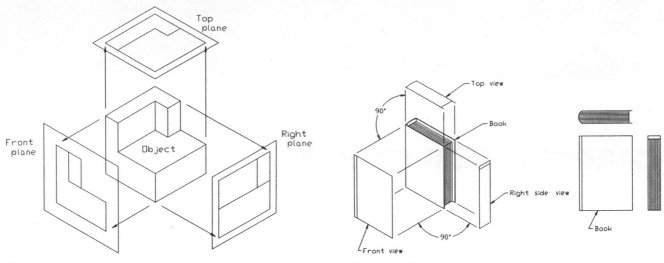

Figure 4-1

Figure 4-2

Normal Surfaces

Normal surfaces are surfaces that are at 90° to each other. Figures 4-3, 4-4, and 4-5 show objects that include only normal surfaces and their orthographic views.

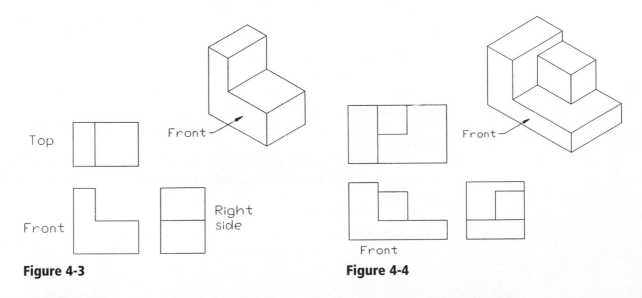

Figure 4-3

Figure 4-4

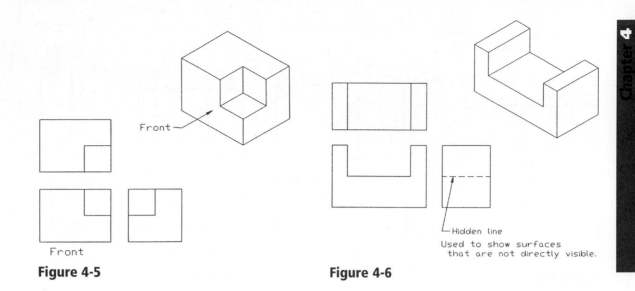

Figure 4-5

Figure 4-6

Hidden line
Used to show surfaces
that are not directly visible.

Hidden Lines

Hidden lines are used to show surfaces that are not directly visible. All surfaces must be shown in all views. If an edge or surface is blocked from view by another feature, it is drawn using a hidden line. Figures 4-6 and 4-7 show objects that require hidden lines in their orthographic views.

Figure 4-8 shows an object that contains an edge line, A-B. In the top view, line A-B is partially hidden and partially visible. The hidden portion of the line is drawn using a hidden-line pattern, and the visible portion of the line is drawn using a solid line.

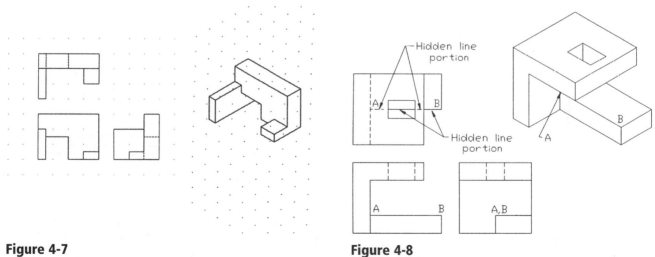

Figure 4-7

Figure 4-8

Figures 4-9 and 4-10 show objects that require hidden lines in their orthographic views.

Precedence of Lines

It is not unusual for one type of line to be drawn over another type of line. Figure 4-11 shows two examples of overlap by different types of lines. Lines are shown on the views in a prescribed order of precedence. A solid

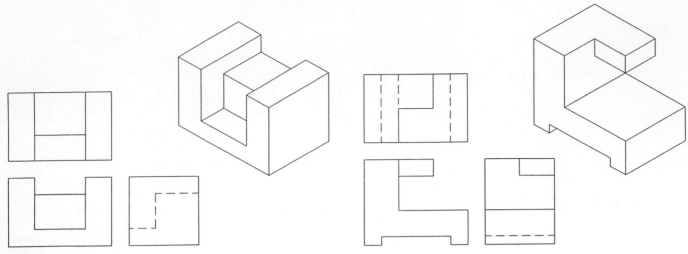

Figure 4-9

Figure 4-10

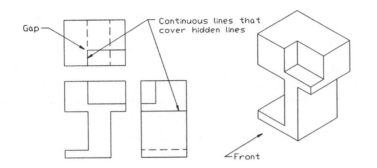

Figure 4-11

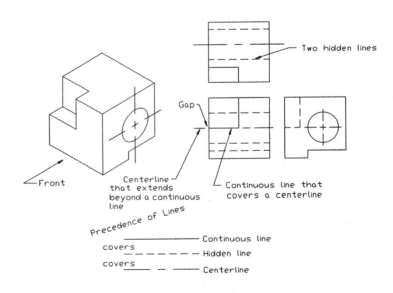

line (object or continuous) takes precedence over a hidden line, and a hidden line takes precedence over a centerline.

Slanted Surfaces

Slanted surfaces are surfaces drawn at an angle to each other. Figure 4-12 shows an object that contains two slanted surfaces. Surface ABCD appears as a rectangle in both the top and front views. Neither rectangle represents the true shape of the surface. Each is smaller that the actual surface.

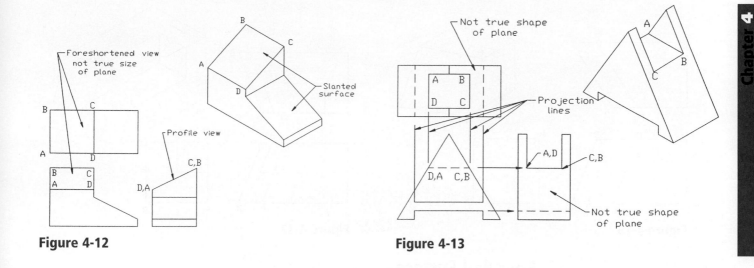

Figure 4-12

Figure 4-13

Also, none of the views show enough of the object to enable the viewer to accurately define the shape of the object. The views must be used together for a correct understanding of the object's shape.

Figures 4-13 and 4-14 show objects that include slanted surfaces. Projection lines have been included to emphasize the importance of correct view location. Information is projected between the front and top views using vertical lines and between the front and side views using horizontal lines.

Compound Lines

A **compound line** is formed when two slanted surfaces intersect. Figure 4-15 shows an object that includes a compound line.

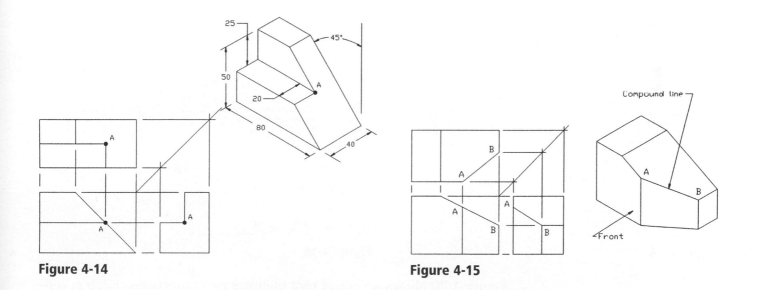

Figure 4-14

Figure 4-15

Oblique Surfaces

An **oblique surface** is a surface that is slanted in two different directions. Figures 4-16 and 4-17 show objects that include oblique surfaces.

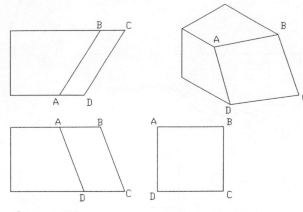

Figure 4-16

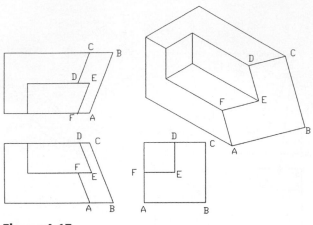

Figure 4-17

Rounded Surfaces

Figure 4-18 shows an object with two rounded surfaces. Note that as with slanted surfaces, an individual view is insufficient to define the shape of a surface. More than one view is needed to accurately define the surface's shape.

Convention calls for a smooth transition between rounded and flat surfaces; that is, no lines are drawn to indicate the tangency. SolidWorks includes a line to indicate tangencies between surfaces in the isometric drawings created using the multiview options but does not include them in the orthographic views. Tangency lines are also not included when models are rendered.

Figure 4-19 shows the drawing conventions for including lines for rounded surfaces. If a surface includes no vertical portions or no tangency, no line is included.

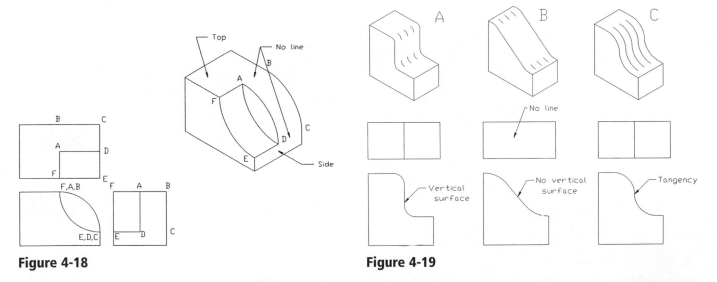

Figure 4-18

Figure 4-19

Figure 4-20 shows an object that includes two tangencies. Each is represented by a line. Note in Figure 4-20 that SolidWorks will add tangent lines to the 3D model. These lines will not appear in the orthographic views.

Figure 4-21 shows two objects with similar configurations; however, the boxlike portion of the lower object blends into the rounded portion exactly on its widest point, so no line is required.

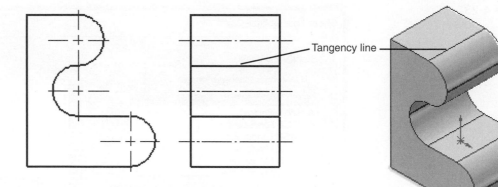

Tangency line

Figure 4-20

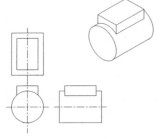

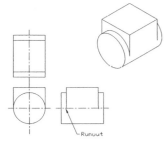

Runout

Figure 4-21

4-3 Drawing Orthographic Views Using SolidWorks

SolidWorks creates orthographic views using the drawing tools found on the **New SolidWorks Document** box. See Figure 4-22.

1 Start a new drawing by clicking the **New** tool.

2 Click the **Drawing** icon on the **New SolidWorks Document** box.

3 Click **OK.**

The **Sheet Format/Size** box will appear. See Figure 4-23. Accept the **A- (ANSI) Landscape** format.

> **TIP**
>
> Drawing sheets, that is, the paper drawings are printed on, are manufactured in standard sizes. For example, in the English unit system an A-size drawing sheet is 8.5 × 11 in. In the metric unit system an A4-size drawing sheet is 210 × 297 mm.

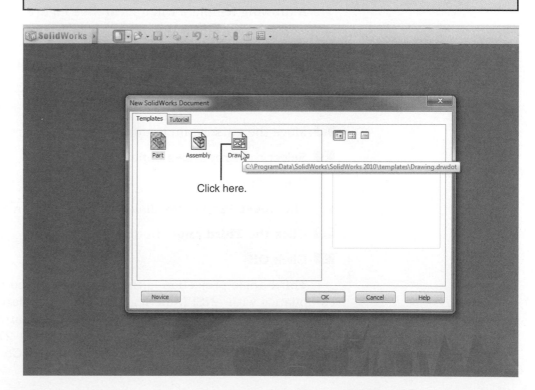

Click here.

C:\ProgramData\SolidWorks\SolidWorks 2010\templates\Drawing.drwdot

Figure 4-22

Figure 4-23

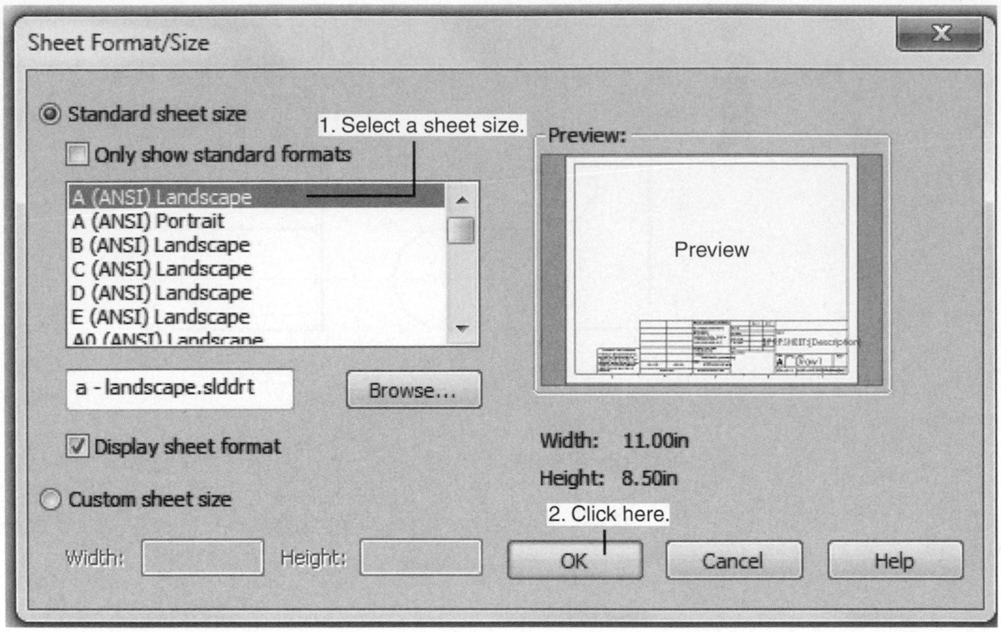

Sheet Format/Size

● Standard sheet size   1. Select a sheet size.   Preview:

☐ Only show standard formats

A (ANSI) Landscape
A (ANSI) Portrait
B (ANSI) Landscape
C (ANSI) Landscape
D (ANSI) Landscape
E (ANSI) Landscape
A0 (ANSI) Landscape

Preview

a - landscape.slddrt   [Browse...]

☑ Display sheet format

Width: 11.00in
Height: 8.50in

○ Custom sheet size   2. Click here.

Width: [   ]   Height: [   ]   [OK]   [Cancel]   [Help]

Standard Drawing Sheet Sizes Inches	Standard Drawing Sheet Sizes Millimeters
A = 8.5 × 11	A4 = 210 × 297
B = 11 × 17	A3 = 297 × 420
C = 17 × 22	A2 = 420 × 594
D = 22 × 34	A1 = 594 × 841
E = 34 × 44	A0 = 841 × 1189

A listing of standard sheet sizes is shown in Figure 4-23.

4 Click **OK**.

A drawing template will appear. See Figure 4-24. The template includes a title block, a release block, a tolerance block, and two other blocks. The template format can be customized, but in this example the default template will be used. The title block will be explained in the next section.

5 Click the **X** mark under the **Model View** heading.

6 Move the cursor into the drawing area and right-click the mouse.

7 Select the **Properties** option.

See Figure 4-25.

The **Sheet Properties** dialog box will appear. See Figure 4-26.

8 Click the **Third angle** button.

9 Click **OK**.

Third-angle projection is the format preferred by U.S. companies in compliance with ANSI (American National Standards Institute) standards. First-angle projection is used by countries that are in compliance with ISO (International Standards Organization). Figure 4-27 shows an L-bracket drawn in both first- and third-angle projection. Compare the differences in the projected views.

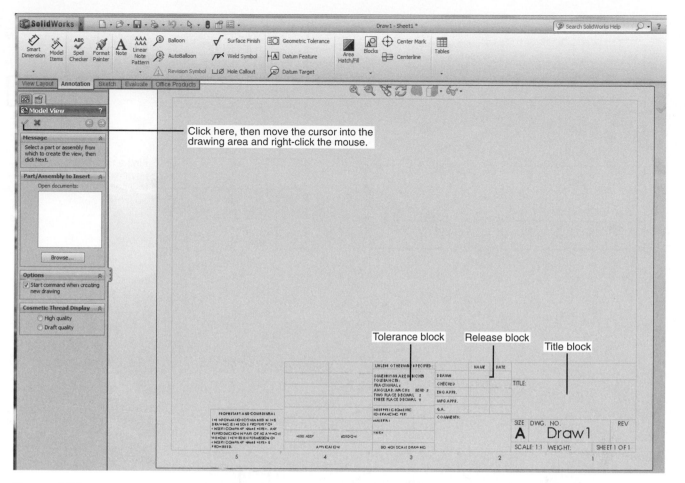

Figure 4-24

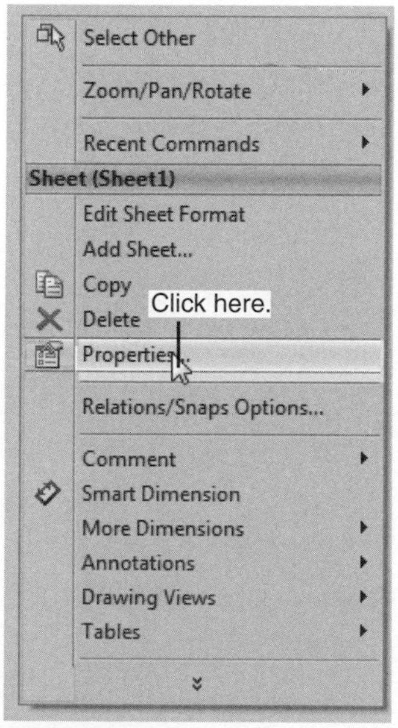

Figure 4-25

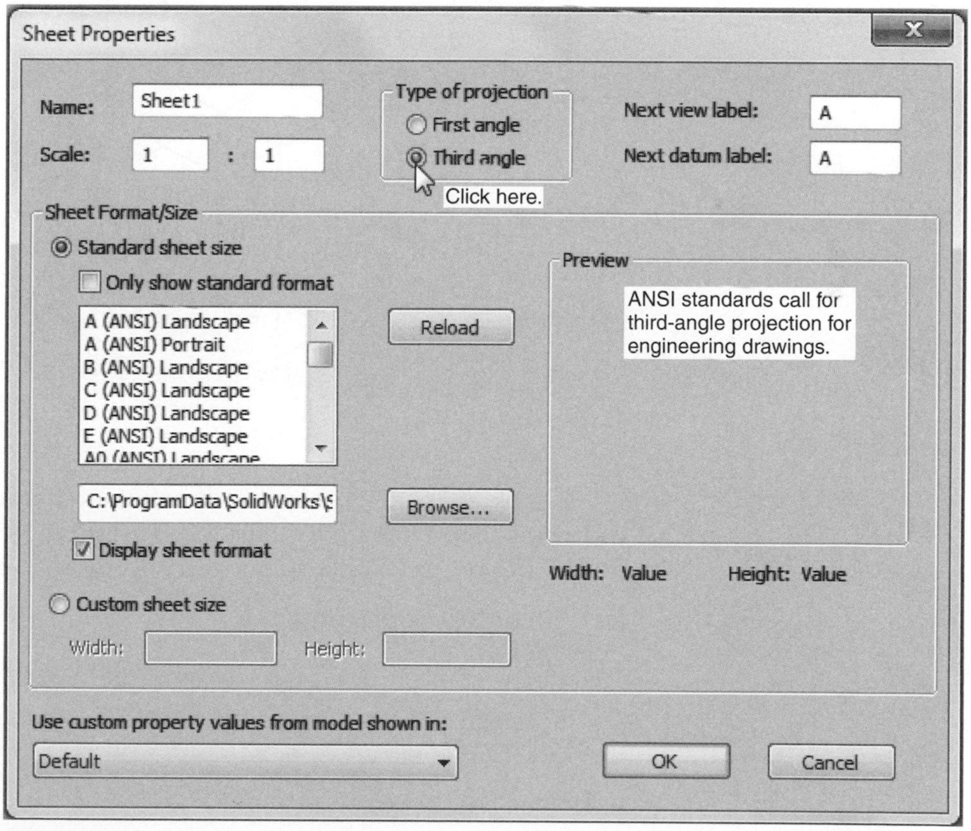

Figure 4-26

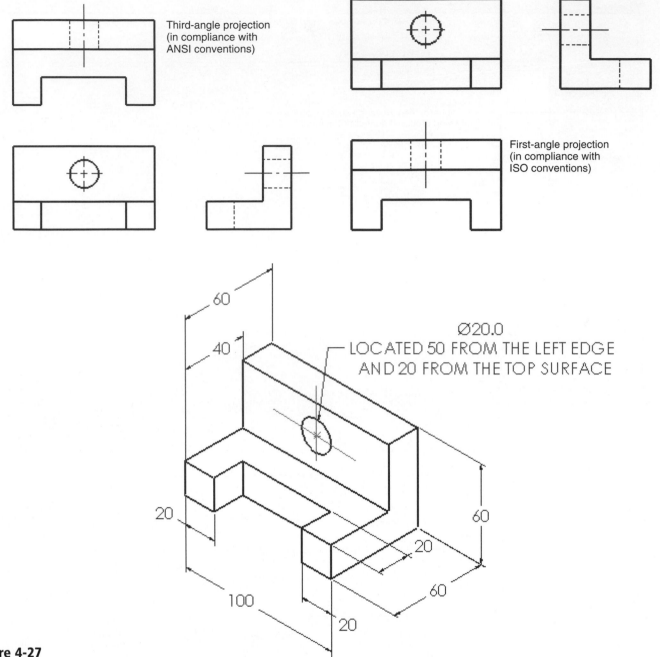

Third-angle projection
(in compliance with
ANSI conventions)

First-angle projection
(in compliance with
ISO conventions)

Ø20.0
LOCATED 50 FROM THE LEFT EDGE
AND 20 FROM THE TOP SURFACE

Figure 4-27

Figure 4-27 also shows a dimensioned isometric drawing of the L-bracket. The bracket was drawn in Section 3-3. If you have not previously drawn the bracket, do so now and save it as **L-bracket.**

10 Click the **View Layout** tab.

11 Click the **Standard 3 View** tool located on the **View Layout** panel.

See Figure 4-28. The **Standard 3 View PropertyManager** will appear on the left side of the screen.

12 Click the **Browse ...** box.

The **Open** box will appear. See Figure 4-29.

Figure 4-28

Click here to create three orthographic views.

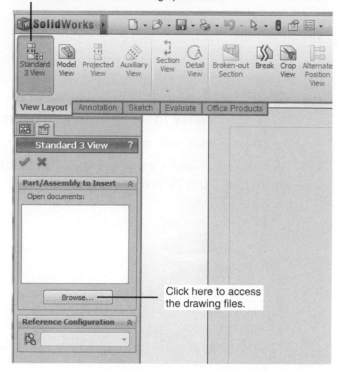

Click here to access the drawing files.

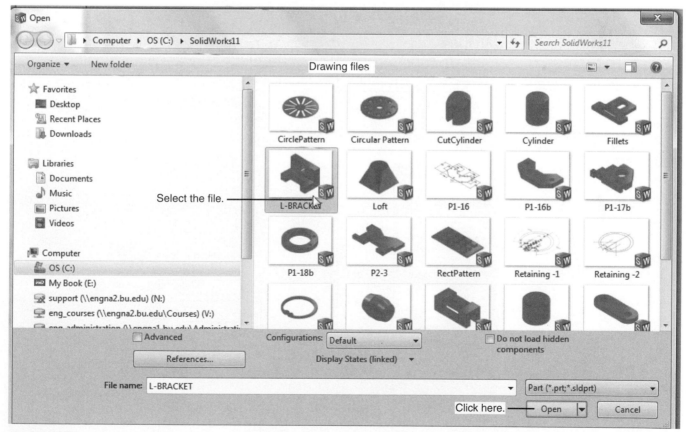

Select the file.

Click here.

Figure 4-29

13 Select the **L-RACKET** file. A rectangle will appear on the screen representing the views.

14 Select the L-bracket, and click **Open.**

Three orthographic views will appear on the screen. They include no hidden lines. The hidden lines must be added. See Figure 4-30.

15 Click the top orthographic view and select the **Hidden Lines Visible** tool in the **Display Style** box of the **Drawing View PropertyManager.**

The hidden lines will appear in the top view.

16 Click the right-side view, then click the **Hidden Lines Visible** tool to add hidden lines to the right-side view.

Figure 4-30

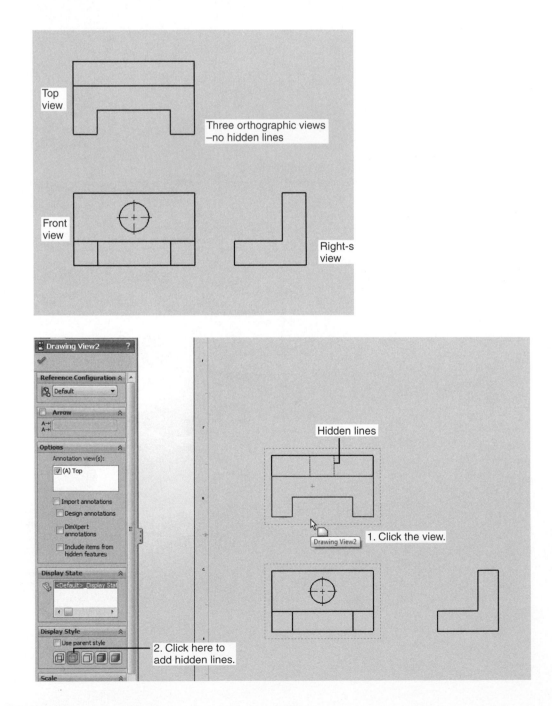

Figure 4-30
(*Continued*)

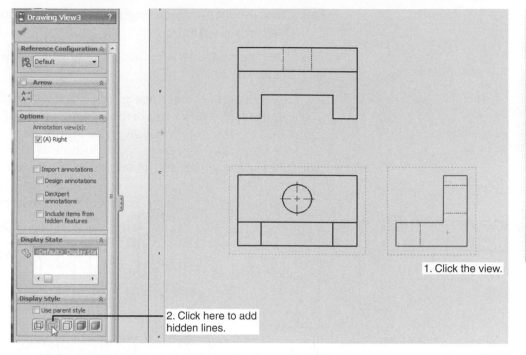

1. Click the view.

2. Click here to add hidden lines.

Notice in the top and right-side views that there are no centerlines for the hole. Centerlines are added using the **Centerline** option found on the **Annotation** tab. See Figure 4-31. The circular view of the hole will automatically generate a set of perpendicular centerlines.

Note the difference between center marks and centerline tools.

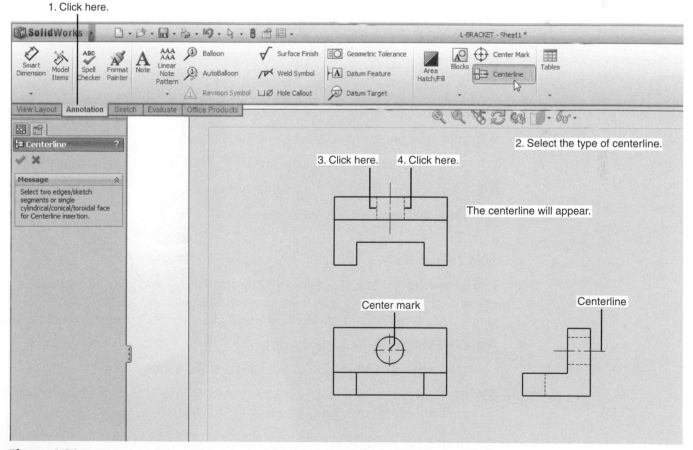

1. Click here.

2. Select the type of centerline.

3. Click here.   4. Click here.

The centerline will appear.

Center mark

Centerline

Figure 4-31

17 Click the arrow on the right side of the **Annotation** box and select the **Centerline** option.

18 Click each of the two parallel lines in the top and side views that define the hole.

The centerlines will appear. See Figure 4-32.

Figure 4-33 shows the orthographic views of another object. The dimensions for the object are given in Figure P4-7. Note the hidden lines in the side view that represent the Ø30 hole. The right vertical line is continuously straight, whereas the left vertical line has a step. Why?

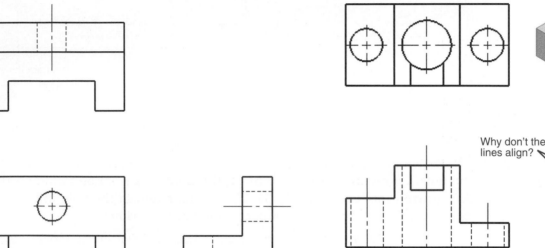

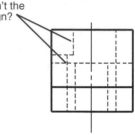

Figure 4-32

Figure 4-33

To Move Orthographic Views

Figure 4-34 shows the orthographic views of the L-bracket generated for Figure 4-32. The views can be moved closer together or farther apart

1 Move the cursor into the area of the top view.

A red boundary line will appear.

2 Click and hold one of the boundary lines.

3 Drag the view to a new location.

To Create Other Views

The **Standard 3 View** tool will generate front, top, and right-side orthographic views of an object. These views are considered the standard three views. Other orthographic views and isometric views can be generated.

1 Click the **Projected View** tool.

The **Projected View** tool is one of the **View Layout** tools.

2 Click the front view and move the cursor to the left of the front view, creating a new orthographic view.

In this example a left-side view was created. Add hidden and centerlines as needed.

Figure 4-34

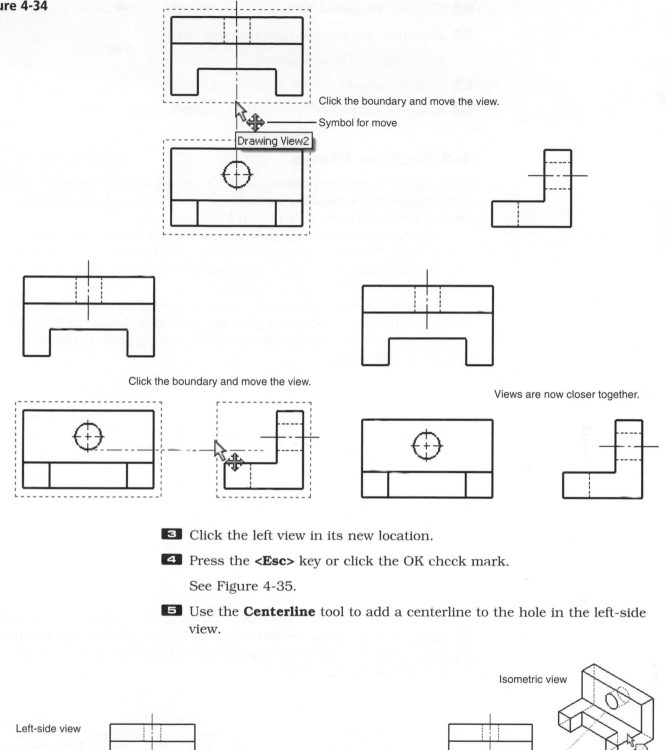

Click the boundary and move the view.

Symbol for move

Drawing View2

Click the boundary and move the view.

Views are now closer together.

3 Click the left view in its new location.

4 Press the **<Esc>** key or click the OK check mark.

See Figure 4-35.

5 Use the **Centerline** tool to add a centerline to the hole in the left-side view.

Isometric view

Left-side view

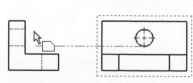

Click the front view and move the cursor to the left, projecting a left-side view.

Click the front view and move to the right and upward to create an isometric view.

Figure 4-35

6 Click the **Projected View** tool and click the front view again.

7 Move the cursor to the right and upward.

An isometric view will appear.

8 Click the isometric view in its new location.

9 Press the **<Esc>** key or click the OK check mark.

4-4 Section Views

Some objects have internal surfaces that are not directly visible in normal orthographic views. **Section views** are used to expose these surfaces. Section views do not include hidden lines.

Any material cut when a section view is defined is hatched using section lines. There are many different styles of hatching, but the general style is evenly spaced 45° lines. This style is defined as ANSI 31 and will be applied automatically by SolidWorks.

Figure 4-36 shows a three-dimensional view of an object. The object is cut by a cutting plane. **Cutting planes** are used to define the location of the section view. Material to one side of the cutting plane is removed, exposing the section view.

Figure 4-36

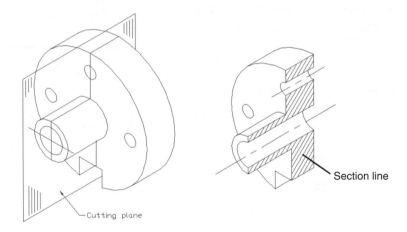

Figure 4-37 shows the same object presented in Figure 4-36 using two orthographic views and a section view. The cutting plane is represented by a cutting plane line. The cutting plane line is defined as A-A, and the section view is defined as view A-A.

Figure 4-37

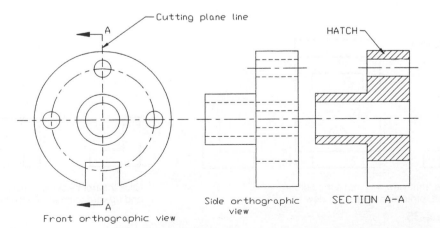

All surfaces directly visible must be shown in a section view. In Figure 4-38 the back portion of the object is not affected by the section view and is directly visible from the cutting plane. The section view must include these surfaces. Note how the rectangular section blocks out part of the large hole. No hidden lines are used on section views.

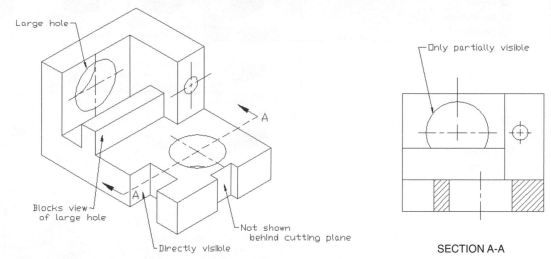

Figure 4-38

4-5 Drawing a Section View Using SolidWorks

This section will show how to draw a section view of an existing model. In this example, the model pictured in Figure 4-33 is used. This is the same as Figure P4-7 in the Chapter Projects.

1 Start a new drawing using the **Drawing** format.

See the previous section on how to create orthographic views using SolidWorks. Select the **A (ANSI)-Landscape** format and select **Third-angle** projection.

> **NOTE**
> See Figures 4-24 to 4-27 for an explanation of how to specify the third-angle format.

2 Click the **Model View** tool on the **View Layout** panel.

> **TIP**
> The **Model View** tool is similar to the **Standard 3 View** tool but creates only one orthographic view rather that three views.

3 In the **Part/Assembly to Insert** box click **Browse. ...**

See Figure 4-39. The **Open** box will appear. See Figure 4-40.

4 Click the model to be used to draw orthographic views, and click **Open.**

In this example the model is called **BLOCK, 3 HOLE.** The dimensions for the BLOCK, 3 HOLE can be found in Figure P4-7.

A rectangular outline will appear defining the boundaries of the orthographic view. By default, this will be a front view. In this example we want a top view.

Figure 4-39

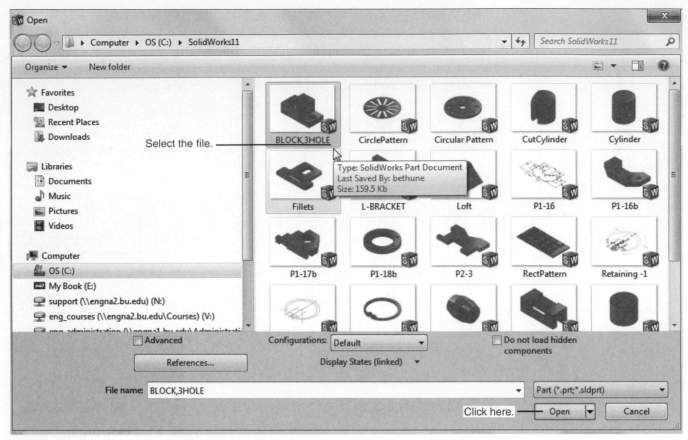

Select the file. ——

Type: SolidWorks Part Document
Last Saved By: bethune
Size: 159.5 Kb

Click here. — Open

Figure 4-40

5 Click the **Top** view tool.

See Figure 4-41.

Figure 4-41

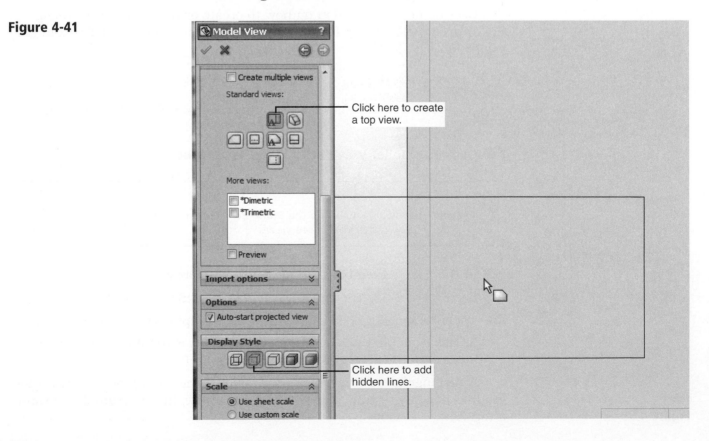

Click here to create
a top view.

Click here to add
hidden lines.

6 Locate the top orthographic view on the drawing screen and click the mouse.

7 Add a center mark to the Ø30 hole.

See Figure 4-42.

Figure 4-42

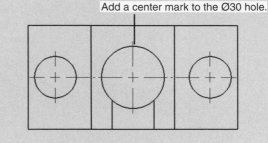

Add a center mark to the Ø30 hole.

8 Click the **View Layout** tab and click the **Section View** tool.

The orthographic view will be outlined by a dotted line.

NOTE

If more than one view was present on the screen, you would first have to select which view you wanted to be used to create the section view.

9 Define the location of the cutting plane line by moving the cursor to the approximate midpoint of the left vertical line of the orthographic view.

The system will automatically jump to the line's midpoint. A filled square icon will appear.

10 Move the cursor horizontally to the left of the view's edge line to the vertical outline of the view.

A dotted line will follow the cursor.

11 Move the cursor horizontally across the view to a point on the right vertical outline edge line.

12 Click the mouse and move the cursor downward.

The section view will appear and move with the cursor. See Figure 4-43.

13 Select an appropriate location and click the mouse.

14 Click the **Flip direction** box.

See Figure 4-44.

NOTE

Section views are always located behind the arrows; that is, the arrows point away from the section view. Think of the arrows as your eyes looking at the section view.

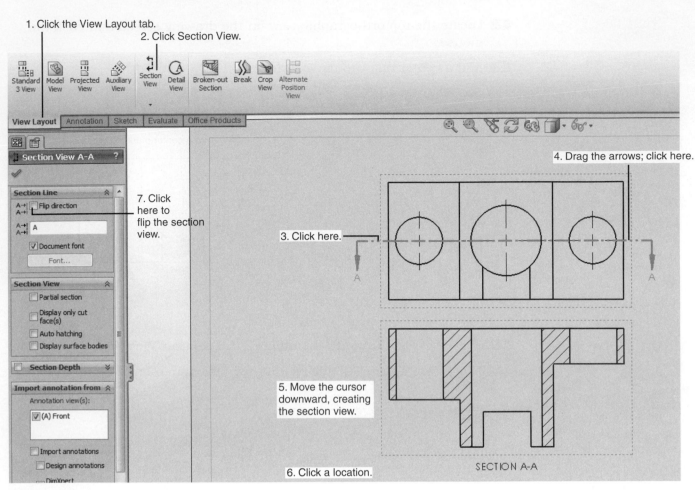

1. Click the View Layout tab.

2. Click Section View.

4. Drag the arrows; click here.

3. Click here.

7. Click here to flip the section view.

5. Move the cursor downward, creating the section view.

6. Click a location.

SECTION A-A

Figure 4-43

Figure 4-44

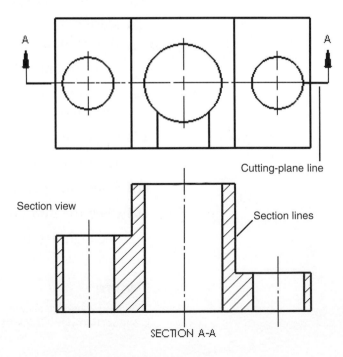

Top view

A   A

Cutting-plane line

Section view

Section lines

SECTION A-A

15 Add centerlines.

16 Click the OK check mark.

More than one section view may be taken from the same model. See Figure 4-45.

Figure 4-45

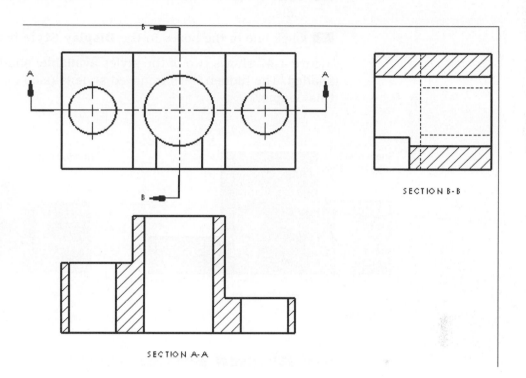

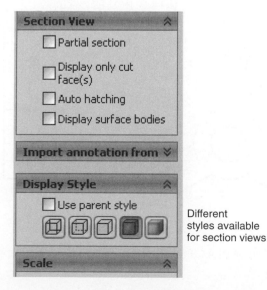

The section views shown in Figure 4-45 use a hatching pattern made from evenly spaced 45° lines. This is the most commonly used hatch pattern for section views and is designated as ANSI 31 in the ANSI hatch patterns. SolidWorks can also draw section views using one of five different styles. See Figure 4-46.

Figure 4-46

Different styles available for section views

To Change the Style of a Section View

1 Move the cursor into the area of the section view and right-click the mouse.

A listing of tools will appear, and the **Display Style** box will appear.

2 Click the mouse again in the section view area to remove the list of tools.

3 Click one of the boxes in the **Display Style** box.

Figure 4-47 shows two of the styles available: shaded with edge lines, and shaded. The hidden lines removed style is used for all other illustrations in this chapter.

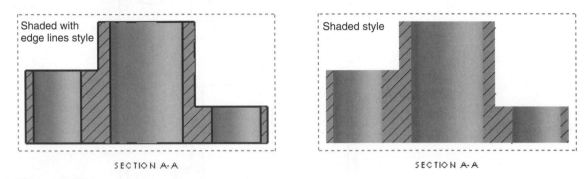

SECTION A-A   SECTION A-A

Figure 4-47

4-6 Aligned Section Views

Figure 4-48 shows an example of an aligned section view. Aligned section views are most often used on circular objects and use an angled cutting plane line to include more features in the section view. Note in Figure 4-48 how section view A-A was created by rotating the cutting plane into a vertical position before projecting the section view.

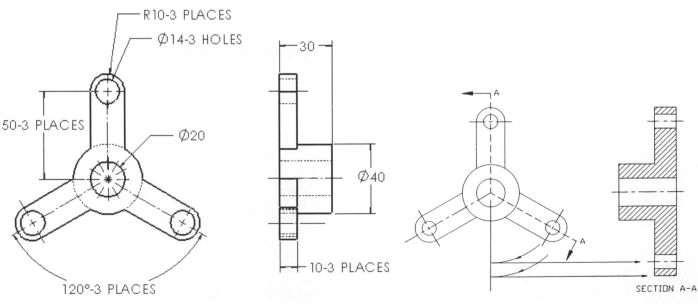

Figure 4-48

Figure 4-49 shows an aligned section view created using SolidWorks. The aligned section view was created as follows.

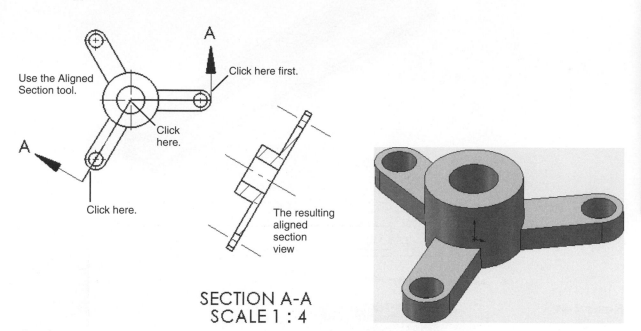

Use the Aligned Section tool.

Click here first.

Click here.

A

A

Click here.

The resulting aligned section view

SECTION A-A
SCALE 1 : 4

Figure 4-49

1 Start a new drawing using the **Drawing** format and click on the model for the aligned section view.

The model was drawn previously using the given dimensions.

2 Access the **Aligned Section View** tool.

The **Aligned Section View** tool is a flyout from the **Section View** tool.

3 Click the edge of the object as shown in Figure 4-49.

4 Click the object's center point.

5 Click the other edge of the object as shown.

6 Move the cursor away from the object.

The aligned section will appear as the cursor is moved.

7 Change the scale of the object if desired and add centerlines.

4-7 Broken Views

It is often convenient to break long continuous shapes so that they take up less drawing space. Figure 4-50 shows a long L-bracket that has a continuous shape; that is, its shape is constant throughout its length.

To Create a Broken View

1 Draw a model of the long L-bracket using the dimensions shown in Figure 4-50. Save the model.

2 Start a new drawing using the **Drawing** format and click on the long L-bracket.

3 Click the **View Layout** tab, and click the **Break** tool.

See Figure 4-51.

Figure 4-50

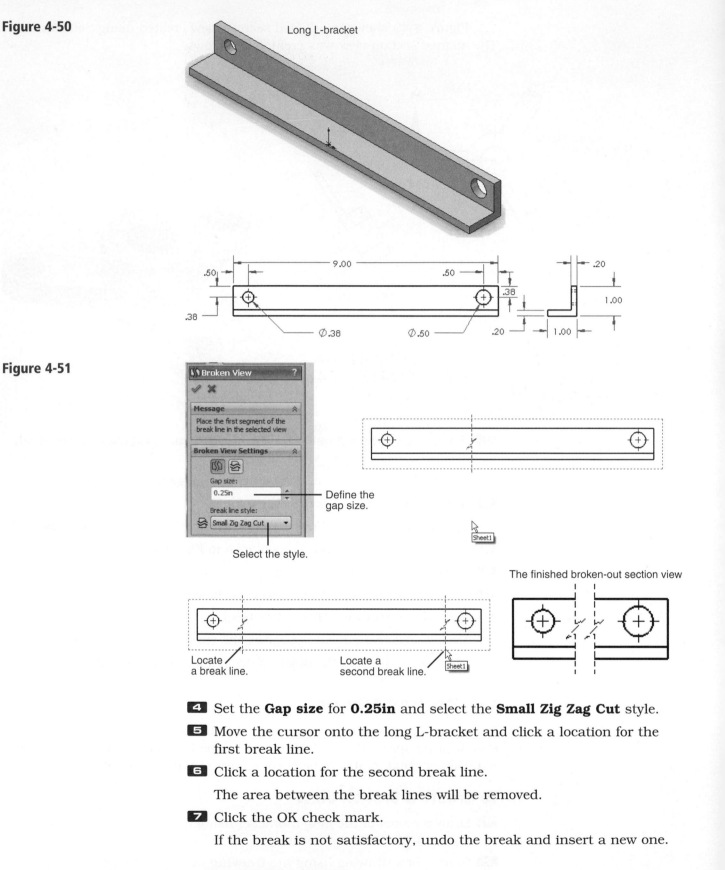

Long L-bracket

Figure 4-51

Define the gap size.

Select the style.

The finished broken-out section view

Locate a break line.

Locate a second break line.

4 Set the **Gap size** for **0.25in** and select the **Small Zig Zag Cut** style.

5 Move the cursor onto the long L-bracket and click a location for the first break line.

6 Click a location for the second break line.

The area between the break lines will be removed.

7 Click the OK check mark.

If the break is not satisfactory, undo the break and insert a new one.

4-8 Detail Views

A *detail view* is used to clarify specific areas of a drawing. Usually, an area is enlarged so that small details are easier to see.

To Draw a Detail View

In this example, the model shown in Figure P4-7 was used.

1 Create a **Part** drawing for the model shown in Figure P4-7. Save the model.

2 Start a new drawing using the **Drawing** format and create front and top orthographic views of a model. Use third-angle projection.

3 Click the **Detail View** tool.

See Figure 4-52.

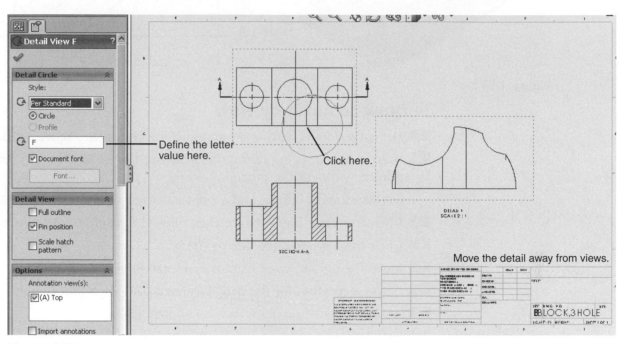

Figure 4-52

4 Locate the center point for a circle that will be used to define the area for the detail view by clicking a point.

In this example the intersection of the top view's front edge line and the right edge line of the slot were selected.

5 Move the cursor away from the point.

A detail view will appear.

6 When the circle is big enough to enclose all the area you wish to display in the detail view, click the mouse.

7 Move the cursor away from the views.

8 Select a location for the detail view and click the mouse.

The scale of the detail view can be changed by changing the values in the **Scale box.** The callout letters are changed using the **Detail Circle box.**

4-9 Auxiliary Views

Auxiliary views are orthographic views used to present true-shaped views of a slanted surface. In Figure 4-53 neither the front or side view shows a true shape of the slanted surface. A top view would show a foreshortened view. Only a view taken 90° to the surface will show its true shape.

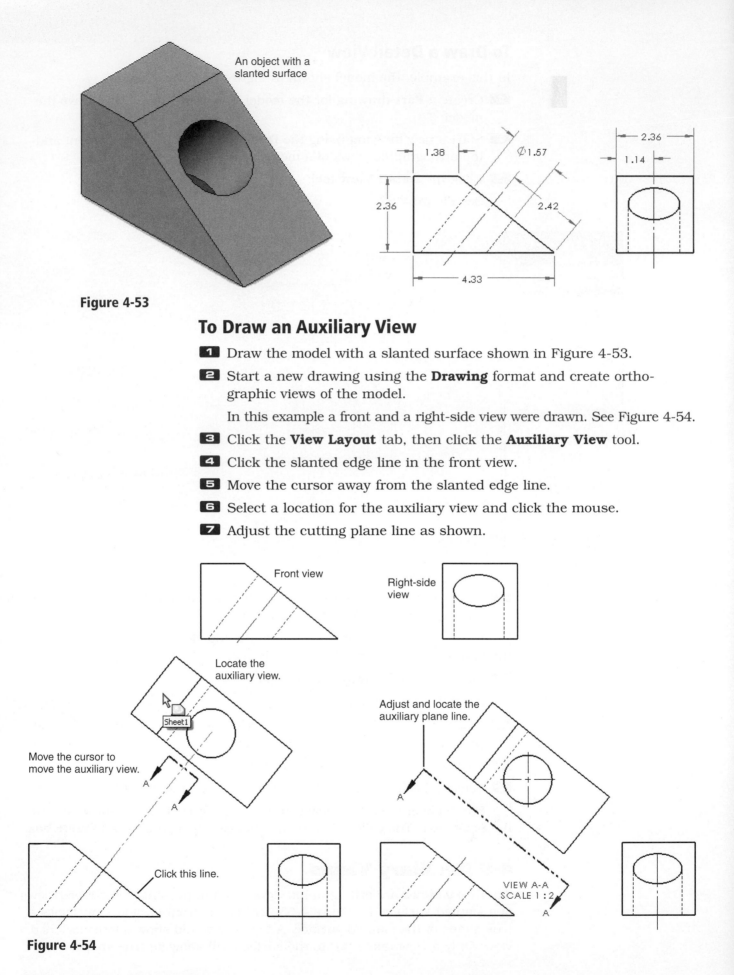

Figure 4-53

An object with a slanted surface

To Draw an Auxiliary View

1 Draw the model with a slanted surface shown in Figure 4-53.

2 Start a new drawing using the **Drawing** format and create orthographic views of the model.

In this example a front and a right-side view were drawn. See Figure 4-54.

3 Click the **View Layout** tab, then click the **Auxiliary View** tool.

4 Click the slanted edge line in the front view.

5 Move the cursor away from the slanted edge line.

6 Select a location for the auxiliary view and click the mouse.

7 Adjust the cutting plane line as shown.

Front view

Right-side view

Locate the auxiliary view.

Sheet1

Move the cursor to move the auxiliary view.

Click this line.

Adjust and locate the auxiliary plane line.

VIEW A-A
SCALE 1:2

Figure 4-54

Chapter Projects

Project 4-1:

Draw a front, a top, and a right-side orthographic view of each of the objects in Figures P4-1 through P4-24. Make all objects from mild steel.

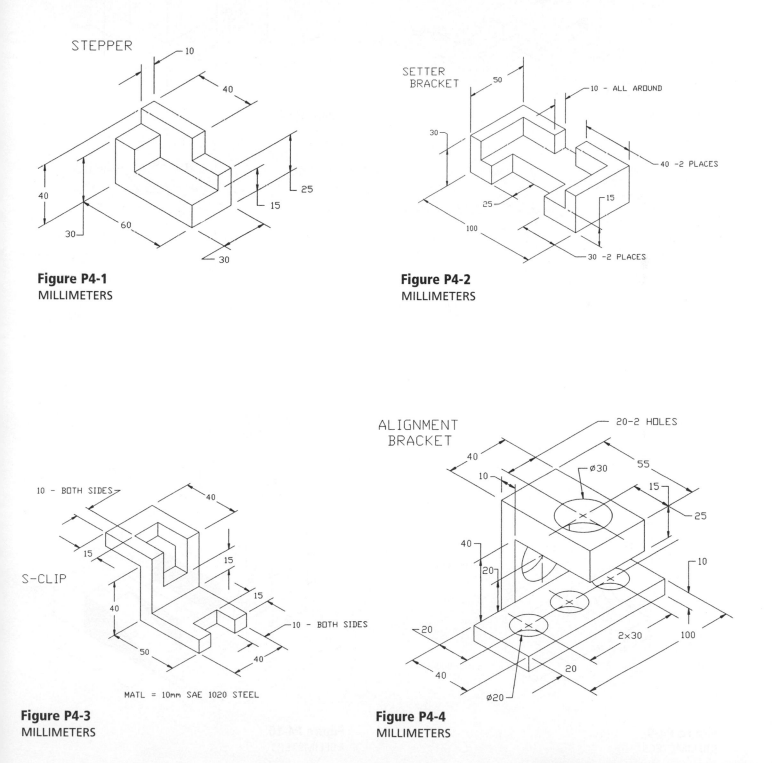

Figure P4-1
MILLIMETERS

Figure P4-2
MILLIMETERS

Figure P4-3
MILLIMETERS

Figure P4-4
MILLIMETERS

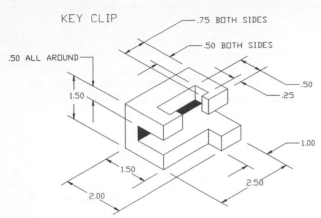

KEY CLIP

.50 ALL AROUND
.75 BOTH SIDES
.50 BOTH SIDES
.50
.25
1.50
1.00
1.50
2.50
2.00

Figure P4-5
INCHES

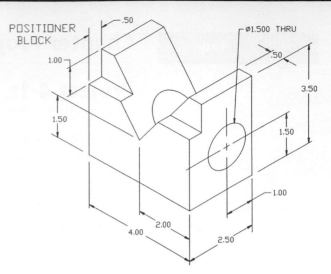

POSITIONER
BLOCK
.50
1.00
Ø1.500 THRU
.50
1.50
3.50
1.50
1.00
4.00
2.00
2.50

Figure P4-6
INCHES

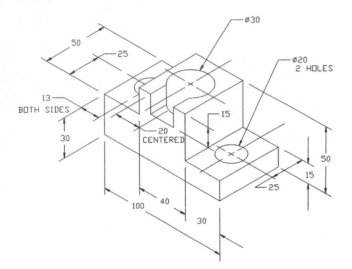

Ø30
50
25
Ø20
2 HOLES
13
BOTH SIDES
15
30
20
CENTERED
50
100
40
25
15
30

Figure P4-7
MILLIMETERS

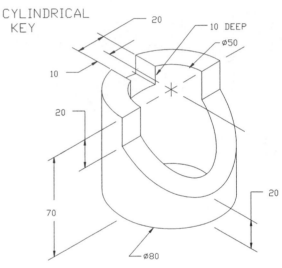

CYLINDRICAL
KEY
20
10 DEEP
Ø50
10
20
20
70
Ø80

Figure P4-8
MILLIMETERS

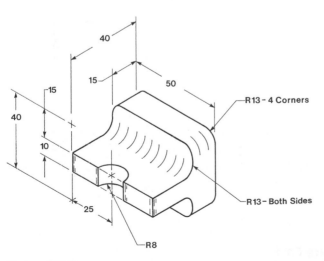

40
15
15
50
R13 – 4 Corners
40
10
R13 – Both Sides
25
R8

Figure P4-9
MILLIMETERS

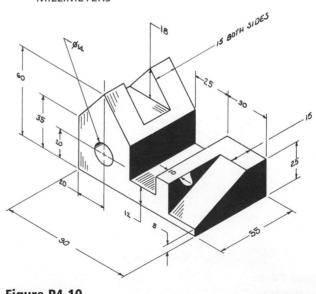

18
15 BOTH SIDES
Ø14
60
25
35
20
30
20
15
20
25
12
8
90
55

Figure P4-10
MILLIMETERS

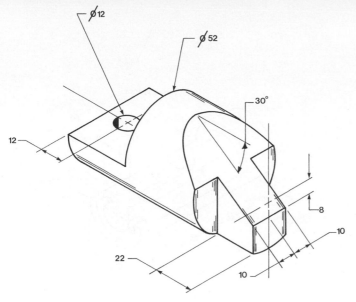

Figure P4-11
MILLIMETERS

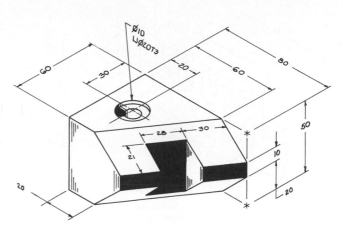

Figure P4-12
MILLIMETERS

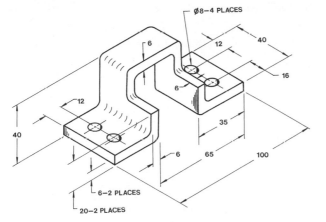

NOTE: ALL FILLETS AND ROUNDS=R3

Figure P4-13
MILLIMETERS

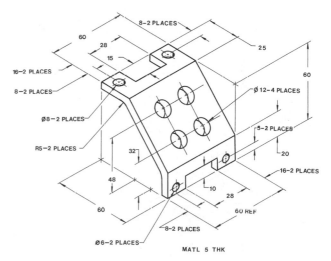

MATL 5 THK

Figure P4-14
MILLIMETERS

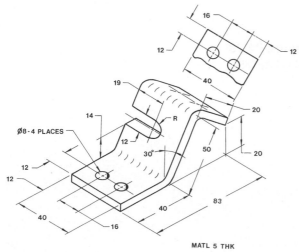

MATL 5 THK

ALL INSIDE BEND RAD 5

Figure P4-15
MILLIMETERS

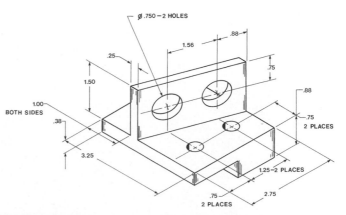

Figure P4-16
INCHES

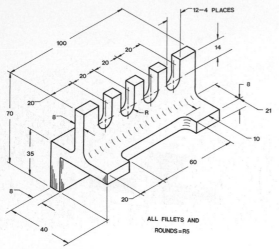

Figure P4-17
MILLIMETERS

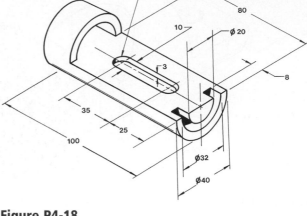

Figure P4-18
MILLIMETERS

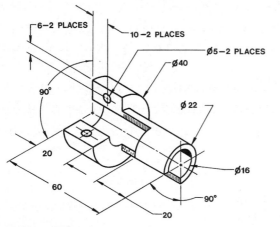

Figure P4-19
MILLIMETERS

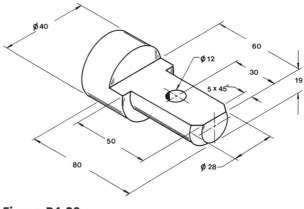

Figure P4-20
MILLIMETERS

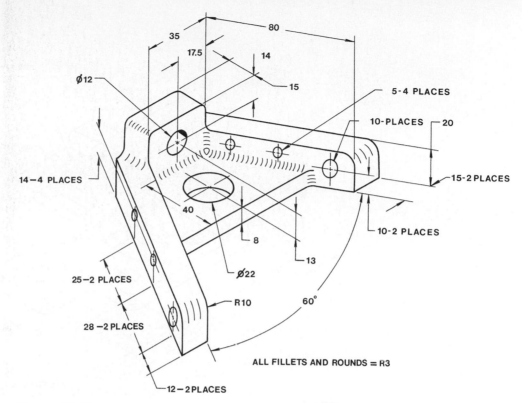

Figure P4-21
MILLIMETERS

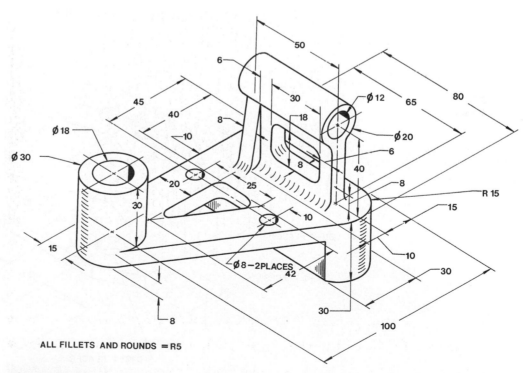

Figure P4-22
MILLIMETERS

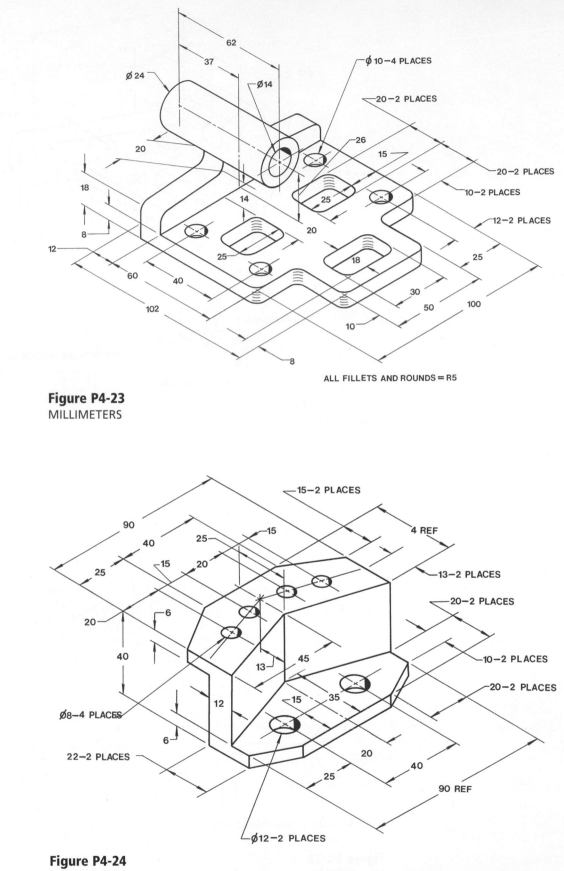

Figure P4-23
MILLIMETERS

Figure P4-24
MILLIMETERS

Project 4-2:

Draw at least two orthographic views and one auxiliary view of each of the objects in Figures P4-25 through P4-36.

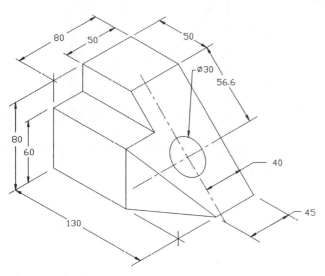

Figure P4-25
MILLIMETERS

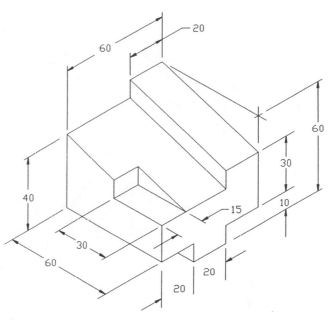

Figure P4-26
MILLIMETERS

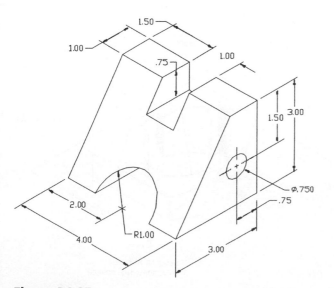

Figure P4-27
INCHES

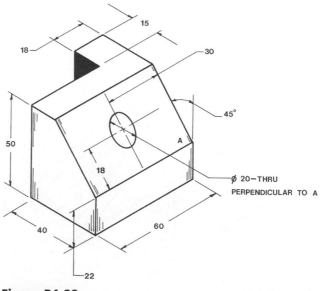

Figure P4-28
MILLIMETERS

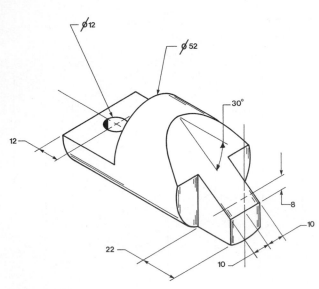

Figure P4-29
MILLIMETERS

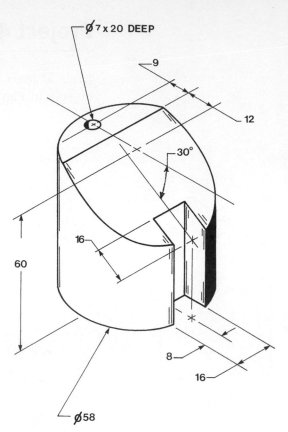

Figure P4-30
MILLIMETERS

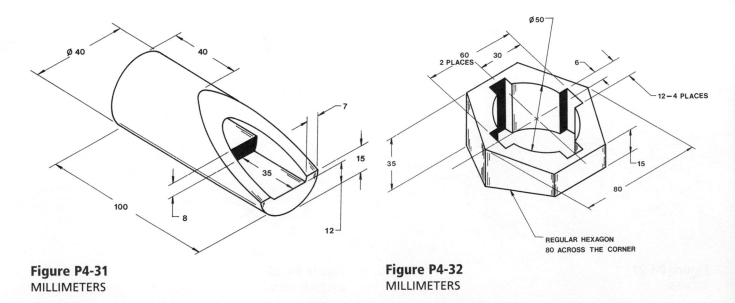

Figure P4-31
MILLIMETERS

Figure P4-32
MILLIMETERS

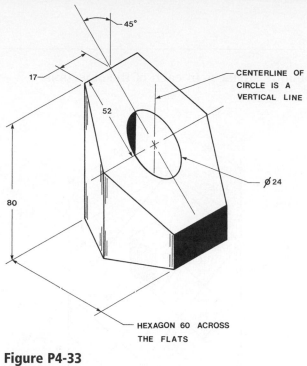

Figure P4-33
MILLIMETERS

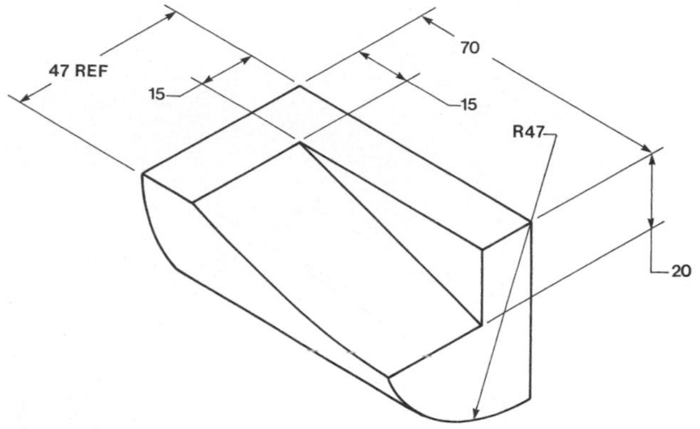

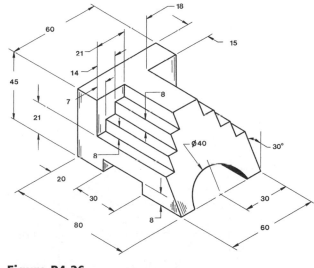

Figure P4-34
MILLIMETERS

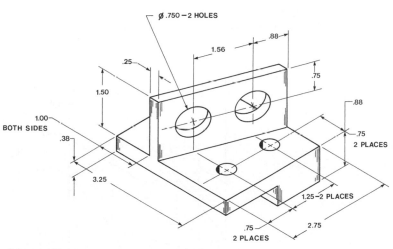

Figure P4-35
INCHES

Figure P4-36
MILLIMETERS

Project 4-3:

Define the true shape of the oblique surfaces in each of the objects is Figures P4-37 through P4-40.

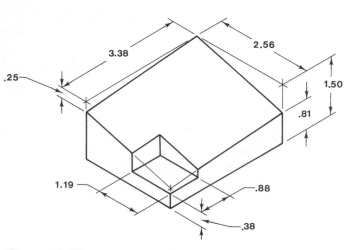

Figure P4-37
INCHES

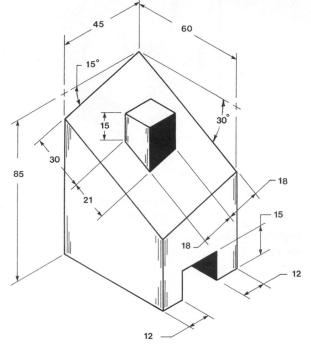

Figure P4-38
MILLIMETERS

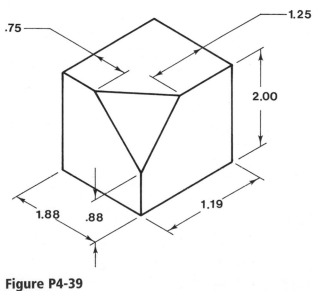

Figure P4-39
INCHES

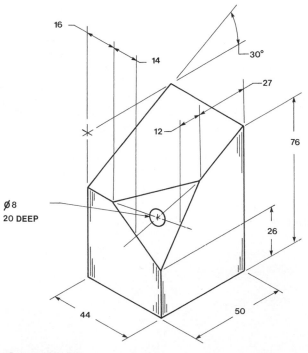

Figure P4-40
MILLIMETERS

Project 4-4:

Draw each of the objects shown in Figures P4-41 through P4-44 as a model, then draw a front view and an appropriate section view of each.

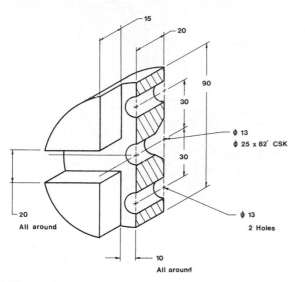

Figure P4-41
MILLIMETERS

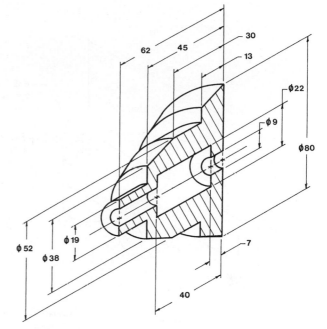

Figure P4-42
MILLIMETERS

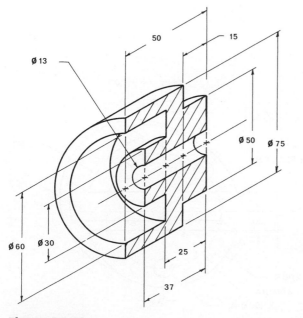

Figure P4-43
MILLIMETERS

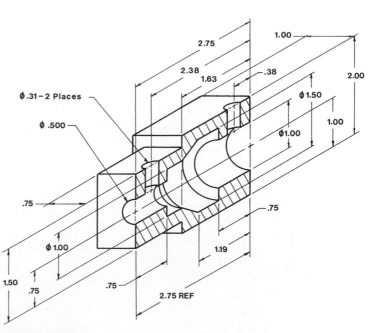

Figure P4-44
INCHES

Project 4-5:

Draw at least one orthographic view and the indicated section view for each object in Figures P4-45 through P4-50.

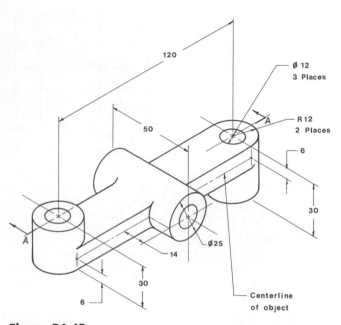

Figure P4-45
MILLIMETERS

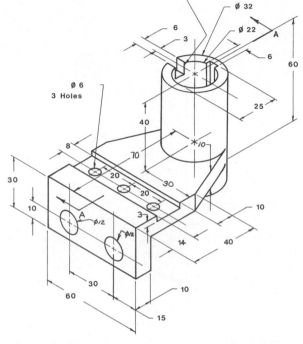

Figure P4-46
MILLIMETERS

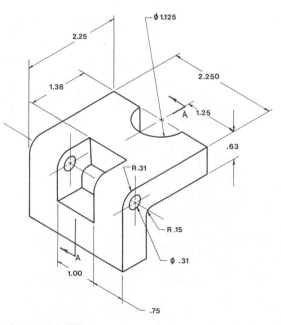

Figure P4-47
INCHES

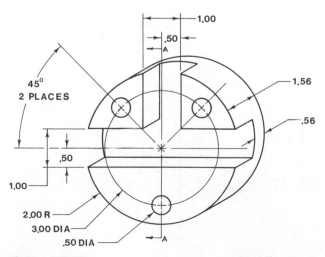

Figure P4-48
INCHES

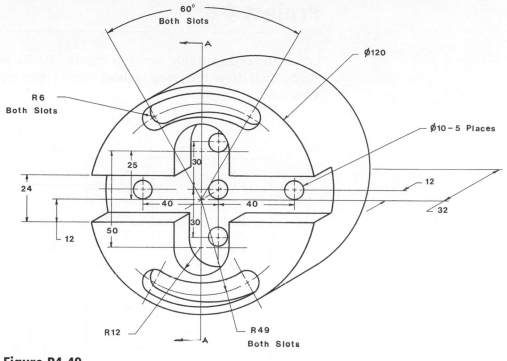

Figure P4-49
MILLIMETERS

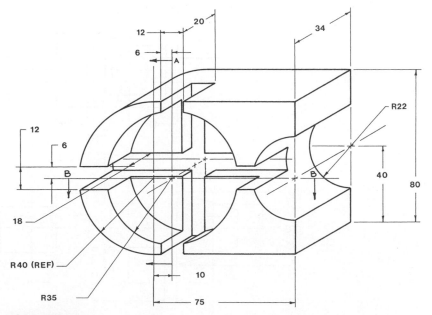

Figure P4-50
MILLIMETERS

Project 4-6:

Given the orthographic views in Figures P4-51 and P4-52, draw a model of each, then draw the given orthographic views and the appropriate section views.

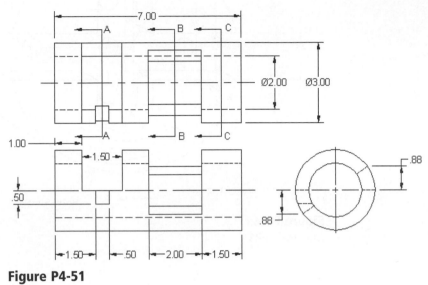

Figure P4-51
INCHES

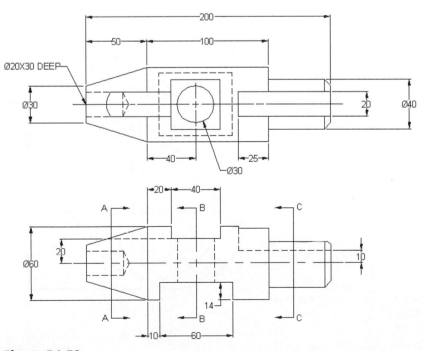

Figure P4-52
MILLIMETERS

Project 4-7:

Draw a 3D model and a set of multiviews for each object shown in Figures P4-53 through P4-60.

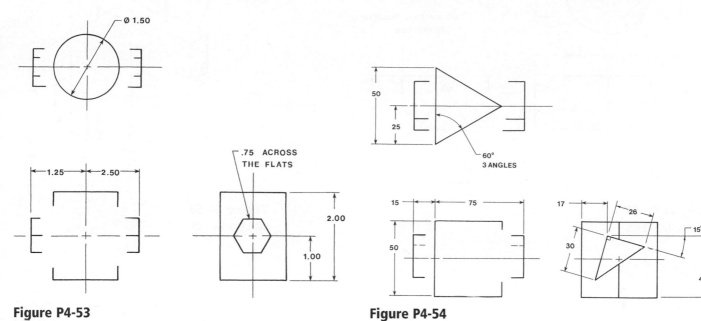

Figure P4-53
INCHES

Figure P4-54
MILLIMETERS

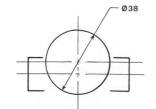

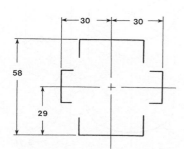

Figure P4-55
MILLIMETERS

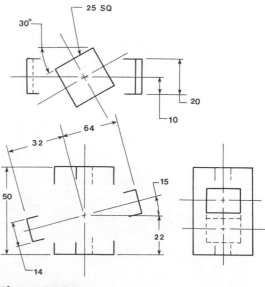

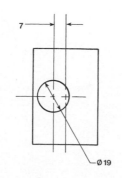

Figure P4-56
MILLIMETERS

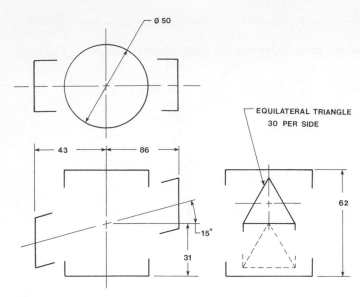

Figure P4-57
MILLIMETERS

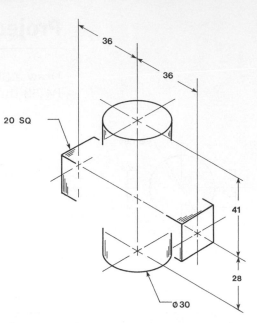

Figure P4-58
MILLIMETERS

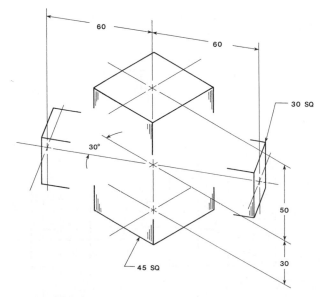

Figure P4-59
MILLIMETERS

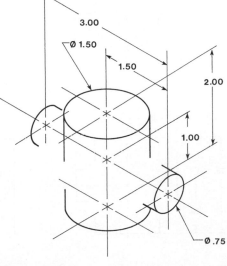

Figure P4-60
INCHES

Project 4-8:

Figures P4-61 through P4-66 are orthographic views. Draw 3D models from the given views. The hole pattern defined in Figure P4-61 also applies to Figure P4-62.

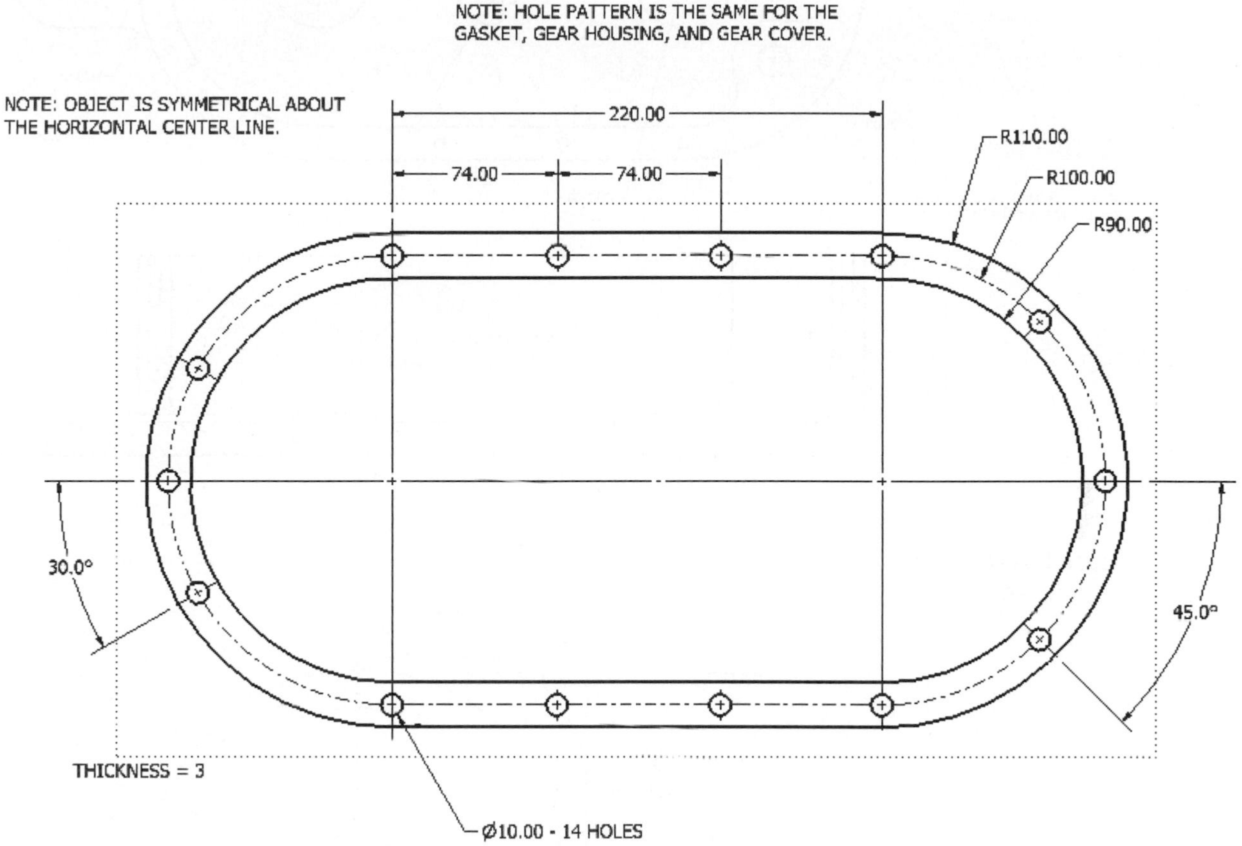

NOTE: HOLE PATTERN IS THE SAME FOR THE GASKET, GEAR HOUSING, AND GEAR COVER.

NOTE: OBJECT IS SYMMETRICAL ABOUT THE HORIZONTAL CENTER LINE.

220.00

74.00   74.00

R110.00

R100.00

R90.00

30.0°

45.0°

THICKNESS = 3

Ø10.00 - 14 HOLES

Figure P4-61
MILLIMETERS

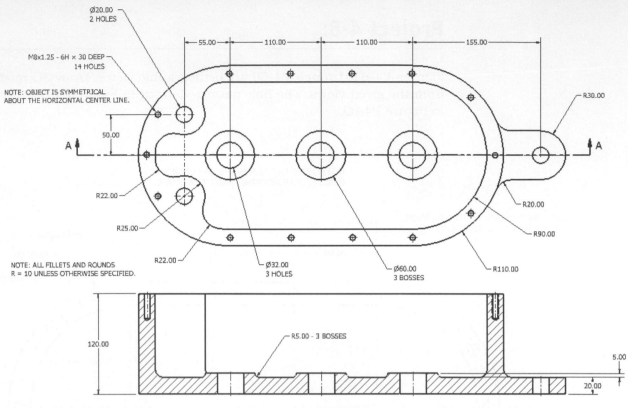

Ø20.00
2 HOLES

M8x1.25 - 6H × 30 DEEP
14 HOLES

NOTE: OBJECT IS SYMMETRICAL
ABOUT THE HORIZONTAL CENTER LINE.

55.00   110.00   110.00   155.00

R30.00

A

50.00

R22.00

R25.00

R22.00

R20.00

R90.00

R110.00

Ø32.00
3 HOLES

Ø60.00
3 BOSSES

NOTE: ALL FILLETS AND ROUNDS
R = 10 UNLESS OTHERWISE SPECIFIED.

120.00

R5.00 - 3 BOSSES

5.00

20.00

SECTION A-A
SCALE 1 / 2

Figure P4-62
MILLIMETERS

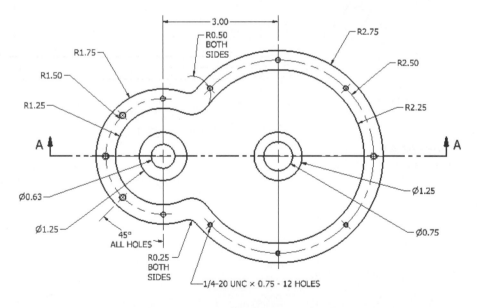

3.00

R0.50
BOTH
SIDES

R2.75

R1.75

R2.50

R1.50

R2.25

R1.25

A

A

Ø0.63

Ø1.25

Ø1.25

Ø0.75

45°
ALL HOLES

R0.25
BOTH
SIDES

1/4-20 UNC × 0.75 - 12 HOLES

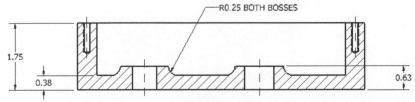

R0.25 BOTH BOSSES

1.75

0.38

0.63

SECTION A-A
SCALE 3 / 4

Figure P4-63
INCHES

Figure P4-64
INCHES

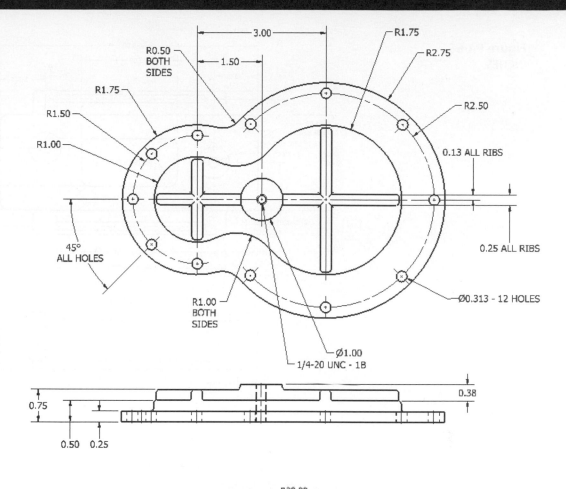

Figure P4-65
MILLIMETERS

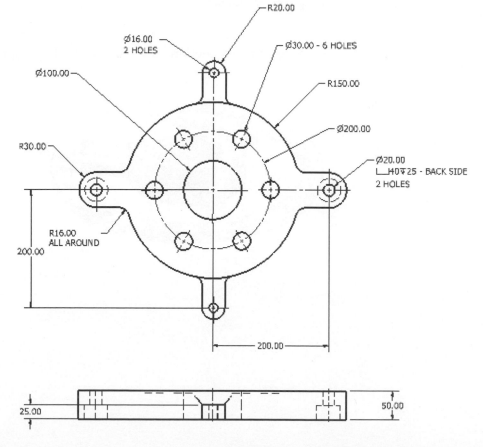

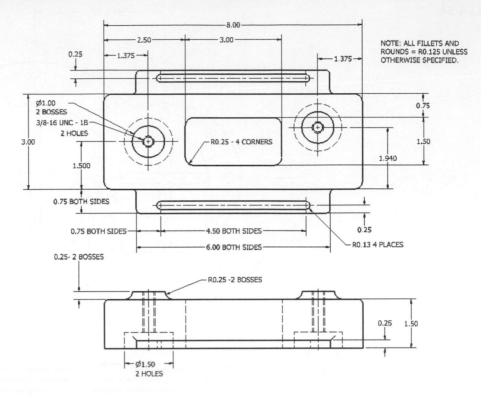

Project 4-9:

Draw an aligned section view as indicated in Figures P4-67 and P4-68.

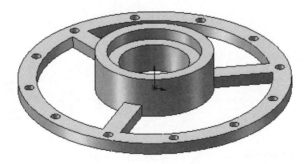

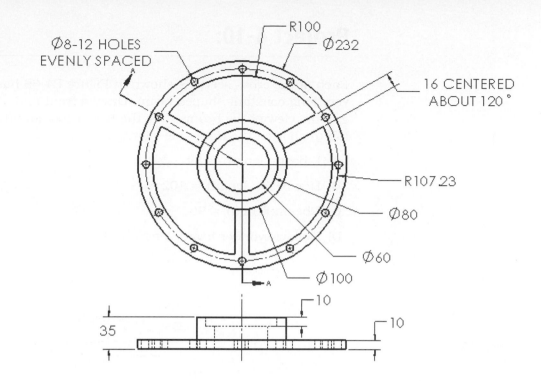

Ø8-12 HOLES
EVENLY SPACED

R100

Ø232

16 CENTERED
ABOUT 120°

R107.23

Ø80

Ø60

Ø100

35

10

10

Figure P4-68
INCHES

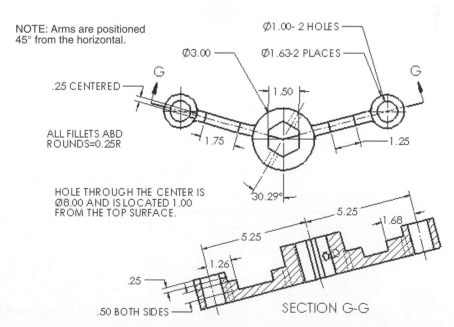

NOTE: Arms are positioned
45° from the horizontal.

Ø1.00- 2 HOLES

Ø3.00

Ø1.63-2 PLACES

G

G

.25 CENTERED

1.50

ALL FILLETS ABD
ROUNDS=0.25R

1.75

1.25

30.29°

HOLE THROUGH THE CENTER IS
Ø8.00 AND IS LOCATED 1.00
FROM THE TOP SURFACE.

5.25

1.68

5.25

5.25

1.26

.25

.50 BOTH SIDES

SECTION G-G

Project 4-10:

Each of the cross sections shown in Figure P4-69 has been extruded to a very long constant-shaped beam. Draw a front and a right-side orthographic view of the beams. Use the **Break** tool found on the **View Layout** tab to shorten the right-side view.

A. L-beam: length = 84

B. Hex beam: length = 102

C. I-beam: length = 96

D. Hollow-cylinder beam: length = 120

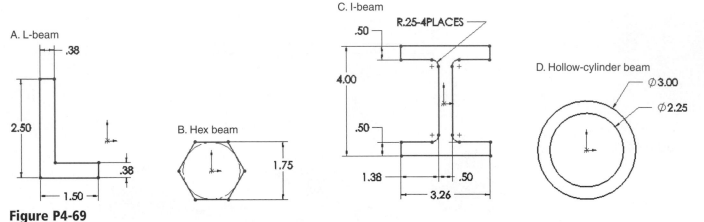

Figure P4-69
INCHES

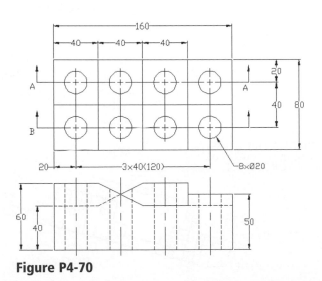

Figure P4-70

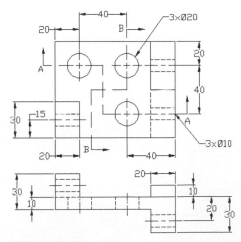

Figure P4-71

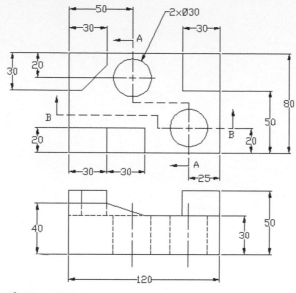

Figure P4-72

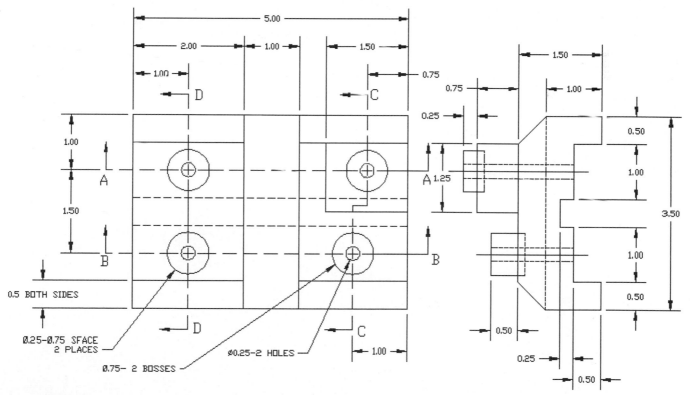

Figure P4-73

5 chapterfive
Assemblies

CHAPTER OBJECTIVES

- Learn how to create assembly drawings
- Learn how to create exploded assembly drawings
- Learn how to create a parts list
- Learn how to animate an assembly
- Learn how to edit a title block

5-1 Introduction

This chapter introduces the **Assembly** tools. These tools are used to create assembly drawings. Assembly drawings can be exploded to form isometric assembly drawings that when labeled and accompanied by a parts list become working drawings. Assembly drawings can be animated.

5-2 Starting an Assembly Drawing

Figure 5-1 shows a test block. The overall dimensions for the block are 80 × 80 × 80 mm. The cutout is 40 × 40 × 80 mm. The test block will be used to help introduce the **Assembly** tools.

1 Start a new drawing.

2 Select the **Assembly** format.

3 Click **OK**.

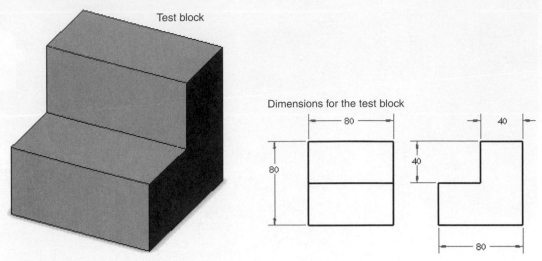

Test block

Dimensions for the test block

Figure 5-1

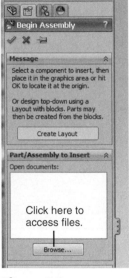

Click here to access files.

Figure 5-2

Draw the block and save it as **BLOCK,TEST.**

The **Begin Assembly PropertyManager** will appear. See Figure 5-2.

4 Click the **Browse. . .** box.

The **Open** box will appear. See Figure 5-3.

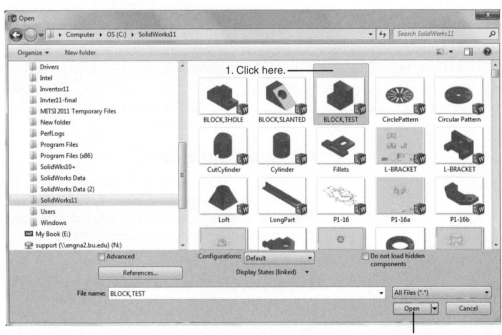

1. Click here.

2. Click here.

Figure 5-3

5 Click **BLOCK,TEST,** then click **Open.**

The test block will appear on the screen. See Figure 5-4.

6 Click the **Insert Components** tool, click the **Browser box,** select the **BLOCK,TEST** and insert a second block.

Figure 5-4

Click here to open a second BLOCK,TEST.

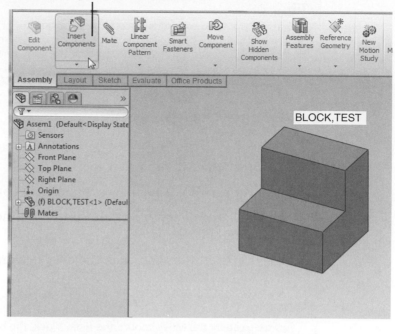

BLOCK,TEST

See Figure 5-5. The first block inserted is fixed in place. In any assembly drawing the first component will automatically be fixed in place. Note the **(f)** notation to the left of **BLOCK,TEST<1>.** See Figure 5-6. As the assembly is created, components will move to the fixed first component.

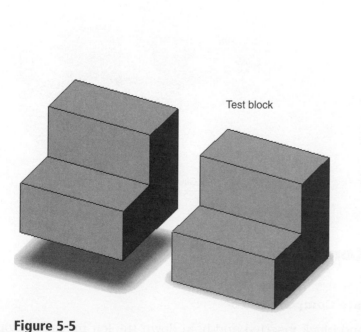

Test block

Figure 5-5

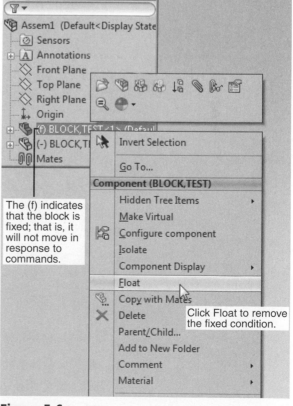

The (f) indicates that the block is fixed; that is, it will not move in response to commands.

Click Float to remove the fixed condition.

Figure 5-6

5-3 Move Component

See Figure 5-7.

1 Click the **Move Component** tool.

2 Click the second block inserted and hold down the left mouse button.

3 While holding down the left button, move the block around the screen by moving the mouse.

4 Release the button and click the OK check mark.

Figure 5-7

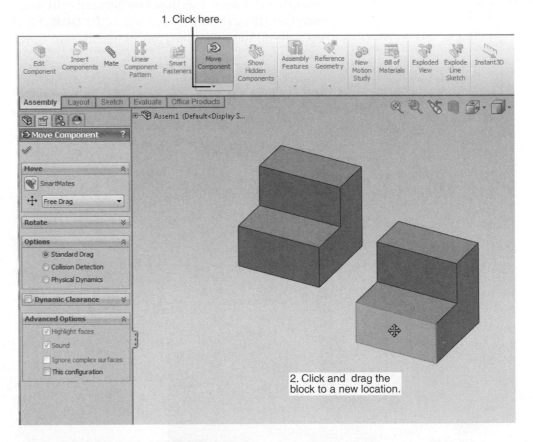

5-4 Rotate Component

See Figure 5-8.

1 Click the **Rotate Component** tool.

2 Click the second block inserted and hold down the left mouse button.

Figure 5-8

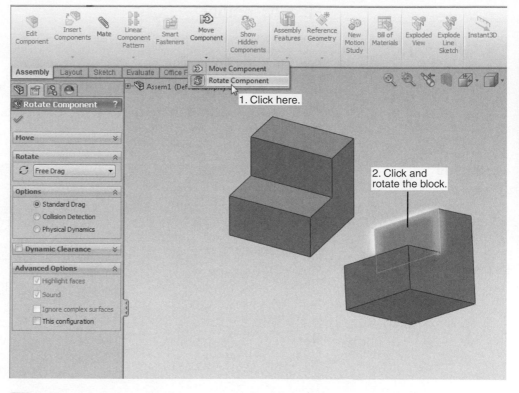

3 While holding down the left button, rotate the block around the screen by moving the mouse.

4 Release the button and click the OK check mark.

5 Use the **Undo** tool to return the block to its original position.

5-5 Mate

The **Mate** tool is used to align components to create assembly drawings. See Figure 5-9.

Figure 5-9

Click the Mate tool.

First Assembly

Mate the two test blocks side by side.

1 Click the **Mate** tool.

2 Click the upper right edge of the first block inserted.

See Figure 5-10. Note that the first block is listed in the **Mate Selections** box after it is selected.

Figure 5-10

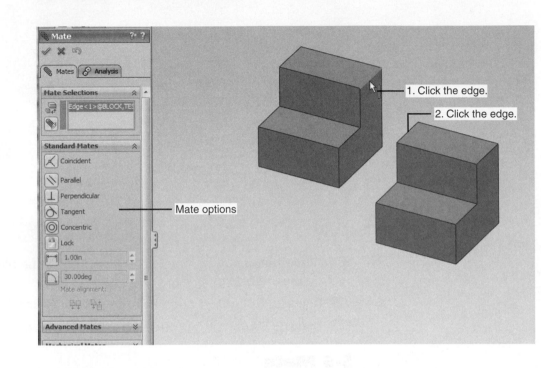

3 Click the upper left edge on the second block.

The edges will align. See Figure 5-11.

Figure 5-11

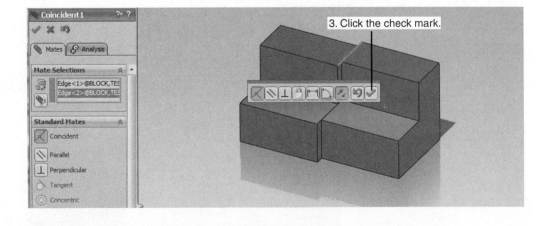

4 Click the OK check mark to clear the tools.

The **Mate Selections** box should be clear.

5 Click the upper front surface of the second block.

6 Click the upper front surface of the first block.

See Figure 5-12. The surfaces will align. See Figure 5-13.

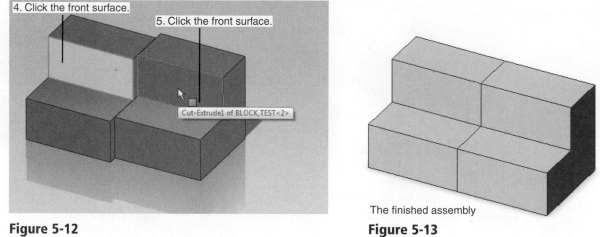

Figure 5-12

The finished assembly

Figure 5-13

Second Assembly

Mate the two test blocks face-to-face.

1 Use the **Undo** tool and return the blocks to their original positions.

See Figure 5-14. The second test block must be rotated into a different position relative to the first test block.

2 Use the **Rotate Component** tool and position the second block as shown.

See Figure 5-15.

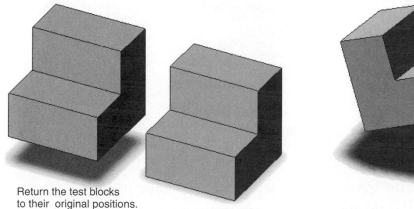

Return the test blocks to their original positions.

Figure 5-14

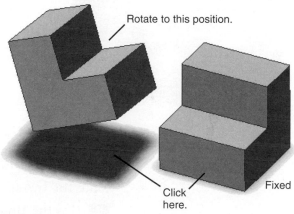

Rotate to this position.

Click here.

Fixed

Figure 5-15

3 Use the **Mate** tool and click the lower front face of each block.

The second block will rotate relative to the first block. See Figure 5-16. Recall that the first block is in the fixed condition, and the second block is in the floating condition.

4 Click the **Add/Finish Mate** check mark on the toolbar, then click the OK check mark.

5 Use the **Mate** tool and click the two faces of the test block as shown.

See Figure 5-17.

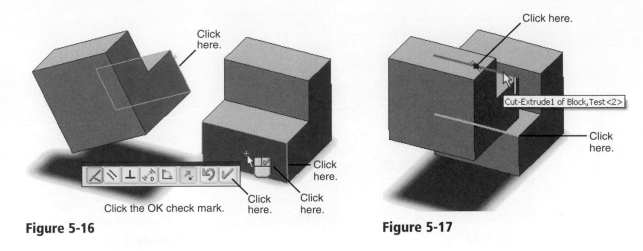

Figure 5-16

Figure 5-17

6 Click the **Add/Finish Mate** check mark on the toolbar, then click the OK check mark.

7 Use the **Mate** tool and click the two edge lines as shown.

See Figure 5-18.

8 Click the **Add/Finish Mate** check mark on the toolbar, then click the OK check mark.

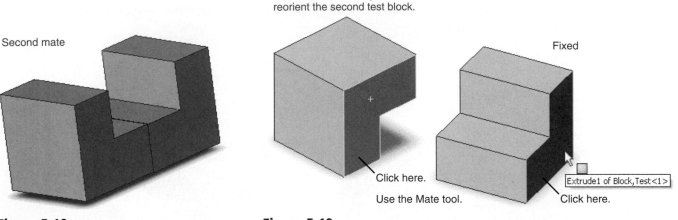

Figure 5-18

Figure 5-19

Third Assembly

Mate the two test blocks to form a rectangular prism.

1 Use the **Undo** tool and return the blocks to their original positions.

See Figure 5-14.

2 Use the **Rotate Component** tool and position the second test block as shown.

See Figure 5-19.

3 Click the **Add/Finish Mate** check mark on the toolbar, then click the OK check mark.

4 Use the **Mate** tool and click the right surfaces of the blocks.

5 Click the **Add/Finish Mate** check mark on the toolbar, then click the OK check mark.

See Figure 5-20.

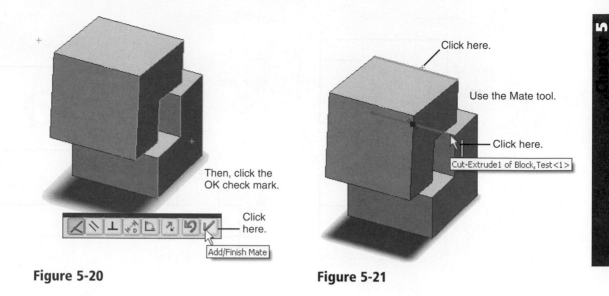

Figure 5-20

Figure 5-21

6 Click the upper edge of the blocks as shown.

See Figure 5-21.

7 Click the **Add/Finish Mate** check mark on the toolbar, then click the OK check mark.

See Figure 5-22.

8 Reorient the blocks so that the bottom surfaces are visible.

See Figure 5-23.

9 Use the **Mate** tool and click the bottom surfaces of the blocks.

Figure 5-24 shows the finished assembly.

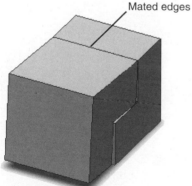

Figure 5-22

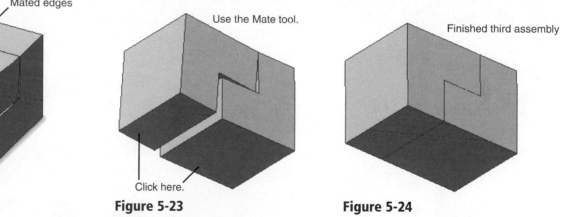

Figure 5-23

Figure 5-24

5-6 Bottom-up Assemblies

Bottom-up assemblies are assemblies that are created for existing parts; that is, the parts have already been drawn as models. In this example the three parts shown in Figure 5-25 have been drawn and saved.

1 Start a new drawing and select the **Assembly** format.

2 Click the **Browse. . .** box, then click the **Block, Bottom** component.

See Figure 5-26. The Block, Bottom will appear on the screen. See Figure 5-27.

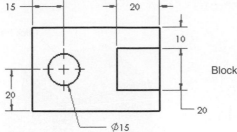

Block, Bottom

Ø15

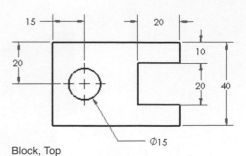

Block, Top

Ø15

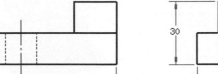

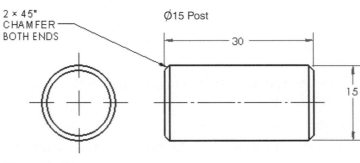

2 × 45°
CHAMFER
BOTH ENDS

Ø15 Post

30

15

Figure 5-25

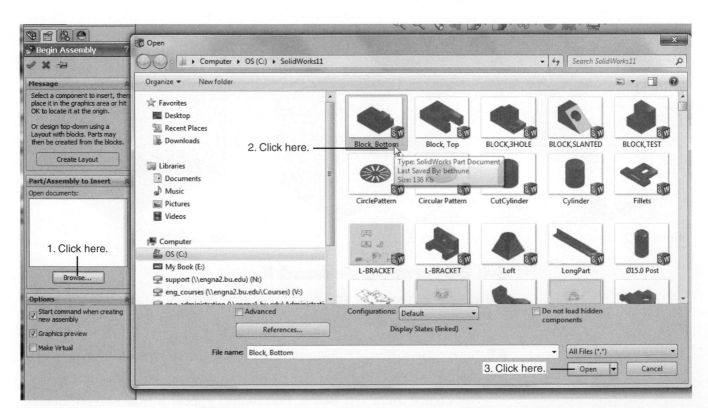

Figure 5-26

Figure 5-27

Click here to return to files to add another component.

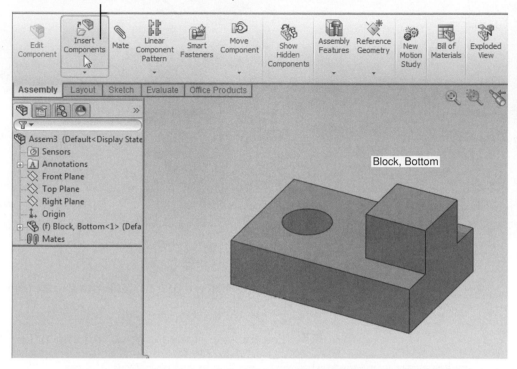

3 Click the **Insert Component** tool, click the **Browse. . .** box, and select **Block, Top.**

4 Repeat the sequence and select **Ø15 Post.**

See Figure 5-28.

> **NOTE**
>
> Note that the Block, Bottom was the first part entered and is fixed in its location, as designated by the **(f)** symbol in the **PropertyManager** box.

Figure 5-28

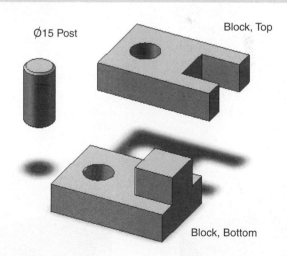

Ø15 Post

Block, Top

Block, Bottom

5 Use the **Mate** tool and click the center point of the edge line of the Block, Bottom and the Block, Top as shown.

See Figure 5-29. A dot will appear when the cursor is on the center point of the edge. Figure 5-30 shows the resulting mate. If the blocks do not align, use the **Mate** tool again to align the blocks by clicking their end surfaces.

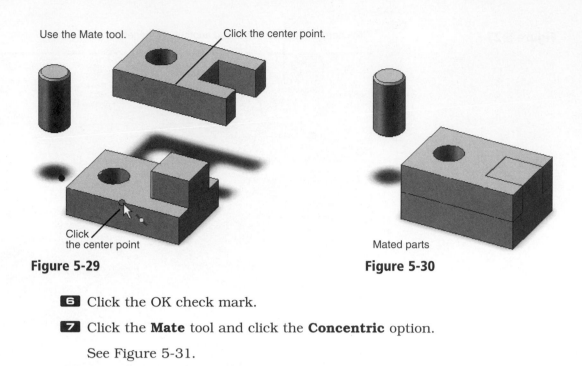

Use the Mate tool.　　　Click the center point.

Click
the center point

Figure 5-29

Mated parts

Figure 5-30

6 Click the OK check mark.

7 Click the **Mate** tool and click the **Concentric** option.

See Figure 5-31.

8 Click the side of the Ø15 Post and the inside of the hole in the Block, Top.

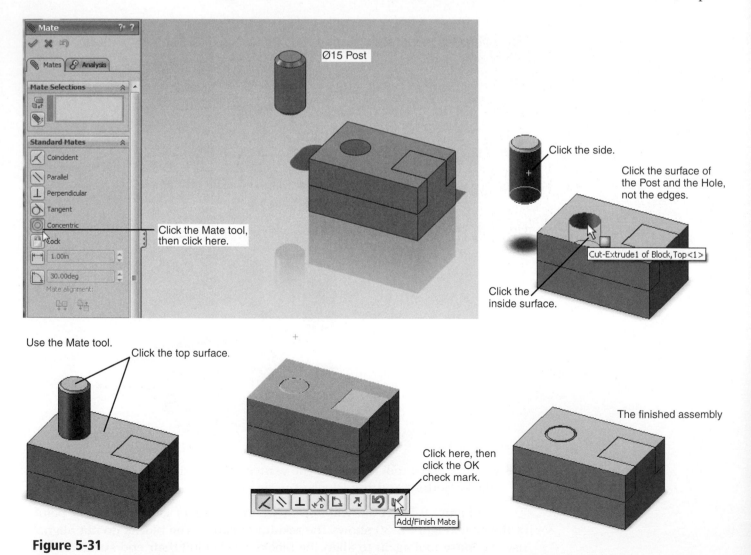

Figure 5-31

NOTE

Click the surface of the components, not their edge lines. Clicking the edge lines would produce different results.

9 Click the **Add/Finish Mate** check mark on the toolbar, then click the OK check mark.

10 Use the **Mate** tool and click the top surface of the Ø15 Post and the top surface of the Block, Top.

11 Click the **Add/Finish Mate** check mark on the toolbar, then click the OK check mark.

5-7 Creating an Exploded Isometric Assembly Drawing

An exploded isometric assembly drawing shows the components of an assembly pulled apart. This makes it easier to see how parts fit together.

1 Click the **Exploded View** tool.

See Figure 5-32.

Figure 5-32

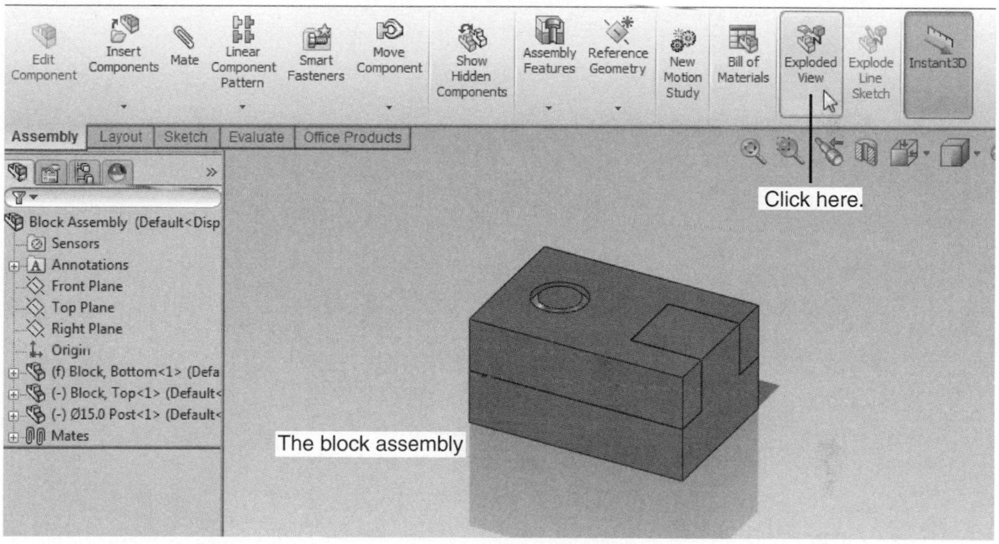

2 Click the top surface of the Ø15 Post.

An axis system icon will appear. See Figure 5-33. The arrow in the Z-direction (the one pointing vertically) will initially be green.

3 Move the cursor onto the Z-direction arrow and hold down the left mouse button.

The arrow will turn yellow when selected.

4 Drag the Ø15 Post to a location above the assembly as shown.

A real-time scale will appear as you drag the Post.

5 Click the OK check mark.

6 Repeat the procedure and drag the Block, Top away from the Block, Bottom.

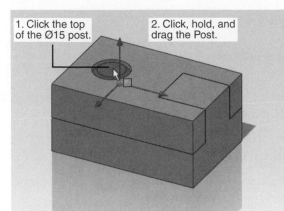

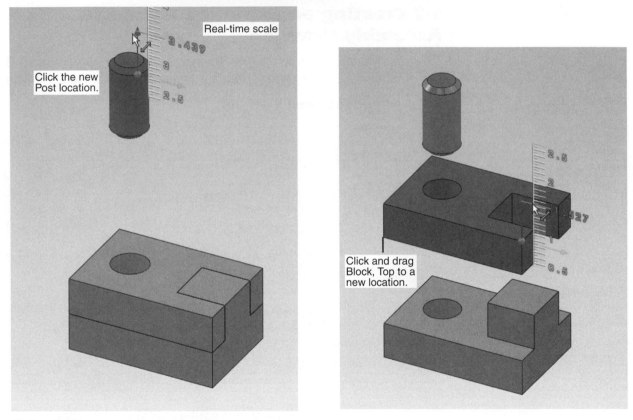

Figure 5-33

7 Click the OK check mark.

8 Save the assembly as **Block Assembly.**

Figure 5-34 shows the final assembly.

5-8 Creating an Exploded Isometric Drawing Using the Drawing Format

1 Create a new drawing using the **Drawing** format.

2 Select the **A-(ANSI)Landscape** sheet format.

3 Click the **Browse. . .** box in the **Model View PropertyManager.**

See Figure 5-35.

Figure 5-34

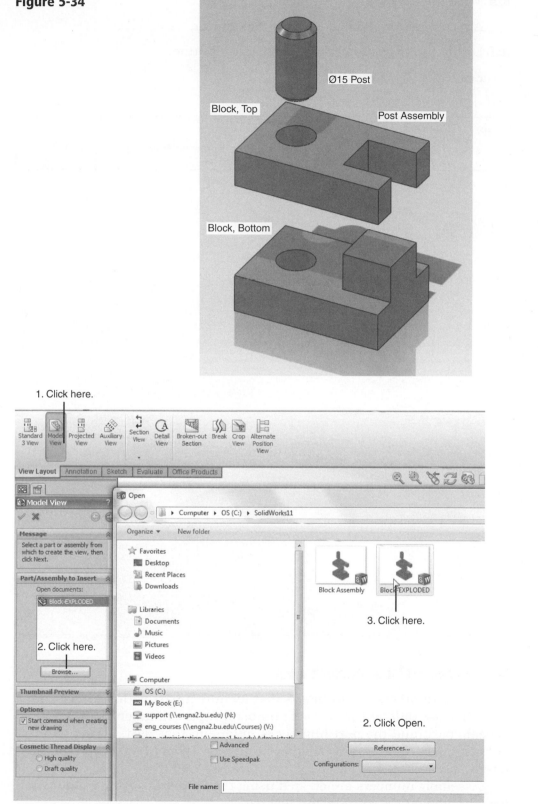

Figure 5-35

Figure 5-36

4. Select **Block-EXPLODED;** click **Open.**

5. Set the **Orientation** for **Isometric** and the **Display Style** for **Hidden Lines Removed.**

See Figure 5-36.

6 Move the cursor into the drawing area.

A rectangular outline of the view will appear.

7 Locate the view and click the left mouse button.

See Figure 5-37.

TIP
As a general rule, hidden lines are not included on isometric drawings.

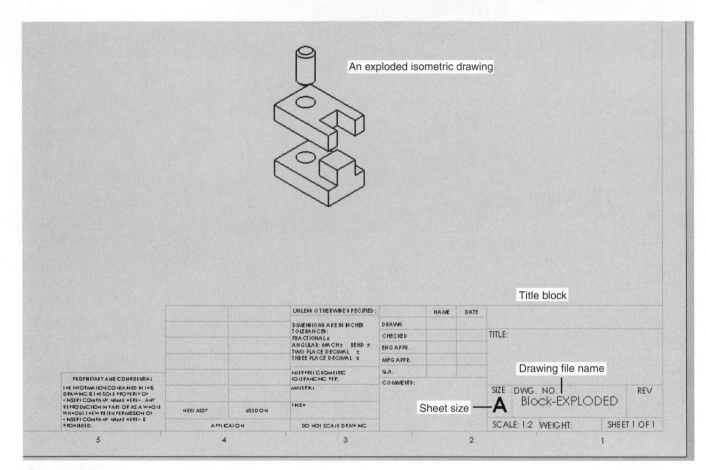

An exploded isometric drawing

Title block

Drawing file name

Sheet size ──A

Block-EXPLODED

Figure 5-37

5-9 Assembly Numbers

Assembly numbers are numbers that identify a part within an assembly. They are different from part numbers. A part number identifies a specific part, and the part number is unique to that part. A part has only one part number but may have different assembly numbers in different assemblies.

Assembly numbers are created using the **Balloon** or **AutoBalloon** tools located on the **Annotation** tool panel.

1 Click the **Annotation** tab.

2 Click the **AutoBalloon** tool.

3 Move the cursor into the Block Assembly area (a red out line will appear) and click the mouse.

Figure 5-38 shows the results. The **AutoBalloon** arrangements may not always be the best presentation. The balloons may be rearranged or applied individually.

Figure 5-38

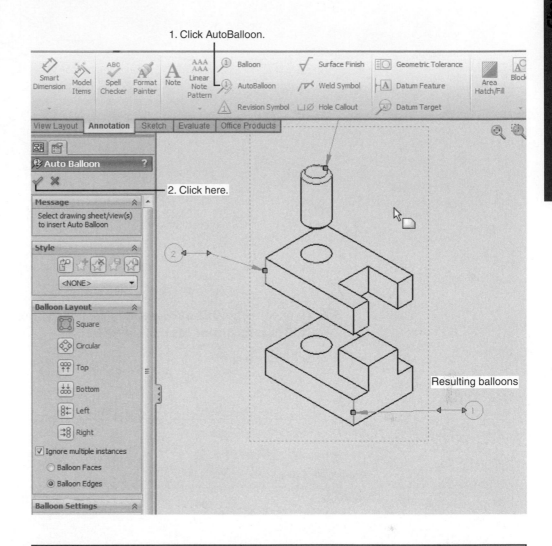

TIP

Balloons can be moved by first clicking them. They will change color. Click and hold either the balloon or the box that will appear on the arrow. Drag either the balloon or the arrow to a new location.

4 Undo the auto balloons.

5 Click the **Balloon** tool.

6 Click each part and locate the balloon.

7 Click the OK check mark.

See Figure 5-39.

5-10 Bill of Materials (BOM or Parts List)

A *bill of materials* is a listing of all parts included in an assembly drawing. A bill of materials may also be called a parts list.

Figure 5-39

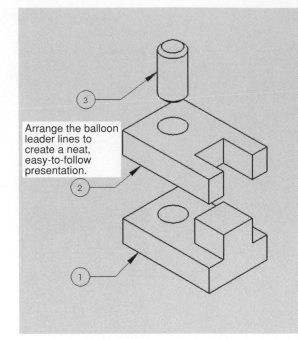

Arrange the balloon leader lines to create a neat, easy-to-follow presentation.

1 To access the **Bill of Materials** tool click the **Annotation** tab, then the **Tables** and **Bill of Materials** tools.

See Figure 5-40.

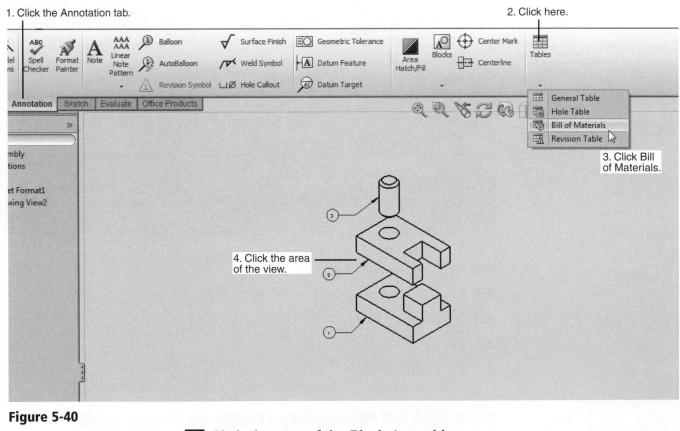

Figure 5-40

2 Click the area of the Block Assembly.

A red box will appear around the Block Assembly. Click within that box.

3 Click the OK check mark.

Pull the cursor back into the drawing area. The BOM will follow. Select a location for the BOM and click the mouse.

See Figure 5-41.

Figure 5-41

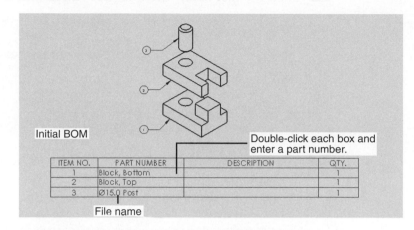

Initial BOM

Double-click each box and enter a part number.

File name

ITEM NO.	PART NUMBER	DESCRIPTION	QTY.
1	Block, Bottom		1
2	Block, Top		1
3	Ø15.0 Post		1

NOTE

Note that the information in the **PART NUMBER** column is each part's file name. These names are directly linked by SolidWorks to the original part drawings. They can be manually edited, but if the assembly is changed and regenerated, the original part names will appear. In this example the original parts were renamed using part numbers as their file names. See Figure 5-42.

Figure 5-42

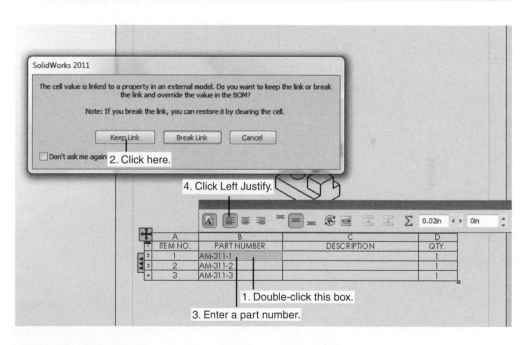

SolidWorks 2011

The cell value is linked to a property in an external model. Do you want to keep the link or break the link and override the value in the BOM?

Note: If you break the link, you can restore it by clearing the cell.

Keep Link   Break Link   Cancel

Don't ask me again   2. Click here.

4. Click Left Justify.

	A	B	C	D
	ITEM NO.	PART NUMBER	DESCRIPTION	QTY.
1	1	AM-311-1		1
2	2	AM-311-2		1
3	3	AM-311-3		1

1. Double-click this box.

3. Enter a part number.

To Edit the BOM

1 Double-click the box directly under the heading **PART NUMBER.**

A warning dialog box will appear.

2 Click the **Keep Link** box.

The **Formatting** dialog box will appear.

3 Type in a part number.

4 Click the **Left Justify** option.

See Figure 5-43.

5 Click the box below the one just edited and enter the part numbers.

Figure 5-43

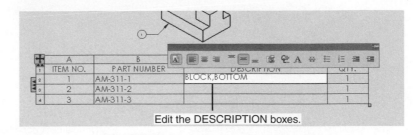

Edit the DESCRIPTION boxes.

6 Click the boxes under the **DESCRIPTION** heading and enter the descriptions.

See Figure 5-44.

Figure 5-44

ITEM NO.	PART NUMBER	DESCRIPTION	QTY.
1	AM-311-1	BLOCK,BOTTOM	1
2	AM-311-2	BLOCK,TOP	1
3	AM-311-3	Ø15 POST	1

To Add Columns to the BOM

1 Right-click the **BLOCK, BOTTOM** box.

See Figure 5-45.

Figure 5-45

1. Right-click this box

	A	B	C	D
1	ITEM NO.	PART NUMBER	DESCRIPTION	QTY.
2	1	AM-311-1	BLOCK,BOTTOM	
3	2	AM-311-2	BLOCK,TOP	
4	3	AM-311-3	Ø15 POST	

Zoom/Pan/Rotate
Recent Commands
Open block, bottom.sldprt
Insert → Column Right
Select → Column Left
Delete → Row Above
Hide → Row Below
Formatting
Split

UNLESS OTHERWISE SPECIFIED:
DIMENSIONS ARE IN INCHES   DRAWN

2. Click here

2 Click the **Insert** option, then click **Column Right.**

A new column will appear to the right of the BLOCK, BOTTOM box. See Figure 5-46.

Figure 5-46

New column

DESCRIPTION		QTY.
BLOCK,BOTTOM		1
BLOCK,TOP		1
Ø15 POST		1

3 Right-click one of the boxes in the new column.

4 Select the **Formatting** option; click **Column Width.**

See Figure 5-47. The **Column Width** dialog box will appear. See Figure 5-48.

5 Enter a new value.

In this example a value of **1.75in** was entered. Figure 5-48 shows the new column width. Edit the other columns if necessary.

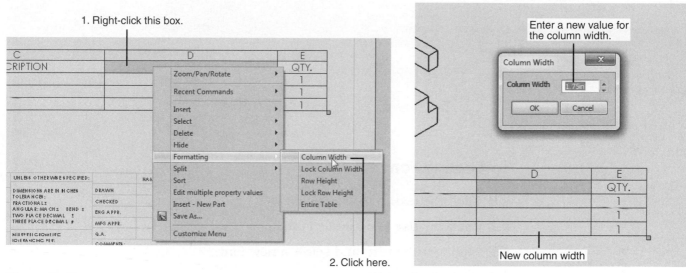

Figure 5-47

Figure 5-48

To Edit a BOM

1 Click the top box of the new 1.75-wide column.

2 Type the heading **MATERIALS.**

3 Center-justify the heading.

See Figure 5-49.

4 Add material specifications as shown in Figure 5-50.

In this example a material specification of SAE 1020 was added. SAE 1020 is a type of mild steel.

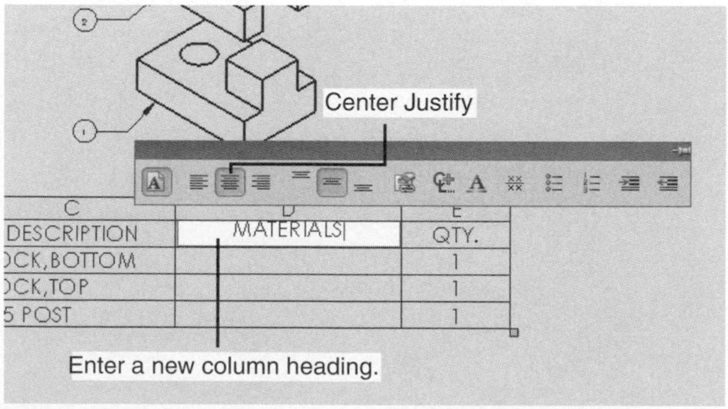

Figure 5-49

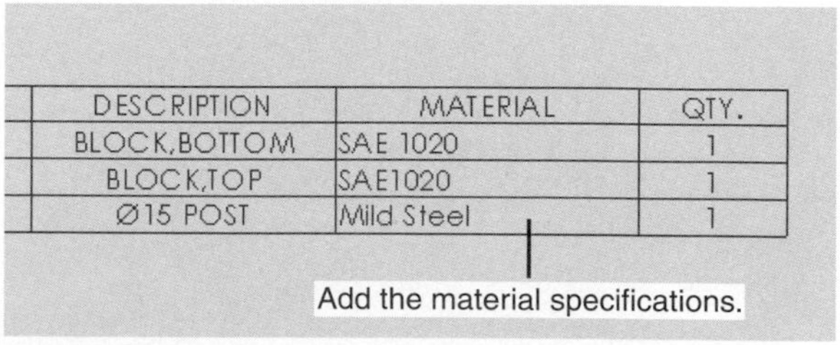

Figure 5-50

The **Formatting** tool can be used to change the row height as well as the column width. The text font can also be changed. In Figure 5-51 the font of the column heads was changed from the default SolidWorks font Century Gothic to Times New Roman and made bold.

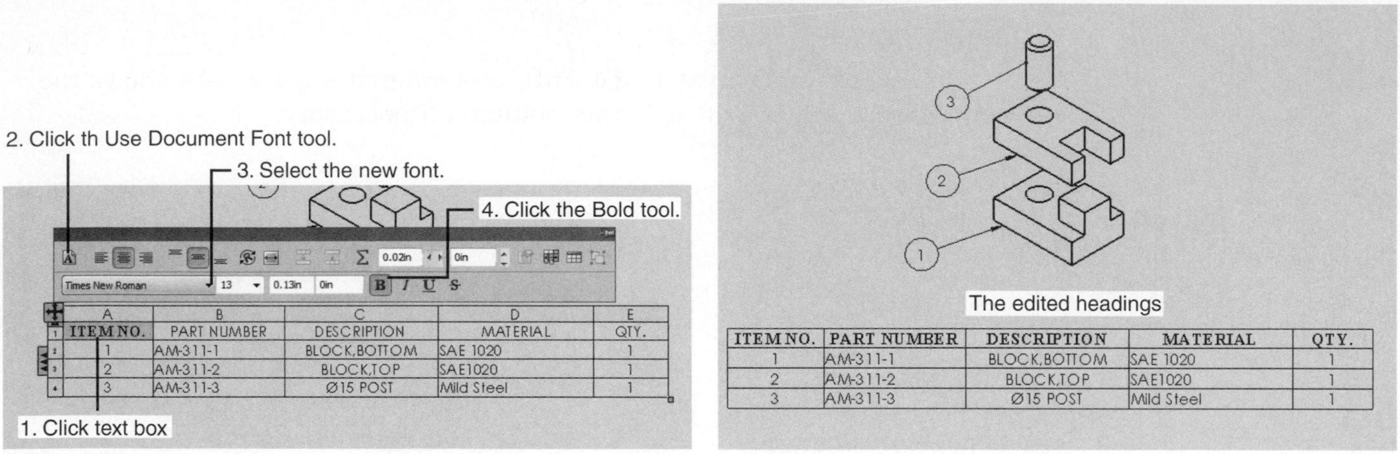

Figure 5-51

To Change Font

1 Click the text to be changed.

2 Click the **Use Document Font** tool

3 Highlight the text, and select a new font.

4 Click the **Bold (B)** tool.

5-11 Title Blocks

A title block contains information about the drawing. See Figure 5-52. The information presented in a title block varies from company to company but usually includes the company's name, the drawing name and part number, the drawing scale, and a revision letter.

Revision Letters

As a drawing goes through its production cycle, changes are sometimes made. The changes may be because of errors but they may also be be-

Figure 5-52

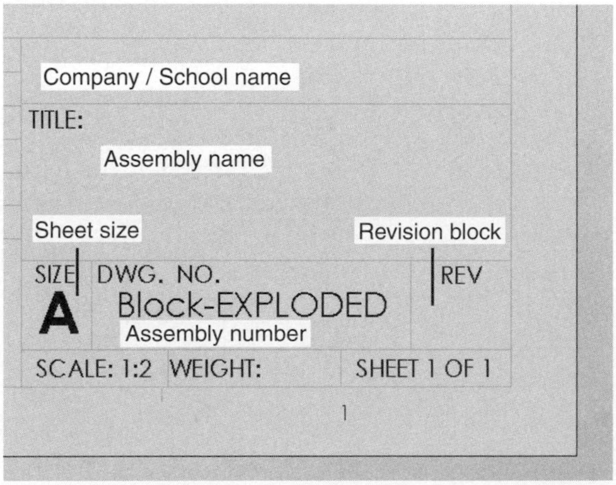

cause of the availability of new materials, manufacturing techniques, or new customer requirements. As the changes are incorporated onto the drawing, a new revision letter is added to the drawing.

To Edit a Title Block

See Figure 5-53.

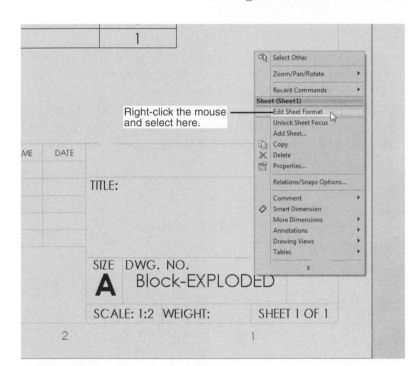

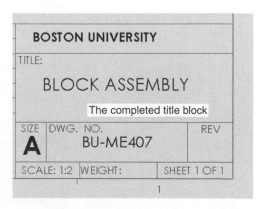

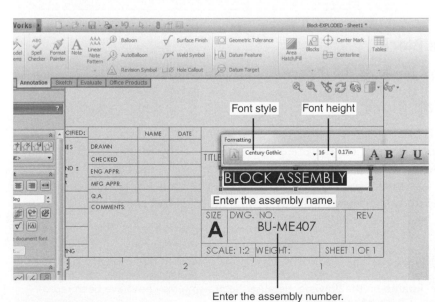

Figure 5-53

1 Right-click the mouse and select the **Edit Sheet Format** option.

2 Click the **Block-EXPLODED** file name.

The **Formatting** dialog box will appear.

3 Change the **DWG. NO.** to **BU-ME407**.

4 Click the **Annotation** tab, locate the note within the title, and enter the drawing name (**BLOCK ASSEMBLY**).

In this example the font height was changed to 16.

5 Use the **Note** tool to add the company name.

In this example "Boston University" was added. Consider using your own school or company name.

Release Blocks

A finished engineering drawing is a legal document that goes through a release process before it becomes final. The release block documents the release process. For example, once you have completed a drawing, you will initial and date the **DRAWN** box located just to the left of the title block. The drawing will then go to a checker, who, after reviewing and incorporating any changes, will sign and date the **CHECKED** box. See Figure 5-54.

Figure 5-54

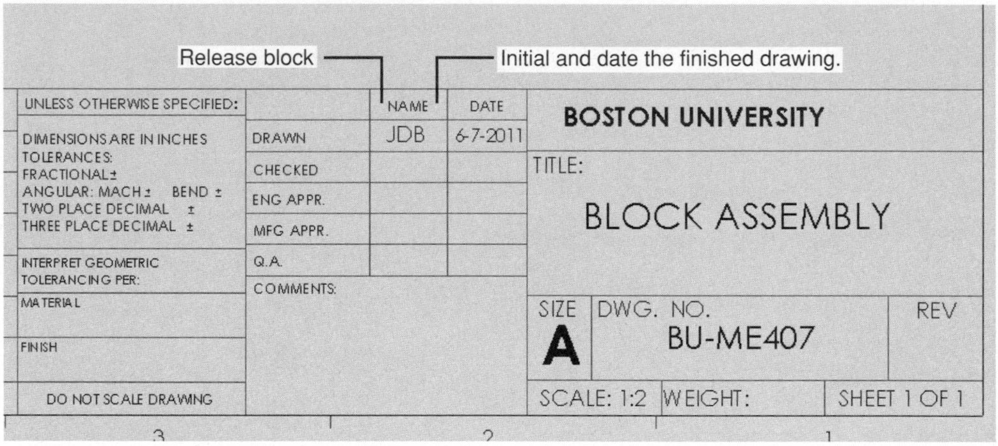

Tolerance Block

The tolerance block will be discussed in Chapter 8, Tolerances.

Application Block

See Figure 5-55.

This block is used to reference closely related drawings. In this example, we know that the block assembly will be used on assembly ME-312A and that it was also used on EK131-46. This information makes it easier to access related drawings that can be checked for interfaces.

> **NOTE**
>
> The note "DO NOT SCALE DRAWING" located at the bottom of the tolerance block is a reminder not to measure the views on the drawing. If a dimension is missing, do not measure the distance on the drawing, because the drawing may not have been reproduced at exactly 100% of the original.

Figure 5-55

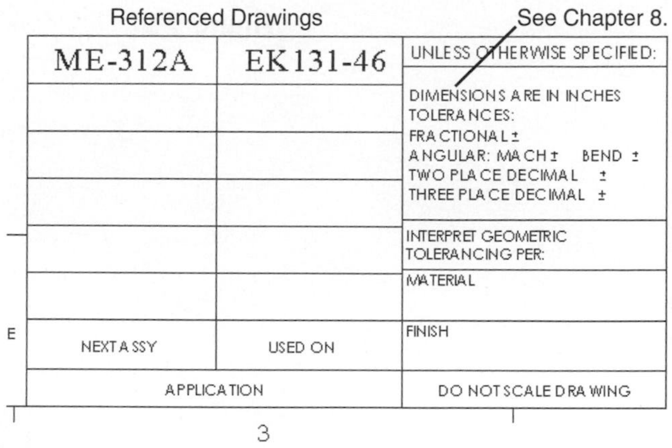

Referenced Drawings		See Chapter 8.
ME-312A	EK131-46	UNLESS OTHERWISE SPECIFIED:
		DIMENSIONS ARE IN INCHES TOLERANCES: FRACTIONAL ± ANGULAR: MACH ± BEND ± TWO PLACE DECIMAL ± THREE PLACE DECIMAL ±
		INTERPRET GEOMETRIC TOLERANCING PER:
		MATERIAL
NEXT ASSY	USED ON	FINISH
APPLICATION		DO NOT SCALE DRAWING

3

5-12 Animate Collapse

Exploded Assembly drawings can be animated. In this example the **Animate collapse** tool will be used.

1 Open the block assembly.

2 Right-click the **BLOCK ASSEMBLY** heading in the **FeatureManager.**

See Figure 5-56.

Figure 5-56

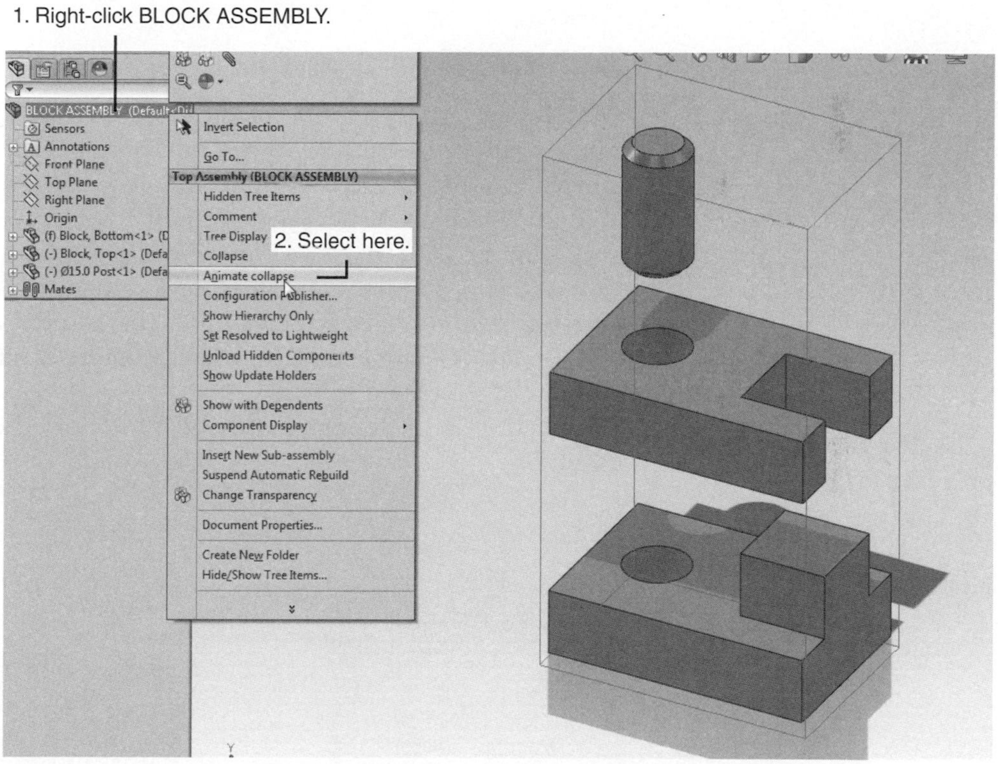

1. Right-click BLOCK ASSEMBLY.

2. Select here.

3 Click the **Animate collapse** option.

The assembly will automatically be animated and start to move. See Figure 5-57.

4 Click the **Stop** button to stop the animation and return the assembly to the exploded position.

5 Close the **Animation Controller.**

Figure 5-57

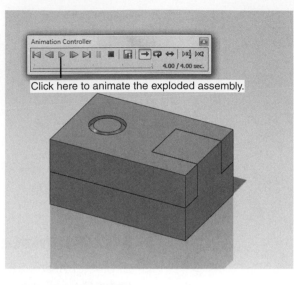

In this example the **Animate collapse** tool was used because the assembly was shown in the exploded position. Had the assembly been in a closed assembled position, the **Animate explode** option would have been used.

5-13 Motion Study

The **Motion Study** tool is used to animate an assembly. Animating an assembly allows the viewer to see and better understand how an assembly moves. The **Motion Study** tool will also display any interferences in the motion. There are four types of motion available: motor, spring, contact, and gravity.

Figure 5-58 shows the **MotionManager.** It is accessed by clicking the **Motion Study** tab at the bottom of the screen. Additional motion studies may be added by clicking the **New Motion Study** tool at the top of the screen.

Section 5-12 demonstrates how to apply the **Motion Study** tool to an assembly.

Figure 5-58

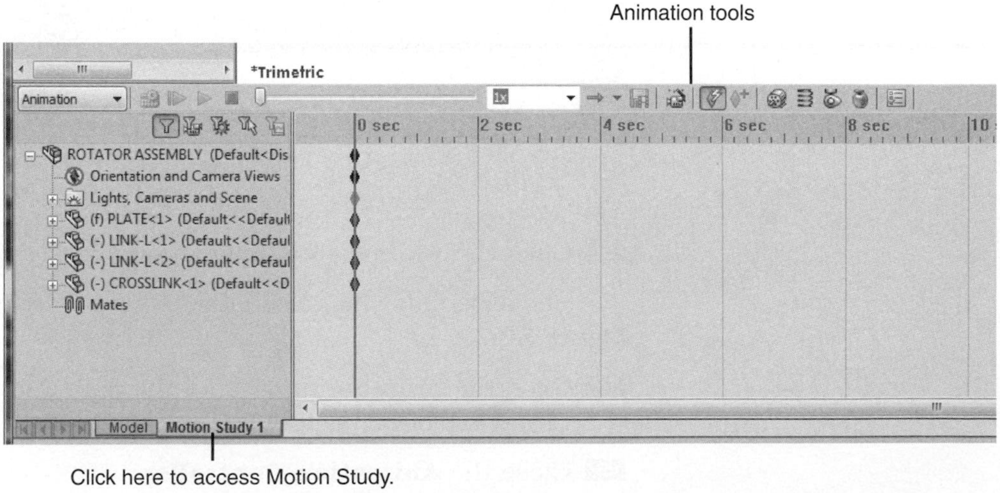

5-14 Sample Problem 5-1: Creating the Rotator Assembly

Figure 5-59 shows the components for the Rotator Assembly. The dimensions for the components can be found in Project P5-10 at the end of the chapter. Draw and save the four Rotator Assembly components as **Part** documents.

1 Start a new **Assembly** document.

2 Insert the PLATE, CROSSLINK and two LINK-Ls into the drawing.

> **NOTE**
> Insert the PLATE first so it will be fixed (f).

Figure 5-59

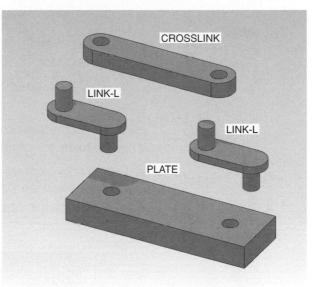

3 Click the **Mate** tool.

4 Click the **Concentric** tool.

5 Click the side of the bottom post of one LINK-L and the inside of the left hole in the PLATE.

See Figure 5-60. The LINK-L and PLATE will align.

> **TIP**
> Click the surfaces of the posts and holes. Do not click the edge lines.

6 Click the OK check mark.

7 Click the **Mate** tool.

8 Click the top surface of the PLATE and the bottom surface of the LINK-L.

See Figure 5-61. Use the **Rotate View** tool to manipulate the view orientation so that the bottom surface of the LINK-L is visible. The part

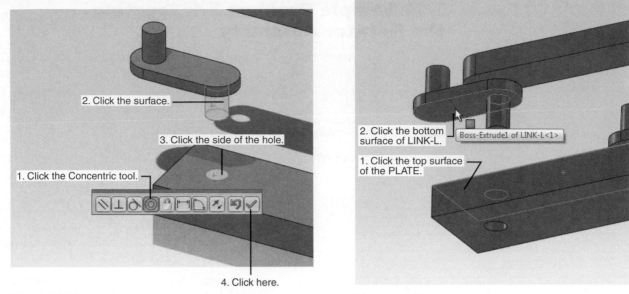

Figure 5-60

Figure 5-61

also can be rotated by holding down the mouse wheel and moving the cursor.

9 Click the **Distance** box and enter a value. In this example a value of **2.0mm** was entered.

See Figure 5-62. The initial offset values may be in inches. Enter the new value of 2.00 followed by **mm,** and the system will automatically change to metric (millimeter) distances.

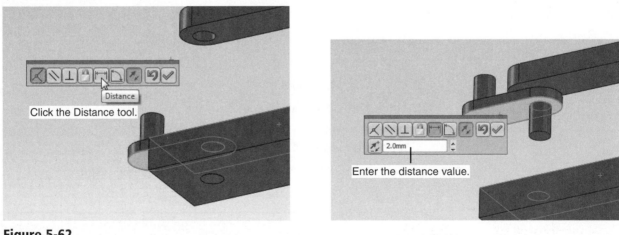

Figure 5-62

10 Click the OK check mark twice.

Figure 5-63 shows the 2-mm offset between the PLATE and the LINK-L.

11 Return the drawing to the **Isometric** orientation.

12 Repeat the procedure for the other LINK-L.

See Figure 5-64.

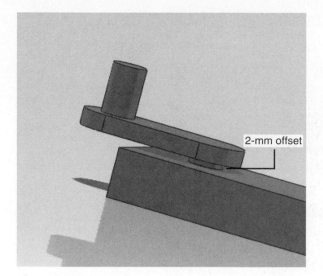

Figure 5-63

Figure 5-64

13 Access the **Mate** tool and use the **Concentric** tool to align the top post of the first LINK-L with the left hole in the CROSSLINK.

14 Use the **Mate** tool and click the top surface of the LINK-L's post and the top surface of the CROSSLINK.

See Figure 5-65.

15 Click the OK check mark.

16 Access the **Mate** tool, click the **Concentric** tool, and align the right hole in the CROSSLINK with the post on the second LINK-L.

See Figure 5-66.

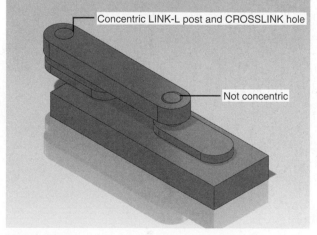

Figure 5-65

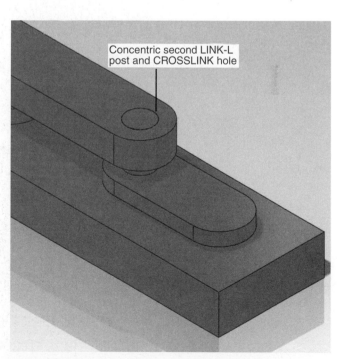

Figure 5-66

17 Locate the cursor on the CROSSLINK and move it around.

The CROSSLINK and two LINK-Ls should rotate about the PLATE.

18 Save the Rotator Assembly.

> **TIP**
> All mates will be listed in the **FeatureManager**.

5-15 Using the SolidWorks Motion Study Tool

1 Access the Rotator Assembly

2 Click the **Mate** tool, then click the **Parallel** tool.

3 Make the front surface line of the CROSSLINK parallel to the front edge of the PLATE.

This step will assure that the CROSSLINK rotates in an orientation parallel to the front edge of the PLATE. See Figure 5-67.

4 Click the **Motion Study** tab at the bottom of the screen.

See Figure 5-68.

Figure 5-67

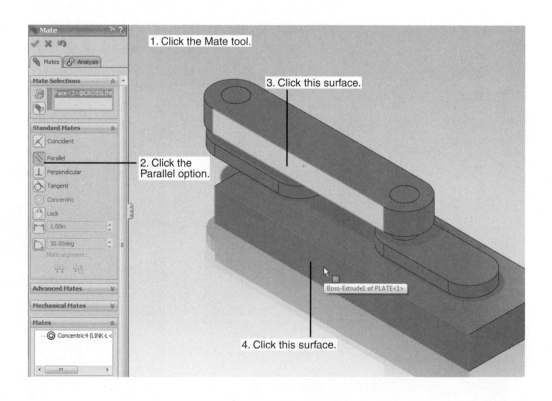

5 Click the **Motor** tool.

The **Motor PropertyManager** box will appear.

See Figure 5-69.

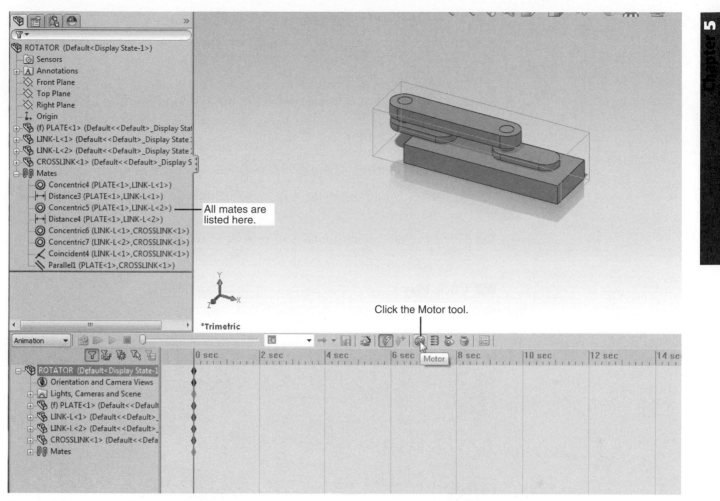

Click the Motor tool.

Figure 5-68

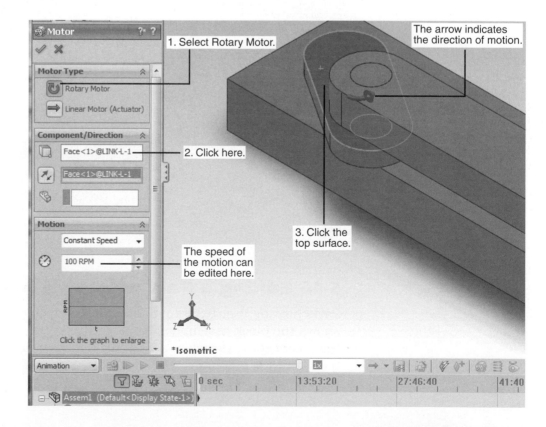

1. Select Rotary Motor.

The arrow indicates the direction of motion.

2. Click here.

3. Click the top surface.

The speed of the motion can be edited here.

Figure 5-69

6 Click the **Rotary Motor** tool.

7 Click the box under the **Component/Direction** heading, then click the top surface of the left LINK-L.

The left LINK-L is now the driver link. An arrow will appear indicating the direction of motion. It will drive the other components.

Motion

1 Go to the **Motion** box and define the assembly's motion.

In this example the default values of **Constant Speed** and **100 RPM** were accepted.

2 Click the OK check mark and return to the **MotionManager.**

See Figure 5-70.

3 Click **Play**.

Figure 5-70

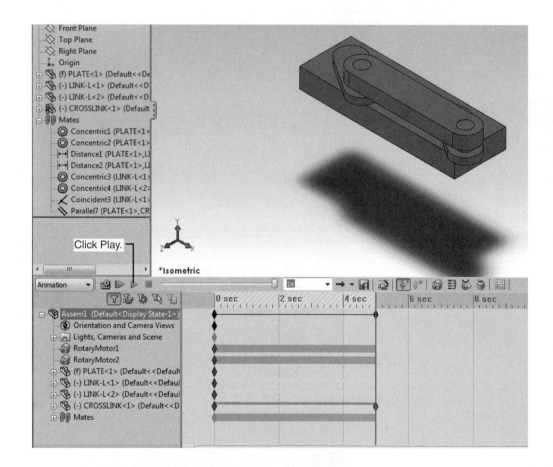

5-16 Editing a Part within an Assembly

Parts already inserted into an assembly drawing can be edited. Figure 5-71 shows the block assembly created earlier in the chapter. The general operating concept is to isolate a part, make the changes, and insert the part back into the assembly.

1 Right-click the **Block, Top.**

Say we wanted to change the hole in the top block.

2 Click the plus sign to the left of the **Block, Top** heading in the **FeatureManager.**

3 Click the **+ sign** to the left of **Cut-Extrusion 1** under the **Block, Top** heading in the **FeatureManager.**

In this example the **Cut-Extrusion 1** is the hole in the top block. See Figure 5-72.

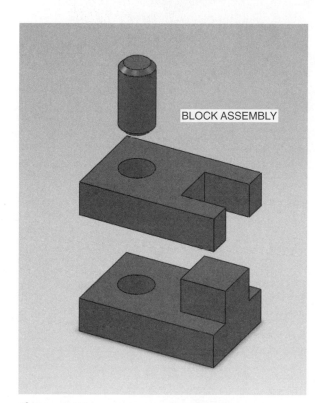

Figure 5-71

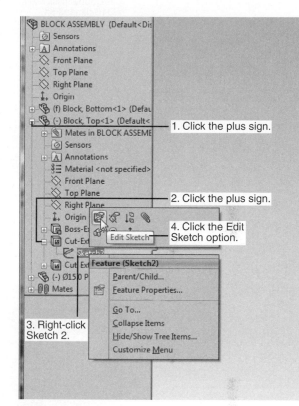

Figure 5-72

4 Right-click the **Sketch2** heading and click the **Edit Sketch** option.

5 Double-click the **Ø15** hole value and enter a new value.

In this example, the value was changed to **Ø20.0.** See Figure 5-73.

6 Click the OK check mark.

7 Click the **Exit Sketch** option.

8 Click the **Edit Assembly** tool located in the upper right corner of the drawing screen.

Figure 5-73

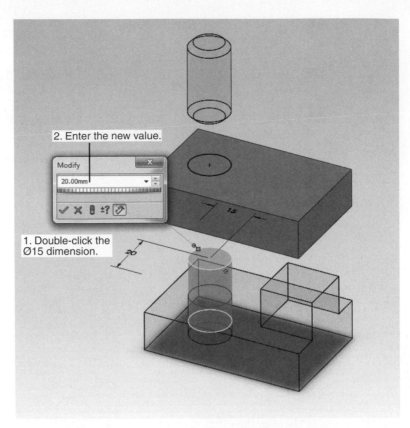

2. Enter the new value.

Modify

20.00mm

1. Double-click the Ø15 dimension.

15

Figure 5-74

The Edit Assembly tool

The edited assembly

Chapter Projects

Project 5-1:

Create a **Part** document of the SQBLOCK using the given dimensions. Create assemblies using two SQBLOCKS, positioning the blocks as shown in Figures P5-1A through P5-1G.

Pages 262 through 264 show a group of parts. These parts are used to create the assemblies presented as problems in this section. Use the given descriptions, part numbers, and materials when creating BOMs for the assemblies.

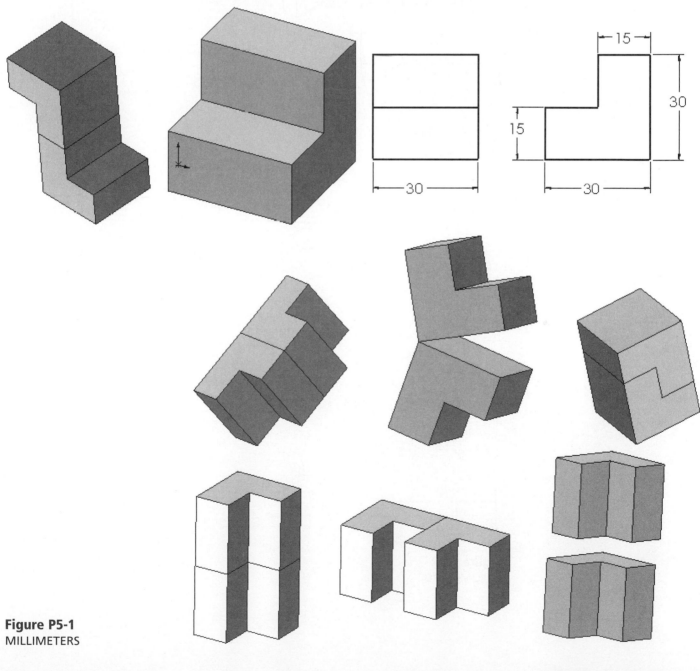

Figure P5-1
MILLIMETERS

Project 5-2:

Redraw the following models and save them as **Standard (mm).ipn** files. All dimensions are in millimeters.

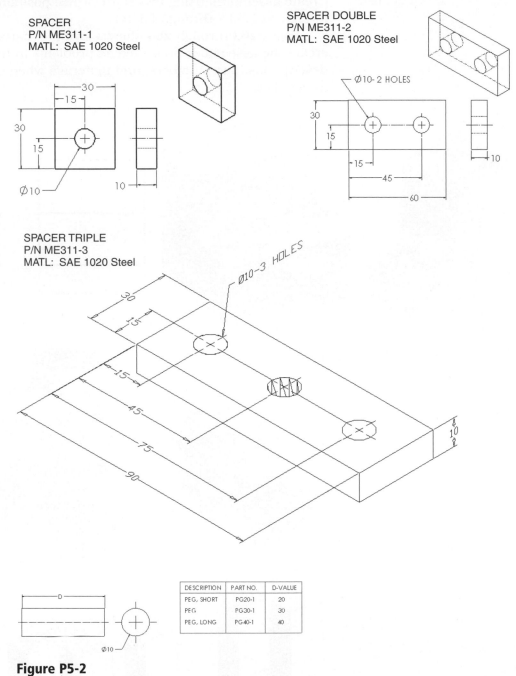

SPACER
P/N ME311-1
MATL: SAE 1020 Steel

SPACER DOUBLE
P/N ME311-2
MATL: SAE 1020 Steel

Ø10- 2 HOLES

SPACER TRIPLE
P/N ME311-3
MATL: SAE 1020 Steel

Ø10-3 HOLES

DESCRIPTION	PART NO.	D-VALUE
PEG, SHORT	PG20-1	20
PEG	PG30-1	30
PEG, LONG	PG40-1	40

Figure P5-2
MILLIMETERS

PEGS
MATL: Steel

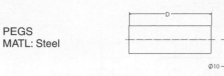

DESCRIPTION	PART NO.	D-VALUE
PEG, SHORT	PG20-1	20
PEG	PG30-1	30
PEG, LONG	PG40-1	40

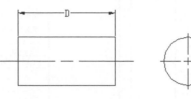

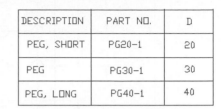

DESCRIPTION	PART NO.	D
PEG, SHORT	PG20-1	20
PEG	PG30-1	30
PEG, LONG	PG40-1	40

ALL DISTANCES IN MILLIMETERS

L-BRACKET
P/N BK20-1
MATL: SAE 1040 Steel

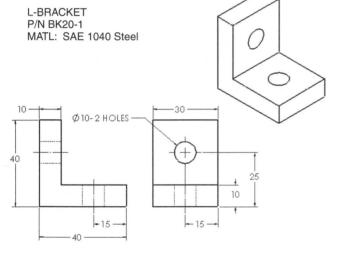

Z-BRACKET
P/N BK20-2
MATL: SAE 1040 Steel

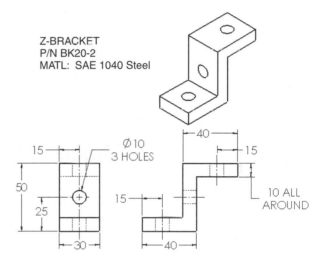

C-BRACKET
P/N BK20-3
MATL: SAE 1040 Steel

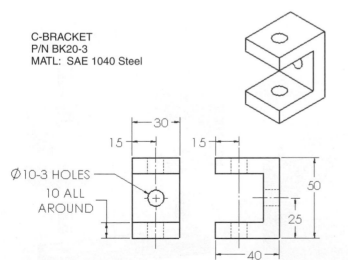

PLATE, QUAD
P/N ME311-4
MATL: SAE 1020 Steel

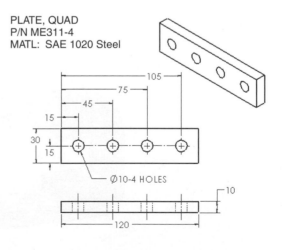

Figure P5-2
(*Continued*)

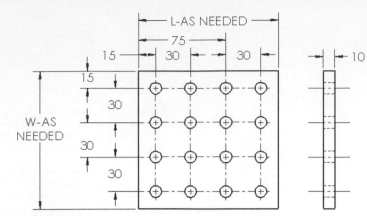

Figure P5-2
(*Continued*)

PART NO.	TOTAL NO. OF HOLES	L	W	HOLE PATTERN
PL110-9	9	90	90	3×3
PL110-16	16	120	120	4×4
PL110-6	6	60	90	2×3
PL110-8	8	60	120	2×4
PL110-4	4	60	60	2×2

Project 5-3:

Draw an exploded isometric assembly drawing of Assembly 1. Create a BOM.

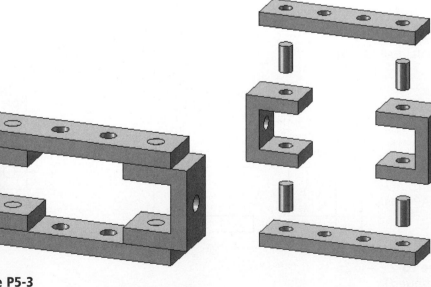

Figure P5-3
MILLIMETERS

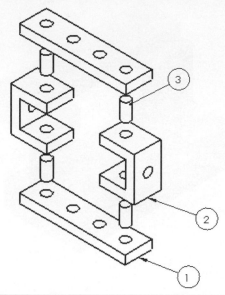

ITEM NO.	PART NUMBER	DESCRIPTION	QTY.
1	ME311-4	PLATE, QUAD	2
2	BK20-3	C-BRACKET	2
3	PG20-1	Ø12×20 PEG	4

Project 5-4:

Draw an exploded isometric assembly drawing of Assembly 2. Create a BOM.

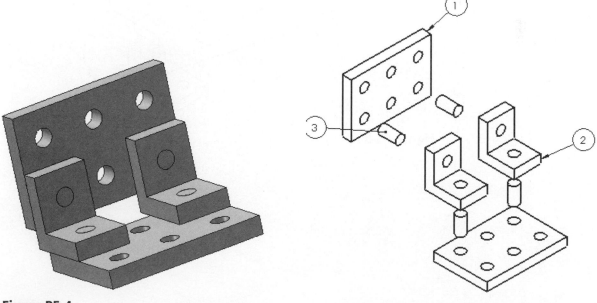

Figure P5-4
MILLIMETERS

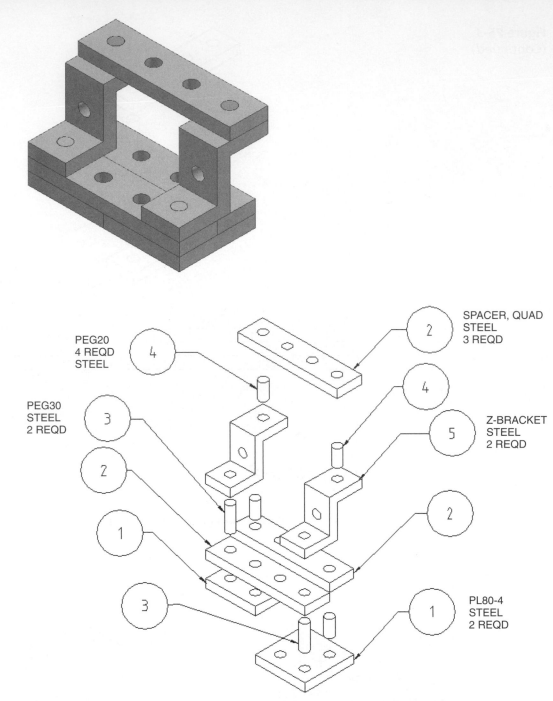

PEG20
4 REQD
STEEL

PEG30
STEEL
2 REQD

SPACER, QUAD
STEEL
3 REQD

Z-BRACKET
STEEL
2 REQD

PL80-4
STEEL
2 REQD

Figure P5-5

Project 5-6:

Draw an exploded isometric assembly drawing of Assembly 3. Create a BOM.

Figure P5-6
MILLIMETERS

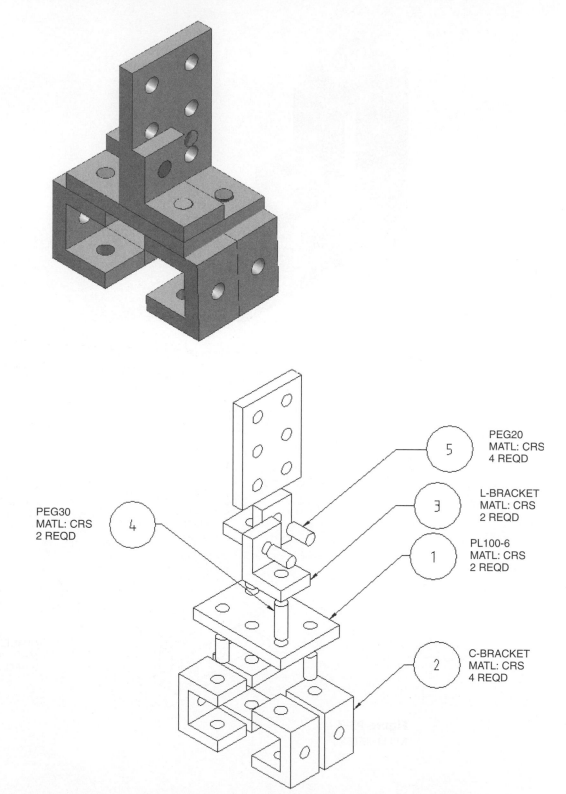

PEG20
MATL: CRS
4 REQD

L-BRACKET
MATL: CRS
2 REQD

PL100-6
MATL: CRS
2 REQD

PEG30
MATL: CRS
2 REQD

C-BRACKET
MATL: CRS
4 REQD

Project 5-7:

Draw an exploded isometric assembly drawing of Assembly 4. Create a BOM.

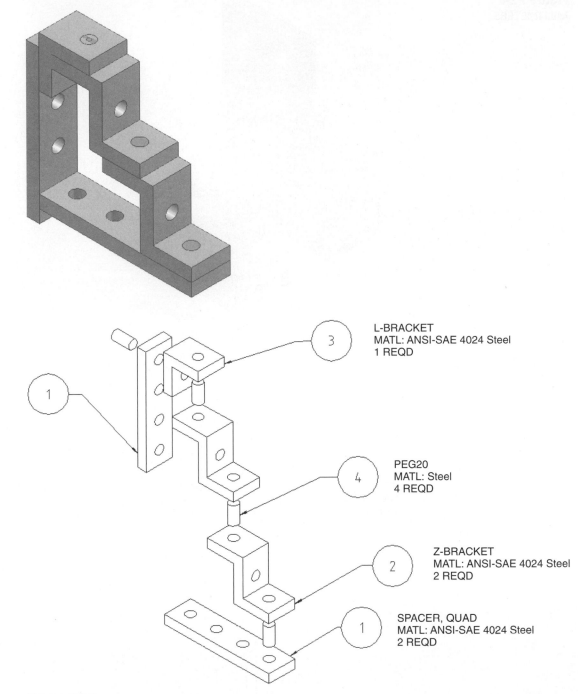

Figure P5-7
MILLIMETERS

Project 5-8:

Draw an exploded isometric assembly drawing of Assembly 5. Create a BOM.

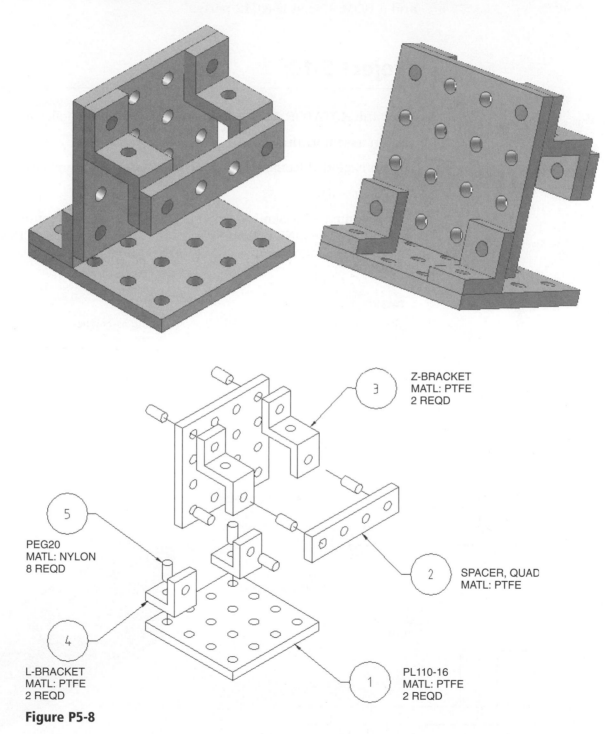

Figure P5-8

Project 5-9:

Create an original assembly based on the parts shown on pages 262–264.
Include a scene, an exploded isometric drawing with assembly numbers,
and a BOM. Use at least 12 parts.

Project 5-10:

Draw the ROTATOR ASSEMBLY shown. Include the following:

A. An assembly drawing

B. An exploded isometric drawing with assembly numbers

C. A parts list

D. An animated assembly drawing; the LINKs should rotate relative to the
   PLATE. The LINKs should carry the CROSSLINK. The CROSSLINK
   should remain parallel during the rotation.

> **NOTE**
> This assembly was used in the section on animating assemblies. See page 253.

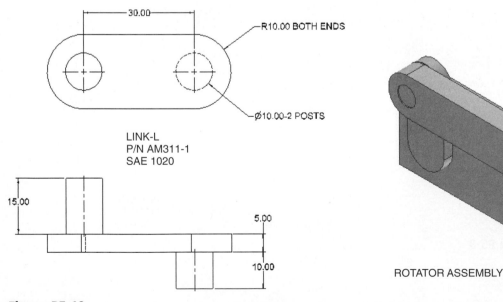

30.00

R10.00 BOTH ENDS

Ø10.00-2 POSTS

LINK-L
P/N AM311-1
SAE 1020

15.00

5.00

10.00

ROTATOR ASSEMBLY

Figure P5-10

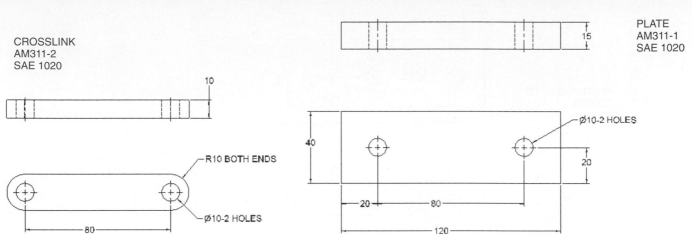

CROSSLINK
AM311-2
SAE 1020

PLATE
AM311-1
SAE 1020

10

R10 BOTH ENDS

Ø10-2 HOLES

80

40

Ø10-2 HOLES

20

20 — 80

120

15

Figure P5-10
(*Continued*)

Project 5-11:

Draw the FLY ASSEMBLY shown. Include the following:

A. An assembly drawing

B. An exploded isometric drawing with assembly numbers

C. A parts list

D. An animated assembly drawing; the FLYLINK should rotate around the SUPPORT base.

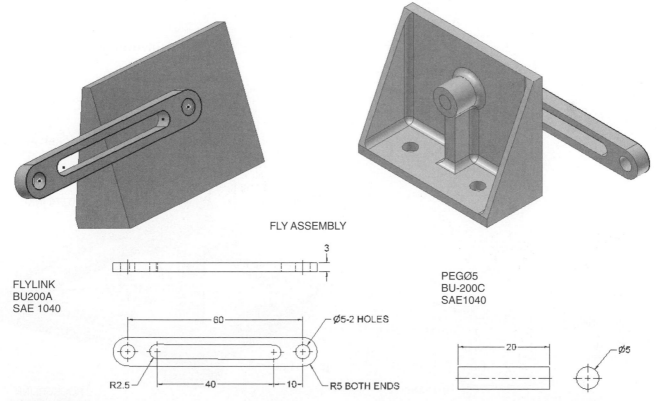

FLY ASSEMBLY

FLYLINK
BU200A
SAE 1040

3

60

Ø5-2 HOLES

R2.5

40

10

R5 BOTH ENDS

PEGØ5
BU-200C
SAE1040

20

Ø5

Figure P5-11

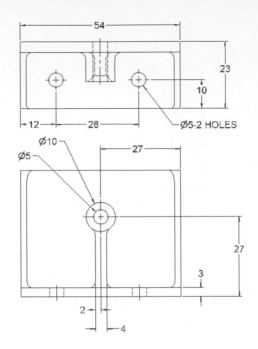

PLATE,SUPPORT
BU200B
SAE 1040

R2.0 FOR ALL FILLETS AND ROUNDS

Figure P5-11
(*Continued*)

Project 5-12:

Draw the ROCKER ASSEMBLY shown. Include the following:

A. An assembly drawing

B. An exploded isometric drawing with assemblynumbers

C. A parts list

D. An animated assembly drawing

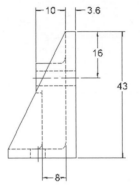

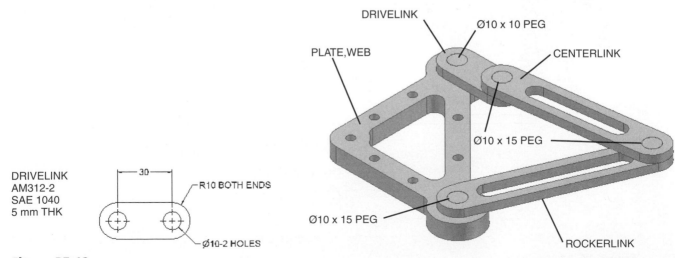

DRIVELINK
AM312-2
SAE 1040
5 mm THK

Figure P5-12

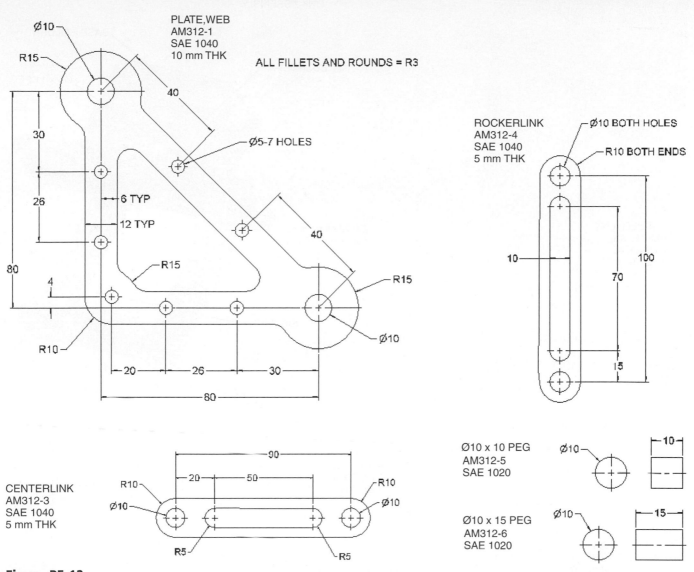

PLATE,WEB
AM312-1
SAE 1040
10 mm THK

ALL FILLETS AND ROUNDS = R3

Ø10
R15
30
26
80
4
R10
6 TYP
12 TYP
R15
40
Ø5-7 HOLES
40
R15
Ø10
20
26
30
80

ROCKERLINK
AM312-4
SAE 1040
5 mm THK

Ø10 BOTH HOLES
R10 BOTH ENDS
10
100
70
15

CENTERLINK
AM312-3
SAE 1040
5 mm THK

90
20
50
R10
R10
Ø10
Ø10
R5
R5

Ø10 x 10 PEG
AM312-5
SAE 1020

Ø10
10

Ø10 x 15 PEG
AM312-6
SAE 1020

Ø10
15

Figure P5-12
(*Continued*)

Project 5-13:

Draw the LINK ASSEMBLY shown. Include the following:

A. An assembly drawing

B. An exploded isometric drawing with assembly numbers

C. A parts list

C. An animated assembly drawing; the HOLDER ARM should rotate between –30° and +30°.

LINK ASSEMBLY

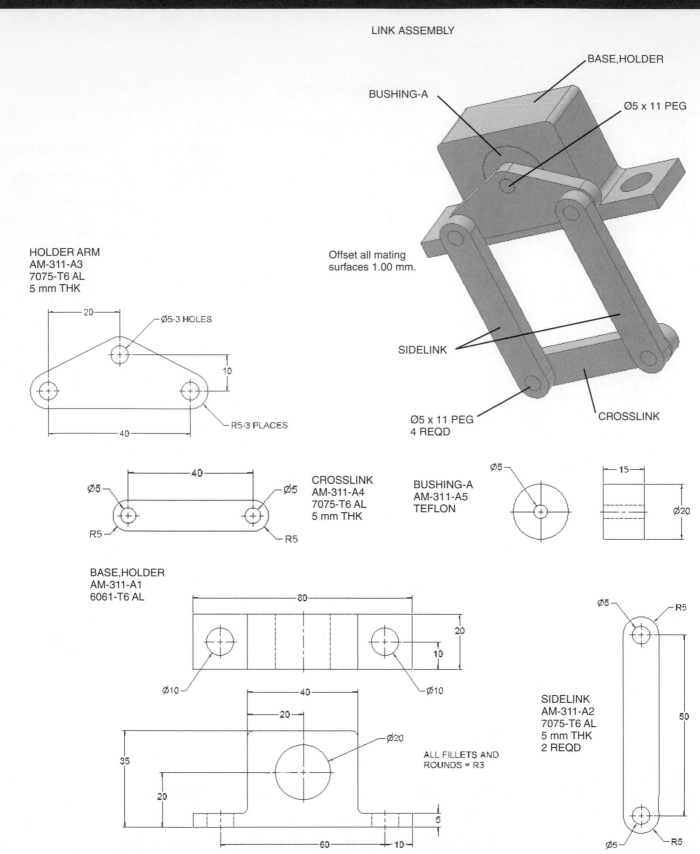

BASE,HOLDER

BUSHING-A

Ø5 x 11 PEG

HOLDER ARM
AM-311-A3
7075-T6 AL
5 mm THK

Offset all mating
surfaces 1.00 mm.

Ø5-3 HOLES

20

10

40

R5-3 PLACES

SIDELINK

Ø5 x 11 PEG
4 REQD

CROSSLINK

CROSSLINK
AM-311-A4
7075-T6 AL
5 mm THK

40

Ø5

Ø5

R5

R5

BUSHING-A
AM-311-A5
TEFLON

Ø5

15

Ø20

BASE,HOLDER
AM-311-A1
6061-T6 AL

80

20

10

Ø10

Ø10

40

20

Ø20

35

20

ALL FILLETS AND
ROUNDS = R3

60

10

5

SIDELINK
AM-311-A2
7075-T6 AL
5 mm THK
2 REQD

Ø5

R5

50

Ø5

R5

Figure P5-13

Project 5-14:

Draw the PIVOT ASSEMBLY shown using the dimensioned components given. Include the following:

A. A 3D exploded isometric drawing

B. A parts list

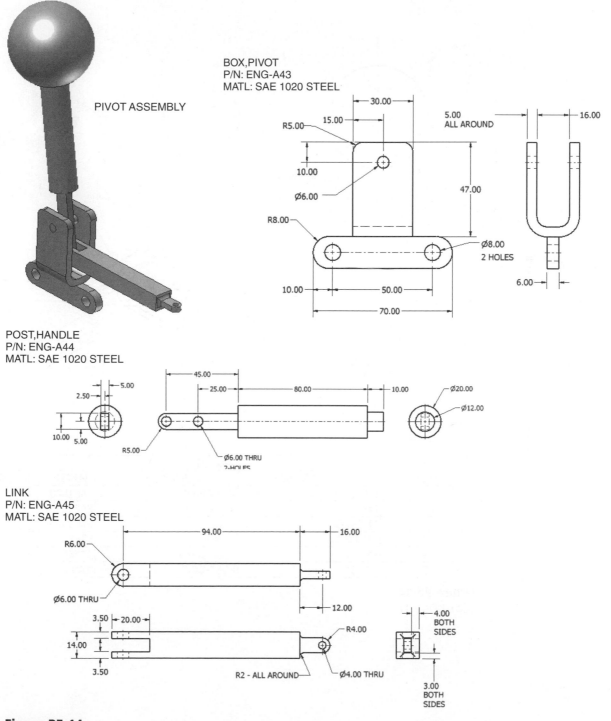

PIVOT ASSEMBLY

BOX,PIVOT
P/N: ENG-A43
MATL: SAE 1020 STEEL

POST,HANDLE
P/N: ENG-A44
MATL: SAE 1020 STEEL

LINK
P/N: ENG-A45
MATL: SAE 1020 STEEL

Figure P5-14
MILLIMETERS

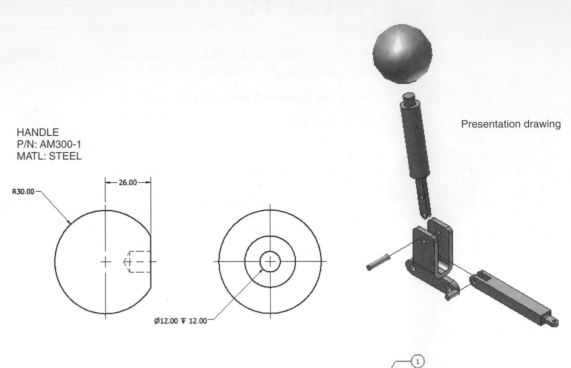

HANDLE
P/N: AM300-1
MATL: STEEL

R30.00

26.00

Ø12.00 ▼ 12.00

Presentation drawing

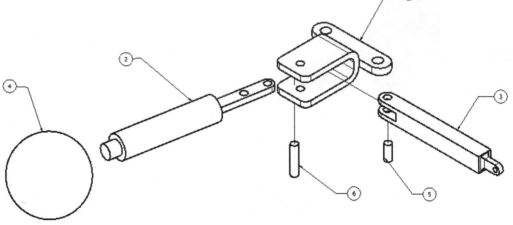

Parts List				
ITEM	PART NUMBER	DESCRIPTION	MATERIAL	QTY
1	ENG-A43	BOX,PIVOT	SAE1020	1
2	ENG-A44	POST,HANDLE	SAE1020	1
3	ENG-A45	LINK	SAE1020	1
4	AM300-1	HANDLE	STEEL	1
5	EK-132	POST-Ø6x14	STEEL	1
6	EK-131	POST-Ø6x26	STEEL	1

Figure P5-14
(*Continued*)

6

chaptersix

Threads and Fasteners

CHAPTER OBJECTIVES

- Learn thread terminology and conventions
- Learn how to draw threads
- Learn how to size both internal and external threads

- Learn how to use standard-sized threads
- Learn how to use and size washers, nuts, and setscrews

6-1 Introduction

This chapter explains how to draw threads, washers, and nuts. It also explains how to select fasteners, washers, nuts, and setscrews.

Internal threads are created using the **Hole Wizard** tool, which is located on the **Features** toolbar. Predrawn fasteners and other standard components may be accessed using the **Design Library.** See Figure 6-1.

> **NOTE**
> The **Design Library** is accessed through a tab in the Task Pane.

All threads in this book are in compliance with ANSI (American National Standards Institute) standards—ANSI Inch and ANSI Metric threads.

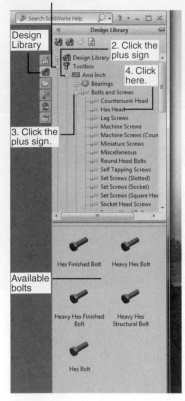

1. Click the plus sign.

2. Click the plus sign

4. Click here.

3. Click the plus sign.

Available bolts

Figure 6-1

6-2 Thread Terminology

Figure 6-2 shows a thread. The peak of a thread is called the **crest,** and the valley portion is called the **root.** The **major diameter** of a thread is the distance across the thread from crest to crest. The **minor diameter** is the distance across the thread from root to root.

The **pitch** of a thread is the linear distance along the thread from crest to crest. Thread pitch is usually referred to in terms of a unit of length such as 20 threads per inch or 1.6 threads per millimeter.

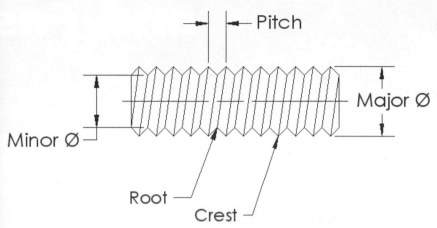

Pitch

Major Ø

Minor Ø

Root

Crest

Figure 6-2

6-3 Thread Callouts—Metric Units

Threads are specified on a drawing using drawing callouts. See Figure 6-3. The M at the beginning of a drawing callout specifies that the callout is for a metric thread. Holes that are not threaded use the Ø symbol.

M10 × 30

Thread length

Major Ø

Figure 6-3

M10 × 1.5 × 30

Thread Pitch

Generally omitted for coarse threads

The number following the M is the major diameter of the thread. An M10 thread has a major diameter of 10 mm. The pitch of a metric thread is assumed to be a coarse thread unless otherwise stated. The callout M10 × 30 assumes a coarse thread, or a thread length of 1.5 mm per thread. The number 30 is the thread length in millimeters. The "×" is read as "by," so the thread is called a "ten by thirty."

The callout M10 × 1.25 × 30 specifies a pitch of 1.25 mm per thread. This is not a standard coarse thread size, so the pitch must be specified.

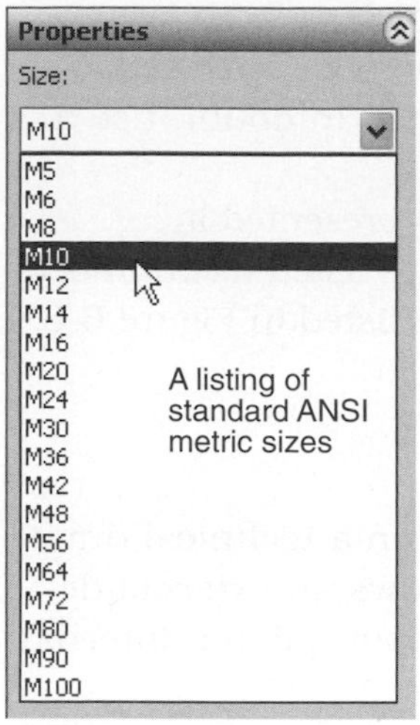

Figure 6-4

Figure 6-4 shows a listing standard metric thread sizes available in the SolidWorks **Design Library** for one type of hex head bolt. The sizes are in compliance with ANSI Metric specifications.

Whenever possible use preferred thread sizes for designing. Preferred thread sizes are readily available and are usually cheaper than nonstandard sizes. In addition, tooling such as wrenches is also readily available for preferred sizes.

6-4 Thread Callouts—ANSI Unified Screw Threads

ANSI Unified Screw Threads (English units) always include a thread form specification. Thread form specifications are designated by capital letters, as shown in Figure 6-6, and are defined as follows:

UNC—Unified National Coarse

UNF—Unified National Fine

UNEF—Unified National Extra Fine

UN—Unified National, or constant-pitch threads

An ANSI (English units) thread callout starts by defining the major diameter of the thread followed by the pitch specification. The callout .500-13 UNC means a thread whose major diameter is .500 in. with 13 threads per inch. The thread is manufactured to the UNC standards.

There are three possible classes of fit for a thread: 1, 2, and 3. The different class specifications specify a set of manufacturing tolerances. A class 1 thread is the loosest and a class 3 the most exact. A class 2 fit is the most common.

The letter A designates an external thread, B an internal thread. The symbol $\times$ means "by" as in 2 $\times$ 4, "two by four." The thread length (3.00) may be followed by the word LONG to prevent confusion about which value represents the length.

Drawing callouts for ANSI (English unit) threads are sometimes shortened, such as in Figure 6-5. The callout .500-13 UNC-2A $\times$ 3.00 LONG is shortened to .500-13 $\times$ 3.00. Only a coarse thread has 13 threads per inch, and it should be obvious whether a thread is internal or external, so

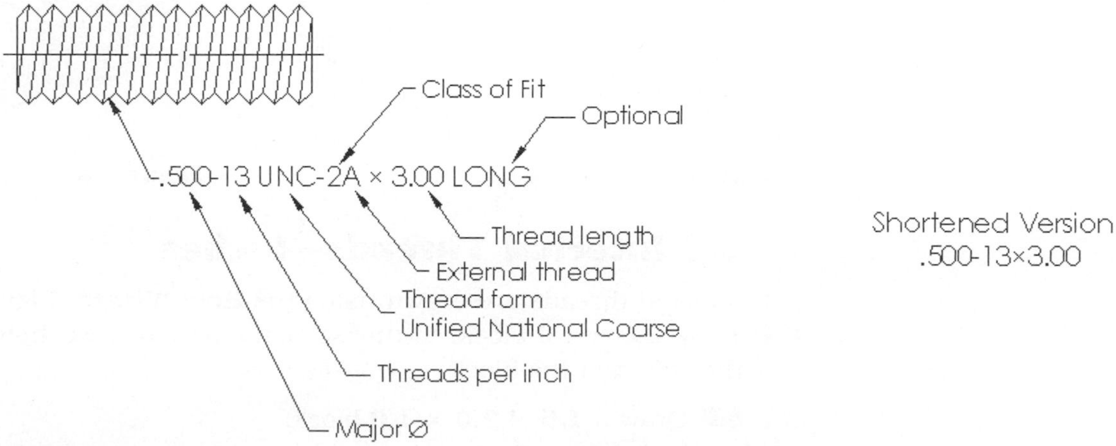

Figure 6-5

Figure 6-6

these specifications may be dropped. Most threads are class 2, so it is tacitly accepted that all threads are class 2 unless otherwise specified. The shortened callout form is not universally accepted. When in doubt, use a complete thread callout.

A listing of standard ANSI (English unit) threads, as presented in SolidWorks, is shown in Figure 6-6. Some of the drill sizes listed use numbers and letters. The decimal equivalents to the numbers are listed in Figure 6-6.

6-5 Thread Representations

There are three ways to graphically represent threads on a technical drawing: detailed, schematic, and simplified. Figure 6-5 shows an external detailed representation, and Figure 6-7 shows both the external and internal simplified and schematic representations.

Figure 6-8 shows an internal and an external thread created using SolidWorks. Note that no thread representations appear. This is called the **Simplified** representation. SolidWorks uses the **Simplified** thread representation as a way to minimize file size. Cosmetic thread representations can be created and will be discussed later in the chapter. Actual threads may be drawn using the **Helix** tool. SolidWorks can also draw a **Schematic** thread representation.

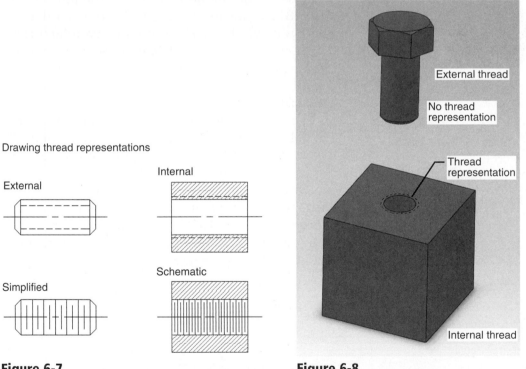

Figure 6-7   **Figure 6-8**

6-6 Internal Threads—Inches

Internal threads are drawn using the **Hole Wizard.** Figure 6-9 shows a 1.5 × 2.0 × 1.0 block. In this section a 3/8-16 UNC hole will be located in the center of the block.

1 Draw a **1.5 × 2.0 × 1.0** block.

2 Orient the block in the **Isometric** view.

3 Click the **Hole Wizard** toolbar on the **Features** toolbar.

4 Define the thread's size and length.

In this example an internal 3/8-16 UNC thread will be created. The thread will go completely through the block. See Figure 6-10.

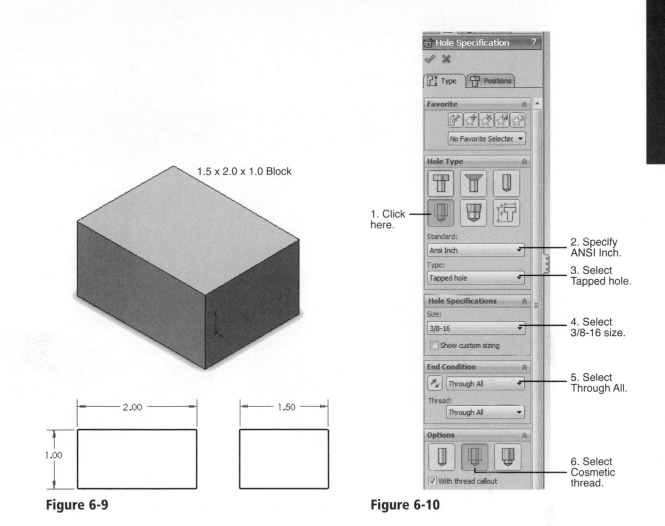

1.5 x 2.0 x 1.0 Block

Figure 6-9

Figure 6-10

5 Select a 3/8-16 thread in the **Hole Specifications** box.

6 Select the **Through All** option in the **End Condition** box.

7 Click the **Cosmetic thread** option.

> **NOTE**
>
> The **Cosmetic thread** option will create a hidden line around the finished hole that serves to indicate that the hole is threaded.

8 Click the **Positions** tab in the **Hole Wizard PropertyManager.**

9 Click a location near the center of the top surface of the block.

See Figure 6-11.

Figure 6-11

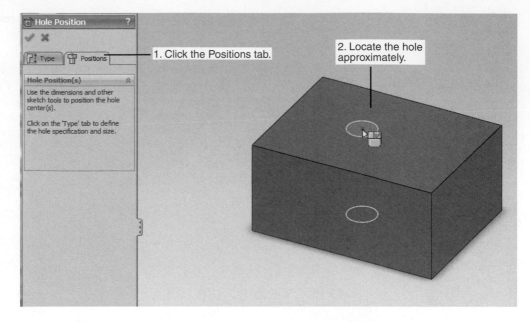

1. Click the Positions tab.

2. Locate the hole approximately.

Use the Smart Dimension tool and locate the hole's center point.

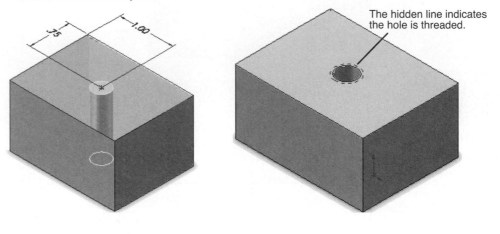

The hidden line indicates the hole is threaded.

10 Use the **Smart Dimension** tool and locate the center point of the hole.

11 Click the OK check mark.

The hidden line surrounding the hole is a cosmetic thread and indicates that the hole is threaded. Note that there are no threads on the inside of the hole.

6-7 Threaded Blind Holes—Inches

A *blind hole* is one that does not go completely though an object. See Figure 6-12.

1 Use the **Undo** tool and remove the hole added to the 1.5 × 2.0 × 1.0 block.

2 Edit the block so that it is **2.00** thick.

3 Click the **Hole Wizard** tool.

4 Size the hole to **3/8-16** and set the **Blind Thread** depth in the **End Condition** box to **1.25in.**

Figure 6-12

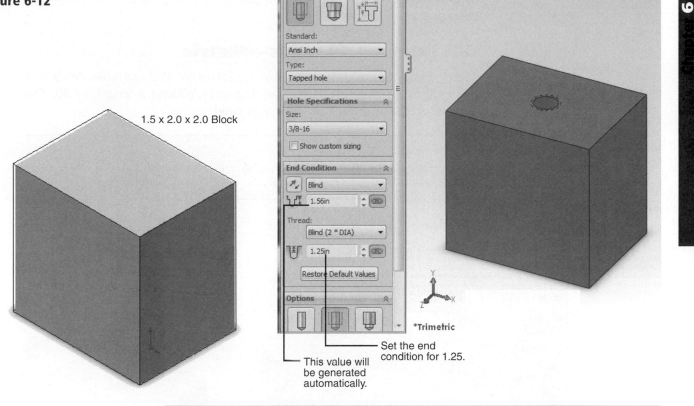

1.5 x 2.0 x 2.0 Block

*Trimetric

Set the end condition for 1.25.

This value will be generated automatically.

NOTE

The tap thread depth is automatically calculated as the hole's thread depth is defined.

In this example the tap thread depth was calculated as 1.56 in.

5 Click the **Positions** tab and locate a center point near the center of the top surface of the block.

6 Use the **Smart Dimension** tool to locate the center point.

7 Click the OK check mark.

Figure 6-13 shows an orthographic view of the block and a section view. Note that the tapping hole extends beyond the end of the threads and

Figure 6-13

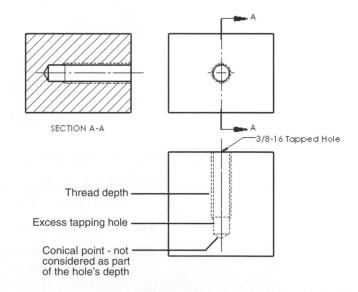

SECTION A-A

3/8-16 Tapped Hole

Thread depth

Excess tapping hole

Conical point - not considered as part of the hole's depth

ends with a conical point. The depth of the tapping hole does not include the conical end point.

6-8 Internal Threads—Metric

Metric threads are designated by the letter M. For example, M10 × 30 is the callout for a metric thread of diameter 10 and a length of 30. The thread is assumed to be a coarse thread.

> **TIP**
> For metric threads drawings the symbol **Ø** indicates a hole or cylinder without threads; the symbol **M** indicates metric threads.

1 Draw a **20 × 30 × 15** block.

See Figure 6-14.

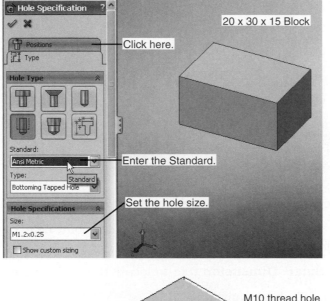

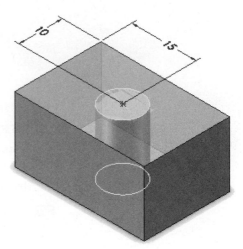
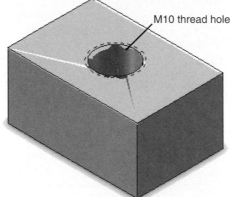

Figure 6-14

2 Click the **Hole Wizard.**

3 Set the **Standard** for **Ansi Metric,** the hole size for **M10 × 1.0,** and the depth for **Through All.**

4 Click the **Cosmetic thread** option.

5 Click the **Positions** tab and locate the center point near the center of the top surface of the block.

6 Use the **Smart Dimension** tool to locate the hole's center point.

7 Click the OK check mark.

6-9 Accessing the Design Library

SolidWorks includes a **Design Library**. The **Design Library** includes a listing of predrawn standard components such as bolts, nuts, and washers. These components may be accessed and inserted into drawings to create assemblies. Figure 6-15 shows how to access hex bolts in the **Design Library**.

Figure 6-15

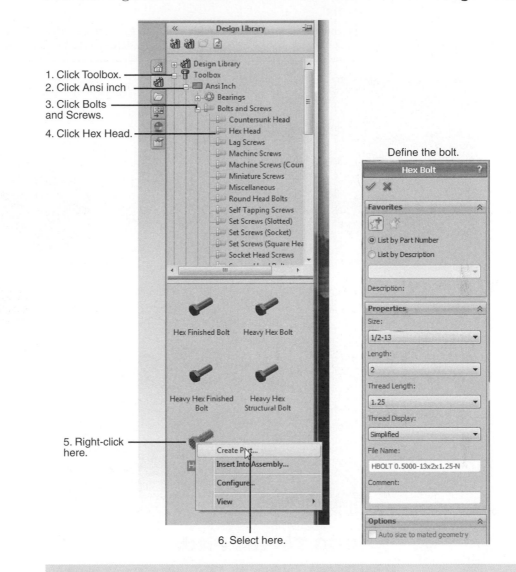

1. Click Toolbox.
2. Click Ansi inch
3. Click Bolts and Screws.
4. Click Hex Head.

Define the bolt.

5. Right-click here.

6. Select here.

NOTE

The **Design Library** is accessed through a tab in the Task Pane.

---

1 Click the **Design Library** tab.

2 Click **Toolbox**.

3 Click **Ansi Inch**.

4 Click **Bolts and Screws**.

5 Click **Hex Head**.

A listing of various types of hex head bolts will appear.

6 Right-click the **Hex Bolt,** and click **Create Part.**

7 Define the needed size and length.

In this example a 1/2-13 UNC × 2.00 HEX HEAD BOLT was created.

8 Define the **Thread Display** style.

9 Click the OK check mark.

> **TIP**
> There are three display styles available for threads: **Schematic, Cosmetic,** and **Simplified.**
> See Figure 6-16. The **Simplified** style was created to use a smaller file size.

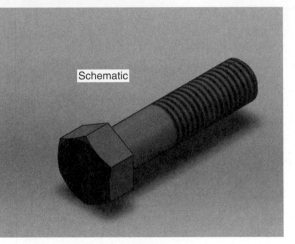

Figure 6-16

6-10 Thread Pitch

Thread pitch for an ANSI Inch fastener is defined as

$$P = \frac{1}{N}$$

where

P = pitch
N = number of threads per inch

In ANSI Inch standards a sample bolt callout is 1/4-20 UNC × length. The 20 value is the number of threads per inch, so the pitch is 1/20 or 0.05. The pitch for a 1/4-28 UNF thread would be 1/28, or 0.036.

A sample thread callout for ANSI Metric is written M10 × 1.0 × 30, where 1.0 is the pitch. No calculation is required to determine the pitch for metric threads. It is included directly in the thread callout.

| M10x1.0 |
| M8x1.25 |
| M8x1.0 |
| M10x1.5 |
| M10x1.0 |
| M10x1.25 |
| M12x1.75 |
| M12x1.25 |
| M12x1.5 |
| M14x1.5 |
| M14x2.0 |
| M16x1.5 |

Different pitch sizes available for M10 thread

Figure 6-17

> **TIP**
> Almost all threads are coarse, so ANSI metric thread callouts omit the pitch designation. A pitch size in included only when a metric thread is not coarse.

Figure 6-17 shows a listing of possible pitch sizes for an M10 thread.

6-11 Determining an External Thread Length—Inches

Figure 6-18 shows three blocks stacked together. Their dimension are given. They are to be held together using a hex bolt, two washers, and a nut. The bolt will be a 3/8-16 UNC. What length should be used?

Figure 6-18

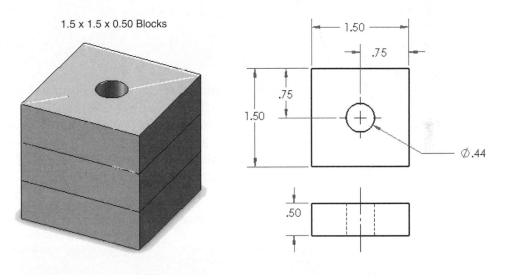

1.5 x 1.5 x 0.50 Blocks

1 Draw a **1.5 × 1.5 × 0.50** block. Draw a **Ø.44** (7/16) hole through the center of the block. Save the block as **BLOCK, BOLT.**

The Ø.44 was selected because it allows for clearance between the bolt and the block.

2 Create an assembly drawing, enter three BLOCK, BOLTs, and assemble them as shown.

3 Save the assembly as **3-BLOCK ASSEMBLY.**

4 Access the **Design Library, Toolbox, Ansi Inch, Washers,** and **Plain Washers (Type A).**

See Figure 6-19.

5 Click and hold the **Preferred-Narrow Flat Washer Type A.**

6 Click the washer and drag-and-drop it into the field of the drawing.

The washer preview will appear in the drawing area.

7 Size the washer by clicking the arrow to the right of the initial size value and selecting a nominal value.

See Figure 6-20.

Figure 6-19

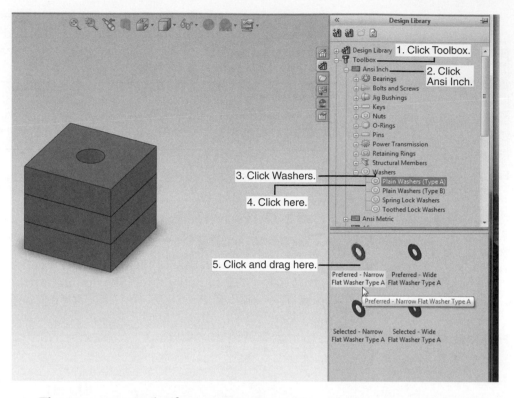

The term *nominal* refers to a starting value. In this case we are going to use a 3/8-16 UNC thread. The 3/8 value is a nominal value. We select a washer with a specified 3/8 nominal inside diameter. The actual inside diameter of the washer is .406. Clearance between the washer and the bolt is created when the washer is manufactured. The fastener will also not measure .375 but will be slightly smaller. The .375 size is the size of the bolt's shaft before the threads were cut.

Note that the washer thickness is .065 (about 1/16).

Figure 6-20

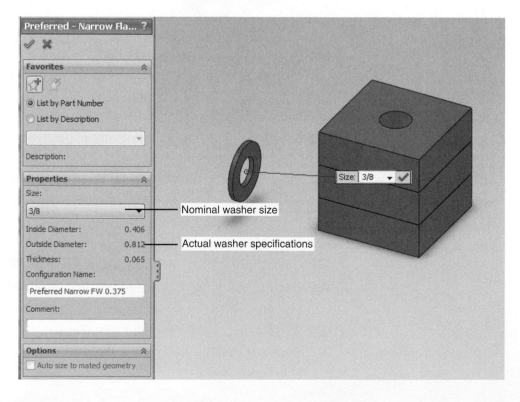

> **NOTE**
>
> Washers are identified using Insider diameter × Outside diameter × Thickness.

8 Click the OK check mark.

9 Add a second washer into the assembly.

10 Use the **Mate Concentric** and **Mate Coincident** tools to position the washers around the block's holes as shown.

See Figure 6-21.

11 Access the **Design Library,** then click **Toolbox, Ansi Inch, Nuts, Hex Nuts, Hex Jam Nut,** and drag and drop the nut into the drawing area.

See Figure 6-22.

Figure 6-21

> Use the Mate tool and position the washers.

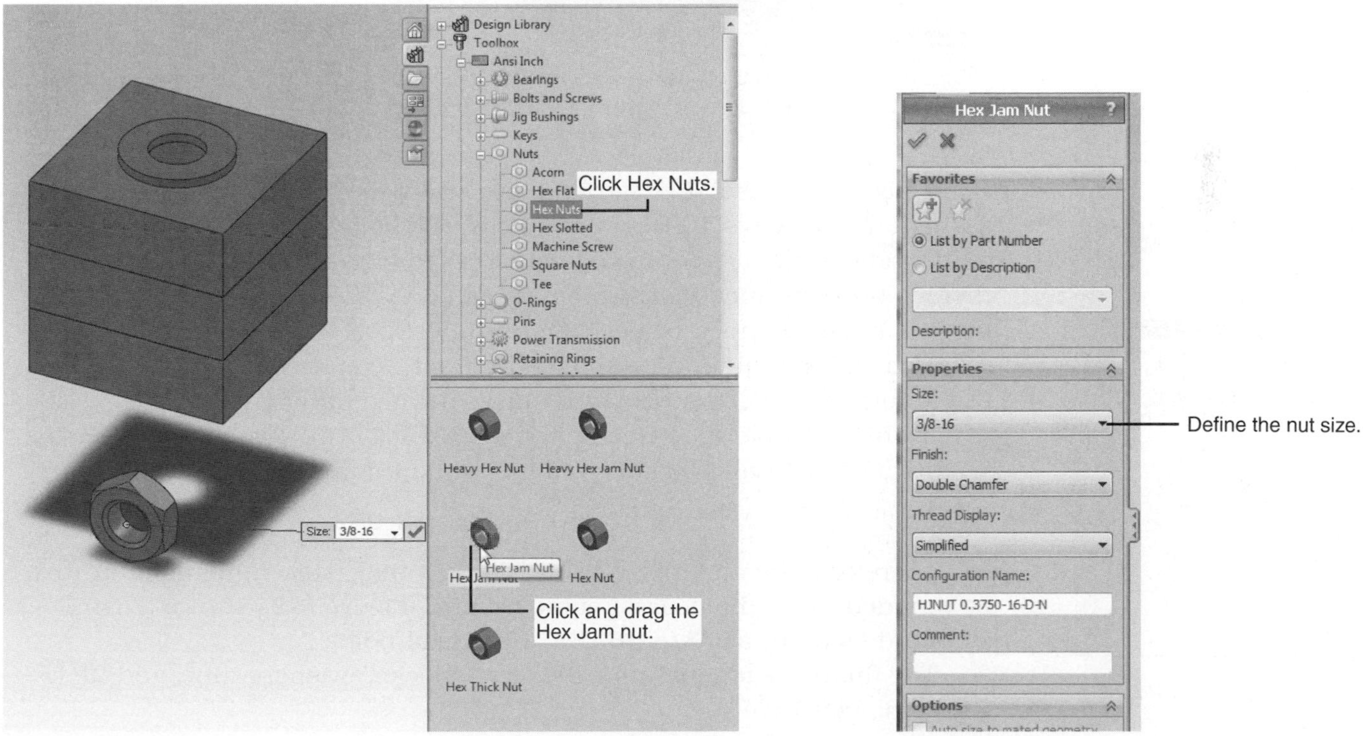

Figure 6-22

12 Size the nut to 3/8-16 UNC. It must match the 3/8-16 UNC thread on the bolt.

13 Use the **Mate** tool and position the nut as shown.

See Figure 6-23.

Figure 6-23

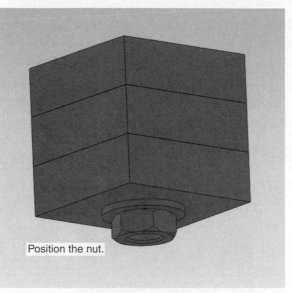

Position the nut.

The nut thickness is .227. This value was obtained by using the **Edit Feature** tool and determining the extrusion value used to create the nut. The nut is defined as 3/8-16 UNC Hex Jam Nut.

So far, the bolt must pass through three blocks (.50 × 3 = 1.50), two washers (.065 × 2 = .13), and one nut (.337). Therefore, the initial bolt length is 1.50 + .13 + .227 = 1.857.

> **NOTE**
>
> Bolt threads must extend beyond the nut to ensure 100% contact with the nut. The extension must be equal to at least two pitches (2P).

Calculations used to determine the strength of a bolt/nut combination assume that there is 100% contact between the bolt and the nut; that is, all threads of the nut are in contact with the threads of the nut. However, there is no assurance that the last thread on a bolt is 360°, so at least two threads must extended beyond the nut to ensure 100% contact. The 2P requirement is a minimum value. More than 2P is acceptable. Solidworks will automatically add at least 4P unless defined otherwise.

In this example the thread pitch is .0625 (1/16). Two pitches (2P) is .125. This value must be added to the initial thread length:

$$1.857 + .125 = 1.982.$$

Therefore, the minimum bolt length is 1.982. This value must in turn be rounded up to the nearest standard size. Figure 6-24 shows a listing of standard sizes for a 1 3/8-16 UNC Hex Head bolt.

The final thread length for the given blocks, washers, nut, and 2P is 2.00. The bolt callout is

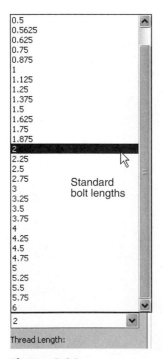

Figure 6-24

3/8-16 UNC × 2.00 Hex Head Bolt

14 Click the **Design Library, Toolbox, Ansi Inch, Bolts and Screws, Hex Head, Hex Bolt,** and click and drag the bolt into the drawing.

15 Define the **Size** as **3/8-16** and the **Length** as **2.**

See Figure 6-25. Note how the bolt extends beyond the nut.

Figure 6-25

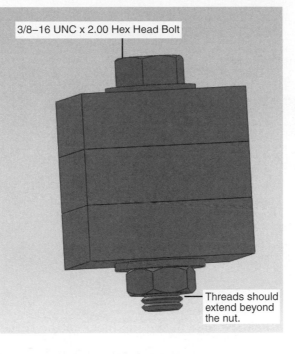

3/8–16 UNC x 2.00 Hex Head Bolt

Threads should extend beyond the nut.

6-12 Smart Fasteners

The **Smart Fasteners** tool will automatically create the correct bolt. Given the three blocks, two washers, and nut shown in Figure 6-26, use the **Smart Fasteners** tool to add the appropriate bolt.

1 Click the **Smart Fasteners** tool located on the **Assembly** toolbar.

A dialog box will appear. See Figure 6-27.

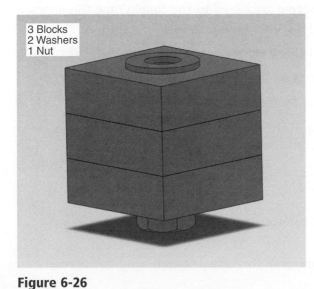

3 Blocks
2 Washers
1 Nut

Figure 6-26

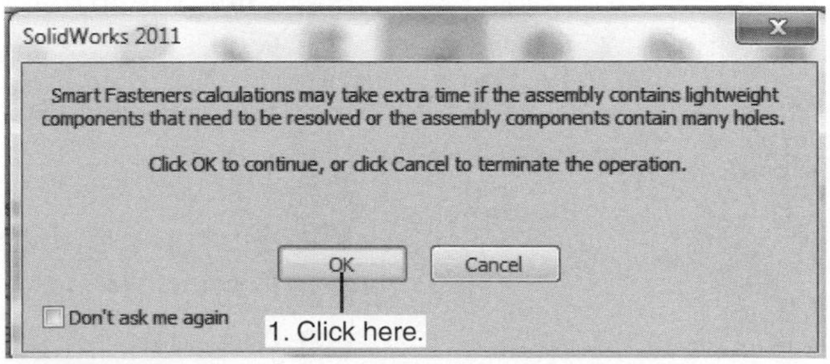

SolidWorks 2011

Smart Fasteners calculations may take extra time if the assembly contains lightweight components that need to be resolved or the assembly components contain many holes.

Click OK to continue, or click Cancel to terminate the operation.

OK   Cancel

☐ Don't ask me again   1. Click here.

Figure 6-27

2 Click OK.

The **Smart Fasteners PropertyManager** will appear. See Figure 6-28.

Figure 6-28

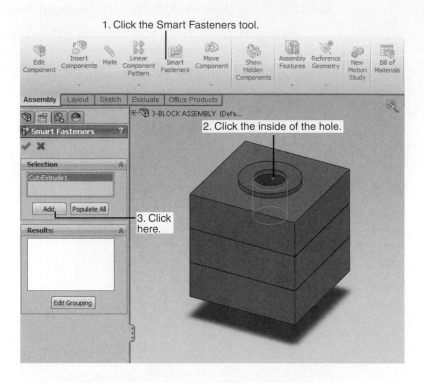

3 Click the hole in the top block of the three blocks.

TIP

Click the hole, that is, a cylindrical-shaped section as shown in Figure 6-28, not the edge of the hole.

The words **Cut-Extrude 1** will appear in the **Selection** box.

4 Click **Add.**

A fastener will appear in the hole. This may take a few seconds. In this example a **Socket Head Cap Screw** appeared in the hole. Once the screw is added to the drawing it can be edited as needed.

5 Right-click the **Socket Head Cap Screw** heading in the **Fastener** box.

6 Click the **Change fastener type** option.

See Figure 6-29. The **Smart Fastener** dialog box will appear.

7 Click the arrow to the right of the **Type** box and select a **Hex Head** type.

See Figure 6-30.

8 Click **OK.**

9 Scroll down the **Smart Fasteners PropertyManager** and access the **Properties** box.

10 Define the thread size, number of threads per inch, and the thread length.

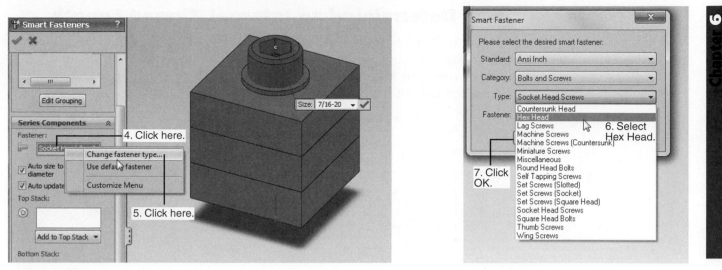

Figure 6-29

Figure 6-30

11 Click the OK check mark.

Note that the fastener extends beyond the nut. See Figure 6-31.

Figure 6-31

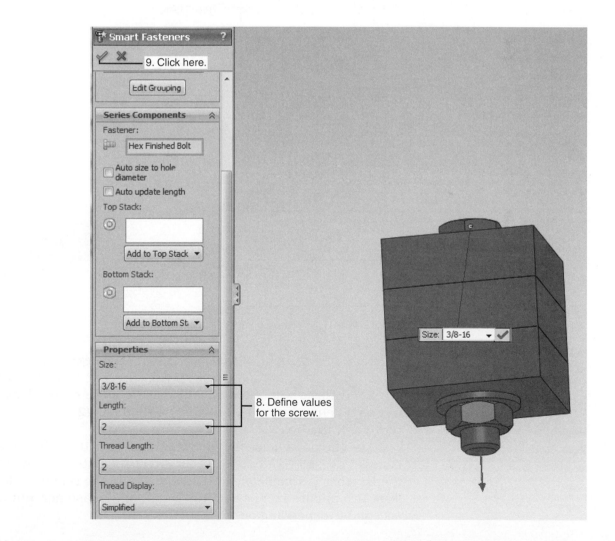

6-13 Determining an Internal Thread Length

Figure 6-32 shows two blocks: Block, Cover and Block, Base. Their dimensions are also shown. The two blocks are to be assembled and held together using an M10 × 1.25 × 25 hex head screw. What should be the threaded hole in the Block, Base?

Figure 6-32

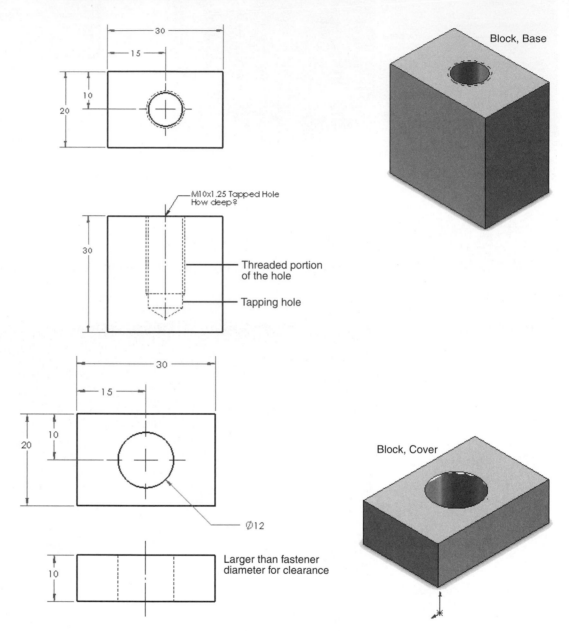

Note in Figure 6-32 that the tapping hole extends beyond the threaded portion of the hole. This is to prevent damage to the tapping bit. SolidWorks will automatically calculate the excess length needed, but as a general rule it is at least two pitches (2P) beyond the threaded portion of the hole.

The threaded hole should always be longer then the fastener so the fastener doesn't "bottom out," that is, hit the bottom of the threads before the fastener is completely in the hole. Again, the general rule is to allow at least two pitches (2P) beyond the length of the fastener, but more are acceptable depending on the situation.

TIP

Metric thread callouts give the pitch directly.

In this example the thread pitch is 1.25. Two pitches = 2.50. The bolt length is 25, but it must initially pass through the 10-thick Block, Cover, so the length of the bolt in the Block, Base is 15. Adding 2.50 to this value yields a minimum thread length of 17.50. Rounding the value up determines that the threaded hole in the Block, Base should be M10 × 1.25 × 18 deep. See Figure 6-33.

Figure 6-33

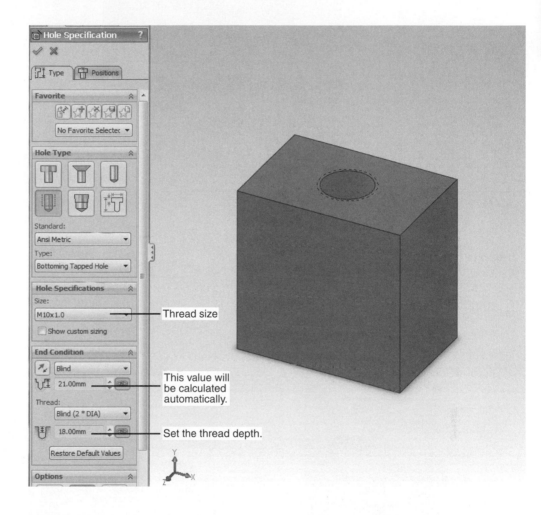

1. Draw the parts as dimensioned in Figure 6-32 and use the **Hole Wizard** to add an M10 × 18 deep hole to the Block, Base.

   See Figure 6-34.

2. Assemble the parts as shown.

3. Access the **Design Library.** Click **Toolbox, Ansi Metric, Bolts and Screws, Hex Head** and access Formed Hex Screw ANSI B18.2.3.2M.

4. Click and drag the bolt onto the screen.

   See Figure 6-35.

5. Define the **Size** of the screw as **M10** and the **Length** as **25.**

Figure 6-34

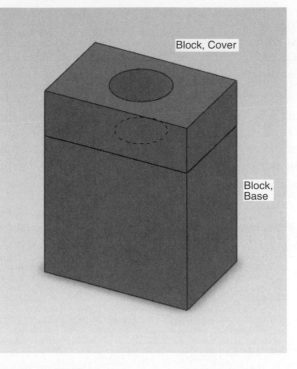

Figure 6-35

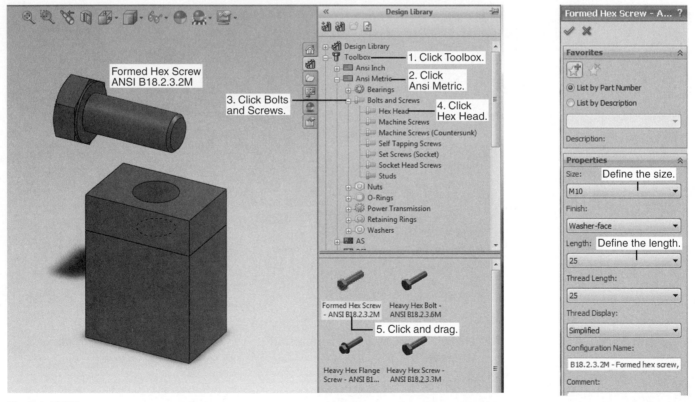

6 Use the **Mate Concentric** and **Mate Coincident** tools to place the screen into the assembly.

7 Save the assembly. See Figure 6-36.

Figure 6-37 shows an isometric view, an orthographic view, and a section view of the internal thread assembly.

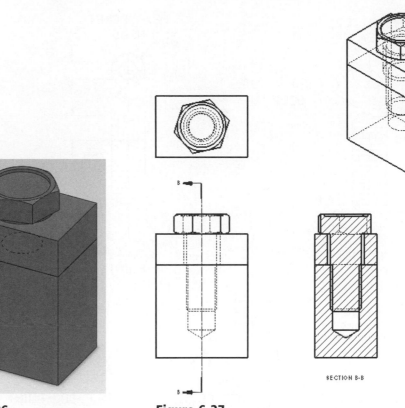

SECTION B-B

Figure 6-36

Figure 6-37

6-14 Set Screws

Set screws are fasteners used to hold parts like gears and pulleys to rotating shafts or other moving objects to prevent slippage between the two objects. See Figure 6-38.

Figure 6-38

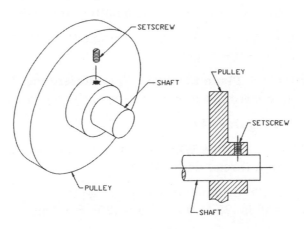

Most set screws have recessed heads to help prevent interference with other parts.

Many different head styles and point styles are available. See Figure 6-39. The dimensions shown in Figure 6-39 are general sizes for use in this book. For actual sizes, see manufacturers' specifications.

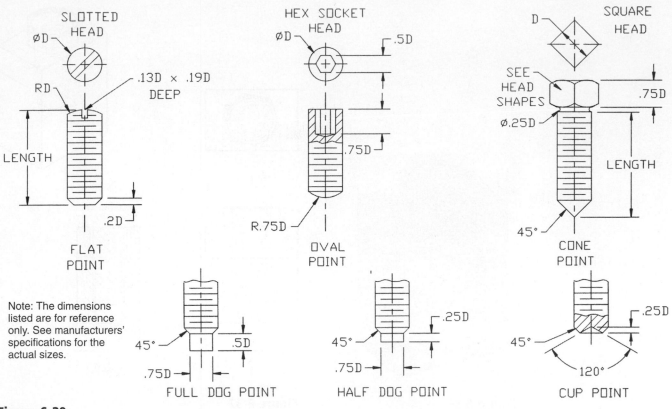

Figure 6-39

Note: The dimensions listed are for reference only. See manufacturers' specifications for the actual sizes.

6-15 Drawing a Threaded Hole in the Side of a Cylinder

Figure 6-40 shows a Ø.75 × Ø1.00 × 1.00 collar with a #10-24 threaded hole. This section will explain how to add a threaded hole through the sides of a cylinder and insert set screws.

1 Draw the collar by drawing a **Ø1.00 × 1.00** cylinder and then drawing a **Ø.75** hole through the length of the cylinder.

See Figure 6-41. In this example the Ø1.00 × 1.00 cylinder was centered about the origin.

2 Use the **Plane** tool flyout from **Reference Geometry** tool and create an offset right plane tangent to the outside edge of the cylinder.

See Figure 6-42.

3 Click the **Hole Wizard** tool and define the **Size** of the hole as **#10-24** with a thread depth of **.38.**

The .38 distance is enough to go through the wall of the collar. The collar wall is .25 (1.00 − .75 = .25). See Figure 6-43.

TIP

Do not use the **Through All** option, as this will create holes in both sides of the collar.

---

4 Use the **View Orientation** tool and create a **Right** view of the collar.

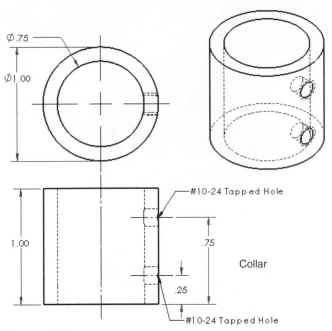

Figure 6-40

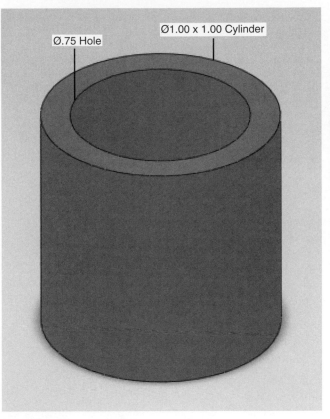

Figure 6-41

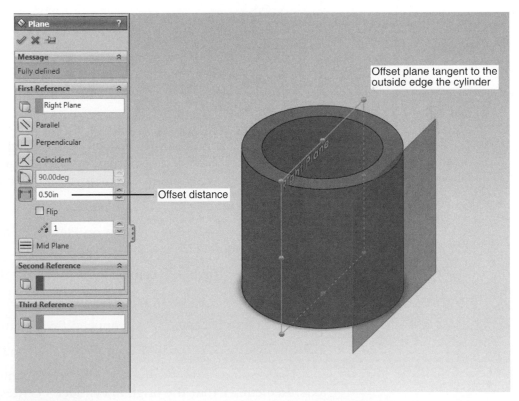

Figure 6-42

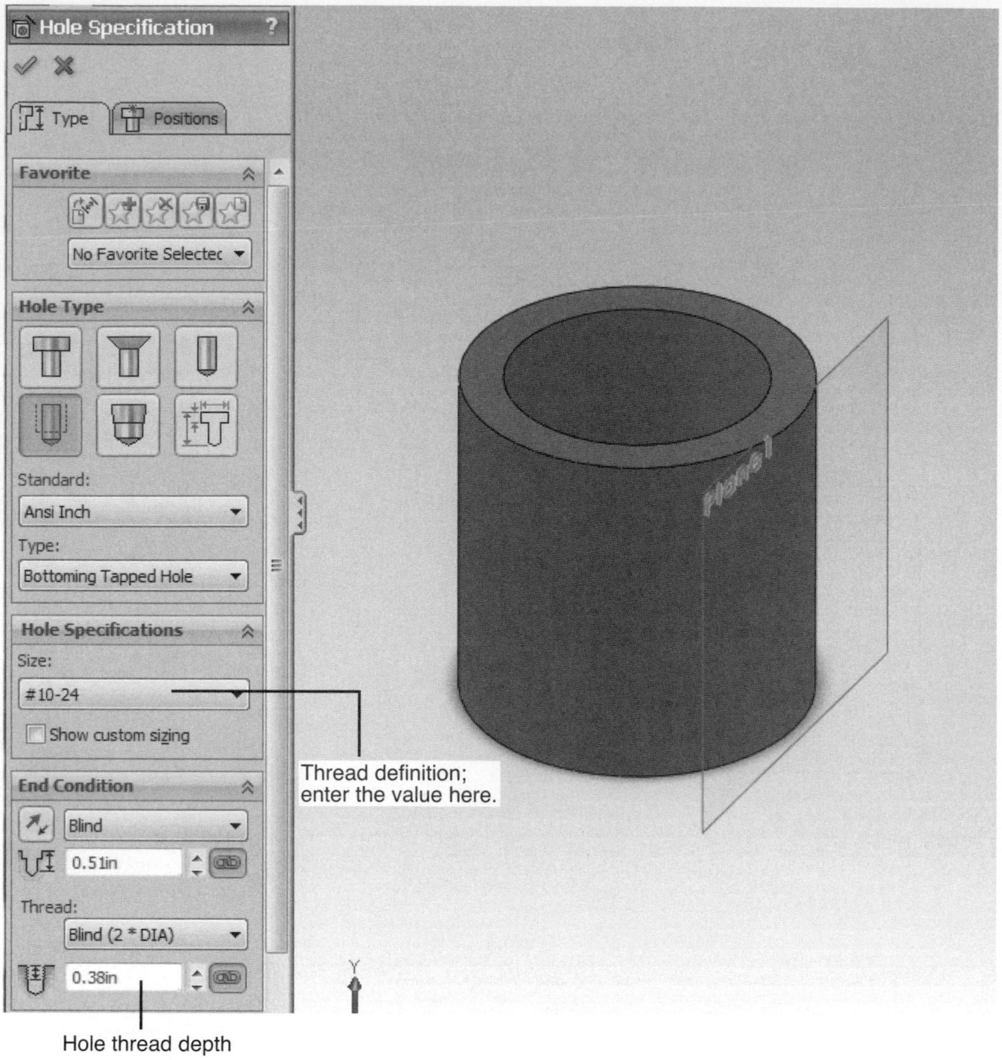

Figure 6-43

This view orientation will give a direct 90° view of Plane 1. See Figure 6-44. The holes must be located at exactly 90° to the cylinder. There are several methods that can be used to achieve this goal. This example will use coordinate values to position the holes.

5 Click the **Positions** tab and locate a hole on Plane 1.

See Figure 6-45. Any location on Plane 1 is acceptable, but try to position the hole near its final location.

6 Right-click the hole's center point and click the **Select** option.

7 Click the hole's center point again.

A listing of parameters will appear. See Figure 6-46.

8 Change the Z value to **0.00** and the Y value to **.25.**

The Z value of 0.00 will locate the hole's center point directly on the Z axis. Remember that the original cylinder's center point is on the origin, so this Z value will locate the hole's center point on the Z axis.

Figure 6-44

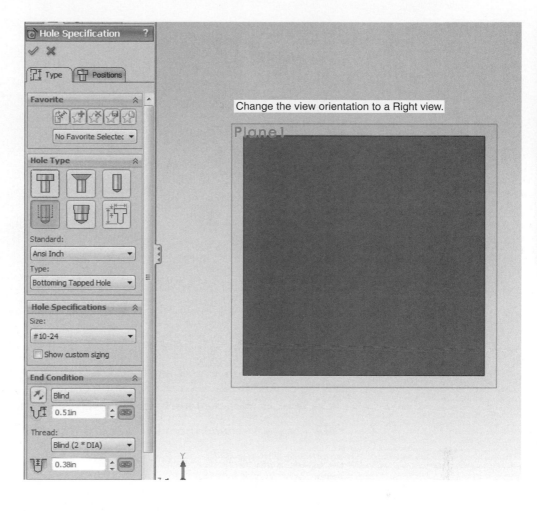

Figure 6-45

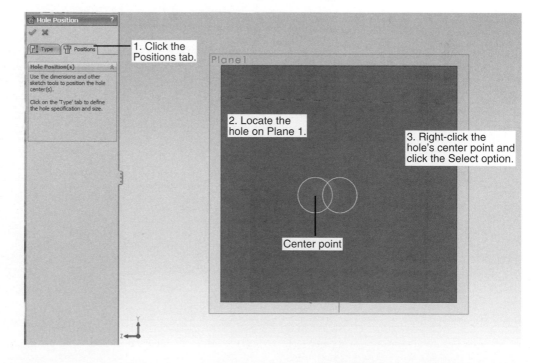

Figure 6-46

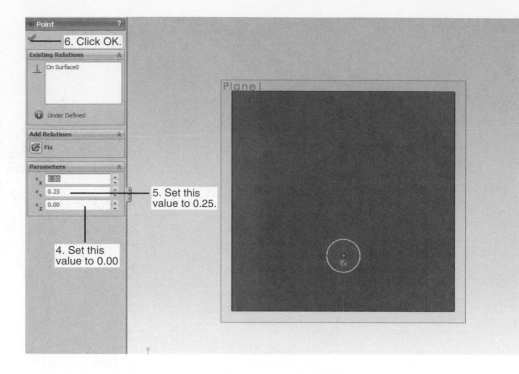

The .25 value comes from the given .25 dimension. See Figure 6-40.

9 Locate a second threaded hole **.75** from the base as shown.

See Figure 6-47.

10 Hide Plane 1.

11 Save the collar as **Ø1.00COLLAR.**

Figure 6-48 shows the resulting holes.

Figure 6-47

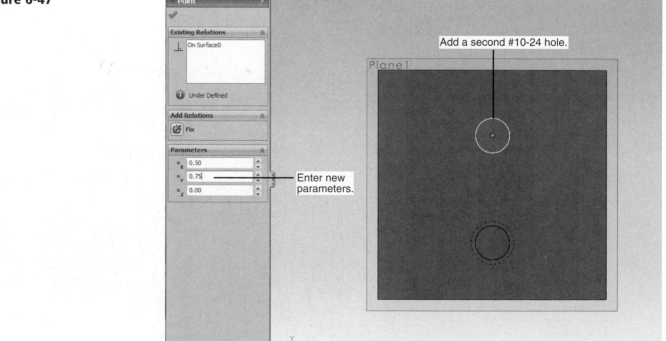

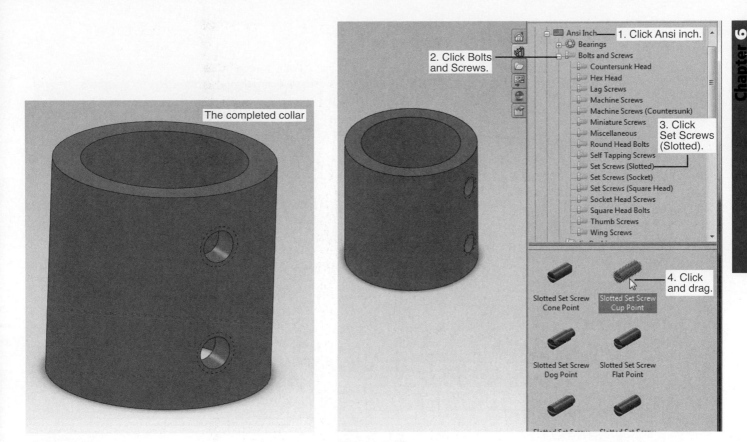

Figure 6-48

Figure 6-49

1. Click Ansi inch.

2. Click Bolts and Screws.

3. Click Set Screws (Slotted).

4. Click and drag.

Ansi Inch
- Bearings
- Bolts and Screws
  - Countersunk Head
  - Hex Head
  - Lag Screws
  - Machine Screws
  - Machine Screws (Countersunk)
  - Miniature Screws
  - Miscellaneous
  - Round Head Bolts
  - Self Tapping Screws
  - Set Screws (Slotted)
  - Set Screws (Socket)
  - Set Screws (Square Head)
  - Socket Head Screws
  - Square Head Bolts
  - Thumb Screws
  - Wing Screws

The completed collar

Slotted Set Screw Cone Point
Slotted Set Screw Cup Point
Slotted Set Screw Dog Point
Slotted Set Screw Flat Point

6-16 Adding Set Screws to the Collar

1 Start a new **Assembly** drawing.

2 Use the **Browse** tool and locate the Ø1.00 COLLAR on the screen.

3 Access the **Design Library,** then click **Toolbox, Ansi Inch, Bolts and Screws,** and **Set Screws (Slotted).**

See Figure 6-48.

4 Select the **Slotted Set Screw Cup Point** option and click and drag the set screw into the drawing.

See Figure 6-49.

5 Define the **Size** of the set screw as **#10-24** and the **Length** as **0.315.**

The 0.315 is a standard length. It is good design practice to use standard lengths whenever possible. See Figure 6-50.

6 Click the OK check mark.

7 Add a second set screw.

8 Use the **Mate** tool and insert the set screws into the collar.

See Figure 6-51.

9 Save the assembly.

Slotted Set Screw Cup... ?

Click here.

Favorites

List by Part Number
List by Description

Description:

Properties

Size: Define the thread.
#10-24

Length: Define the length.
0.315

Thread Display:
Simplified

Configuration Name:
SSCUPSLT 0.19-24x0.315-N

Comment:

Figure 6-50

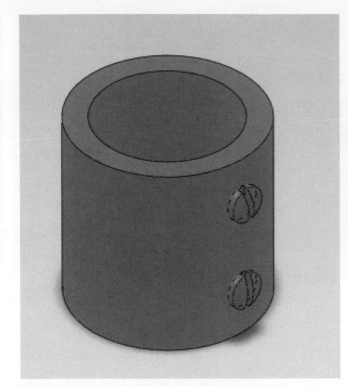

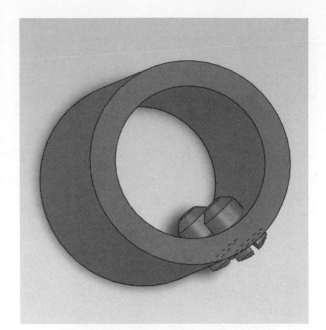

Figure 6-51

Chapter Projects

Project 6-1: Millimeters

Figure P6-1 shows three blocks. Assume that the blocks are each 30 × 30 × 10 and that the hole is Ø9. Assemble the three blocks so that their holes are aligned and they are held together by a hex head bold secured by an appropriate hex nut. Locate a washer between the bolt head and the top block and between the nut and the bottom block. Create all drawings using either an A4 or A3 drawing sheet, as needed. Include a title block on all drawing sheets.

    A. Define the bolt.
    B. Define the nut.
    C. Definc the washers.
    D. Draw an assembly drawing including all componcnts.
    E. Create a BOM for the assembly.
    F. Create an isometric exploded drawing of the assembly.
    G. Create an animation drawing of the assembly.

Figure P6-1

Three blocks, each 30 x 30 x 30 with a centered Ø9 hole.
P/N AM311-10M

Assemble the three blocks using a hex head nut, a hex nut, and two plain narrow washers.

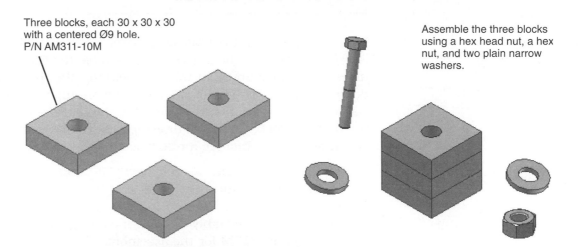

Project 6-2: Millimeters

Figure P6-2 shows three blocks, one 30 × 30 × 50 block with a centered M8 threaded hole, and two 30 × 30 × 10 blocks with centered Ø9 holes. Join the two 30 × 30 × 10 blocks to the 30 × 30 × 50 block using an M8 hex head bolt. Locate a regular plain washer under the bolt head.

    A. Define the bolt.
    B. Define the thread depth.
    C. Define the hole depth.
    D. Define the washers.
    E. Draw an assembly drawing including all components.
    F. Create a BOM for the assembly.
    G. Create an isometric exploded drawing of the assembly.
    H. Create an animation drawing of the assembly.

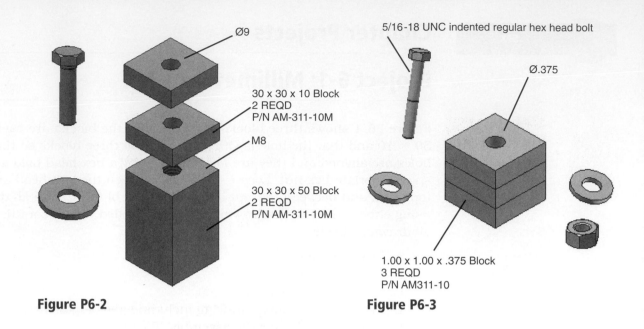

Figure P6-2

Figure P6-3

Project 6-3: Inches

Figure P6-3 shows three blocks. Assume that each block is 1.00 × 1.00 × .375 and that the hole is Ø.375. Assemble the three blocks so that their holes are aligned and that they are held together by a 5/16-18 UNC indented regular hex head bolt secured by an appropriate hex nut. Locate a washer between the bolt head and the top block and between the nut and the bottom block. Create all drawings using either an A4 or A3 drawing sheet, as needed. Include a title block on all drawing sheets.

    A.   Define the bolt.
    B.   Define the nut.
    C.   Define the washers.
    D.   Draw an assembly drawing including all components.
    E.   Create a BOM for the assembly.
    F.   Create an isometric exploded drawing of the assembly.
    G.   Create an animation drawing of the assembly.

Project 6-4: Inches

Figure P6-4 shows three blocks, one 1.00 × 1.00 × 2.00 with a centered threaded hole, and two 1.00 × 1.00 × .375 blocks with centered Ø.375 holes. Join the two 1.00 × 1.00 × .375 blocks to the 1.00 × 1.00 × 2.00 block using a 5/16-18 UNC hex head bolt. Locate a regular plain washer under the bolt head.

    A.   Define the bolt.
    B.   Define the thread depth.
    C.   Define the hole depth.
    D.   Define the washer.

E. Draw an assembly drawing including all components.
F. Create a BOM for the assembly.
G. Create an isometric exploded drawing of the assembly.
H. Create an animation drawing of the assembly.

Figure P6-4

1.00 x 1.00 x .375 Block
2 REQD
P/N AM311-10

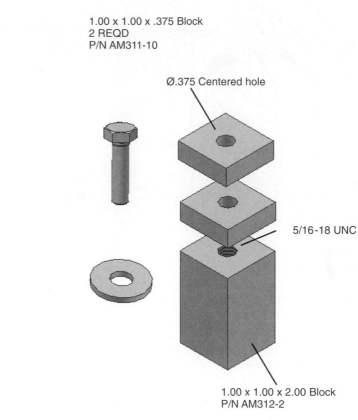

Ø.375 Centered hole

5/16-18 UNC

1.00 x 1.00 x 2.00 Block
P/N AM312-2

Project 6-5: Inches or Millimeters

Figure P6-5 shows a centering block. Create an assembly drawing of the
block and insert three set screws into the three threaded holes so that they
extend at least .25 in. or 6 mm into the center hole.

A. Use the inch dimensions.
B. Use the millimeter dimensions.
C. Define the set screws.
D. Draw an assembly drawing including all components.
E. Create a BOM for the assembly.
F. Create an isometric exploded drawing of the assembly.
G. Create an animation drawing of the assembly.

Centering Block
P/N BU2004-5
SAE 1020 Steel

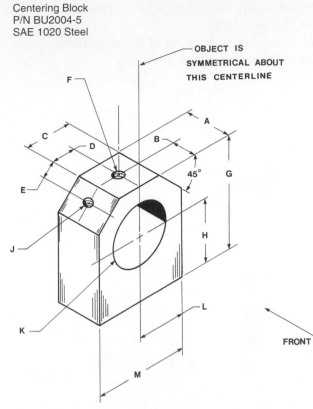

OBJECT IS
SYMMETRICAL ABOUT
THIS CENTERLINE

FRONT

Figure P6-5

DIMENSION	INCHES	mm
A	1.00	26
B	.50	13
C	1.00	26
D	.50	13
E	.38	10
F	.190–32 UNF	M8X1
G	2.38	60
H	1.38	34
J	.164–36 UNF	M6
K	Ø1.25	Ø30
L	1.00	26
M	2.00	52

Project 6-6: Millimeters

Figure P6-6 shows two parts: a head cylinder and a base cylinder. The head cylinder has outside dimensions of Ø40 × 20, and the base cylinder has outside dimensions of Ø40 × 50. The holes in both parts are located on a Ø24 bolt circle. Assemble the two parts using hex head bolts.

    A. Define the bolt.
    B. Define the holes in the head cylinder, the counterbore diameter and depth, and the clearance hole diameter.
    C. Define the thread depth in the base cylinder.
    D. Define the hole depth in the base cylinder.
    E. Draw an assembly drawing including all components.
    F. Create a BOM for the assembly.
    G. Create an isometric exploded drawing of the assembly.
    H. Create an animation drawing of the assembly.

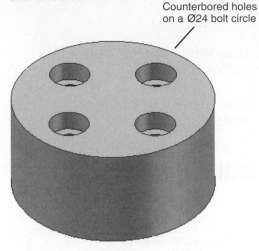

Cylinder Head
P/N EK130-1
SAE 1040 Steel

Counterbored holes
on a Ø24 bolt circle

Cylinder Base
P/N EK130-2
SAE 1040 Steel

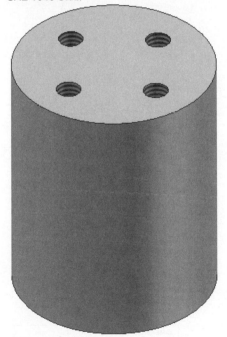

Figure P6-6

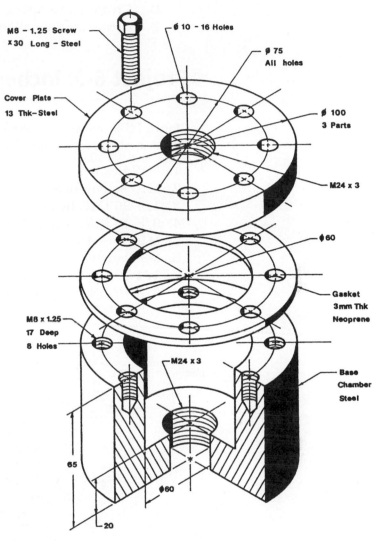

M8 – 1.25 Screw
×30 Long – Steel

Ø 10 – 16 Holes

Ø 75
All holes

Cover Plate
13 Thk–Steel

Ø 100
3 Parts

M24 x 3

Ø 60

M8 x 1.25
17 Deep
8 Holes

Gasket
3mm Thk
Neoprene

M24 x 3

Base
Chamber
Steel

65

20

Ø60

Figure P6-7

Project 6-7: Millimeters

Figure P6-7 shows a pressure cylinder assembly.

    A.   Draw an assembly drawing including all components.

    B.   Create a BOM for the assembly.

    C.   Create an isometric exploded drawing of the assembly.

    D.   Create an animation drawing of the assembly.

Project 6-8: Millimeters

Figure P6-7 shows a pressure cylinder assembly.

    A. Revise the assembly so that it uses M10 × 35 hex head bolts.
    B. Draw an assembly drawing including all components.
    C. Create a BOM for the assembly.
    D. Create an isometric exploded drawing of the assembly.
    E. Create an animation drawing of the assembly.

Project 6-9: Inches and Millimeters

Figure P6-9 shows a C-block assembly.
Use one of the following fasteners assigned by your instructor.

1. M12 hex head
2. M10 square head
3. 1/4-20 UNC hex head
4. 3/8-16 UNC square head
5. M10 socket head
6. M8 slotted head
7. 1/4-20 UNC slotted head
8. 3/8-16 UNC socket head

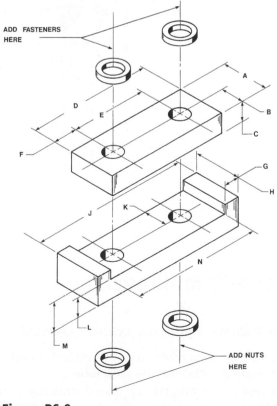

DIMENSION	INCHES	mm
A	1.25	32
B	.63	16
C	.50	13
D	3.25	82
E	2.00	50
F	.63	16
G	.38	10
H	1.25	32
J	4.13	106
K	.63	16
L	.50	13
M	.75	10
N	3.38	86

Figure P6-9

A. Define the bolt.
B. Define the nut.
C. Define the washers.
D. Draw an assembly drawing including all components.
E. Create a BOM for the assembly.
F. Create an isometric exploded drawing of the assembly.
G. Create an animation drawing of the assembly.

Project 6-10: Millimeters

Figure P6-10 shows an exploded assembly drawing. There are no standard parts, so each part must be drawn individually.

A. Draw an assembly drawing including all components.
B. Create a BOM for the assembly.
C. Create an isometric exploded drawing of the assembly.
D. Create an animation drawing of the assembly.

Project 6-11: Millimeters

Figure P6-11 shows an exploded assembly drawing.

A. Draw an assembly drawing including all components.
B. Create a BOM for the assembly.

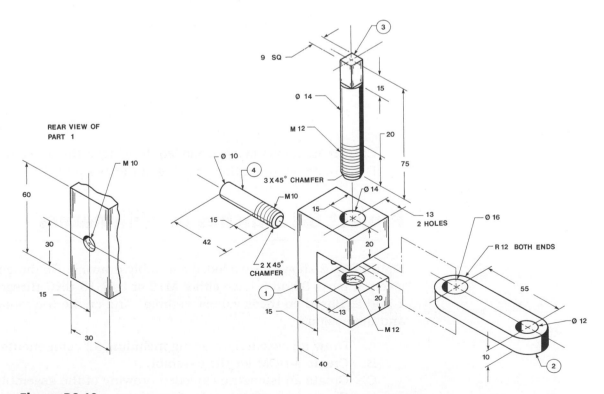

Figure P6-10

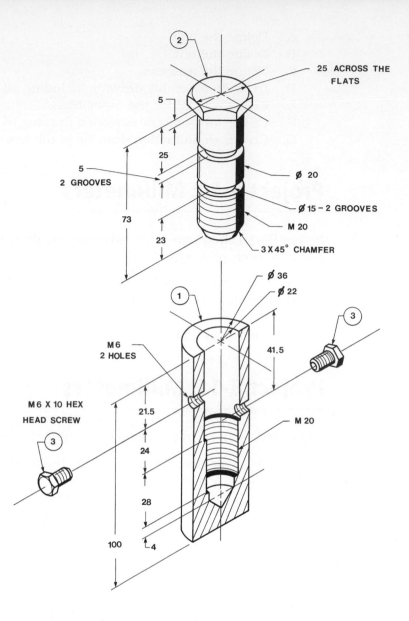

C. Create an isometric exploded drawing of the assembly.

D. Create an animation drawing of the assembly.

Project 6-12: Inches or Millimeters

Figure P6-12 shows an exploded assembly drawing. No dimensions are given. If parts 3 and 5 have either M10 or 3/8-16 UNC threads, size parts 1 and 2. Based on these values, estimate and create the remaining sizes and dimensions.

A. Draw an assembly drawing including all components.

B. Create a BOM for the assembly.

C. Create an isometric exploded drawing of the assembly.

D. Create an animation drawing of the assembly.

Figure P6-12

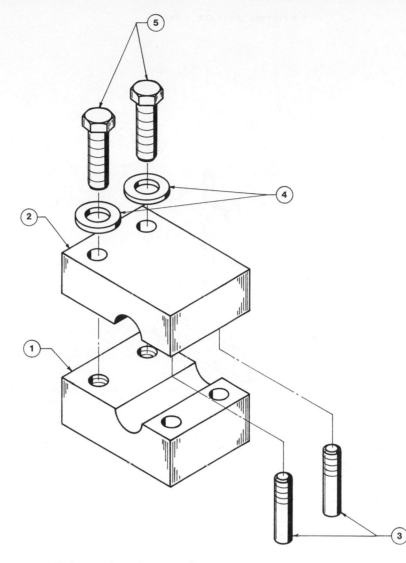

Project 6-13: Inches

Figure P6-13 shows an assembly drawing and detail drawings of a surface gauge.

    A.   Draw an assembly drawing including all components.
    B.   Create a BOM for the assembly.
    C.   Create an isometric exploded drawing of the assembly.
    D.   Create an animation drawing of the assembly.

Project 6-14: Millimeters

Figure P6-14 shows an assembly made from parts defined on pages 313–315. Assemble the parts using M10 threaded fasteners.

    A.   Define the bolt.
    B.   Define the nut.

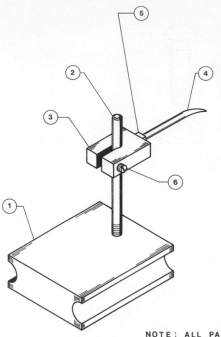

NOTE: ALL PARTS MADE
FROM SAE 1020 STEEL

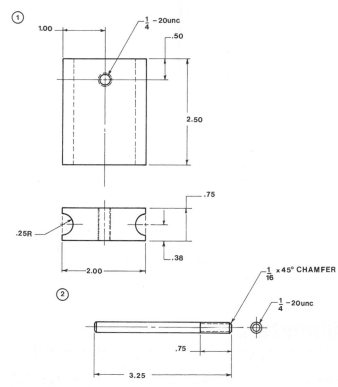

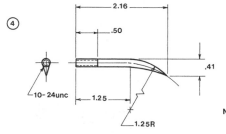

NOTE: START TAPER
.88 FROM END

Figure P6-13

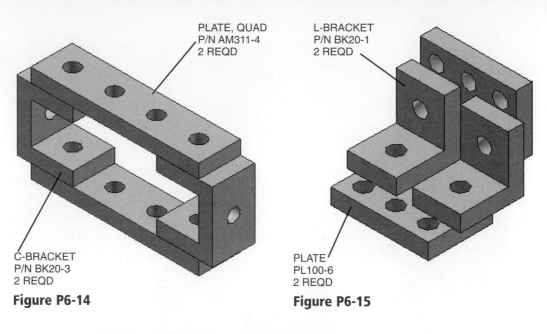

PLATE, QUAD
P/N AM311-4
2 REQD

L-BRACKET
P/N BK20-1
2 REQD

C-BRACKET
P/N BK20-3
2 REQD

PLATE
PL100-6
2 REQD

Figure P6-14

Figure P6-15

C. Draw an assembly drawing including all components.
D. Create a BOM for the assembly.
E. Create an isometric exploded drawing of the assembly.
F. Create an animation drawing of the assembly.
G. Consider possible interference between the nuts and ends of the fasteners both during and after assembly. Recommend an assembly sequence.

Project 6-15: Millimeters

Figure P6-15 shows an assembly made from parts defined on page 315. Assemble the parts using M10 threaded fasteners.

A. Define the bolt.
B. Define the nut.
C. Draw an assembly drawing including all components.
D. Create a BOM for the assembly.
E. Create an isometric exploded drawing of the assembly.
F. Create an animation drawing of the assembly.
G. Consider possible interference between the nuts and ends of the fasteners both during and after assembly. Recommend an assembly sequence.

Project 6-16: Millimeters

Figure P6-16 shows an assembly made from parts defined on pages 315–316. Assemble the parts using M10 threaded fasteners.

A. Define the bolt.
B. Define the nut.

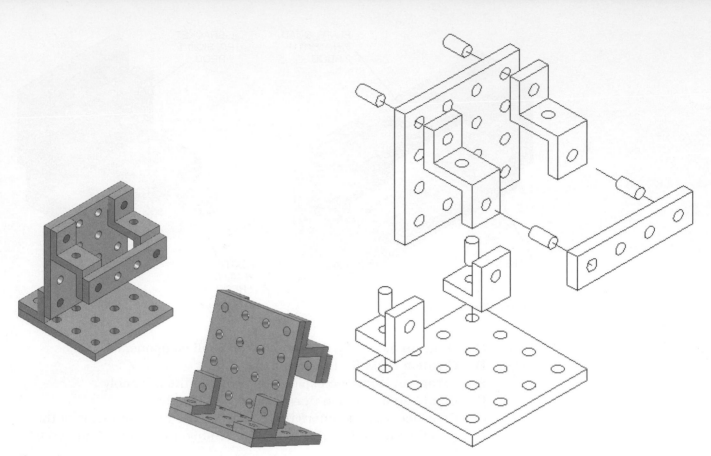

Figure P6-16

C. Draw an assembly drawing including all components.
D. Create a BOM for the assembly.
E. Create an isometric exploded drawing of the assembly.
F. Create an animation drawing of the assembly.
G. Consider possible interference between the nuts and ends of the fasteners both during and after assembly. Recommend an assembly sequence.

Project 6-17: Access Controller

Design an access controller based on the information given in Figure P6-17. The controller works by moving an internal cylinder up and down within the base so the cylinder aligns with output holes A and B. Liquids will enter the internal cylinder from the top, then exit the base through holes A and B. Include as many holes in the internal cylinder as necessary to create the following liquid-exit combinations.

1. A open, B closed
2. A open, B open
3. A closed, B open

INTERNAL CYLINDER

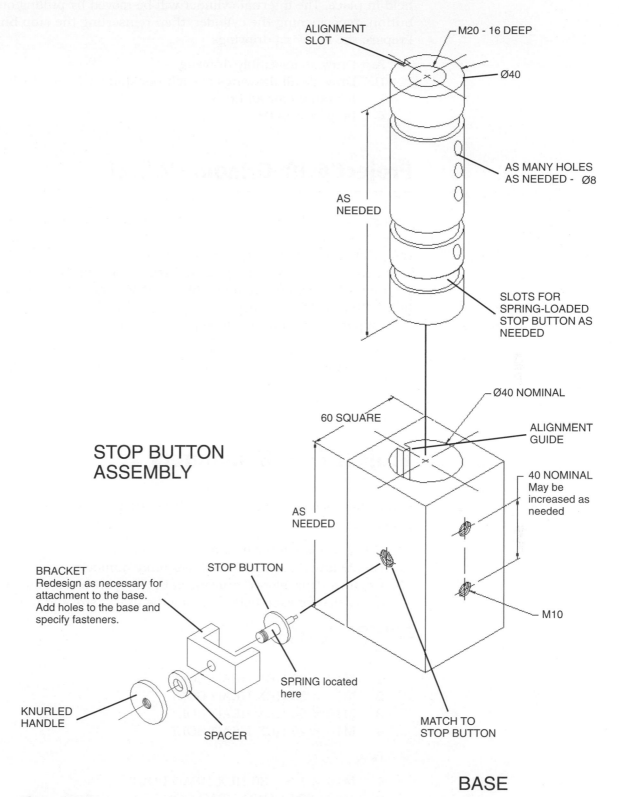

ALIGNMENT SLOT

M20 - 16 DEEP

Ø40

AS NEEDED

AS MANY HOLES AS NEEDED - Ø8

SLOTS FOR SPRING-LOADED STOP BUTTON AS NEEDED

Ø40 NOMINAL

60 SQUARE

ALIGNMENT GUIDE

STOP BUTTON ASSEMBLY

AS NEEDED

40 NOMINAL
May be increased as needed

BRACKET
Redesign as necessary for attachment to the base. Add holes to the base and specify fasteners.

STOP BUTTON

M10

SPRING located here

KNURLED HANDLE

SPACER

MATCH TO STOP BUTTON

BASE

Figure P6-17

The internal cylinder is to be held in place by an alignment key and a stop button. The stop button is to be spring-loaded so that it will always be held in place. The internal cylinder will be moved by pulling out the stop button, repositioning the cylinder, then reinserting the stop button. Prepare the following drawings.

    A. Draw an assembly drawing.
    B. Draw detail drawings of each nonstandard part. Include positional tolerances for all holes.
    C. Prepare a BOM.

Project 6-18: Grinding Wheel

Design a hand-operated grinding wheel as shown in Figure P6-18 specifically for sharpening a chisel. The chisel is to be located on an adjustable rest while it is being sharpened. The mechanism should be able to be clamped to a table during operation using two thumbscrews. A standard grinding wheel is 6.00 in. and 1/2 in. thick, and has an internal mounting hole with a 50.00±.03 bore.

Prepare the following drawing.

    A. Draw an assembly drawings.
    B. Draw detail drawings of each nonstandard part. Include positional tolerances for all holes.
    C. Prepare a BOM.

Project 6-19: Millimeters

Given the assembly shown in Figure P6-19 on page 320, add the following fasteners.

1. Create an assembly drawing.
2. Create a parts list including assembly numbers.
3. Create a dimensioned drawing of the support block and specify a dimension for each hole including the thread size and the depth required.

Fasteners:

    A.

    1. M10 × 35 HEX HEAD BOLT
    2. M10 × 35 HEX HEAD BOLT
    3. M10 × 30 HEX HEAD BOLT
    4. M10 × 25 HEX HEAD BOLT

    B.

    1. M10 × 1.5 × 35 HEX HEAD BOLT
    2. M8 × 35 ROUND HEAD BOLT
    3. M10 × 30 HEXAGON SOCKET HEAD CAP SCREW
    4. M6 × 30 SQUARE BOLT

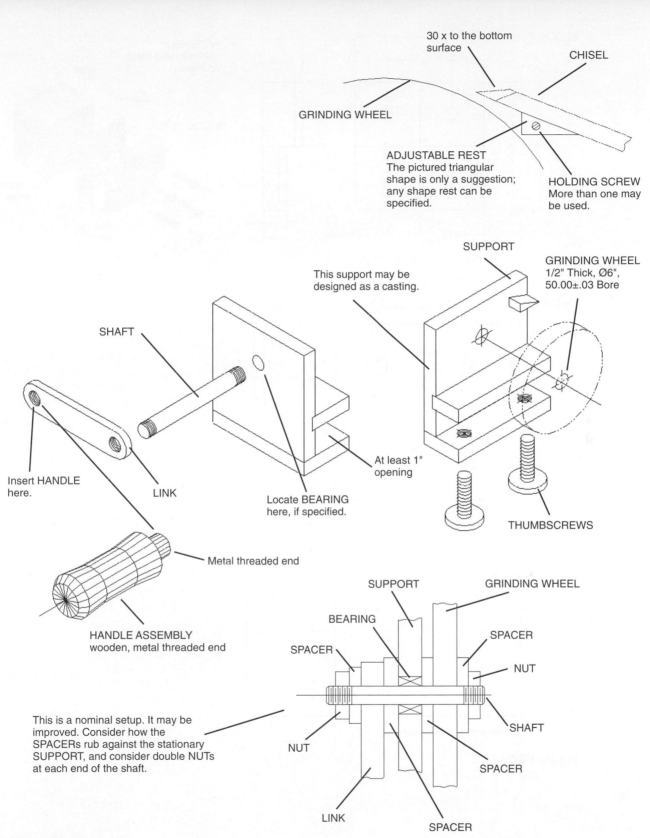

30 x to the bottom surface

CHISEL

GRINDING WHEEL

ADJUSTABLE REST
The pictured triangular shape is only a suggestion; any shape rest can be specified.

HOLDING SCREW
More than one may be used.

SUPPORT

GRINDING WHEEL
1/2" Thick, Ø6", 50.00±.03 Bore

This support may be designed as a casting.

SHAFT

Insert HANDLE here.

LINK

Locate BEARING here, if specified.

At least 1" opening

THUMBSCREWS

Metal threaded end

HANDLE ASSEMBLY
wooden, metal threaded end

SUPPORT

GRINDING WHEEL

BEARING

SPACER

SPACER

NUT

SPACER

SHAFT

This is a nominal setup. It may be improved. Consider how the SPACERs rub against the stationary SUPPORT, and consider double NUTs at each end of the shaft.

NUT

LINK

SPACER

SPACER

Figure P6-18

BLOCK, TOP

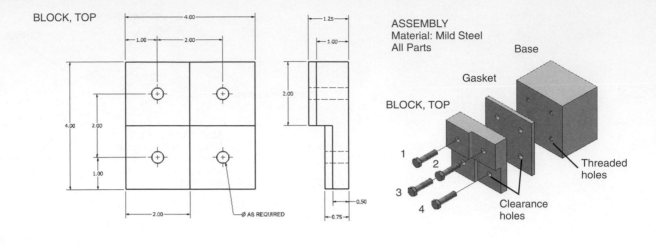

ASSEMBLY
Material: Mild Steel
All Parts

GASKET

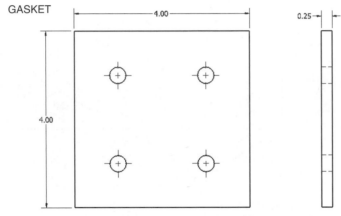

HOLE PATTERN TO MATCH BLOCK,TOP

BASE

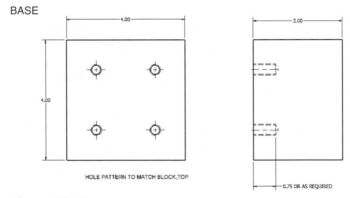

HOLE PATTERN TO MATCH BLOCK,TOP

Figure P6-19

Project 6-20: Inches

1. Create an assembly drawing.
2. Create a BOM including assembly numbers.
3. Create a dimensioned drawing of the base and specify a dimension for each hole including the thread size and the depth required.

Fasteners:

A.
1. 3/8-16 UNC × 2.50 HEX HEAD BOLT
2. 1/4-20 UNC × 2.00 HEX HEAD BOLT
3. 7/16-14 UNC × 1.75 HEX HEAD BOLT
4. 5/16-18 UNC × 2.25 HEX HEAD BOLT

B.
1. 1/4-28 UNF × 2.00 HEX HEAD BOLT
2. #8.(.164)-32 UNC × 2.00 HEX HEAD BOLT
3. 3/8-16 UNC × 1.75 PAN HEAD MACHINE BOLT
4. 5/16-18 UNC × 1.75 HEXAGON SOCKET HEAD CAP BOLT

Project 6-21: Millimeters

Given the collar shown in Figure P6-21, add the following set screws.

1. Create an assembly drawing.
2. Create a BOM.
3. Create a dimensioned drawing of the collar. Specify a thread specification for each hole as required by the designated set screw.

A.
1. M4 × 6 ANSI B18.3.5M SOCKET SET SCREW - HALF DOG POINT
2. M3 × 3 SOCKET SET SCREW - OVAL POINT
3. M2.5 × 4 B18.3.6M SOCKET SET SCREW - FLAT POINT
4. M4 × 5 B18.3.1M SOCKET HEAD CAP SCREW

B.
1. M2 × 4 B18.3.4M SOCKET BUTTON HEAD CAP SCREW
2. M3 × 6 B18.3.6M SOCKET SET SCREW -CONE POINT
3. M4 × 5 B18.3.6M SOCKET SET SCREW - FLAT POINT
4. M1.6 × 4 B18.3.6M SOCKET SET SCREW - CUP POINT

Project 6-22: Inches

Given the collar shown in Figure P6-22, add the following set screws.

1. Create an assembly drawing.
2. Create a BOM.
3. Create a dimensioned drawing of the collar. Specify a thread specification for each hole as required by the designated set screw.

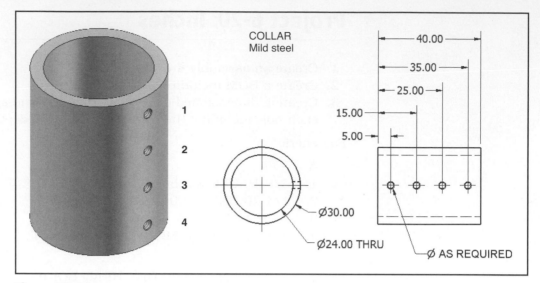

Figure P6-21

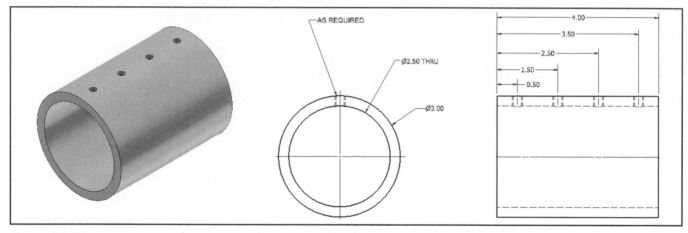

Figure P6-22

Holes:

A.

1. #10 (0.190) × .375 SQUARE HEAD SET SCREW - HALF DOG POINT-INCH
2. #6 (0.138) × .125 SLOTTED HEADLESS SET SCREW-FLAT POINT-INCH
3. #8 (0.164) × 3.75 SOCKET SET SCREW-CUP POINT-INCH
4. #5 (0.126) × .45 HEXAGON SOCKET SET SCREW-CONE POINT-INCH

B.

1. #6 (0.138) × .25 TYPE D-SOCKET SET SCREW-CUP POINT-INCH
2. #8 (0.164) × .1875 SLOTTED HEADLESS SET SCREW-DOG POINT-INCH
3. #10 (0.190) × .58 HEXAGON SOCKET SET SCREW-FLAT POINT-INCH
4 #6 (0.138) × .3125 SOCKET SET SCREW-HALF-DOG POINT-INCH

Project 6-23: Millimeters

Given the components shown in Figure P6-23:

1. Create an assembly drawing.
2. Animate the drawing.
3. Create an exploded isometric drawing.
4. Create a BOM.

Project 6-24: Inches

Given the assembly drawing shown in Figure P6-24:

1. Create an assembly drawing.
2. Animate the drawing.
3. Create an exploded isometric drawing.
4. Create a BOM.

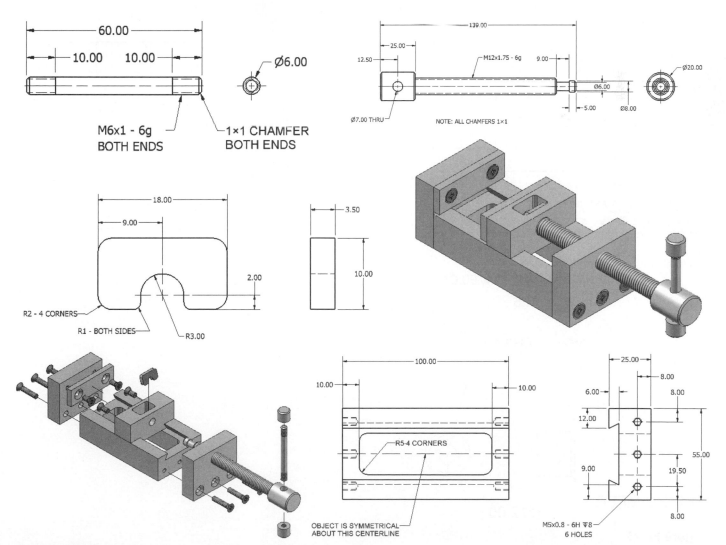

Figure P6-23

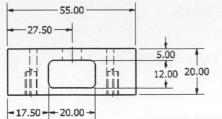

NOTE: ALL FILLETS = R2

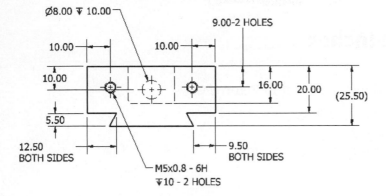

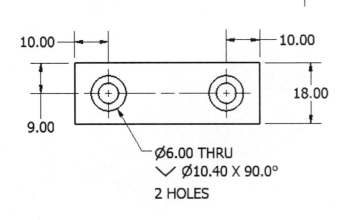

Ø6.00 THRU
∨ Ø10.40 X 90.0°
2 HOLES

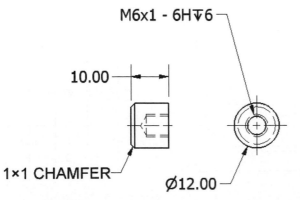

M6x1 - 6H▼6

10.00

1×1 CHAMFER

Ø12.00

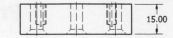

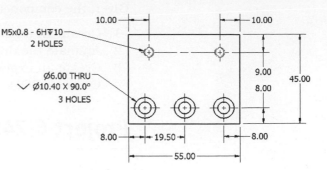

M5x0.8 - 6H▼10
2 HOLES

Ø6.00 THRU
∨ Ø10.40 X 90.0°
3 HOLES

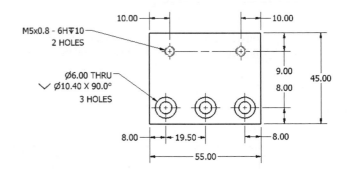

M5x0.8 - 6H▼10
2 HOLES

Ø6.00 THRU
∨ Ø10.40 X 90.0°
3 HOLES

Figure P6-23
(*Continued*)

ADJUSTABLE ASSEMBLY

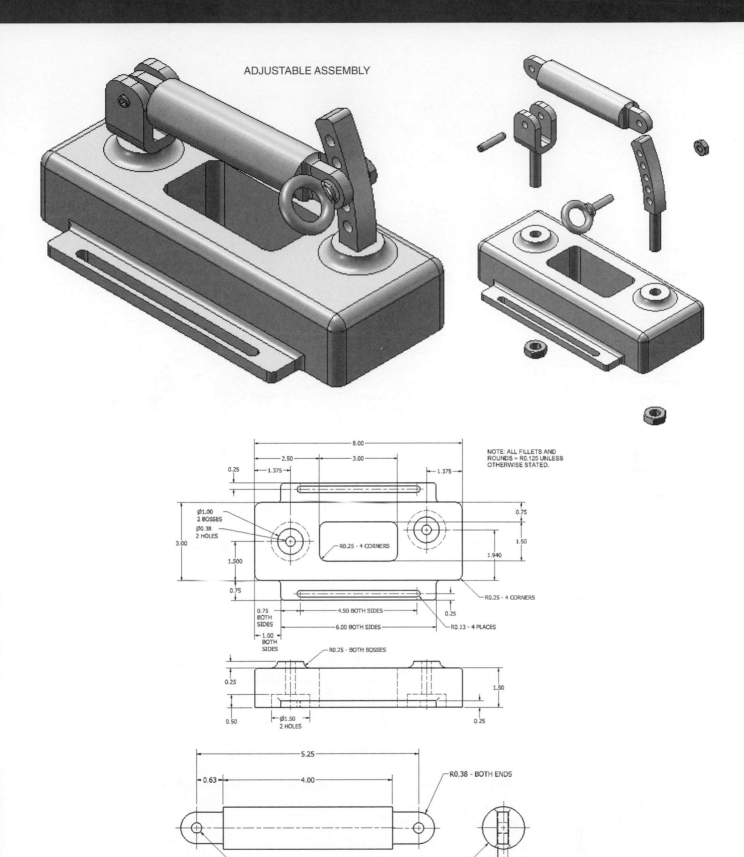

NOTE: ALL FILLETS AND ROUNDS = R0.125 UNLESS OTHERWISE STATED.

Ø1.00 2 BOSSES
Ø0.38 2 HOLES
R0.25 - 4 CORNERS
R0.25 - 4 CORNERS
R0.13 - 4 PLACES

8.00
2.50
3.00
1.375
0.25
1.375
0.75
3.00
1.500
1.50
1.940
0.75
0.75 BOTH SIDES
4.50 BOTH SIDES
0.25
6.00 BOTH SIDES
1.00 BOTH SIDES

R0.25 - BOTH BOSSES
0.25
1.50
0.50
Ø1.50 2 HOLES
0.25

5.25
0.63
4.00
R0.38 - BOTH ENDS
Ø0.25 +0.00 +0.02 - 2 HOLES
Ø1.00
0.12 BOTH ENDS
0.25 BOTH ENDS

NOTE: ALL FILLETS = R 0.125

Figure P6-24

NOTE: ALL FILLETS = R0.125

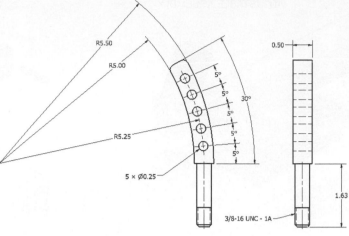

R5.50

R5.00

R5.25

5°
5°
5°
5°
5°

30°

5 × Ø0.25

0.50

1.63

3/8-16 UNC - 1A

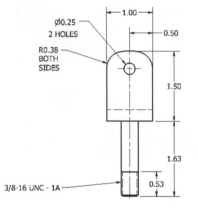

Ø0.25
2 HOLES

R0.38
BOTH
SIDES

1.00

0.50

1.50

1.63

0.53

3/8-16 UNC - 1A

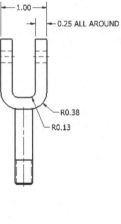

1.00

0.25 ALL AROUND

R0.38

R0.13

ITEM NO.	PART NUMBER	DESCRIPTION	MATL	QTY.
1	SP6-24a	BASE, CAST #4	CAST IRON	1
2	SP6-24c	SUPPORT, ROUND	SAE 1020	1
3	SP6-24d	POST, ADJUSTABLE	SAE 1020	1
4	SP6-24b	YOKE	SAE 1040	1
5	AI 18.15_type2 0.25x2.22-N-0.75	EYEBOLT, TYPE 2 FORGED	STEEL	1
6	SPS 0.25x1.125	PIN, SPRING, SLOTTED	STEEL	1
7	HHJNUT 0.2500-20-D-N	HEX NUT	STEEL	1
8	HHJNUT 0.3750-16-D-N	HEX NUT	STEEL	2

Figure P6-24
(*Continued*)

Project 6-25: Inches

Given the assembly shown in Figure P6-25:

1. Create an assembly drawing.
2. Animate the drawing.
3. Create an exploded isometric drawing.
4. Create a BOM.

Figure P6-25

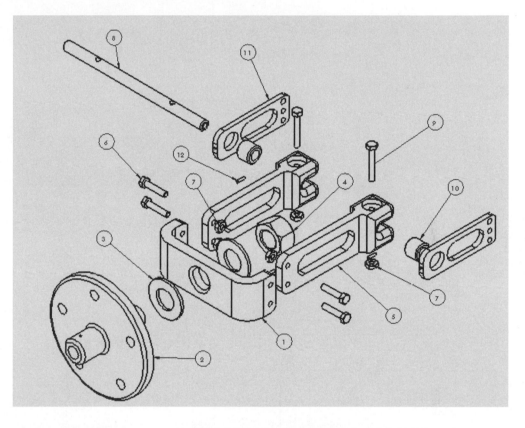

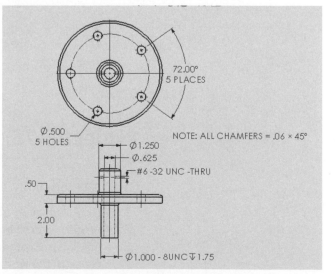

ITEM NO.	PART NUMBER	DESCRIPTION	QTY.
1	ME 311-1	WHEEL BRACKET	1
2	ME 311-2	WHEEL SUPPORT	1
3		1.00 × 1.75 × .06 PLAIN WASHER	2
4		1 × 8 UNC HEX NUT	1
5	ME 311-3	SUPPORT ARM	2
6		1/4 - 28 UNF × 1.25 HEX HEAD	4
7		1/4 - 28 UNF × 1.75 HEX HEAD	2
8		1/4 - 28 UNF HEX NUT	6
9	ME 311-4	PIVOT SHAFT	1
10		.500 × .875 .750 BEARING	2
11	ME 311-5	STATIONARY ARM	2
12		#6-32 × .560 UNC SET SCREW CONE POINT	2

Figure P6-25
(*Continued*)

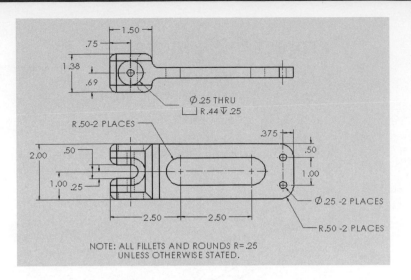

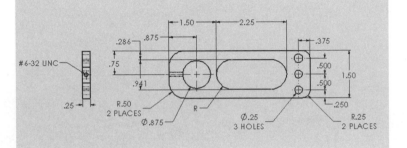

NOTE: ALL FILLETS AND ROUNDS R=.25
UNLESS OTHERWISE STATED.

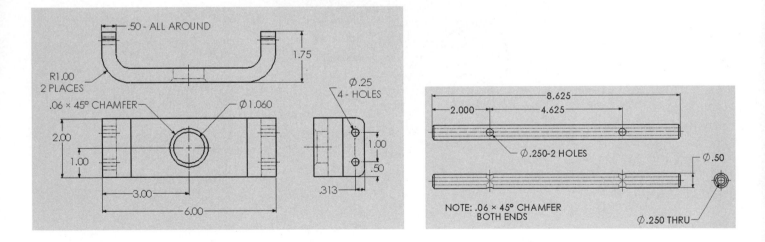

Project 6-26: Inches

Given the assembly shown in Figure P6-26:

1. Create an assembly drawing.
2. Animate the drawing.
3. Create an exploded isometric drawing.
4. Create a BOM.

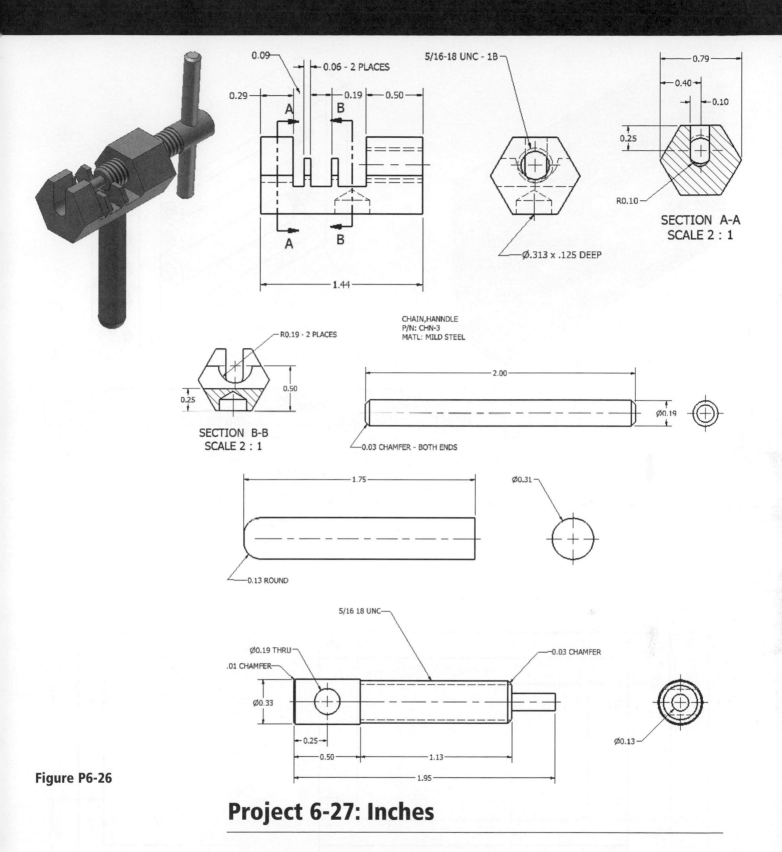

Figure P6-26

Project 6-27: Inches

Given the assembly shown in Figure P6-27:

1. Create an assembly drawing.
2. Animate the drawing.
3. Create an exploded isometric drawing.
4. Create a BOM.

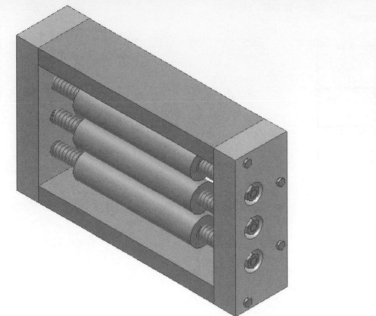

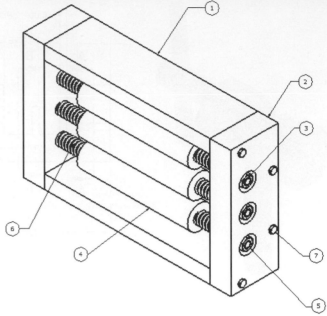

Parts List				
ITEM	PART NUMBER	DESCRIPTION	MATERIAL	QTY
1	AM311-1	BASE	Steel, Mild	1
2	AM311-2	PLATE,END	Steel, Mild	2
3	AM311-3	POST, GUIDE	Steel, Mild	3
4	EK-152	WEIGHT	Steel, Mild	3
5	AS 2465 - 1/2 UNC	HEX NUT	Steel, Mild	6
6		COMPRESSION SPRING	Steel, Mild	6
7	AS 2465 - 1/4 x 2 1/2 UNC	HEX BOLT	Steel, Mild	8

BASE
P/N AM311-1
MILD STEEL
1 REQD

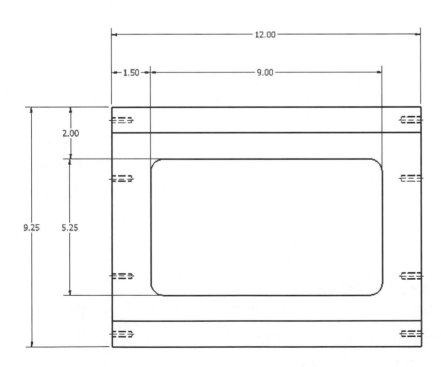

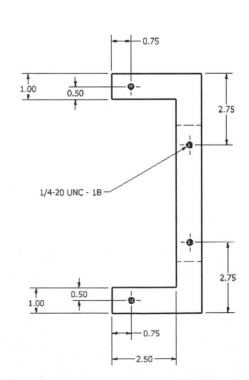

Figure P6-27

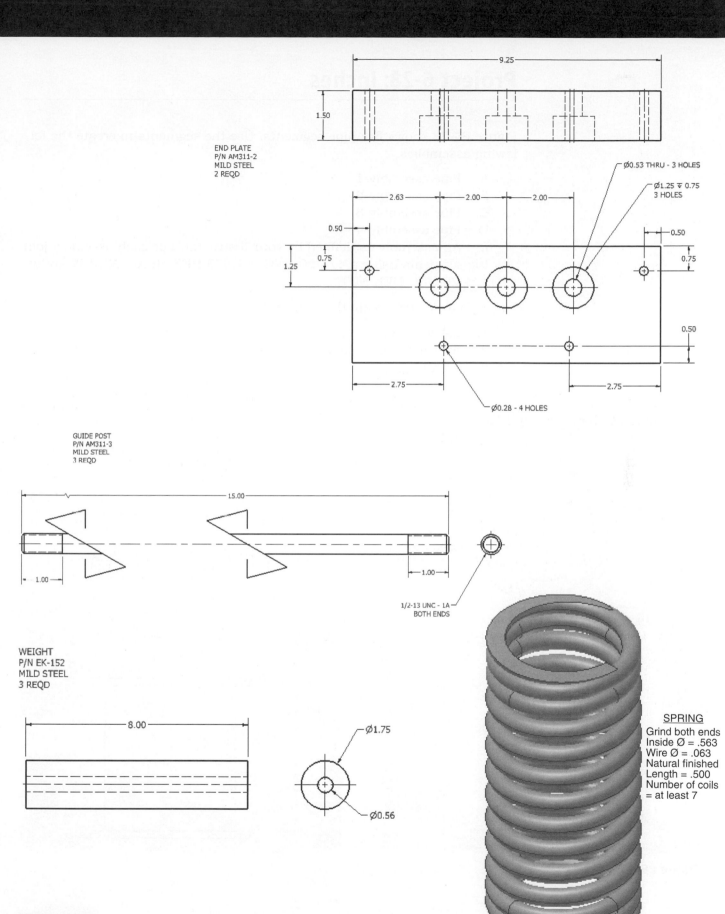

END PLATE
P/N AM311-2
MILD STEEL
2 REQD

9.25

1.50

Ø0.53 THRU - 3 HOLES

Ø1.25 ▼ 0.75
3 HOLES

2.63

2.00

2.00

0.50

0.50

0.75

0.75

1.25

0.50

2.75

2.75

Ø0.28 - 4 HOLES

GUIDE POST
P/N AM311-3
MILD STEEL
3 REQD

15.00

1.00

1.00

1/2-13 UNC - 1A
BOTH ENDS

WEIGHT
P/N EK-152
MILD STEEL
3 REQD

8.00

Ø1.75

Ø0.56

SPRING
Grind both ends
Inside Ø = .563
Wire Ø = .063
Natural finished
Length = .500
Number of coils
= at least 7

Figure P6-27
(Continued)

Project 6-28: Inches

Figure P6-28 shows five pipe segments. Use the segments to create the following assemblies.

A. Pipe assembly-1
B. Pipe assembly-2
C. Pipe assembly-3
D. Pipe assembly-4
E. An assembly as defined by your instructor. For each assembly join the segments using a 1/4-20 UNC × 1.375 HEX HEAD SCREW and a 1/4-20 UNC HEX NUT.

For each assembly create the following.

1. Assembly drawing
2. An isometric exploded drawing
3. A BOM

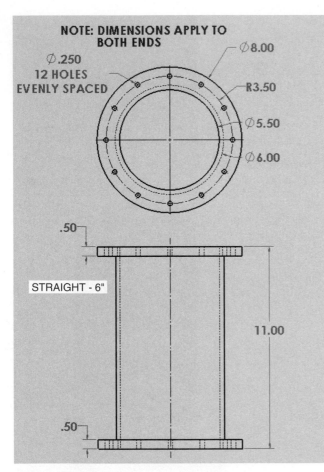

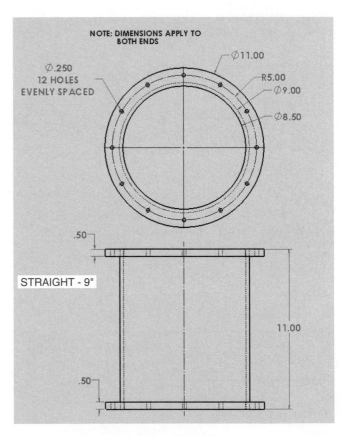

Figure P6-28

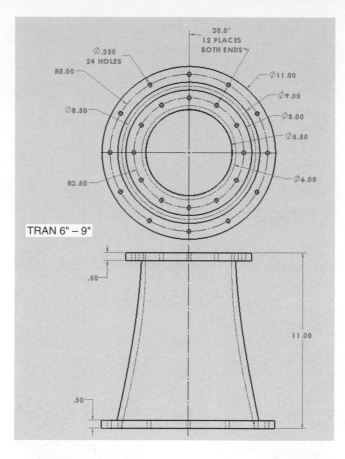

TRAN 6" – 9"

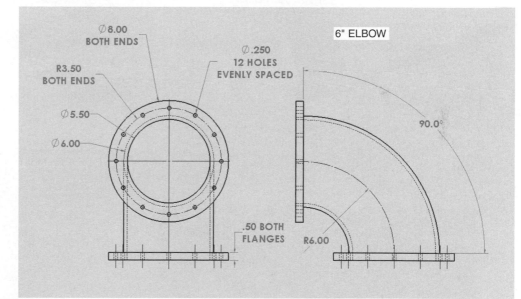

6" ELBOW

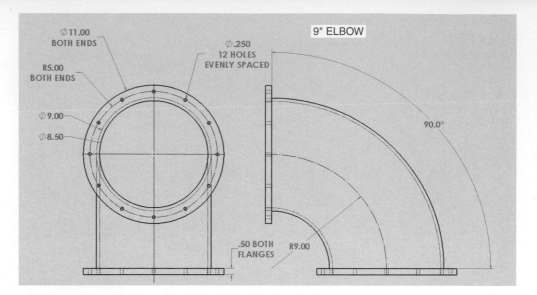

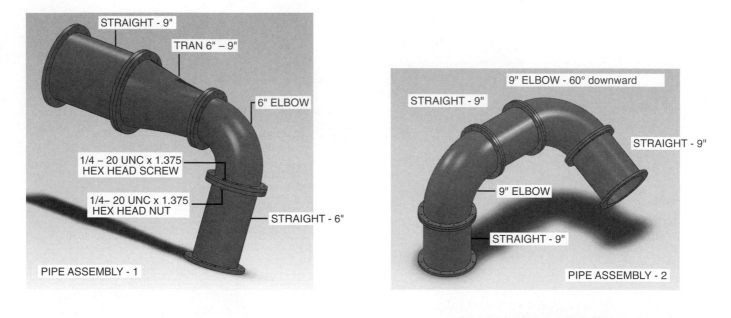

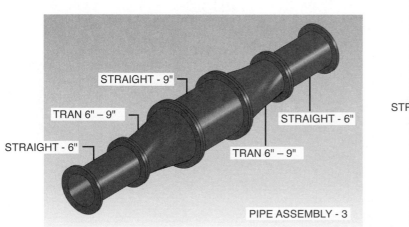

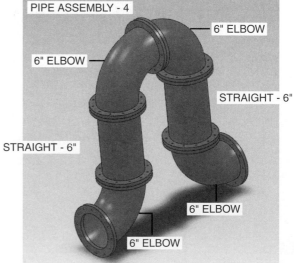

CHAPTER OBJECTIVES

- Learn how to dimension objects
- Learn about ANSI standards and conventions
- Learn how to dimension different shapes and features
- Learn the fundamentals of 3D dimensioning

7-1 Introduction

Dimensions are added to SolidWorks on **Drawing** documents. Dimensions will appear in **Part** documents, but these are construction dimensions. These sketch dimensions are used to create a part and are used when a sketch is edited. They may be modified as the part is being created using the **Smart Dimension** tool. They will not appear on the finished model or in assembly drawings.

Figure 7-1 shows a dimensioned shape. The upper drawing in Figure 7-1 shows the sketching dimensions that were created as the part was being created. The lower drawing in Figure 7-1 shows dimensions that were created using the **Smart Dimension** tool in a **Drawing** document. These are defining dimensions and will appear on the working drawings. This chapter will show how to apply these types of dimensions.

SolidWorks has ANSI Inch and ANSI Metric dimensions available. Other dimensioning systems such as ISO, are also available. This text is in compliance with ANSI standards.

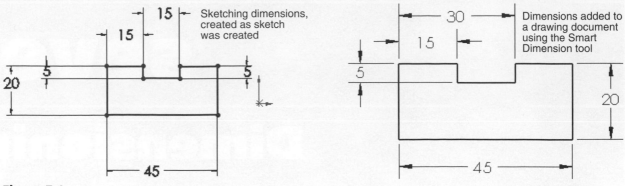

Figure 7-1

7-2 Terminology and Conventions—ANSI

Some Common Terms

Figure 7-2 shows both ANSI and ISO style dimensions. The terms apply to both styles.

Dimension lines: In mechanical drawings, lines between extension lines that end with an arrowhead and include a numerical dimensional value located within the line.

Extension lines: Lines that extend away from an object and allow dimensions to be located off the surface of an object.

Leader lines: Lines drawn at an angle, not horizontal or vertical, that are used to dimension specific shapes such as holes. The start point of a leader line includes an arrowhead. Numerical values are drawn at the end opposite the arrowhead.

Linear dimensions: Dimensions that define the straight-line distance between two points.

Angular dimensions: Dimensions that define the angular value, measured in degrees, between two straight lines.

Some Dimensioning Conventions

See Figure 7-3.

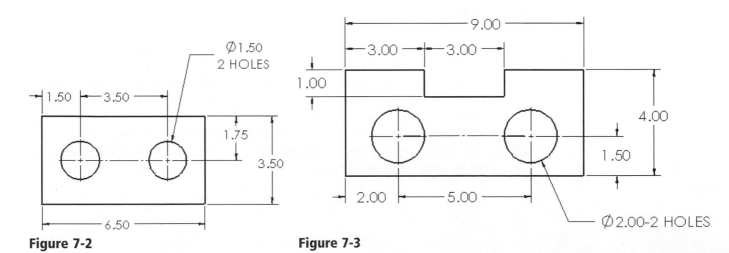

Figure 7-2

Figure 7-3

1 Dimension lines should be drawn evenly spaced; that is, the distance between dimension lines should be uniform. A general rule of thumb is to locate dimension lines about 1/2 in. or 15 mm apart.

2 There should a noticeable gap between the edge of a part and the beginning of an extension line. This serves as a visual break between the object and the extension line. The visual difference between the line types can be enhanced by using different colors for the two types of lines.

3 Leader lines are used to define the size of holes and should be positioned so that the arrowhead points toward the center of the hole.

4 Centerlines may be used as extension lines. No gap is used when a centerline is extended beyond the edge lines of an object.

5 Align dimension lines whenever possible to give the drawing a neat, organized appearance.

Some Common Errors to Avoid

See Figure 7-4.

1 Avoid crossing extension lines. Place longer dimensions farther away from the object than shorter dimensions.

2 Do not locate dimensions within cutouts; always use extension lines.

3 Do not locate any dimension close to the object. Dimension lines should be at least 1/2 in. or 15 mm from the edge of the object.

4 Avoid long extension lines. Locate dimensions in the same general area as the feature being defined.

7-3 Adding Dimensions to a Drawing

Figure 7-5 shows a part that includes two holes. This section will explain how to add dimensions to the part. The part was drawn as a **Part** document and saved as **Block, 2 Holes**. See Figure 7-9 for the part's dimensions. The part is 0.50 thick.

Some common errors

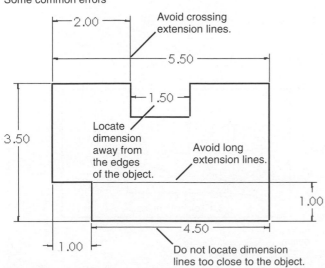

Figure 7-4

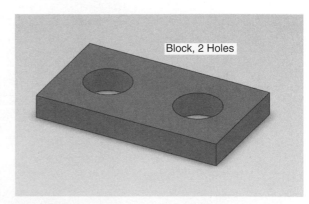

Figure 7-5

1 Click **New, Drawing, OK** and start a new drawing.

2 Create a top view of the Block, 2 Holes.

In this example we will work with only one view.

3 Click the **Annotation** tab and select the **Center Mark** option. In the **Center Mark PropertyManager**, click the **Linear Center Mark** tool.

4 Add a centerline between the two holes by clicking the outside edge of each circle.

The holes now have the same horizontal centerline, so only one vertical dimension can be used to define the hole's location.

TIP

Centerlines can be extended by first clicking them and then dragging an endpoint to a new location.

---

5 Click the **Smart Dimension** tool, click the top end of the left hole's vertical centerline and the upper left corner of the block. Click the drawing screen to complete the dimension.

See Figure 7-6.

6 Use the **Smart Dimension** tool and add the horizontal and vertical dimensions as shown.

See Figure 7-7.

Note that the dimension values for the vertical dimensions are written horizontally. This is in compliance with ANSI standards.

RULE

Keep dimension lines aligned and evenly spaced.

Figure 7-6

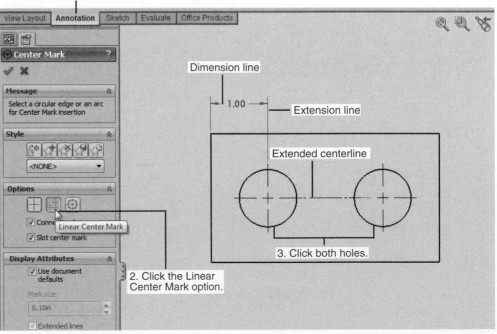

Figure 7-7

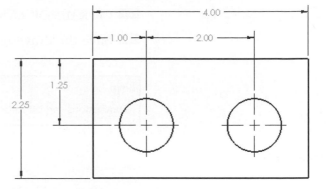

7 Click the **Smart Dimension** tool, click the edge of the left hole, and move the cursor away from the hole.

Note that the leader arrow always points at the center of the hole.

8 Select a location off the surface of the part and click the mouse.

> **RULE**
>
> Never locate dimensions on the surface of the part.

9 Go to the **Dimension PropertyManager** at the left of the screen and locate the cursor in the **Dimension Text** box, and click the mouse.

The text already in the box defines the hole's diameter. See Figure 7-8.

10 Move the cursor to the end of the existing text line, press **<Enter>** to start a new text line, and type **2 HOLES.**

Figure 7-8

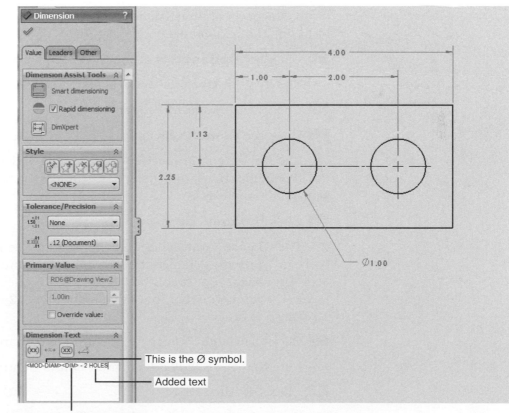

This is the dimension value.

11 Click the OK check mark.

12 Save the drawing.

TIP
Dimensions can be relocated by clicking and dragging the dimension text.

Figure 7-9

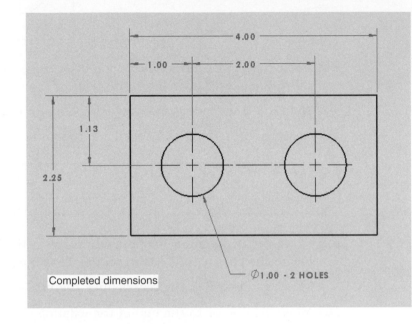

Completed dimensions

Ø1.00 - 2 HOLES

Controlling Dimensions

Various aspects of dimensions can be edited, such as text height, arrow location, and text values.

1 Click the **Options** tool at the top of the screen.

The **System Options-General** dialog box will appear. See Figure 7-10.

2 Click the **Document Properties** tab.

3 Click the **Dimensions** option.

The **Document Properties-Dimensions** dialog box can be used to edit the style and form of dimensions. It can also be used to change the way arrows are applied.

4 Click the **Font** option.

The **Choose Font** dialog box will appear. See Figure 7-11. This dialog box can be used to change the font, font style, and height of dimension text. The height of text can be measured in inches, millimeters, or points. *Point* is a printer's term that equals about 1/72 of an inch. (There are 12 points to a *pica*.)

5 Click the **Height: Units** radio button and change the height to **0.250in.**

Note that the SolidWorks default font is Century Gothic.

6 Click **OK,** then OK.

Figure 7-11 shows the enlarged dimensions.

Figure 7-10

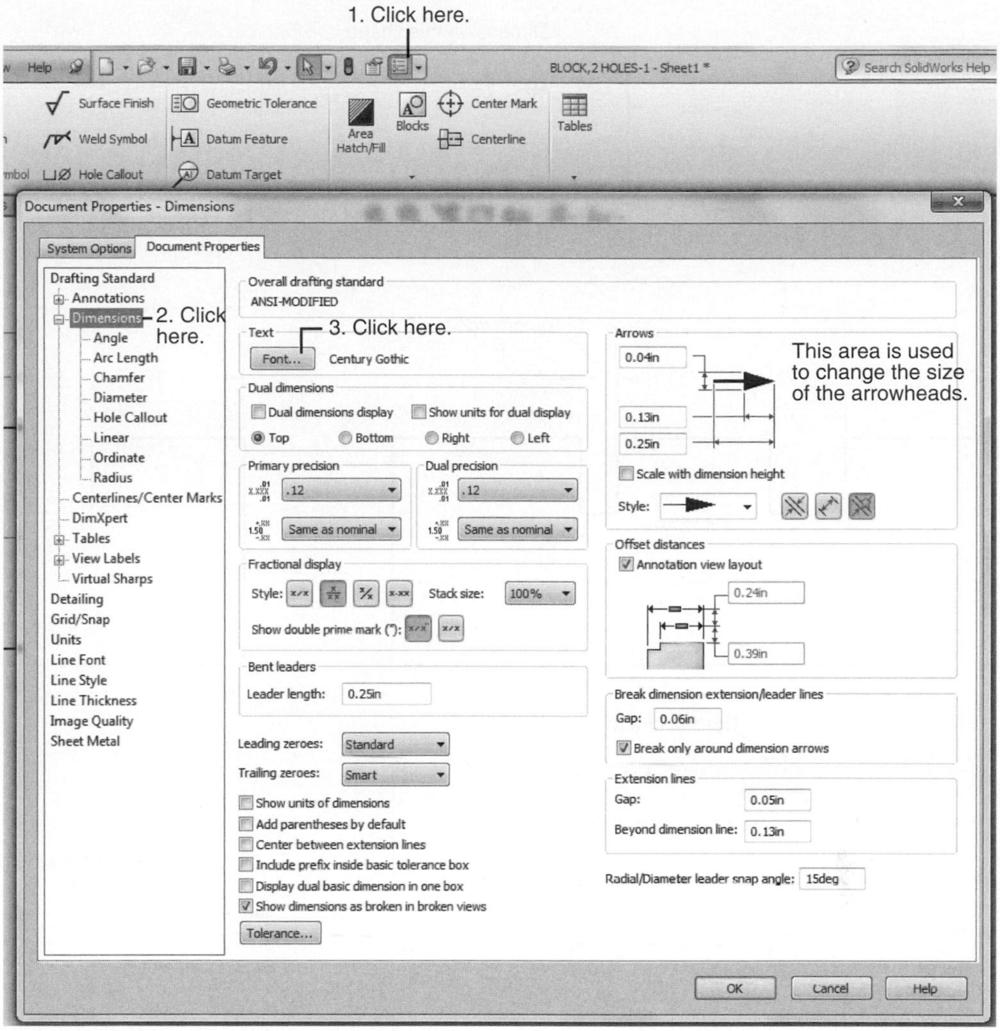

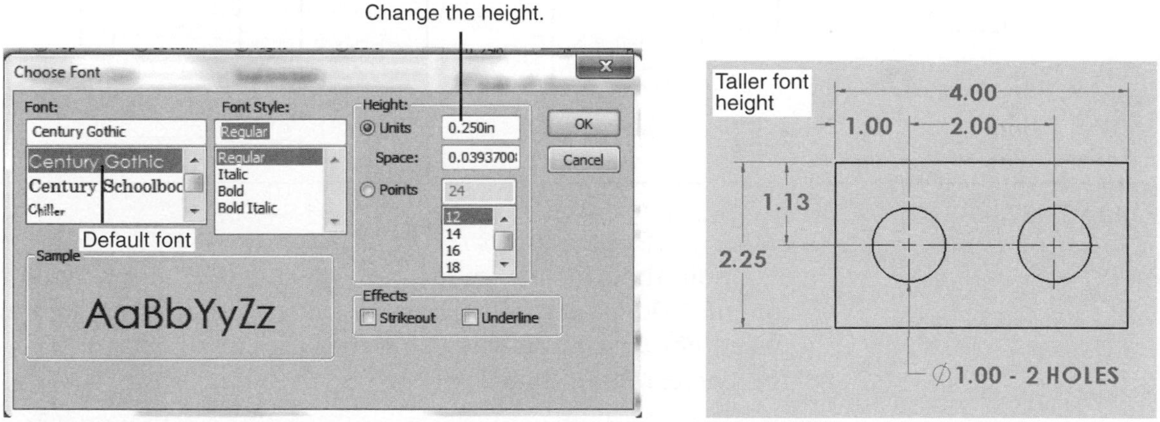

1. Click here.

Document Properties - Dimensions

System Options | Document Properties

Drafting Standard
⊕ Annotations
⊕ Dimensions — 2. Click here.
    Angle
    Arc Length
    Chamfer
    Diameter
    Hole Callout
    Linear
    Ordinate
    Radius
  Centerlines/Center Marks
  DimXpert
⊕ Tables
⊕ View Labels
    Virtual Sharps
Detailing
Grid/Snap
Units
Line Font
Line Style
Line Thickness
Image Quality
Sheet Metal

Overall drafting standard
ANSI-MODIFIED

Text — 3. Click here.
Font... | Century Gothic

Dual dimensions
☐ Dual dimensions display   ☐ Show units for dual display
◉ Top   ○ Bottom   ○ Right   ○ Left

Primary precision   Dual precision
.12   .12
1.50 Same as nominal   1.50 Same as nominal

Fractional display
Style: [x/x] [x/xx] [%] [x-xx]   Stack size: [100%]

Show double prime mark ("): [x/x] [x/x]

Bent leaders
Leader length: 0.25in

Leading zeroes: Standard
Trailing zeroes: Smart

☐ Show units of dimensions
☐ Add parentheses by default
☐ Center between extension lines
☐ Include prefix inside basic tolerance box
☐ Display dual basic dimension in one box
☑ Show dimensions as broken in broken views

Tolerance...

Arrows
0.04in
0.13in
0.25in
This area is used to change the size of the arrowheads.

☐ Scale with dimension height

Style: [→] [X] [✎] [X]

Offset distances
☑ Annotation view layout
0.24in
0.39in

Break dimension extension/leader lines
Gap: 0.06in
☑ Break only around dimension arrows

Extension lines
Gap: 0.05in
Beyond dimension line: 0.13in

Radial/Diameter leader snap angle: 15deg

OK | Cancel | Help

Change the height.

Choose Font

Font:
Century Gothic
[Century Gothic]
Century Schoolboc
Chiller
  └ Default font

Font Style:
Regular
[Regular]
Italic
Bold
Bold Italic

Height:
◉ Units   0.250in
  Space: 0.0393700
○ Points 24
  [12]
  14
  16
  18

OK
Cancel

Sample
AaBbYyZz

Effects
☐ Strikeout   ☐ Underline

Taller font height

4.00
1.00 2.00
1.13
2.25
Ø1.00 - 2 HOLES

Figure 7-11

Dimensioning Short Distances

Figure 7-12 shows an object that includes several short distances. We will start by using the standard dimensions settings and show how to edit them for a particular situation.

1 Use the **Smart Dimension** tool and add dimensions to the drawing.

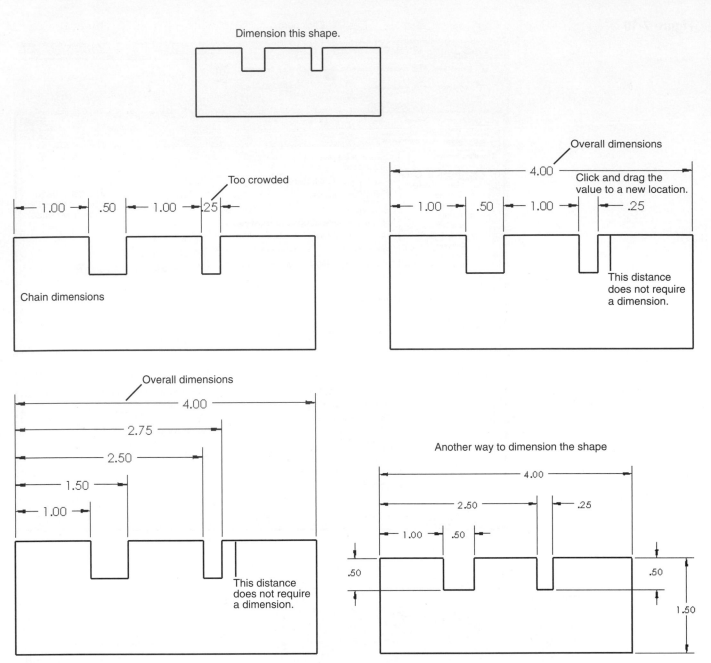

Figure 7-12

Note that the arrows for the .50 dimension are aligned with the arrows for the 1.00 dimensions. Dimensions that are aligned in a single row are called **chain dimensions.** Note that the .25 dimension is crowded between the two extension lines.

> **RULE**
>
> Never squeeze dimension values. Dimension values should always be presented clearly and should be easy to read.

There are several possible solutions to the crowded .25 value.

 Click and drag the .25 dimension to the right outside the extension lines.

 Add the **4.00** overall dimension.

Dimensions that define the total length and width of an object are called **overall dimensions**. In this example the dimension 4.00 defines the total length of the part, so it is an overall dimension. Overall dimensions are located farthest away from the edge of the part.

The right edge of the part, the section below the .25 does not need a dimension. The reason for this will be discussed in the next chapter, on tolerances.

> **TIP**
>
> To delete an existing dimension, click the dimension and press the <Del> key.

Figure 7-12 shows two other options for dimensioning. The first is the baseline method, in which all dimensions are taken from the same datum line. The second method is a combination of chain and baseline dimensions.

> **RULE**
>
> Never dimension the same distance twice. This is called double dimensioning.

Figure 7-13 shows an example of double dimensioning. The top edge distance is dimensioned twice: once using the 1.00 + .50 + 1.00 + .25 + 1.25 dimensions, and a second time using the 4.00 dimension. One of the dimensions must be omitted. Double dimensioning will be explained in more detail in the next chapter.

Figure 7-13

ERROR - double dimensions

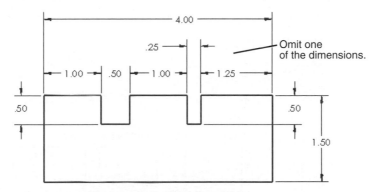

The top edge is dimensioned twice.

Autodimension Tool

The **Autodimension** tool will automatically add dimensions to a drawing.

> **WARNING**
>
> The dimensions created using the **Autodimension** tool are not always in the best locations. The dimensions must be relocated to be in compliance with ANSI conventions.

Figure 7-14 shows a shape to be dimensioned using the **Autodimension** tool.

 Click the arrow on the **Annotation** tab, then click the **Autodimension** tab.

Figure 7-14

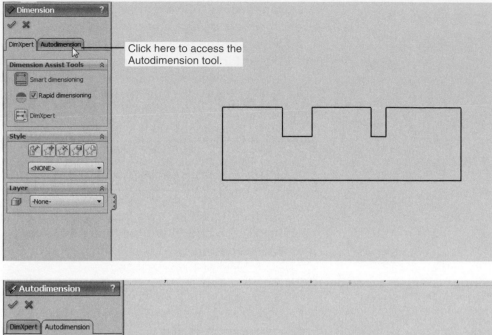

Click here to access the Autodimension tool.

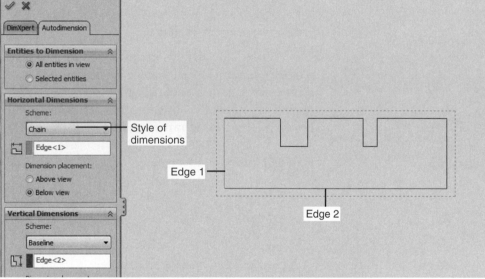

Style of dimensions

Edge 1

Edge 2

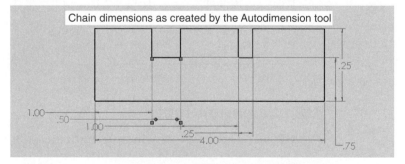

Chain dimensions as created by the Autodimension tool

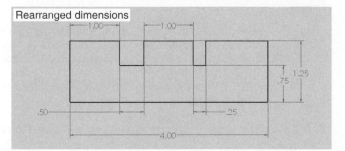

Rearranged dimensions

The **Entities to Dimension** dialog box will appear.

2 Select the **Chain Scheme,** define **Edge 1** and **Edge 2,** click the **Apply** box, and click the OK check mark.

Solidworks will automatically pick edges 1 and 2. If it does not, or the edges selected are not the ones you want, click the **Edge** box, then click the edge. The word **Edge<1>** should appear in the box.

Figure 7-14 shows the dimensions applied using the **Autodimension** tool. They are not in acceptable positions.

3 Rearrange the dimensions to comply with standard conventions.

Figure 7-15 shows the shape shown in Figure 7-14 dimensioned using the baseline scheme, which are created as follows.

Figure 7-15

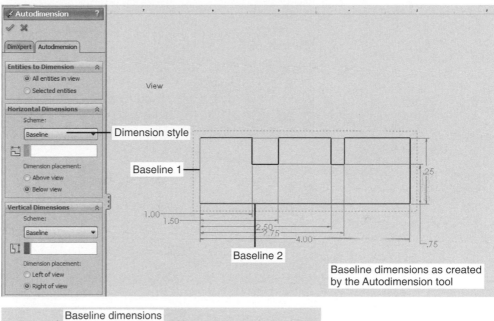

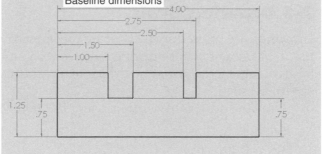

To Create Baseline Dimensions

1 Access the **Autodimension** tool and select the **Baseline Scheme.**

2 Select **Edge 1** and **Edge 2.**

3 Click **Apply.**

4 Click the OK check mark.

Figure 7-15 shows the dimensions created by the **Autodimension** tool and how the dimensions can be rearranged.

Figure 7-16 shows the object dimensioned using the **Ordinate Scheme** of the **Autodimension** tool. Some of the created dimensions are located on the surface of the part. This is a violation of the convention that states that dimensions should never be located on the surface of the part. Figure 7-16 shows how the ordinate dimensions were rearranged.

Figure 7-16

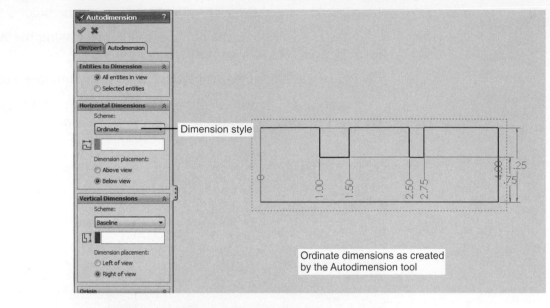

Ordinate dimensions as created by the Autodimension tool

Ordinate dimensions

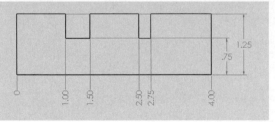

7-4 Drawing Scale

Drawings are often drawn "to scale" because the actual part is either too big to fit on a sheet of drawing paper or too small to be seen. For example, a microchip circuit must be drawn at several thousand times its actual size to be seen.

Drawing scales are written using the following formats:

SCALE: 1=1

SCALE: FULL

SCALE: 1000=1

SCALE: .25=1

In each example the value on the left indicates the scale factor. A value greater than 1 indicates that the drawing is larger than actual size. A value smaller than 1 indicates that the drawing is smaller than actual size.

Regardless of the drawing scale selected the dimension values must be true size. Figure 7-17 shows the same rectangle drawn at two different scales. The top rectangle is drawn at a scale of 1 = 1, or its true size. The bottom rectangle is drawn at a scale of 2 = 1, or twice its true size. In both examples the 3.00 dimension remains the same.

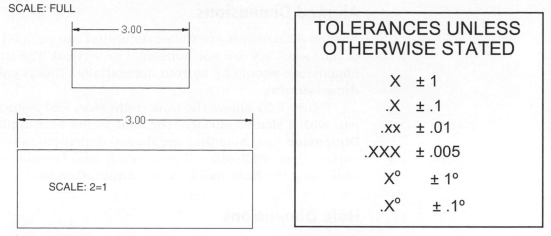

SCALE: FULL

3.00

3.00

SCALE: 2=1

Figure 7-17

TOLERANCES UNLESS OTHERWISE STATED	
X	± 1
.X	± .1
.xx	± .01
.XXX	± .005
X°	± 1°
.X°	± .1°

Figure 7-18

7-5 Units

It is important to understand that dimension values are not the same as mathematical units. Dimension values are manufacturing instructions and always include a tolerance, even if the tolerance value is not stated. Manufacturers use a predefined set of standard dimensions that are applied to any dimensional value that does not include a written tolerance. Standard tolerance values differ from organization to organization. Figure 7-18 shows a chart of standard tolerances.

In Figure 7-19 a distance is dimensioned twice: once as 5.50 and a second time as 5.5000. Mathematically these two values are equal, but they are not the same manufacturing instruction. The 5.50 value could, for example, have a standard tolerance of ±.01, whereas the 5.5000 value could have a standard tolerance of ±.0005. A tolerance of 6.0005 is more difficult and therefore more expensive to manufacture than a tolerance of ±.01.

Figure 7-20 shows examples of units expressed in millimeters and in decimal inches. A zero is not required to the left of the decimal point for decimal inch values less than one. Millimeter values do not require zeros to the right of the decimal point. Millimeter and decimal inch values never include symbols; the units will be defined in the title block of the drawing.

These dimensions are not the same. They have different tolerance requirements.

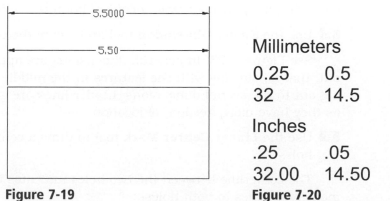

5.5000

5.50

Figure 7-19

Millimeters

| 0.25 | 0.5 | 0.033 |
| 32 | 14.5 | 3 |

Zero required

Inches

No zero required

| .25 | .05 | .033 |
| 32.00 | 14.50 | 3.000 |

Figure 7-20

Aligned Dimensions

Aligned dimensions are dimensions that are parallel to a slanted edge or surface. They are not horizontal or vertical. The units for aligned dimensions should be written horizontally. This is called *unidirectional dimensioning.*

Figure 7-21 shows the front, right side, and isometric views of an a part with a slanted surface. The dimensions were applied using the **Smart Dimension** tool. Note that the slanted dimension, aligned with the slanted surface, has unidirectional (horizontal) text. The hole dimension was created using the **Note** tool from the **Annotation** tab.

Hole Dimensions

Figure 7-22 shows an object that has two holes, one blind, and one completely through. The object has filleted corners. In this section we will add dimensions to the views.

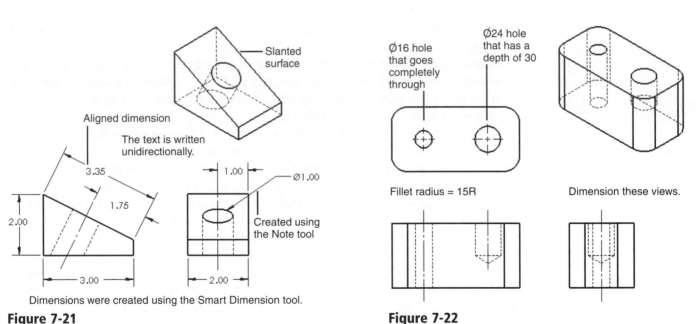

Figure 7-21

Figure 7-22

The holes were drawn using the **Hole Wizard** tool. The **Hole Wizard** tool will automatically create a conical point to a blind hole.

1 Use the **Smart Dimension** tool and locate the two holes.

See Figure 7-23. In general, dimensions are applied from the inside out, that is, starting with the features in the middle of the part and working out to the overall dimensions. Leader lines are generally applied last, as they have more freedom of location.

2 Use the **Linear Center Mark** tool to draw a centerline between the two holes.

The centerline between the two holes indicates that the vertical 30 dimension applies to both holes.

Figure 7-23

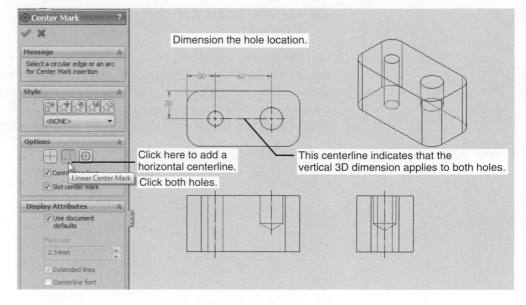

Change the arrows on the 30 dimensions (both the horizontal and vertical) so that they are inside the extension lines.

3 Click the **Options** tool at the top of the screen.

4 Click the **Document Properties** tab, click **Dimensions,** then click the **Inside** button in the **Arrows** box.

See Figure 7-24. The arrows for the 30 dimensions are located within the extension lines. All dimensions will now have their arrows located inside the extension lines.

Figure 7-24

5 Use the **Smart Dimension** tool and add a dimension to one of the filleted corners.

Note that the arrow is on the outside of the arc. The direction of the arrow that defines the arc can be changed by clicking the **Options** tool, **Document Properties** tab, **Radius** option, and selecting the **Broken Leader, Horizontal Text** option. See Figure 7-25. The arrow for the radius dimension will be located outside the fillet, pointing inward.

Figure 7-25

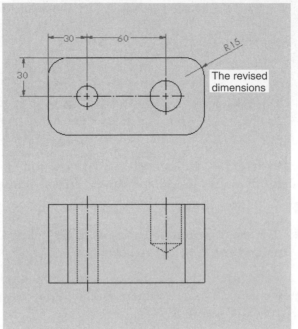

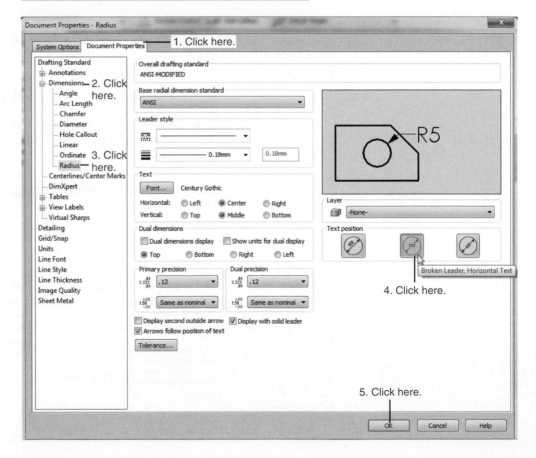

TIP

The dimension options found on the **Document PropertyManager** will change all dimensions. Clicking a dimension and using the **Dimension PropertyManager** allows you to change just that dimension.

6 Click the fillet dimension again, go to the **Dimension Text** block on the **Dimension PropertyManager,** and type **4 CORNERS** as shown.

See Figure 7-26.

Figure 7-26

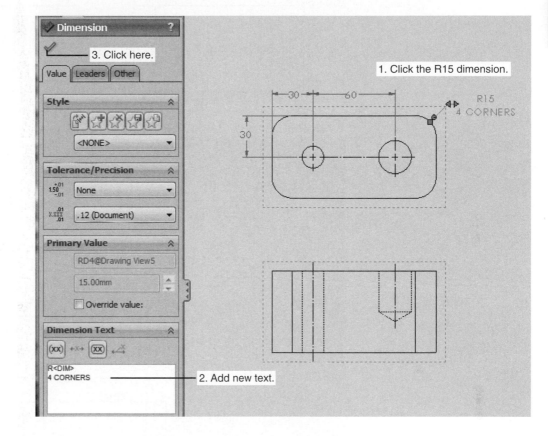

7 Click **OK, Apply,** and OK.

8 Use the **Smart Dimension** tool and dimension the Ø16 hole.

The Ø16 hole goes completely through the part, so no depth specification is required.

See Figure 7-27.

9 Dimension the Ø24 hole.

Initially, just the hole's diameter value will appear. The hole does not go completely through the part, so a depth specification is required.

10 Click the Ø24 dimension.

The **Dimension PropertyManager** will appear. See Figure 7-28. Use the **Dimension Text** box to modify the dimension.

Figure 7-27

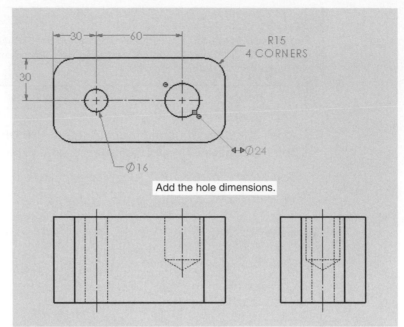

Add the hole dimensions.

Figure 7-28

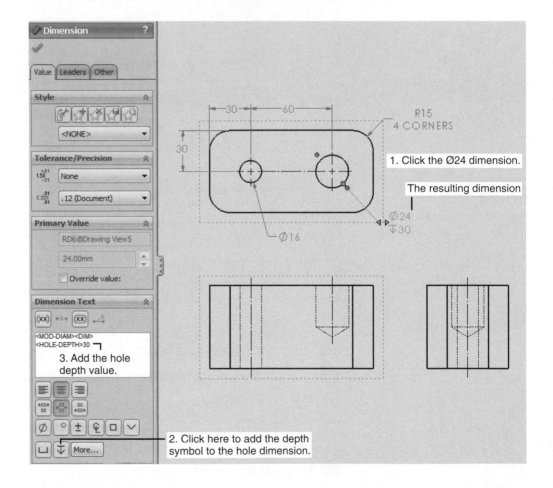

1. Click the Ø24 dimension.

The resulting dimension

3. Add the hole depth value.

2. Click here to add the depth symbol to the hole dimension.

11 Locate the cursor to the right of the existing dimension, click the **Hole Depth** symbol, and enter the depth value of **30.** Click the OK check mark.

12 Complete the dimensions.

See Figure 7-29.

Figure 7-29

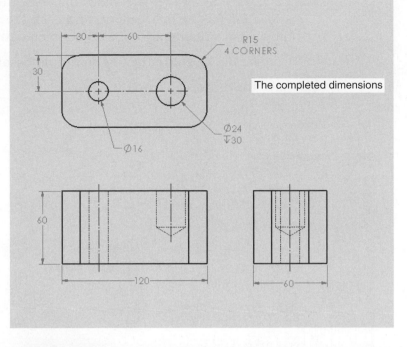

The completed dimensions

NOTE

If the **Hole Callout** tool had been used, and if this hole had been created using the **Hole Wizard,** the depth dimension would appear automatically. The **Hole Callout** tool will be demonstrated in the next section.

7-6 Dimensioning Holes and Fillets

A *blind hole* is a hole that does not go completely through an object. It has a depth requirement. Figure 7-30 shows a 2.00 × 2.00 × 2.00 block with a blind Ø0.50 × 1.18 DEEP hole. It was created as follows.

Dimensioning a Blind Hole

1 Draw the block.

2 Click the **Hole Wizard** tool.

3 Click the **Hole** tool in the **Hole Type** box. Define the hole using the **Ansi Inch** standard with a diameter of **1/2** and a depth of **1.18in.**

4 Click the **Positions** tab.

5 Locate the hole as shown.

The initial location is an approximation. Use the **Smart Dimension** tool to specify the exact location of the hole's centerpoint.

6 Click the OK check mark.

7 Save the drawing as **Block, Blind.**

8 Start a new **Drawing** document and create a front and a top orthographic view of the **Block, Blind**.

9 Add dimensions to the views.

10 Click the **Annotation** tab and click the **Hole Callout** option.

11 Click the edge of the hole, move the cursor away from the hole, define a location for the hole callout, and click the mouse. The hole callout dimension will initially appear as a rectangular box.

Change the height of the text font if necessary.

12 Save the drawing.

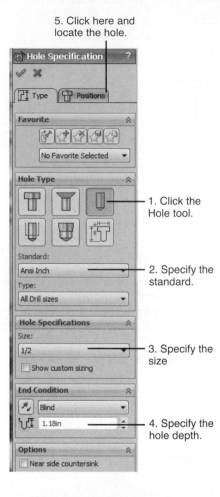

5. Click here and locate the hole.

1. Click the Hole tool.

2. Specify the standard.

3. Specify the size

4. Specify the hole depth.

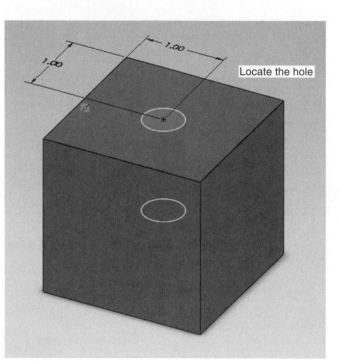

Locate the hole

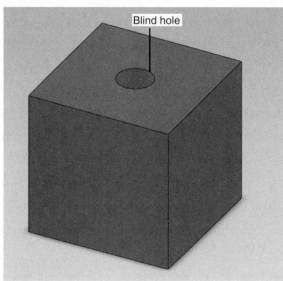

Blind hole

Figure 7-30

Figure 7-30
(*Continued*)

Chapter 7

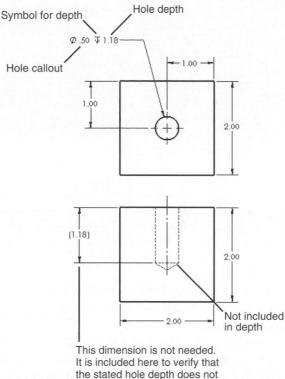

Note that the hole includes a conical point. Holes manufactured using twist drills will have conical points. The conical point is not included in the hole's depth dimension. A special drill bit can be used to create a flat-bottomed hole.

Figure 7-31 shows three different methods that can be used to dimension a blind hole.

Figure 7-32 shows three methods of dimensioning holes in section views. The single line note version is the preferred method.

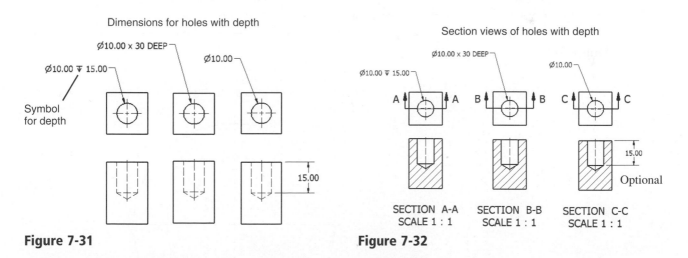

Figure 7-31

Figure 7-32

Dimensioning Hole Patterns

Figure 7-33 shows two different hole patterns dimensioned. The circular pattern includes the note Ø10-4 HOLES. This note serves to define all four holes within the object.

Figure 7-33

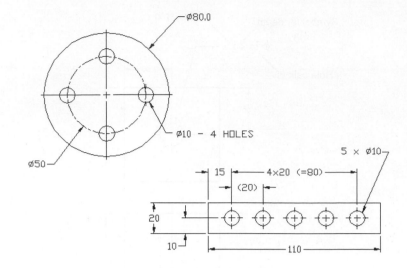

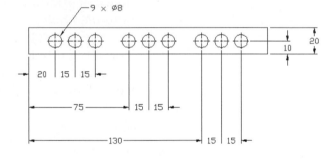

Figure 7-33 also shows a rectangular object that contains five holes of equal diameter, equally spaced from one another. The notation 5 × Ø10 specifies five holes of 10 diameter. The notation 4 × 20 (=80) means four equal spaces of 20. The notation (=80) is a reference dimension and is included for convenience. Reference dimensions are explained in Chapter 9.

Figure 7-34 shows two additional methods for dimensioning repeating hole patterns. Figure 7-35 shows a circular hole pattern that includes two

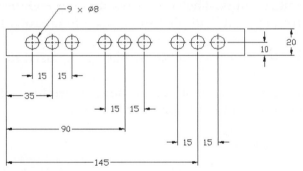

Figure 7-34

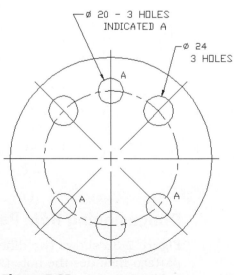

Figure 7-35

different hole diameters. The hole diameters are not noticeably different and could be confused. One group is defined by indicating letter (A); the other is dimensioned in a normal manner.

7-7 Dimensioning Counterbored and Countersunk Holes

Counterbored holes are dimensioned in the sequence of their manufacture. First the hole's diameter is given, then the counterbore diameter, then the depth of the counterbore.

Figure 7-36 shows a part that contains two counterbored holes; one goes completely through and the other is blind. Dimensions will applied to both.

Figure 7-36

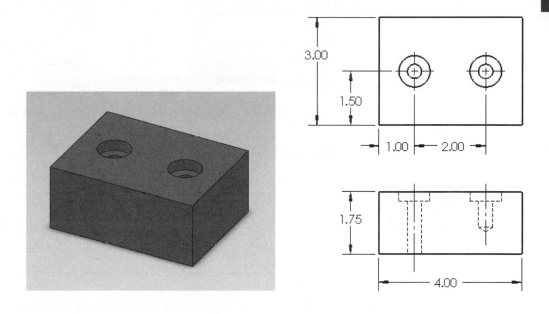

1 Draw a **3.00 × 4.00 × 1.75** block.

2 Click the **Hole Wizard** tool, click the **Counterbore** option, and draw the counterbored holes.

Remember that one hole goes completely through the block, and the other is blind and has a depth of 1.00.

3 Specify a **Hex Screw** with a **3/8** diameter.

See Figure 7-37. SolidWorks will automatically select the diameter for the counterbored hole that will accommodate a Ø3/8 Hex Screw.

Note that the counterbored hole has a small chamfer added. This can be changed by changing the values in the **Options** box.

4 Locate the holes using the given dimensions.

5 Access the **Near side** countersink option and change the distance value to **0.0in.** This will remove the countersink

6 Save the block as **Block, Cbore.**

7 Start a new **Drawing** document and create a front and a top orthographic view of the **Block, Cbore.**

Figure 7-37

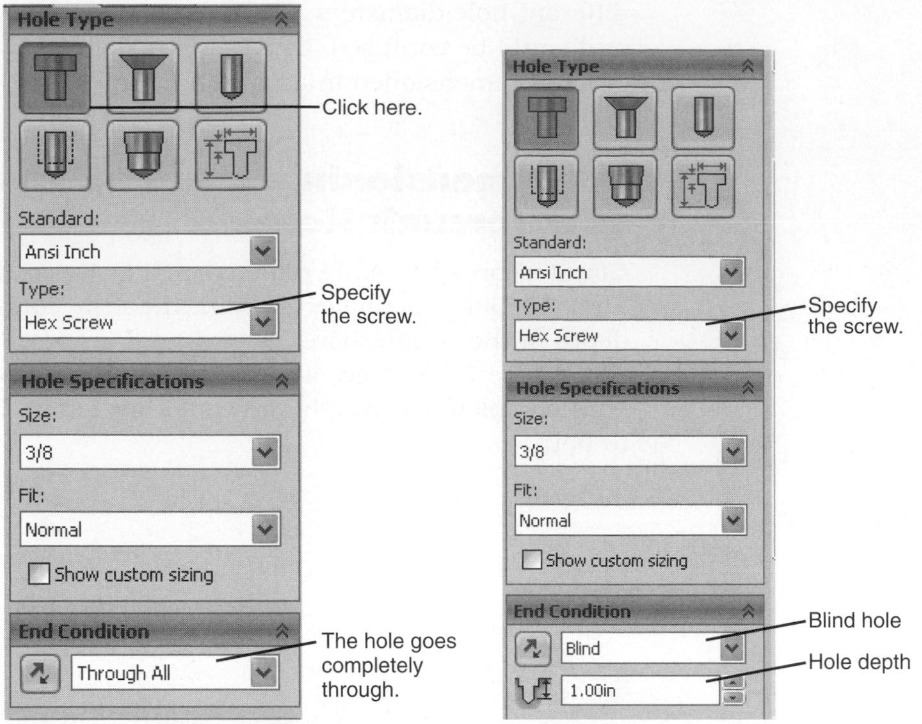

Click here.
Specify the screw.
The hole goes completely through.

Specify the screw.
Blind hole
Hole depth

8 Add all dimensions other than the hole dimensions.

9 Click the **Annotation** tab and select the **Hole Callout** tool.

See Figure 7-37.

10 Click the edge of each hole, move the cursor away from the hole, and click the mouse when a suitable location is found.

The counterbored hole's dimension note is interpreted as shown in Figure 7-38.

Figure 7-39 shows the Block, Cbore assembled with hex head screws. SolidWorks will automatically generate the correct size counterbored hole for a specified screw. The counterbore depth will align the top of the screw head with the top surface of the part and will define a hole diameter that includes clearance between the fastener and the hole. In this example the Ø.40 is .02 larger than the specified .38 fastener diameter

If a clearance is required between the top of the screw and the top surface of the part, check the **Head clearance** box under **Options** on the **Hole Specification** section of the **Hole Wizard PropertyManager.** See Figure 7-40.

Note also that the diameter of the counterbored hole is larger than the head of the screw. This is a tool allowance; that is, the hole is large enough to allow a socket wrench to fit over the head of the fastener and still fit within the hole.

Counterbored Hole with Threads

Figure 7-41 shows a 3.00 × 4.00 × 2.00 block with two counterbored holes. Both holes are threaded.

1 Draw the block.

2 Click the **Hole Wizard** and specify a **3/8 -16 UNC** thread that goes completely through.

Figure 7-38

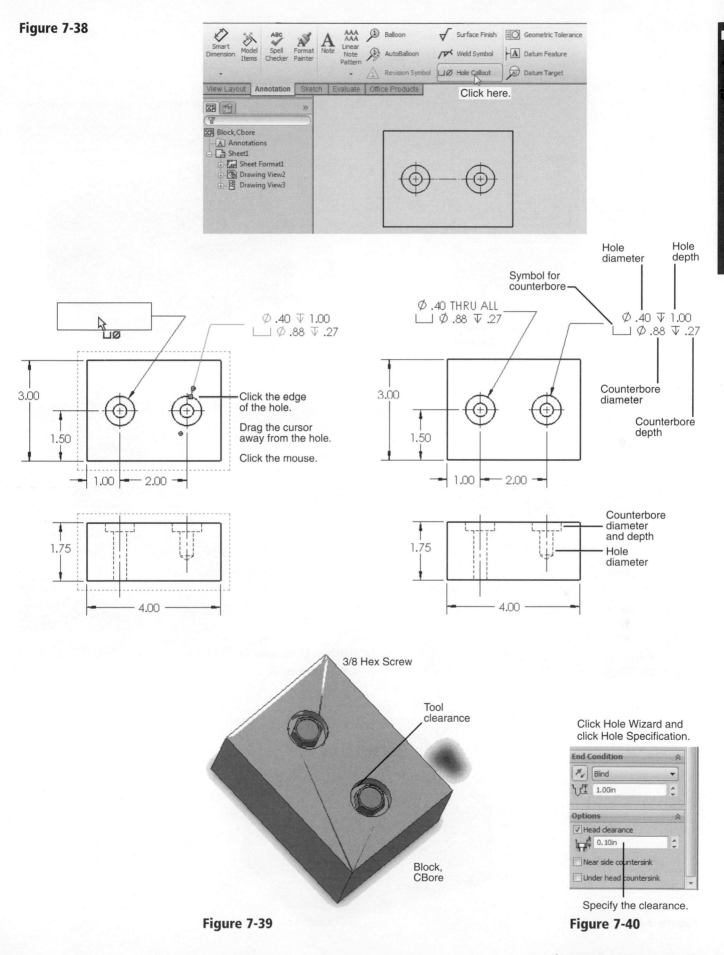

Click here.

Hole diameter
Hole depth

Symbol for counterbore

Click the edge of the hole.

Drag the cursor away from the hole.

Click the mouse.

Ø .40 ⊤ 1.00
⊔ Ø .88 ⊤ .27

3.00

1.50

1.00   2.00

1.75

4.00

Ø .40 THRU ALL
⊔ Ø .88 ⊤ .27

Ø .40 ⊤ 1.00
Ø .88 ⊤ .27

Counterbore diameter

Counterbore depth

3.00

1.50

1.00   2.00

Counterbore diameter and depth

Hole diameter

1.75

4.00

3/8 Hex Screw

Tool clearance

Block, CBore

Figure 7-39

Click Hole Wizard and click Hole Specification.

End Condition

Blind

1.00in

Options

☑ Head clearance

0.10in

☐ Near side countersink

☐ Under head countersink

Specify the clearance.

Figure 7-40

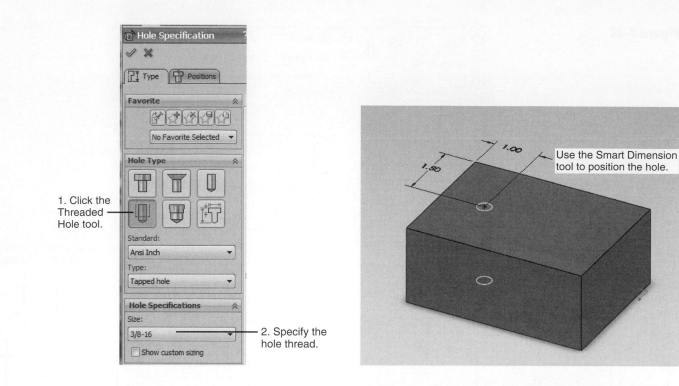

1. Click the Threaded Hole tool.

2. Specify the hole thread.

Use the Smart Dimension tool to position the hole.

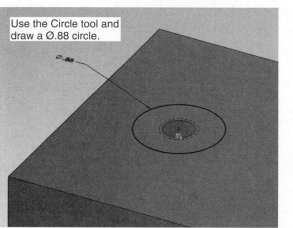

Use the Circle tool and draw a Ø.88 circle.

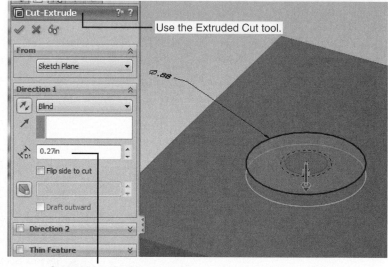

Use the Extruded Cut tool.

Counterbore depth

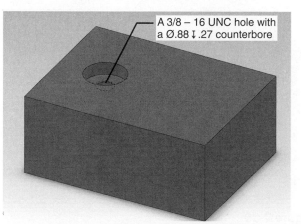

A 3/8 – 16 UNC hole with a Ø.88 ↧ .27 counterbore

Figure 7-41

3 Click the **Positions** tab and locate the hole.

4 Click the OK check mark.

This will locate a 3/8-16 UNC thread hole in the block. Now, we add the counterbore.

5 Click the top surface of the block and click the **Sketch** option.

6 Click the **Circle** tool and draw a **Ø0.88** circle on the top surface centered on the same center point as the Ø3/8-16 hole.

The dimension for this example came from Figure 7-38.

7 Click the **Features** tab, click the **Extruded Cut** tool, and specify a cut depth of **0.27.**

8 Click the OK check mark.

9 Repeat the procedure adding a second hole with a thread to a depth of **0.85.**

TIP

For an internal thread the thread depth is measured from the top surface of the part.

See Figure 7-42.

10 Save the block as **Block, Threads.**

11 Create a new **Drawing** document and create front and top orthographic views of the Block, Threads.

12 Add centerlines to the front view and add dimensions as shown.

See Figure 7-43.

13 Use the **Smart Dimension** tool and click the left threaded hole.

14 Locate the text and click the mouse.

15 Click the Ø.88 text and modify the callout to include the thread and counterbore callouts.

Specify the threaded hole depth.

Figure 7-42

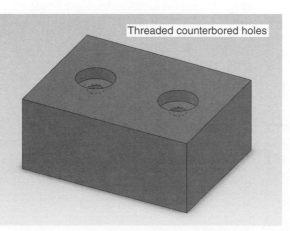

Threaded counterbored holes

The thread callout is modified using the **Dimension Text** box and appropriate symbols.

16 Click the OK check mark.

17 Click the right hole.

18 Locate the text and click the mouse.

19 Click the Ø.88 text and modify the callout to include the thread callout as shown.

Figure 7-44 shows dimensioned counterbored holes using metric units. The **Hole Callout** tool was used to dimension the counterbored holes.

To Draw and Dimension Countersunk Holes

Countersunk holes are used with flat head screws to create assemblies in which the fasteners do not protrude above the surfaces.

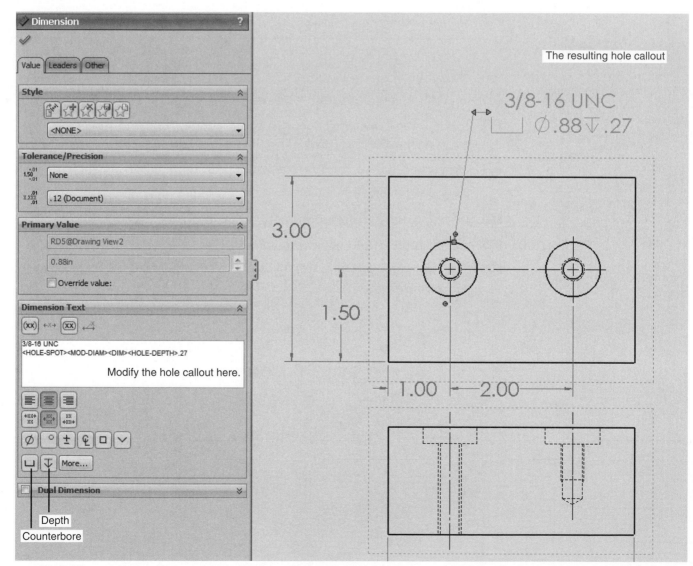

Figure 7-43

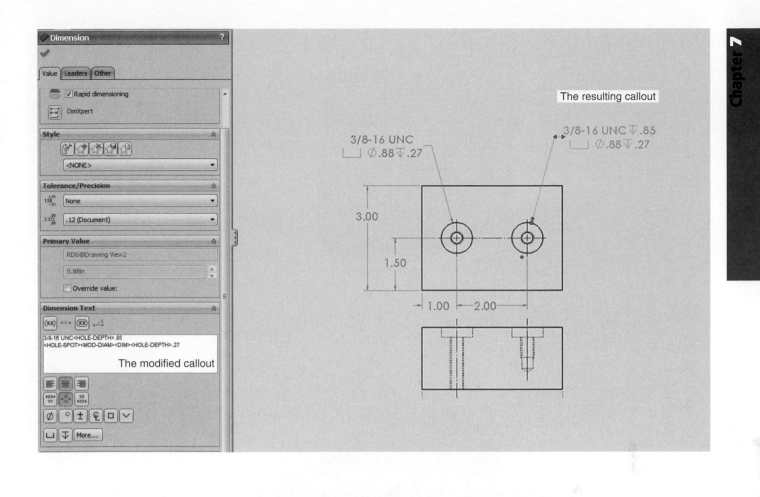

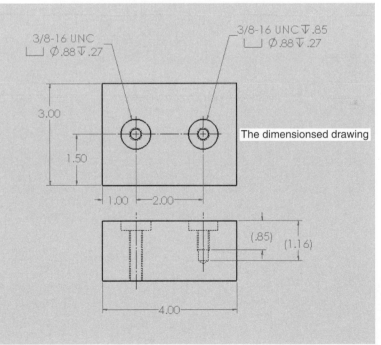

Figure 7-43
(*Continued*)

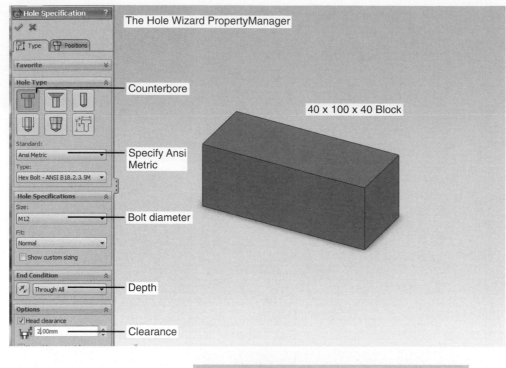

The Hole Wizard PropertyManager

Counterbore

Specify Ansi Metric

Bolt diameter

Depth

Clearance

40 x 100 x 40 Block

Specification for hole depth

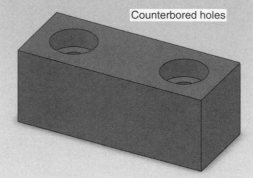

Counterbored holes

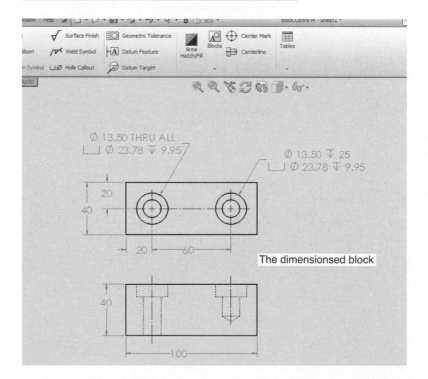

Ø 13.50 THRU ALL
⊔ Ø 23.78 ▽ 9.95

Ø 13.50 ▽ 25
⊔ Ø 23.78 ▽ 9.95

The dimensionsed block

Figure 7-44

Figure 7-45 shows a part with two countersunk holes; one goes completely through, the other has a depth specification.

1 Draw a 40 × 80 × 60 block.

2 Use the **Hole Wizard** tool, click the **Countersink** type, specify the **Ansi Metric** standard, select an **M10** size for a flat head screw, and a hole that goes all the way through. Define a head clearance of **2.00.**

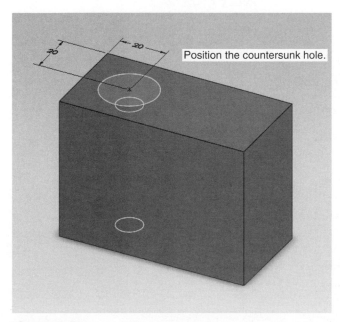

Figure 7-45

Hole Specification

Type | Positions — 6. Click here

Favorite

Hole Type — 1. Click here.

Standard:
Ansi Metric — 2. Click here.

Type:
Flat Head Screw – ANSI B18.6

Hole Specifications

Size:
M10 — 3. Click here-
specify the diameter and

Fit:
Normal
☐ Show custom sizing

End Condition
Through All — 4. Click here.

Options
☑ Head clearance
2.00mm — 5. Specify the clearance.

Hole Specification

Type | Positions

Favorite

Hole Type

Standard:
Ansi Metric

Type:
Flat Head Screw – ANSI B18.6

Hole Specifications

Size:
M10

Fit:
Normal
☐ Show custom sizing

End Condition
Blind
25.00mm

Options
☑ Head clearance
2.00mm

Specify the depth.

Position the countersunk hole.

Two countersunk holes

3 Click the **Positions** tab and position the countersunk hole's center point as shown using the **Smart Dimension** tool.

4 Click the OK check mark.

5 Click the **Hole Wizard** tool, click the **Countersink** type, specify the **Ansi Metric** standard, select an **M10** size for a flat head screw, and specify the depth requirement for a blind hole. Define a head clearance of **2.00.**

In this example the depth is 25.0 mm.

6 Click the **Positions** tab and locate the hole as shown.

7 Click the OK check mark.

8 Save the drawing as **Block, CSink.**

To Dimension the Block

1 Create a new **Drawing** document with a front and top orthographic view of the Block, CSink.

2 Use the **Smart Dimension** tool and add the appropriate dimensions.

3 Use the **Center Mark** tool to add a centerline between the two holes indicating they are aligned.

4 Click the **Annotation** tab, click the **Hole Callout** tool, and dimension the two countersunk holes.

See Figure 7-46

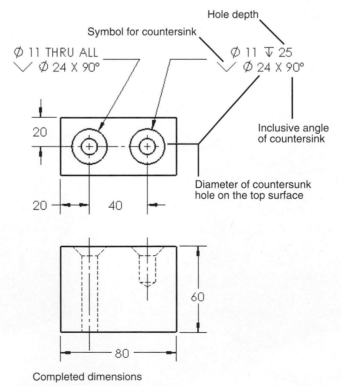

Completed dimensions

Figure 7-46

7-8 Angular Dimensions

Figure 7-47 shows a model that includes a slanted surface and dimensioned orthographic views of the model. The dimension values are located beyond the model between two extension lines. Locating dimensions between extension lines is preferred to locating the value between an extension line and the edge of the model.

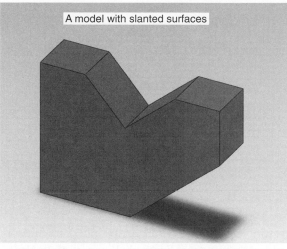

A model with slanted surfaces

Figure 7-47

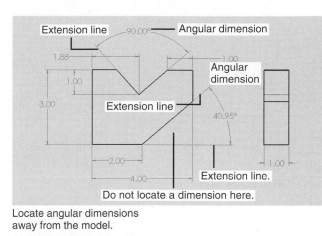

Locate angular dimensions away from the model.

Figure 7-48 shows a shape that includes a slanted surface dimensioned in two different ways. The shape on the left uses an angular dimension; the one on the right does not. Both are acceptable.

Figure 7-49 shows two objects dimensioned using angular dimensions. One has an evenly spaced hole pattern, the other has an uneven hole pattern.

To Dimension an Evenly Spaced Hole Pattern

1 Start a new drawing of the object and create a view as shown.

The object will automatically include horizontal and vertical centerlines.

2 Right-click each centerline and select the **Hide** option.

3 Click the **Center Mark** tool on the **Annotation** toolbar.

4 Click the **Circular Center Mark** option and click each of the six holes.

Figure 7-48

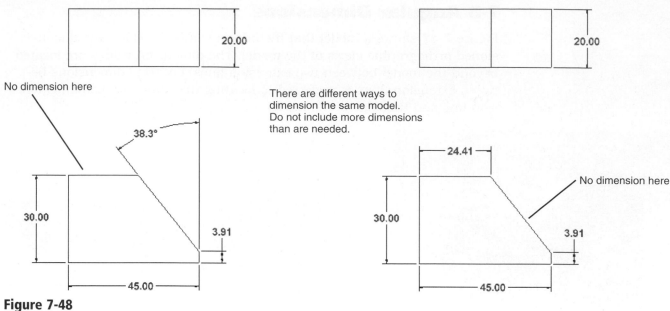

No dimension here

There are different ways to dimension the same model. Do not include more dimensions than are needed.

Figure 7-48
(*Continued*)

This option will generate a circular centerline that can be used to dimension the hole pattern. This circular centerline is called a *bolt circle*. Note that the center marks are not horizontal and vertical but point at the center point of the pattern.

5 Add dimensions to the pattern and the object.

The six holes are evenly spaced and are all the same size, so only one angular dimension and a note are needed, as shown. All the holes are the same distance from the center point, so the circular centerline needs only one dimension that will include the six holes.

Figure 7-49 shows a similar object but with an uneven hole pattern. Each hole must be dimensioned separately.

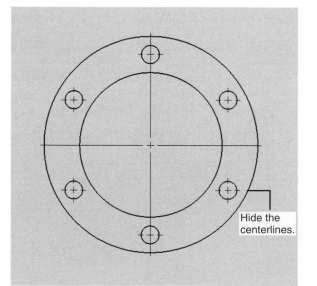

Hide the centerlines.

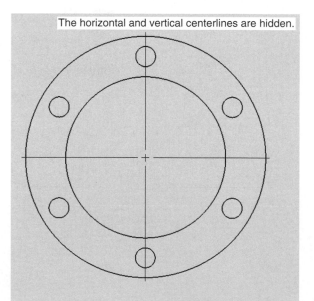

The horizontal and vertical centerlines are hidden.

Figure 7-49

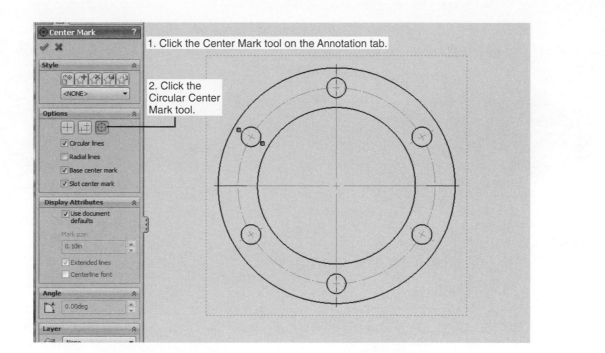

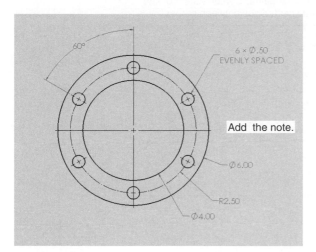

Figure 7-49
(*Continued*)

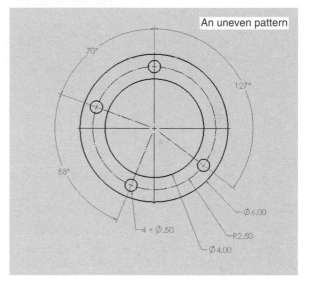

7-9 Ordinate Dimensions

Ordinate dimensions are dimensions based on an X,Y coordinate system. Ordinate dimensions do not include extension lines, dimension lines, or arrowheads but simply horizontal and vertical leader lines drawn directly from the features of the object. Ordinate dimensions are particularly useful when dimensioning an object that includes many small holes.

Figure 7-50 shows a part that is to be dimensioned using ordinate dimensions. Ordinate dimensions values are calculated from the X,Y origin, which, in this example, is the lower left corner of the front view of the model.

To Create Ordinate Dimensions

See Figure 7-51.

1 Start a new **Drawing** document and create a top orthographic view of the part.

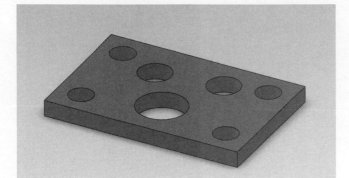
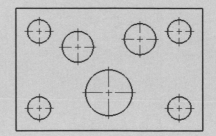

Figure 7-50

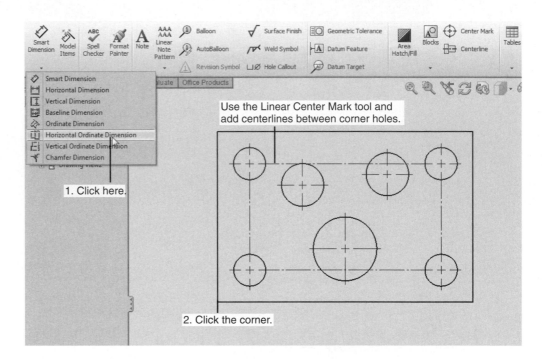

Use the Linear Center Mark tool and add centerlines between corner holes.

1. Click here.

2. Click the corner.

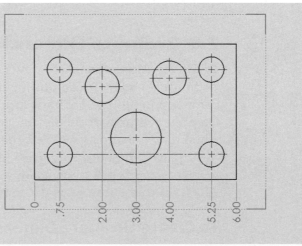

3. Drag 0 away from the corner.

4. Click the lower end of each hole's centerline and the edge line and drag the ordinate value away from the object.

Figure 7-51

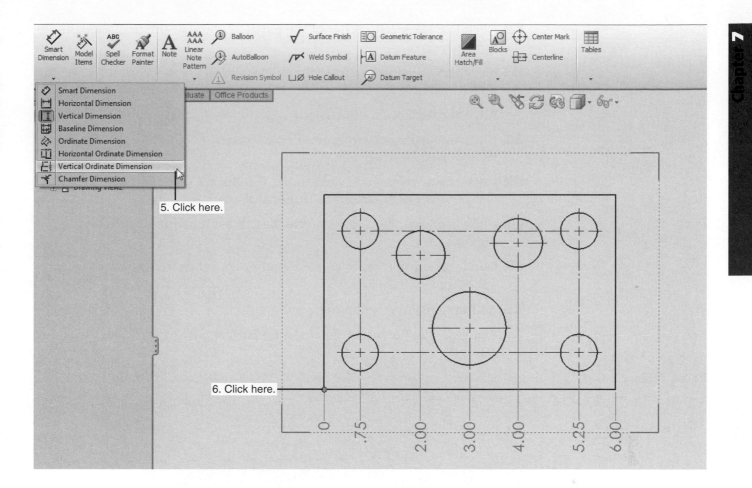

5. Click here.

6. Click here.

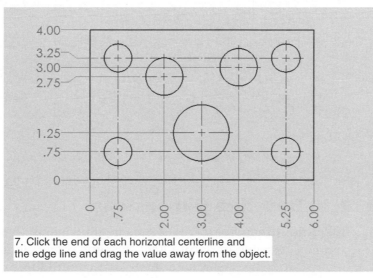

7. Click the end of each horizontal centerline and the edge line and drag the value away from the object.

Figure 7-51
(Continued)

Use the dimensions shown in either Figure 7-51 or 7-53.

2 Use the **Linear Center Mark** tool and add connection centerlines between the four corner holes.

3 Click the arrowhead located under the **Smart Dimension** tool and click the **Horizontal Ordinate Dimension** option.

4 Click the lower left corner of the part to establish the origin for the dimensions.

5 Move the cursor away from the origin and define a location for the "0" dimension.

All other horizontal dimensions will align with this location.

6 Click the lower portion of each hole's vertical centerline and the lower right corner of the part.

7 Click the arrowhead located under the **Smart Dimension,** tool and click the **Vertical Ordinate Dimension** option.

8 Click the lower left corner of the part to establish the origin for the dimensions.

9 Click the left portion of each hole's horizontal centerline and the upper left corner of the part.

10 Add dimensions for the holes.

Figure 7-52 shows the dimensioned part.

Figure 7-52

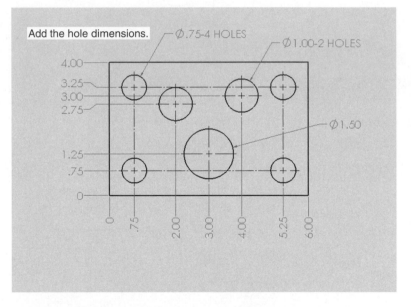

7-10 Baseline Dimensions

Baseline dimensions are a series of dimensions that originate from a common baseline or datum line. Baseline dimensions are very useful because they help eliminate the tolerance buildup that is associated with chain-type dimensions.

To Create Baseline Dimensions

See Figure 7-53.

1 Start a new **Drawing** document and create a top orthographic view of the part.

2 Use the **Linear Center Mark** tool and add connection centerlines between the four corner holes.

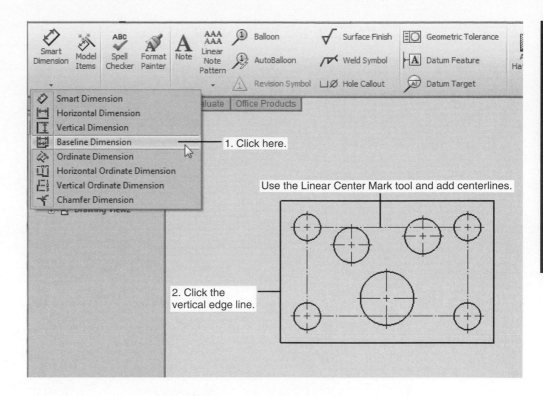

1. Click here.

Use the Linear Center Mark tool and add centerlines.

2. Click the vertical edge line.

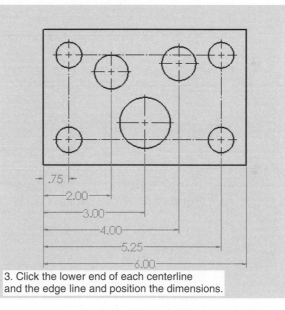

.75

2.00

3.00

4.00

5.25

6.00

3. Click the lower end of each centerline and the edge line and position the dimensions.

Figure 7-53

 Click the arrowhead under the **Smart Dimension** tool and click the **Baseline Dimension** option.

4 Click the left vertical edge of the part and the lower portion of the first vertical centerline.

This will establish the baseline.

5 Click the lower portion of each vertical centerline and the right vertical edge line and locate the dimensions.

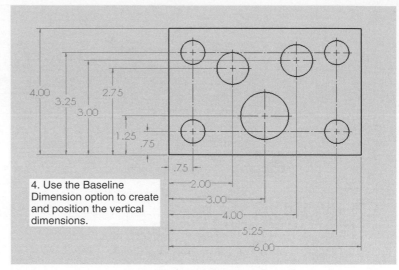

4. Use the Baseline Dimension option to create and position the vertical dimensions.

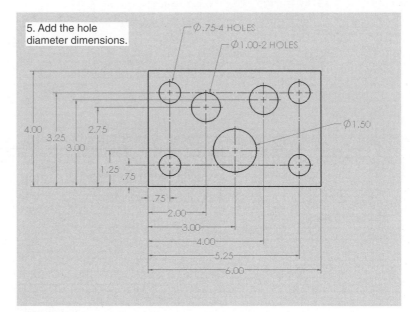

5. Add the hole diameter dimensions.

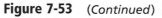

Figure 7-53 *(Continued)*

NOTE

The distance between the dimension lines can be changed in the **Offset distances** box under **Dimensions** on the **Document Properties** tab of the **Options** tool.

---

6 Click the arrowhead under the **Smart Dimension** tool and click the **Baseline Dimension** option.

7 Click the lower horizontal edge of the part and the left end of the first horizontal centerline.

8 Click the left end of each horizontal centerline and the right top horizontal edge line.

The alignment of the vertical dimension lines can be changed by right-clicking the individual dimension and selecting the **Break Alignment** option.

9 Add the hole dimensions.

Hole Tables

Hole tables are a method for dimensioning parts that have large numbers of holes where standard dimensioning may be cluttered and difficult to read. See Figure 7-54.

1 Start a new **Drawing** document and create a top orthographic view of the part.

2 Use the **Linear Center Mark** tool and add connection centerlines between the four corner holes.

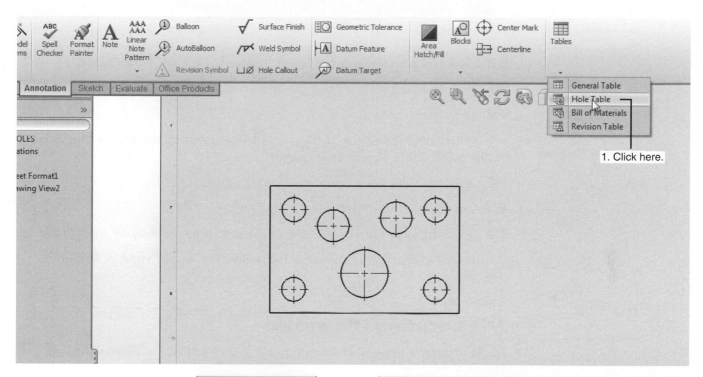

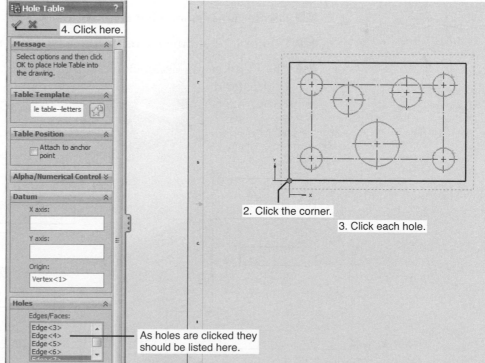

Figure 7-54

Figure 7-54
(*Continued*)

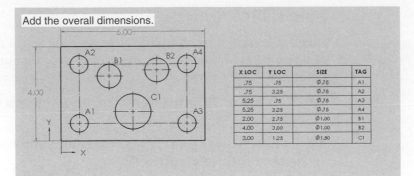

Add the overall dimensions.

X LOC	Y LOC	SIZE	TAG
.75	.75	Ø.75	A1
.75	3.25	Ø.75	A2
5.25	.75	Ø.75	A3
5.25	3.25	Ø.75	A4
2.00	2.75	Ø1.00	B1
4.00	3.00	Ø1.00	B2
3.00	1.25	Ø1.50	C1

3 Click the **Annotation** tab, click **Tables,** and click **Hole Table.**

4 Click the lower left corner of the part to establish an orign.

5 Click each hole.

As the holes are clicked they should be listed in the **Holes** box located in the **Hole Table PropertyManager.**

6 Click the OK check mark and locate the hole table.

7 Add the overall dimensions.

8 Move the hole tags as needed to present a clear, easy-to-read drawing.

In this example all tags were located to the upper right of the holes they define.

7-11 Locating Dimensions

There are eight general rules concerning the location of dimensions. See Figure 7-55.

1 Locate dimensions near the features they are defining.

2 Do not locate dimensions on the surface of the object.

3 Align and group dimensions so that they are neat and easy to understand.

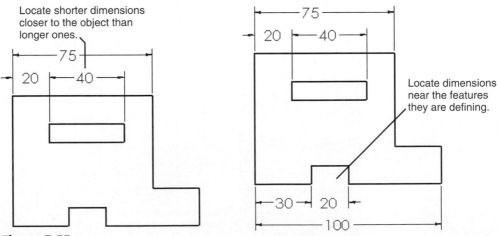

Figure 7-55

DO NOT LOCATE DIMENSIONS ON
THE SURFACE OF THE OBJECT.

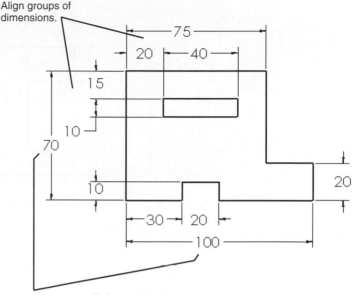

Align groups of
dimensions.

Locate overall dimensions the
farthest away from the object.

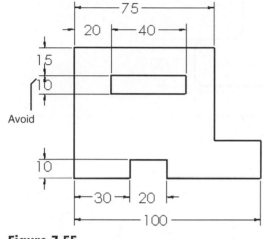

Avoid

Figure 7-55
(*Continued*)

4 Avoid crossing extension lines.

Sometimes it is impossible not to cross extension lines because of the complex shape of the object, but whenever possible, avoid crossing extension lines.

5 Do not cross dimension lines.

6 Locate shorter dimensions closer to the object than longer ones.

7 Always locate overall dimensions the farthest away from the object.

8 Do not dimension the same distance twice. This is called double dimensioning and will be discussed in Chapter 8.

7-12 Fillets and Rounds

Fillets and rounds may be dimensioned individually or by a note. In many design situations all the fillets and rounds are the same size, so a note as shown in Figure 7-56 is used. Any fillets or rounds that have a different radius from that specified by the note are dimensioned individually.

7-13 Rounded Shapes—Internal

Internal rounded shapes are called *slots.* Figure 7-57 shows three different methods for dimensioning slots. The end radii are indicated by the note R - 2 PLACES, but no numerical value is given. The width of the slot is dimensioned, and it is assumed that the radius of the rounded ends is exactly half of the stated width.

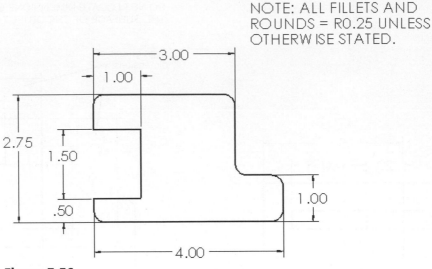

NOTE: ALL FILLETS AND ROUNDS = R0.25 UNLESS OTHERWISE STATED.

Figure 7-56

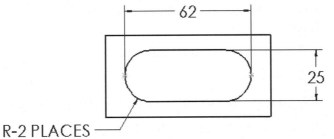

Figure 7-57

7-14 Rounded Shapes—External

Figure 7-58 shows two shapes with external rounded ends. As with internal rounded shapes, the end radii are indicated, but no value is given. The width of the object is given, and the radius of the rounded end is assumed to be exactly half of the stated width.

The second example shown in Figure 7-58 shows an object dimensioned using the object's centerline. This type of dimensioning is done when the distance between the holes is more important than the overall length of the object; that is, the tolerance for the distance between the holes is more exact than the tolerance for the overall length of the object.

The overall length of the object is given as a reference dimension (100). This means the object will be manufactured based on the other dimensions, and the 100 value will be used only for reference.

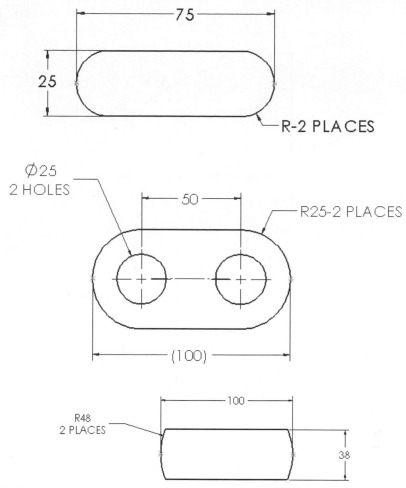

Figure 7-58

Objects with partially rounded edges should be dimensioned as shown in Figure 7-58. The radii of the end features are dimensioned. The center point of the radii is implied to be on the object centerline. The overall dimension is given; it is not referenced unless specific radii values are included.

7-15 Irregular Surfaces

There are three different methods for dimensioning irregular surfaces: tabular, baseline, and baseline with oblique extension lines. Figure 7-59 shows an irregular surface dimensioned using the tabular method. An XY axis is defined using the edges of the object. Points are then defined relative to the XY axis. The points are assigned reference numbers, and the reference numbers and XY coordinate values are listed in chart form as shown.

Figure 7-60 shows an irregular curve dimensioned using baseline dimensions. The baseline method references all dimensions to specified baselines. Usually there are two baselines, one horizontal and one vertical.

It is considered poor practice to use a centerline as a baseline. Centerlines are imaginary lines that do not exist on the object and would make it more difficult to manufacture and inspect the finished objects.

Baseline dimensioning is very common because it helps eliminate tolerance buildup and is easily adaptable to many manufacturing processes.

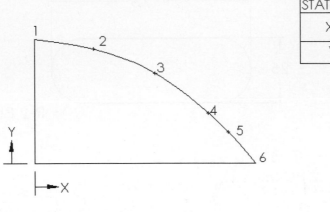

STATION	1	2	3	4	5	6
X	0	20	40	55	62	70
Y	40	38	30	16	10	0

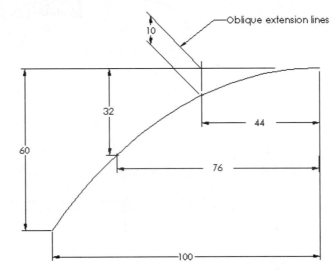

Figure 7-59

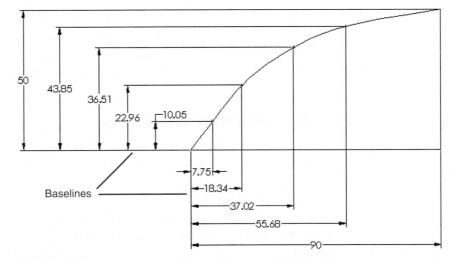

Figure 7-60

7-16 Polar Dimensions

Polar dimensions are similar to polar coordinates. A location is defined by a radius (distance) and an angle. Figure 7-61 shows an object that includes polar dimensions. The holes are located on a circular centerline, and their positions from the vertical centerline are specified using angles.

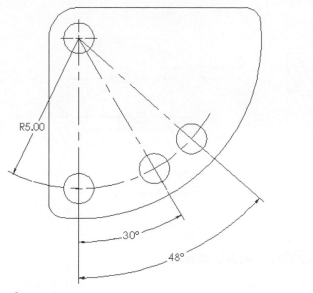

Figure 7-61

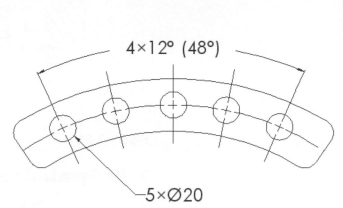

Figure 7-62

Figure 7-62 shows an example of a hole pattern dimensioned using polar dimensions.

7-17 Chamfers

Chamfers are angular cuts made on the edges of objects. They are usually used to make it easier to fit two parts together. They are most often made at 45° angles but may be made at any angle. Figure 7-63 shows two objects with chamfers between surfaces 90° apart and two examples between surfaces that are not 90° apart. Either of the two types of dimensions shown for the 45° dimension may be used. If an angle other than 45° is used, the angle and setback distance must be specified.

Figure 7-64 shows two examples of internal chamfers. Both define the chamfer using an angle and diameter. Internal chamfers are very similar to countersunk holes.

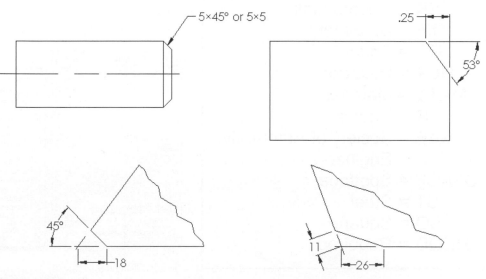

Figure 7-63

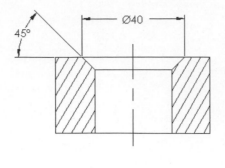

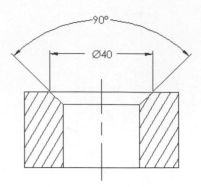

Figure 7-64

7-18 Symbols and Abbreviations

Symbols are used in dimensioning to help accurately display the meaning of the dimension. Symbols also help eliminate language barriers when reading drawings.

Abbreviations should be used very carefully on drawings. Whenever possible, write out the full word including correct punctuation. The dimension manager includes a group of symbols and words commonly used on technical drawings. Figure 7-65 lists several standard abbreviations used on technical drawings.

Figure 7-66 shows a list of symbols available the **Dimension Value ProopertyManager.**

TIP
To access the **Dimension Value PropertyManager**, click an existing dimension.

```
         AL = Aluminum
    C'BORE = Counterbore
       CRS = Cold Rolled Steel
       CSK = Countersink
       DIA = Diameter
        EQ = Equal
       HEX = Hexagon
     MAT'L = Material
         R = Radius
       SAE = Society of Automotive
             Engineers
     SFACE = Spotface
        ST = Steel
        SQ = Square
      REQD = Required
```

Figure 7-65

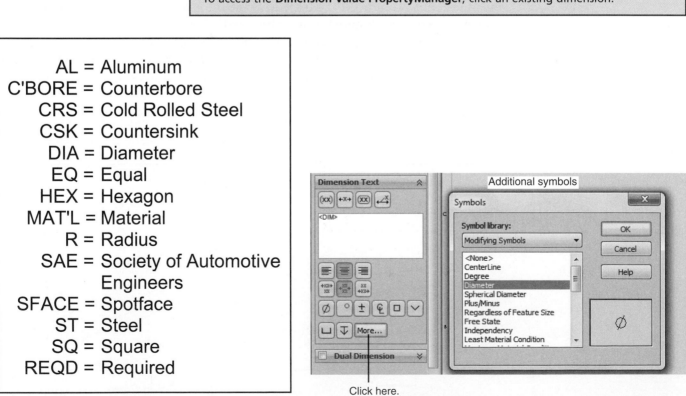

Click here.

Figure 7-66

More symbols are available by clicking the **More** box. A list of available symbols will appear. Click a new symbol. A preview will appear of the selected symbol. Click **OK** and the symbol will appear on the drawing next to the existing symbol.

7-19 Symmetrical and Centerline Symbols

An object is symmetrical about an axis when one side is an exact mirror image of the other. Figure 7-67 shows a symmetrical object. The two short parallel lines symbol or the note OBJECT IS SYMMETRICAL ABOUT THIS AXIS (centerline) may be used to designate symmetry.

If an object is symmetrical, only half the object need be dimensioned. The other dimensions are implied by the symmetry note or symbol.

Centerlines are slightly different from the axis of symmetry. An object may or may not be symmetrical about its centerline. See Figure 7-67. Centerlines are used to define the center of both individual features and entire objects. Use the centerline symbol when a line is a centerline, but do not use it in place of the symmetry symbol.

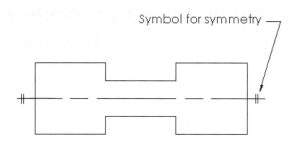

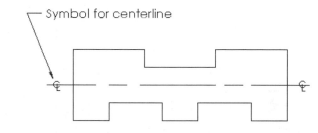

Figure 7-67

7-20 Dimensioning to a Point

Curved surfaces can be dimensioned using theoretical points. See Figure 7-68. There should be a small gap between the surface of the object and the lines used to define the theoretical point. The point should be defined by the intersection of at least two lines.

There should also be a small gap between the extension lines and the theoretical point used to locate the point.

7-21 Dimensioning Section Views

Section views are dimensioned, as are orthographic views. See Figure 7-69. The section lines should be drawn at an angle that allows the viewer to clearly distinguish between the section lines and the extension lines.

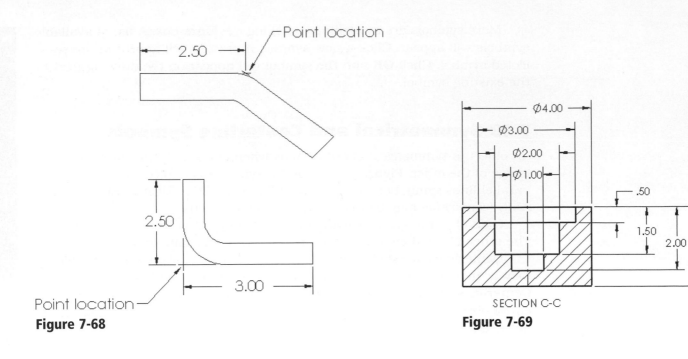

Figure 7-68

Figure 7-69

7-22 Dimensioning Orthographic Views

Dimensions should be added to orthographic views where the features appear in contour. Holes should be dimensioned in their circular views. Figure 7-70 shows three views of an object that has been dimensioned.

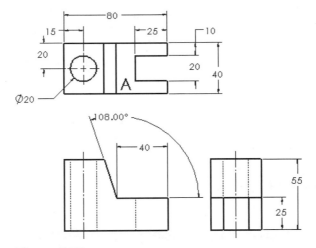

Figure 7-70

The hole dimensions are added to the top view, where the hole appears circular. The slot is also dimensioned in the top view because it appears in contour. The slanted surface is dimensioned in the front view.

The height of surface A is given in the side view rather than run along extension lines across the front view. The length of surface A is given in the front view. This is a contour view of the surface.

It is considered good practice to keep dimensions in groups. This makes it easier for the viewer to find dimensions.

Be careful not to double-dimension a distance. A distance should be dimensioned only once. If a 30 dimension were added above the 25 dimension on the right-side view, it would be an error. The distance would be double-dimensioned: once with the 25 + 30 dimension and again with the 55 overall dimension. The 25 + 30 dimensions are mathematically equal to the 55 overall dimension, but there is a distinct difference in how they affect the manufacturing tolerances. Double dimensions are explained more fully in Chapter 8.

Dimensions Using Centerlines

Figure 7-71 shows an object dimensioned from its centerline. This type of dimensioning is used when the distance between the holes relative to each other is critical.

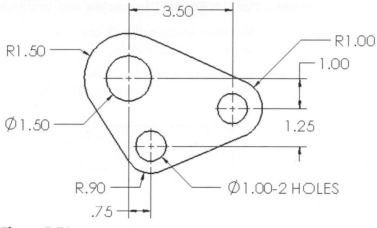

Figure 7-71

Chapter Projects

Project 7-1:

Measure and redraw the shapes in Figures P7-1 through P7-24. The dotted grid background has either .50-in. or 10-mm spacing. All holes are through holes. Specify the units and scale of the drawing. Use the **Part** template to create a model. Use the grid background pattern to determine the dimensions. Use the **Drawing** template to create the orthographic view shown. Use the **Smart Dimension** tool to dimension the view.

    A.   Measure using millimeters.

    B.   Measure using inches.

        All dimensions are within either .25 in. or 5 mm. All fillets and rounds are R.50 in., R.25 in. or R10 mm, R5 mm.

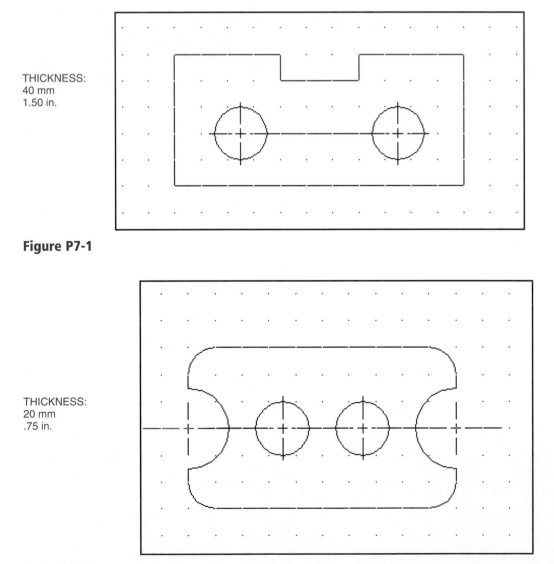

THICKNESS:
40 mm
1.50 in.

Figure P7-1

THICKNESS:
20 mm
.75 in.

Figure P7-2

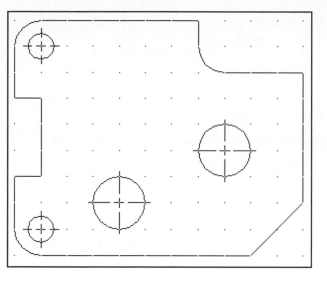

THICKNESS:
35 mm
1.25 in.

Figure P7-3

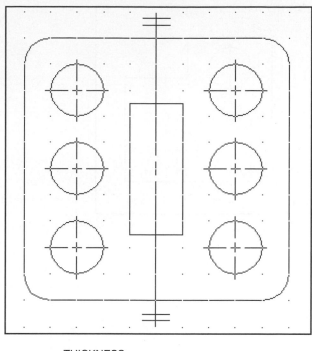

THICKNESS:
15 mm
.50 in.

Figure P7-4

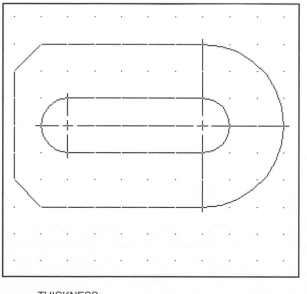

THICKNESS:
10 mm
.50 in.

Figure P7-5

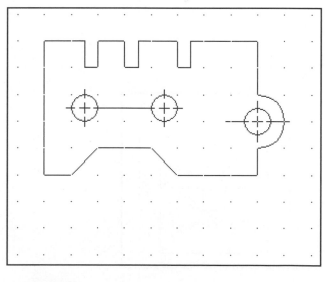

THICKNESS:
5 mm
.25 in.

Figure P7-6

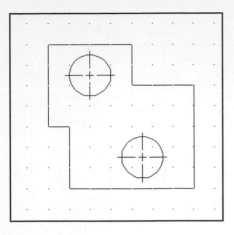

THICKNESS:
12 mm
.50 in.

Figure P7-7

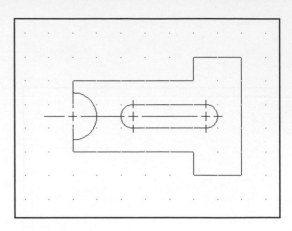

THICKNESS:
25 mm
1.00 in.

Figure P7-8

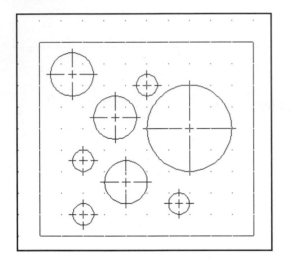

THICKNESS:
5 mm
.25 in.

Figure P7-9

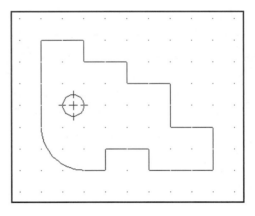

THICKNESS:
20 mm
.75 in.

Figure P7-10

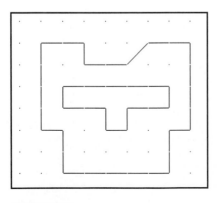

THICKNESS:
18 mm
.625 in.

Figure P7-11

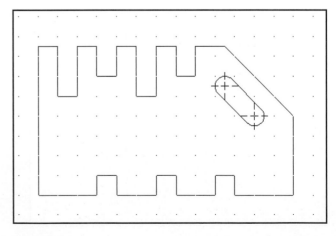

THICKNESS:
24 mm
1.00 in.

Figure P7-12

Figure P7-13

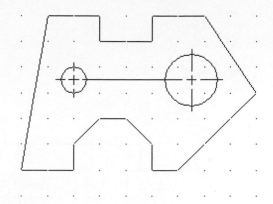

THICKNESS:
10 mm
.25 in.

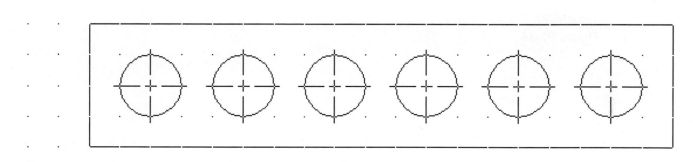

THICKNESS:
8 mm
.25 in.

Figure P7-14

Figure P7-15

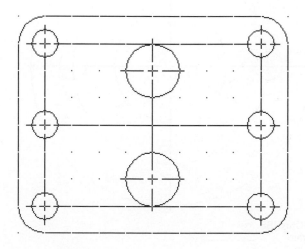

THICKNESS:
20 mm
.75 in.

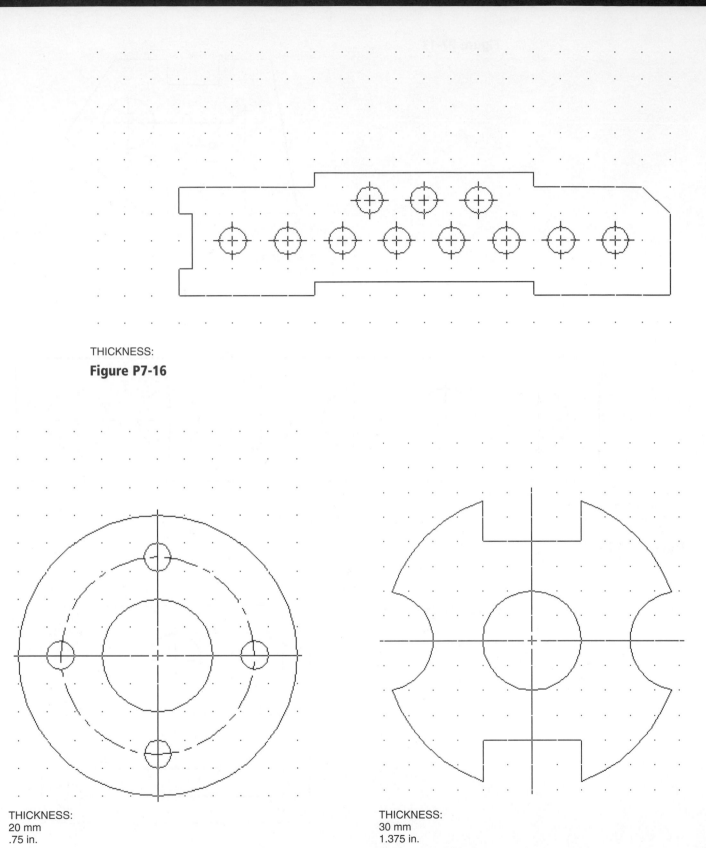

THICKNESS:

Figure P7-16

THICKNESS:
20 mm
.75 in.

Figure P7-17

THICKNESS:
30 mm
1.375 in.

Figure P7-18

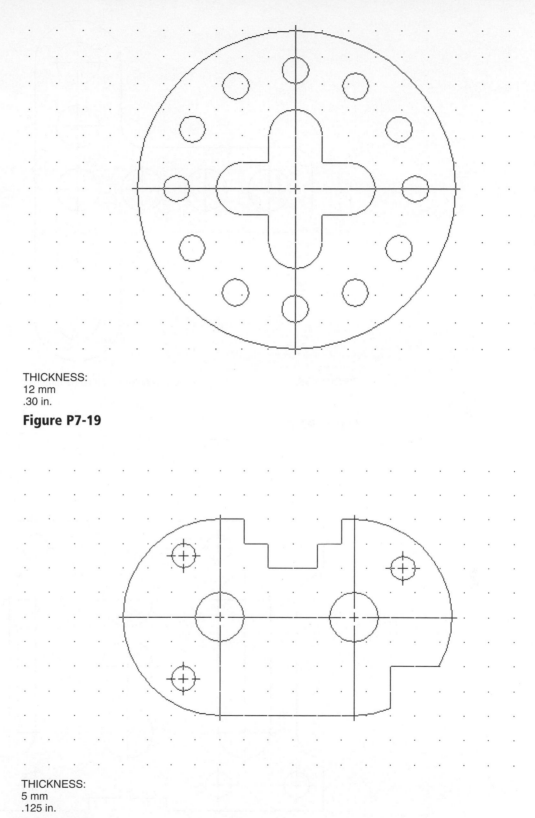

THICKNESS:
12 mm
.30 in.

Figure P7-19

THICKNESS:
5 mm
.125 in.

Figure P7-20

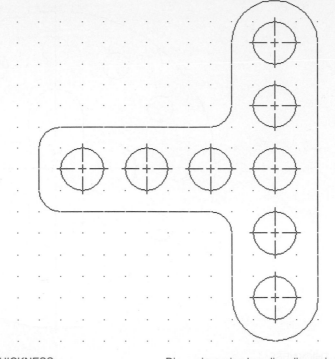

THICKNESS:
10 mm
.25 in.

Dimension using baseline dimensions.

Figure P7-21

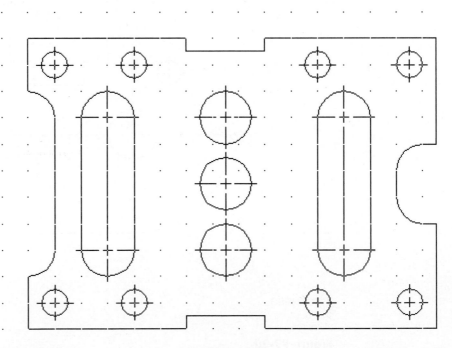

THICKNESS:
15 mm
.50 in.

Dimension using
A. Baseline dimensions.   C. Chain dimensions.
B. Ordinate dimensions.   D. Hole table.

Figure P7-22

Figure P7-23

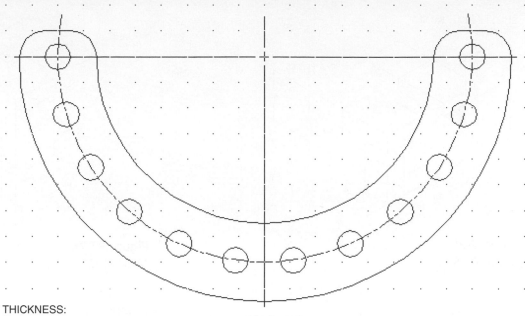

THICKNESS:
5 mm
.19 in.

Figure P7-24

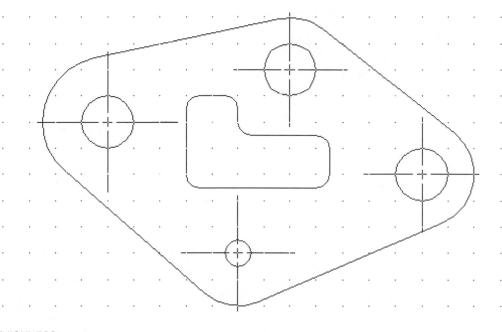

THICKNESS:
15 mm
.625 in.

Project 7-2:

Use the **Part** template to draw models of the objects shown in Figures P7-25 through P7-42.

1 Create orthographic views of the objects. Dimension the orthographic views.

2 Create 3D models of the objects. Dimension the 3D models.

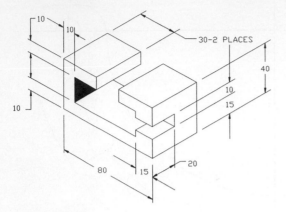

Figure P7-25
MILLIMETERS

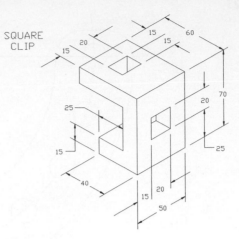

Figure P7-26
MILLIMETERS

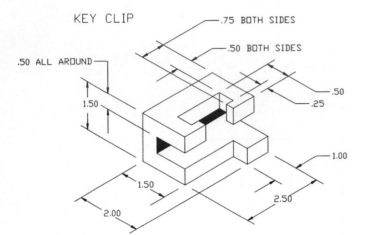

Figure P7-27
INCHES

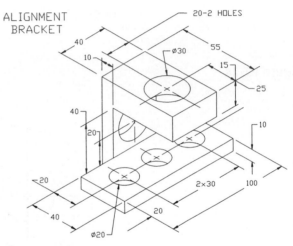

Figure P7-28
MILLIMETERS

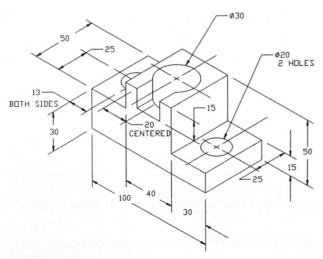

Figure P7-29
MILLIMETERS

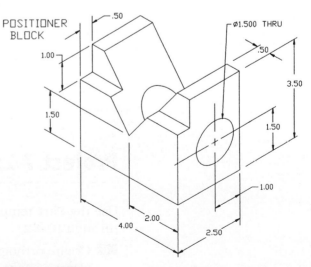

Figure P7-30
INCHES

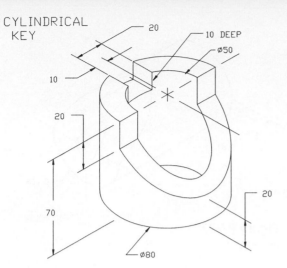

CYLINDRICAL KEY

10 DEEP
Ø50
20
10
20
70
20
Ø80

Figure P7-31
MILLIMETERS

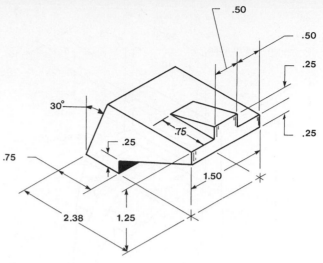

.50
.50
.25
.25
30°
.75
.25
.75
1.50
2.38
1.25

Figure P7-32
INCHES

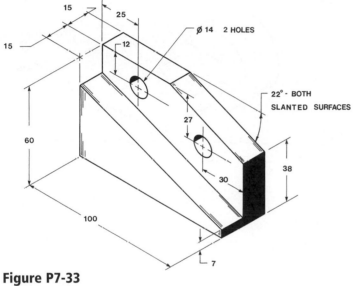

15
25
15
12
Ø 14   2 HOLES
27
22° - BOTH
SLANTED SURFACES
60
30
38
100
7

Figure P7-33
MILLIMETERS

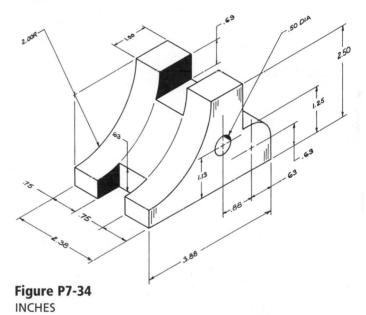

2.00R
1.00
.69
.50 DIA
2.50
.63
1.25
.75
1.13
.63
.75
.63
.88
2.38
3.88

Figure P7-34
INCHES

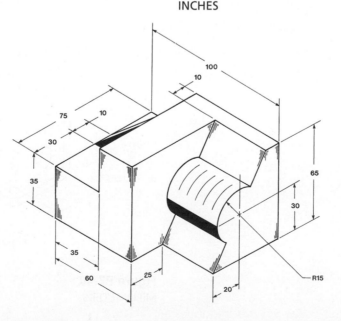

100
10
75
10
30
65
35
30
35
60
25
20
R15

Figure P7-35
MILLIMETERS

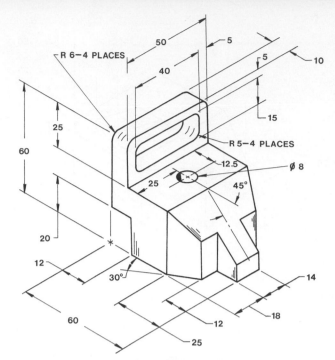

Figure P7-36
MILLIMETERS

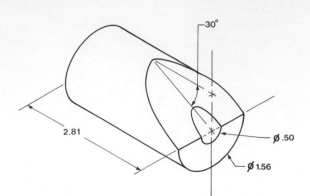

Figure P7-37
INCHES

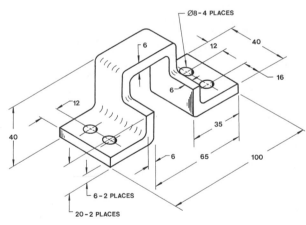

NOTE: ALL FILLET AND ROUNDS=R3

Figure P7-38
MILLIMETERS

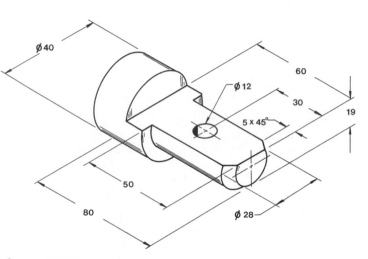

Figure P7-39
MILLIMETERS

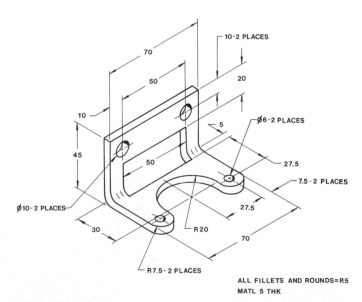

ALL FILLETS AND ROUNDS=R5
MATL 5 THK

Figure P7-40
MILLIMETERS

Figure P7-41
MILLIMETERS

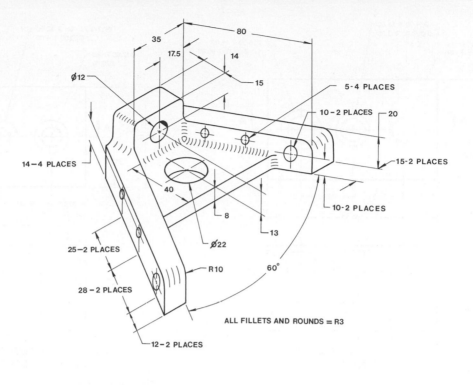

Figure P7-42
MILLIMETERS

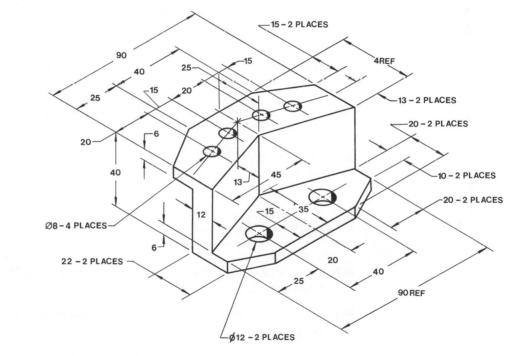

Project 7-3:

1 Draw a 3D model from the given top orthographic and section views in Figure P7-43.

2 Draw a top orthographic view and a section view of the object and add dimensions.

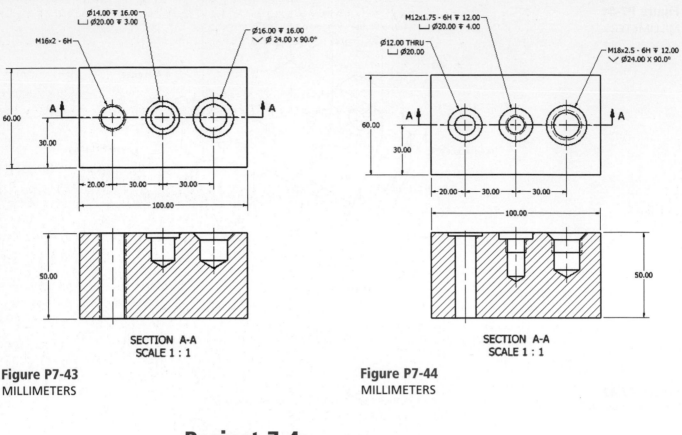

Figure P7-43
MILLIMETERS

Figure P7-44
MILLIMETERS

Project 7-4:

1 Draw a 3D model from the given top orthographic and section views in Figure P7-44.

2 Draw a top orthographic view and a section view of the object and add dimensions.

Project 7-5:

1 Draw a 3D model from the given top orthographic and section views in Figure P7-45.

2 Draw a top orthographic view and a section view of the object and add dimensions.

Project 7-6:

1 Draw a 3D model from the given top orthographic and section views in Figure P7-46.

2 Draw a top orthographic view and a section view of the object and add dimensions.

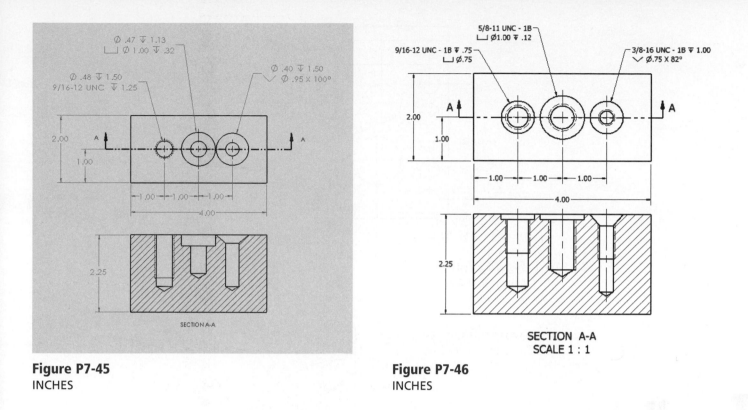

Figure P7-45
INCHES

Figure P7-46
INCHES

Redraw the given shape and dimension it using the following dimension styles.

1 Baseline

2 Ordinate

3 Hole Table

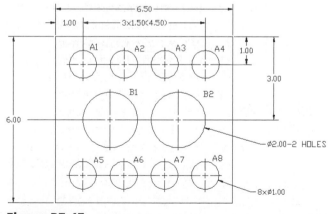

Figure P7-47
INCHES

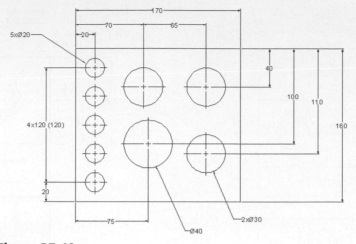

Figure P7-48
MILLIMETERS

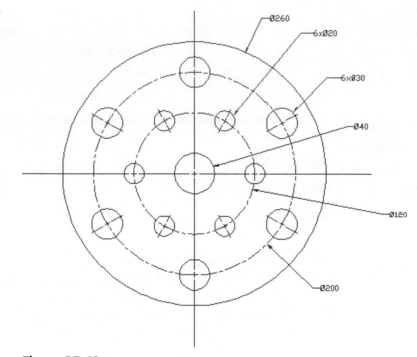

Figure P7-49
INCHES

8 chapter eight
Tolerancing

CHAPTER OBJECTIVES

- Understand tolerance conventions
- Understand the meaning of tolerances
- Learn how to apply tolerances
- Understand geometric tolerances
- Understand positional tolerances

8-1 Introduction

Tolerances define the manufacturing limits for dimensions. All dimensions have tolerances either written directly on the drawing as part of the dimension or implied by a predefined set of standard tolerances that apply to any dimension that does not have a stated tolerance.

This chapter explains general tolerance conventions and how they are applied using SolidWorks. It includes a sample tolerance study and an explanation of standard fits and surface finishes.

8-2 Direct Tolerance Methods

There are two methods used to include tolerances as part of a dimension: *plus and minus,* and *limits.* Plus and minus tolerances can be expressed in either bilateral (deviation) or unilateral (symmetric) form.

A **bilateral tolerance** has both a plus and a minus value, whereas a **unilateral tolerance** has either the plus or the minus value equal to 0. Figure 8-1 shows a horizontal dimension of 60 mm that includes a bilateral

Figure 8-1

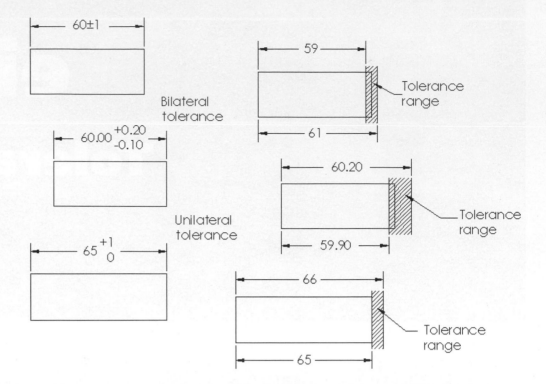

tolerance of plus or minus 1 and another dimension of 60.00 mm that includes a bilateral tolerance of plus 0.20 or minus 0.10. Figure 8-1 also shows a dimension of 65 mm that includes a unilateral tolerance of plus 1 or minus 0.

> **NOTE**
>
> Bilateral tolerance are called *symmetric* in SolidWorks. Unilateral tolerances are called *deviation.*

Plus or minus tolerances define a range for manufacturing. If inspection shows that all dimensioned distances on an object fall within their specified tolerance range, the object is considered acceptable; that is, it has been manufactured correctly.

The dimension and tolerance of 60±0.1 means that the part must be manufactured within a range no greater than 60.1 nor less than 59.9. The dimension and tolerance 65 +1/−0 defines the tolerance range as 65 to 66.

Figure 8-2 shows some bilateral and unilateral tolerances applied using decimal inch values. Inch dimensions and tolerances are written using a slightly different format than millimeter dimensions and tolerances, but they also define manufacturing ranges for dimension values. The horizontal bilateral dimension and tolerance 2.50±.02 defines the longest acceptable distance as 2.52 in. and the shortest as 2.48. The unilateral dimension 2.50 +.02/−.00 defines the longest acceptable distance as 2.52 and the shortest as 2.50.

8-3 Tolerance Expressions

Dimension and tolerance values are written differently for inch and millimeter values. See Figure 8-3. Unilateral dimensions for millimeter values specify a zero limit with a single 0. A zero limit for inch values must include

Figure 8-2

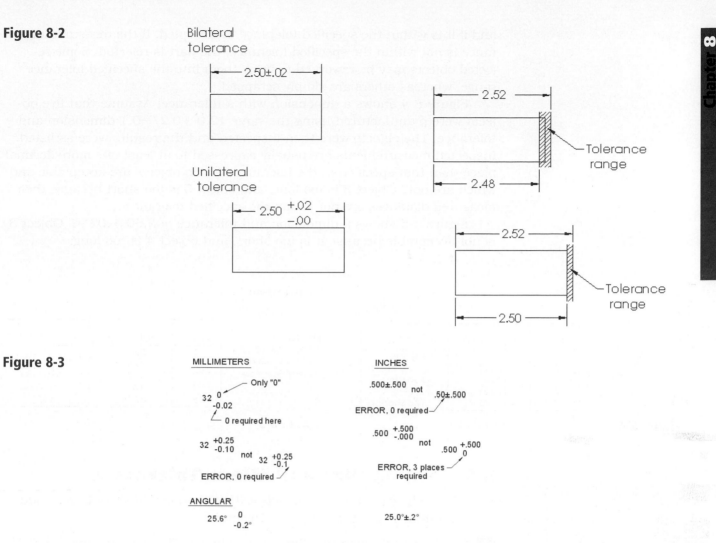

Bilateral tolerance

Unilateral tolerance

MILLIMETERS

INCHES

ANGULAR

the same number of decimal places given for the dimension value. In the example shown in Figure 8-3, the dimension value .500 has a unilateral tolerance with minus zero tolerance. The zero limit is written as .000, three decimal places for both the dimension and the tolerance.

Both values in a bilateral tolerance for inch values must contain the same number of decimal places; for millimeter values the tolerance values need not include the same number of decimal places as the dimension value. In Figure 8-3 the dimension value 32 is accompanied by tolerances of +0.25 and −0.10. This form is not acceptable for inch dimensions and tolerances. An equivalent inch dimension and tolerance would be written $32.00^{+.25}_{-.10}$.

Degree values must include the same number of decimal places in both the dimension value and the tolerance values for bilateral tolerances. A single 0 may be used for unilateral tolerances.

8-4 Understanding Plus and Minus Tolerances

A millimeter dimension and tolerance of 12.0 +0.2/−0.1 means the longest acceptable distance is 12.2000 . . . 0, and the shortest is 11.9000 . . . 0. The total range is 0.3000 . . . 0.

After an object is manufactured, it is inspected to ensure that the object has been manufactured correctly. Each dimensioned distance is measured, and if it is within the specified tolerance, is accepted. If the measured distance is not within the specified tolerance, the part is rejected. Some rejected objects may be reworked to bring them into the specified tolerance range, whereas others are simply scrapped.

Figure 8-4 shows a dimension with a tolerance. Assume that five objects were manufactured using the same 12.0 +0.2/−0.1 dimension and tolerance. The objects were then inspected and the results were as listed. Inspected measurements are usually expressed to at least one more decimal place than that specified in the tolerance. Which objects are acceptable and which are not? Object 3 is too long, and object 5 is too short because their measured distances are not within the specified tolerances.

Figure 8-5 shows a dimension and tolerance of 3.50 +.02 in. Object 3 is not acceptable because it is too short, and object 4 is too long.

GIVEN (mm):

MEANS:
TOL MAX = 12.2
TOL MIN = 11.9
TOTAL TOL = 0.3

OBJECT	AS MEASURED	ACCEPTABLE ?
1	12.160	OK
2	12.020	OK
3	12.203	Too Long
4	11.920	OK
5	11.895	Too Short

Figure 8-4

GIVEN (inches):

3.50±.02

MEANS:
TOL MAX = 3.52
TOL MIN = 3.48
TOTAL TOL = .04

OBJECT	AS MEASURED	ACCEPTABLE ?
1	3.520	OK
2	3.486	OK
3	3.470	Too Short
4	3.521	Too Long
5	3.515	OK

Figure 8-5

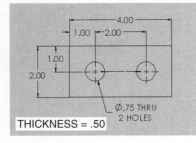

Figure 8-6

8-5 Creating Plus and Minus Tolerances

Figure 8-6 shows a dimensioned view. This section will show how to add plus and minus to the existing dimensions.

1 Create a part using the dimensions shown. The part thickness is 0.50.

2 Save the part as **BLOCK, TOL.**

3 Create a **Drawing** document of the BLOCK, TOL and create an orthographic view as shown.

4 Add dimensions as shown.

See Figure 8-7.

5 Click the horizontal **2.00** dimension.

Click the arrow in the **Tolerance/Precision** box as shown.

6 Select the **Bilateral** option.

7 Enter a plus tolerance of **0.02** and a minus tolerance of **0.01.**

See Figure 8-8.

8 Click the OK check mark.

To Add Plus and Minus Symmetric Tolerances Using the Dimension Text Box

See Figure 8-9.

1 Click the vertical **1.00** dimension.

Figure 8-7

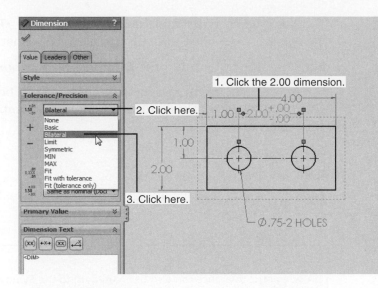

Figure 8-8

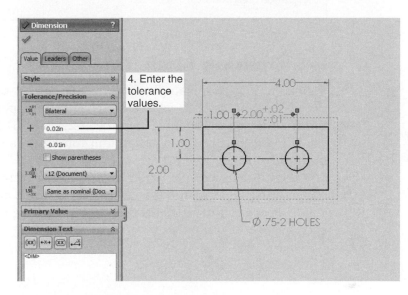

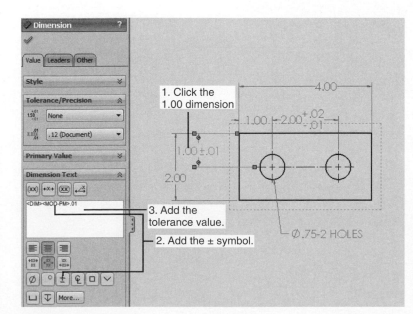

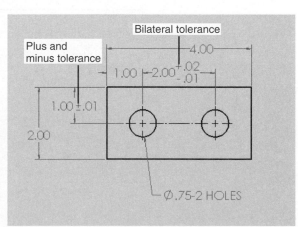

Figure 8-9

Note the entry in the **Dimension Text** box: **<DIM>.** This represents the existing text value taken from the part's construction dimensions.

2 Move the cursor into the **Dimension Text** box and click the ± symbol.

Note that the entry in the **Dimension Text** box now reads **<DIM><MOD-PM>.** This indicates that the ± symbol has been added to the dimension text.

3 Type **.01** after <MOD-PM>.

4 Click the OK check mark.

5 Save the **BLOCK, TOL** drawing.

> **TIP**
> A symmetric tolerance can also be created using the **Symmetric** option in the **Tolerance/Precision** box.

8-6 Creating Limit Tolerances

Figure 8-10 shows examples of limit tolerances. Limit tolerances replace dimension values. Two values are given: the upper and lower limits for the dimension value. The limit tolerance 62.1 and 61.9 is mathematically equal to 62±0.1, but the stated limit tolerance is considered easier to read and understand.

Limit tolerances define a range for manufacture. Final distances on an object must fall within the specified range to be acceptable.

This section uses the **BLOCK, TOL** drawing created in the previous section. See Figure 8-11.

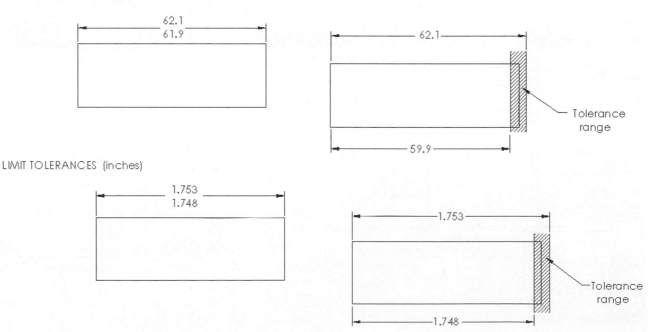

LIMIT TOLERANCES (millimeters)

LIMIT TOLERANCES (inches)

Figure 8-10

Figure 8-11

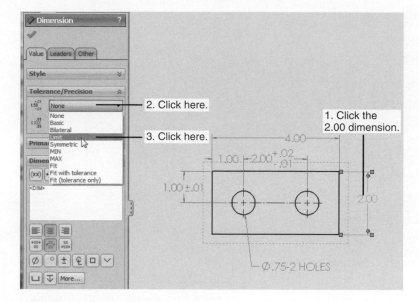

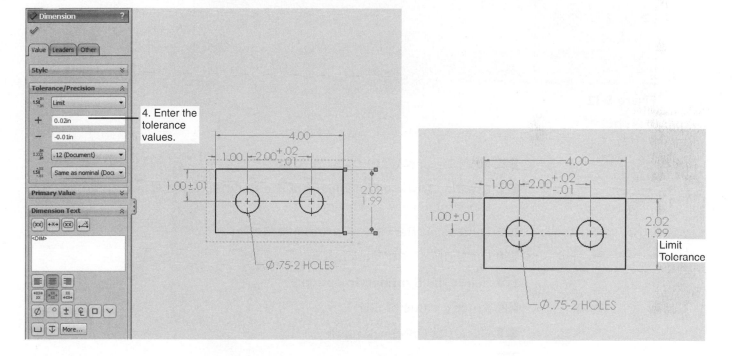

1️⃣ Click the vertical **2.00** dimension

2️⃣ Select the **Limit** option as shown.

3️⃣ Set the upper limit for **.02** and the lower limit for **.01.**

4️⃣ Click the OK check mark.

8-7 Creating Angular Tolerances

Figure 8-12 shows an example of an angular dimension with a symmetric tolerance. The procedures explained for applying different types of tolerances to linear dimensions also apply to angular dimensions.

See Figure 8-12.

1️⃣ Draw the part shown in Figure 8-12. Extrude the part to a thickness of **.50.**

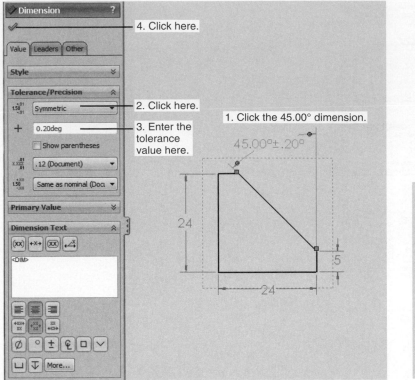

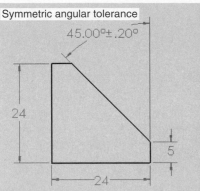

Figure 8-12

2 Save the part as **BLOCK, ANGLE**

3 Create a **Drawing** document of the **BLOCK, ANGLE** and create an orthographic view as shown.

4 Dimension the view.

5 Click the **45.00°** dimension.

6 Select the **Symmetric** option.

7 Enter a value of **.20.**

8 Click the OK check mark

9 Save the drawing.

8-8 Standard Tolerances

Most manufacturers establish a set of standard tolerances that are applied to any dimension that does not include a specific tolerance. Figure 8-13 shows some possible standard tolerances. Standard tolerances vary from company to company. Standard tolerances are usually listed on the first page of a drawing to the left of the title block, but this location may vary.

The X value used when specifying standard tolerances means any X stated in that format. A dimension value of 52.00 would have an implied tolerance of ±.01 because the stated standard tolerance is .XX ±.01. Thus, any dimension value with two decimal places has a standard implied tolerance of ±.01. A dimension value of 52.000 would have an implied tolerance of ±.001.

Figure 8-13

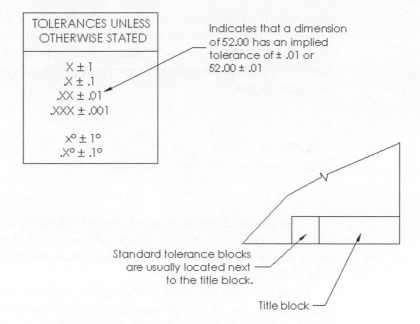

TOLERANCES UNLESS
OTHERWISE STATED

X ± 1
X ± .1
.XX ± .01
.XXX ± .001

X° ± 1°
.X° ± .1°

Indicates that a dimension
of 52.00 has an implied
tolerance of ± .01 or
52.00 ± .01

Standard tolerance blocks
are usually located next
to the title block.

Title block

8-9 Double Dimensioning

It is an error to dimension the same distance twice. This mistake is called
double dimensioning. Double dimensioning is an error because it does
not allow for tolerance buildup across a distance.

Figure 8-14 shows an object that has been dimensioned twice across
its horizontal length, once using three 30-mm dimensions and a second
time using the 90-mm overall dimension. The two dimensions are mathematically equal but are not equal when tolerances are considered. Assume
that each dimension has a standard tolerance of ±1 mm. The three 30-mm

Figure 8-14

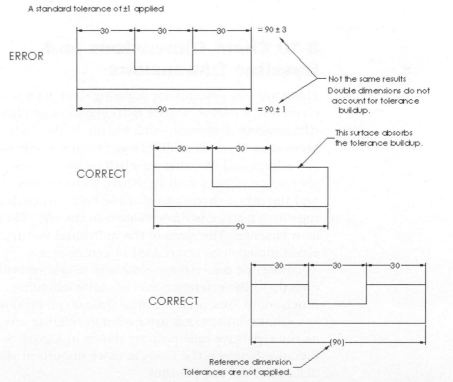

A standard tolerance of ±1 applied

ERROR

30   30   30   = 90 ± 3

90   = 90 ± 1

Not the same results
Double dimensions do not
account for tolerance
buildup.

This surface absorbs
the tolerance buildup.

CORRECT

30   30

90

CORRECT

30   30   30

(90)

Reference dimension
Tolerances are not applied.

dimensions could create an acceptable distance of 90±3 mm, or a maximum distance of 93 and a minimum distance of 87. The overall dimension of 90 mm allows a maximum distance of 91 and a minimum distance of 89. The two dimensions yield different results when tolerances are considered.

> **NOTE**
> Never dimension the same distance twice.

The size and location of a tolerance depends on the design objectives of the object, how it will be manufactured, and how it will be inspected. Even objects that have similar shapes may be dimensioned and toleranced very differently.

One possible solution to the double dimensioning shown in Figure 8-14 is to remove one of the 30-mm dimensions and allow that distance to "float," that is, absorb the cumulated tolerances. The choice of which 30-mm dimension to eliminate depends on the design objectives of the part. For this example the far-right dimension was eliminated to remove the double-dimensioning error.

Another possible solution to the double-dimensioning error is to retain the three 30-mm dimensions and to change the 90-mm overall dimension to a reference dimension. A reference dimension is used only for mathematical convenience. It is not used during the manufacturing or inspection process. A reference dimension is designated on a drawing using parentheses: (90).

If the 90-mm dimension was referenced, then only the three 30-mm dimensions would be used to manufacture and inspect the object. This would eliminate the double- dimensioning error.

8-10 Chain Dimensions and Baseline Dimensions

There are two systems for applying dimensions and tolerances to a drawing: chain and baseline. Figure 8-15 shows examples of both systems. *Chain dimensions* dimension each feature to the feature next to it. *Baseline dimensions* dimension all features from a single baseline or datum.

Chain and baseline dimensions may be used together. Figure 8-15 also shows two objects with repetitive features; one object includes two slots, and the other, three sets of three holes. In each example, the center of the repetitive feature is dimensioned to the left side of the object, which serves as a baseline. The sizes of the individual features are dimensioned using chain dimensions referenced to centerlines.

Baseline dimensions eliminate tolerance buildup and can be related directly to the reference axis of many machines. They tend to take up much more area on a drawing than do chain dimensions.

Chain dimensions are useful in relating one feature to another, such as the repetitive hole pattern shown in Figure 8-15. In this example the distance between the holes is more important than the individual hole's distance from the baseline.

Figure 8-15

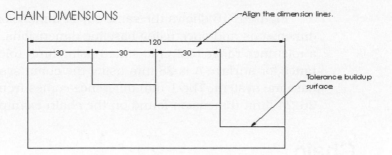

CHAIN DIMENSIONS

Align the dimension lines.

Tolerance buildup
surface

BASELINE DIMENSIONS

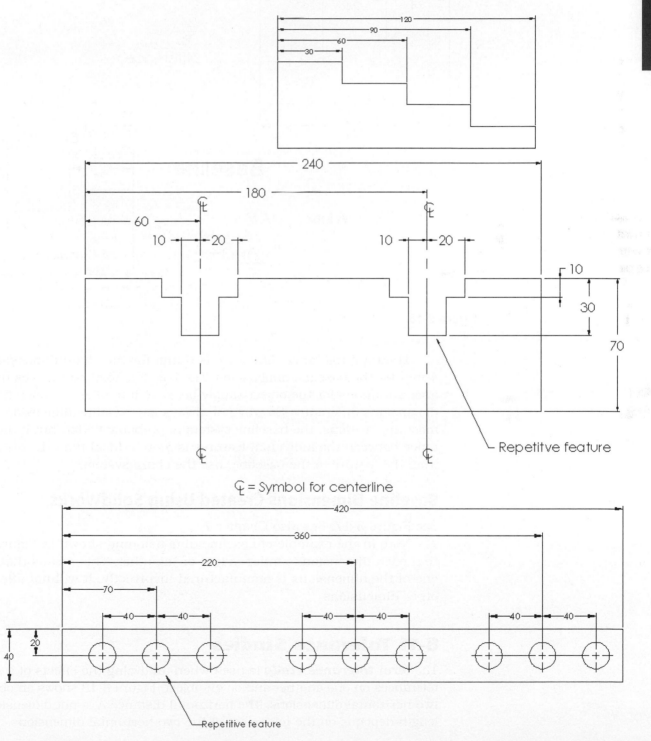

Repetitve feature

Ȼ = Symbol for centerline

Repetitive feature

Figure 8-16 shows the same object dimensioned twice, once using chain dimensions and once using baseline dimensions. All distances are assigned a tolerance range of 2 mm, stated using limit tolerances. The maximum distance for surface A is 28 mm using the chain system and 27 mm using the baseline system. The 1-mm difference comes from the elimination of the first 26–24 limit dimension found on the chain example but not on the baseline.

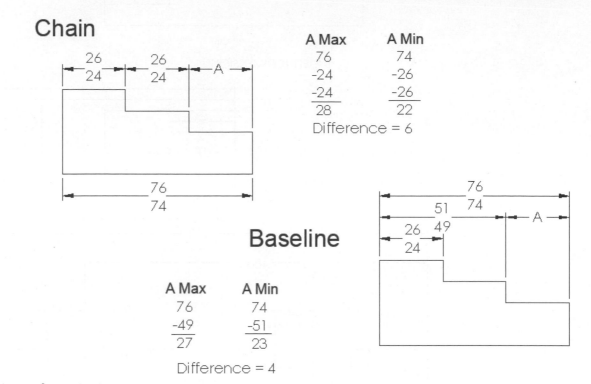

Figure 8-16

The total tolerance difference is 6 mm for the chain dimensions and 4 mm for the baseline dimensions. The baseline method reduces the tolerance variations for the object simply because it applies the tolerances and dimensions differently. So why not always use baseline dimensions? For most applications, the baseline system is probably better, but if the distance between the individual features is more critical than the distance from the feature to the baseline, use the chain system.

Baseline Dimensions Created Using SolidWorks

See Figure 8-17. See also Chapter 7.

Note in the example of baseline dimensioning shown in Figure 8-17 that each dimension is independent of the other. This means that if one of the dimensions is manufactured incorrectly, it will not affect the other dimensions.

8-11 Tolerance Studies

The term **tolerance study** is used when analyzing the effects of a group of tolerances on one another and on an object. Figure 8-18 shows an object with two horizontal dimensions. The horizontal distance A is not dimensioned. Its length depends on the tolerances of the two horizontal dimensions.

Figure 8-17

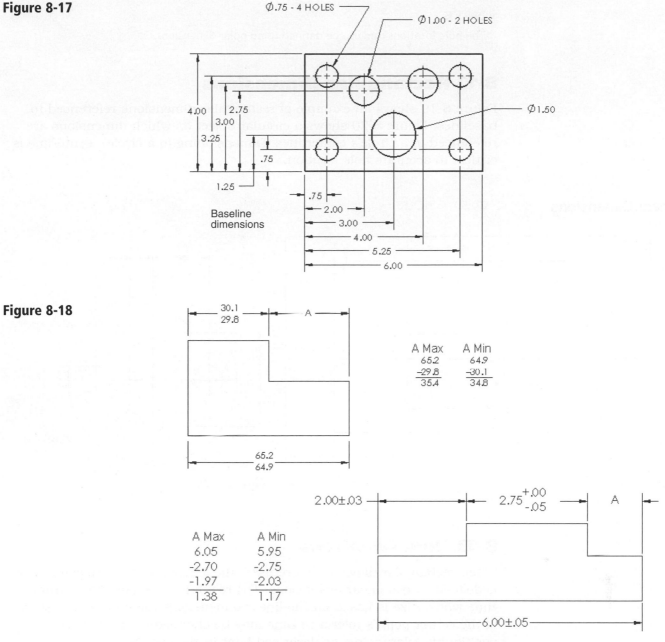

Figure 8-18

Calculating the Maximum Length of A

Distance A will be longest when the overall distance is at its longest and the other distance is at its shortest.

$$
\begin{array}{r}
65.2 \\
- \ 29.8 \\
\hline
35.4
\end{array}
$$

Calculating the Minimum Length of A

Distance A will be shortest when the overall length is at its shortest and the other length is at its longest.

$$
\begin{array}{r}
64.9 \\
- \ 30.1 \\
\hline
34.8
\end{array}
$$

NOTE

The hole locations can also be defined using polar dimensions.

8-12 Rectangular Dimensions

Figure 8-19 shows an example of rectangular dimensions referenced to baselines. Figure 8-20 shows a circular object on which dimensions are referenced to a circle's centerlines. Dimensioning to a circle's centerline is critical to accurate hole location.

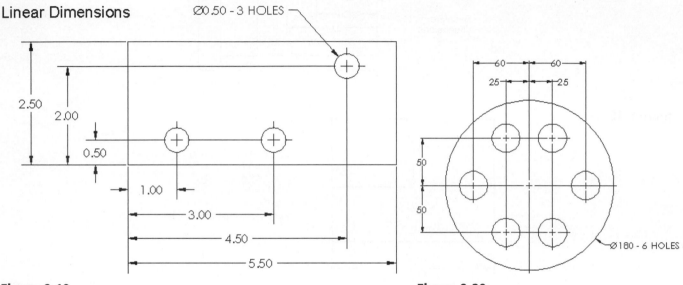

Linear Dimensions

Figure 8-19   Figure 8-20

8-13 Hole Locations

When rectangular dimensions are used, the location of a hole's center point is defined by two linear dimensions. The result is a rectangular tolerance zone whose size is based on the linear dimension's tolerances. The shape of the center point's tolerance zone may be changed to circular using positioning tolerancing, as described later in the chapter.

Figure 8-21 shows the location and size dimensions for a hole. Also shown are the resulting tolerance zone and the overall possible hole shape. The center point's tolerance is .2 by .3 based on the given linear locating tolerances.

The hole diameter has a tolerance of ±.05. This value must be added to the center point location tolerances to define the maximum overall possible shape of the hole. The maximum possible hole shape is determined by drawing the maximum radius from the four corner points of the tolerance zone.

This means that the left edge of the hole could be as close to the vertical baseline as 12.75 or as far as 13.25. The 12.75 value was derived by subtracting the maximum hole diameter value 12.05 from the minimum linear distance 24.80 (24.80 − 12.05 = 12.75). The 13.25 value was derived by subtracting the minimum hole diameter 11.95 from the maximum linear distance 25.20 (25.20 − 11.95 = 13.25).

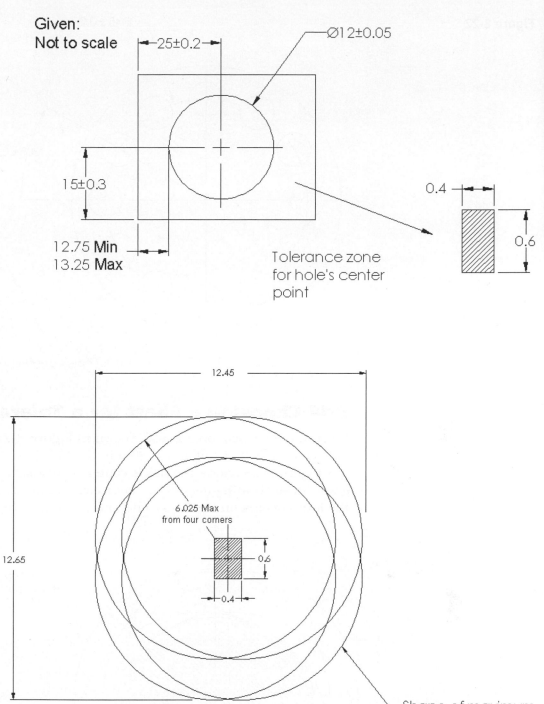

Given:
Not to scale

25±0.2

Ø12±0.05

15±0.3

12.75 Min
13.25 Max

Tolerance zone
for hole's center
point

0.4

0.6

12.45

12.65

6.025 Max
from four corners

0.6

0.4

Shape of maximum
tolerance zone

Figure 8-21

Figure 8-22 shows a hole's tolerance zone based on polar dimensions. The zone has a sector shape, and the possible hole shape is determined by locating the maximum radius at the four corner points of the tolerance zone.

Figure 8-22

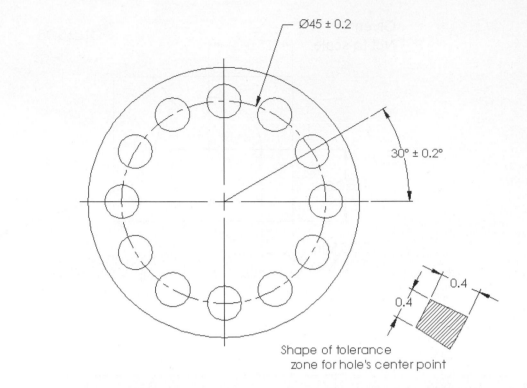

Ø45 ± 0.2

30° ± 0.2°

0.4

0.4

Shape of tolerance
zone for hole's center point

8-14 Choosing a Shaft for a Toleranced Hole

Given the hole location and size shown in Figure 8-21, what is the largest diameter shaft that will always fit into the hole?

Figure 8-23 shows the hole's center point tolerance zone based on the given linear locating tolerances. Four circles have been drawn centered at the four corners on the linear tolerance zone that represents the smallest

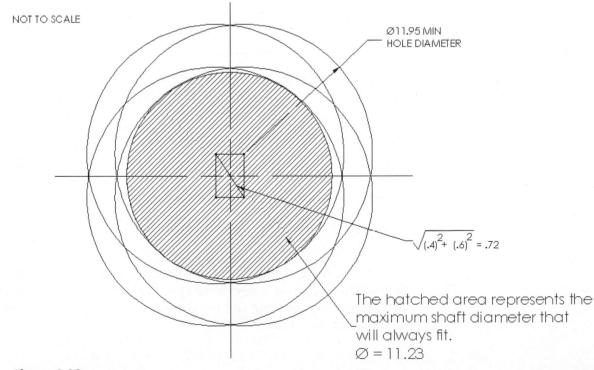

NOT TO SCALE

Ø11.95 MIN
HOLE DIAMETER

$$\sqrt{(.4)^2 + (.6)^2} = .72$$

The hatched area represents the maximum shaft diameter that will always fit.
Ø = 11.23

Figure 8-23

possible hole diameter. The circles define an area that represents the maximum shaft size that will always fit into the hole, regardless of how the given dimensions are applied.

The diameter size of this circular area can be calculated by subtracting the maximum diagonal distance across the linear tolerance zone (corner to corner) from the minimum hole diameter.

The results can be expressed as a formula.

For Linear Dimensions and Tolerances

$$S_{max} = H_{min} - DTZ$$

where

S_{max} = maximum shaft diameter
H_{min} = minimum hole diamter
DTZ = diagonal distance across the tolerance zone

In the example shown the diagonal distance is determined using the Pythagorean theorem:

$$DTZ = \sqrt{(.4)^2 + (.6)^2}$$

$$= \sqrt{.16 + .36}$$

$$DTZ = .72$$

This means that the maximum shaft diameter that will always fit into the given hole is 11.23:

$$S_{max} = H_{min} - DTZ$$

$$= 11.95 - .72$$

$$S_{max} = 11.23$$

This procedure represents a restricted application of the general formula presented later in the chapter for positioning tolerances.

NOTE

Linear tolerances generate a square or rectangular tolerance zone.

Once the maximum shaft size has been established, a tolerance can be applied to the shaft. If the shaft had a total tolerance of .25, the minimum shaft diameter would be $11.23 - .25$, or 10.98. Figure 8-23 shows a shaft dimensioned and toleranced using these values.

The formula presented is based on the assumption that the shaft is perfectly placed on the hole's center point. This assumption is reasonable if two objects are joined by a fastener and both objects are free to move. When both objects are free to move about a common fastener, they are called *floating objects.*

8-15 Sample Problem SP8-1

Parts A and B in Figure 8-24 are to be joined by a common shaft. The total tolerance for the shaft is to be .05. What are the maximum and minimum shaft diameters?

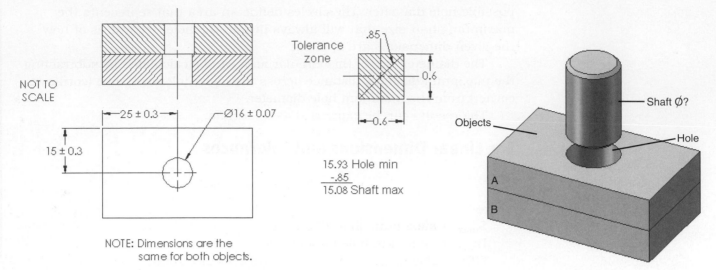

Figure 8-24

Both objects have the same dimensions and tolerances and are floating relative to each other.

$$S_{max} = H_{min} - DTZ$$

$$= 15.93 - .85$$

$$S_{max} = 15.08$$

The shaft's minimum diameter is found by subtracting the total tolerance requirement from the calculated maximum diameter:

$$15.08 - .05 = 15.03$$

Therefore,
Shaft max = 5.08
Shaft min = 5.03

8-16 Sample Problem SP8-2

The procedure presented in Sample Problem SP8-1 can be worked in reverse to determine the maximum and minimum hole size based on a given shaft size.

Objects AA and BB as shown in Figure 8-25 are to be joined using a bolt whose maximum diameter is .248. What is the minimum hole size for objects that will always accept the bolt? What is the maximum hole size if the total hole tolerance is .005?

$$S_{max} = H_{min} - DTZ$$

In this example H_{min} is the unknown factor, so the equation is rewritten as

$$H_{min} = S_{max} + DTZ$$

$$= .248 + .010$$

$$H_{min} = .258$$

Figure 8-25

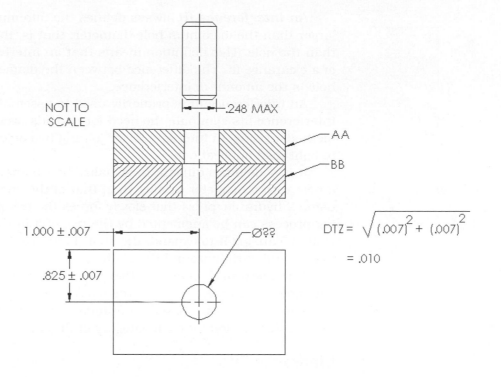

NOT TO
SCALE

.248 MAX

AA

BB

1.000 ± .007

.825 ± .007

Ø??

$$DTZ = \sqrt{(.007)^2 + (.007)^2}$$
$$= .010$$

This is the minimum hole diameter, so the total tolerance requirement is added to this value:

$$.258 + .005 = .263$$

Therefore,
Hole max = .263
Hole min = .258

8-17 Nominal Sizes

The term **nominal** refers to the approximate size of an object that matches a common fraction or whole number. A shaft with a dimension of 1.500 + .003 is said to have a nominal size of "one and a half inches." A dimension of 1.500 +.000/−.005 is still said to have a nominal size of one and a half inches. In both examples 1.5 is the closest common fraction.

8-18 Standard Fits (Metric Values)

Calculating tolerances between holes and shafts that fit together is so common in engineering design that a group of standard values and notations has been established. These values may be calculated using the **Limits and Fits** option of the **Design Library**.

There are three possible types of fits between a shaft and a hole: clearance, transitional, and interference. There are several subclassifications within each of these categories.

A **clearance fit** always defines the maximum shaft diameter as smaller than the minimum hole diameter. The difference between the two diameters is the amount of clearance. It is possible for a clearance fit to be defined with zero clearance; that is, the maximum shaft diameter is equal to the minimum hole diameter.

An *interference fit* always defines the minimum shaft diameter as larger than the maximum hole diameter; that is, the shaft is always bigger than the hole. This definition means that an interference fit is the converse of a clearance fit. The difference between the diameter of the shaft and the hole is the amount of interference.

An interference fit is primarily used to assemble objects together. Interference fits eliminate the need for threads, welds, or other joining methods. Using an interference for joining two objects is generally limited to light load applications.

It is sometimes difficult to visualize how a shaft can be assembled into a hole with a diameter smaller than that of the shaft. It is sometimes done using a hydraulic press that slowly forces the two parts together. The joining process can be augmented by the use of lubricants or heat. The hole is heated, causing it to expand, the shaft is inserted, and the hole is allowed to cool and shrink around the shaft.

A *transition fit* may be either a clearance or an interference fit. It may have a clearance between the shaft and the hole or an interference.

The notations are based on Standard International Tolerance values. A specific description for each category of fit follows.

Clearance Fits

H11/c11or C11/h11 = loose running fit

H8/d8 or D8/h8 = free running fit

H8/f7 or F8/h7 = close running fit

H7/g6 or G7/h6 = sliding fit

H7/h6 = locational clearance fit

Transitional Fits

H7/k6 or K7/h6 = locational transition fit

H7/n6 or N7/h6 = locational transition fit

Interference Fits

H7/p6 or P7/h6 = locational transition fit

H7/s6 or S7/h6 = medium drive fit

H7/u6 or U7/h6 = force fit

8-19 Standard Fits (Inch Values)

Inch values are accessed in the **Design Library** by selecting the **Ansi-Inch** standards.

Fits defined using inch values are classified as follows:

RC = running and sliding fits

LC = clearance locational fits

LT = transitional locational fits

LN = interference fits

FN = force fits

Each of these general categories has several subclassifications within it defined by a number, for example, Class RC1, Class RC2, through Class RC8. The letter designations are based on International Tolerance Standards, as are metric designations.

> **TIP**
> Charts of tolerance values can be found in the appendix.

To Add a Fit Callout to a Drawing

Figure 8-26 shows a block and post. Figure 8-27 shows a drawing containing a front and a top orthographic view of the block and post assembly.

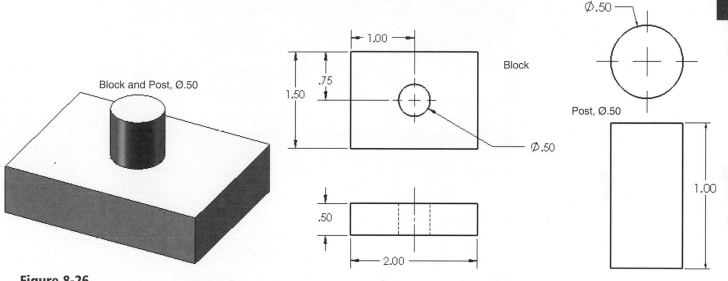

Block

Post, Ø.50

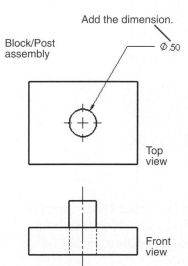

Figure 8-26

Figure 8-27

1 Draw the block and post and create an assembly drawing as shown in Figure 8-26.

2 Draw a front and a top orthographic view of the assembly as shown.

3 Add a **Ø.50** dimension to the top view.

4 Click the **Ø.50** dimension.

The **Dimension Value PropertyManager** will appear. See Figure 8-28.

5 Select the **Fit** option from the **Tolerance/Precision** box as shown.

6 Select a **Clearance** fit.

7 Select an **H5** tolerance for the hole.

8 Select the **g4** tolerance for the shaft.

9 Change the number of decimal places in the Ø.50 dimension to four places, **Ø.5000.**

10 Click the OK check mark.

Reading Fit Tables

There are several fit tables in the appendix for both English units and metric units. The metric tables can be read directly, as they state hole and

Figure 8-28

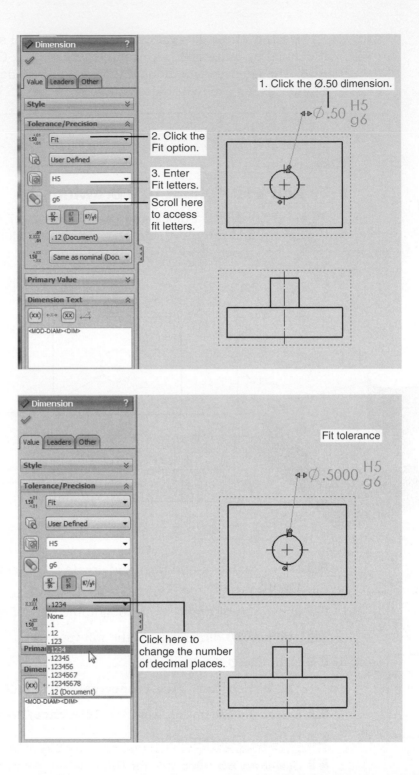

shaft dimension. For example, the tolerance for a Preferred Clearance Fit for a 10mm nominal hole using a loose running fit is 10.090/10.000 for the hole and 9.920/9.830 for the shaft. The tolerance callout would be H11/c11. English unit tables require interpretation.

Figure 8-29 shows the table values for a .5000 nominal hole using an H5/g4 tolerance. The tolerance values are in thousands of an inch; that is, a listed value of 0.25 equals 0.0025 in. The Ø.5000 nominal value is in the 0.40–0.71 size range, so the tolerance values are as shown. These values can be applied to the detail drawings of the block and shaft. See Figure 8-30.

Figure 8-29

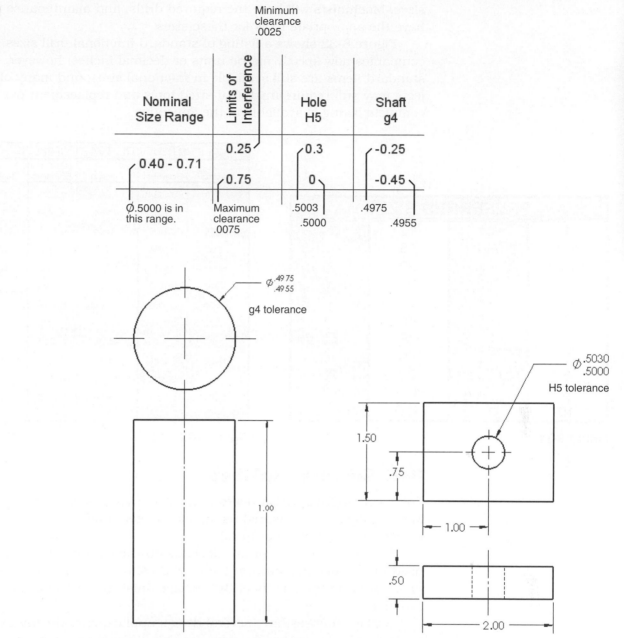

Nominal Size Range	Limits of Interference	Hole H5	Shaft g4
0.40 - 0.71	0.25	0.3	-0.25
	0.75	0	-0.45

Minimum clearance .0025

Ø.5000 is in this range.

Maximum clearance .0075

.5003
.5000

.4975
.4955

Figure 8-30

Ø .4975 / .4955
g4 tolerance

1.00

Ø .5030 / .5000
H5 tolerance

1.50
.75
1.00

.50
2.00

8-20 Preferred and Standard Sizes

It is important that designers always consider preferred and standard sizes when selecting sizes for designs. Most tooling is set up to match these sizes, so manufacturing is greatly simplified when preferred and standard sizes are specified. Figure 8-31 shows a listing of preferred sizes for metric values.

Consider the case of design calculations that call for a 42-mm-diameter hole. A 42-mm-diameter hole is not a preferred size. A diameter of 40 mm is the closest preferred size, and a 45-mm diameter is a second choice. A 42-mm hole could be manufactured but would require an unusual drill size that might not be available. It would be wise to reconsider the design to see if a 40-mm-diameter hole could be used, and if not, possibly a 45-mm-diameter hole.

A production run of a very large quantity could possibly justify the cost of special tooling, but for smaller runs it is probably better to use preferred sizes. Machinists will have the required drills, and maintenance people will have the appropriate tools for these sizes.

Figure 8-32 shows a listing of standard fractional drill sizes. Most companies now specify metric units or decimal inches; however, many standard items are still available in fractional sizes, and many older objects may still require fractional-sized tools and replacement parts. A more complete listing is available in the appendix.

PREFERRED SIZES

1	1.1	12	14
1.2	1.4	16	18
1.6	1.8	20	22
2	2.2	25	28
2.5	2.8	30	35
3	3.5	40	45
4	4.5	50	55
5	5.5	60	70
6	7	80	90
8	9	100	110
10	11	120	140

Figure 8-31

STANDARD TWIST DRILL SIZES

Fraction	Decimal Equivalent	Fraction	Decimal Equivalent	Fraction	Decimal Equivalent
7/16	0.1094	21/64	0.3281	11/16	0.6875
1/8	0.1250	11/64	0.3438	3/4	0.7500
9/64	0.1406	23/64	0.3594	13/16	0.8125
5/32	0.1562	3/8	0.3750	7/8	0.8750
11/64	0.1719	25/64	0.3906	15/16	0.9375
3/16	0.1875	13/32	0.4062	1	1.0000
13/64	0.2031	27/64	0.4219		
7/32	0.2188	7/16	0.4375		
1/4	0.2500	29/64	0.4531		
17/64	0.2656	15/32	0.4688		
9/32	0.2812	1/2	0.5000		
19/64	0.2969	9/16	0.5625		
5/16	0.3125	5/8	0.6250		

Figure 8-32

8-21 Surface Finishes

The term **surface finish** refers to the accuracy (flatness) of a surface. Metric values are measured using micrometers (µm), and inch values are measured in microinches (µin.).

The accuracy of a surface depends on the manufacturing process used to produce the surface. Figure 8-33 shows a listing of manufacturing processes and the quality of the surface finish they can be expected to produce.

Surface finishes have several design applications. **Datum surfaces,** or surfaces used for baseline dimensioning, should have fairly accurate

Surface Roughness Average Obtained by Common Production Methods											
	Roughness Height Rating - microinches, micromillimeters										
Process — µmm	50	25	12.5	6.3	3.2	1.6	0.8	0.4	0.2	0.1	0.05
µin	2000	1000	500	250	125	63	32	16	8	4	2
Flame Cutting											
Snagging											
Sawing											
Planing & Shaping											
Drilling											
Chemical Milling											
Electric Discharge											
Milling											
Broaching											
Reaming											
Electron Beam											
Laser											

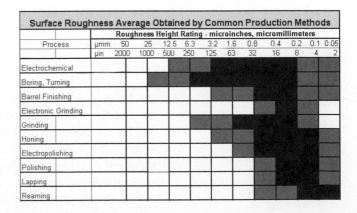

Figure 8-33

Figure 8-33
(*Continued*)

Surface Roughness Average Obtained by Common Production Methods												
	Roughness Height Rating - microinches, micromillimeters											
Process	µmm	50	25	12.5	6.3	3.2	1.6	0.8	0.4	0.2	0.1	0.05
	µin	2000	1000	500	250	125	63	32	16	8	4	2
Sand Casting												
Hot Rolling												
Forging												
Perm Mold Casting												
Investment Casting												
Extrusion												
Cold Rolling, Drawing												
Polishing	Die Casting											

surface finishes to help assure accurate measurements. Bearing surfaces should have good-quality surface finishes for better load distribution, and parts that operate at high speeds should have smooth finishes to help reduce friction. Figure 8-34 shows a screw head sitting on a very wavy surface. Note that the head of the screw is actually in contact with only two wave peaks, meaning all the bearing load is concentrated on the two peaks. This situation could cause stress cracks and greatly weaken the surface. A better-quality surface finish would increase the bearing contact area.

Bearing Load

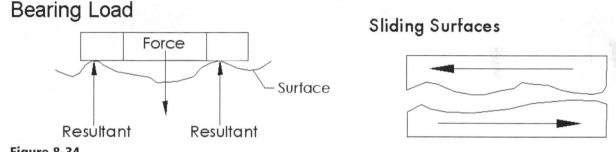

Figure 8-34

Sliding Surfaces

Figure 8-34 also shows two very rough surfaces moving in contact with each other. The result will be excess wear to both surfaces because the surfaces touch only on the peaks, and these peaks will tend to wear faster than flatter areas. Excess vibration can also result when interfacing surfaces are too rough.

Surface finishes are classified into three categories: surface texture, roughness, and lay. **Surface texture** is a general term that refers to the overall quality and accuracy of a surface.

Roughness is a measure of the average deviation of a surface's peaks and valleys. See Figure 8-35.

Figure 8-35

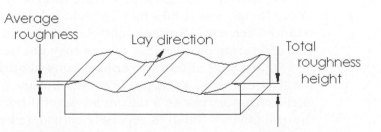

Lay refers to the direction of machine marks on a surface. See Figure 8-36. The lay of a surface is particularly important when two moving objects are in contact with each other, especially at high speeds.

Figure 8-36

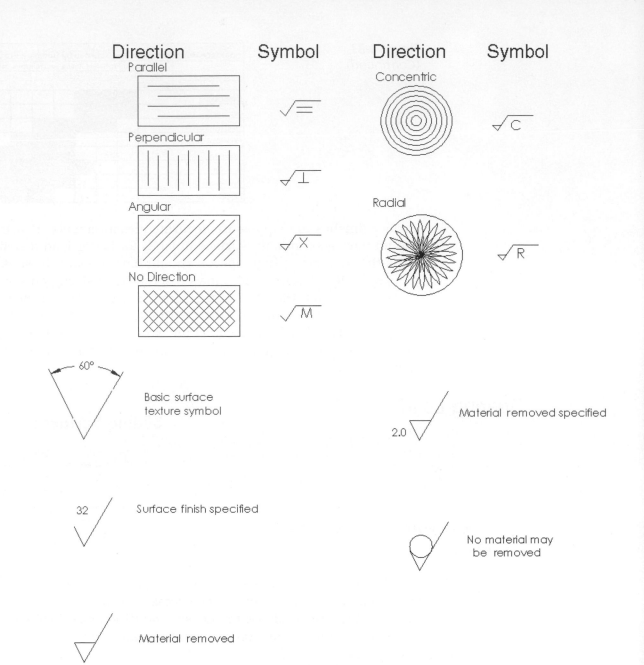

8-22 Surface Control Symbols

Surface finishes are indicated on a drawing using surface control symbols. See Figure 8-37. The general surface control symbol looks like a check mark. Roughness values may be included with the symbol to specify the required accuracy. Surface control symbols can also be used to specify the manufacturing process that may or may not be used to produce a surface.

Figure 8-37 shows two applications of surface control symbols. In the first example, a 0.8-μm (32 μin.) surface finish is specified on the surface that serves as a datum for several horizontal dimensions. A 0.8-μm surface finish is generally considered the minimum acceptable finish for datums.

A second finish mark with a value of 0.4 μm is located on an extension line that refers to a surface that will be in contact with a moving object. The extra flatness will help prevent wear between the two surfaces.

Figure 8-37

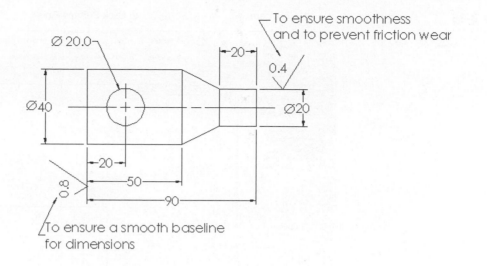

8-23 Applying Surface Control Symbols

Figure 8-38 shows a dimensioned orthographic view. Surface symbols will be added to this view.

Figure 8-38

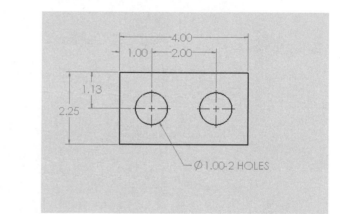

1 Click the **Annotation** tab and select the **Surface Finish** tool.

See Figure 8-39.

2 Select the **Basic** symbol and enter a value of **32.**

3 Move the cursor into the drawing area and locate the surface control symbol on an extension line as shown.

4 Click the **<Esc>** key.

5 Click the OK check mark

6 Save the drawing.

To Add a Lay Symbol to a Drawing

Use the same drawing as in Figure 8-39.

1 Click the **Annotation** tab and select the **Surface Finish** tool.

Figure 8-39

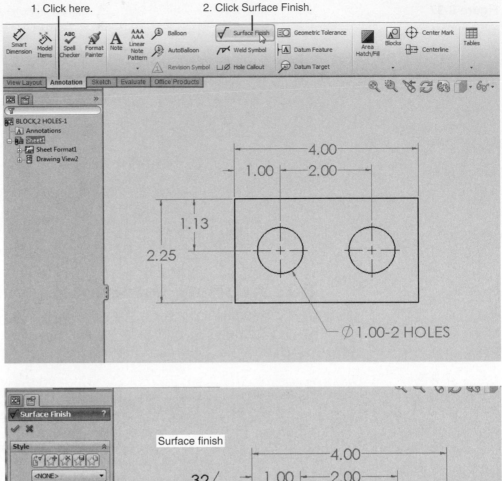

1. Click here. 2. Click Surface Finish.

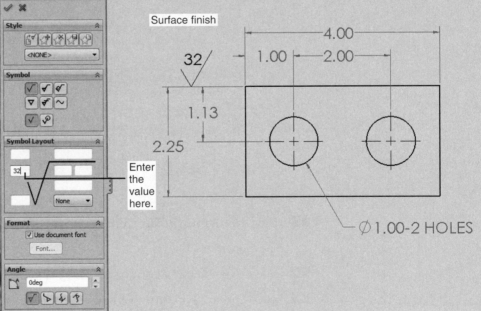

See Figure 8-40.

2 Click the **Lay Direction** box and select the **Multi-Directional** option.

3 Click the **Machine Required** symbol box.

4 Move the cursor into the drawing area and locate the surface control symbol on an extension line as shown.

5 Click the **<Esc>** key.

6 Click the OK check mark.

Figure 8-40

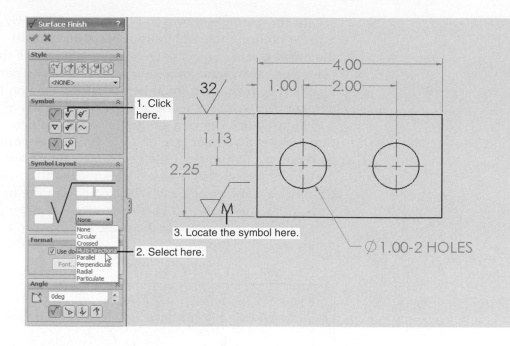

8-24 Design Problems

Figure 8-41 shows two objects that are to be fitted together using a fastener such as a screw-and-nut combination. For this example a cylinder will be used to represent a fastener. Only two nominal dimensions are given. The dimensions and tolerances were derived as follows.

The distance between the centers of the holes is given as 50 nominal. The term *nominal* means that the stated value is only a starting point. The final dimensions will be close to the given value but do not have to equal it.

Assigning tolerances is an iteration process; that is, a tolerance is selected and other tolerance values are calculated from the selected initial values. If the results are not satisfactory, go back and modify the initial value and calculate the other values again. As your experience grows you will become better at selecting realistic initial values.

Figure 8-41

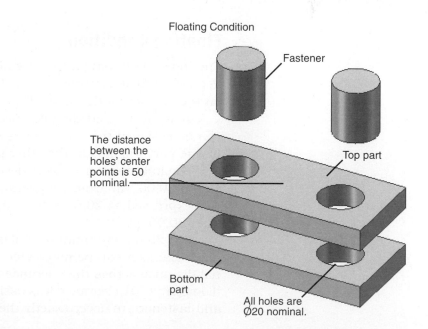

In the example shown in Figure 8-41, start by assigning a tolerance of ±.01 to both the top and bottom parts for both the horizontal and vertical dimensions used to locate the holes. This means that there is a possible center point variation of .02 for both parts. The parts must always fit together, so tolerances must be assigned based on the worst-case condition, or when the parts are made at the extreme ends of the assigned tolerances.

Figure 8-42 shows a greatly enlarged picture of the worst-case condition created by a tolerance of ±.01. The center points of the holes could be as much as .028 apart if the two center points were located at opposite corners of the tolerance zones. This means that the minimum hole diameter must always be at least .028 larger than the maximum stud diameter. In addition, there should be a clearance tolerance assigned so that the hole and stud are never exactly the same size. Figure 8-43 shows the resulting tolerances.

> **TIP**
> The tolerance zones in this section are created by line dimensions that generated square tolerance zones.

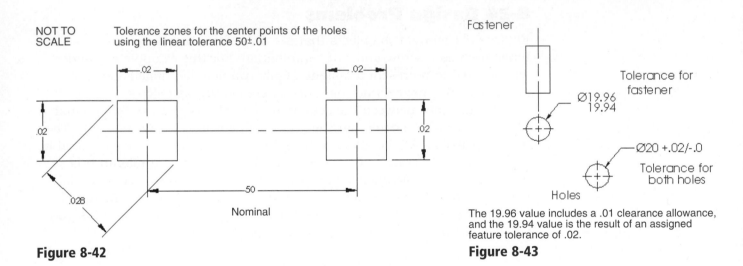

Figure 8-42

Figure 8-43

The 19.96 value includes a .01 clearance allowance, and the 19.94 value is the result of an assigned feature tolerance of .02.

Floating Condition

The top and bottom parts shown in Figure 8-41 are to be joined by two independent fasteners; that is, the location of one fastener does not depend on the location of the other. This situation is called a ***floating condition.***

This means that the tolerance zones for both the top and bottom parts can be assigned the same values and that a fastener diameter selected to fit one part will also fit the other part.

The final tolerances were developed by first defining a minimum hole size of 20.00. An arbitrary tolerance of .02 was assigned to the hole and was expressed as 20.00 +.02/−0, so the hole can never be any smaller than 20.00.

The 20.00 minimum hole diameter dictates that the maximum fastener diameter can be no greater than 19.97, or .03 (the rounded-off diagonal distance across the tolerance zone—.028) less than the minimum hole diameter. A .01 clearance was assigned. The clearance ensures that the hole and fastener are never exactly the same diameter. The resulting maximum allowable diameter for the fastener is 19.96. Again, an arbitrary tolerance of .02 was assigned to the fastener. The final fastener dimensions are therefore 19.96 to 19.94.

The assigned tolerances ensure that there will always be at least .01 clearance between the fastener and the hole. The other extreme condition occurs when the hole is at its largest possible size (20.02) and the fastener is at its smallest (19.94). This means that there could be as much as .08 clearance between the parts. If this much clearance is not acceptable, then the assigned tolerances will have to be reevaluated.

Figure 8-44 shows the top and bottom parts dimensioned and toleranced. Any dimensions that do not have assigned tolerances are assumed to have standard tolerances.

Figure 8-44

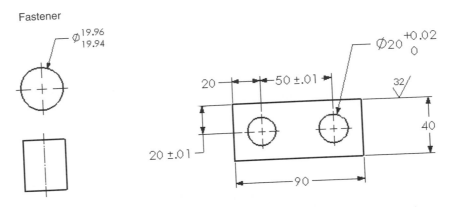

Note, in Figure 8-44, that the top edge of each part has been assigned a surface finish. This was done to help ensure the accuracy of the 20±.01 dimension. If this edge surface was rough, it could affect the tolerance measurements.

This example will be done later in the chapter using geometric tolerances. Geometric tolerance zones are circular rather than rectangular.

Fixed Condition

Figure 8-45 shows the same nominal conditions presented in Figure 8-41, but the fasteners are now fixed to the top part. This situation is called the *fixed condition.* In analyzing the tolerance zones for the fixed condition, two position tolerances must be considered: the positional tolerances for the holes in the bottom part, and the positional tolerances for the fixed

Figure 8-45

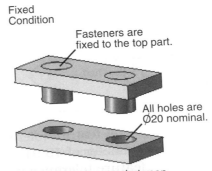

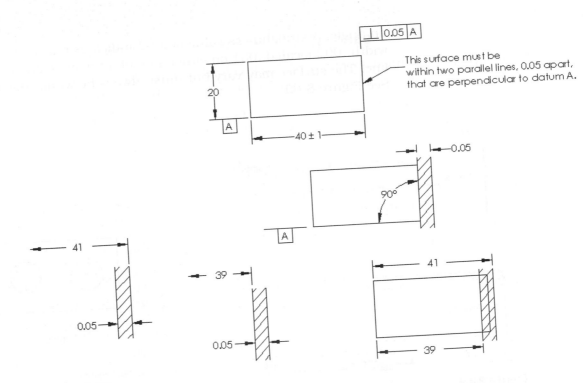

Figure 8-70

datum A, and the right vertical edge is toleranced so that it must be perpendicular within a limit of 0.05 to datum A. The perpendicularity tolerance defines a tolerance zone 0.05 wide between two parallel planes that
are perpendicular to datum A.

The object also includes a horizontal dimension and tolerance of 40±1.
This tolerance is called a *locational tolerance* because it serves to locate the
right edge of the object. As with rectangular coordinate tolerances, discussed earlier in the chapter, the 40±1 controls the location of the edge—
how far away or how close it can be to the left edge—but does not directly
control the shape of the edge. Any shape that falls within the specified tolerance range is acceptable. This may in fact be sufficient for a given design, but if a more controlled shape is required, a perpendicularity tolerance must be added. The perpendicularity tolerance works within the
locational tolerance to ensure that the edge is not only within the locational tolerance but is also perpendicular to datum A.

Figure 8-70 shows the two extreme conditions for the 40±1 locational
tolerance. The perpendicularity tolerance is applied by first measuring the
surface and determining its maximum and minimum lengths. The difference between these two measurements must be less than 0.05. Thus, if
the measured maximum distance is 41, then no other part of the surface
may be less then $41 - 0.05 = 40.95$.

Tolerances of perpendicularity serve to complement locational tolerances, to make the shape more exact, so tolerances of perpendicularity
must always be smaller than tolerances of location. It would be of little
use, for example, to assign a perpendicularity tolerance of 1.5 for the object shown in Figure 8-71. The locational tolerance would prevent the variation from ever reaching the limits specified by such a large perpendicularity tolerance.

Figure 8-72 shows a perpendicularity tolerance applied to cylindrical
features: a shaft and a hole. The figure includes examples of both RFS and

Figure 8-71

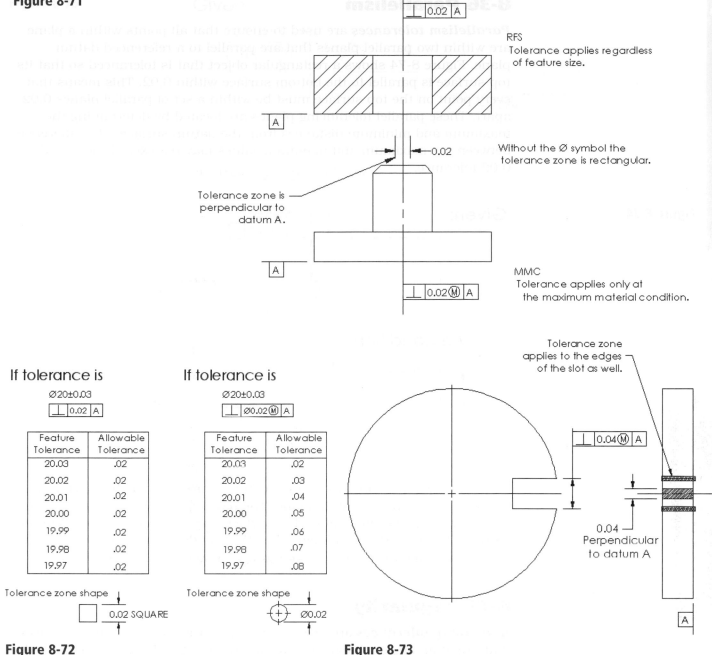

RFS
Tolerance applies regardless
of feature size.

Without the Ø symbol the
tolerance zone is rectangular.

Tolerance zone is
perpendicular to
datum A.

MMC
Tolerance applies only at
the maximum material condition.

Tolerance zone
applies to the edges
of the slot as well.

If tolerance is

Ø20±0.03

Feature Tolerance	Allowable Tolerance
20.03	.02
20.02	.02
20.01	.02
20.00	.02
19.99	.02
19.98	.02
19.97	.02

Tolerance zone shape

0.02 SQUARE

Figure 8-72

If tolerance is

Ø20±0.03

Feature Tolerance	Allowable Tolerance
20.03	.02
20.02	.03
20.01	.04
20.00	.05
19.99	.06
19.98	.07
19.97	.08

Tolerance zone shape

Ø0.02

0.04
Perpendicular
to datum A

Figure 8-73

MMC applications. As with straightness tolerances applied at MMC, perpendicularity tolerances applied about a hole or shaft's centerline allow the tolerance zone to vary as the feature size varies.

The inclusion of the Ø symbol in a geometric tolerance is critical to its interpretation. See Figure 8-73. If the Ø symbol is not included, the tolerance applies only to the view in which it is written. This means that the tolerance zone is shaped like a rectangular slice, not a cylinder, as would be the case if the Ø symbol were included. In general it is better to always include the Ø symbol for cylindrical features because it generates a tolerance zone more like that used in positional tolerancing.

Figure 8-73 shows a perpendicularity tolerance applied to a slot, a noncylindrical feature. Again, the MMC specification is always for variations in the tolerance zone.

Figure 8-77

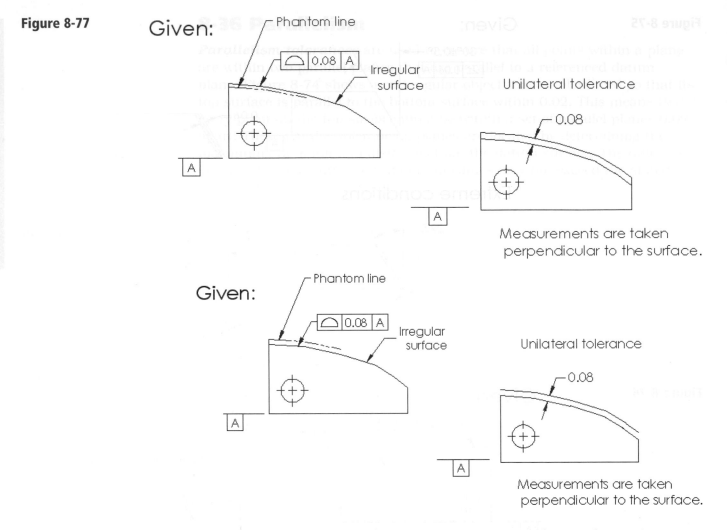

Given:

Phantom line

⌒ 0.08 A

Irregular surface

A

Unilateral tolerance

0.08

A

Measurements are taken perpendicular to the surface.

Given:

Phantom line

⌒ 0.08 A

Irregular surface

A

Unilateral tolerance

0.08

A

Measurements are taken perpendicular to the surface.

Surface and line profile tolerances are somewhat analogous to flatness and straightness tolerances. Flatness and surface profile tolerances are applied across an entire surface, whereas straightness and line profile tolerances are applied only along a single line across the surface.

Given:

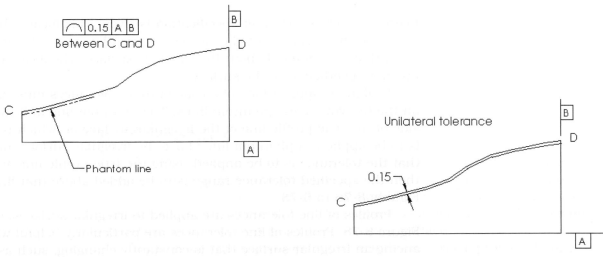

⌒ 0.15 A B
Between C and D

B

D

C

A

Phantom line

Unilateral tolerance

B

D

0.15

C

A

Figure 8-78

8-39 Runouts

A *runout tolerance* is used to limit the variations between features of an object and a datum. More specifically, they are applied to surfaces around a datum axis such as a cylinder or to a surface constructed perpendicular to a datum axis. There are two types of runout tolerances: circular and total.

Figure 8-79 shows a cylinder that includes a circular runout tolerance. The runout requirements are checked by rotating the object about its longitudinal axis or datum axis while holding an indicator gauge in a fixed position on the object's surface.

Runout tolerances may be either bilateral or unilateral. A runout tolerance is assumed to be bilateral unless otherwise indicated. If a runout tolerance is to be unilateral, a phantom line is used to indicate the side of the object's true surface to which the tolerance is to be applied. See Figure 8-80.

Runout tolerances may be applied to tapered areas of cylindrical objects, as shown in Figure 8-81. The tolerance is checked by rotating the object about a datum axis while holding an indicator gauge in place.

A total runout tolerance limits the variation across an entire surface. See Figure 8-82. An indicator gauge is not held in place while the object is rotated, as it is for circular runout tolerances, but is moved about the rotating surface.

Figure 8-83 shows a circular runout tolerance that references two datums. The two datums serve as one datum. The object can then be rotated about both datums simultaneously as the runout tolerances are checked.

Figure

RUNOUT tolerance

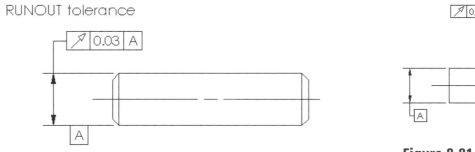

Figure 8-79

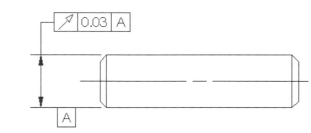

Figure 8-81

RUNOUT tolerance

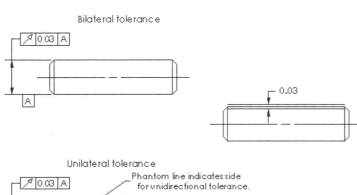

Bilateral tolerance

Figure 8-82

Unilateral tolerance

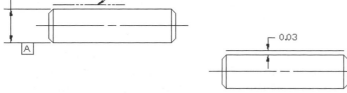

Figure 8-80

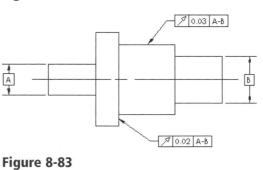

Figure 8-83

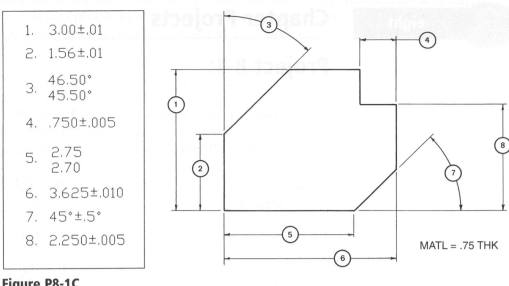

1.	3.00±.01
2.	1.56±.01
3.	46.50° 45.50°
4.	.750±.005
5.	2.75 2.70
6.	3.625±.010
7.	45°±.5°
8.	2.250±.005

MATL = .75 THK

Figure P8-1C
INCHES

Fig

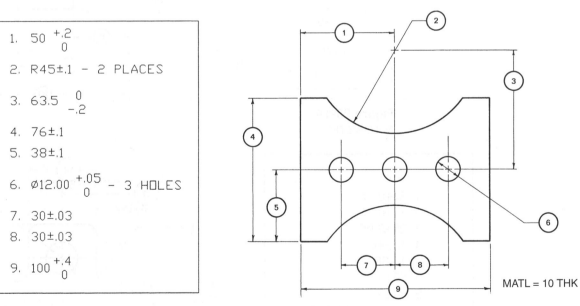

1.	50 $^{+.2}_{\ \ 0}$
2.	R45±.1 – 2 PLACES
3.	63.5 $^{\ \ 0}_{-.2}$
4.	76±.1
5.	38±.1
6.	Ø12.00 $^{+.05}_{\ \ \ 0}$ – 3 HOLES
7.	30±.03
8.	30±.03
9.	100 $^{+.4}_{\ \ 0}$

MATL = 10 THK

Figure P8-1D
MILLIMETERS

Project 8-2:

Redraw the object shown in Figure P8-2, including the given dimensions and tolerances. Calculate and list the maximum and minimum distances for surface A.

MATL = 25 THK

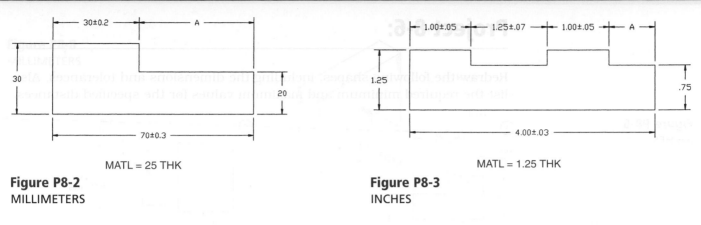

Figure P8-2
MILLIMETERS

MATL = 1.25 THK

Figure P8-3
INCHES

Project 8-3:

A. Redraw the object shown in Figure P8-3, including the dimensions and tolerances. Calculate and list the maximum and minimum distances for surface A.
B. Redraw the given object and dimension it using baseline dimensions. Calculate and list the maximum and minimum distances for surface A.

Project 8-4:

Redraw the object shown in Figure P8-4, including the dimensions and tolerances. Calculate and list the maximum and minimum distances for surfaces D and E.

Project 8-5:

Dimension the object shown in Figure P8-5 twice, once using chain dimensions and once using baseline dimensions. Calculate and list the maximum and minimum distances for surface D for both chain and baseline dimensions. Compare the results.

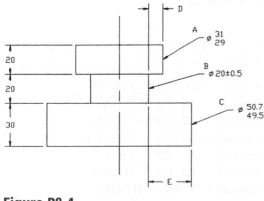

Figure P8-4
MILLIMETERS

MATL = 20 THK

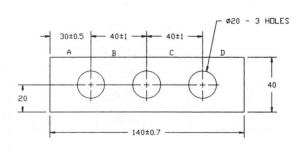

Figure P8-5
MILLIMETERS

D. Nominal = 0.75, Fit = Class RC3, H7/f6
E. Nominal = 1.75, Fit = Class RC6, H9/e8
F. Nominal = .500, Fit = Class LT2, H8/js7
G. Nominal = 1.25, Fit = Class LT5, H7/n6
H. Nominal = 1.38, Fit = Class LN3, J7/h6
I. Nominal = 1.625, Fit = Class FN, H7/s6
J. Nominal = 2.00, Fit = Class FN4, H7/u6

Figure P8-9
INCHES

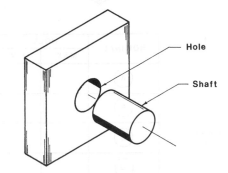

half space

NOMINAL	HOLE		SHAFT		CLEARANCE	
	MAX	MIN	MAX	MIN	MAX	MIN
A						
B						
C						
D						
E						

3.75
6 equal spaces

1.5   6.0 − 6 equal spaces

NOMINAL	HOLE		SHAFT		INTERFERENCE	
	MAX	MIN	MAX	MIN	MAX	MIN
F						
G						
H						
I						
J						

Use the same dimensions given above

Project 8-10:

Draw the chart shown and add the appropriate values based on the dimensions and tolerances given in Figures P8-10A through P8-10D.

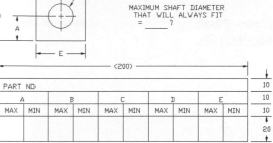

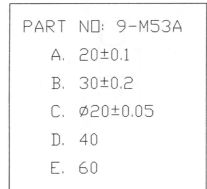

Figure P8-10A
MILLIMETERS

Project

Draw a fro
sions and t

Project

Given the f
and AM312
orientation.
the assembl
with an ope

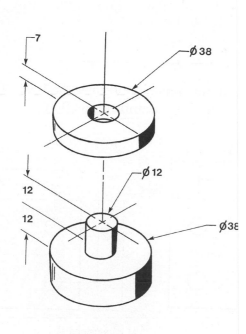

FINAL CONDITION

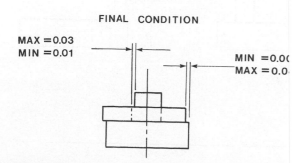

Figure P8-13
MILLIMETERS

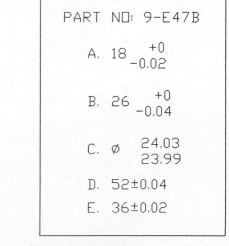

Figure P8-10B
MILLIMETERS

Figure P8-10C
MILLIMETERS

Figure P8-10D
MILLIMETERS

Proje ~~ct 8-11:~~

Prepare
the give

Proje

Redraw t
and toler

Maximum al

Project 8-15:

Given the following rail assembly, add dimensions and tolerances so that the parts always fit together as shown in the assembled position.

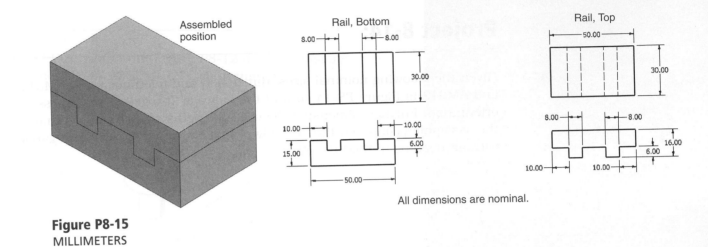

Assembled position

Rail, Bottom

8.00 — 8.00

30.00

10.00 — 10.00
15.00 — 6.00

50.00

Rail, Top

50.00

30.00

8.00 — 8.00

16.00
6.00

10.00 — 10.00

All dimensions are nominal.

Figure P8-15
MILLIMETERS

Project 8-16:

Given the following peg assembly, add dimensions and tolerances so that the parts always fit together as shown in the assembled position.

Nominal dimensi

1.00

1.00

1.00

.50

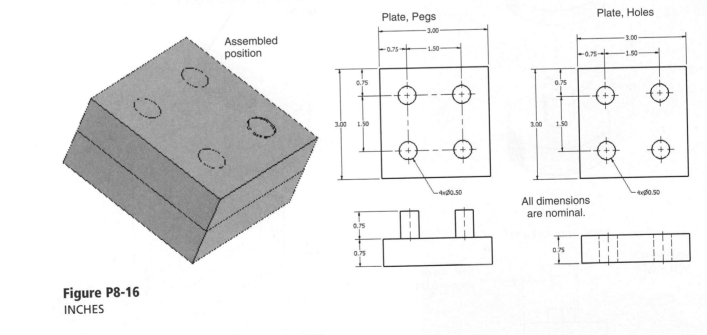

Assembled position

Plate, Pegs

3.00
0.75 — 1.50
0.75
3.00   1.50

4xØ0.50

0.75
0.75

Plate, Holes

3.00
0.75 — 1.50
0.75
3.00   1.50

4xØ0.50

All dimensions are nominal.

0.75

Figure P8-16
INCHES

Project 8-17:

Given the following collar assembly, add dimensions and tolerances so that the parts always fit together as shown in the assembled position.

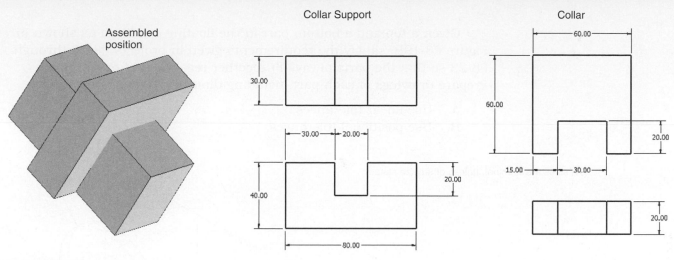

Figure P8-17
MILLIMETERS

Project 8-18:

Given the following vee-block assembly, add dimensions and tolerances so that the parts always fit together as shown in the assembled position. The total height of the assembled blocks must be between 4.45 and 4.55 in.

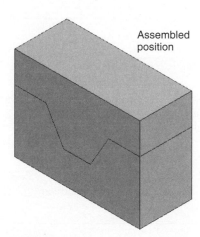

Figure P8-18
INCHES

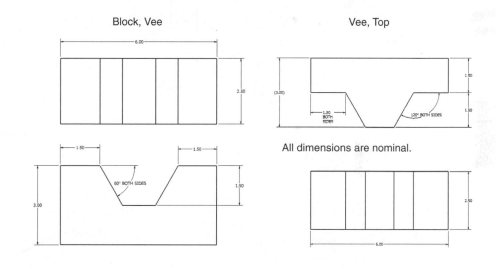

All dimensions are nominal.

Project 8-19:

Design a bracket that will support the three Ø100 wheels shown in Figure P8-19A. The wheels will utilize three Ø5.00±0.01 shafts attached to the bracket. The bottom of the bracket must be a minimum of 10 mm from the ground. The wall thickness of the bracket must always be at least 5 mm, and the minimum bracket opening must be at least 15 mm.

1. Prepare a front and a side view of the bracket.
2. Draw the wheels in their relative positions using phantom lines.
3. Add all appropriate dimensions and tolerances.

Given a top and a bottom part in the floating condition as shown in Figure P8-19B, satisfy the requirements given in projects P8-20 through P8-23 so that the parts always fit together regardless of orientation. Prepare drawings of each part including dimensions and tolerances.

A. Use linear tolerances.
B. Use positional tolerances.

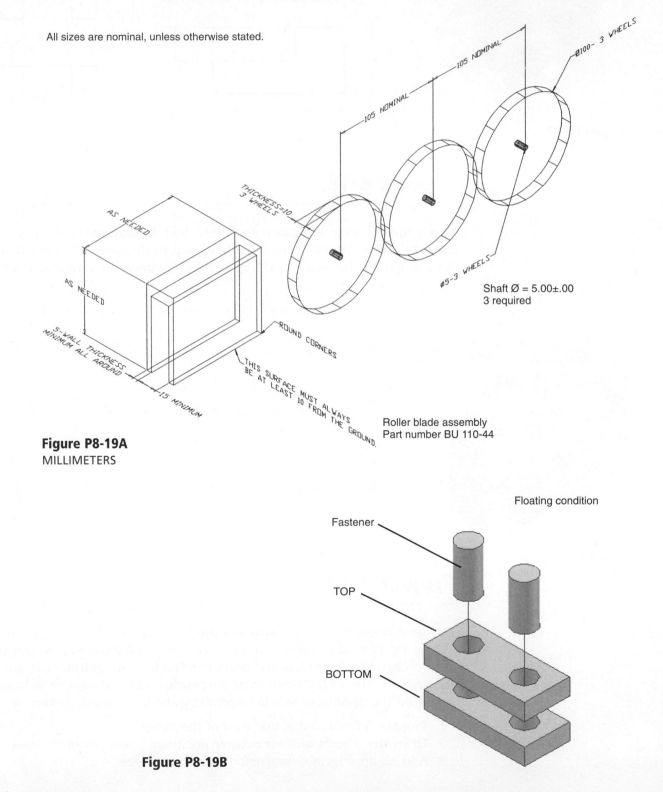

All sizes are nominal, unless otherwise stated.

105 NOMINAL

105 NOMINAL

Ø100– 3 WHEELS

THICKNESS=10
3 WHEELS

Ø5–3 WHEELS

Shaft Ø = 5.00±.00
3 required

AS NEEDED

AS NEEDED

5–WALL THICKNESS
MINIMUM ALL AROUND

15 MINIMUM

ROUND CORNERS

THIS SURFACE MUST ALWAYS
BE AT LEAST 10 FROM THE GROUND.

Roller blade assembly
Part number BU 110-44

Figure P8-19A
MILLIMETERS

Floating condition

Fastener

TOP

BOTTOM

Figure P8-19B

Project 8-20: Inches

A. The distance between the holes' center points is 2.00 nominal.
B. The holes are Ø.375 nominal.
C. The fasteners have a tolerance of .001.
D. The holes have a tolerance of .002.
E. The minimum allowable clearance between the fasteners and the holes is .003.
F. The positional tolerance is .001.

Project 8-21: Millimeters

A. The distance between the holes' center points is 80 nominal.
B. The holes are Ø12 nominal.
C. The fasteners have a tolerance of 0.05.
D. The holes have a tolerance of 0.03.
E. The minimum allowable clearance between the fasteners and the holes is 0.02.
F. The positional tolerance is .01.

Project 8-22: Inches

A. The distance between the holes' center points is 3.50 nominal.
B. The holes are Ø.625 nominal.
C. The fasteners have a tolerance of .005.
D. The holes have a tolerance of .003.
E. The minimum allowable clearance between the fasteners and the holes is .002.
F. The positional tolerance is .002.

Project 8-23: Millimeters

A. The distance between the holes' center points is 65 nominal.
B. The holes are Ø16 nominal.
C. The fasteners have a tolerance of 0.03.
D. The holes have a tolerance of 0.04.
E. The minimum allowable clearance between the fasteners and the holes is 0.03.
F. The positional tolerance is .02.

Given a top and a bottom part in the fixed condition as shown in Figure P8-23, satisfy the requirements given in projects P8-24 through P8-27 so that the parts fit together regardless of orientation. Prepare drawings of each part including dimensions and tolerances.

A. Use linear tolerances
B. Use positional tolerances.

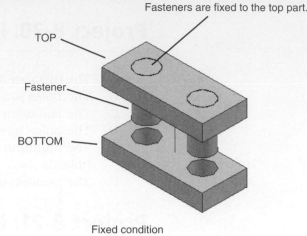

TOP

Fasteners are fixed to the top part.

Fastener

BOTTOM

Fixed condition

Project 8-24: Millimeters

A. The distance between the holes' center points is 60 nominal.
B. The holes are Ø10 nominal.
C. The fasteners have a tolerance of 0.04.
D. The holes have a tolerance of 0.02.
E. The minimum allowable clearance between the fasteners and the holes is 0.02.
F. The positional tolerance is 0.01.

Project 8-25: Inches

A. The distance between the holes' center points is 3.50 nominal.
B. The holes are Ø.563 nominal.
C. The fasteners have a tolerance of .005.
D. The holes have a tolerance of .003.
E. The minimum allowable clearance between the fasteners and the holes is .002.
F. The positional tolerance is .001.

Project 8-26: Millimeters

A. The distance between the holes' center points is 100 nominal.
B. The holes are Ø18 nominal.
C. The fasteners have a tolerance of 0.02.
D. The holes have a tolerance of 0.01.
E. The minimum allowable clearance between the fasteners and the holes is 0.03
F. The positional tolerance is 0.02.

Project 8-27: Inches

A. The distance between the holes' center points is 1.75 nominal.
B. The holes are Ø.250 nominal.
C. The fasteners have a tolerance of .002.
D. The holes have a tolerance of .003.
E. The minimum allowable clearance between the fasteners and the holes is .001.
F. The positional tolerance is .002.

Project 8-28: Millimeters

Dimension and tolerance the rotator assembly shown in Figure P8-28. Use the given dimensions as nominal and add sleeve bearings between the LINKs and both the CROSS-LINK and the PLATE. Create drawings of each part. Modify the dimensions as needed and add the appropriate tolerances. Specify the selected sleeve bearing.

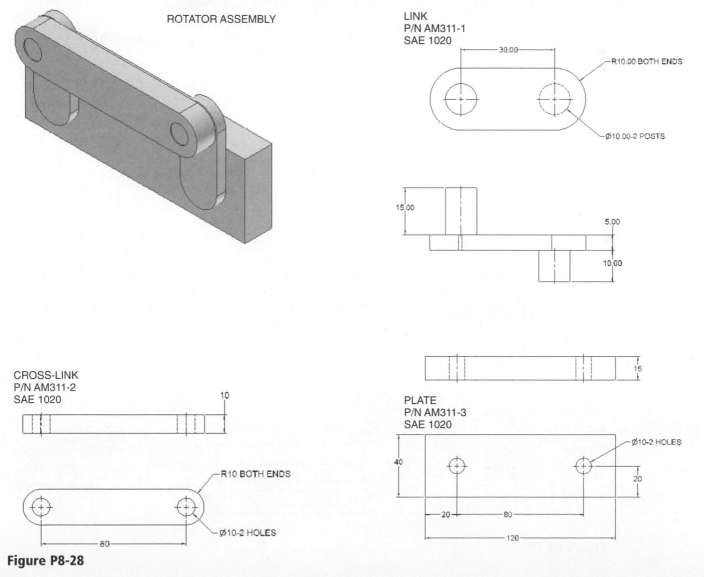

Figure P8-28

Project 8-29:

Dimension and tolerance the rocker assembly shown in Figure P8-29. Use the given dimensions as nominal, and add sleeve bearings between all moving parts. Create drawings of each part. Modify the dimensions as needed and add the appropriate tolerances. Specify the selected sleeve bearing.

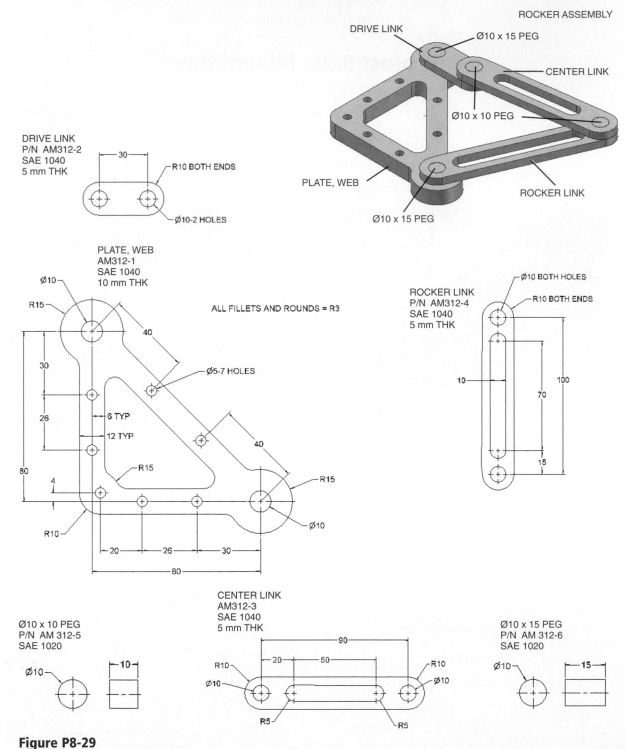

Figure P8-29

Project 8-30:

Draw the model shown in Figure P8-30, create a drawing layout with the appropriate views, and add the specified dimensions and tolerances.

Project 8-31:

Redraw the shaft shown in Figure P8-31, create a drawing layout with the appropriate views, and add a feature dimension and tolerance of 36±0.1 and a straightness tolerance of 0.07 about the centerline at MMC.

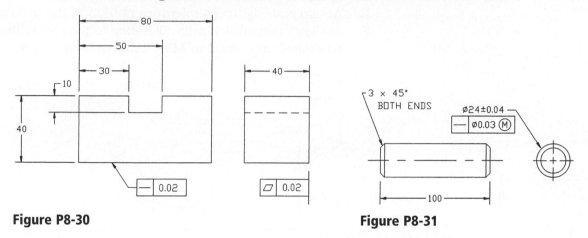

Figure P8-30   **Figure P8-31**

Project 8-32:

    A. Given the shaft shown in Figure P8-32, what is the minimum hole diameter that will always accept the shaft?

    B. If the minimum clearance between the shaft and a hole is equal to 0.02, and the tolerance on the hole is to be 0.6, what are the maximum and minimum diameters for the hole?

Project 8-33:

    A. Given the shaft shown in Figure P8-33, what is the minimum hole diameter that will always accept the shaft?

    B. If the minimum clearance between the shaft and a hole is equal to .005, and the tolerance on the hole is to be .007, what are the maximum and minimum diameters for the hole?

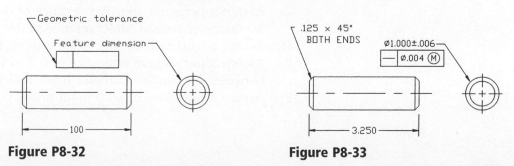

Figure P8-32   **Figure P8-33**

Project 8-34:

Draw a front and a right-side view of the object shown in Figure P8-34 and add the appropriate dimensions and tolerances based on the following information. Numbers located next to an edge line indicate the length of the edge.

    A. Define surfaces A, B, and C as primary, secondary, and tertiary datums, respectively.
    B. Assign a tolerance of ±0.5 to all linear dimensions.
    C. Assign a feature tolerance of 12.07–12.00 to the protruding shaft.
    D. Assign a flatness tolerance of 0.01 to surface A.
    E. Assign a straightness tolerance of 0.03 to the protruding shaft.
    F. Assign a perpendicularity tolerance to the centerline of the protruding shaft of 0.02 at MMC relative to datum A.

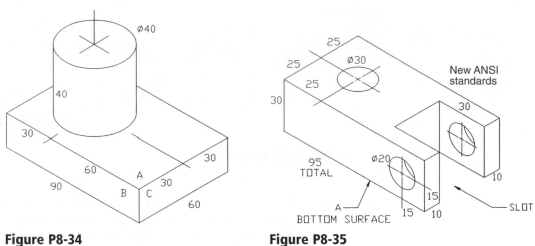

Figure P8-34　　　　　　　**Figure P8-35**

Project 8-35:

Draw a front and a right-side view of the object shown in Figure P8-35 and add the following dimensions and tolerances.

    A. Define the bottom surface as datum A.
    B. Assign a perpendicularity tolerance of 0.4 to both sides of the slot relative to datum A.
    C. Assign a perpendicularity tolerance of 0.2 to the centerline of the 30 diameter hole at MMC relative to datum A.
    D. Assign a feature tolerance of ±0.8 to all three holes.
    E. Assign a parallelism tolerance of 0.2 to the common centerline between the two 20 diameter holes relative to datum A.
    F. Assign a tolerance of ±0.5 to all linear dimensions.

Project 8-36:

Draw a circular front and the appropriate right-side view of the object shown in Figure P8-36 and add the following dimensions and tolerances.

- A. Assign datum A as indicated.
- B. Assign the object's longitudinal axis as datum B.
- C. Assign the object's centerline through the slot as datum C.
- D. Assign a tolerance of ±0.5 to all linear tolerances.
- E. Assign a tolerance of ±0.5 to all circular features.
- F. Assign a parallelism tolerance of 0.01 to both edges of the slot.
- G. Assign a perpendicularity tolerance of 0.01 to the outside edge of the protruding shaft.

Project 8-37:

Given the two objects shown in Figure P8-37, draw a front and a side view of each. Assign a tolerance of ±0.5 to all linear dimensions. Assign a feature tolerance of ±0.4 to the shaft, and also assign a straightness tolerance of 0.2 to the shaft's centerline at MMC.

Tolerance the hole so that it will always accept the shaft with a minimum clearance of 0.1 and a feature tolerance of 0.2. Assign a perpendicularity tolerance of 0.05 to the centerline of the hole at MMC.

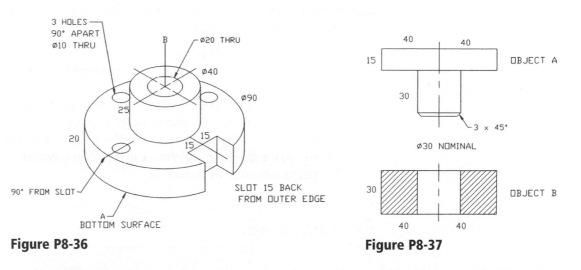

Figure P8-36

Figure P8-37

Project 8-38:

Given the two objects shown in Figure P8-38, draw a front and a side view of each. Assign a tolerance of ±.005 to all linear dimensions. Assign a feature tolerance of ±.004 to the shaft, and also assign a straightness tolerance of .002 to the shaft's centerline at MMC.

Tolerance the hole so that it will always accept the shaft with a minimum clearance of .001 and a feature tolerance of .002.

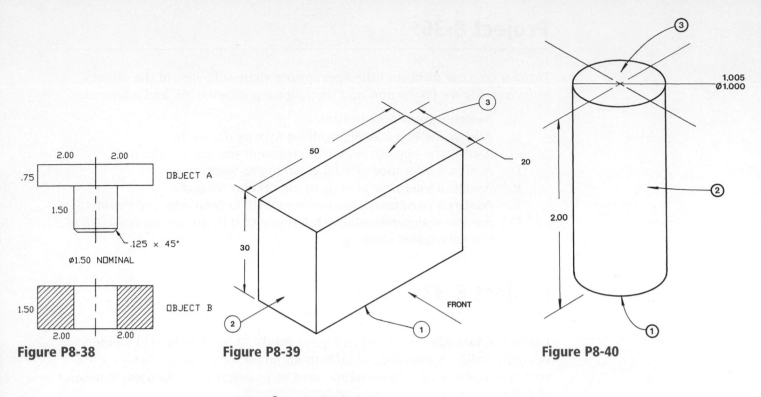

Figure P8-38

Figure P8-39

Figure P8-40

Project 8-39:

Draw a model of the object shown in Figure P8-39, then create a drawing layout including the specified dimensions. Add the following tolerances and specifications to the drawing.

- A. Surface 1 is datum A.
- B. Surface 2 is datum B and is perpendicular to datum A within 0.1 mm.
- C. Surface 3 is datum C and is parallel to datum A within 0.3 mm.
- D. Locate a 16-mm diameter hole in the center of the front surface that goes completely through the object. Use positional tolerances to locate the hole. Assign a positional tolerance of 0.02 at MMC perpendicular to datum A.

Project 8-40:

Draw a model of the object shown in Figure P8-40, then create a drawing layout including the specified dimensions. Add the following tolerances and specifications to the drawing.

- A. Surface 1 is datum A.
- B. Surface 2 is datum B and is perpendicular to datum A within .003 in.
- C. Surface 3 is parallel to datum A within .005 in.
- D. The cylinder's longitudinal centerline is to be straight within .001 in. at MMC.
- E. Surface 2 is to have circular accuracy within .002 in.

Project 8-41:

Draw a model of the object shown in Figure P8-41, then create a drawing layout including the specified dimensions. Add the following tolerances and specifications to the drawing.

A. Surface 1 is datum A.
B. Surface 4 is datum B and is perpendicular to datum A within 0.08 mm.
C. Surface 3 is flat within 0.03 mm.
D. Surface 5 is parallel to datum A within 0.01 mm.
E. Surface 2 has a runout tolerance of 0.2 mm relative to surface 4.
F. Surface 1 is flat within 0.02 mm.
G. The longitudinal centerline is to be straight within 0.02 at MMC and perpendicular to datum A.

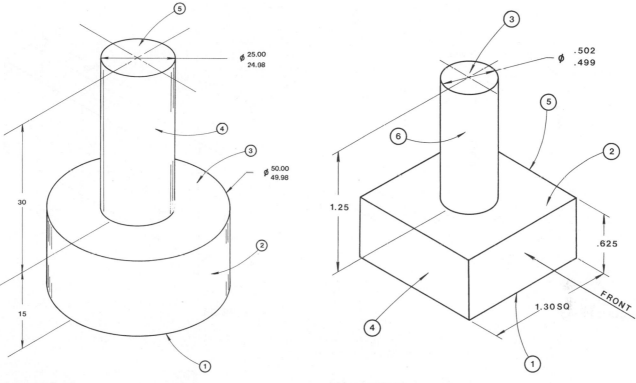

Figure P8-41   **Figure P8-42**

Project 8-42:

Draw a model of the object shown in Figure P8-42, then create a drawing layout including the specified dimensions. Add the following tolerances and specifications to the drawing.

A. Surface 2 is datum A.
B. Surface 6 is perpendicular to datum A with .000 allowable variance at MMC but with a .002 in. MAX variance limit beyond MMC.
C. Surface 1 is parallel to datum A within .005.
D. Surface 4 is perpendicular to datum A within .004 in.

Project 8-43:

Draw a model of the object shown in Figure P8-43, then create a drawing layout including the specified dimensions. Add the following tolerances and specifications to the drawing.

A. Surface 1 is datum A.
B. Surface 2 is datum B.
C. The hole is located using a true position tolerance value of 0.13 mm at MMC. The true position tolerance is referenced to datums A and B.
D. Surface 1 is to be straight within 0.02 mm.
E. The bottom surface is to be parallel to datum A within 0.03 mm.

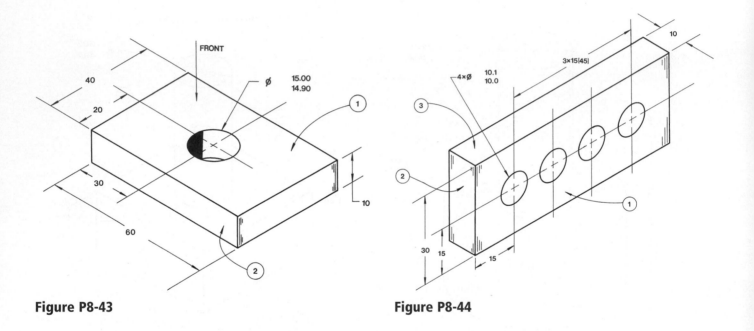

Figure P8-43   **Figure P8-44**

Project 8-44:

Draw a model of the object shown in Figure P8-44, then create a drawing layout including the specified dimensions. Add the following tolerances and specifications to the drawing.

A. Surface 1 is datum A.
B. Surface 2 is datum B.
C. Surface 3 is perpendicular to surface 2 within 0.02 mm.
D. The four holes are to be located using a positional tolerance of 0.07 mm at MMC referenced to datums A and B.
E. The centerlines of the holes are to be straight within 0.01 mm at MMC.

Project 8-45:

Draw a model of the object shown in Figure P8-45, then create a drawing layout including the specified dimensions. Add the following tolerances and specifications to the drawing.

- A. Surface 1 has a dimension of .378–.375 in. and is datum A. The surface has a dual primary runout with datum B to within .005 in. The runout is total.
- B. Surface 2 has a dimension of 1.505–1.495 in. Its runout relative to the dual primary datums A and B is .008 in. The runout is total.
- C. Surface 3 has a dimension of 1.000±.005 and has no geometric tolerance.
- D. Surface 4 has no circular dimension but has a total runout tolerance of .006 in. relative to the dual datums A and B.
- E. Surface 5 has a dimension of .500–.495 in. and is datum B. It has a dual primary runout with datum A within .005 in. The runout is total.

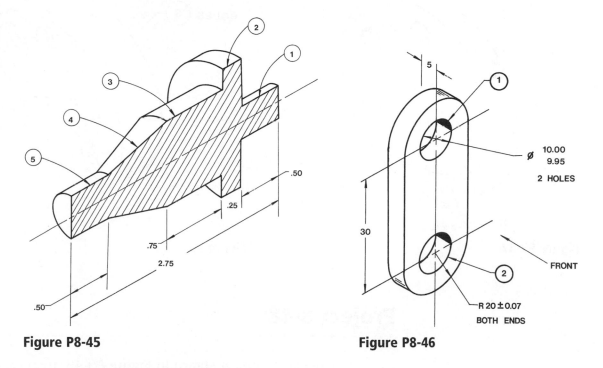

Figure P8-45   **Figure P8-46**

Project 8-46:

Draw a model of the object shown in Figure P8-46, then create a drawing layout including the specified dimensions. Add the following tolerances and specifications to the drawing.

- A. Hole 1 is datum A.
- B. Hole 2 is to have its circular centerline parallel to datum A within 0.2 mm at MMC when datum A is at MMC.
- C. Assign a positional tolerance of 0.01 to each hole's centerline at MMC.

Project 8-47:

Draw a model of the object shown in Figure P8-47, then create a drawing layout including the specified dimensions. Add the following tolerances and specifications to the drawing.

    A.   Surface 1 is datum A.
    B.   Surface 2 is datum B.
    C.   The six holes have a diameter range of .502–.499 in. and are to be located using positional tolerances so that their centerlines are within .005 in. at MMC relative to datums A and B.
    D.   The back surface is to be parallel to datum A within .002 in.

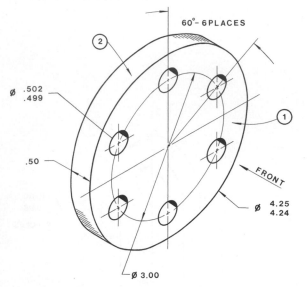

Figure P8-47

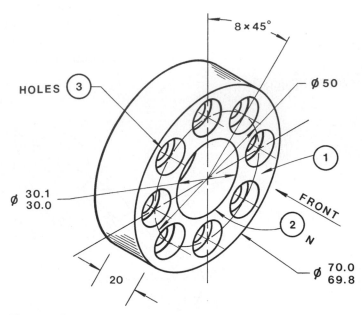

Figure P8-48

Project 8-48:

Draw a model of the object shown in Figure P8-48, then create a drawing layout including the specified dimensions. Add the following tolerances and specifications to the drawing.

    A.   Surface 1 is datum A.
    B.   Hole 2 is datum B.
    C.   The eight holes labeled 3 have diameters of 8.4−8.3 mm with a positional tolerance of 0.15 mm at MMC relative to datums A and B. Also, the eight holes are to be counterbored to a diameter of 14.6−14.4 mm and to a depth of 5.0 mm.
    D.   The large center hole is to have a straightness tolerance of 0.2 at MMC about its centerline.

Project 8-49:

Draw a model of the object shown in Figure P8-49, then create a drawing layout including the specified dimensions. Add the following tolerances and specifications to the drawing.

- A. Surface 1 is datum A.
- B. Surface 2 is datum B.
- C. Surface 3 is datum C.
- D. The four holes labeled 4 have a dimension and tolerance of 8 +0.3/−0 mm. The holes are to be located using a positional tolerance of 0.05 mm at MMC relative to datums A, B, and C .
- E. The six holes labeled 5 have a dimension and tolerance of 6 +0.2/ −0 mm. The holes are to be located using a positional tolerance of 0.01 mm at MMC relative to datums A, B, and C .

Figure P8-49

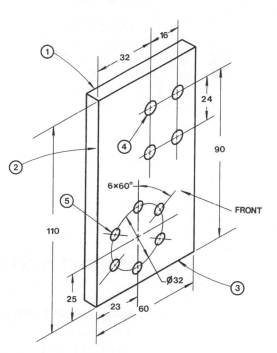

Project 8-50:

The objects in Figure P8-50B labeled A and B are to be toleranced using four different tolerances as shown. Redraw the charts shown in Figure P8-50A and list the appropriate allowable tolerance for "as measured" increments of 0.1 mm or .001 in. Also include the appropriate geometric tolerance drawing called out above each chart.

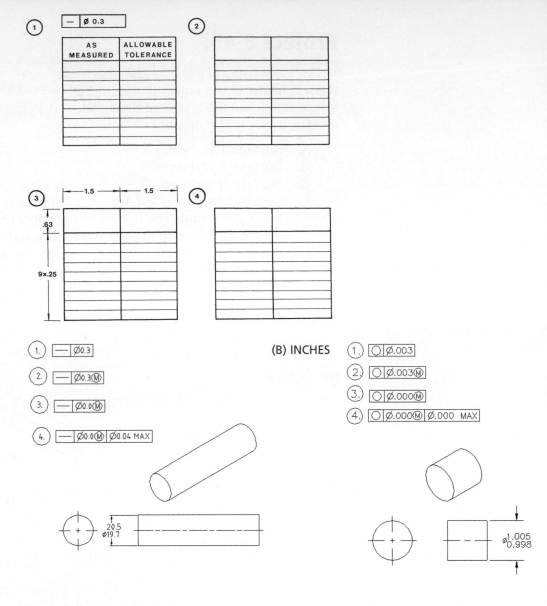

Figure P8-50B
(A) (MILLIMETERS)

(B) INCHES

Project 8-51:

Assume that there are two copies of the part in Figure P8-51 and that these parts are to be joined together using four fasteners in the floating condition. Draw front and top views of the object, including dimensions and tolerances. Add the following tolerances and specifications to the drawing, then draw front and top views of a shaft that can be used to join the two objects. The shaft should be able to fit into any of the four holes.

- A. Surface 1 is datum A.
- B. Surface 2 is datum B.
- C. Surface 3 is perpendicular to surface 2 within 0.02 mm.
- D. Specify the positional tolerance for the four holes applied at MMC.
- E. The centerlines of the holes are to be straight within 0.01 mm at MMC.
- F. The clearance between the shafts and the holes is to be 0.05 minimum and 0.10 maximum.

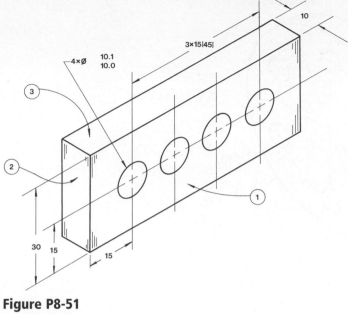

Figure P8-51
MILLIMETERS

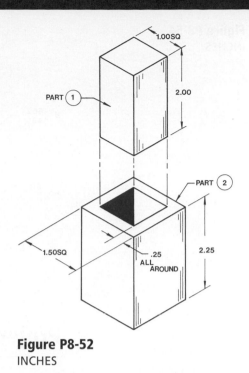

Figure P8-52
INCHES

Project 8-52:

Dimension and tolerance parts 1 and 2 of Figure P8-52 so that part 1 always fits into part 2 with a minimum clearance of .005 in. The tolerance for part 1's outer matching surface is .006 in.

Project 8-53:

Dimension and tolerance parts 1 and 2 of Figure P8-53 so that part 1 always fits into part 2 with a minimum clearance of 0.03 mm. The tolerance for part 1's diameter is 0.05 mm. Take into account the fact that the interface is long relative to the diameters.

Project 8-54:

Assume that there are two copies of the part in Figure P8-54 and that these parts are to be joined together using six fasteners in the floating condition. Draw front and top views of the object, including dimensions and tolerances. Add the following tolerances and specifications to the drawing, then draw front and top views of a shaft that can be used to join the two objects. The shaft should be able to fit into any of the six holes.

A. Surface 1 is datum A .
B. Surface 2 is round within .003.
C. Specify the positional tolerance for the six holes applied at MMC.
D. The clearance between the shafts and the holes is to be .001 minimum and .003 maximum.

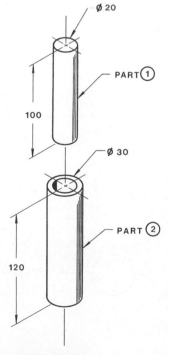

Figure P8-53
MILLIMETERS

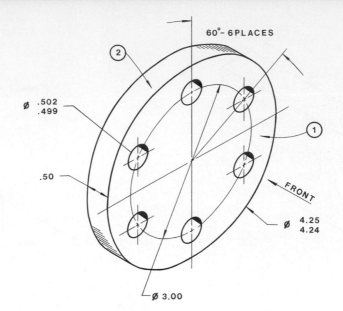

Project 8-55:

The assembly shown in Figure P8-55 is made from parts defined in Chapter 5.

    A. Draw an exploded assembly drawing.
    B. Draw a BOM.
    C. Use the drawing layout mode and draw orthographic views of each part. Include dimensions and geometric tolerances. The pegs should have a minimum clearance of 0.02. Select appropriate tolerances

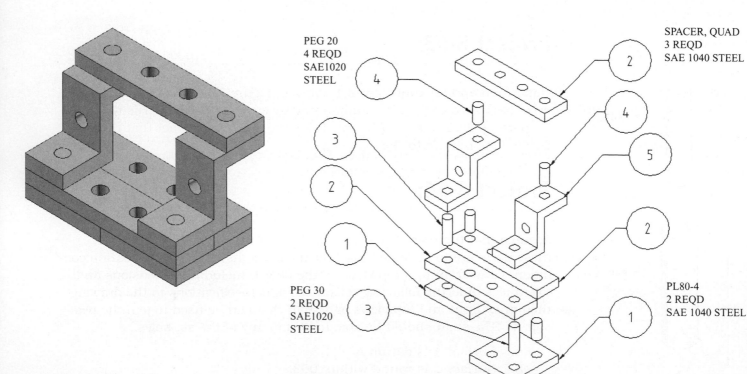

Figure P8-55
MILLIMETERS

9 chapter nine

Bearings and Fit Tolerances

CHAPTER OBJECTIVES

- Learn about sleeve and ball bearings
- Learn about fits
- Learn how fits are applied to bearings and shafts
- Learn about tolerances for bearings

9-1 Introduction

This text deals with two types of bearings: sleeve bearings or *bushings* and ball bearings. See Figure 9-1. **Sleeve bearings**, or jig bushings are hollow cylinders made from a low-friction material such as Teflon or impregnated bronze. Sleeve bearings may have flanges. **Ball bearings** include spherical bearings in an internal race that greatly reduce friction. In general, sleeve bearings are cheaper than ball bearings, but ball bearings can take heavier loads at faster speeds. A listing of ball bearings is included in the **Design Library**.

Figure 9-1

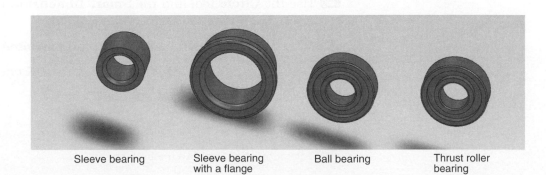

Sleeve bearing   Sleeve bearing with a flange   Ball bearing   Thrust roller bearing

9-2 Sleeve Bearings

Sleeve bearings are identified by the following callout format:

> Inside diameter × Outside Diameter × Thickness

> For example,

> .375 × .750 × .500   or   3/8 × 3/4 × 1/2

To Draw a Sleeve Bearing

Draw a .500 × 1.000 × 1.000 sleeve bearing. See Figure 9-2

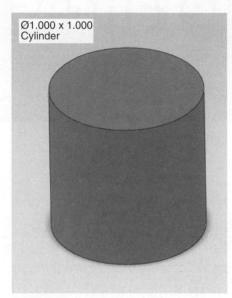
Ø1.000 x 1.000 Cylinder

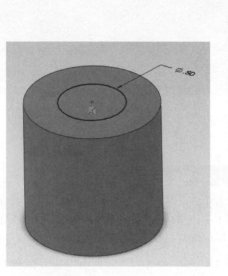
Ø.50

Use the Extruded Cut tool to create a hole.

Figure 9-2

1 Start a new **Part** document.

2 Select the **Front Plane** orientation.

3 Click the **Sketch** group, then click the **Circle** tool.

4 Draw a Ø**1.000** circle. Use the **Smart Dimension** tool to size the circle.

5 Click the **Features** tab, then click the **Extruded Boss/Base** tool.

6 Define the thickness of the extrusion as **1.00 in**.

7 Click the OK check mark.

8 Right-click the front surface of the cylinder and select the **Sketch** tool.

9 Use the **Circle** tool and the **Smart Dimension** tool to draw a Ø**.5000** circle on the front surface of the cylinder.

10 Click the **Features** tab and select the **Extruded Cut** tool.

11 Define the Ø.500 to be cut and click the OK check mark.

12 Save the drawing as **.50 BEARING.**

NOTE

No tolerance are assigned to the bushing.

To Use a Sleeve Bearing in an Assembly Drawing

See Figures 9-3 and 9-4.

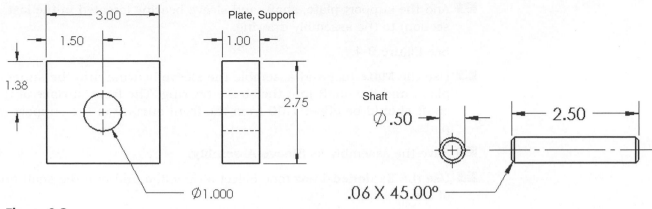

Figure 9-3

Figure 9-4

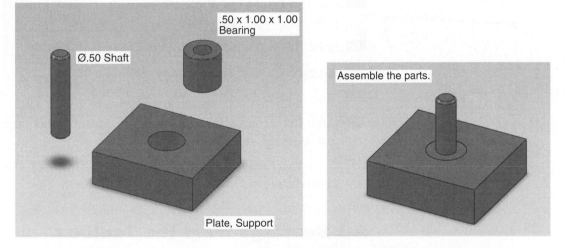

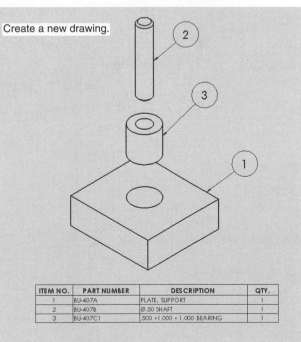

ITEM NO.	PART NUMBER	DESCRIPTION	QTY.
1	BU-407A	PLATE, SUPPORT	1
2	BU-407B	Ø .50 SHAFT	1
3	BU-407C1	.500 ×1.000 × 1.000 BEARING	1

1 Draw the support plate and Ø.500 × 2.500 shaft defined in Figure 9-3. Save the drawings.

2 Create a new **Assembly** drawing.

3 Add the support plate, shaft, and sleeve bearing (created in the last section) to the assembly drawing.

See Figure 9-4.

4 Use the **Mate** tool and assemble the sleeve bearing into the support plate, and the shaft into the sleeve bearing. The front surface of the shaft should be offset **1.50** from the front surface of the support plate.

5 Save the assembly as **Sleeve Assembly**.

6 Use the **Exploded View** tool. Select a direction and pull the shaft out of the assembly.

See Figure 5-33 for instructions on how to use the **Exploded View** tool.

7 Use the **Exploded View** tool to pull the bearing away from the support plate.

8 Save the exploded drawing as **Sleeve Assembly**.

Replace the old **Sleeve Assembly** drawing.

9 Start a new drawing.

10 Click the **Annotation** tab, click the **Balloon** tool, and add the assembly numbers as shown.

11 Click the **Annotation** tab, click the **Tables** tool, click the **Bill of Materials** tool, and add a BOM to the drawing.

9-3 Bearings from the Toolbox

The SolidWorks **Toolbox** includes many different sizes and styles of bearings. In this example we will use the PLATE, SUPPORT, and Ø.50 SHAFT with a bearing from the **Toolbox** to create an assembly.

1 Create a new assembly drawing and add the **PLATE, SUPPORT** and **Ø.50 SHAFT** to the drawing.

See Figure 9-5.

Figure 9-5

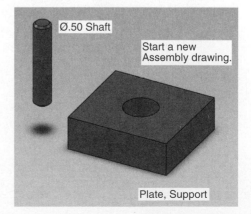

Ø.50 Shaft

Start a new Assembly drawing.

Plate, Support

Figure 9-5
(*Continued*)

Chapter **9**

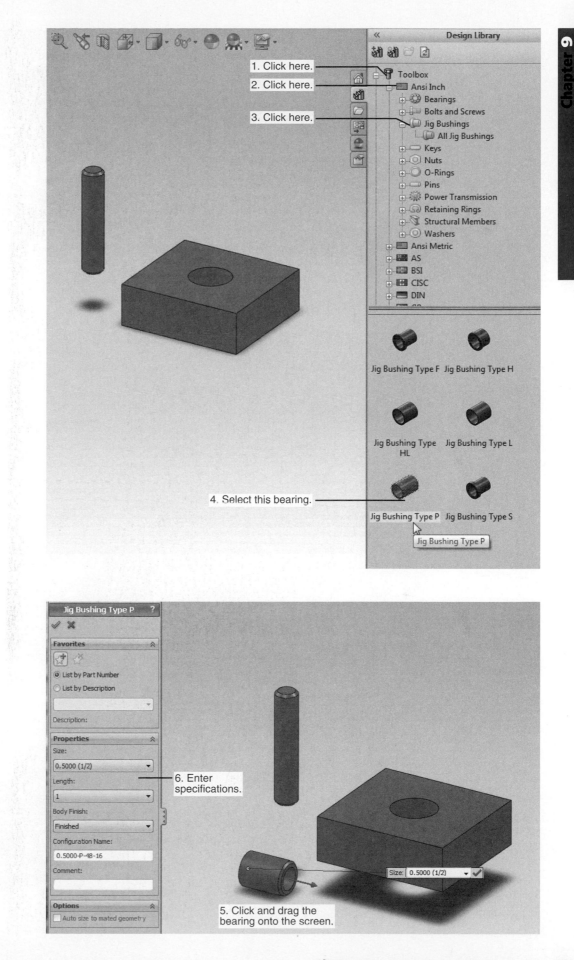

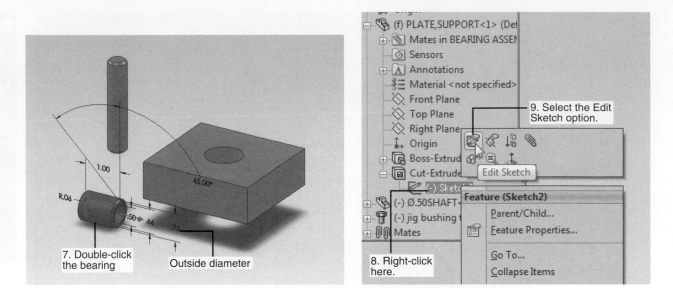

7. Double-click the bearing

Outside diameter

9. Select the Edit Sketch option.

8. Right-click here.

Edit Sketch

Feature (Sketch2)

Parent/Child...

Feature Properties...

Go To...

Collapse Items

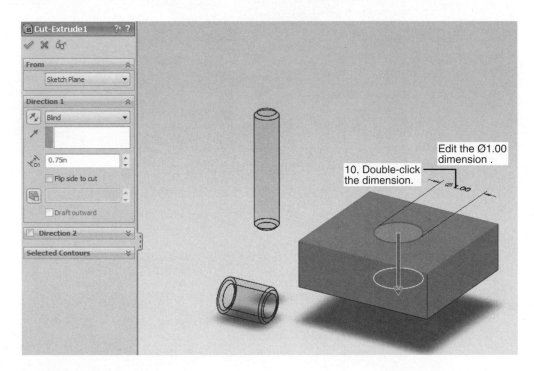

10. Double-click the dimension.

Edit the Ø1.00 dimension.

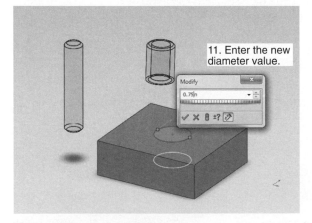

11. Enter the new diameter value.

12. Complete the assembly.

Figure 9-5
(*Continued*)

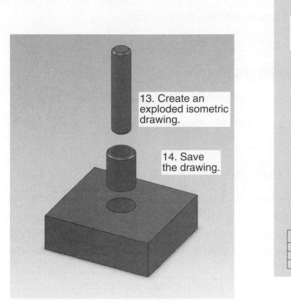

13. Create an exploded isometric drawing.

14. Save the drawing.

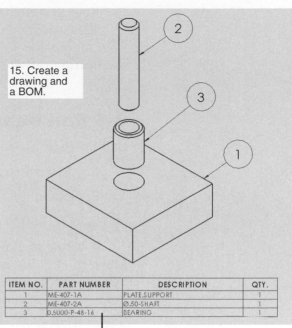

15. Create a drawing and a BOM.

ITEM NO.	PART NUMBER	DESCRIPTION	QTY.
1	ME-407-1A	PLATE,SUPPORT	1
2	ME-407-2A	Ø.50-SHAFT	1
3	0.5000-P-48-16	BEARING	1

Manufacturer's part number

Figure 9-5
(*Continued*)

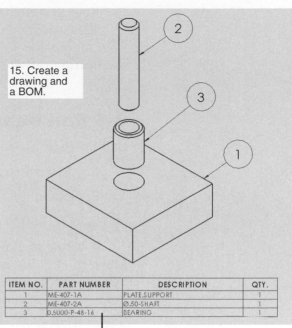

2 Save the assembly as **BEARING ASSEMBLY.**

3 Click the **Toolbox** and access the **Jig Bushings** tool.

4 Select a **Jig Bushing Type P** and drag it onto the drawing screen.

We know the shaft diameter is **.500**, so we will size the bearing's inside diameter to match the shaft diameter. Tolerances are not considered. They will be included in later examples.

5 Select a **.5000 × 1.000** bearing and click the **OK** check mark.

What is the outside diameter of the bearing? To answer this question, double-click the bearing on the drawing screen. The dimensions used to create the bearing will become visible.

The outside diameter is defined as **.75,** so the Ø1.00 hole in the Plate, Support is not acceptable. It must be edited.

6 Click the drawing screen to remove the bearing's dimensions and click the + sign next to the **PLATE, SUPPORT** heading in the **FeatureManager**.

7 Click the + sign next to the **Cut-Extrusion** heading and click the **Sketch 2** heading.

8 Click the **Edit Sketch** option.

The dimension for the Ø1.00 hole will appear.

9 Double-click the **1.00** dimension and change the diameter from 1.00 to **.75;** click the **OK** check mark.

10 Return to the assembly drawing and assemble the components.

11 Create an exploded assembly drawing of the assembly.

12 Create a drawing of the exploded assembly and add a BOM.

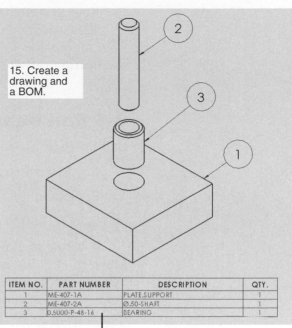

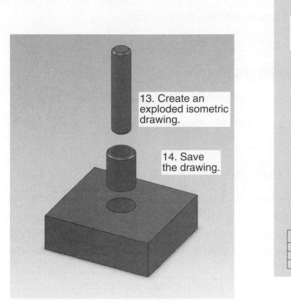

Note that the bearing's part number, 0.5000-P-48-16, was used as is. This is a vendor item; that is, we did not make it but purchased it from an outside source, so we used the manufacturer's part number for the bearing rather than creating a new one.

9-4 Ball Bearings

Ball bearings are identified by the following callout format:

Inside Diameter × Outside Diameter × Thickness

For example,

.375 × .750 × .500 or 3/8 × 3/4 × 1/2

A listing of standard ball bearing sizes can be found in the **Design Library**. For this example a .5000 × .8750 × .2188 instrument ball bearing will be used and will be inserted into a counterbored hole. Only nominal dimensions will be considered. Tolerances will be defined later in the chapter.

Figure 9-6 shows a ball bearing support plate.

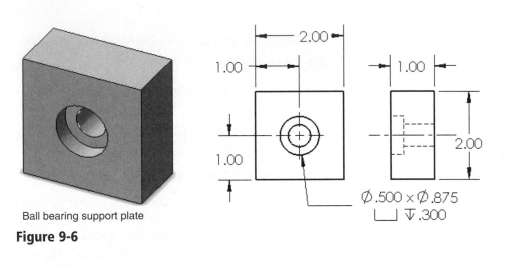

Ball bearing support plate

Figure 9-6

1 Draw and save the ball bearing support plate.

2 Draw and save a **Ø.500 × 2.50** shaft with **.03** chamfers at each end.

3 Start a new **Assembly** drawing and insert the ball bearing support plate and Ø.500 × 2.50 shaft.

See Figure 9-7.

4 Access the **Design Library, Toolbox, Ansi Inch, Bearings, Ball Bearings,** and select **Instrument Ball Bearing – AFBMA 12.2.**

5 Click and drag the bearing into the drawing screen and set the properties as shown.

In this example a 0.5000 − 0.8750 − 0.2188 was used. See the values in the **Instrument Ball Bearing PropertyManager**.

6 Insert the ball bearing into the counterbored hole.

7 Insert the shaft into the bearing.

8 Create a new drawing showing the assembly drawing and a BOM.

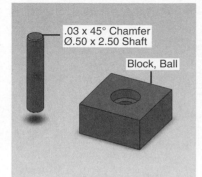

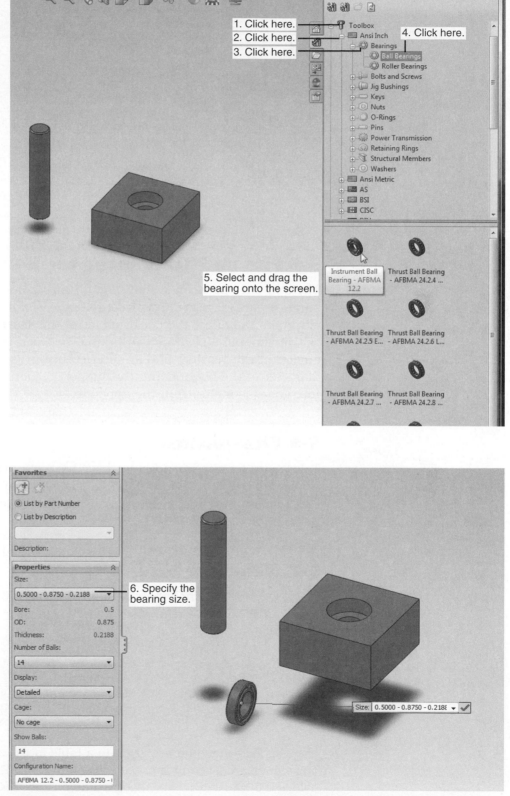

Figure 9-7

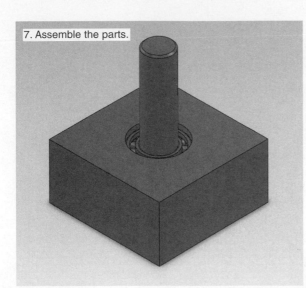

7. Assemble the parts.

Figure 9-7
(Continued)

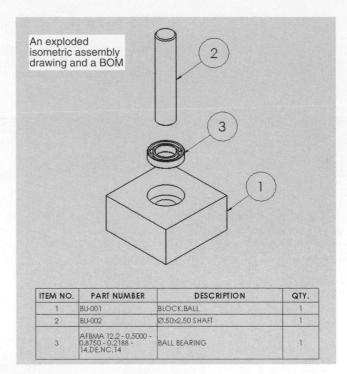

An exploded isometric assembly drawing and a BOM

ITEM NO.	PART NUMBER	DESCRIPTION	QTY.
1	BU-001	BLOCK,BALL	1
2	BU-002	Ø.50x2.50 SHAFT	1
3	AFBMA 12.2 - 0.5000 - 0.8750 - 0.2188 - 14,DE,NC,14	BALL BEARING	1

9-5 Fits and Tolerances for Bearings

The tolerance between a shaft and a bearing and between a bearing and a support part is critical. Incorrect tolerances can cause excessive wear or vibration and affect the performance of the assembly.

In general, a clearance fit is used between the shaft and the inside diameter of the bearing, and an interference fit is used between the outside diameter of the bearing and the support structure. A listing of standard fit tolerances is included in the appendix.

9-6 Fits—Inches

Tolerances for shafts and holes have been standardized and are called *fits*. An example of a fit callout is H7/g6. The hole tolerance is always given first using an uppercase letter, and the shaft tolerance is given second using a lowercase letter.

9-7 Clearance Fits

Say a Ø0.500 nominal shaft is to be inserted into a Ø0.500 nominal hole using an H7/g6 clearance fit, which is also referred to as a Class LC5 Clearance fit.

> **NOTE**
>
> The term *nominal* refers to a starting value for the shaft and hole. It is not the final dimension.

The following data are given in a table in the appendix. See Figure 9-8. The values are given in thousandths of an inch. The nominal value for the hole is 0.5000, so the +0.7 table value means .5007 in. The −0.25 table

Figure 9-8

Class LC5			
Nominal Size Range	Limits of Clearance	Standard Limits	
		Hole H7	Shaft g6
0.40 – 0.71	0.25 1.35	+0.7 0	–0.25 –0.65

Hole basis

value for the 0.5000 nominal shaft means 0.49975 in. The limits of clearance values are the differences between the hole minimum value and the shaft maximum value, 0.00 and −0.25, or 0.25 absolute, and between the maximum hole value and the minimum shaft value, +0.7 and −0.65, or 1.35.

9-8 Hole Basis

The 0 value for the hole's minimum indicates that the tolerances were derived using **hole basis** calculations; that is, the tolerances were applied starting with the minimum hole value. Tolerances applied starting with the shaft are called **shaft basis**.

9-9 Shaft Basis

The limits of clearance values would be applied starting with the minimum shaft diameter. If the H7/g6 tolerances were applied using the shaft basis, the resulting tolerance values for the shaft would be 0.50000 to 0.50040, and for the hole would be 0.50065 (.50040 + .00025) to 0.50135. These values maintain the limits of tolerance, 0.50135 to 0.00135, and the individual tolerances for the hole (0.50135 − 0.50065 = 0.0007) and the shaft (0.50040 − 0.50000 = .00040).

9-10 Sample Problem SP10-2

Say a shaft with nominal values of Ø.750 × 3.00 is to be fitted into a bearing with an inside diameter bore, nominal, of 0.7500 using Class LC5 fit, hole basis. What are the final dimensions for the shaft and bearing's bore? The table values for the hole are 0/+0.5, yielding a hole tolerance of .7500 to .7505, and the shaft values for the hole are 0/−0.4, yielding a shaft tolerance of .7500 to .7496.

> **NOTE**
> The fact that both the hole and the shaft could be .7500 is called **locational fit**.

See Figure 9-9.

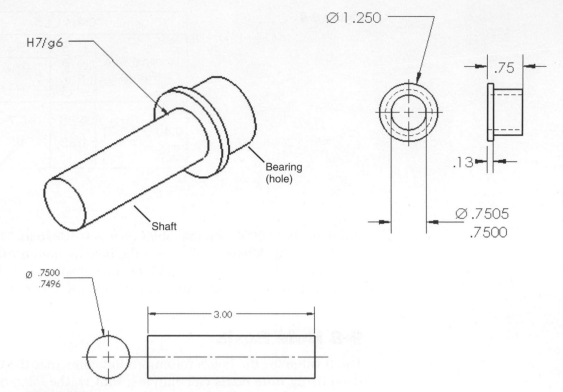

Figure 9-9

9-11 Interference Fits

When the shaft is equal to or larger in diameter than the hole, the fit is called an ***interference fit***. Interference fits are sometimes used to secure a shaft into a hole rather than using a fastener or adhesive. For example, an aluminum shaft with a nominal diameter of .250 in. inserted into a hole in a steel housing with a Ø.250 nominal hole using .0006 in. interference would require approximately 123 in.-lb of torque to turn the shaft.

In this example a sleeve bearing with a nominal outside diameter (O.D.) of .875 is to be inserted into a Ø.875 nominal hole using an LN1 Interference Locational fit. The hole and shaft (bearing O.D.) specifications are H6/n5. The following values were derived from a table in the appendix. See Figure 9-10.

Figure 9-10

Class LN1			
Nominal Size Range	Limits of Interference	Standard Limits	
		Hole	Shaft
0.71 – 1.19	0	+0.5	+1.0
	1.0	0	+0.5

Hole basis

All stated values are in thousandths of an inch. The 0 in the column for the hole indicates that it is a hole basis calculation (see the explanation in the previous section). Given the .875 nominal value for both the hole and the shaft, the hole and shaft tolerances are as follows. See Figure 9-11.

Hole: Ø.8755/.875 Shaft: Ø.8760/.8755

2.00
1.00
.50
Ø.8760
.8755
2.00
.50
1.00
Ø.8755
.8750
Ø.500
H6/n5

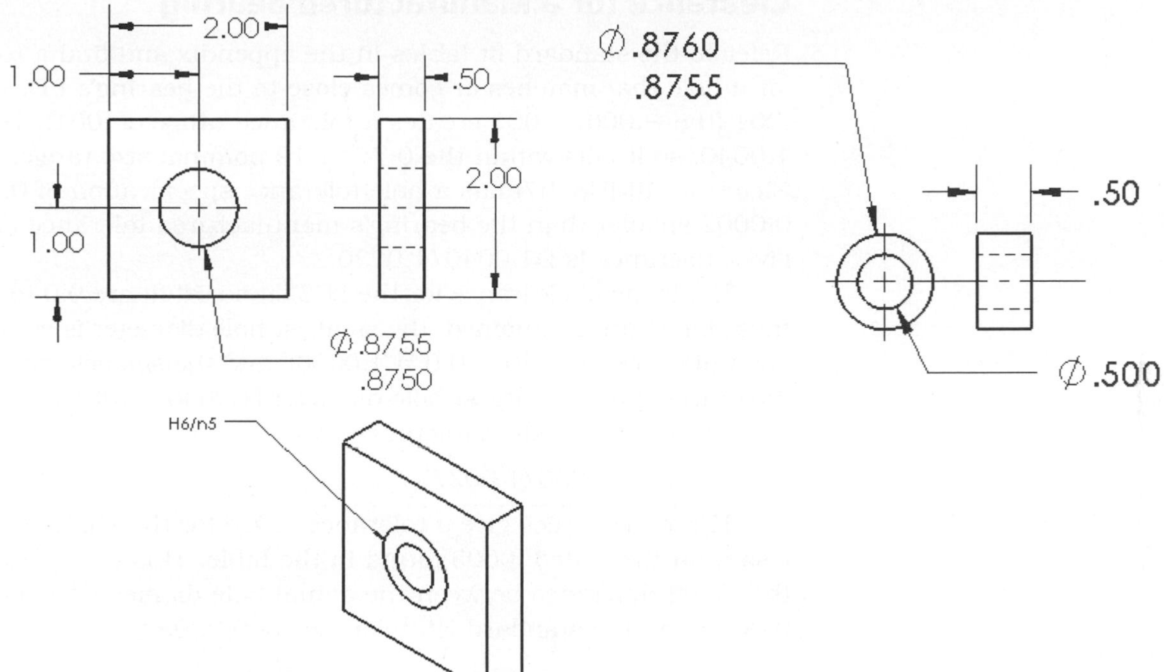

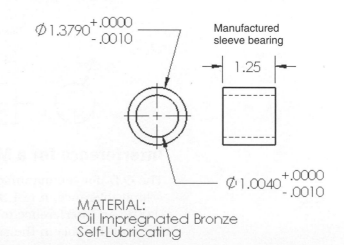

Figure 9-11

9-12 Manufactured Bearings

Most companies do not manufacture their own bearings but, rather, purchase them from a bearing manufacturer. This means that tolerances must be assigned to assemblies based on existing given tolerances for the purchased bearings.

> **NOTE**
>
> Companies that manufacture bearings usually also manufacture shafts that match the bearings; that is, the tolerances for the bearings and shafts are coordinated.

Figure 9-12 shows a typical manufactured sleeve bearing. The dimensions and tolerances are included. The inside diameter (bore or I.D.) of the bearing is matched to the shaft using a clearance fit, and the O.D. is to be

Figure 9-12

Ø1.3790 +.0000 -.0010
Manufactured
sleeve bearing
1.25
Ø1.0040 +.0000 -.0010
MATERIAL:
Oil Impregnated Bronze
Self-Lubricating

matched to the support using an interference fit. The procedure is to find standard fits that are closest to the bearing's manufactured dimensions and apply the limits of tolerance to create the needed tolerances.

Clearance for a Manufactured Bearing

Refer to the standard fit tables in the appendix and find a tolerance range for a hole that matches or comes close to the bearing's I.D. tolerance of .001 (the +.000/−.001 creates a tolerance range of .001). The given I.D. is 1.0040, so it falls within the 0.71−1.19 nominal size range. An LC2 Clearance fit (H8/h7) has a hole tolerance specification of 0.0 to 0.0008, 0.0002 smaller than the bearing's manufactured tolerance of .0010. The given tolerance is Ø1.0040/1.0030.

The limits of clearance for the LC2 standard fit are 0.0 to 0.0013. If these limits are maintained, the smallest hole diameter is equal to the largest shaft diameter (1.0030 − 0.0 = 1.0030), and the smallest shaft diameter is .0013 less than the largest hole diameter (1.0040 − .0013 = 1.0027).

Therefore, the shaft tolerances are

Shaft: Ø1.0030/1.0027

These tolerances give a tolerance range for the shaft of .0003, or .0002 less than the stated .0005 found in the table. This difference makes up for the .0002 difference between the actual hole diameter's tolerance range of 0.0010 and the standard H8 tolerance of 0.0008.

To Apply a Clearance Fit Tolerance Using SolidWorks

Figure 9-13 shows a shaft with a nominal diameter of 1.0040. Enter the required 1.0030/1.0027 tolerance.

1 Click the **Limit** option in the **Tolerance/Precision** box.

2 Set the upper limit for **−0.0010** and the lower limit for **−0.0013**.

3 Click the OK check mark.

Figure 9-13

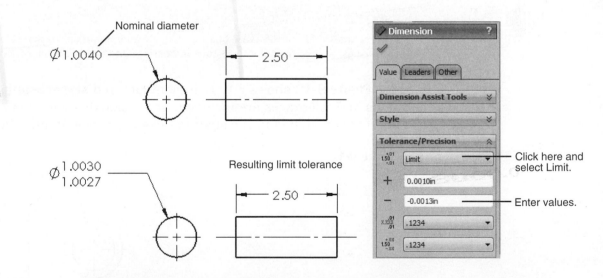

Interference for a Manufactured Bearing

The O.D. for the manufactured bearing is 1.379 +.000/−.001. Written as a limit tolerance, it is 1.3790/1.3780. The tolerance range for the O.D. is 0.001. An interference tolerance is required between the O.D. of the bearing and the hole in the support.

NOTE

An interference fit is also called a *press fit*.

A search of the Standard Fit tables in the appendix for a shaft (the O.D. of the bearing acts like a shaft in this condition) tolerance range of 0.001 finds that an LN2 (H7/p6) shaft range is .0008, or .0002 less than manufactured tolerance.

The limits of interference for the LN2 standard fit are 0.0 to 0.0013. If these limits are maintained, the smallest shaft diameter is equal to the largest hole diameter (1.3780 + 0.0 = 1.3780), and the largest shaft diameter is .0013 greater than the smallest hole diameter (1.3790 − .0013 = 1.3777).

Therefore, the shaft tolerances are

Shaft: Ø1.3780/1.3777

These tolerances give a tolerance range for the shaft of .0003, or .0002 less than the stated .0005 found in the table. This difference makes up for the .0002 difference between the actual hole diameter's tolerance range of 0.0010 and the standard H7 tolerance of 0.0008.

To Apply an Interference Fit Tolerance Using SolidWorks

Figure 9-14 shows a support with a nominal diameter of 1.3780. Enter the required 1.3780/1.3777 tolerance. See Chapter 8 for further explanation on how to apply tolerances.

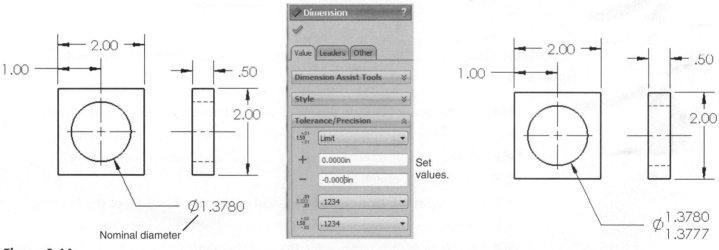

Figure 9-14

1 Click the **Limit** option in the **Tolerance/Precision** box.

2 Set the upper limit for **+0.0000** and the lower limit for **−0.0003**.

3 Click the OK check mark.

Using SolidWorks to Apply Standard Fit Tolerances to an Assembly Drawing

Figure 9-15 shows the assembly of the shaft and support toleranced in the previous section with the manufactured bearing. The standard tolerance callouts are added as follows.

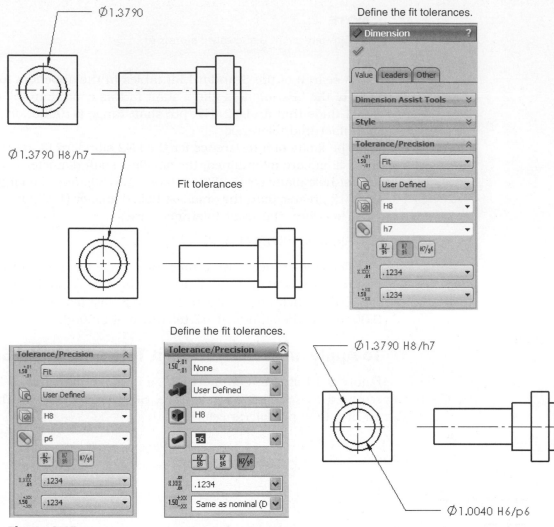

Define the fit tolerances.

Ø1.3790

Ø1.3790 H8/h7

Fit tolerances

Ø1.3790 H8/h7

Define the fit tolerances.

Ø1.0040 H6/p6

Figure 9-15

1 Use the **Smart Dimension** tool and dimension the O.D. of the bearing.

2 Access the **Tolerance/Precision** box and select the **Fit** option.

3 Set the hole fit tolerance for **H8** and the shaft fit tolerance for **h7**.

4 Click the OK check mark.

5 Use the **Smart Dimension** tool and dimension the I.D. of the bearing.

6 Access the **Tolerance/Precision** box and select the **Fit** option.

7 Set the hole fit tolerance for **H6** and the shaft fit tolerance for **p6**.

9-13 Fit Tolerances—Millimeters

The appendix also includes tables for preferred fits using metric values. These tables are read directly. For example, the values for a Close Running Preferred Clearance fit H8/f7 for a nominal shaft diameter of 16 is as follows:

Hole: Ø16.027/16.000   Shaft: Ø15.984/15.966

Fit (limits of fits): 0.016

The value 16.000 indicates that the hole basis condition was used to calculate the tolerances. Metric fits are applied in the same manner as English unit values.

Chapter Projects

Figure P9-1 shows a support plate with three holes. A dimensioned drawing of the support plate is included. The holes are lettered. Three shafts are also shown. All shafts are 3.00 long. For Projects 9-1 to P9-8:

A. Create dimensioned and tolerances drawings for the support plate and shafts.

B. Specify tolerances for both the support plate holes and the shaft's diameters based on the given fit information.

Figure P9-1

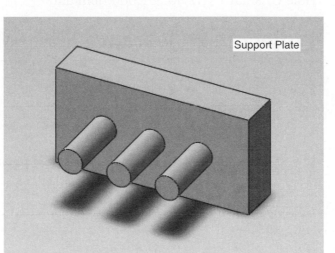

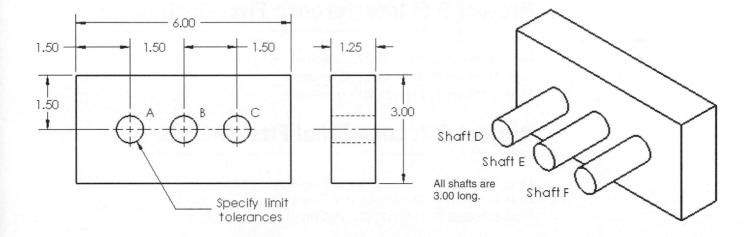

Project 9-1: Clearance Fits—Inches

Hole A/Shaft D: H7/h6, Ø.125 nominal
Hole B/Shaft E: H6/h5, Ø.750 nominal
Hole C/Shaft F: H9/f8, Ø.250 nominal

Project 9-2: Clearance Fits—Inches

Hole A/Shaft D: H10/d9, Ø1.123 nominal
Hole B/Shaft E: H7/h6, Ø.500 nominal
Hole C/Shaft F: H5/g4, Ø.625 nominal

Project 9-3: Clearance Fits—Inches

Hole A/Shaft D: H9/f8, Ø.500 nominal
Hole B/Shaft E: H8/e7, Ø.635 nominal
Hole C/Shaft F: H7/f6, Ø1.000 nominal

Project 9-4: Clearance Fits—Millimeters

Hole A/Shaft D: D9/h9, Ø10.0 nominal
Hole B/Shaft E: H7/h6, Ø16.0 nominal
Hole C/Shaft F: C11/h11, Ø20.0 nominal

Project 9-5: Interference Fits—Inches

Hole A/Shaft D: H6/n5, Ø.250 nominal
Hole B/Shaft E: H7/p6, Ø.750 nominal
Hole C/Shaft F: H7/r6, Ø.250 nominal

Project 9-6: Interference Fits—Inches

Hole A/Shaft D: FN2, Ø.375 nominal
Hole B/Shaft E: FN3, Ø1.500 nominal
Hole C/Shaft F: FN4, Ø.250 nominal

Project 9-7: Locational Fits—Inches

Hole A/Shaft D: H8/k7, Ø.4375 nominal
Hole B/Shaft E: H7/k6, Ø.7075 nominal
Hole C/Shaft F: H8/js7, Ø1.155 nominal

Project 9-8: Interference Fits—Millimeters

Hole A/Shaft D: H7/k6, Ø12.0 nominal
Hole B/Shaft E: H7/p6, Ø25.0 nominal
Hole C/Shaft F: N7/h6, Ø8.0 nominal

Figure P9-2 Shows a U-bracket, four sleeve bearings, and two shafts. A dimensioned drawing of the U-bracket is also included. For Projects 9-9 to 9-12:

Figure P9-2

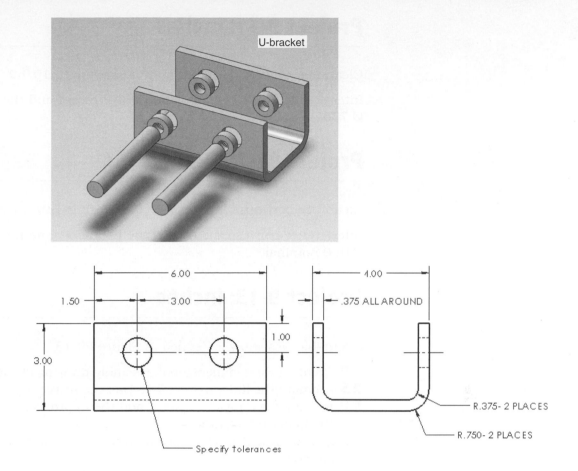

A. Create dimensioned and toleranced drawings for the U-bracket, sleeve bearings, and shafts. All shafts are 5.00 long.
B. Specify tolerances for the shaft diameter and the outside diameter of the sleeve bearings based on the given interference fits.
C. Specify tolerances for the holes in the U-bracket and the outside diameter of the sleeve bearings based on the sizes given in the appendix.
D. Create new links for parts 7, 8, and 9, and note the changes in motion created.

Project 9-9: Inches

Clearance between shaft and bearing: H9/f8, Ø.875 nominal

Interference between the hole in the U-bracket and the bearing: H7/p6, Ø.375 nominal

Project 9-10: Inches

Clearance between the shaft and the bearing: H9/f8, Ø.875 nominal

Interference between the hole in the U-bracket and the bearing: Class FN2, Ø1.125 nominal

Project 9-11: Inches

Clearance between the shaft and the bearing: H10/h9, Ø.500 nominal

Interference between the hole in the U-bracket and the bearing: H7/r6, Ø.750 nominal

Project 9-12: Millimeters

Clearance between the shaft and the bearing: H9/d9, Ø10.0 nominal

Interference between the hole in the U-bracket and the bearing: H7/p6, Ø16.0 nominal

Project 9-13: Inches

A four-bar assembly is defined in Figure P9-13.

1 Create a three-dimensional assembly drawing of the four-bar assembly.
2 Animate the links using LINK-1 as the driver.
3 Redraw the individual parts, add the appropriate dimensions, and add the following tolerances:
A. Assign an LN1 interference fit between the links and the needle roller bearing.
B. Assign an LC2 clearance between the holder posts, both regular and long posts, and the inside diameter of the needle roller bearing.
C. Assign an LC3 clearance between the holder posts, both regular and long posts, and the spacers.

Project 9-14 Inches

Redraw the crank assembly shown in Figure P9-14. Create the following drawings.
A. An exploded isometric drawing with balloons and a BOM.
B. Dimensioned drawings of each part.
C. Animate the assembly drawing.
D. Change the length of the links and note the differences in motion.

Four Bar Assembly

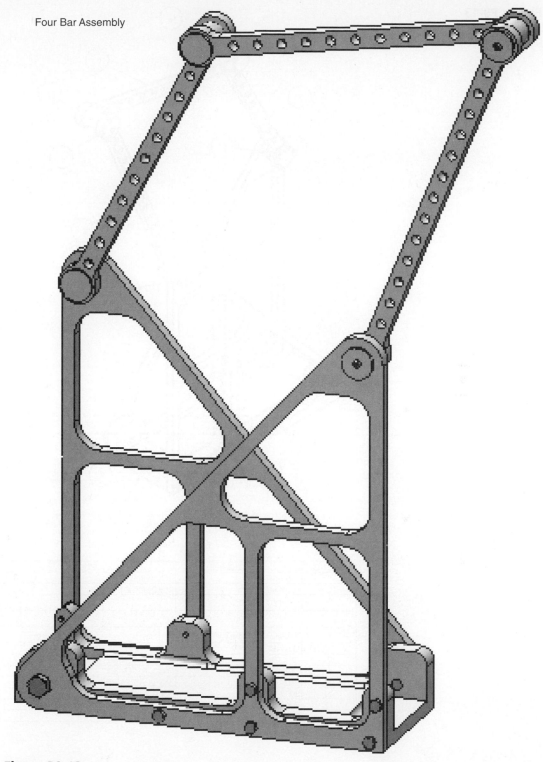

Figure P9-13

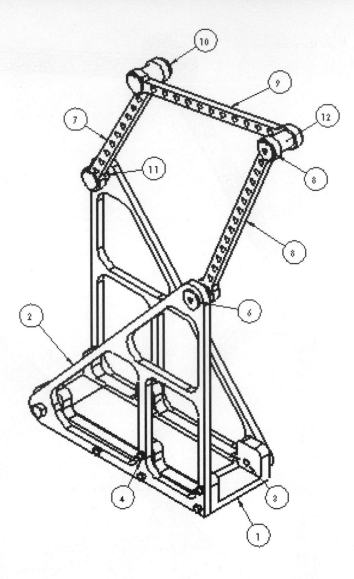

ITEM NO.	PART NUMBER	DESCRIPTION	QTY.
1	BU09-ME1	HOLDER, BASE	1
2	BU09-ME2	HOLDER, SIDE	2
3	HBOLT 0.5000-13x1.25x1.25-N		2
4	HBOLT 0.2500-20x1x1-N		11
5	HBOLT 0.2500-20x1.25x1.25-N		1
6	BU09-P1	POST, PIVOT, SHORT	2
7	LINK-01	LINK1, ASSEMBLY	1
8	LINK-03	LINK3, ASSEMBLY	1
9	LINK-02	LINK 2, ASSEMBLY	1
10	BU09-P2	POST, PIVOT, LONG	2
11	BU09-S1	SPACER, SHORT	2
12	BU09-S2	SPACER, LONG	2

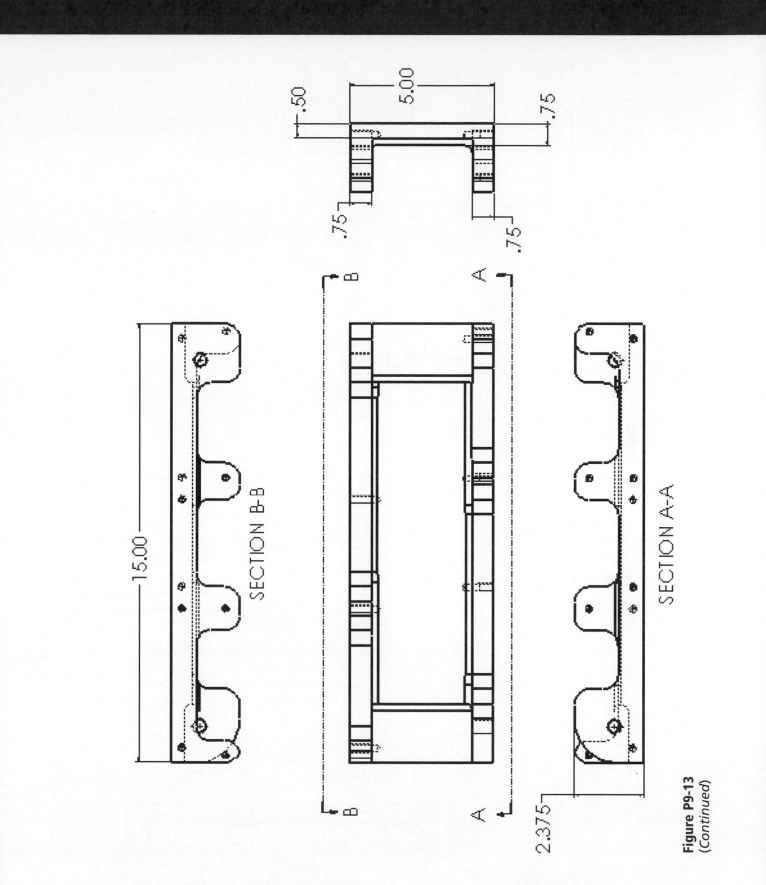

Figure P9-13
(Continued)

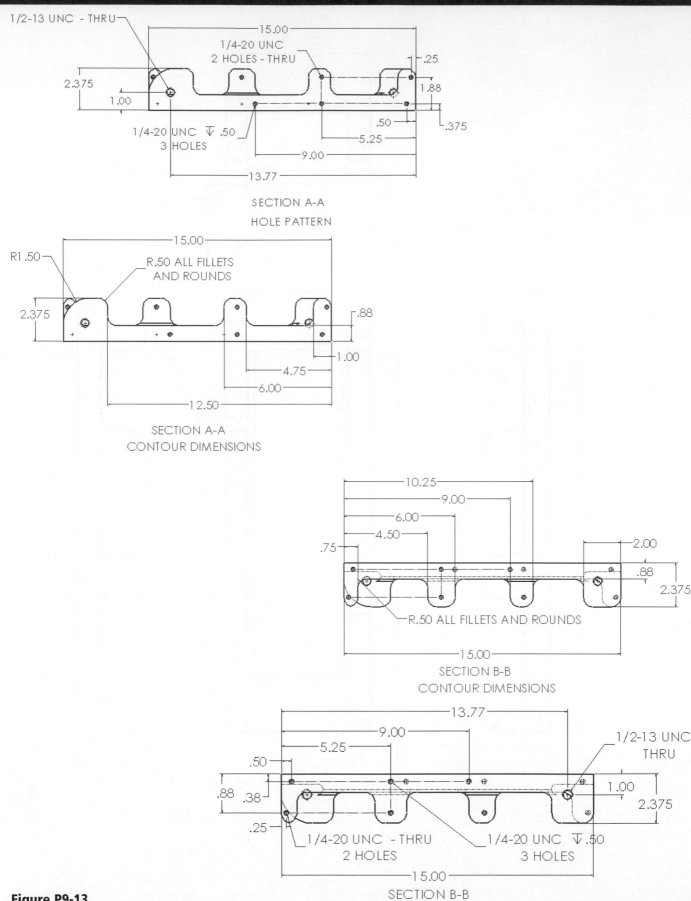

1/2-13 UNC - THRU

15.00

1/4-20 UNC
2 HOLES - THRU

.25

2.375

1.88

1.00

1/4-20 UNC ▽ .50
3 HOLES

.50

.375

5.25

9.00

13.77

SECTION A-A
HOLE PATTERN

15.00

R1.50

R.50 ALL FILLETS
AND ROUNDS

2.375

.88

1.00

4.75

6.00

12.50

SECTION A-A
CONTOUR DIMENSIONS

10.25

9.00

6.00

4.50

.75

2.00

.88

2.375

R.50 ALL FILLETS AND ROUNDS

15.00

SECTION B-B
CONTOUR DIMENSIONS

13.77

9.00

5.25

.50

1/2-13 UNC
THRU

.88

.38

1.00

2.375

.25

1/4-20 UNC - THRU
2 HOLES

1/4-20 UNC ▽ .50
3 HOLES

15.00

SECTION B-B
HOLE PATTERN

Figure P9-13
(Continued)

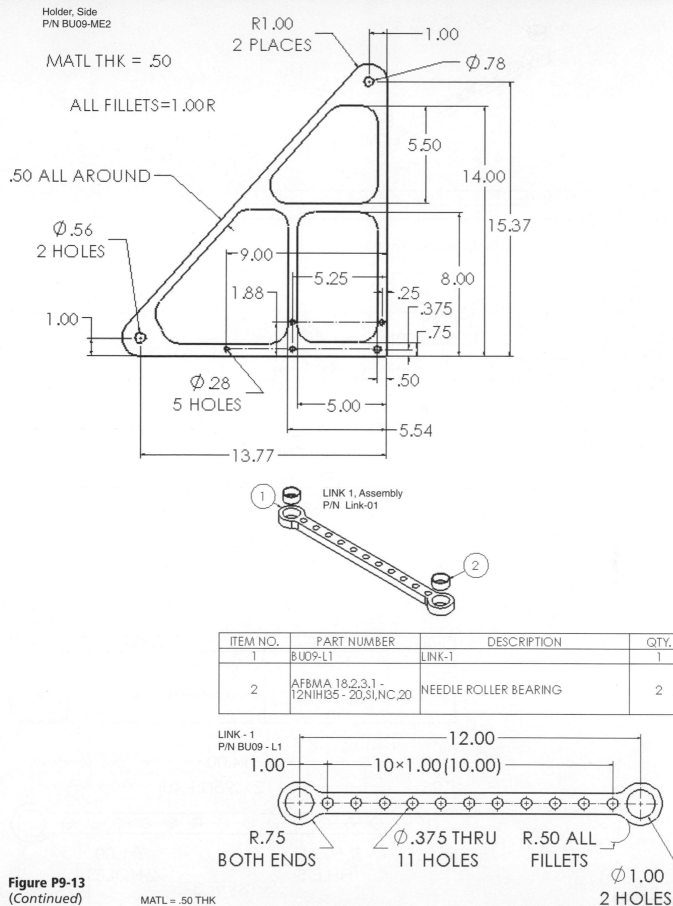

Holder, Side
P/N BU09-ME2

MATL THK = .50

ALL FILLETS=1.00R

R1.00
2 PLACES

⌀.78

.50 ALL AROUND

⌀.56
2 HOLES

⌀.28
5 HOLES

LINK 1, Assembly
P/N Link-01

ITEM NO.	PART NUMBER	DESCRIPTION	QTY.
1	BU09-L1	LINK-1	1
2	AFBMA 18.2.3.1 - 12NIHI35 - 20,SI,NC,20	NEEDLE ROLLER BEARING	2

LINK - 1
P/N BU09 - L1

12.00

1.00

10×1.00(10.00)

R.75
BOTH ENDS

⌀.375 THRU
11 HOLES

R.50 ALL
FILLETS

⌀1.00
2 HOLES

Figure P9-13
(*Continued*)   MATL = .50 THK

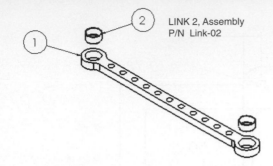

LINK 2, Assembly
P/N Link-02

ITEM NO.	PART NUMBER	DESCRIPTION	QTY.
1	BU09-L2	LINK - 2	1
2	AFBMA 18.2.3.1 - 12NIHB5 - 20,SI,NC,20	NEEDLE ROLLER BEARING	2

Link - 2
P/N BU09 - L2

13.00

1.50

10 × 1.00(10.00)

Holes

∅1.00
2 HOLES

MATL = .50 THK

R.50 ALL
FILLETS

R.75
BOTH ENDS

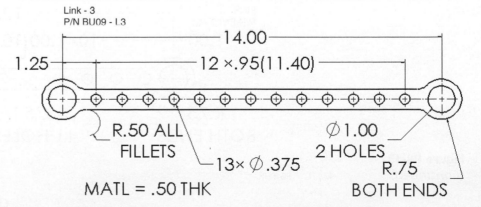

LINK 3, Assembly
P/N Link - 03

ITEM NO.	PART NUMBER	DESCRIPTION	QTY.
1	BU09-L3	LINK-3	1
2	AFBMA 18.2.3.1 - 12NIHB5 - 20,SI,NC,20	NEEDLE ROLLER BEARING	2

Link - 3
P/N BU09 - L3

14.00

1.25

12 ×.95(11.40)

R.50 ALL
FILLETS

13× ∅.375

∅1.00
2 HOLES

R.75
BOTH ENDS

MATL = .50 THK

Figure P9-13
(*Continued*)

Short Post
Assembly

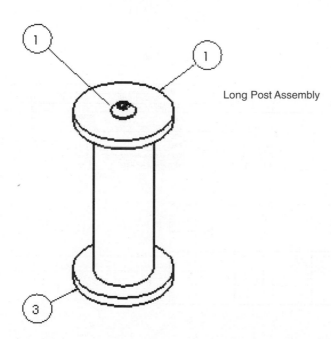

Post, Holder
P/N BU09 - 07

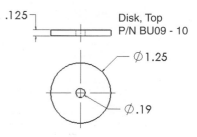

∅ .14 ▽ .66
8-32 UNC ▽ .50

∅.75

.125

1.69

.125

Disk, Top
P/N BU09 - 10

∅1.25

∅.19

ITEM NO.	PART NUMBER	DESCRIPTION	QTY.
1	BU09-07	POST, HOLDER	1
2	BU09--10	DISK, TOP	1
3	SBHC SCREW 0.164-32x0.4375-HX-N	SOCKET BUTTON HEAD CAP SCREW	1

Long Post Assembly

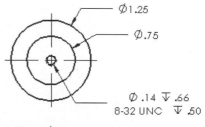

∅1.25

∅.75

∅ .14 ▽ .66
8-32 UNC ▽ .50

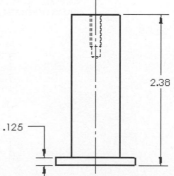

2.38

.125

ITEM NO.	PART NUMBER	DESCRIPTION	QTY.
1	BU09-10	DISK, TOP	1
2	SBHC SCREW 0.164-32x0.4375-HX-N	SOCKET BUTTON HEAD CAP SCREW	1
3	BU09-08	POST, HOLDER, LONG	1

Figure P9-13
(*Continued*)

517

Figure P9-13
(*Continued*)

Spacer, Long
P/N BU09 - S2

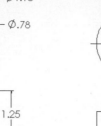

Ø1.13
Ø.78

1.25

Spacer, Short
P/N BU09 - S1

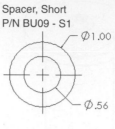

Ø1.00
Ø.56

.44

Figure P9-14

Crank Assembly

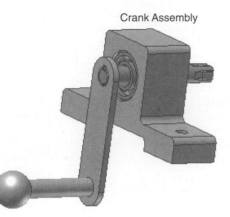

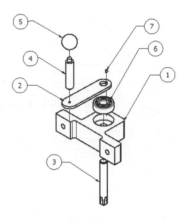

Parts List				
ITEM	PART NUMBER	DESCRIPTION	MATERIAL	QTY
1	EK131-1	SUPPORT	STEEL	1
2	EK131-2	LINK	STEEL	1
3	EK131-3	SHAFT,DRIVE	STEEL	1
4	EK131-4	POST, THREADED	STEEL	1
5	EK131-5	BALL	STEEL	1
6	BS 292 - BRM 3/4	Deep Groove Ball Bearings	STEEL,MILD	1
7	3/16x1/8x1/4	RECTANGULAR KEY	STEEL	1

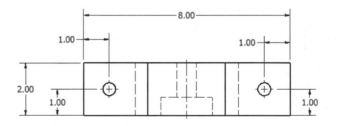

8.00
1.00
1.00
2.00
1.00
1.00
1.00

NOTE: ALL FILLETS AND ROUNDS R=0.250
UNLESS OTHERWISE STATED.

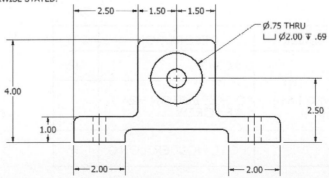

2.50
1.50
1.50

Ø.75 THRU
Ø2.00 ▼ .69

4.00
2.50
1.00
2.00
2.00

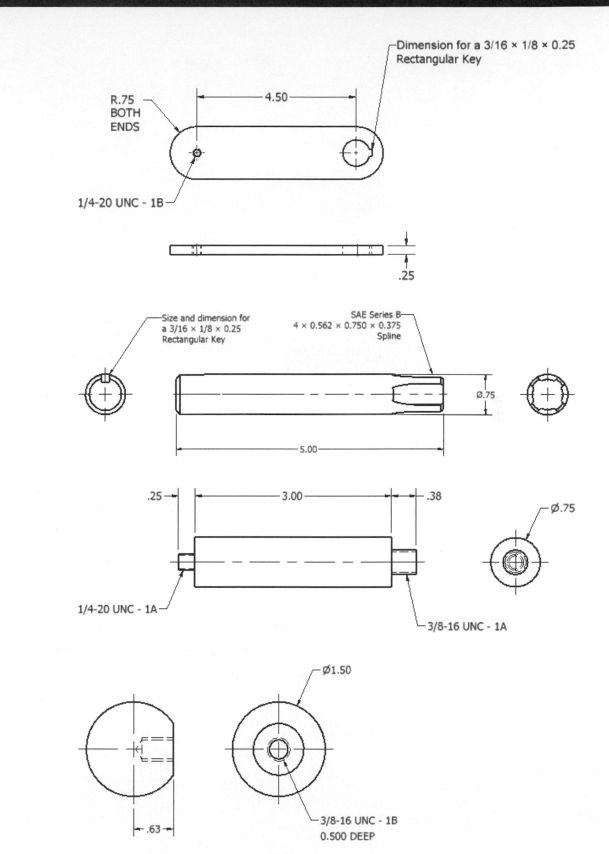

R.75
BOTH
ENDS

Dimension for a 3/16 × 1/8 × 0.25
Rectangular Key

4.50

1/4-20 UNC - 1B

.25

Size and dimension for
a 3/16 × 1/8 × 0.25
Rectangular Key

SAE Series B
4 × 0.562 × 0.750 × 0.375
Spline

Ø.75

5.00

.25

3.00

.38

Ø.75

1/4-20 UNC - 1A

3/8-16 UNC - 1A

Ø1.50

.63

3/8-16 UNC - 1B
0.500 DEEP

10 chapter ten

Gears

CHAPTER OBJECTIVES

- Learn the concept of power transmission
- Learn the fundamentals of gears

- Learn how to draw and animate gears

10-1 Introduction

Gears, pulleys, and chains are part of a broader category called ***power transmission.*** Power comes from a source such as an engine, motor, or windmill. The power is then transferred to a mechanism that performs some function. For example an automobile engine transmits power from the engine to the wheels via a gear box. Bicyclists transmit the power of their legs to wheels via a chain and sprocket.

This section explains how gears, pulleys, and chains are drawn using SolidWorks and how the finished drawings can be animated. There is also a discussion of how speed is transferred and changed using gears, pulleys, and chains. Figure 10-1 shows a spur gear drawn using SolidWorks.

10-2 Gear Terminology

Pitch Diameter (*D*): The diameter used to define the spacing of gears. Ideally, gears are exactly tangent to each other along their pitch diameters.

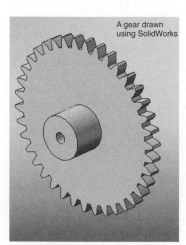

A gear drawn using SolidWorks

Figure 10-1

Diametral Pitch (P): The number of teeth per inch. Meshing gears must have the same diametral pitch. Manufacturers' gear charts list gears with the same diametral pitch.

Module (M): The pitch diameter divided by the number of teeth. The metric equivalent of diametral pitch.

Number of Teeth (N): The number of teeth of a gear.

Circular Pitch (CP): The circular distance from a fixed point on one tooth to the same position on the next tooth as measured along the pitch circle. The circumference of the pitch circle divided by the number of teeth.

Preferred Pitches: The standard sizes available from gear manufacturers. Whenever possible, use preferred gear sizes.

Center Distance (CD): The distance between the center points of two meshing gears.

Backlash: The difference between a tooth width and the engaging space on a meshing gear.

Addendum (a): The height of a tooth above the pitch diameter.

Dedendum (d): The depth of a tooth below the pitch diameter.

Whole Depth: The total depth of a tooth. The addendum plus the dedendum.

Working Depth: The depth of engagement of one gear into another. Equal to the sum of the two gears' addendeums.

Circular Thickness: The distance across a tooth as measured along the pitch circle.

Face Width (F): The distance from front to back along a tooth as measured perpendicular to the pitch circle.

Outside Diameter: The largest diameter of the gear. Equal to the pitch diameter plus the addendum.

Root Diameter: The diameter of the base of the teeth. The pitch diameter minus the dedendum.

Clearance: The distance between the addendum of the meshing gear and the dedendum of the mating gear.

Pressure Angle: The angle between the line of action and a line tangent to the pitch circle. Most gears have pressure angles of either 14.5° or 20°

See Figure 10-2.

10-3 Gear Formulas

Figure 10-3 shows a chart of formulas commonly associated with gears. The formulas are for spur gears.

10-4 Creating Gears Using SolidWorks

In this section we will create two gears and then create an assembly that includes a support plate and two posts to hold the gears in place. The specifications for the two gears are as follows. See Figure 10-4.

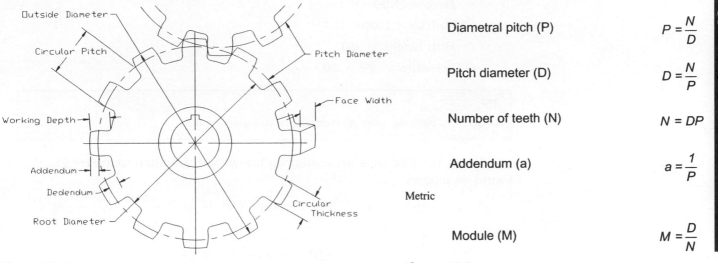

Figure 10-2

Diametral pitch (P) $P = \dfrac{N}{D}$

Pitch diameter (D) $D = \dfrac{N}{P}$

Number of teeth (N) $N = DP$

Addendum (a) $a = \dfrac{1}{P}$

Metric

Module (M) $M = \dfrac{D}{N}$

Figure 10-3

Gear 1: Diametral pitch = **24**
    Number of teeth = **30**
    Face thickness = **.50**
    Bore = ∅**.50**
    Hub ∅ = **1.00**
    Hub height = **.50**
    Pressure angle = **20**

Gear 2: Diametral pitch = **24**
    Number of teeth = **60**
    Face thickness = **.50**

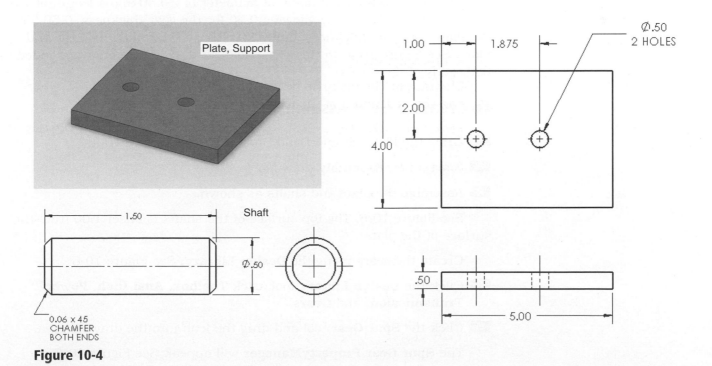

Figure 10-4

Bore = $\varnothing$**.50**

Hub $\varnothing$ = **1.00**

Hub height = **.50**

Pressure angle = **20**

> **TIP**
>
> Gears must have the same diametral pitch to mesh properly.

Using the formulas presented we know that the pitch diameter is found as follows:

$$D = N/P$$

So

$$D1 = 30/24 = 1.25 \text{ in.}$$
$$D2 = 60/24 = 2.50 \text{ in.}$$

The center distance between gears is found from the relation $(D1 + D2)/2$:

$$\frac{1.25 + 2.50}{2} = 1.875 \text{ in.}$$

This center distance data was used to create the Plate, Support shown in Figure 10-4.

The bore for the gears is defined as 0.50, so shafts that hold the gears will be $\varnothing$0.50, and the holes in the Plate, Support will also be 0.50.

> **NOTE**
>
> Tolerances for gears, shafts, and support plates will be discussed in Chapter 10, Bearings and Fit Tolerances.

The shafts will have a nominal diameter of $\varnothing$0.50 and a length of 1.50. The length was derived by allowing 0.50 for the gear thickness, 0.50 for the Plate, Support thickness, and 0.50 clearance between the gear and the plate. See Figure 10-4. In this example 0.06 × 45° chamfers were added to both ends of the shafts.

To Create a Gear Assembly

1 Draw the Plate, Support and Shaft shown in Figure 10-4.

2 Start a new **Assembly** drawing.

3 Assemble the plate and shafts as shown.

See Figure 10-5. The top surface of the shafts is offset 1.00 from the surface of the plate.

Create the gears using the **Design Library.** See Figure 10-6.

4 Click the **Design Library** tool, click **Toolbox, Ansi Inch, Power Transmission,** and **Gears.**

5 Click the **Spur Gear** tool and drag the icon into the drawing area.

The **Spur Gear PropertyManager** will appear. See Figure 10-7.

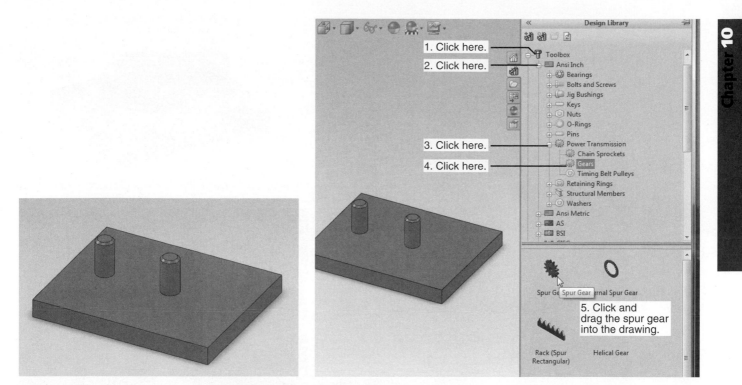

1. Click here.
2. Click here.
3. Click here.
4. Click here.

5. Click and drag the spur gear into the drawing.

Figure 10-5

Figure 10-6

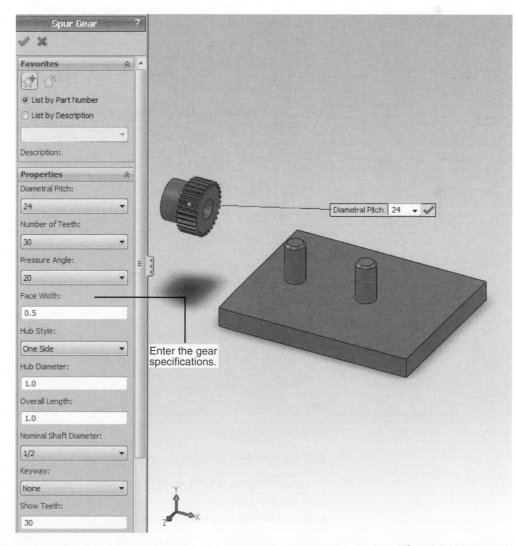

Figure 10-7

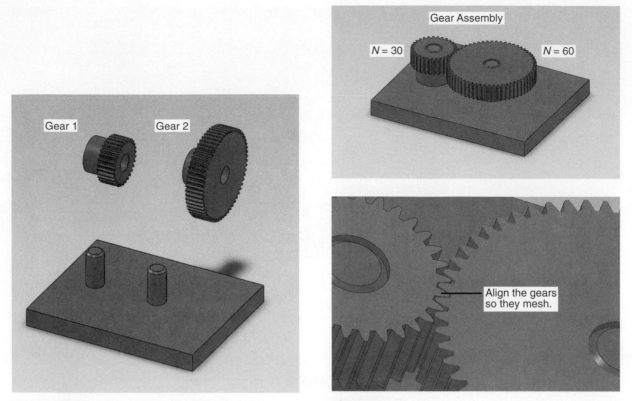

Figure 10-8

Figure 10-9

6 Enter the gear values as presented earlier for Gears 1 and 2 and create the two gears.

See Figure 10-8.

7 Use the **Mate** tool and assemble the gears onto the shafts so that they mesh. First, use the **Mate/Concentric** tool to align the gears' bores with the shafts, then use the **Mate/Parallel** tool to align the top surface of the shafts with the top surfaces of the gears.

See Figure 10-9.

8 Zoom in on the gear teeth and align them so they mesh.

> **TIP**
> Gears can be meshed by rotating one of the gears using the cursor.

9 Click the **Mate** tool.

10 Click **Mechanical Mates.**

11 Select the **Gear** option.

See Figure 10-10.

12 Define the gear mate by clicking the inside bore of the two gears.

See Figure 10-11.

13 Define the ratio between the gears.

See Figure 10-12. In this example the ratio between the two gears is 2:1; that is, the smaller 30-tooth gear goes around twice for every revolution of the 60-tooth larger gear.

Figure 10-10

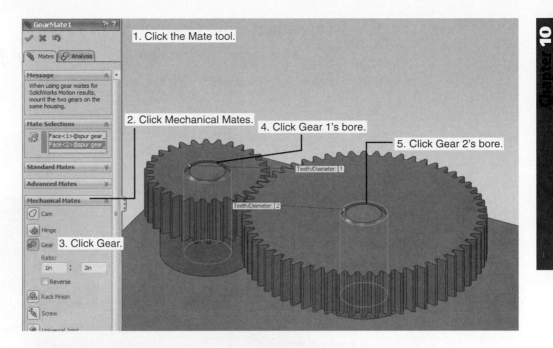

1. Click the Mate tool.

2. Click Mechanical Mates.

4. Click Gear 1's bore.

5. Click Gear 2's bore.

3. Click Gear.

Figure 10-11

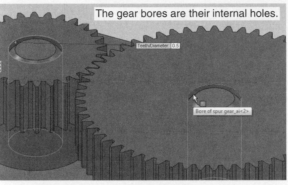

The gear bores are their internal holes.

Figure 10-12

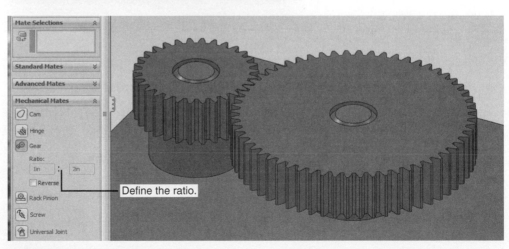

Define the ratio.

14 Click the OK check mark.

15 Locate the cursor on the smaller gear and rotate the gears.

> **TIP**
>
> If the gears were not aligned, step 8, an error message would appear stating that the gears interfere with each other. The gears will turn relative to each other even if they interfere, but it is better to go back and align the gears.

To Animate the Gears

1 Click the **Motion Study** tab at the bottom of the screen.

2 Click the **Motor** tool.

See Figure 10-13.

Figure 10-13

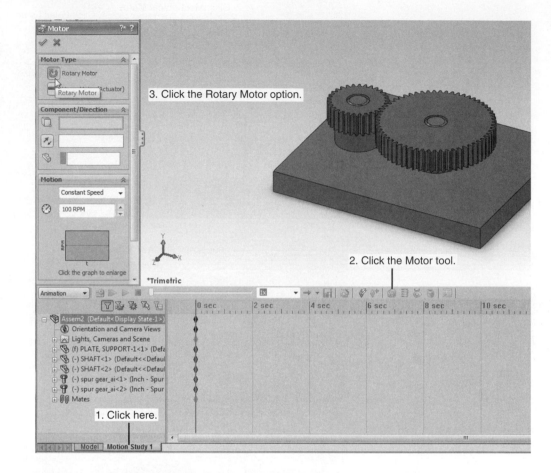

3. Click the Rotary Motor option.

2. Click the Motor tool.

1. Click here.

3 Click the **Rotary Motor** option in the **Motor PropertyManager.**

4 Click the smaller 30-tooth gear.

A red arrow will appear on the gear, and the gear will be identified in the **Component/Direction** box. See Figure 10-14.

Figure 10-14

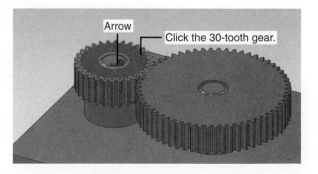

Arrow

Click the 30-tooth gear.

5 Click the OK check mark.

Click the **Play** button and the gears will animate. See Figure 10-15.

6 Save the gear assembly.

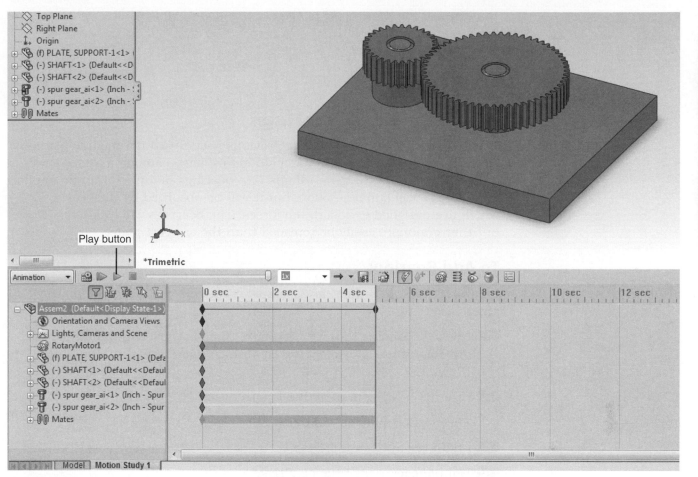

Play button

*Trimetric

Figure 10-15

10-5 Gear Ratios

Gear ratios are determined by the number of teeth of each gear. In the previous example a gear with 30 teeth was meshed with a gear that has 60 teeth. Their gear ratio is 2:1, that is, the smaller gear turns twice for every one revolution of the larger gear. Figure 10-16 shows a group of four gears. A grouping of gears is called a ***gear train.*** The gear train shown contains two gears with 30 teeth and two gears with 90 teeth. One the 30-tooth gears is mounted on the same shaft as one of the 90-tooth gears. The gear ratio for the gear train is found as follows:

$$\left(\frac{3}{1}\right)\left(\frac{3}{1}\right) = \frac{9}{1}$$

Figure 10-16

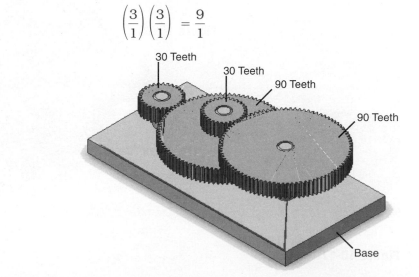

30 Teeth

30 Teeth

90 Teeth

90 Teeth

Base

Thus, if the leftmost 30-tooth gear turns at 1750 RPM, the rightmost 90-tooth gear turns at

$$\frac{1750}{9} = 199.4 \text{ RPM}$$

10-6 Gears and Bearings

The gear assembly created in the previous section did not include bearings. As gears rotate they rub against a stationary part, causing friction. It would be better to mount the gears' shafts into bearings mounted into the support plate. There will still be friction, but it will be absorbed by the bearings, which are designed to absorb the forces. The bearings will eventually wear, but they can more easily be replaced than the support plate.

To Add Bearings

Figure 10-17 shows the gear assembly created in the last section. The shafts are ∅.50.

1 Click the **Design Library, Toolbox, Ansi Inches, Jig Bushings, All Jig Bushings**, and select **Jig Bushing Type P** and drag it onto the drawing.

2 Size the bearing to **.5** with a length of **.5.**

The support plate is .50 thick.

3 Add a second bearing.

4 Double-click one of the bearings.

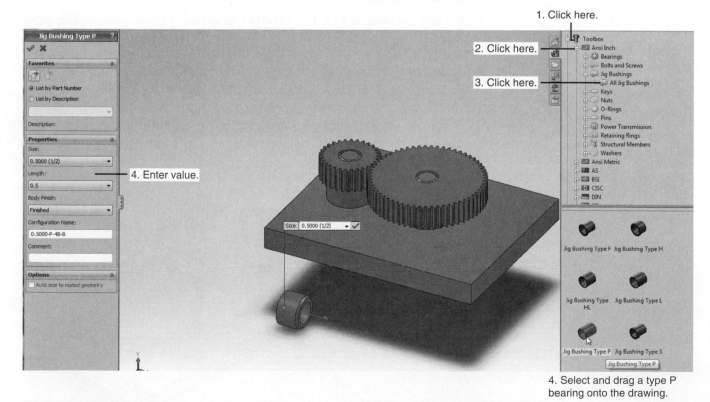

Figure 10-17

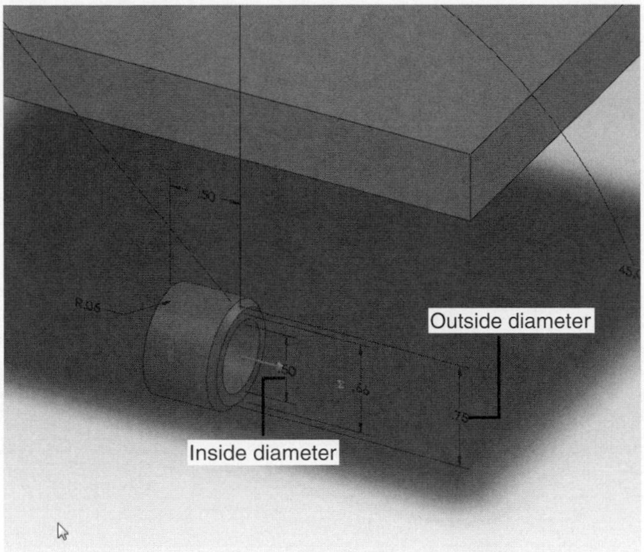

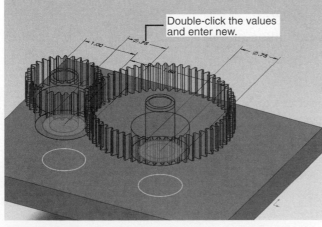

Figure 10-18

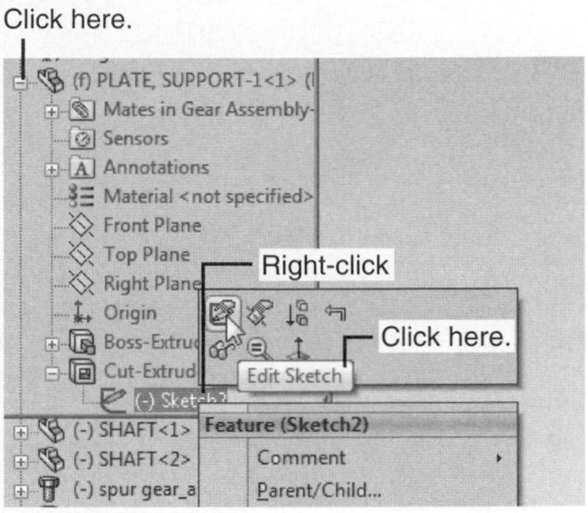

Outside diameter

Inside diameter

Click here.

(f) PLATE, SUPPORT-1<1> (
Mates in Gear Assembly-
Sensors
Annotations
Material <not specified>
Front Plane
Top Plane
Right-click
Right Plane
Origin
Boss-Extrud
Cut-Extrud
Click here.
Edit Sketch
(-) Sketch2
(-) SHAFT<1> Feature (Sketch2)
(-) SHAFT<2> Comment
(-) spur gear_a Parent/Child...

Figure 10-19

The dimensions used to create the bearing will appear. See Figure 10-18. The outside diameter of the bearing is .75. The holes in the support plate must be edited to ∅.75.

5 Click the **+** sign to the left of the **PLATE, SUPPORT** heading in the **FeatureManager.**

6 Right-click the **Sketch 2** heading under the **Cut-Extrude 1** heading and select the **Edit Sketch** option.

See Figure 10-19.

7 Double-click the holes' **.50** diameter dimensions and change them to **.75.**

See Figure 10-20.

8 Rotate the entire assembly so that the bottom surface of the support plate is visible.

9 Use the **Mate** tool to position the bearings onto the bottoms of the shafts.

Figure 10-21 shows an exploded isometric drawing of the assembly with a BOM.

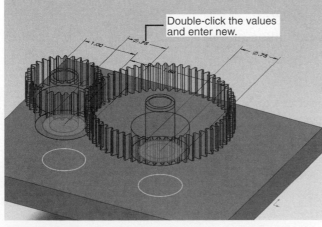

Double-click the values and enter new.

Figure 10-20

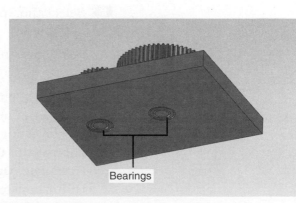

Bearings

Figure 10-21

Figure 10-22

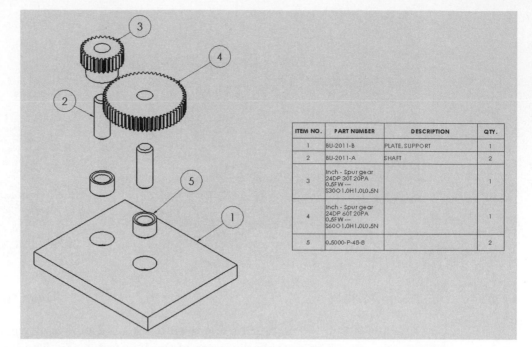

ITEM NO.	PART NUMBER	DESCRIPTION	QTY.
1	BU-2011-B	PLATE, SUPPORT	1
2	BU-2011-A	SHAFT	2
3	Inch - Spur gear 24DP 30T 20PA 0.5FW --- S30O1.0H1.0L0.5N		1
4	Inch - Spur gear 24DP 60T 20PA 0.5FW --- S60O1.0H1.0L0.5N		1
5	0.5000-P-48-8		2

10-7 Power Transmission—Shaft to Gear

When a gear is mounted on a shaft there must be a way to transfer the power from the shaft to the gear and from the gear to the shaft. Three common ways to achieve this transfer are to use set screws, keys, and splines. This section shows how to add set screws and keyways to gears. Splines will not be included.

10-8 Set Screws and Gear Hubs

This section shows how add a hub to a gear and then how to create a threaded hole in the hub that will accept a set screw.

1 Start a new **Part** drawing and create the ∅**0.50** × **2.25** shaft shown in Figure 10-23. Save the part.

2 Start a new **Assembly** drawing.

3 Use the **Insert Components** tool and add the ∅0.50 × 2.25 shaft to the drawing.

4 Access the **Design Library** and click **Toolbox, Ansi Inch, Power Transmission,** and **Gears.**

5 Select the **Spur Gear** option and click and drag a gear onto the drawing screen.

See Figure 10-24.

6 Set the gear's properties as follows. See Figure 10-25.
Diametral pitch: **24**
Number of teeth: **36**
Pressure angle: **14.5**
Face width: **0.5**
Hub style: **One Side**
Hub Diameter: **1.00**
Overall length: **1.00**

Ø.50

2.25

.06 x 45°
CHAMFER
BOTH ENDS

Figure 10-23

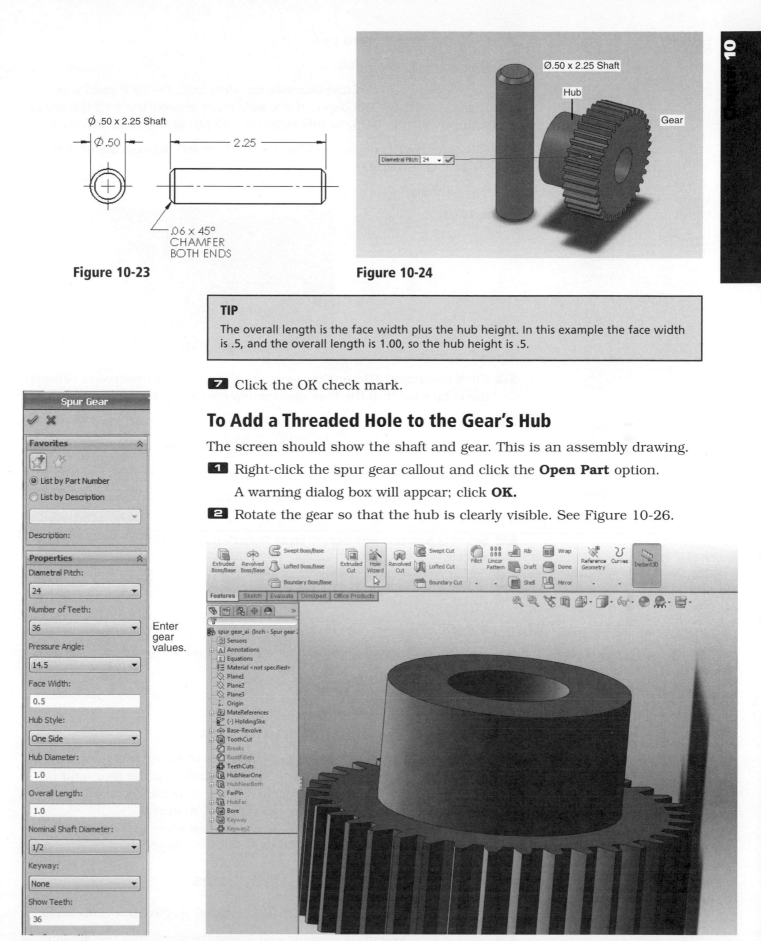

Ø.50 x 2.25 Shaft

Hub

Gear

Diametral Pitch: 24

Figure 10-24

TIP

The overall length is the face width plus the hub height. In this example the face width is .5, and the overall length is 1.00, so the hub height is .5.

---

7 Click the OK check mark.

To Add a Threaded Hole to the Gear's Hub

The screen should show the shaft and gear. This is an assembly drawing.

1 Right-click the spur gear callout and click the **Open Part** option.

A warning dialog box will appear; click **OK.**

2 Rotate the gear so that the hub is clearly visible. See Figure 10-26.

Spur Gear

Favorites

○ List by Part Number
○ List by Description

Description:

Properties

Diametral Pitch:
24

Number of Teeth:
36

Pressure Angle:
14.5

Face Width:
0.5

Hub Style:
One Side

Hub Diameter:
1.0

Overall Length:
1.0

Nominal Shaft Diameter:
1/2

Keyway:
None

Show Teeth:
36

Enter gear values.

Figure 10-25

Figure 10-26

Figure 10-27

3 Click the **Hole Wizard** tool.

4 Define the **Type** of hole.

See Figure 10-27. In this example an ANSI Inch #6-32 thread was selected for the hole. The depth of the hole must exceed the wall thickness of the hub, which is 0.25. In this example a depth of 0.50 was selected.

5 Click the **Positions** tab and locate the threaded hole on the outside surface of the hub.

See Figure 10-28.

Figure 10-28

6 Click the **Smart Dimension** tool and create a **0.25** dimension between the center point of the hole and the top surface of the gear teeth.

7 Click the OK check mark.

8 Save the reversal drawing as **GEAR, SET SCREW**.

9 Click the **Close** tool.

10 Access the **Design Library**, click **Toolbox, Ansi Inch, Bolts and Screws**, and **Set Screws (Slotted)**.

11 Select a **Slotted Set Screw Oval Point** and drag it onto the drawing screen.

12 Define the **Properties** of the set screw as **#6-32, 0.263** long; click the OK check mark.

See Figure 10-29.

13 Use the **Mate** tool and assemble the shaft and set screw into the gear as shown.

See Figure 10-30.

10-9 Keys, Keyseats, and Gears

Keys are used to transfer power from a drive shaft to an entity such as a gear or pulley. A *keyseat* is cut into both the shaft and the gear, and the key is inserted between them. See Figure 10-31. The SolidWorks **Design Library** contains two types of keys: parallel and Woodruff.

In this section we will insert a parallel key between a ∅0.50 × 3.00 shaft and a gear. Both the shaft and gear will have keyseats.

To Define and Create Keyseats in Gears

1 Draw a **∅0.50 × 3.00** shaft and save the shaft as **∅0.50 × 3.00 SHAFT**.

2 Start a new **Assembly** drawing and insert the shaft into the drawing.

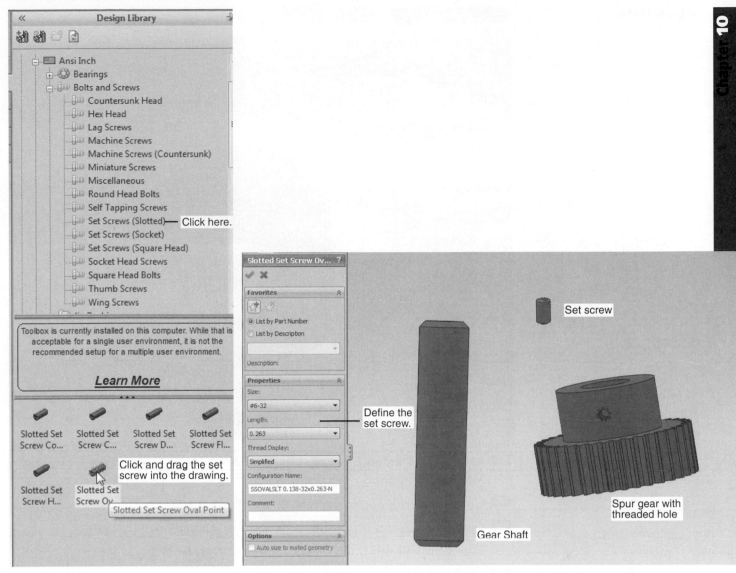

Figure 10-29

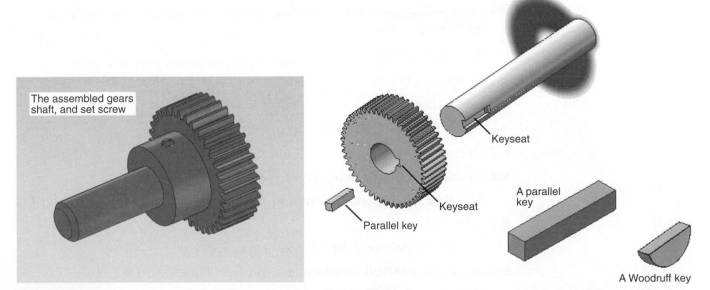

Figure 10-30

Figure 10-31

Figure 10-32

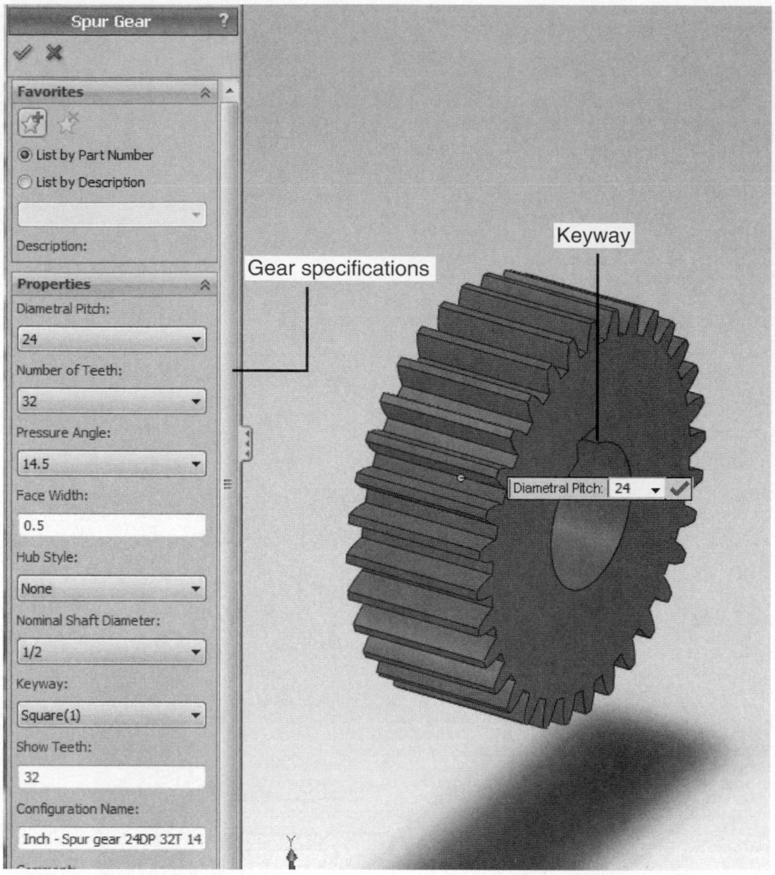

3 Access the **Design Library, Toolbox, Ansi Inch, Power Transmission,** and **Gears** options.

4 Click and drag a spur gear into the drawing area.

5 Define the gear's properties as shown in Figure 10-32.

This gear will not have a hub. Define a **Square(1)** keyway.

6 Click the OK check mark.

> **NOTE**
>
> The gear will automatically have a keyseat cut into it. The size of the keyseat is based on the gear's bore diameter.

The key will also be sized according to the gear's bore diameter, but say we wish to determine the exact keyway size. See Figure 10-33.

1 Right-click the gear and select the **Open Part** option.

A warning dialog box will appear.

2 Click **OK.**

3 Click the **Make Drawing from Part/Assembly** tool.

The **New SolidWorks Document** dialog box will appear.

4 Click **OK.**

The **Sheet Format/Size** dialog box will appear.

5 Select the **B(ANSI) Landscape** sheet size; click OK.

The system will switch to the **Drawing** format.

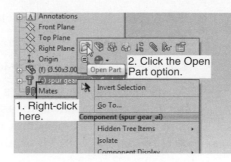

2. Click the Open Part option.

1. Right-click here.

3. Click here.

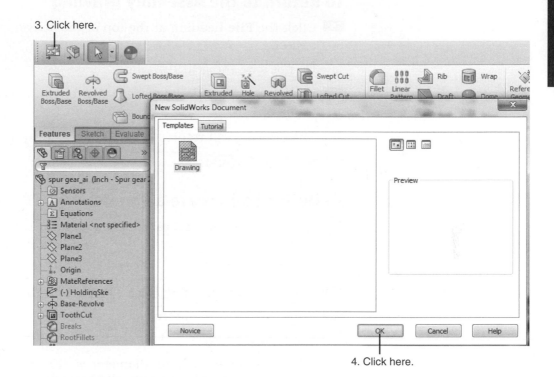

4. Click here.

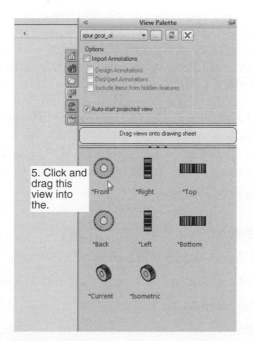

5. Click and drag this view into the.

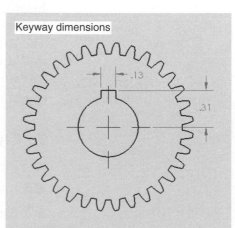

Keyway dimensions

Figure 10-33

6 Click and drag a front view of the gear into the drawing area.

7 Use the **Center Mark** tool to add a centerline to the gear's bore.

8 Use the **Smart Dimension** tool and dimension the keyseat.

Notice that the keyseat's width is .13, or a little more than .125. The height of the keyseat is measured from the bore's center point. The height is defined as .31. Therefore, the height of the keyseat is .31 − .25 (the radius of the bore) = .06, or about half the width.

To Return to the Assembly Drawing

1 Click the **File** heading at the top of the screen, and select the **Close** option.

Do not save the gear drawing.

2 Again, click the **File** heading at the top of the screen, and select the **Close** option.

The drawing will return to the assembly drawing.

See Figure 10-34.

To Define and Create a Parallel Key

1 Access the **Design Library, Toolbox, Ansi Inch, Keys,** and **Parallel Keys.**

See Figure 10-35.

2 Click and drag the **Key (B17.1)** icon onto the drawing screen.

3 Enter the shaft diameter value and the key's length.

See Figure 10-36.

In this example the shaft diameter is .50, or 1/2 inch (8/16). This value is between 7/16 and 9/16. The key's length is .50.

Note that key dimensions are also given as .125 × .125 and a keyseat depth of .0625. Define the key length as .50. The key size automatically matches the keyway in the gear. The width of the gear's keyseat was .13, or .005 larger than the key. A rule of thumb is to make the height of the keyseat in both the shaft and the gear equal to a little more than the key's height. The height of the keyseat in the gear was .06, so the depth of the keyway in the shaft will be .07, for a total keyway height of .06 + .07 = .13. The calculation does not take into account the tolerances between the shaft and the gear or the tolerances between the key and the keyseat. For exact tolerance values refer to *Machinery's Handbook* or some equivalent source.

4 Click the OK check mark.

To Create a Keyseat in the Shaft

The keyway for the shaft will be .13 × .07.

1 Click the top surface of the ∅0.50 × 3.00 shaft.

2 Click the **Normal To** tool.

See Figure 10-37. The top surface of the shaft will become normal to the drawing screen.

Figure 10-34

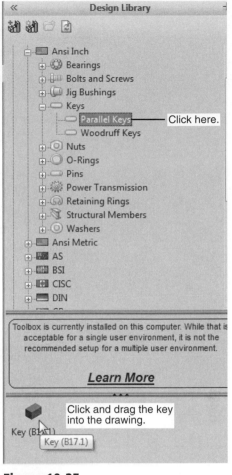

Figure 10-35

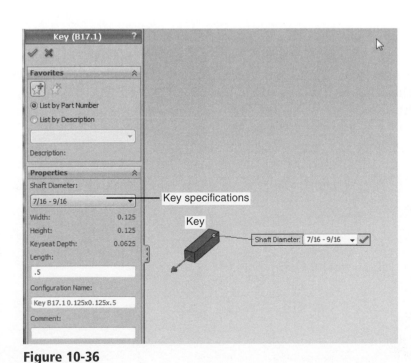

Figure 10-36

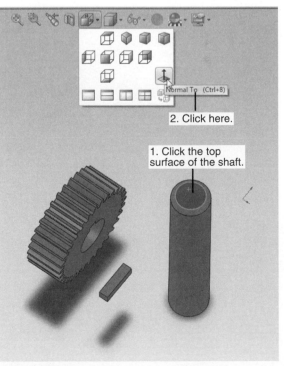

Figure 10-37

3 Right-click the normal surface again and select the **Sketch** option.

4 Click the **Sketch** tab, then click the **Line** tool and draw a vertical line from the center point of the shaft as shown.

This vertical line is for construction purposes. It will be used to center the keyway.

See Figure 10-38.

5 Click the **Sketch** tab, then the **Rectangle** tool and draw a rectangle as shown.

Draw the rectangle so that the top horizontal line is above the edge of the shaft.

6 Use the **Smart Dimension** tool to locate the left vertical line of the rectangle .065 from the vertical construction line.

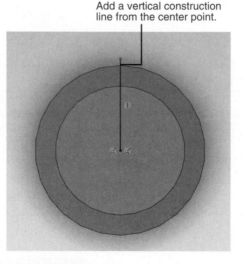

Add a vertical construction line from the center point.

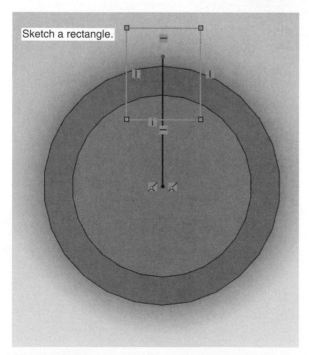

Sketch a rectangle.

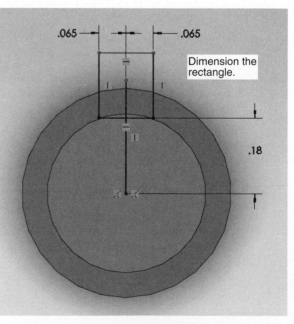

.065   .065

Dimension the rectangle.

.18

Figure 10-38

7 Use the **Smart Dimension** tool and dimension the rectangle as shown.

To Create the Keyseat

1 Access the **Extruded Cut** tool on the **Features** tab and click the dimensioned rectangle.

See Figure 10-39.

2 Define the cut length for **0.50 in;** click the OK check mark.

The keyseat will end with an arc-shaped cut. The radius of the arc is equal to the depth of the keyseat. The arc shape is generated by the **Extruded Cut** tool used to create the keyseat.

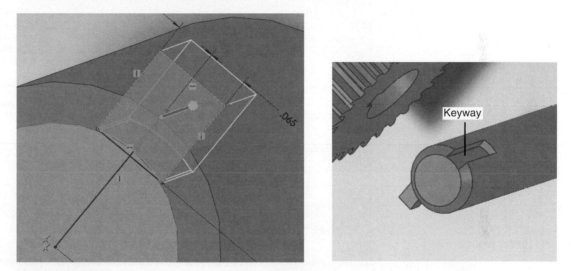

Figure 10-39

To Create the Arc-Shaped End of a Keyseat

1 Right-click the inside vertical surface of the keyseat and click the **Sketch** tab.

2 Use the **Circle** tool and draw a circle centered about the end of the keyseat on the surface of the shaft and using the lower corner of the keyway to define the radius value.

See Figure 10-40.

3 Use the **Extruded Cut** tool to cut the arc-shaped end surface.

The length of the cut equals the width of the keyway, or .13.

4 Assembly the parts as shown. See Figures 10-41 and 10-42.

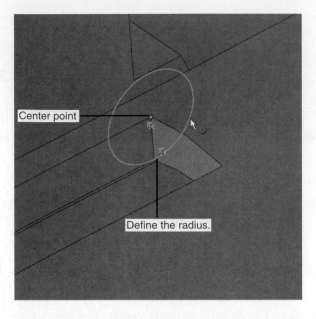

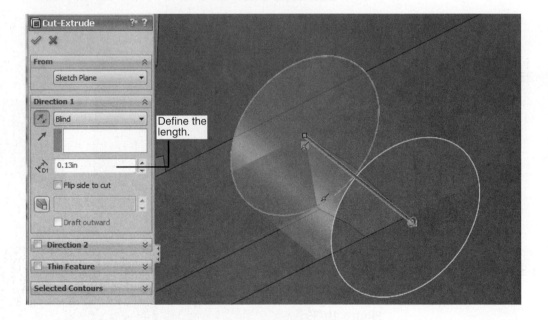

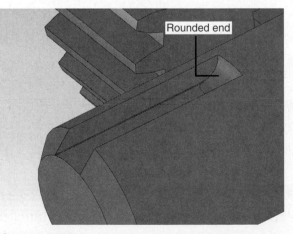

Figure 10-40

Assembly with key in keyway

Figure 10-41

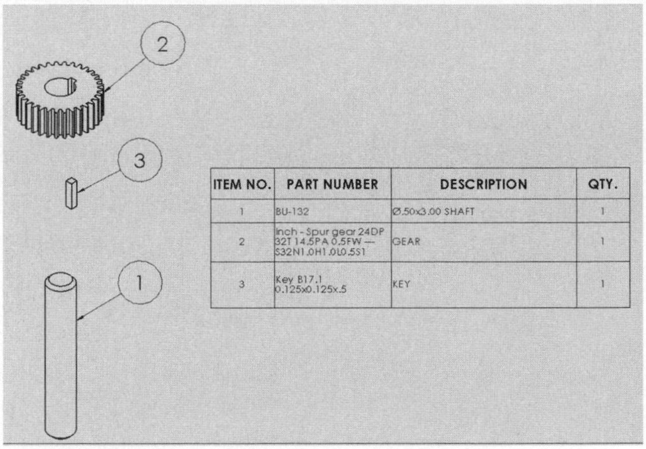

ITEM NO.	PART NUMBER	DESCRIPTION	QTY.
1	BU-132	Ø.50x3.00 SHAFT	1
2	Inch - Spur gear 24DP 32T 14.5PA 0.5FW --- S32N1.0H1.0L0.5S1	GEAR	1
3	Key B17.1 0.125x0.125x.5	KEY	1

Figure 10-42

Figure 10-43

10-10 Sample Problem 10-1—Support Plates

This exercise explains how to determine the size of plates used to support spur gears and their shafts.

Say we wish to design a support plate that will support four spur gears. The gear specifications are as follows. See Figure 10-43.

Gear 1

Diametral Pitch = **24**

Number of Teeth = **20**

Pressure Angle = **14.5°**

Face Width = **0.375**

Hub Style = **One Side**

Hub Diameter = **0.75**

Overall Length = **.875**

Nominal Shaft Diameter = **1/2**

Keyway = **None**

Gear 2

Diametral pitch = **24**

Number of teeth = **60**

Pressure angle = **14.5°**

Face width = **0.375**

Hub style = **One Side**

Hub diameter = **0.75**

Overall length = **.875**

Nominal shaft diameter = **1/2**

Keyway = **None**

To Determine the Pitch Diameter

The pitch diameter of the gears is determined by

$$D = \frac{N}{P}$$

where

> D = pitch diameter
> N = number of teeth
> P = diametral pitch

Therefore, for Gear 1

$$D = \frac{20}{24} = .83$$

For Gear 2

$$D = \frac{60}{24} = 2.50$$

The center distance (CD) between the gears is calculated as follows.

$$CD = \frac{.83 + 2.50}{2} = 1.67$$

The radius of the gears is .46 and 1.25, respectively.

Figure 10-44 shows a support plate for the gears. The dimensions for the support plate were derived from the gear pitch diameters and an allowance of about .50 between the gear pitch diameters and the edge of the support plate. For example, the pitch diameter of the larger gear is 2.50. Allowing .50 between the top edge and the bottom edge gives .50 + 2.50 + .50 = 3.50.

The pitch diameter for the smaller gear is .83. Adding the .50 edge distance gives a distance of 1.33 from the smaller gear's center point. In this example the distance was rounded up to 1.50. The center distance between the gears is 1.67. Therefore, the total length of the support plate is 1.50 + 1.67 + 1.67 + 1.75 = 6.59, or about 6.75. The height will be 3.50.

Each of the gears has a 1/2 nominal shaft diameter. For this example a value of .50 will be assigned to both the gear bores and the holes in the support plate. Bearings are not included in this example.

Figure 10-45 shows a $\varnothing.50 \times 2.00$ shaft that will be used to support the gears.

Create an **Assembly** drawing using the support plate, three $\varnothing.50 \times 2.00$ shafts, and the four gears. The gears were created using the given

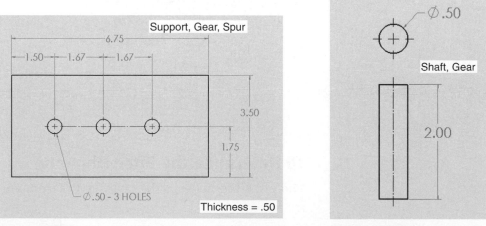

Figure 10-44

Figure 10-45

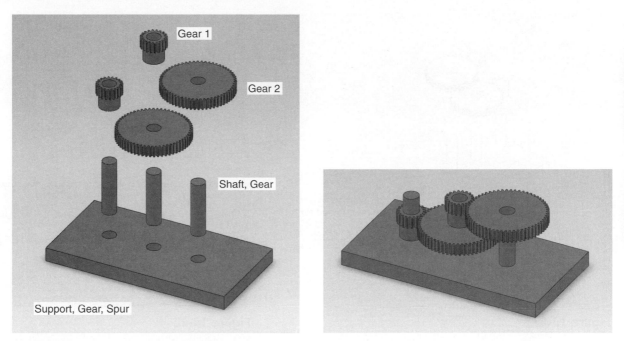

Gear 1

Gear 2

Shaft, Gear

Support, Gear, Spur

Figure 10-46

information. Figure 10-46 shows the components in their assembled position. Save the assembly as **ASSEMBLY, THREE GEAR.** The gears are offset .60 from the support and from each other on the gear shafts.

Create an exploded drawing using the three-gear assembly in the **Isometric** orientation with no hidden lines. See Figure 10-47. Access the **Annotation** menu, add balloons, click the **Tables** tool, and select the **Bill of Materials** tool. Locate the bill of materials (BOM) as shown.

The PART NUMBER column does not show part numbers but lists the file names assigned to each part and, in the case of the gears, a listing of gear parameters.

To Edit the Bill of Materials

See Figure 10-47. SolidWorks will automatically insert the part's file name as its part number.

1 Double-click the first cell under the heading **DESCRIPTION.**

A warning dialog box will appear. See Figure 10-48.

2 Click **Break Link.**

An editing text box will appear in the cell. See Figure 10-49.

3 Type in the part description.

In this example the file name SUPPORT, GEAR, SPUR was used, and the text was left aligned.

> **NOTE**
> The description was typed using only uppercase letters. Uppercase letters are the preferred convention.

4 Complete the editing of the DESCRIPTION column.

5 Click the PART NUMBER column and add part numbers as shown.

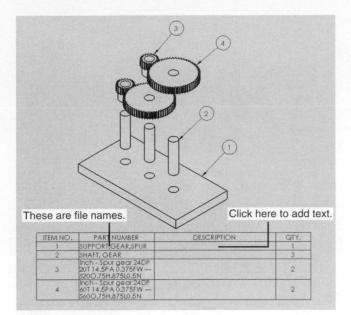

These are file names.

Click here to add text.

ITEM NO.	PART NUMBER	DESCRIPTION	QTY.
1	SUPPORT,GEAR,SPUR		1
2	SHAFT, GEAR		3
3	Inch - Spur gear 24DP 20T 14.5PA 0.375FW — S20O.75H.875L0.5N		2
4	Inch - Spur gear 24DP 60T 14.5PA 0.375FW — S60O.75H.875L0.5N		2

Figure 10-47

SolidWorks 2011

The cell value is linked to a property in a read-only external model. Do you want to break the link and override the value in the BOM?

Note: If you break the link, you can restore it by clearing the cell.

Break Link   No

☐ Don't ask me again   Click here.

Figure 10-48

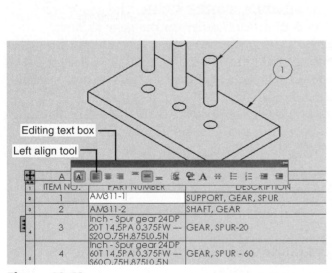

Editing text box

Left align tool

ITEM NO.	PART NUMBER	DESCRIPTION
1	AM311-1	SUPPORT, GEAR, SPUR
2	AM311-2	SHAFT, GEAR
3	Inch - Spur gear 24DP 20T 14.5PA 0.375FW — S20O.75H.875L0.5N	GEAR, SPUR-20
4	Inch - Spur gear 24DP 60T 14.5PA 0.375FW — S60O.75H.875L0.5N	GEAR, SPUR - 60

Figure 10-49

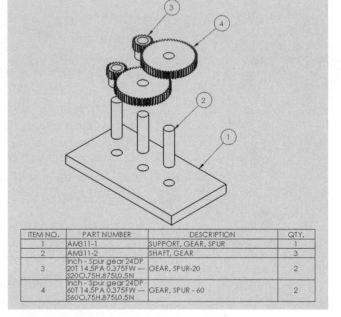

ITEM NO.	PART NUMBER	DESCRIPTION	QTY.
1	AM311-1	SUPPORT, GEAR, SPUR	1
2	AM311-2	SHAFT, GEAR	3
3	Inch - Spur gear 24DP 20T 14.5PA 0.375FW — S20O.75H.875L0.5N	GEAR, SPUR-20	2
4	Inch - Spur gear 24DP 60T 14.5PA 0.375FW — S60O.75H.875L0.5N	GEAR, SPUR - 60	2

Figure 10-50

NOTE

Part numbers differ from item numbers (assembly numbers). The support plate is item number 1 and has a part number of AM311-1. If the plate was to be used in another assembly, it might have a different item number, but it will always have the same AM311-1 part number.

The gears' part numbers were accepted as is because they are standard numbers assigned to each gear. In general, manufacturers' part numbers are used directly. See Figure 10-50.

The Three Gear Assembly can be animated using the **Mechanical Mates** tool.

1 Click the **Mate** tool.

2 Click the **Mechanical Mates** heading.

3 Click the **Gear** tool.

4 Click the edge of **Gear 1.**

The gear name should appear in the **Mate Selections** box.

5 Click **Gear 2.**

6 Set the gear ratio to **1:2**

See Figure 10-51.

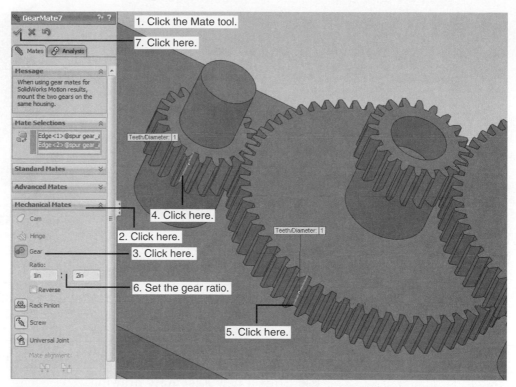

Figure 10-51

7 Create a **Gear Mate** between Gear 2 and the second Gear 1, located on the same shaft, and set the gear ratio for **1:1.**

The gears are on the same shaft, so they will rotate at the same speed.

8 Create a **Gear Mate** between the second Gear 1 and the second Gear 2 and set the gear ratio for **1:2.**

Figure 10-52 shows mates used to create the animated assembly.

9 Use the cursor to rotate Gear 1.

The gears should rotate.

The total gear ratio is

$$\left(\frac{3}{1}\right)\left(\frac{3}{1}\right) = \frac{9}{1}$$

Therefore, if the first Gear 1 rotates at 1750 RPM, the second Gear 2 will rotate at 194.4RPM:

1750/9 = 194.4 RPM

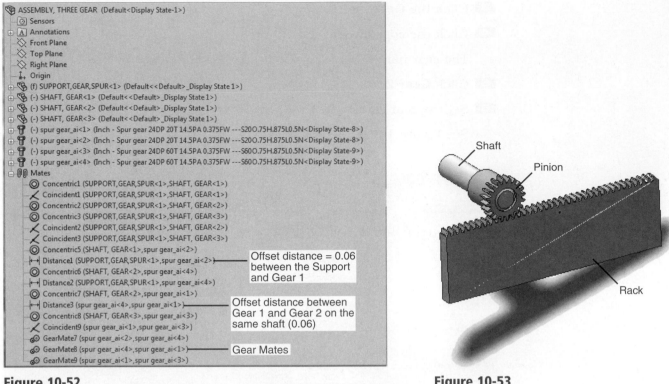

Figure 10-52

Figure 10-53

10-11 Rack and Pinion Gears

Figure 10-53 shows a rack and pinion gear setup. It was created using the **Assembly** format starting with a ∅.50 × 2.25 shaft and with a rack and pinion gear from the **Design Library.**

1 Draw a ∅**.50 × 2.25** shaft with a **0.30** chamfer at each end.

2 Start a new **Assembly** drawing.

3 Insert the ∅.50 × 2.25 shaft.

The shaft will serve as a base for the gears and a reference for animation.

4 Access the **Design Library, Toolbox, Ansi inches, Power Transmission, Gears,** and click and drag a **Rack (Spur Rectangular)** into the drawing area.

5 Set the rack's properties as shown in Figure 10-54.

6 Click and drag a spur gear into the drawing area.

The spur gear will become the pinion.

7 Set the pinion's properties as shown in Figure 10-55.

8 Reorient the components and use the **Mate** tool to insert the pinion onto the shaft.

See Figure 10-56.

Remember that the shaft was entered into the assembly first, so its position is fixed. Use the **Float** option to move the shaft.

9 Use the **Mate** tool to make the top surface of the pinion parallel with the front flat surface of the rack.

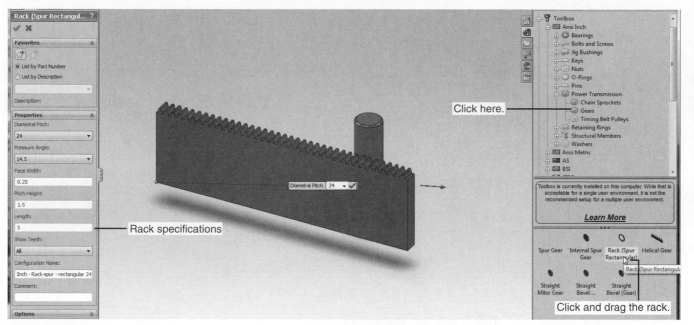

Figure 10-54

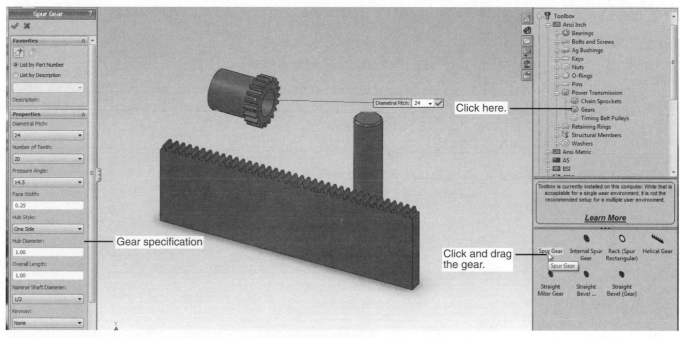

Figure 10-55

10 Use the **Mate** tool and align the top surface (not an edge) of one of the pinion's teeth with the bottom surface of one of the rack's teeth.

See Figure 10-57.

11 Adjust the pinion as needed to create a proper fit between the pinion and the rack by locating the cursor on the pinion and rotating the pinion.

To Animate the Rack and Pinion

See Figure 10-58. This animation is based on the rack and pinion setup created in the previous section.

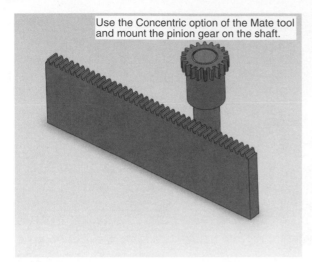

Use the Concentric option of the Mate tool and mount the pinion gear on the shaft.

Figure 10-56

Mate the pinion gear to the rack teeth.

Figure 10-57

1 Click the **Mate** tool.

2 Click **Mechanical Mates.**

3 Click the **Rack Pinion** option.

4 Click the front edge of the rack's teeth.

5 Click the pinion gear (not an edge).

6 Click the **Reverse** box so that a check mark appears.

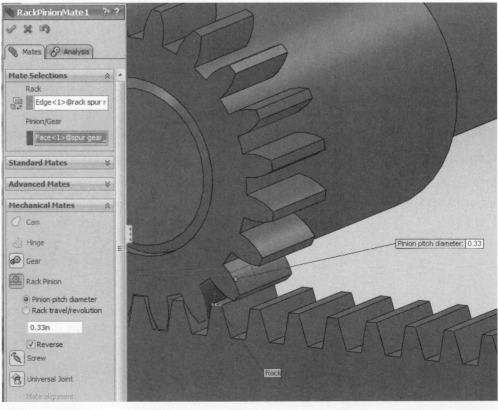

Figure 10-58

7 Click the OK check mark.

8 Use the cursor to rotate the pinion.

The rack will slide back and forth as the pinion is moved.

10-12 Metric Gears

Gears created using the metric system are very similar to gears created using English units with one major exception. Gears in the English system use the term *pitch* to refer to the number of teeth per inch. Gears in the metric system use the term **module** to refer to the pitch diameter divided by the number of teeth. As meshing gears in the English system must have the same pitch, so meshing gears in the metric system must have the same module.

To Create a Metric Gear

See Figure 10-59

1 Start a new **Part** document and set the units for **MMGS.**

2 Draw a Ø**16 × 60** millimeter shaft. Save the shaft as Ø**16 × 60.**

3 Start a new **Assembly** drawing and insert the Ø16 × 60 shaft.

4 Access the **Design Library.**

5 Click **Toolbox, Ansi Metric, Power Transmission,** and **Gears.**

6 Click and drag a spur gear into the drawing area.

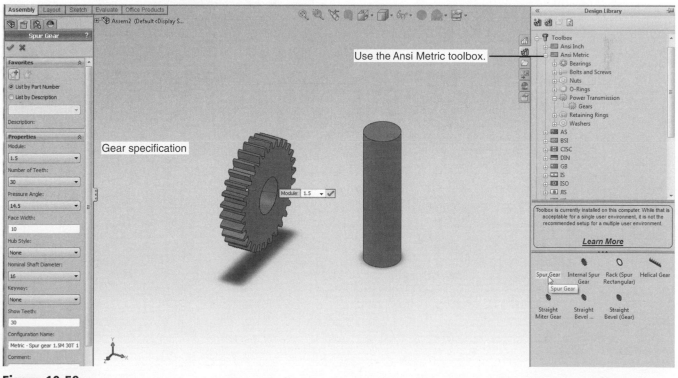

Figure 10-59

7 Define the gear's properties as follows:

   a. Module = **1.5**

   b. Number of Teeth = **30**

   c. Pressure Angle = **14.5**

   d. Face Width = **10**

   e. Hub Style = **None**

   f. Nominal Shaft Diameter = **16**

   g. Keyway = **None**

8 Use the **Mate** tool and assemble the gear onto the shaft.

Figure 10-60 shows the gear assembled on to the shaft.

Figure 10-60

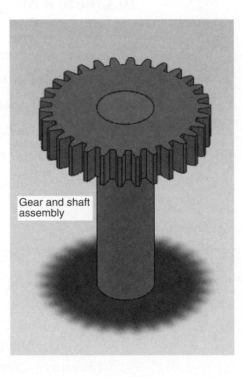

Gear and shaft assembly

Chapter Projects

Project 10-1: Inches

See Figure P10-1.

  1. Create a Ø.375 × 1.75 shaft.

    A. Create a spur gear based on the following specifications:

      Diametral Pitch = **32**

      Number of Teeth = **36**

      Pressure Angle = **14.5**

      Face Width = **.250**

      Hub Style = **None**

      Nominal Shaft Diameter = **3/8**

      Keyway = **None**

    B. Assemble the gear onto the shaft with a .25 offset from the end of the shaft.

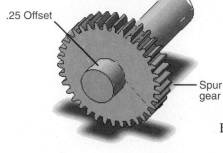

Ø.375 x 1.75 Shaft

.25 Offset

Spur gear

Figure P10-1

Project 10-2: Inches

    A. Create a Ø.250 × 1.50 shaft.

    B. Create a spur gear based on the following specifications:

      Diametral Pitch = **40**

      Number of Teeth = **56**

      Pressure Angle = **14.5**

      Face Width = **.125**

      Hub Style = **None**

      Nominal Shaft Diameter = **1/4**

      Keyway = **None**

    C. Assemble the gear onto the shaft with a .125 offset from the end of the shaft.

Project 10-3: Inches

    A. Create a Ø1.00 × 4.00 shaft.

    B. Create a spur gear based on the following specifications:

      Diametral Pitch = **8**

      Number of Teeth = **66**

      Pressure Angle = **14.5**

      Face Width = **.625**

Hub Style = **None**

Nominal Shaft Diameter = **1**

Keyway = **None**

C. Assemble the gear onto the shaft with a 0.00 offset from the end of the shaft.

Project 10-4: Millimeters

A. Create a Ø8.0 × 30 shaft.

B. Create a spur gear based on the following specifications:

Module = **2**

Number of Teeth = **40**

Pressure Angle = **14.5**

Face Width = **12**

Hub Style = **None**

Nominal Shaft Diameter = **8**

Keyway = **None**

C. Assemble the gear onto the shaft with a 5.0 offset from the end of the shaft.

Project 10-5: Inches

See Figure P10-5.

A. Create a Ø.625 × 4.00 shaft.

Figure P10-5

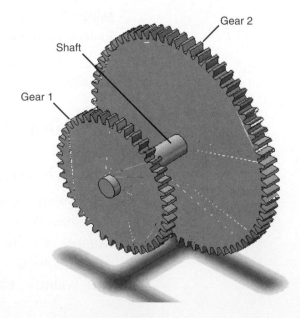

Gear 2

Shaft

Gear 1

B. Create a spur gear based on the following specifications:

Gear 1:

Diametral Pitch = **10**

Number of Teeth = **42**

Pressure Angle = **14.5**

Face Width = **.375**

Hub Style = **None**

Nominal Shaft Diameter = **5/8**

Keyway = **None**

C. Create a second gear based on the following specifications:

Gear 2:

Diametral Pitch = **10**

Number of Teeth = **68**

Pressure Angle = **14.5**

Face Width = **.500**

Hub Style = **None**

Nominal Shaft Diameter = **5/8**

Keyway = **None**

D. Assemble the gears onto the shaft with Gear 1 offset .25 from the front end of the shaft and Gear 2 offset 3.00 from the front end of the shaft.

Project 10-6: Inches

A. Create a Ø.25 × 2.75 shaft.

B. Create a spur gear based on the following specifications:

Gear 1:

Diametral Pitch = **40**

Number of Teeth = **18**

Pressure Angle = **14.5**

Face Width = **.125**

Hub Style = **None**

Nominal Shaft Diameter = **1/4**

Keyway = **None**

C. Create a second gear based on the following specifications:

Gear 2:

Diametral Pitch = **40**

Number of Teeth = **54**

Pressure Angle = **14.5**

Face Width = **.125**

Hub Style = **None**

Nominal Shaft Diameter = **1/4**

Keyway = **None**

D. Assemble the gears onto the shaft with Gear 1 offset .125 from the front end of the shaft and Gear 2 offset 2.00 from the front end of the shaft.

Project 10-7: Millimeters

A. Create a Ø12 × 80 shaft.

B. Create a spur gear based on the following specifications:

Gear 1:

Module = **1.0**

Number of Teeth = **16**

Pressure Angle = **14.5**

Face Width = **8**

Hub Style = **None**

Nominal Shaft Diameter = **12**

Keyway = **None**

C. Create a second gear based on the following specifications:

Gear 2:

Module = **1.0**

Number of Teeth = **48**

Pressure Angle = **14.5**

Face Width = **10**

Hub Style = **None**

Nominal Shaft Diameter = **12**

Keyway = **None**

D. Assemble the gears onto the shaft with Gear 1 offset 5 from the front end of the shaft and Gear 2 offset 50 from the front end of the shaft.

Project 10-8: Inches

See Figure P10-8.

A. Create a Ø.375 × 2.75 shaft. Save the shaft.

B. Create a spur gear based on the following specifications:

Gear 1:

Diametral Pitch = **10**

Number of Teeth = **22**

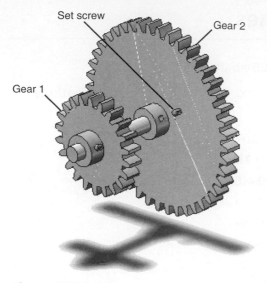

Set screw

Gear 2

Gear 1

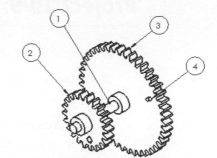

ITEM NO.	PART NUMBER	DESCRIPTION	QTY.
1	AM-311-A1	Ø.375 × 2.75 SHAFT	1
2	AM311-A2	GEAR 1 - N22	1
3	AM311-A3	GEAR 2 - N44	1
4	#6-32 UNC	SET SCREW	2

Figure P10-8

Pressure Angle = **14.5**

Face Width = **.375**

Hub Style = **One Side**

Hub Diameter = **.75**

Overall Length = **.75**

Nominal Shaft Diameter = **3/8**

Keyway = **None**

C. Create another spur gear based on the following specifications:

Gear 2:

Diametral Pitch = **10**

Number of Teeth = **44**

Pressure Angle = **14.5**

Face Width = **.375**

Hub Style = **One Side**

Hub Diameter = **.75**

Overall Length = **.75**

Nominal Shaft Diameter = **3/8**

Keyway = **None**

D. Add #6-32 threaded holes to each gear hub .19 from the top hub surface.

E. Assemble the gears onto the shaft with Gear 1 offset .25 from the front end of the shaft and Gear 2 offset 2.25 from the front end of the shaft.

F. Insert a #6-32 Slotted Set Screw with an Oval Point into each hole.

G. Create an exploded assembly drawing.

H. Create a bill of materials.

I. Animate the assembly.

Project 10-9: Inches

A. Create a Ø.375 × 3.25 shaft. Save the shaft.

B. Create a spur gear based on the following specifications:

Gear 1:

Diametral Pitch = **20**

Number of Teeth = **18**

Pressure Angle = **14.5**

Face Width = **.25**

Hub Style = **One Side**

Hub Diameter = **.50**

Overall Length = **.50**

Nominal Shaft Diameter = **3/8**

Keyway = **None**

C. Create another spur gear based on the following specifications:

Gear 2:

Diametral Pitch = **20**

Number of Teeth = **63**

Pressure Angle = **14.5**

Face Width = **.25**

Hub Style = **One Side**

Hub Diameter = **.50**

Overall Length = **.50**

Nominal Shaft Diameter = **3/8**

Keyway = **None**

D. Add #4-40 threaded holes to each gear hub .19 from the top hub surface.

E. Assemble the gears onto the shaft with Gear 1 offset .25 from the front end of the shaft and Gear 2 offset 2.63 from the front end of the shaft.

Project 10-10: Millimeters

A. Create a 24 × 120 shaft. Save the shaft.

B. Create a spur gear based on the following specifications:

Gear 1:

Module = **1.5**

Number of Teeth = **18**

Pressure Angle = **14.5**

Face Width = **12**

Hub Style = **One Side**

Hub Diameter = **32**

Overall Length = **30**

Nominal Shaft Diameter = **16**

Keyway = **None**

C. Create another spur gear based on the following specifications:

Gear 2:

Module = **1.5**

Number of Teeth = **70**

Pressure Angle = **14.5**

Face Width = **12**

Hub Style = **One Side**

Hub Diameter = **40**

Overall Length = **30**

Nominal Shaft Diameter = **16**

Keyway = **None**

D. Add M3.0 threaded holes to each gear hub 10 from the top hub surface.

E. Assemble the gears onto the shaft with Gear 1 offset 4.0 from the front end of the shaft and Gear 2 offset 80.0 from the front end of the shaft.

F. Insert an M3 Socket Set Screw with a Cup Point into each hole.

G. Create an exploded assembly drawing.

H. Create a bill of materials.

I. Animate the assembly.

Project 10-11: Inches

See Figure P10-11.

A. Draw three Ø.375 × 3.00 shafts.

B. Draw the support plate shown.

C. Access the **Design Library** and create two Gear 1s and two Gear 2s.

The gears are defined as follows:

Gear 1:

Diametral Pitch = **16**

Number of Teeth = **24**

Pressure Angle = **14.5**

Face Width = **.25**

Hub Style = **One Side**

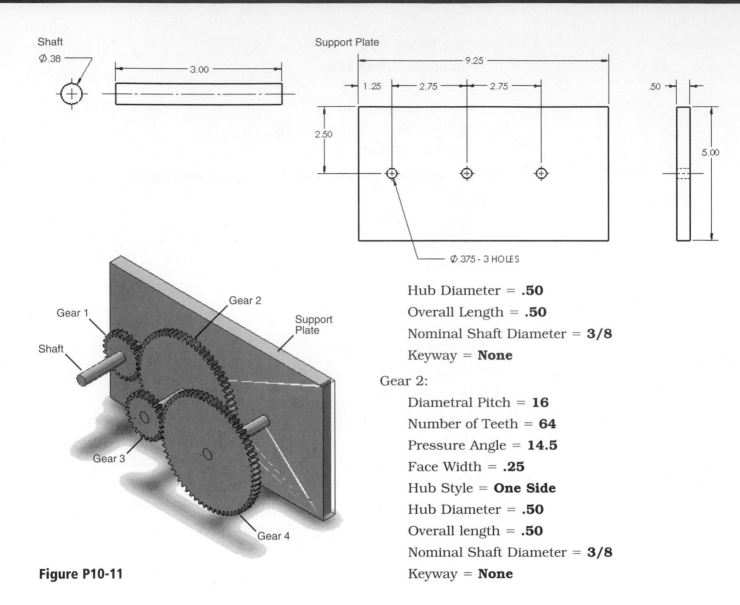

Shaft

⌀.38

3.00

Support Plate

9.25

1.25   2.75   2.75

2.50

.50

5.00

⌀.375 - 3 HOLES

Gear 1

Shaft

Gear 3

Gear 2

Support Plate

Gear 4

Figure P10-11

Hub Diameter = **.50**

Overall Length = **.50**

Nominal Shaft Diameter = **3/8**

Keyway = **None**

Gear 2:

Diametral Pitch = **16**

Number of Teeth = **64**

Pressure Angle = **14.5**

Face Width = **.25**

Hub Style = **One Side**

Hub Diameter = **.50**

Overall length = **.50**

Nominal Shaft Diameter = **3/8**

Keyway = **None**

D. Add #6-32 threaded holes to each gear hub .19 from the top hub surface.

E. Assemble the gears onto the shafts so that Gear 1 and Gear 2 are offset .50 from the support plate, and Gear 3 and Gear 4 are parallel to the ends of the shafts.

F. Insert a #6-32 Slotted Set Screw with an Oval Point into each hole.

G. Create an exploded assembly drawing.

H. Create a bill of materials.

I. Animate the assembly.

Project 10-12: Inches—Design Problem

Based on Figure P10-11 define a support plate and shafts that support the following gears. Use two of each gear.

Parameters:

Plate: .50 thick, a distance of at least .50 beyond the other edge of the gears to the edge of the plate.

Shafts: Diameters that match the gear's bore diameter; minimum offset between the plate and the gear is .50 or greater.

Gear 1:

Diametral Pitch = **10**

Number of Teeth = **24**

Pressure Angle = **14.5**

Face Width = **.375**

Hub Style = **One Side**

Hub Diameter = **1.00**

Overall Length = **.875**

Nominal Shaft Diameter = **7/16**

Keyway = **None**

A. Create another spur gear based on the following specifications:

Gear 2:

Diametral Pitch = **10**

Number of Teeth = **96**

Pressure Angle = **14.5**

Face Width = **.375**

Hub Style = **One Side**

Hub Diameter = **1.00**

Overall Length = **.875**

Nominal Shaft Diameter = **7/16**

Keyway = **None**

B. Add #6-32 threaded holes to each gear hub .19 from the top hub surface.

C. Assemble the gears onto the shafts so that Gear 1 and Gear 2 are offset .50 from the support plate, and Gear 3 and Gear 4 are parallel to the ends of the shafts.

D. Insert a #6-32 Slotted Set Screw with an Oval Point into each hole.

E. Create an exploded assembly drawing.

F. Create a bill of materials.

G. Animate the assembly.

Project 10-13: Inches—Design Problem

Based on Figure P10-11 define a support plate and shafts that support the following gears. Use two of each gear.

Parameters:

Plate: .50 thick, a distance of at least .50 beyond the other edge of the gears to the edge of the plate.

Shafts: Diameters that match the gear's bore diameter: minimum offset between the plate and the gear is .50 or greater.

Gear 1:

Diametral Pitch = **6**

Number of Teeth = **22**

Pressure Angle = **14.5**

Face Width = **.500**

Hub Style = **One Side**

Hub Diameter = **1.50**

Overall Length = **1.25**

Nominal Shaft Diameter = **.75**

Keyway = **None**

Gear 2:

Diametral Pitch = **6**

Number of Teeth = **77**

Pressure Angle = **14.5**

Face Width = **.50**

Hub Style = **One Side**

Hub Diameter = **1.50**

Overall Length = **1.25**

Nominal Shaft Diameter = **.75**

Keyway = **None**

A. Add 1/4-20 UNC threaded holes to each gear hub 0.25 from the top hub surface.

B. Assemble the gears onto the shafts so that Gear 1 and Gear 2 are offset .50 from the support plate, and Gear 3 and Gear 4 are parallel to the ends of the shafts.

C. Insert a 1/4-20 UNC Slotted Set Screw with an Oval Point into each hole.

D. Create an exploded assembly drawing.

E. Create a bill of materials.

F. Animate the assembly.

Project 10-14: Millimeters—Design Problem

Based on Figure P10-11 define a support plate and shafts that support the following gears. Use two of each gear.

Parameters:

Plate: 20 thick, a distance of at least 25 beyond the other edge of the gears to the edge of the plate.

Shafts: Diameters that match the gear's bore diameter; minimum offset between the plate and the gear is 20 or greater.

Gear 1:

Module = **2.5**

Number of Teeth = **20**

Pressure Angle = **14.5**

Face Width = **16**

Hub Style = **One Side**

Hub Diameter = **26**

Overall Length = **30**

Nominal Shaft Diameter = **20**

Keyway = **None**

Gear 2:

Module = **2.5**

Number of Teeth = **50**

Pressure Angle = **14.5**

Face Width = **16**

Hub Style = **One Side**

Hub Diameter = **30**

Overall Length = **30**

Nominal Shaft Diameter = **20**

Keyway = **None**

A. Add M4 threaded holes to each gear hub 12 from the top hub surface.

B. Assemble the gears onto the shafts so that Gear 1 and Gear 2 are offset 10 from the support plate, and Gear 3 and Gear 4 are parallel to the ends of the shafts.

C. Insert an M4 Slotted Set Screw with an Oval Point into each hole.

D. Create an exploded assembly drawing.

E. Create a bill of materials.

F. Animate the assembly.

Project 10-15: Inches

See Figure P10-15.

A. Draw four Ø.375 × 3.00 shafts.

B. Draw the support plate shown in Figure P10-15.

C. Access the **Design Library** and create three Gear 1s and three Gear 2s.

The gears are defined as follows:

Gear 1:

Diametral Pitch = **16**

Number of Teeth = **24**

Pressure Angle = **14.5**

Face Width = **.25**

Hub Style = **One Side**

Hub Diameter = **.50**

Overall Length = **.50**

Nominal Shaft Diameter = **3/8**

Keyway = **None**

Figure P10-15

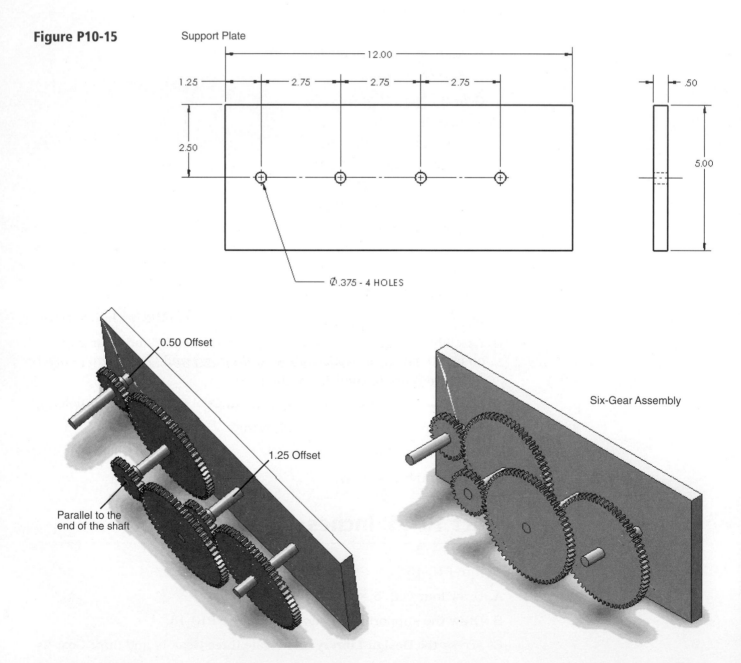

Support Plate

Six-Gear Assembly

Gear 2:

    Diametral Pitch = **16**

    Number of Teeth = **64**

    Pressure Angle = **14.5**

    Face Width = **.25**

    Hub Style = **One Side**

    Hub Diameter = **.50**

    Overall Length = **.50**

    Nominal Shaft Diameter = **3/8**

    Keyway = **None**

D. Add #6-32 threaded holes to each gear hub 0.19 from the top hub surface.

E. Assemble the gears onto the shafts so that the offset between the support plate and the gears is as defined in Figure P10-15.

F. Insert a #6-32 Slotted Set Screw with an Oval Point into each hole.

G. Create an exploded assembly drawing.

H. Create a bill of materials.

I. Animate the assembly.

Project 10-16: Inches—Design Problem

Based on Figure P10-15 define a support plate and shafts that support the following gears. Use two of each gear.

Parameters:

Plate: .50 thick, a distance of at least .50 beyond the other edge of the gears to the edge of the plate.

Shafts: Diameters that match the gear's bore diameter; minimum offset between the plate and the gear is .50 or greater.

Gear 1:

    Diametral Pitch = **6**

    Number of Teeth = **22**

    Pressure Angle = **14.5**

    Face Width = **.500**

    Hub Style = **One Side**

    Hub Diameter = **1.50**

    Overall Length = **1.25**

    Nominal Shaft Diameter = **.75**

    Keyway = **None**

Gear 2:

> Diametral Pitch = **6**
>
> Number of Teeth = **77**
>
> Pressure Angle = **14.5**
>
> Face Width = **.50**
>
> Hub Style = **One Side**
>
> Hub Diameter = **1.50**
>
> Overall Length = **1.25**
>
> Nominal Shaft Diameter = **.75**
>
> Keyway = **None**

A. Add 1/4-20 UNC threaded holes to each gear hub .25 from the top hub surface.

B. Assemble the gears onto the shafts so that Gear 1 and Gear 2 are offset .50 from the support plate, and Gear 3 and Gear 4 are parallel to the ends of the shafts.

C. Insert a 1/4-20 UNC Slotted Set Screw with an Oval Point into each hole.

D. Create an exploded assembly drawing.

E. Create a bill of materials.

F. Animate the assembly.

Project 10-17: Millimeters—Design Problem

Based on Figure P10-15 define a support plate and shafts that support the following gears. Use two of each gear.

Parameters:

> Plate: 20 thick, a distance of at least 25 beyond the other edge of the gears to the edge of the plate.
>
> Shafts: Diameters that match the gear's bore diameter; minimum offset between the plate and the gear is 20 or greater.

Gear 1:

> Module = **2.5**
>
> Number of Teeth = **20**
>
> Pressure Angle = **14.5**
>
> Face Width = **16**
>
> Hub Style = **One Side**
>
> Hub Diameter = **26**
>
> Overall Length = **30**
>
> Nominal Shaft Diameter = **20**
>
> Keyway = **None**

Gear 2:

 Module = **2.5**

 Number of Teeth = **50**

 Pressure Angle = **14.5**

 Face Width = **16**

 Hub Style = **One Side**

 Hub Diameter = **30**

 Overall Length = **30**

 Nominal Shaft Diameter = **20**

 Keyway = **None**

A. Add M4 threaded holes to each gear hub 12 from the top hub surface.

B. Assemble the gears onto the shafts so that Gear 1 and Gear 2 are offset 10 from the support plate, and Gear 3 and Gear 4 are parallel to the ends of the shafts.

C. Insert an M4 Slotted Set Screw with an Oval Point into each hole.

D. Create an exploded assembly drawing.

E. Create a bill of materials.

F. Animate the assembly.

Project 10-18: Inches—Design Problem

Redraw the following gear assembly. Create the following:

A. An assembly drawing

B. An exploded isometric drawing

Figure P10-18

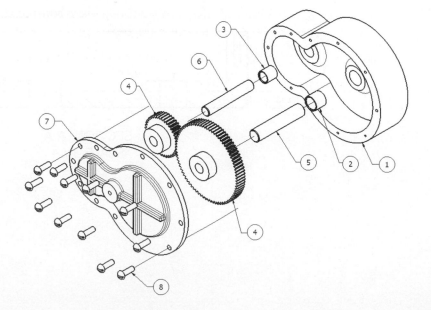

C. A BOM

D. Dimensioned drawings of each part

Parts from the **Toolbox** do not need drawings but should be listed on the BOM.

Figure P10-18
(*Continued*)

		Parts List		
ITEM	PART NUMBER	DESCRIPTION	MATERIAL	QTY
1	ENG-453-A	GEAR, HOUSING	CAST IRON	1
2	BU-1123	BUSHING Ø0.75	Delrin, Black	1
3	BU-1126	BUSHING Ø0.625	Delrin, Black	1
4	ASSEMBLY-6	GEAR ASSEEMBLY	STEEL	1
5	AM-314	SHAFT, GEAR Ø.625	STEEL	1
6	AM-315	SHAFT, GEAR Ø.0.500	STEEL	1
7	ENG -566-B	COVER, GEAR	CAST IRON	1
8	ANSI B18.6.2 - 1/4-20 UNC - 0.75	Slotted Round Head Cap Screw	Steel, Mild	12

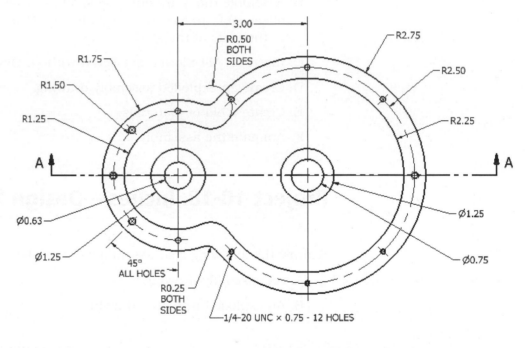

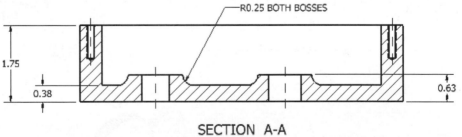

SECTION A-A
SCALE 3 / 4

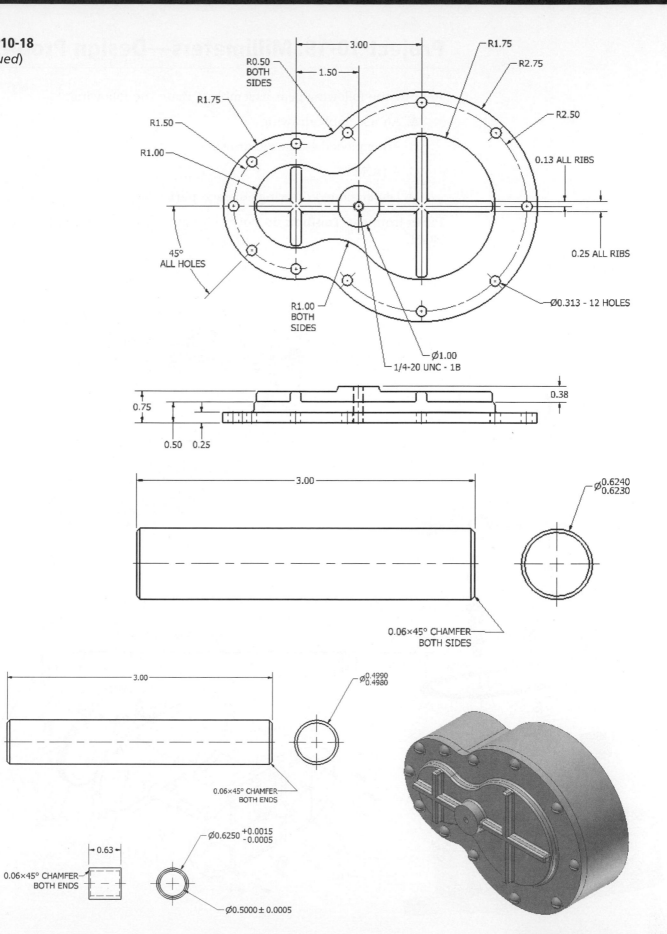

Project 10-19: Millimeters—Design Problem

Redraw the following gear assembly. Create the following:

    A. An assembly drawing

    B. An exploded isometric drawing

    C. A BOM

    D. Dimensioned drawings of each part

Parts from the **Toolbox** do not need drawings but should be listed on the BOM.

Figure P10-19

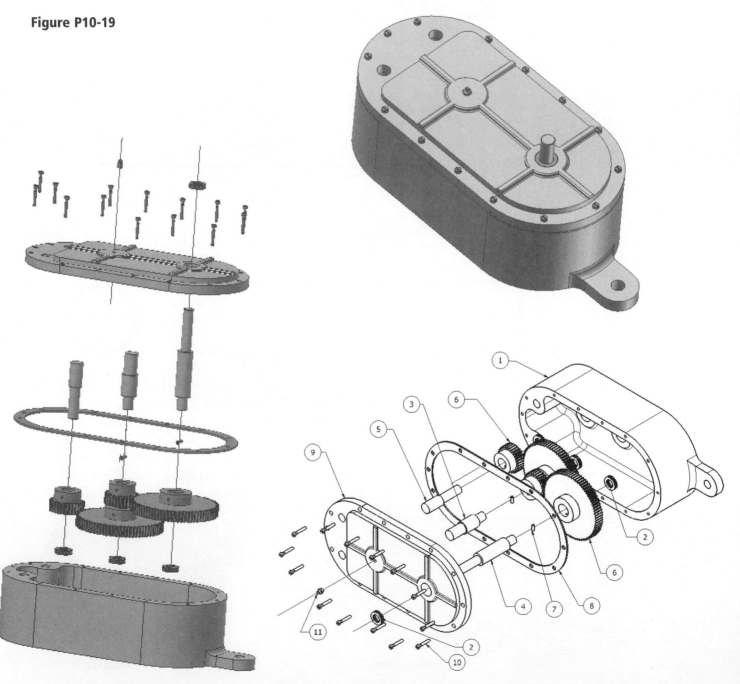

		Parts List		
ITEM	PART NUMBER	DESCRIPTION	MATERIAL	QTY
1	ENG-311-1	4-GEAR HOUSING	CAST IRON	1
2	BS 5989: Part 1 - 0 10 - 20x32x8	Thrust Thrust Ball Bearing	Steel, Mild	4
3	SH-4002	SHAFT, NEUTRAL	STEEL	1
4	SH-4003	SHAFT, OUTPUT	STEEL	1
5	SH-4004A	SHAFT, INPUT	STEEL	1
6	4-GEAR-ASSEMBLY		STEEL	2
7	CSN 02 1181 - M6 x 16	Slotted Headless Set Screw - Flat Point	Steel, Mild	2
8	ENG-312-1	GASKET	Brass, Soft Yellow	1
9	COVER			1
10	CNS 4355 - M 6 x 35	Slotted Cheese Head Screw	Steel, Mild	14
11	CSN 02 7421 - M10 x 1coned short	Lubricating Nipple, coned Type A	Steel, Mild	1

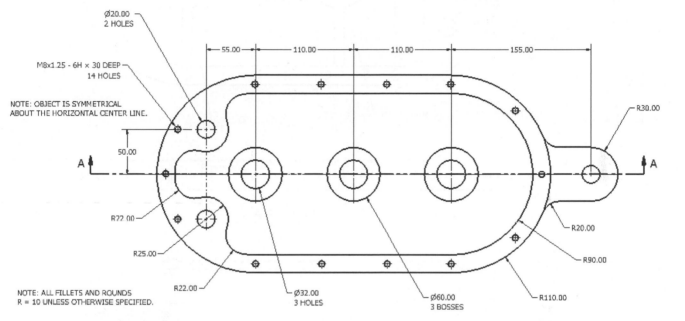

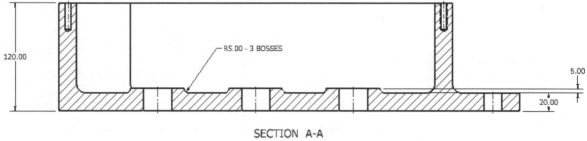

SECTION A-A
SCALE 1 / 2

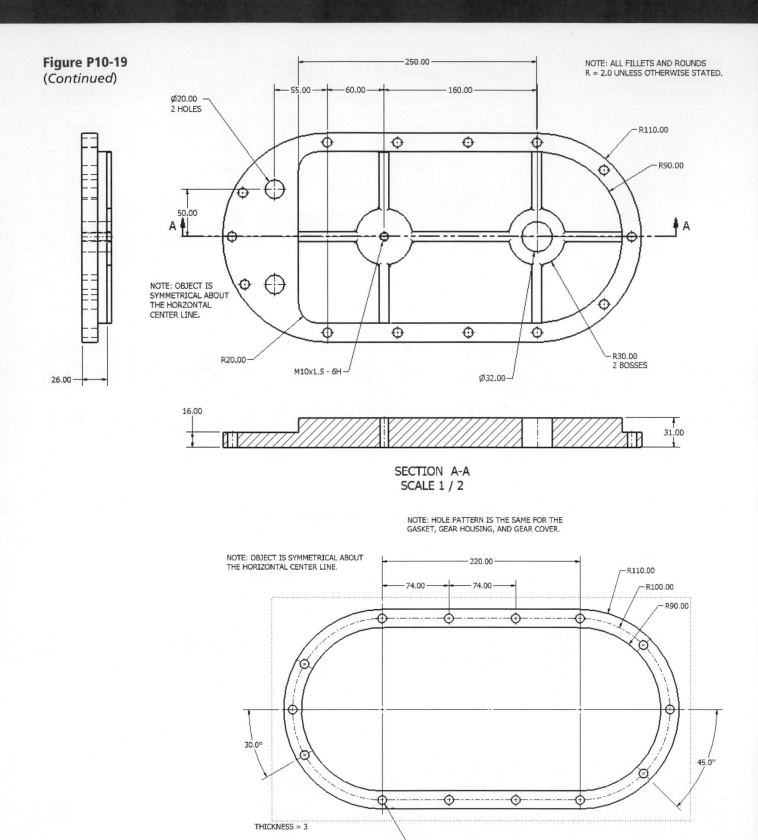

NOTE: ALL FILLETS AND ROUNDS
R = 2.0 UNLESS OTHERWISE STATED.

Ø20.00
2 HOLES

R110.00

R90.00

250.00

55.00

60.00

160.00

50.00

A

A

NOTE: OBJECT IS
SYMMETRICAL ABOUT
THE HORZONTAL
CENTER LINE.

R20.00

M10x1.5 - 6H

Ø32.00

R30.00
2 BOSSES

26.00

16.00

31.00

SECTION A-A
SCALE 1 / 2

NOTE: HOLE PATTERN IS THE SAME FOR THE
GASKET, GEAR HOUSING, AND GEAR COVER.

NOTE: OBJECT IS SYMMETRICAL ABOUT
THE HORIZONTAL CENTER LINE.

220.00

74.00

74.00

R110.00

R100.00

R90.00

30.0°

45.0°

THICKNESS = 3

Ø10.00 - 14 HOLES

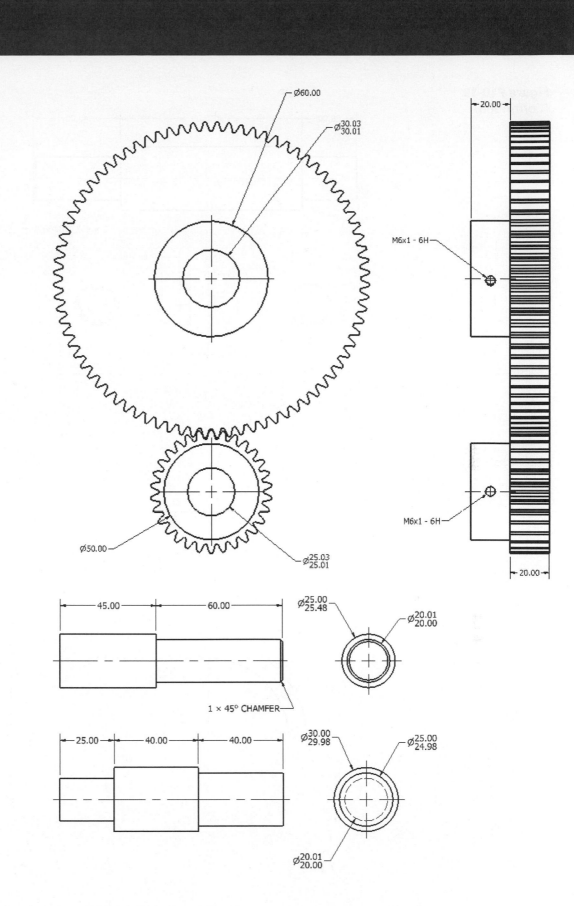

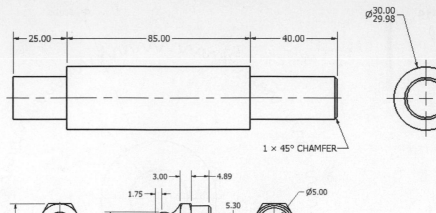

1 × 45° CHAMFER

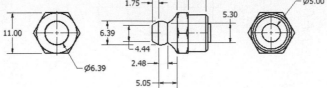

CHAPTER OBJECTIVES

- Learn to draw belts and pulleys
- Understand the use of standard sizes for designs using belts and pulleys

11-1 Introduction

Belts and pulleys are another form of power transmission. They are cheaper than gears, require less stringent tolerances, can be used to cover greater distances, and can absorb shock better. However, belts cannot take as much load as gears and can slip or creep, and operate at slower speeds.

11-2 Belt and Pulley Standard Sizes

There are many different-sized belts and pulleys. Listed here are belt designations, belt overall thicknesses, belt widths, and pulley widths that can be used to create assemblies within the context of this text. For other belt and pulley properties see manufacturers' specifications.

Standard Belt Sizes—Single-Sided Belt Thickness
Mini Extra Light: MXL (0.080)—0.045
Extra Light: XL (0.200)—0.09
Light: L (0.375)—0.14
Heavy: H (0.500)—0.16
Extra Heavy: XL (0.875)—0.44
Double Extra Heavy: XXL (1.250)—0.62

Standard Pulley Widths
MXL: 0.25
XL: 0.38
L: 0.50, 0.75, 1.00
H: 1.00, 1.50, 2.00, 3.00
XH: 2.00, 3.00, 4.00
XXH: 2.00, 3.00, 4.00, 5.00

Standard Belt Widths
XXL—0.12, 0.19, 0.25
XL—0.25, 0.38
L—0.50, 0.75, 1.00
H—0.75, 1.00, 1.50, 2.00, 3.00,
XH—2.00, 3.00, 4.00
XXH—2.00, 3.00, 4.00, 5.00

To Draw a Belt and Pulley Assembly

Figure 11-1 shows dimensioned drawings of the support plate and shaft.

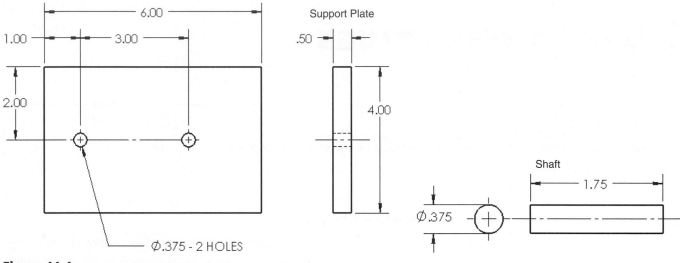

Figure 11-1

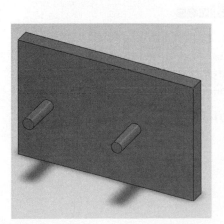

Figure 11-2

1 Create **Part** documents of the support plate and the shaft

2 Assemble two shafts into the support plate. The shafts should extend **1.25** beyond the support plate.

See Figure 11-2.

3 Access the **Design Library** and click **Toolbox, Ansi Inch, Power Transmission,** and **Timing Belts.**

4 Click and drag a **Timing Belt Pulley** into the drawing area.

5 Set the properties as follows: Belt Pitch = **(0.200)** = **XL,** Belt Width = **0.38,** Pulley Style = **Flanged,** Number of grooves = **20,** Hub Diameter = **.500,** Overall Length = **.500,** Keyway = **None,** Nominal Shaft Diameter = **3/8.**

See Figure 11-3.

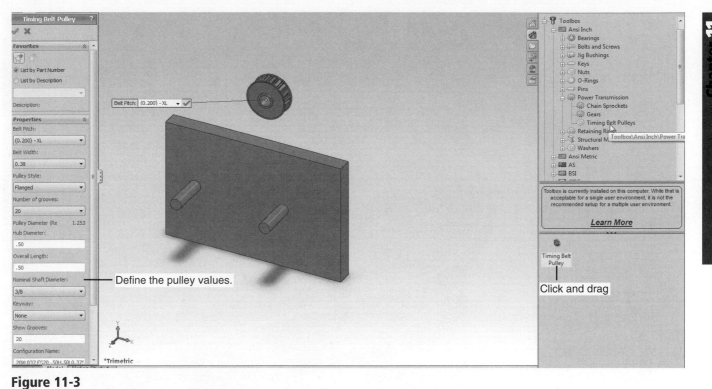

Figure 11-3

6 Create two pulleys.

7 Assemble the pulleys onto the ends of the shafts.

See Figure 11-4.

8 Click the **Insert** tool at the top of the screen, click **Assembly Feature,** then **Belt/Chain.**

See Figure 11-5.

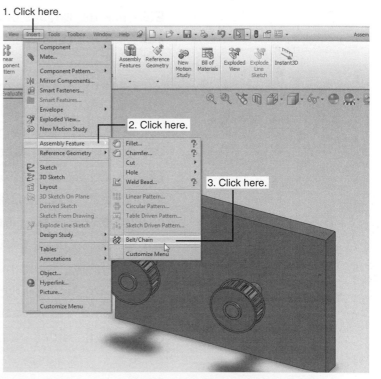

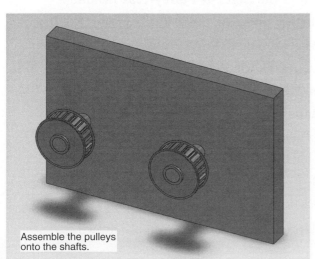

Figure 11-4

Figure 11-5

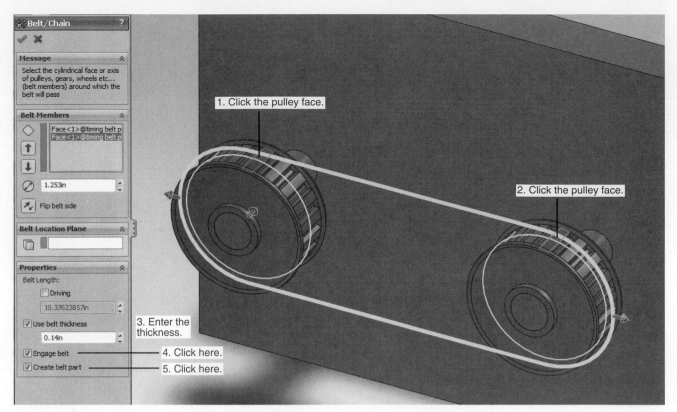

Figure 11-6

9. Select the **Belt Members** by clicking the top surfaces on the pulleys' teeth as shown.

See Figure 11-6.

10. Scroll down the **Belt/Chain PropertyManager,** click the **Use belt thickness** box, and set the thickness for **0.14in.**

11. Click the **Engage belt** box.

12. Click the **Create belt part** box.

13. Click the OK check mark.

14. Click the + sign to the left of the **Belt1** heading in the **FeatureManager.**

15. Click the + sign to the left of the **Belt1-9 Pulley-test** heading.

Your headings may be slightly different. See Figure 11-7.

16. Right-click **Sketch 2** and select the **Edit Sketch** option.

17. Click the **Features** tab to access the **Features** tools.

18. Click the **Extruded Boss/Base** tool.

The **Extrude PropertyManager** will appear. See Figure 11-8.

19. Set **Direction 1** for **Mid Plane.**

20. Set the belt width value for **0.42in.**

This width keeps the belt inside the flanges.

21. Click the **Thin Feature** option and set the thickness for **0.14in.**

22. Click the OK check mark and return to the assembly drawing.

See Figure 11-9.

23. Save the assembly as **Belt Assembly.**

Figure 11-7

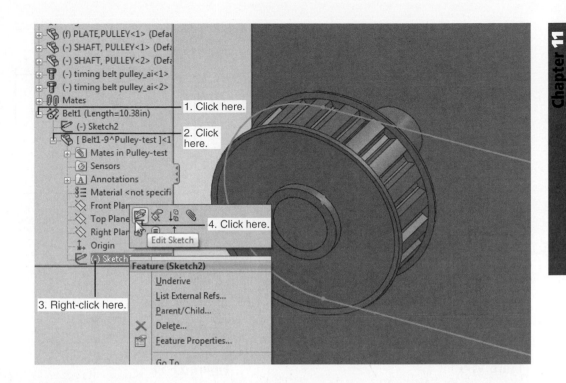

Figure 11-8

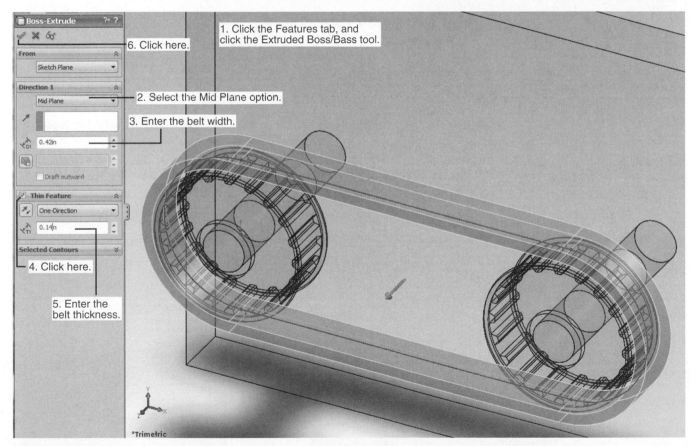

11-3 Pulleys and Keys

Figure 11-10 shows a dimensioned drawing of the support plate defined in Figure 11-1 and a shaft. The shaft includes a keyway defined to accept a .125 × .125 × .250 square key.

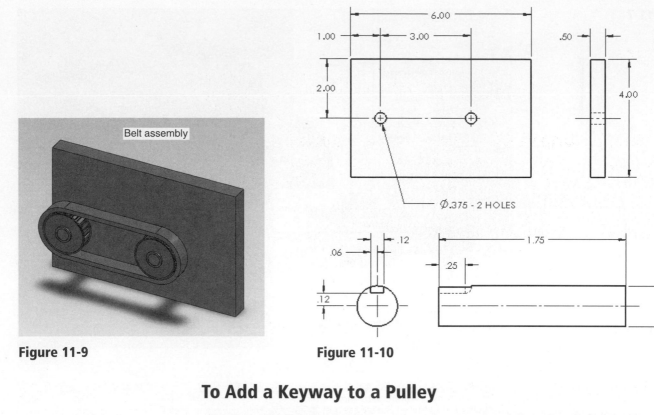

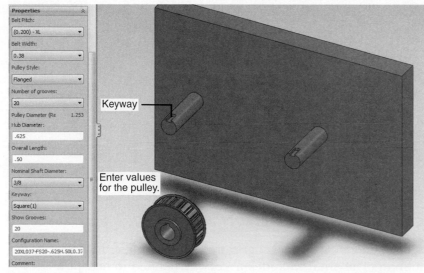

Figure 11-9

Figure 11-10

To Add a Keyway to a Pulley

1 Access the **Design Library,** click **Toolbox, Ansi Inch, Power Transmission,** and **Timing Belt Pulley.**

2 Click and drag a pulley into the drawing area.

3 Set the values as shown in Figure 10-60. Set the **Keyway** for **Square 1.**

See Figure 11-11.

4 Create a second pulley identical to the first and click the OK check mark.

5 Assemble the pulleys onto the shafts.

See Figure 11-12.

Figure 11-11

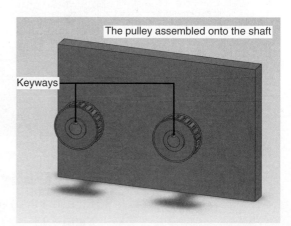

Figure 11-12

Enter the values for key.

Click and drag

Figure 11-13

---

6 Access the **Design Library,** click **Toolbox, Ansi Inch, Keys,** and **Parallel Keys.**

7 Click and drag a key into the drawing area.

See Figure 11-13.

8 Set the key's **Properties** values for a shaft diameter of **7/16 − 9/16.** Set the **Length** for **.25.**

9 Create a second key and click the OK check mark.

10 Assemble the keys into the keyways and add a timing belt as defined in the last section.

See Figure 11-14.

11-4 Multiple Pulleys

More than one pulley can be included in an assembly. Figure 11-15 shows drawings for a support plate and shaft.

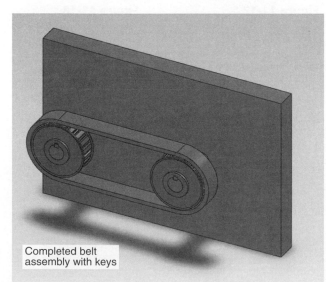

Completed belt assembly with keys

Figure 11-14

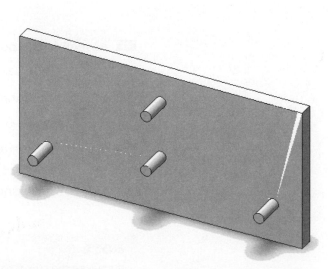

Figure 11-15

To Create a Multi-Pulley Assembly

1 Create an **Assembly** drawing of the support plate and shafts with the shafts inserted into the support plate so that the shafts extend 1.00 beyond the surface of the support plate.

See Figure 11-16.

2 Create two XL pulleys with the properties specified in Figure 11-17.

3 Create two L pulleys with the properties specified in Figure 11-18.

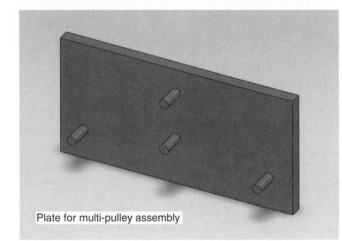

Plate for multi-pulley assembly

Figure 11-16

XL pulley properties

Properties	⌃
Belt Pitch:	
(0.200) - XL ▾	
Belt Width:	
0.38 ▾	
Pulley Style:	
Flanged ▾	
Number of grooves:	
20 ▾	
Pulley Diameter (Re	1.253
Hub Diameter:	
.50	
Overall Length:	
.50	
Nominal Shaft Diameter:	
3/8 ▾	
Keyway:	
None ▾	
Show Grooves:	
20	

Figure 11-17

L pulley properties

Properties	⌃
Belt Pitch:	
(0.375) - L ▾	
Belt Width:	
0.5 ▾	
Pulley Style:	
Flanged ▾	
Number of grooves:	
20 ▾	
Pulley Diameter (Re	2.357
Hub Diameter:	
.50	
Overall Length:	
.50	
Nominal Shaft Diameter:	
3/8 ▾	
Keyway:	
None ▾	
Show Grooves:	
20	

Figure 11-18

4 Assemble the pulleys onto the shafts as shown.

See Figure 11-5.

5 Click **Insert, Assembly Feature,** and **Belt/Chain.**

See Figure 11-5.

6 Click the top surface of the pulley's teeth to identify the belt location. Use the belt position shown. Use the **Flip belt side** tool if necessary.

Figure 11-20 shows the assembly with a belt profile.

> **NOTE**
> If you use the cursor to rotate the edge line of one of the pulleys, they will all rotate.

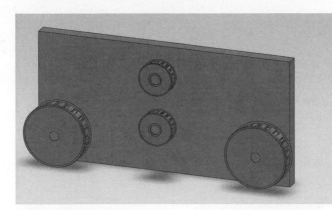

Figure 11-19

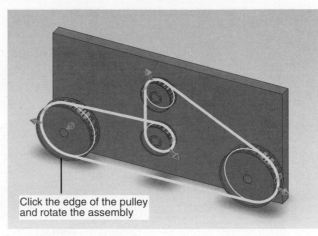

Click the edge of the pulley
and rotate the assembly

Figure 11-20

11-5 Chains and Sprockets

SolidWorks creates chains and sprockets in a manner similar to that used to create belts and pulleys. The resulting chain is a representation of a chain but looks like a belt representation.

Figure 11-21 shows a support plate and a shaft that will be used to create a chain and sprocket assembly.

To Create a Chain and Sprocket Assembly

1 Draw the support plate and shaft shown in Figure 11-21 and create an **Assembly** drawing. The shafts should extend 3.00 beyond the top surface of the support plate.

See Figure 11-22.

2 Access the **Design Library** and click **Toolbox, Ansi Inch, Power Transmission,** and **Chain Sprockets.**

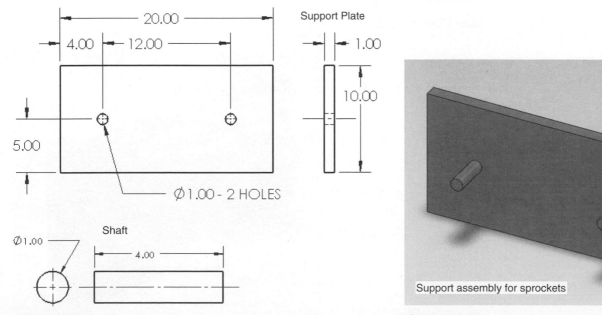

Support assembly for sprockets

Figure 11-21

Figure 11-22

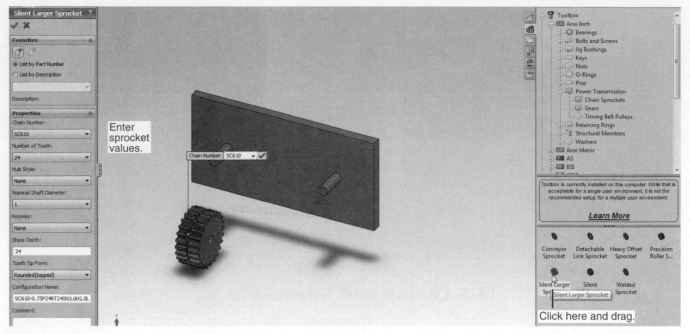

Figure 11-23

Click **Silent Larger Sprocket** and drag the icon into the field of the drawing.

See Figure 11-23.

Set the following chain property values:

Chain Number = **SC610**

Number of Teeth = **24**

Hub Style = **None**

Nominal Shaft Diameter = **1**

Keyway = **None**

Create a second Silent Larger Sprocket and assemble the sprockets onto the shafts.

See Figure 11-24.

Figure 11-24

Assemble the sprockets.

6 Click **Insert** at the top of the screen, then **Assembly Feature,** and **Belt/Chain.**

See Figure 11-5.

7 Click the bottom surface of a sprocket tooth, as shown, on both sprockets.

See Figure 11-25.

8 Click the OK check mark.

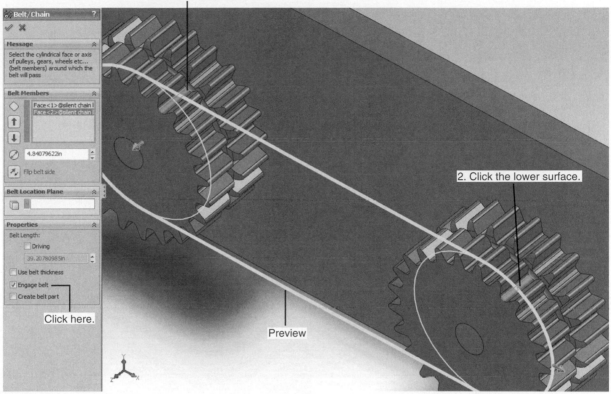

1. Click the lower surface.

2. Click the lower surface.

Preview

Click here.

Figure 11-25

To Add Thickness and Width to the Chain

1 Right-click **Belt1** in the **FeatureManager** and select the **Edit Feature** option.

2 In the **Belt1** box scroll down and click the **Create belt part** box.

3 Click the OK check mark.

4 Save the assembly as **Sprocket Assembly.**

5 Click the + sign to the left of the **Belt1** heading in the **FeatureManager.** Click the + sign to the left of the **[Belt1, Assem . .]** heading, right-click the **Sketch2** heading, and select the **Edit Part** option.

See Figure 11-26.

6 Left-click the upper horizontal segment of the belt (chain) and select the **Edit Sketch** option.

7 Click the **Extrude Boss/Base** tool on the **Features** toolbar.

Set **Direction 1** for **Blind, D1** for **2.00in,** and **Thin Feature** value for **0.125in.**

See Figures 11-27 and Figure 11-28.

Figure 11-26

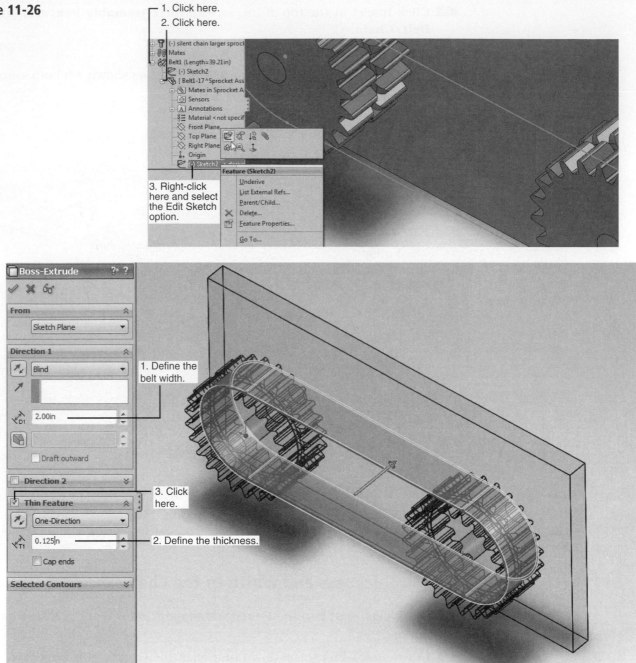

1. Click here.
2. Click here.

(-) silent chain larger sproc
Mates
Belt1 (Length=39.21in)
  (-) Sketch2
  [Belt1-17^Sprocket Ass
  Mates in Sprocket A
  Sensors
  Annotations
  Material <not specif
  Front Plane
  Top Plane
  Right Plane
  Origin
  (-) Sketch2

3. Right-click here and select the Edit Sketch option.

Feature (Sketch2)

Underive
List External Refs...
Parent/Child...
Delete...
Feature Properties...

Go To...

Boss-Extrude

From
Sketch Plane

Direction 1
Blind

2.00in

Draft outward

Direction 2

Thin Feature
One-Direction

0.125in

Cap ends

Selected Contours

1. Define the belt width.

3. Click here.

2. Define the thickness.

Figure 11-27

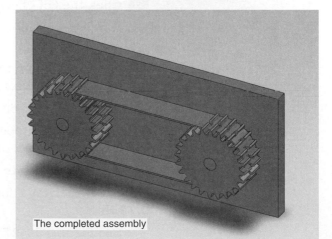

The completed assembly

Figure 11-28

Chapter Projects

Project 11-1: Inches

See Figure P11-1.

    A.   Create a Ø.375 × 2.00 shaft.

    B.   Create the support plate shown.

    C.   Access the **Design Library** and create two pulleys.

The pulleys are defined as follows:

        Pulley 1:
            Belt Pitch = **(.375)–L**
            Belt Width = **.5**
            Pulley Style = **Flanged**
            Number of Grooves = **20**

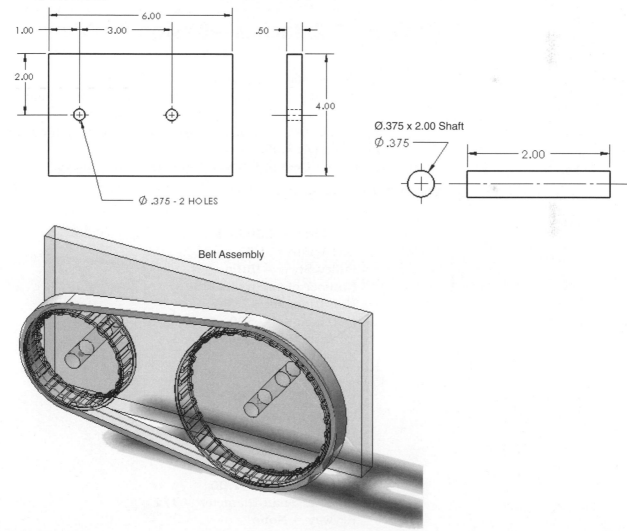

Figure P11-1

Hub Diameter = **.375**
Overall Length = **.500**
Nominal Shaft Diameter = **3/8**
Keyway = **None**

Pulley 2:
Belt Pitch = **(.375)–L**
Belt Width = **.5**
Pulley Style = **Flanged**
Number of Grooves = **32**
Hub Diameter = **.375**
Overall Length = **.500**
Nominal Shaft Diameter = **3/8**
Keyway = **None**

D. Assemble the shafts into the support plate.
E. Assemble the pulleys onto the shafts.
F. Add a timing belt between the pulleys. Make the belt a thin feature with a .14 thickness. Make the width of the belt .42.

Project 11-2: Inches—Design Problem

A. Create a Ø.500 × 3.50 shaft.
B. Create a support plate so that the center distance between the pulleys' center points is 5.52 and the distance between the outside edge of the pulleys and the edge of the support plate is at least .50 but less than 1.00.
C. Access the **Design Library** and create two pulleys.

The pulleys are defined as follows:

Pulley 1:
Belt Pitch = **(.500)–H**
Belt Width = **1.5**
Pulley Style = **Unflanged**
Number of Grooves = **26**
Hub Diameter = **.500**
Hub Length = **.500**
Nominal Shaft Diameter = **1/2**
Keyway = **None**

Pulley 2:
Belt Pitch = **(.500)–H**
Belt Width = **1.5**
Pulley Style = **Unflanged**
Number of Grooves = **44**
Hub Diameter = **.75**
Overall Length = **1.00**
Nominal Shaft Diameter = **1/2**
Keyway = **None**

D. Assemble the shafts into the support plate.

E. Assemble the pulleys onto the shafts.

F. Add a timing belt between the pulleys. Make the belt a thin feature with a .16 thickness. Make the width of the belt 1.50 in.

Project 11-3: Inches—Design Problem

A. Create a Ø.500 × 4.50 shaft.

B. Create a support plate so that the center distance between the pulleys' center points is 21.50 and the distance between the outside edge of the pulleys and the edge of the support plate is at least .50 but less than 1.00.

C. Access the **Design Library** and create two pulleys.

The pulleys are defined as follows:

Pulley 1:
    Belt Pitch = **(.875)–XH**
    Belt Width = **2**
    Pulley Style = **Unflanged**
    Number of Grooves = **30**
    Hub Diameter = **1.00**
    Overall Length = **4.00**
    Nominal Shaft Diameter = **1/2**
    Keyway = **None**

Pulley 2:
    Belt Pitch = **(.875)–XH**
    Belt Width = **2.0**
    Pulley Style = **Unflanged**
    Number of Grooves = **48**
    Hub Diameter = **1.00**
    Overall Length = **4.00**
    Nominal Shaft Diameter = **1/2**
    Keyway = **None**

D. Assemble the shafts into the support plate.

E. Assemble the pulleys onto the shafts.

F. Add a #10-24 threaded hole to each pulley hub and insert a #10-24 UNC Slotted Set Screw Dog Point into each threaded hole.

G. Add a timing belt between the pulleys. Make the belt a thin feature with a .44 thickness. Make the width of the belt 2.00.

Project 11-4: Inches

Create a support plate and shaft as defined in Figure P11-4.

A. Create three Ø.375 × 3.00 shafts.

B. Create three identical pulleys as defined below.

C. Assemble the shafts into the support plate.

D. Assemble the pulleys onto the shafts.

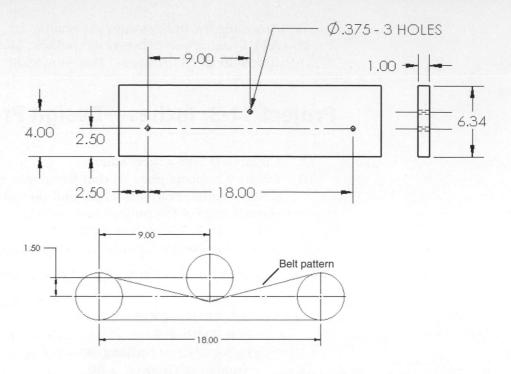

E.   Add a timing belt between the pulleys in the pattern shown. Make the belt a thin feature with a .14 thickness. Make the width of the belt .42.

Pulley Properties:
        Belt Pitch = **(.375)–L**
        Belt Width = **.5**
        Pulley Style = **Flanged**
        Number of Grooves = **32**
        Hub Diameter = **.375**
        Overall Length = **.500**
        Nominal Shaft Diameter = **3/8**
        Keyway = **None**

Project 11-5: Inches

A.   Create a support plate and shaft as defined in Figure P11-5.
B.   Create four Ø.375 × 3.00 shafts.
C.   Create three identical pulleys as defined below.
D.   Assemble the shafts into the support plate.
E.   Assemble the pulleys onto the shafts.
F.   Add a timing belt between the pulleys in the pattern shown. Make the belt a thin feature with a .14 thickness. Make the width of the belt .42.

Pulley Properties:
        Belt Pitch = **(0.375)–L**
        Belt Width = **.5**
        Pulley Style = **Flanged**

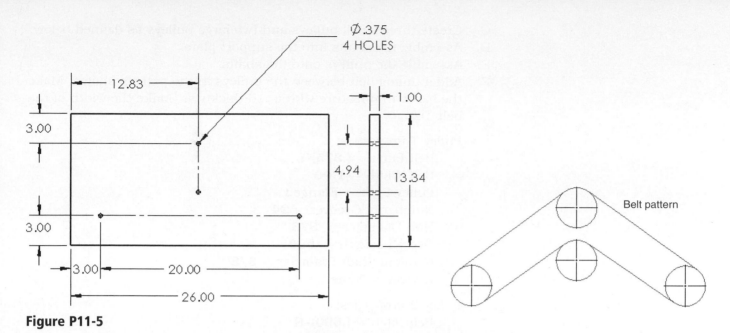

Figure P11-5

Number of Grooves = **32**
Hub Diameter = **.375**
Overall Length = **.500**
Nominal Shaft Diameter = **3/8**
Keyway = **None**

Project 11-6: Inches

A. Create a support plate and shaft as defined in Figure P11-6. Holes labeled A are Ø.375, and holes labeled B are Ø.500.
B. Create three Ø.375 × 3.00 shafts and two Ø.500 × 3.00 shafts.

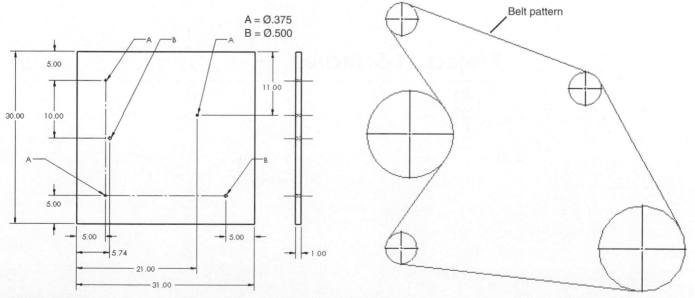

Figure P11-6

C. Create three small pulleys and two large pulleys as defined below.

D. Assemble the shafts into the support plate.

E. Assemble the pulleys onto the shafts.

F. Add a timing belt between the pulleys in the pattern shown. Make the belt a thin feature with a .16 thickness. Make the width of the belt .92.

Pulley 1 Properties:
    Belt Pitch = **(.375)–L**
    Belt Width = **1.00**
    Pulley Style = **Flanged**
    Number of Grooves = **24**
    Hub Diameter = **.375**
    Overall Length = **.500**
    Nominal Shaft Diameter = **3/8**
    Keyway = **None**

Pulley 2 Properties:
    Belt Pitch = **(.500)–H**
    Belt Width = **1.00**
    Pulley Style = **Flanged**
    Number of Grooves = **48**
    Hub Diameter = **.500**
    Overall Length = **.500**
    Nominal Shaft Diameter = **1/2**
    Keyway = **None**

chaptertwelve

Cams

CHAPTER OBJECTIVES

- Learn how to draw cams using SolidWorks
- Learn how to draw displacement diagrams
- Understand the relationship between cams and followers

12-1 Introduction

Cams are mechanical devices used to translate rotary motion into linear motion. Traditionally, cam profiles are designed by first defining a displacement diagram and then transferring the displacement diagram information to a base circle. Figure 12-1 shows a cam and a displacement diagram.

12-2 Base Circle

Cam profiles are defined starting with a base circle. The diameter of the base circle will vary according to the design situation. The edge of the base circle is assumed to be the 0.0 displacement line on the displacement diagram.

12-3 Trace Point

The trace point is the center point of the roller follower. SolidWorks defines the shape of the cam profile by defining the path of the trace point.

Figure 12-1

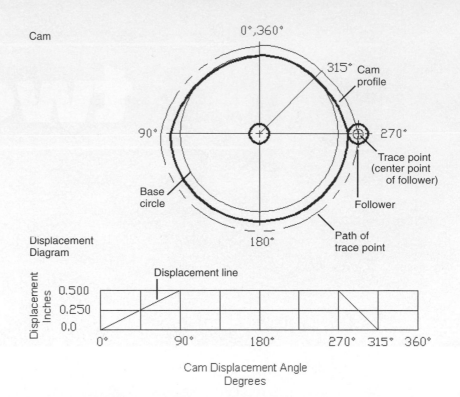

12-4 Dwell, Rise, and Fall

In the displacement diagram shown in Figure 12-1, the displacement line rises .500 in. in the first 90°. This type of motion is called *rise*.

The displacement line then remains at .500 from 90° to 270°. This type of motion is called *dwell*.

> **TIP**
>
> A circle is a shape of constant radius. If a circle was used as a cam, the follower would not go up or down but would remain in the same position, because a circle's radius is constant.

The displacement line falls 0.500 from 270° to 315°. This type of motion is called *fall*. The displacement line dwells between 315° and 360°.

Shape of the Rise and Fall Lines

The shape of the cam's surface during either a rise or a fall is an important design consideration. The shape of the profile will affect the acceleration and deceleration of the follower, and that will in turn affect the forces in both the cam and the follower. SolidWorks includes 13 different types of motions.

Cam Direction

Note that the 90° reference is located on the left side of the cam. This indicates clockwise direction.

12-5 Creating Cams in SolidWorks

Cams are created in SolidWorks by working from existing templates. There are templates for circular and linear cams and for internal and external cams. The templates allow you to work directly on the cam profile and eliminate the need for a displacement diagram. In the following example a circular cam with a 4.00-in. base circle and a profile that rises 0.5 in. in 90° using harmonic motion, dwells for 180°, falls 0.50 in. in 45° using harmonic motions, and dwells for 45°. See the approximate shape of the cam presented in Figure 12-1.

To Access the Cam Tools

1 Create a new **Part** document.

2 Select a **Front Plane** orientation.

3 Click the **Toolbox** heading at the top of the screen.

NOTE

You may have to configure the **Toolbox** as use the **Add-Ins...** feature under the **Tools** heading to add the **Cam** features to your system.

---

4 Click the **Cams** tool.

See Figure 12-2. The **Cam - Circular** toolbox will appear. See Figure 12-3.

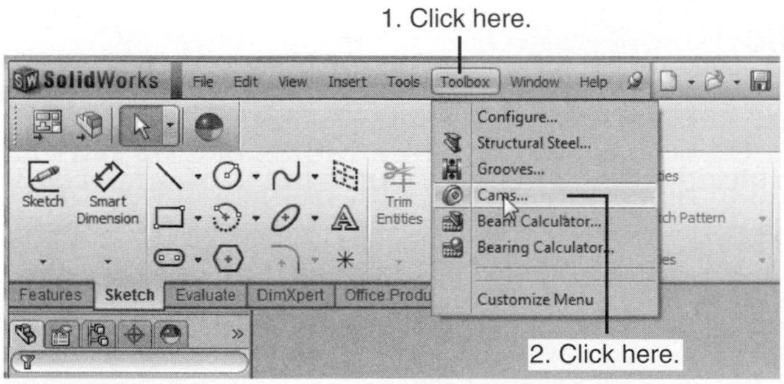

Figure 12-2

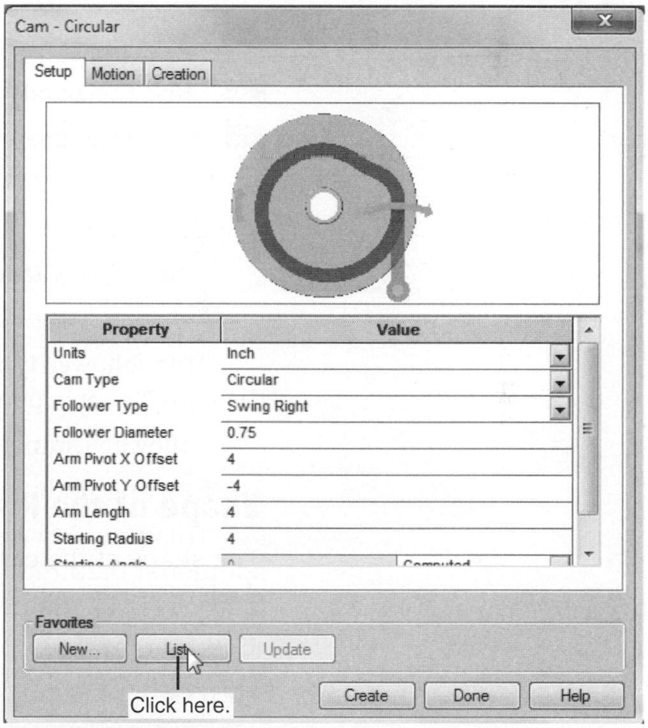

Figure 12-3

12-6 Cam - Circular Setup Tab

1 Click the **List** option on the **Setup** tab of the **Cam - Circular** toolbox.

The **Favorites** dialog box will appear. See Figure 12-4. This box includes a listing of cam templates that can be modified to create a different cam.

2 Click the **Sample 2 - Inch Circular** option.

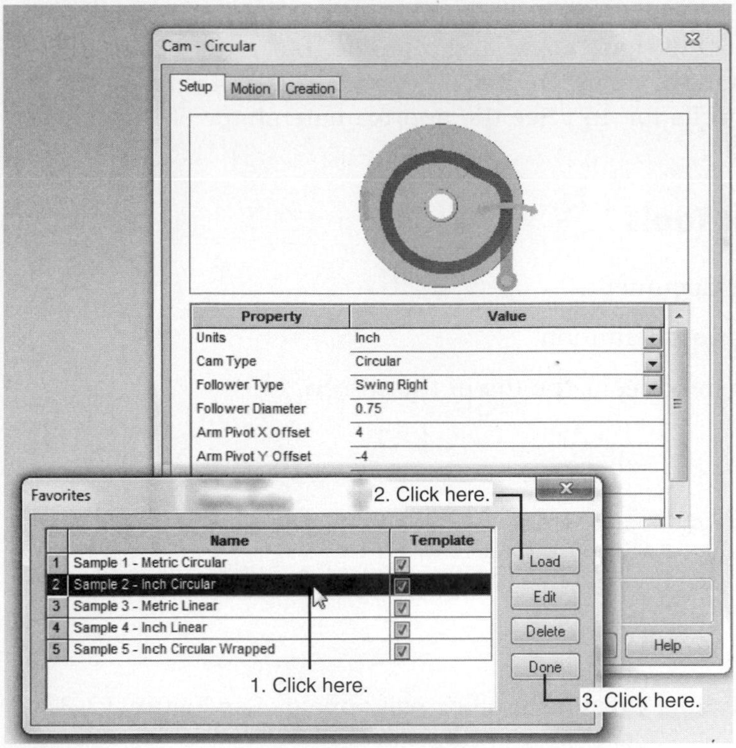

Figure 12-4

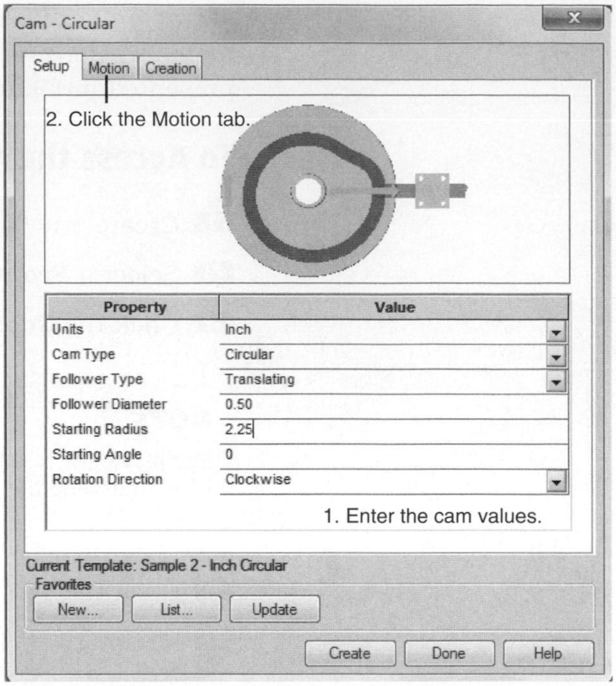

Figure 12-5

3 Click the **Load** box, then click the **Done** box.

4 Define the properties needed for the cam setup.

See Figure 12-5. The properties for the example cam are as follows:

Units: **Inch**

Cam Type: **Circular**

Follower Type: **Translating**

This follower type will locate the follower directly inline with a ray from the cam's center point.

Follower Diameter: **0.50**

Starting Radius: **2.25**

This property defines a Ø4.00 base circle with a radius of 2.00 plus an additional 0.25 radius value to reach the center point of the follower. The follower has a diameter of 0.5.

> **NOTE**
>
> The cam profile is defined by the *path of the trace point*. The trace point is the center point of the circular follower. In this example the trace point at the 0.0° point on the cam is located 2.00 + 0.25 from the center point of the cam.

Starting Angle: **0**

This property defines the ray between the cam's center point and the follower's center point as 0.0°.

Rotation Direction: **Clockwise**

See Figure 12-5.

> **TIP**
>
> Some of the **Value** boxes include other options. SolidWorks will generate real-time previews as these options are clicked. Those interested are encouraged to click and study the various options available.

12-7 Cam - Circular Motion Tab

1 Click the **Motion** tab on the **Cam - Circular** dialog box. See Figure 12-6.

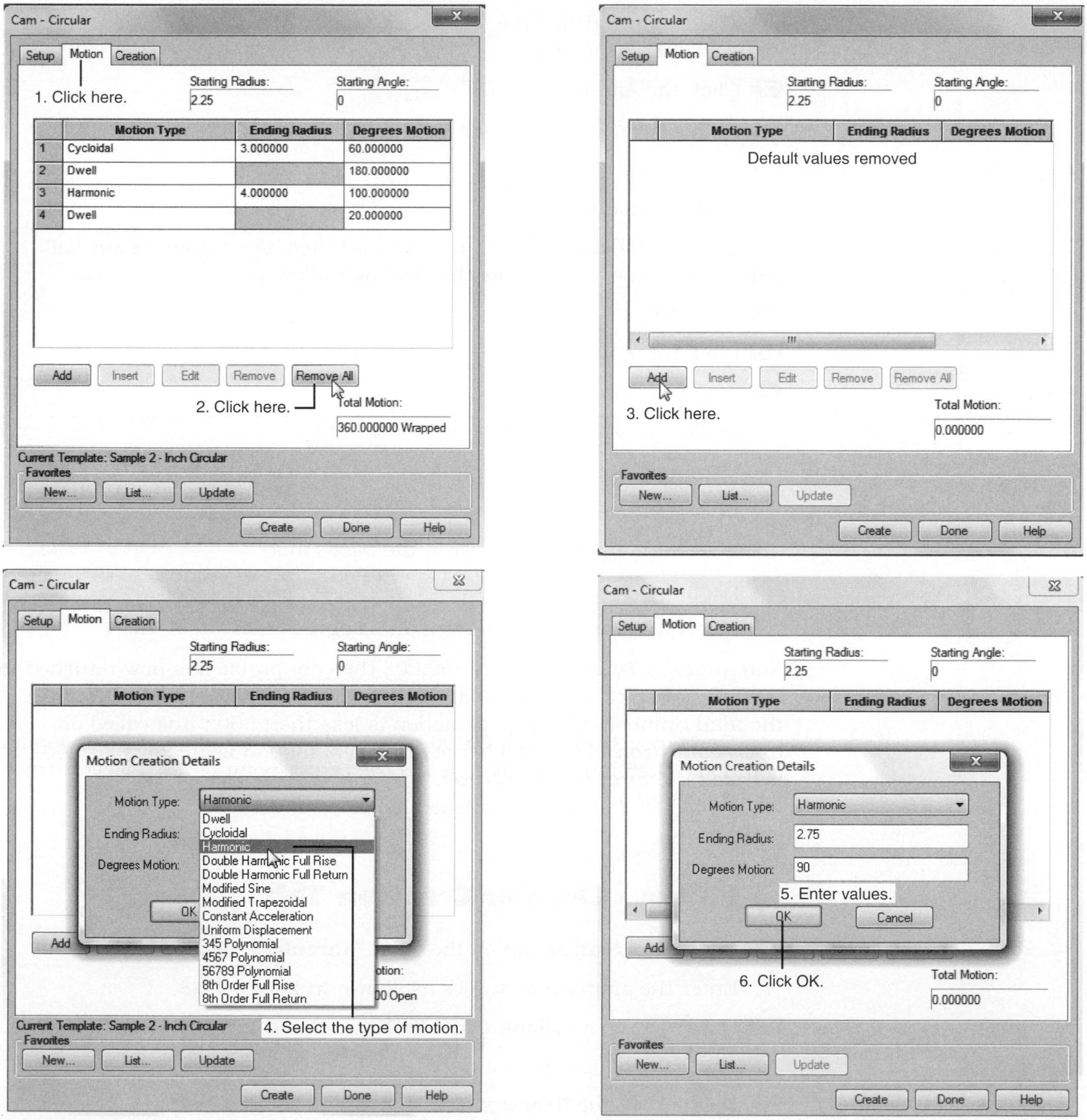

Figure 12-6

2 Click the **Remove All** box.

This step will remove all existing motion types and enable you to define a new cam.

3 Click the **Add** box.

The **Motion Creation Details** dialog box will appear.

4 Click the arrowhead to the right of the **Motion Type** box.

5 Define the **Motion Type** as **Harmonic**.

6 Define the **End Radius** as **2.75** and the **Degrees Motion** as **90**.

These values define the follower rise as 0.50 in. over a distance of 90° using harmonic motion.

7 Click the **Add** box again.

8 Define the following details:

Motion Type: **Dwell**

Degrees Motion: **180.**

Because the dwell motion type was selected, the ending radius will automatically be the same as the starting radius.

9 Click **OK**.

10 Click the **Add** box again.

11 Set the motion as follows:

Motion Type: **Harmonic**

Ending Radius: **2.25**

Degrees Motion: **45.00**

This will return the follower to the base circle.

12 Click the **Add** box again.

13 Select a **Motion Type** of **dwell** and **Degrees Motion** of **45**.

Note that the **Total Motion** is 360.00. The cam profile has now returned to the original starting point of 0.0°. This is called the **closed condition**. If the total number of degrees of motion is less than 360°, it is called an **open condition**. If the number of degrees of motion is greater that 360° it is called the **wrapped condition**.

Figure 12-7 shows the finished **Motion** tab box.

12-8 Cam - Circular Creation Tab

1 Click the **Creation** tab on the **Cam - Circular** dialog box.

Enter the appropriate values as shown in Figure 12-8.

2 Define the cam's **Blank Outside Dia** as **6** and the **Thickness** as **.50** in.

This cam will not have a hub.

3 Define both the **Near** and **Far Hub Dia & Length** as **0**.

4 Define the **Blank Fillet Rad & Chamfer** as **0**.

Cam - Circular

Setup | Motion | Creation

8. Click here.

Starting Radius: 2.25

Starting Angle: 0

	Motion Type	Ending Radius	Degrees Motion
1	Harmonic	2.750000	90.000000
2	Dwell		180.000000
3	Harmonic	2.250000	45.000000
4	Dwell		45.000000

7. Add remaining values needed to define the cam.

Add | Insert | Edit | Remove | Remove All

Total Motion: 360.000000 Closed

Favorites
New... | List... | Update

Create | Done | Help

Figure 12-7

Cam - Circular

Setup | Motion | Creation

CLOSED ONLY

Property	Value	
Near Hub Dia & Length	0	0
Far Hub Dia & Length	0	0
Blank Fillet Rad & Chamfer	0	.040
Thru Hole Dia	0.5	
Track Type & Depth	Thru	.8
Resolution Type & Value	Chordal Tolerance	0.01
Track Surfaces	Inner	
Arcs	✓	

9. Add values.

Favorites
New... | List... | Update

Create | Done | Help

10. Click Creat. — 11. Click Done.

Figure 12-8

5 Define the **Thru Hole Dia** as **0.5**.

6 Define the **Track Type & Depth** as **Thru**.

7 Click the **Arcs** box so that a check mark appears.

8 Set the **Track Surfaces** for **Inner**.

Accept all the other default values.

9 Click the **Create** box.

10 Click the **Done** box.

11 Click the **Top Plane** orientation.

Accept all other default values. Figure 12-9 shows the finished cam. Figure 12-10 shows a top view of the cam. It also shows the cam with the original Ø4.00 base circle superposed onto the surface. Note how the cam profile rises, dwells, falls, and dwells. Figure 12-10 also shows the relationship between the cam profile and the path of the trace point.

Figure 12-9

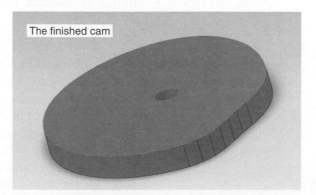

The finished cam

Figure 12-10

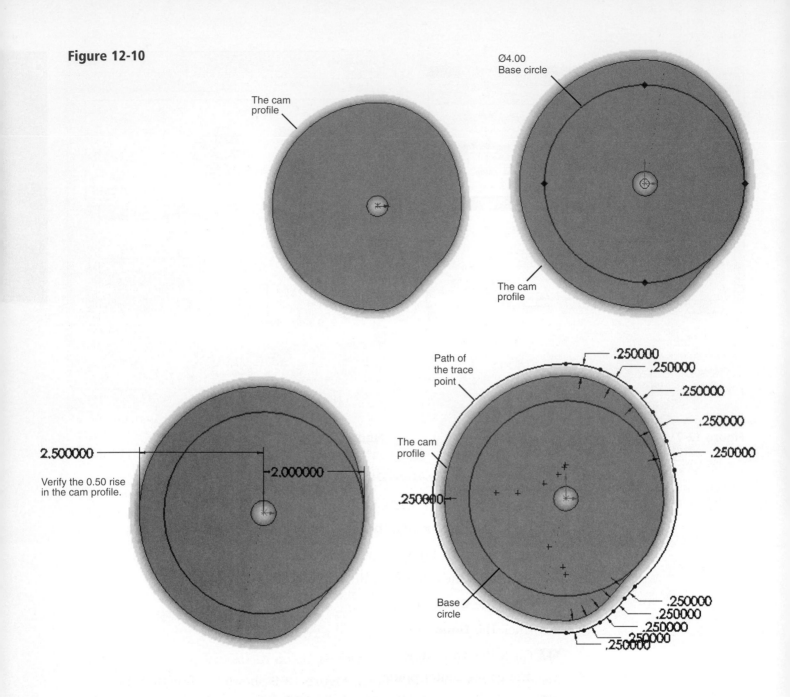

12-9 Hubs on Cams

There are two methods for creating hubs on cams: add the hub directly using the **Cam - Circular** dialog box, or create a hub on an existing cam using the **Sketch** and **Features** tools.

Using the Cam - Circular Dialog Box to Create a Hub

Figure 12-11 shows the **Creation** tab portion of the **Cam - Circular** dialog box that was originally presented in Figure 12-8. The values shown in Figure 12-11 include values for the **Near Hub**. The diameter is to be **Ø1.0** and the length **.75**. All other values are the same as used to create the cam shown in Figure 12-9.

A value of **0.5** has also been entered in the **Thru Hole Dia** box. This will generate a Ø0.5 hole through the hub diameter. The hole will go through the hub and through the cam. All other values are the same.

Figure 12-11

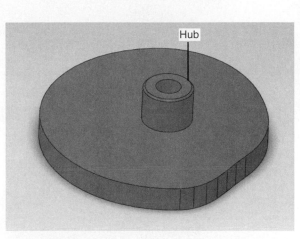

Figure 12-12

Figure 12-12 shows the modified cam that includes the hub. Note that the dimensions match those values entered in the **Cam - Circular** dialog box.

A second, far-side, hub could also be added by entering the appropriate values in the **Far Hub Dia & Length** box on the **Cam - Circular** dialog box.

Using the Sketch and Features Tools to Create a Hub

Figure 12-13 shows the cam created in the first part of this chapter. A hub can be added as follows.

1 Right-click the mouse and select the **Sketch** tool.

2 Use the **Circle** tool and add a circle on the sketch plan centered on the cam's center point.

3 Use the **Smart Dimension** tool and size the circle to **Ø1.00**.

4 Use the **Extruded Boss/Base** tool to extrude the Ø1.00 circle **0.75**.

5 Right-click the mouse and add a new sketch to the top surface of the hub.

6 Use the **Sketch** and **Features** tools to create a **Ø0.50** circle on the top surface of the hub.

7 Use the **Extruded Cut** tool and cut the circle through both the hub and the cam a distance of **1.25 in**.

To Add a Threaded Hole to a Cam's Hub

Threaded holes are added to a cam's hub to accept set screws that hold a cam in place against a rotating shaft. Use the cam created in Section 12-9 with the **Cam-Circular** dialog box to create a **Hub** option.

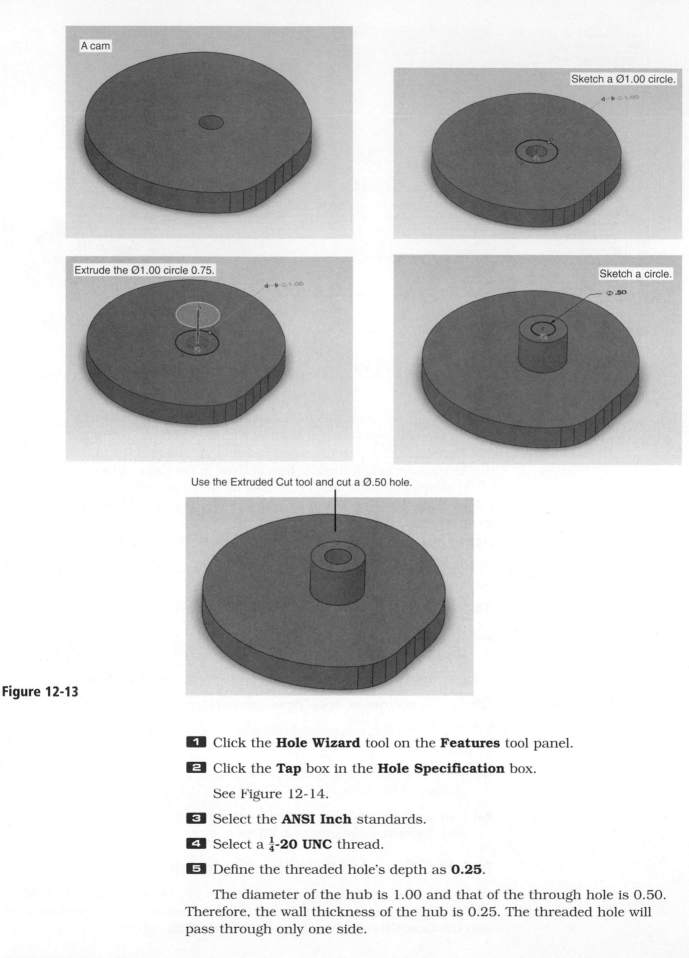

Figure 12-13

1 Click the **Hole Wizard** tool on the **Features** tool panel.

2 Click the **Tap** box in the **Hole Specification** box.

See Figure 12-14.

3 Select the **ANSI Inch** standards.

4 Select a $\frac{1}{4}$-**20 UNC** thread.

5 Define the threaded hole's depth as **0.25**.

The diameter of the hub is 1.00 and that of the through hole is 0.50. Therefore, the wall thickness of the hub is 0.25. The threaded hole will pass through only one side.

The threaded hole can be added anywhere on the hub's surface by clicking the **Positions** tab on the **Hole Wizard PropertyManager** and then clicking a point on the hub's outside surface, but say we wish to locate the threaded hole at a specific location and orientation. See Figure 12-14.

Figure 12-14

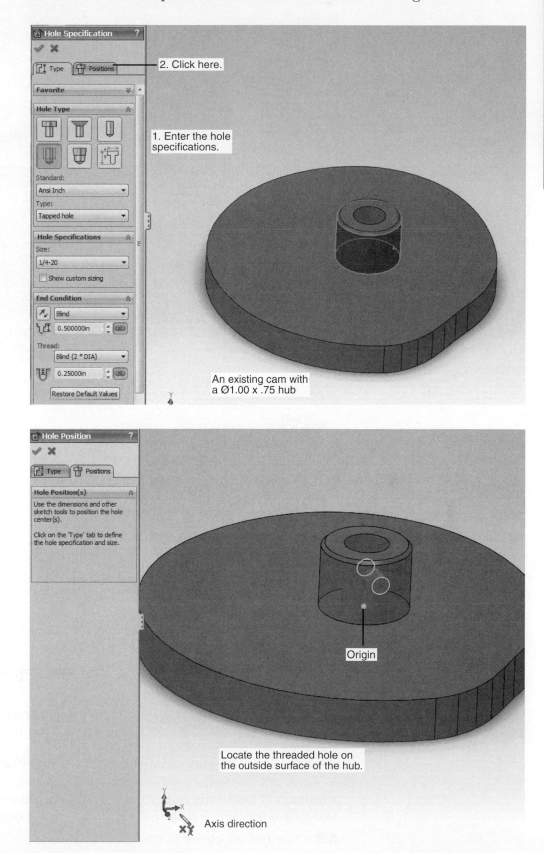

2. Click here.

1. Enter the hole specifications.

An existing cam with a Ø1.00 x .75 hub

Locate the threaded hole on the outside surface of the hub.

Origin

Axis direction

Figure 12-14
(*Continued*)

1. Click the Smart Dimension tool.

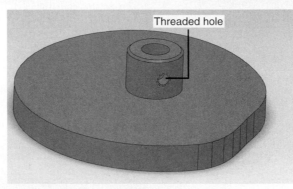

2. Click the hole's center point.

3. Enter values to locate the hole's center point.

Threaded hole

6 Click the **Positions** tab and locate the threaded hole on the surface of the hub.

7 Click the **Smart Dimension** tool, and click the threaded hole's center point.

8 Use the **Parameters** values in the **Point PropertyManager** to locate the threaded hole.

The origin for the XYZ axis is located as shown in Figure 12-14. Note that the directions for the XYZ axes are defined by the orientation icon in the lower left portion of the screen.

The values for this example are **X = 0.00, Y = 3.75, Z = .50.** The X-value will locate the center point on the vertical construction line, the Y-value will locate the center point halfway up the hub, and the Z-value will locate the center point tangent to the hub's outside surface.

9 Click the OK check mark.

To Add a Keyway to Cam

Keys can also be used to hold a cam in place against a drive shaft. Keyways may be cut through the cam hub or just through the cam.

Figure 12-15 shows the cam created earlier in the chapter. A keyway for a $\frac{1}{4} \times \frac{1}{4}$-in. square key is created as follows.

1 Right-click the front surface of the cam, and click the **Sketch** tool.

2 Change the orientation to a view looking directly at the front surface.

3 Draw two construction lines from the cam's center point, one vertical and one horizontal.

4 Use the **Rectangle** tool and draw a rectangle as shown.

5 Use the **Smart Dimension** tool and size the rectangle to accept a $\frac{1}{4} \times \frac{1}{4}$-in. square key.

Tolerances for keys and keyways can be found in Chapter 9.

6 Use the **Extruded Cut** tool and cut the keyway into the cam.

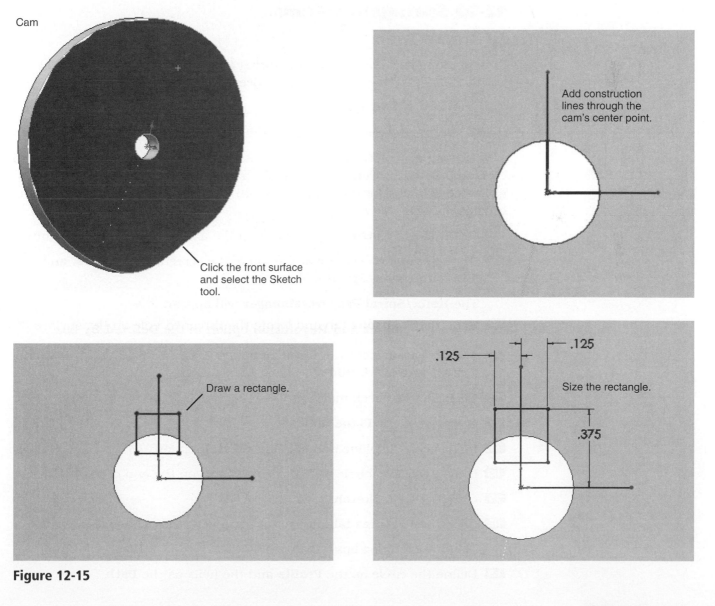

Cam

Click the front surface and select the Sketch tool.

Add construction lines through the cam's center point.

Draw a rectangle.

.125 .125

Size the rectangle.

.375

Figure 12-15

Figure 12-14
(Continued)

Use the Extruded Cut
tool and cut the keyway.

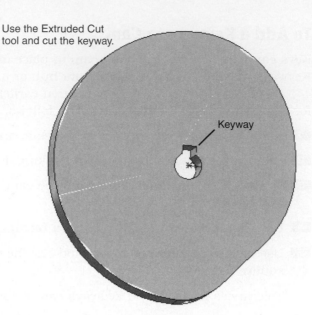

Keyway

12-10 Springs for Cams

To Draw a Spring

This section shows how to draw a spring that will be used in the next section as part of the cam assembly. See Figure 12-16.

1 Start a new **Part** document.

2 Select the top plane and draw a **Ø0.500** circle centered on the origin.

The value Ø0.500 will define the outside diameter of the helix. A Ø0.125 circle will be swept along the helical path to form the spring. This generates an inside diameter for the spring of Ø0.437 (0.500 − 0.063 = 0.437) and an outside diameter of Ø0.563.

3 Select the **Dimetric** orientation from the axis orientation icon menu.

4 Click the **Insert** heading at the top of the screen, click **Curve**, and select the **Helix/Spiral** tool.

The **Helix/Spiral PropertyManager** will appear.

5 Select the **Height and Revolution** option in the **Defined By** box.

6 Set the **Parameters** values for **Height = 1.75 in., 6 Revolutions,** and a **Start angle** of **0.00deg .**

7 Click the OK check mark.

8 Click the **Right Plane** option.

9 Right-click the plane and click the **Sketch** option.

10 Draw a **Ø0.125** circle with its center point on the end of the helix.

11 Click the **Exit Sketch** option.

12 Click the **Features** tab and select the **Swept Boss/Base** tool.

The **Sweep** dialog box will appear.

13 Define the circle as the **Profile** and the helix as the **Path**.

Figure 12-16

Chapter **12**

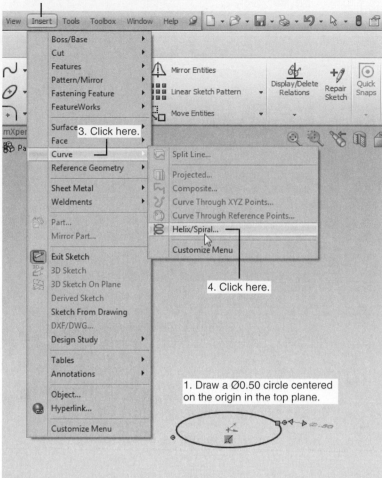

2. Click here.

3. Click here.

4. Click here.

1. Draw a Ø0.50 circle centered on the origin in the top plane.

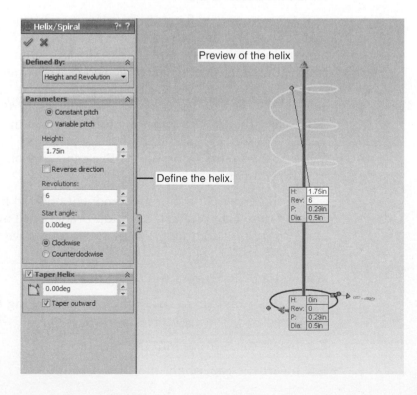

Preview of the helix

Define the helix.

Figure 12-16
(*Continued*)

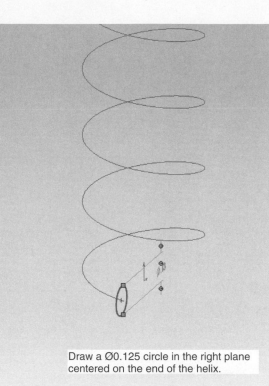

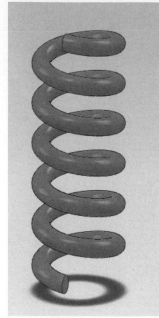

Use the Swept Boss/Base tool to create the spring. The Ø0.125 circle is the profile, and the helix is the path.

Draw a Ø0.125 circle in the right plane centered on the end of the helix.

14 Click the OK check mark.

15 Save the spring as **Cam Spring**.

12-11 Sample Problem SP12-1—Cams in Assemblies

In this section we will create an assembly drawing that includes a cam. The cam will include a keyway. See Figure 12-15. The support shaft will also include a keyway, and a $\frac{1}{4} \times \frac{1}{4} \times \frac{1}{2}$-in. square key will be inserted between the shaft and cam. Dimensioned drawings for the components used in the assembly are shown in Figure 12-17. The cam is the same as was developed earlier in the chapter. See Figures 12-6 to 12-9.

1 Start a new **Assembly** document.

2 Use the **Insert Component Browse**... option and insert the appropriate components.

In this example the first component entered into the assembly drawing screen is the cam bracket. The cam bracket will automatically be fixed in place so that all additional components will move to the bracket. See Figure 12-18.

3 Add a bearing from the **Design Library**.

In this example an **Instrument Ball Bearing 0.5000-1.1250-0.2500** was selected.

4 Insert the bearing into the cam bracket.

5 Insert the cam shaft into the bearing.

Bracket, Cam

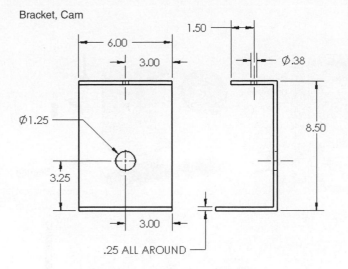

1.50

Ø.38

8.50

.25 ALL AROUND

Shaft, Cam

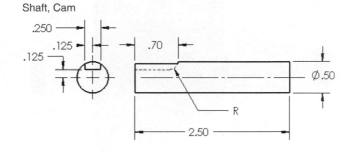

R

2.50

Ø.50

Bracket, Cam Follower

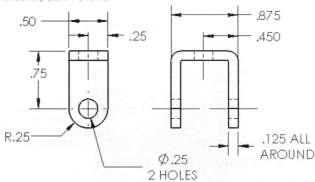

R.25

Ø.25
2 HOLES

.125 ALL AROUND

Figure 12-17

Roller, Cam

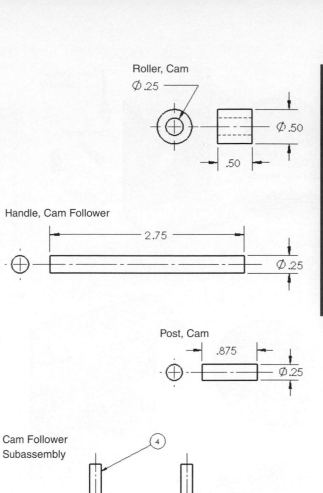

Ø.25

Ø.50

.50

Handle, Cam Follower

2.75

Ø.25

Post, Cam

.875

Ø.25

Cam Follower
Subassembly

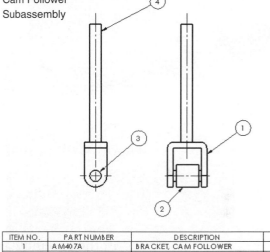

ITEM NO.	PART NUMBER	DESCRIPTION	QTY.
1	AM407A	BRACKET, CAM FOLLOWER	1
2	EK407B	ROLLER, CAM	1
3	AM347A1	POST, CAM	1
4	MN78	HANDLE, CAM FOLLOWER	1

Insert the shaft so that it extends 1.50 from the front surface of the bracket.

6 Assemble the cam onto the shaft.

7 Align the keyway in the cam with the keyway in the shaft.

8 Select a $\frac{1}{4} \times \frac{1}{4} \times \frac{1}{2}$ square key from the **Design Library**.

NOTE

A $\frac{1}{4} \times \frac{1}{4} \times \frac{1}{2}$ key can be drawn as an individual component.

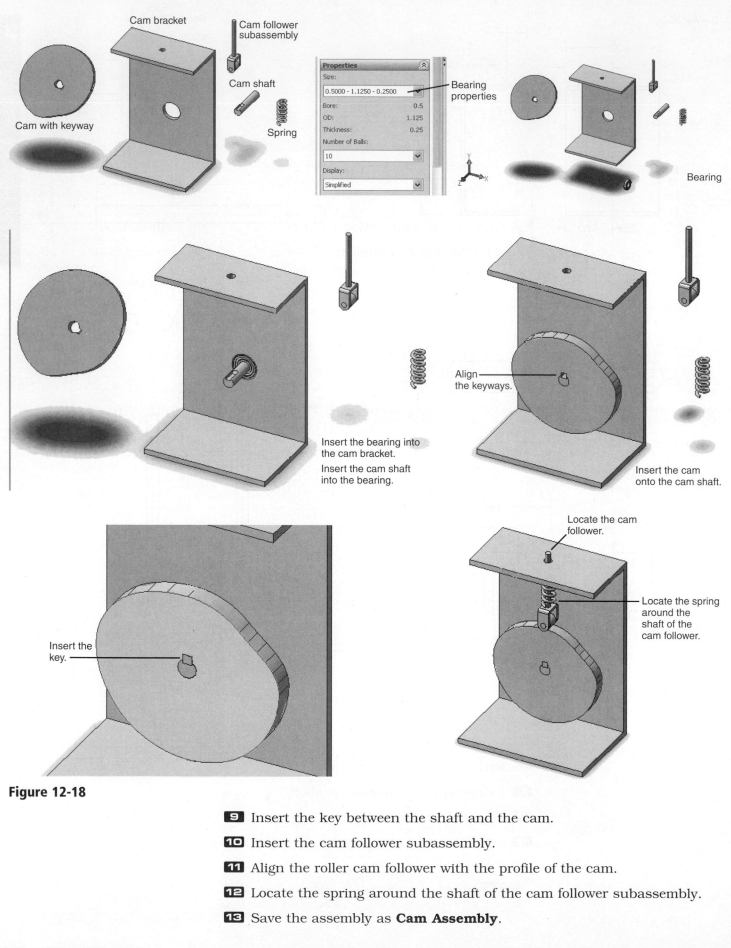

Figure 12-18

9. Insert the key between the shaft and the cam.

10. Insert the cam follower subassembly.

11. Align the roller cam follower with the profile of the cam.

12. Locate the spring around the shaft of the cam follower subassembly.

13. Save the assembly as **Cam Assembly**.

Creating an Orthographic Drawing and a Bill of Materials

1 Start a new **Drawing** document.

2 Use third-angle projection and create a front and a right-side orthographic view of the cam assembly.

3 Click on the **Annotation** tab and add the appropriate centerlines.

See Figure 12-19.

4 Click on the **Annotation** tab and select the **AutoBalloon** tool.

Note that balloon numbers (assembly numbers) have been added to all parts including the parts of the cam follower subassembly.

5 Click on the **Annotation** tab, then **Tables,** and add the bill of materials to the drawing.

Note that the balloon numbers have changed, so that the cam follower subassembly is now identified as item number 5. All components of the subassembly are labeled as 5.

Note also that the part names are listed under the PART NUMBER heading, because the BOM lists file names as part numbers. The BOM must be edited.

6 Edit the BOM by double-clicking a cell and either entering new information or modifying the existing information.

Use the format noun, modifier when entering part names. Use uppercase letters. Justify the cell inputs to the left.

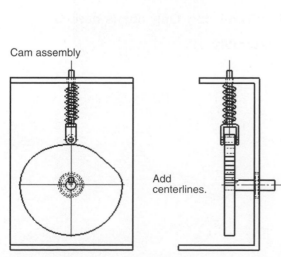

Cam assembly

Add centerlines.

Orthographic views (third-angle projection)

Figure 12-19

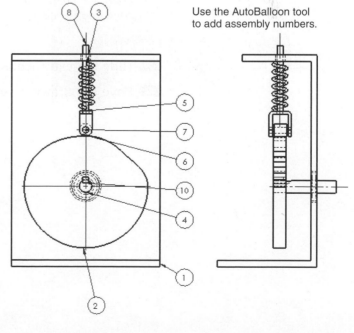

Use the AutoBalloon tool to add assembly numbers.

An edited BOM

ITEM NO.	PART NUMBER	DESCRIPTION	QTY.
1	EK-407A	BRACKET, CAM	1
2	EK-407B	CAM - KEYWAY	1
3	AM311-A2	SPRING, CAM	1
4	MN402-1	SHAFT, CAM	1
5	BU-2009S	FOLLOWER, CAM SUB-ASSEMBLY	1
6	AFBMA 12.2 - 0.5000 - 1.1250 - 0.2500 - 10.SI.NC.10		1
7	DR42	KEY, CAM	1

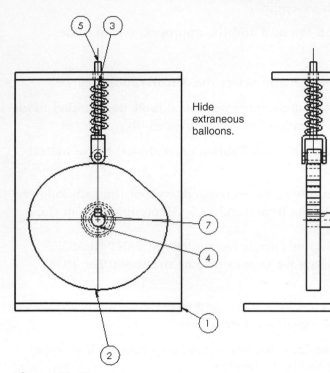

Hide extraneous balloons.

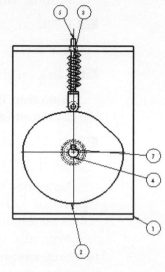

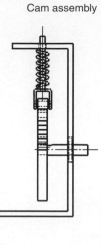

Cam assembly

ITEM NO.	PART NUMBER	DESCRIPTION	QTY.
1	EK-407A	BRACKET, CAM	1
2	EK-407B	CAM - KEYWAY	1
3	AM311-A2	SPRING, CAM	1
4	MN402-1	SHAFT, CAM	1
5	BU-2009S	FOLLOWER, CAM SUB-ASSEMBLY	1
6	AFBMA 12.2 - 0.5000 - 1.1250 - 0.2500 - 10.SI.NC.10		1
7	DR42	KEY, CAM	1

Figure 12-19
(*Continued*)

> **NOTE**
>
> The part number of the bearing selected from the **Design Library** will automatically be inserted into the BOM.

7 Hide the extraneous number 5 balloons. Only one is needed.

8 Save the drawing as **Cam Assembly.**

Chapter Projects

Draw the cams as specified in Projects 12-1 through 12-6.

Project 12-1: Inches

See Figure P12-1.

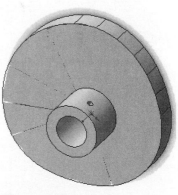

  Units = Inches
  Cam Type = Circular
  Follower Type = Translating
  Follower Diameter = .375
  Starting Radius = 1.4375
  Starting Angle = 0°
  Rotation Direction = Clockwise

  Starting Radius = 1.4375
  Dwell = 45°
  Rise 0.375, Harmonic Motion, 135°
  Dwell = 90°
  Fall 0.375, Harmonic Motion, 90°

  Blank Outside Dia = 2.8675
  Thickness = .375
  No Hub
  Thru Hole Dia = 0.625

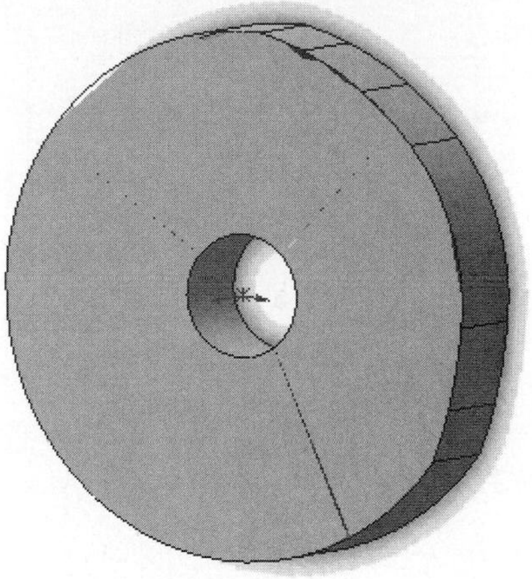

Figure P12-1

Project 12-2: Inches

See Figure P12-2.

  Units = Inches
  Cam Type = Circular
  Follower Type = Translating
  Follower Diameter = .50
  Starting Radius = 2.00
  Starting Angle = 0°
  Rotation Direction = Clockwise

  Starting Radius = 2.00
  Dwell = 45°
  Rise 0.438, Modified Trapezoidal Motion, 90°
  Dwell = 90°
  Fall 0.375, Modified Trapezoidal Motion, 90°
  Dwell = 45°

Figure P12-2

  Blank Outside Dia = 4.876
  Thickness = 0.500
  Near Hub Dia & Length = 1.25, 1.00
  Thru Hole Dia = 0.75

Add a #6-32 threaded hole 0.50 from the top of the hub.

Project 12-3: Design Problem

Use a base circle of Ø4.00 in.
The follower has a Ø0.50 in.
Cam motion:

> Dwell = 45°
> Rise 0.25 in. using Uniform Displacement for 45°
> Dwell = 45°
> Rise 0.25 in. using Uniform Displacement for 45°
> Dwell = 45°
> Fall 0.25 in. using Uniform Displacement for 45°
> Dwell = 45°
> Fall 0.25 in. using Uniform Displacement for 45°

The hub has a diameter of 1.50 in. and extends 1.50 in. from the surface of the cam.
The cam bore is Ø0.75 in.
The hub includes a #10-32 threaded hole.

Project 12-4: Millimeters

See Figure P12-4.

> Units = Metric
> Cam Type = Circular
> Follower Type = Translating
> Follower Diameter = 20
> Starting Radius = 40
> Starting Angle = 0°
> Rotation Direction = Clockwise
>
> Starting Radius = 40
> Dwell = 45°
> Rise 10, Harmonic Motion, 135°
> Dwell = 90°
> Fall 10, Harmonic Motion, 90°
>
> Blank Outside Dia = 100
> Thickness = 20
> No Hub
> Thru Hole Dia = 16.0

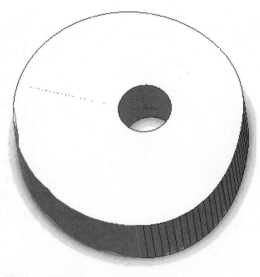

Figure P12-4

Project 12-5:

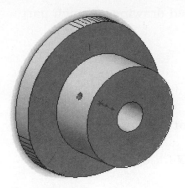

Figure P12-5

See Figure P12-5.

Units = Metric
Cam Type = Circular
Follower Type = Translating
Follower Diameter = 16
Starting Radius = 50.0
Starting Angle = 0°
Rotation Direction = Clockwise

Starting Radius = 50.0
Dwell = 45°
Rise 8.0, Modified Trapezoidal Motion, 90°
Dwell = 90°
Fall 8.0, Modified Trapezoidal Motion, 90°
Dwell = 45°

Blank Outside Dia = 108
Thickness = 12.0
Near Hub Dia & Length = 60, 30
Thru Hole Dia = 18.00

Add an M4 threaded hole 15 from the top of the hub.

Project 12-6: Design Problem

Use a base circle of Ø80.0 mm.
The follower has a Ø12.0 mm.
Cam motion:

Dwell = 45°
Rise 10.0 mm using Uniform Displacement for 45°
Dwell = 45°
Rise 5.0 mm using Uniform Displacement for 45°
Dwell = 45°
Fall 5.0 mm using Uniform Displacement for 45°
Dwell = 45°
Fall 10.0 mm using Uniform Displacement for 45°

The hub has a diameter of 30.0 mm and extends 26.0 mm from the surface of the cam.
The cam bore is Ø16.0 mm.
The hub includes an M6 threaded hole.

Project 12-7: Design Problem

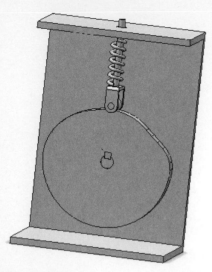

Figure P12-7

Figure P12-7 shows a cam assembly. Dimensioned drawings of each part are shown in Figure 12-17.

1. Draw the assembly.

2. Insert the following cam:
   Cam parameters:

   > Base circle = Ø5.00 in.
   > Follower Diameter = 0.50 in.
   > Select a bearing from the **Design Library**.

   Cam motion:

   > Dwell = 45°
   > Rise 0.250 in. using Uniform Displacement for 45°
   > Dwell = 45°
   > Rise 0.250 in. using Uniform Displacement for 45°
   > Dwell = 45°
   > Fall 0.250 in. using Uniform Displacement for 45°
   > Dwell = 45°
   > Fall 0.250 in. using Uniform Displacement for 45°

3. Create a keyway in both the cam and the cam shaft that will accept a 0.375 × 0.375 × 0.500-in. square key.

4. Calculate the distance between the top surface of the cam follower bracket and the underside of the top flange on the cam bracket, and create a spring to fit into the space.

P12-8: Millimeters

Draw a 3D solid model of the following assembly.

1. Create an exploded isometric assembly drawing with assembly (item) numbers.

2. Create a BOM for the assembly.

3. Create dimensioned drawings of each individual part.

   Cam parameters:

   > Base circle = Ø146
   > Face width = 16
   > Motion: rise 10 using harmonic motion over 90°, dwell for 180°, fall 10 in 90°.
   > Bore = Ø16.0
   > Keyway = 2.3 × 5 × 16
   > Follower = Ø16
   > Follower width = 4
   > Square key = 5 × 5 × 16
   > Bearing overall dimensions

Select an appropriate bearing from the **Design Library** or manufacturer's website.

Bearing 1: 17 × 40 × 10 (D × OD × THK)
Bearing 2: 4 × 13 × 4
Bearing 3: 8 × 18 × 5

Spring parameters:

Wire Ø = 1.5
Inside Ø = 9.0
Length = 20
Coil Direction = Right
Coils = 10

Consider creating a spring with ground ends. See Chapter 3.

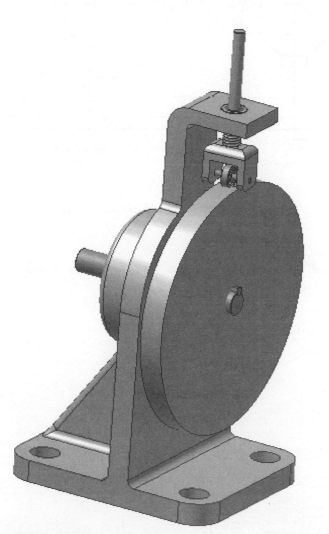

Figure P12-8

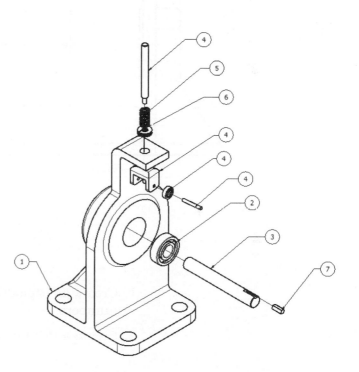

Parts List			
ITEM	QTY	PART NUMBER	DESCRIPTION
1	1	ENG-2008-A	BASE, CAST
2	1	DIN625 - SKF 6203	Single row ball bearings
3	1	SHF-4004-16	SHAFT: Ø16×120,WITH 2.3×5×16 KEYWAY
4	1		SUB-ASSEMBLY, FOLLOWER
5	1	SPR-C22	SPRING,COMPRESSION
6	1	GB 273.2-87 - 7/70 - 8 x 18 x 5	Rolling bearings - Thrust bearings - Plan of boundary dimensions
7	1	IS 2048 - 1983 - Specification for Parallel Keys and Keyways B 5 x 5 x 16	Specification for Parallel Keys and Keyways

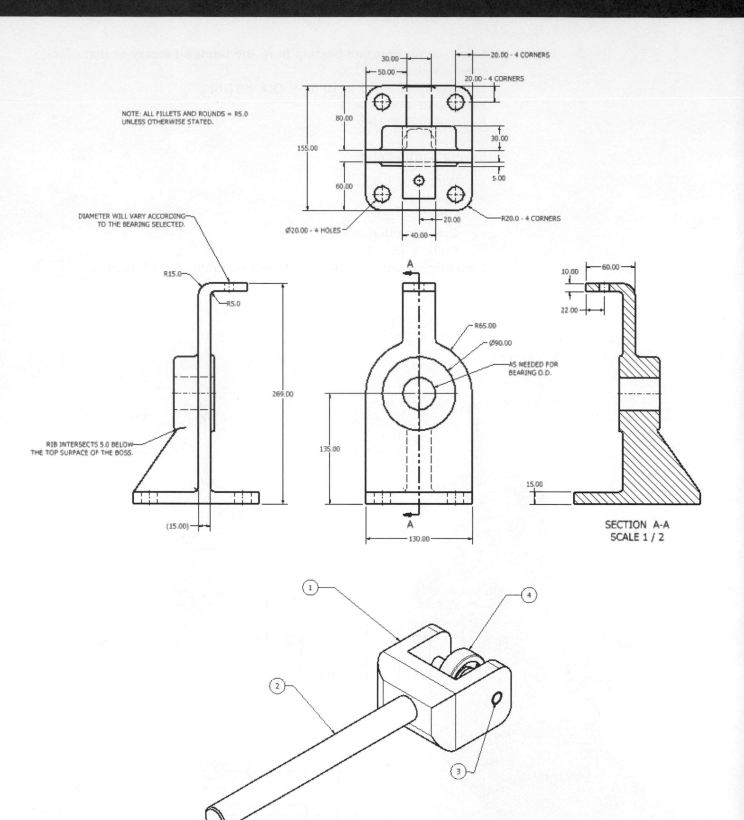

NOTE: ALL FILLETS AND ROUNDS = R5.0
UNLESS OTHERWISE STATED.

30.00
50.00
20.00 - 4 CORNERS
20.00 - 4 CORNERS
80.00
30.00
155.00
5.00
60.00
R20.0 - 4 CORNERS
20.00
Ø20.00 - 4 HOLES
40.00

DIAMETER WILL VARY ACCORDING
TO THE BEARING SELECTED.

R15.0
R5.0
269.00
A
R65.00
Ø90.00
AS NEEDED FOR
BEARING O.D.
10.00
60.00
22.00
135.00
RIB INTERSECTS 5.0 BELOW
THE TOP SURFACE OF THE BOSS.
15.00
(15.00)
A
130.00

SECTION A-A
SCALE 1 / 2

1
4
2
3

Parts List				
ITEM	PART NUMBER	DESCRIPTION	MATERIAL	QTY
1	AM-232	HOLDER	STEEL	1
2	AM-256	POST, FOLLOWER	STEEL	1
3	BS 1804-2 - 4 x 30	Parallel steel dowel pins - metric series	Steel, Mild	1
4	DIN625- SKF 634	Single row ball bearings	Steel, Mild	1

Figure P12-8
(*Continued*)

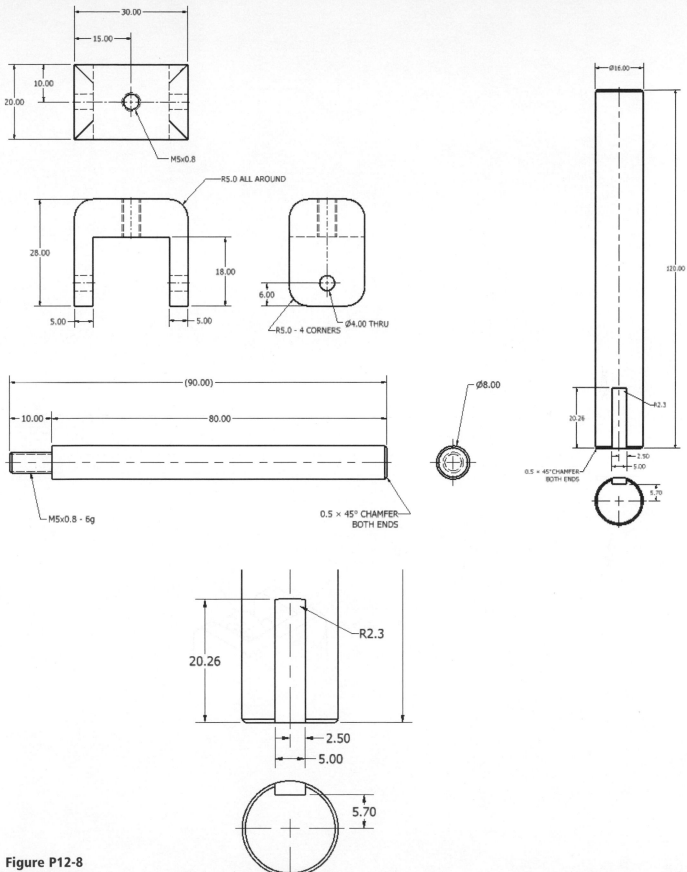

30.00
15.00
10.00
20.00
M5x0.8

R5.0 ALL AROUND
28.00
18.00
5.00   5.00

6.00
R5.0 - 4 CORNERS   Ø4.00 THRU

(90.00)
10.00   80.00
Ø8.00
M5x0.8 - 6g
0.5 × 45° CHAMFER
BOTH ENDS

Ø16.00
120.00
20.26   R2.3
2.50
5.00
0.5 × 45° CHAMFER
BOTH ENDS
5.70

20.26   R2.3
2.50
5.00
5.70

Figure P12-8
(*Continued*)

Wire and Sheet Metal Gauges

Gauge		Thickness	Gauge	Thickness
000	000	0.5800	18	0.0403
00	000	0.5165	19	0.0359
0	000	0.4600	20	0.0320
	000	0.4096	21	0.0285
	00	0.3648	22	0.0253
	0	0.3249	23	0.0226
	1	0.2893	24	0.0201
	2	0.2576	25	0.0179
	3	0.2294	26	0.0159
	4	0.2043	27	0.0142
	5	0.1819	28	0.0126
	6	0.1620	29	0.0113
	7	0.1443	30	0.0100
	8	0.1285	31	0.0089
	9	0.1144	32	0.0080
	10	0.1019	33	0.0071
	11	0.0907	34	0.0063
	12	0.0808	35	0.0056
	13	0.0720	36	0.0050
	14	0.0641	37	0.0045
	15	0.0571	38	0.0040
	16	0.0508	39	0.0035
	17	0.0453	40	0.0031

Figure A-1

American Standard Clearance Locational Fits

Nominal Size Range Inches (Over – To)	Class LC1			Class LC2			Class LC3			Class LC4		
	Limits of Clearance	Hole H6	Shaft h5	Limits of Clearance	Hole H7	Shaft h6	Limits of Clearance	Hole H8	Shaft h7	Limits of Clearance	Hole H10	Shaft h9
0 – 0.12	0 / 0.45	+0.25 / 0	0 / -0.2	0 / 0.65	+0.4 / 0	0 / -0.25	0 / 1	+0.6 / 0	0 / -0.4	0 / 2.6	+1.6 / 0	0 / -1.0
0.12 – 0.24	0 / 0.5	+0.3 / 0	0 / -0.2	0 / 0.8	+0.5 / 0	0 / -0.3	0 / 1.2	+0.7 / 0	0 / -0.5	0 / 3.0	+1.8 / 0	0 / -1.2
0.24 – 0.40	0 / 0.65	+0.4 / 0	0 / -0.25	0 / 1.0	+0.6 / 0	0 / -0.4	0 / 1.5	+0.9 / 0	0 / -0.6	0 / 3.6	+2.2 / 0	0 / -1.4
0.40 – 0.71	0 / 0.7	+0.4 / 0	0 / -0.3	0 / 1.1	+0.7 / 0	0 / -0.4	0 / 1.7	+1.0 / 0	0 / -0.7	0 / 4.4	+2.8 / 0	0 / -1.6
0.71 – 1.19	0 / 0.9	+0.5 / 0	0 / -0.4	0 / 1.3	+0.8 / 0	0 / -0.5	0 / 2	+1.2 / 0	0 / -0.8	0 / 5.5	+3.5 / 0	0 / -2.0
1.19 – 1.97	0 / 1.0	+0.6 / 0	0 / -0.4	0 / 1.6	+1.0 / 0	0 / -0.6	0 / 2.6	+1.6 / 0	0 / -1.0	0 / 6.5	+4.0 / 0	0 / -2.5

Figure A-2A

Nominal Size Range Inches (Over – To)	Class LC5			Class LC6			Class LC7			Class LC8		
	Limits of Clearance	Hole H7	Shaft g6	Limits of Clearance	Hole H9	Shaft f8	Limits of Clearance	Hole H10	Shaft e9	Limits of Clearance	Hole H10	Shaft d9
0 – 0.12	0.1 / 0.75	+0.4 / 0	-0.1 / -0.35	0.3 / 1.9	+1.0 / 0	-0.3 / -0.9	0.6 / 3.2	+1.6 / 0	-0.6 / -1.6	1.0 / 3.6	+1.6 / 0	-1.0 / -2.0
0.12 – 0.24	0.15 / 0.95	+0.5 / 0	-0.15 / -0.45	0.4 / 2.3	+1.2 / 0	-0.4 / -1.1	0.8 / 3.8	+1.8 / 0	-0.8 / -2.0	1.2 / 4.2	+1.8 / 0	-1.2 / -2.4
0.24 – 0.40	0.2 / 1.2	+0.6 / 0	-0.2 / -0.6	0.5 / 2.8	+1.4 / 0	-0.5 / -1.4	1.0 / 4.6	+2.2 / 0	-1.0 / -2.4	1.6 / 5.2	+2.2 / 0	-1.6 / -3.0
0.40 – 0.71	0.25 / 1.35	+0.7 / 0	-0.25 / -0.65	0.6 / 3.2	+1.6 / 0	-0.6 / -1.6	1.2 / 5.6	+2.8 / 0	-1.2 / -2.8	2.0 / 6.4	+2.8 / 0	-2.0 / -3.6
0.71 – 1.19	0.3 / 1.6	+0.8 / 0	-0.3 / -0.8	0.8 / 4.0	+2.0 / 0	-0.8 / -2.0	1.6 / 7.1	+3.5 / 0	-1.6 / -3.6	2.5 / 8.0	+3.5 / 0	-2.5 / -4.5
1.19 – 1.97	0.4 / 2.0	+1.0 / 0	-0.4 / -1.0	1.0 / 5.1	+2.5 / 0	-1.0 / -2.6	2.0 / 8.5	+4.0 / 0	-2.0 / -4.5	3.0 / 9.5	+4.0 / 0	-3.0 / -5.5

Figure A-2B

American Standard Running and Sliding Fits
(Hole Basis)

Nominal Size Range Inches		Class RC1				Class RC2				Class RC3				Class RC4		
		Limits of Clearance	Standard Limits		Limits of Clearance	Standard Limits			Limits of Clearance	Standard Limits			Limits of Clearance	Standard Limits		
Over	To		Hole H5	Shaft g4		Hole H6	Shaft g5			Hole H7	Shaft f6			Hole H8	Shaft f7
0 – 0.12		0.1 / 0.45	+0.2 / 0	−0.1 / −0.25	0.1 / 0.55	+0.25 / 0	−0.1 / −0.3		0.3 / 0.95	+0.4 / 0	−0.3 / −0.55		0.3 / 1.3	+0.6 / 0	−0.3 / −0.7
0.12 – 0.24		0.15 / 0.5	+0.2 / 0	−0.15 / −0.3	0.15 / 0.65	+0.3 / 0	−0.15 / −0.35		0.4 / 1.12	+0.5 / 0	−0.4 / −0.7		0.4 / 1.5	+0.7 / 0	−0.4 / −0.0
0.24 – 0.40		0.2 / 0.6	+0.25 / 0	−0.2 / −0.35	0.2 / 0.85	+0.4 / 0	−0.2 / −0.45		0.5 / 1.5	+0.6 / 0	−0.5 / −0.9		0.5 / 2.0	+0.9 / 0	−0.5 / −1.1
0.40 – 0.71		0.25 / 0.75	+0.3 / 0	−0.25 / −0.45	0.25 / 0.95	+0.4 / 0	−0.25 / −0.55		0.6 / 1.7	+0.7 / 0	−0.6 / −1.0		0.6 / 2.3	+1.0 / 0	−0.6 / −1.3
0.71 – 1.19		0.3 / 0.95	+0.4 / 0	−0.3 / −0.55	0.3 / 1.2	+0.5 / 0	−0.3 / −0.7		0.8 / 2.1	+0.8 / 0	−0.8 / −1.3		0.8 / 2.8	+1.2 / 0	−0.8 / −1.6
1.19 – 1.97		0.4 / 1.1	+0.4 / 0	−0.4 / −0.7	0.4 / 1.4	+0.6 / 0	−0.4 / −0.8		1.0 / 2.6	+1.0 / 0	−1.0 / −1.6		1.0 / 3.6	+1.6 / 0	−1.0 / −2.0

Figure A-3A

Nominal Size Range Inches		Class RC5				Class RC6				Class RC7				Class RC8		
		Limits of Clearance	Standard Limits		Limits of Clearance	Standard Limits			Limits of Clearance	Standard Limits			Limits of Clearance	Standard Limits		
Over	To		Hole H8	Shaft e7		Hole H9	Shaft e8			Hole H9	Shaft d8			Hole H10	Shaft c9
0 – 0.12		0.6 / 1.6	+0.6 / 0	−0.6 / −1.0	0.6 / 2.2	+1.0 / 0	−0.6 / −1.2		1.0 / 2.6	+1.0 / 0	−1.0 / −1.6		2.5 / 5.1	+1.6 / 0	−2.5 / −3.5
0.12 – 0.24		0.8 / 2.0	+0.7 / 0	−0.8 / −1.3	0.8 / 2.7	+1.2 / 0	−0.8 / −1.5		1.2 / 3.1	+1.2 / 0	−1.2 / −1.9		2.8 / 5.8	+1.8 / 0	−2.8 / −4.0
0.24 – 0.40		1.0 / 2.5	+0.9 / 0	−1.0 / −1.6	1.0 / 3.3	+1.4 / 0	−1.0 / −1.9		1.6 / 3.9	+1.4 / 0	−1.6 / −2.5		3.0 / 6.6	+2.2 / 0	−3.0 / −4.4
0.40 – 0.71		1.2 / 2.9	+1.0 / 0	−1.2 / −1.9	1.2 / 3.8	+1.6 / 0	−1.2 / −2.2		2.0 / 4.6	+1.6 / 0	−2.0 / −3.0		3.5 / 7.9	+2.8 / 0	−3.5 / −5.1
0.71 – 1.19		1.6 / 3.6	+1.2 / 0	−1.6 / −2.4	1.6 / 4.8	+2.0 / 0	−1.6 / −2.8		2.5 / 5.7	+2.0 / 0	−2.5 / −3.7		4.5 / 10.0	+3.5 / 0	−4.5 / −6.5
1.19 – 1.97		2.0 / 4.6	+1.6 / 0	−2.0 / −3.0	2.0 / 6.1	+2.5 / 0	−2.0 / −3.6		3.0 / 7.1	+2.5 / 0	−3.0 / −4.6		5.0 / 11.5	+4.0 / 0	−5.0 / −7.5

Figure A-3B

American Standard Transition Locational Fits

Nominal Size Range Inches Over To	Class LT1				Class LT2				Class LT3		
	Fit	Standard Limits		Fit	Standard Limits			Fit	Standard Limits		
		Hole H7	Shaft js6		Hole H8	Shaft js7			Hole H7	Shaft k6	
0 - 0.12	-0.10 +0.50	+0.4 0	+0.10 -0.10	-0.2 +0.8	+0.6 0	+0.2 -0.2				
0.12 - 0.24	-0.15 -0.65	+0.5 0	+0.15 -0.15	-0.25 +0.95	+0.7 0	+0.25 -0.25				
0.24 - 0.40	-0.2 +0.5	+0.6 0	+0.2 -0.2	-0.3 +1.2	+0.9 0	+0.3 -0.3	-0.5 +0.5	+0.6 0	+0.5 +0.1
0.40 - 0.71	-0.2 +0.9	+0.7 0	+0.2 -0.2	-0.35 +1.35	+1.0 0	+0.35 -0.35	-0.5 +0.6	+0.7 0	+0.5 +0.1
0.71 - 1.19	-0.25 +1.05	+0.8 0	+0.25 -0.25	-0.4 +1.6	+1.2 0	+0.4 -0.4	-0.6 +0.7	+0.8 0	+0.6 +0.1
1.19 - 1.97	-0.3 +1.3	+1.0 0	+0.3 -0.3	-0.5 +2.1	+1.6 0	+0.5 -0.5	-0.7 +0.1	+1.0 0	+0.7 +0.1

Figure A-4A

Nominal Size Range Inches Over To	Class LT4				Class LT5				Class LT6		
	Fit	Standard Limits		Fit	Standard Limits			Fit	Standard Limits		
		Hole H8	Shaft k7		Hole H7	Shaft n6			Hole H7	Shaft n7	
0 - 0.12				-0.5 +0.15	+0.4 0	+0.5 +0.25	-0.65 +0.15	+0.4 0	+0.65 +0.25
0.12 - 0.24				-0.6 +0.2	+0.5 0	+0.6 +0.3	-0.8 +0.2	+0.5 0	+0.8 +0.3
0.24 - 0.40	-0.7 +0.8	+0.9 0	+0.7 +0.1	-0.8 +0.2	+0.6 0	+0.8 +0.4	-1.0 +0.2	+0.6 0	+1.0 +0.4
0.40 - 0.71	-0.8 +0.9	+1.0 0	+0.8 +0.1	-0.9 +0.2	+0.7 0	+0.9 +0.5	-1.2 +0.2	+0.7 0	+1.2 +0.5
0.71 - 1.19	-0.9 +1.1	+1.2 0	+0.9 +0.1	-1.1 +0.2	+0.8 0	+1.1 +0.6	-1.4 +0.2	+0.8 0	+1.4 +0.6
1.19 - 1.97	-1.1 +1.5	+1.6 0	+1.1 +0.1	-1.3 +0.3	+1.0 0	+1.3 +0.7	-1.7 +0.3	+1.0 0	+1.7 +0.7

Figure A-4B

American Standard Interference Locational Fits

Nominal Size Range Inches Over – To	Limits of Interference (LN1)	Class LN1 Standard Limits Hole H6	Shaft n5	Limits of Interference (LN2)	Class LN2 Standard Limits Hole H7	Shaft p6	Limits of Interference (LN3)	Class LN3 Standard Limits Hole H7	Shaft r6
0 – 0.12	0 / 0.45	+0.25 / 0	+0.45 / +0.25	0 / 0.65	+0.4 / 0	+0.63 / +0.4	0.1 / 0.75	+0.4 / 0	+0.75 / +0.5
0.12 – 0.24	0 / 0.5	+0.3 / 0	+0.5 / +0.3	0 / 0.8	+0.5 / 0	+0.8 / +0.5	0.1 / 0.9	+0.5 / 0	+0.9 / +0.6
0.24 – 0.40	0 / 0.65	+0.4 / 0	+0.65 / +0.4	0 / 1.0	+0.6 / 0	+1.0 / +0.6	0.2 / 1.2	+0.6 / 0	+1.2 / +0.8
0.40 – 0.71	0 / 0.8	+0.4 / 0	+0.8 / +0.4	0 / 1.1	+0.7 / 0	+1.1 / +0.7	0.3 / 1.4	+0.7 / 0	+1.4 / +1.0
0.71 – 1.19	0 / 1.0	+0.5 / 0	+1.0 / +0.5	0 / 1.3	+0.8 / 0	+1.3 / +0.8	0.4 / 1.7	+0.8 / 0	+1.7 / +1.2
1.19 – 1.97	0 / 1.1	+0.6 / 0	+1.1 / +0.6	0 / 1.6	+1.0 / 0	+1.6 / +1.0	0.4 / 2.0	+1.0 / 0	+2.0 / +1.4

Figure A-5

American Standard Force and Shrink Fits

Nominal Size Range Inches Over – To	Limits of Interference (FN1)	Class FN 1 Standard Limits Hole	Shaft	Limits of Interference (FN2)	Class FN 2 Standard Limits Hole	Shaft	Limits of Interference (FN3)	Class FN 3 Standard Limits Hole	Shaft	Limits of Interference (FN4)	Class FN 4 Standard Limits Hole	Shaft
0 – 0.12	0.05 / 0.5	+0.25 / 0	+0.5 / +0.3	0.2 / 0.85	+0.4 / 0	+0.85 / +0.6				0.3 / 0.95	+0.4 / 0	+0.95 / +0.7
0.12 – 0.24	0.1 / 0.6	+0.3 / 0	+0.6 / +0.4	0.2 / 1.0	+0.5 / 0	+1.0 / +0.7				0.4 / 1.2	+0.5 / 0	+1.2 / +0.9
0.24 – 0.40	0.1 / 0.75	+0.4 / 0	+0.75 / +0.5	0.4 / 1.4	+0.6 / 0	+1.4 / +1.0				0.6 / 1.6	+0.6 / 0	+1.6 / +1.2
0.40 – 0.56	0.1 / 0.8	+0.4 / 0	+0.8 / +0.5	0.5 / 1.6	+0.7 / 0	+1.6 / +1.2				0.7 / 1.8	+0.7 / 0	+1.8 / +1.4
0.56 – 0.71	0.2 / 0.9	+0.4 / 0	+0.9 / +0.6	0.5 / 1.6	+0.7 / 0	+1.6 / +1.2				0.7 / 1.8	+0.7 / 0	+1.8 / +1.4
0.71 – 0.95	0.2 / 1.1	+0.5 / 0	+1.1 / +0.7	0.6 / 1.9	+0.8 / 0	+1.9 / +1.4				0.8 / 2.1	+0.8 / 0	+2.1 / +1.6
0.95 – 1.19	0.3 / 1.2	+0.5 / 0	+1.2 / +0.8	0.6 / 1.9	+0.8 / 0	+1.9 / +1.4	0.8 / 2.1	+0.8 / 0	+2.1 / +1.6	1.0 / 2.3	+0.8 / 0	+2.1 / +1.8
1.19 – 1.58	0.3 / 1.3	+0.6 / 0	+1.3 / +0.9	0.8 / 2.4	+1.0 / 0	+2.4 / +1.8	1.0 / 2.6	+1.0 / 0	+2.6 / +2.0	1.5 / 3.1	+1.0 / 0	+3.1 / +2.5
1.58 – 1.97	0.4 / 1.4	+0.6 / 0	+1.4 / +1.0	0.8 / 2.4	+1.0 / 0	+2.4 / +1.8	1.2 / 2.8	+1.0 / 0	+2.8 / +2.2	1.8 / 3.4	+1.0 / 0	+3.4 / +2.8

Figure A-6

Preferred Clearance Fits — Cylindrical Fits
(Hole Basis; ANSI B4.2)

Basic Size		Loose Running			Free Running			Close Running			Sliding			Locational Clear.		
		Hole H11	Shaft c11	Fit	Hole H9	Shaft d9	Fit	Hole H8	Shaft f7	Fit	Hole H7	Shaft g6	Fit	Hole H7	Shaft h6	Fit
4	Max	4.075	3.930	0.220	4.030	3.970	0.090	4.018	3.990	0.040	4.012	3.996	0.024	4.012	4.000	0.020
	Min	4.000	3.855	0.070	4.000	3.940	0.030	4.000	3.978	0.010	4.000	3.988	0.004	4.000	3.992	0.000
5	Max	5.075	4.930	0.220	5.030	4.970	0.090	5.018	4.990	0.040	5.012	4.996	0.024	5.012	5.000	0.020
	Min	5.000	4.855	0.070	5.000	4.940	0.030	5.000	4.978	0.010	5.000	4.988	0.004	5.000	4.992	0.000
6	Max	6.075	5.930	0.220	6.030	5.970	0.090	6.018	5.990	0.040	6.012	5.996	0.024	6.012	6.000	0.020
	Min	6.000	5.885	0.070	6.000	5.940	0.030	6.000	5.978	0.010	6.000	5.988	0.004	6.000	5.992	0.000
8	Max	8.090	7.920	0.260	8.036	7.960	0.112	8.022	7.987	0.050	8.015	7.995	0.029	8.015	8.000	0.024
	Min	8.000	7.830	0.080	8.000	7.924	0.040	8.000	7.972	0.013	8.000	7.986	0.005	8.000	7.991	0.000
10	Max	10.090	9.920	0.026	10.036	9.960	0.112	10.022	9.987	0.050	10.015	9.995	0.029	10.015	10.000	0.024
	Min	10.000	9.830	0.080	10.000	9.924	0.040	10.000	9.972	0.013	10.000	9.986	0.005	10.000	9.991	0.000
12	Max	12.112	11.905	0.315	12.043	11.950	0.136	12.027	11.984	0.061	12.018	11.994	0.035	12.018	12.000	0.029
	Min	12.000	11.795	0.095	12.000	11.907	0.050	12.000	11.966	0.016	12.000	11.983	0.006	12.000	11.989	0.000
16	Max	16.110	15.905	0.315	16.043	15.950	0.136	16.027	15.984	0.061	16.018	15.994	0.035	16.018	16.000	0.029
	Min	16.000	15.795	0.095	16.000	15.907	0.050	16.000	15.966	0.016	16.000	15.983	0.006	16.000	15.989	0.000
20	Max	20.130	19.890	0.370	20.052	19.935	0.169	20.033	19.980	0.074	20.021	19.993	0.041	20.021	20.000	0.034
	Min	20.000	19.760	0.110	20.000	19.883	0.065	20.000	19.959	0.020	20.000	19.980	0.007	20.000	19.987	0.000
25	Max	25.130	24.890	0.370	25.052	24.935	0.169	25.033	24.980	0.074	25.021	24.993	0.041	25.021	25.000	0.034
	Min	25.000	24.760	0.110	25.000	24.883	0.065	25.000	24.959	0.020	25.000	24.980	0.007	25.000	24.987	0.000
30	Max	30.130	29.890	0.370	30.052	29.935	0.169	30.033	29.980	0.074	30.021	29.993	0.041	30.021	30.000	0.034
	Min	30.000	29.760	0.110	30.000	29.883	0.065	30.000	29.959	0.020	30.000	29.980	0.007	30.000	29.987	0.000

Figure A-7

Preferred Transition and Interference Fits — Cylindrical Fits
(Hole Basis; ANSI B4.2)

Basic Size		Locational Trans. Hole H7	Shaft k6	Fit	Locational Trans. Hole H7	Shaft n6	Fit	Locational Inter. Hole H7	Shaft p6	Fit	Medium Drive Hole H7	Shaft s6	Fit	Force Hole H7	Shaft u6	Fit
4	Max	4.012	4.009	0.011	4.012	4.016	0.004	4.012	4.020	0.000	4.012	4.027	-0.007	4.012	4.031	-0.011
	Min	4.000	4.001	-0.009	4.000	4.008	-0.016	4.000	4.012	-0.020	4.000	4.019	-0.027	4.000	4.023	-0.031
5	Max	5.012	5.009	0.011	5.012	5.016	0.004	5.012	5.020	0.000	5.012	5.027	-0.007	5.012	5.031	-0.011
	Min	5.000	5.001	-0.009	5.000	5.008	-0.016	5.000	5.012	-0.020	5.000	5.019	-0.027	5.000	5.023	-0.031
6	Max	6.012	6.009	0.011	6.012	6.016	0.004	6.012	6.020	0.000	6.012	6.027	-0.007	6.012	6.031	-0.011
	Min	6.000	6.001	-0.009	6.000	6.008	-0.016	6.000	6.012	-0.020	6.000	6.019	-0.027	6.000	6.023	-0.031
8	Max	8.015	8.010	0.014	8.015	8.019	0.005	8.015	8.024	0.000	8.015	8.032	-0.008	8.015	8.037	-0.013
	Min	8.000	8.001	-0.010	8.000	8.010	-0.019	8.000	8.015	-0.024	8.000	8.023	-0.032	8.000	8.028	-0.037
10	Max	10.015	10.010	0.014	10.015	10.019	0.005	10.015	10.024	0.000	10.015	10.032	-0.008	10.015	10.037	-0.013
	Min	10.000	10.001	-0.010	10.000	10.010	-0.019	10.000	10.015	-0.024	10.000	10.023	-0.032	10.000	10.028	-0.037
12	Max	12.018	12.012	0.017	12.018	12.023	0.006	12.018	12.029	0.000	12.018	12.039	-0.010	12.018	12.044	-0.015
	Min	12.000	12.001	-0.012	12.000	12.012	-0.023	12.000	12.018	-0.029	12.000	12.028	-0.039	12.000	12.033	-0.044
16	Max	16.018	16.012	0.017	16.018	16.023	0.006	16.018	16.029	0.000	16.018	16.039	-0.010	16.018	16.044	-0.015
	Min	16.000	16.001	-0.012	16.000	16.012	-0.023	16.000	16.018	-0.029	16.000	16.028	-0.039	16.000	16.033	-0.044
20	Max	20.021	20.015	0.019	20.021	20.028	0.006	20.021	20.035	-0.001	20.021	20.048	-0.014	20.021	20.054	-0.020
	Min	20.000	20.002	-0.015	20.000	20.015	-0.028	20.000	20.022	-0.035	20.000	20.035	-0.048	20.000	20.041	-0.054
25	Max	25.021	25.015	0.019	25.021	25.028	0.006	25.021	25.035	-0.001	25.021	25.048	-0.014	25.021	25.061	-0.027
	Min	25.000	25.002	-0.015	25.000	25.015	-0.028	25.000	25.022	-0.035	25.000	25.035	-0.048	25.000	25.048	-0.061
30	Max	30.021	30.015	0.019	30.021	30.028	0.006	30.021	30.035	-0.001	30.021	30.048	-0.014	30.021	30.061	-0.027
	Min	30.000	30.002	-0.015	30.000	30.015	-0.028	30.000	30.022	-0.035	30.000	30.035	-0.048	30.000	30.048	-0.061

Figure A-8

Preferred Clearance Fits — Cylindrical Fits
(Shaft Basis; ANSI B4.2)

Basic Size		Loose Running			Free Running			Close Running			Sliding			Locational Clear.		
		Hole C11	Shaft h11	Fit	Hole D9	Shaft h9	Fit	Hole F8	Shaft h7	Fit	Hole G7	Shaft h6	Fit	Hole H7	Shaft h6	Fit
4	Max	4.145	4.000	0.220	4.060	4.000	0.090	4.028	4.000	0.040	4.016	4.000	0.024	4.012	4.000	0.020
	Min	4.070	3.925	0.070	4.030	3.970	0.030	4.010	3.988	0.010	4.004	3.992	0.004	4.000	3.992	0.000
5	Max	5.145	5.000	0.220	5.060	5.000	0.090	5.028	5.000	0.040	5.016	5.000	0.024	5.012	5.000	0.020
	Min	5.070	4.925	0.070	5.030	4.970	0.030	5.010	4.988	0.010	5.004	4.992	0.004	5.000	4.992	0.000
6	Max	6.145	6.000	0.220	6.060	6.000	0.090	6.028	6.000	0.040	6.016	6.000	0.024	6.012	6.000	0.020
	Min	6.070	5.925	0.070	6.030	5.970	0.030	6.010	5.988	0.010	6.004	5.992	0.004	6.000	5.992	0.000
8	Max	8.170	8.000	0.260	8.076	8.000	0.112	8.035	8.000	0.050	8.020	8.000	0.029	8.015	8.000	0.024
	Min	8.080	7.910	0.080	8.040	7.964	0.040	8.013	7.985	0.013	8.005	7.991	0.005	8.000	7.991	0.000
10	Max	10.170	10.000	0.260	10.076	10.000	0.112	10.035	10.000	0.050	10.020	10.000	0.029	10.015	10.000	0.024
	Min	10.080	9.910	0.080	10.040	9.964	0.040	10.013	9.985	0.013	10.005	9.991	0.005	10.000	9.991	0.000
12	Max	12.205	12.000	0.315	12.093	12.000	0.136	12.043	12.000	0.061	12.024	12.000	0.035	12.018	12.000	0.029
	Min	12.095	11.890	0.095	12.050	11.957	0.050	12.016	11.982	0.016	12.006	11.989	0.006	12.000	11.989	0.000
16	Max	16.205	16.000	0.315	16.093	16.000	0.136	16.043	16.000	0.061	16.024	16.000	0.035	16.018	16.000	0.029
	Min	16.095	15.890	0.095	16.050	15.957	0.050	16.016	15.982	0.016	16.006	15.989	0.006	16.000	15.989	0.000
20	Max	20.240	20.000	0.370	20.117	20.000	0.169	20.053	20.000	0.074	20.028	20.000	0.041	20.021	20.000	0.034
	Min	20.110	19.870	0.110	20.065	19.948	0.065	20.020	19.979	0.020	20.007	19.987	0.007	20.000	19.987	0.000
25	Max	25.240	25.000	0.370	25.117	25.000	0.169	25.053	25.000	0.074	25.028	25.000	0.041	25.021	25.000	0.034
	Min	25.110	24.870	0.110	25.065	24.948	0.065	25.020	24.979	0.020	25.007	24.987	0.007	25.000	24.987	0.000
30	Max	30.240	30.000	0.370	30.117	30.000	0.169	30.053	30.000	0.074	30.028	30.000	0.041	30.021	30.000	0.034
	Min	30.110	29.870	0.110	30.065	29.948	0.065	30.020	29.979	0.020	30.007	29.987	0.007	30.000	29.987	0.000

Figure A-9

Preferred Transition and Interference Fits — Cylindrical Fits
(Shaft Basis; ANSI B4.2)

Basic Size		Locational Trans.			Locational Trans.			Locational Inter.			Medium Drive			Force		
		Hole K7	Shaft h6	Fit	Hole N7	Shaft h6	Fit	Hole P7	Shaft h6	Fit	Hole S7	Shaft h6	Fit	Hole U7	Shaft h6	Fit
4	Max	4.003	4.000	0.011	3.996	4.000	0.004	3.992	4.000	0.000	3.985	4.000	-0.007	3.981	4.000	-0.011
	Min	3.991	3.992	-0.009	3.984	3.992	-0.016	3.980	3.992	-0.020	3.973	3.992	-0.027	3.969	3.992	-0.031
5	Max	5.003	5.000	0.011	4.996	5.000	0.004	4.992	5.000	0.000	4.985	5.000	-0.007	4.981	5.000	-0.011
	Min	4.991	4.992	-0.009	4.984	4.992	-0.016	4.980	4.992	-0.020	4.973	4.992	-0.027	4.969	4.992	-0.031
6	Max	6.003	6.000	0.011	5.996	6.000	0.004	5.992	6.000	0.000	5.985	6.000	-0.007	5.981	6.000	-0.011
	Min	5.991	5.992	-0.009	5.984	5.992	-0.016	5.980	5.992	-0.020	5.973	5.992	-0.027	5.969	5.992	-0.031
8	Max	8.005	8.000	0.014	7.996	8.000	0.005	7.991	8.000	0.000	7.983	8.000	-0.008	7.978	8.000	-0.013
	Min	7.990	7.991	-0.010	7.981	7.991	-0.019	7.976	7.991	-0.024	7.968	7.991	-0.032	7.963	7.991	-0.037
10	Max	10.005	10.000	0.014	9.996	10.000	0.005	9.991	10.000	0.000	9.983	10.000	-0.008	9.978	10.000	-0.013
	Min	9.990	9.991	-0.010	9.981	9.991	-0.019	9.976	9.991	-0.024	9.968	9.991	-0.032	9.963	9.991	-0.037
12	Max	12.006	12.000	0.017	11.995	12.000	0.006	11.989	12.000	0.000	11.979	12.000	-0.010	11.974	12.000	-0.015
	Min	11.988	11.989	-0.012	11.977	11.989	-0.023	11.971	11.989	-0.029	11.961	11.989	-0.039	11.956	11.989	-0.044
16	Max	16.006	16.000	0.017	15.995	16.000	0.006	15.989	16.000	0.000	15.979	16.000	-0.010	15.974	16.000	-0.015
	Min	15.988	15.989	-0.012	15.977	15.989	-0.023	15.971	15.989	-0.029	15.961	15.989	-0.039	15.956	15.989	-0.044
20	Max	20.006	20.000	0.019	19.993	20.000	0.006	19.986	20.000	-0.001	19.973	20.000	-0.014	19.967	20.000	-0.020
	Min	19.985	19.987	-0.015	19.972	19.987	-0.028	19.965	19.987	-0.035	19.952	19.987	-0.048	19.946	19.987	-0.054
25	Max	25.006	25.000	0.019	24.993	25.000	0.006	24.986	25.000	-0.001	24.973	25.000	-0.014	24.960	25.000	-0.027
	Min	24.985	24.987	-0.015	24.972	24.987	-0.028	24.965	24.987	-0.035	24.952	24.987	-0.048	24.939	24.987	-0.061
30	Max	30.006	30.000	0.019	29.993	30.000	0.006	29.986	30.000	-0.001	29.973	30.000	-0.014	29.960	30.000	-0.027
	Min	29.985	29.987	-0.015	29.972	29.987	-0.028	29.965	29.987	-0.035	29.952	29.987	-0.048	29.939	29.987	-0.061

Figure A-10

Metric Threads—Preferred Sizes			
First Choice	Second Choice	First Choice	Second Choice
1	1.1	12	14
1.2	1.4	16	18
1.6	1.8	20	22
2	2.2	25	28
2.5	2.8	30	35
3	3.5	40	45
4	4.5	50	55
5	5.5	60	70
6	7	80	90
8	9	100	110
10	11	120	140

Figure A-11

Standard Thread Lengths—Inches														
	3/16	1/4	3/8	1/2	5/8	3/4	7/8	1	1 1/4	1 1/2	1 3/4	2	2 1/2	3
#2 - 5	√	√	√	√	√	√	√	√						
#4 - 40		√	√	√	√	√	√	√	√	√				
#6 - 32		√	√	√	√	√		√	√	√	√	√	√	√
#8 - 32		√	√	√	√	√		√	√	√	√	√	√	√
#10 - 24		√	√	√	√	√		√	√	√	√	√	√	√
#10 - 32		√	√	√		√		√	√	√	√	√	√	√
#12 - 24			√	√	√	√		√	√	√	√	√	√	√
1/4 20				√	√	√	√	√	√	√	√	√	√	√
5/16 18				√	√	√	√	√	√	√	√	√	√	√
3/8 16				√	√	√	√	√	√	√	√	√	√	√
1/2 13						√	√	√	√	√	√	√	√	√
5/8 11							√	√	√	√	√	√	√	√
3/4 10										√		√		√

Figure A-12

American National Standard Plain Washers					
Nominal Washer Size		Series	Inside Diameter	Outside Diameter	Thickness
No. 0	0.060	N	0.068	0.125	0.025
		R	0.068	0.188	0.025
		W	0.068	0.250	0.025
No. 1	0.073	N	0.084	0.156	0.025
		R	0.084	0.219	0.025
		W	0.084	0.281	0.032
No. 2	0.086	N	0.094	0.188	0.025
		R	0.094	0.250	0.032
		W	0.094	0.344	0.032
No. 3	0.099	N	0.109	0.219	0.025
		R	0.109	0.312	0.032
		W	0.109	0.406	0.040
No. 4	0.112	N	0.125	0.250	0.032
		R	0.125	0.375	0.040
		W	0.125	0.438	0.040
No. 5	0.125	N	0.141	0.281	0.032
		R	0.141	0.406	0.040
		W	0.141	0.500	0.040
No. 6	1.380	N	0.156	0.312	0.032
		R	0.156	0.438	0.040
		W	0.156	0.562	0.040
No. 8	0.164	N	0.188	0.375	0.040
		R	0.188	0.500	0.040
		W	0.188	0.633	0.063
No. 10	0.190	N	0.203	0.406	0.040
		R	0.203	0.562	0.040
		W	0.203	0.734	0.063
No. 12	0.216	N	0.234	0.438	0.040
		R	0.234	0.625	0.063
		W	0.234	0.875	0.063
1/4	0.250	N	0.281	0.500	0.063
		R	0.281	0.734	0.063
		W	0.281	1.000	0.063
5/16	0.312	N	0.344	0.625	0.063
		R	0.344	0.875	0.063
		W	0.344	1.125	0.063
3/8	0.375	N	0.406	0.734	0.063
		R	0.406	1.000	0.063
		W	0.406	1.250	0.100
7/16	0.438	N	0.469	0.875	0.063
		R	0.469	1.125	0.063
		W	0.469	1.469	0.100
1/2	0.500	N	0.531	1.000	0.063
		R	0.531	1.2.5	0.100
		W	0.531	1.125	0.100

Figure A-13

American National Standard Plain Washers					
Nominal Washer Size		Series	Inside Diameter	Outside Diameter	Thickness
9/16	0.562	N R W	0.594 0.594 0.594	1.125 1.469 2.000	0.063 0.100 0.100
5/8	0.625	N R W	0.656 0.656 0.656	1.250 1.750 2.250	0.100 0.100 0.160
3/4	0.750	N R W	0.812 0.812 0.812	1.375 2.000 2.500	0.100 0.100 0.160
7/8	0.875	N R W	0.938 0.938 0.938	1.469 2.250 2.750	0.100 0.160 0.160
1	1.000	N R W	1.062 1.062 1.062	1.750 2.500 3.000	0.100 0.160 0.160

Figure A-13
(*Continued*)

Index